INTERNATIONAL
LAW REPORTS

VOLUME 114

Volumes published under the title:

ANNUAL DIGEST AND REPORTS
OF PUBLIC INTERNATIONAL LAW CASES

Vol. 1 (1919-22) } Edited by Sir John Fischer Williams, K.C.,
                     and H. Lauterpacht, LL.D.
Vol. 2 (1923-24)

Vol. 3 (1925-26) } Edited by Arnold D. McNair, C.B.E., LL.D.,
                     and H. Lauterpacht, LL.D.
Vol. 4 (1927-28)

Vol. 5 (1929-30)
Vol. 6 (1931-32)
Vol. 7 (1933-34)
Vol. 8 (1935-37)
Vol. 9 (1938-40)
Vol. 10 (1941-42)
Vol. 11 (1919-42) } Edited by H. Lauterpacht, Q.C., LL.D., F.B.A.
Vol. 12 (1943-45)
Vol. 13 (1946)
Vol. 14 (1947)
Vol. 15 (1948)
Vol. 16 (1949)

Volumes published under the title:

INTERNATIONAL LAW REPORTS

Vol. 17 (1950)
Vol. 18 (1951)
Vol. 19 (1952)
Vol. 20 (1953) } Edited by Sir Hersch Lauterpacht, Q.C., LL.D.,
                    F.B.A.
Vol. 21 (1954)
Vol. 22 (1955)
Vol. 23 (1956)
Vol. 24 (1957)   Edited by Sir Hersch Lauterpacht, Q.C., LL.D.,
                    F.B.A., and E. Lauterpacht

Vol. 25 (1958-I) }
                    Edited by E. Lauterpacht, Q.C.
Vol. 26 (1958-II)

Vols. 27—68 *and* Consolidated Tables and Index to Vols. 1—35 *and* 36—45
                    Edited by E. Lauterpacht, Q.C.
Vols. 69—114 *and* Consolidated Index and Consolidated Tables of Cases and
                    Treaties to Vols. 1—80 *and* Vols. 81—100
                    Edited by Sir Elihu Lauterpacht, C.B.E., Q.C.,
                    and C. J. Greenwood

Lauterpacht Research Centre for International Law
University of Cambridge

INTERNATIONAL LAW REPORTS

VOLUME
114

Edited by

SIR ELIHU LAUTERPACHT, CBE QC
Honorary Professor of International Law, University of Cambridge
Bencher of Gray's Inn

C. J. GREENWOOD
Professor of International Law
London School of Economics and Political Science

and

A. G. OPPENHEIMER
Associate Editor: Civil Law Jurisdictions
Fellow of the Lauterpacht Research Centre for International Law, University of Cambridge

GROTIUS PUBLICATIONS

CAMBRIDGE
UNIVERSITY PRESS

CAMBRIDGE
UNIVERSITY PRESS

University Printing House, Cambridge CB2 8BS, United Kingdom

Published in the United States of America by Cambridge University Press, New York

Cambridge University Press is part of the University of Cambridge.

It furthers the University's mission by disseminating knowledge in the pursuit of education, learning and research at the highest international levels of excellence.

www.cambridge.org
Information on this title: www.cambridge.org/ 9780521642446

© Sir Elihu Lauterpacht 1999

First published 1999
Reprinted 2013
3rd printing 2017

Printed in Singapore by Markono Print Media Pte Ltd

A catalogue record for this publication is available from the British Library

ISBN 978-0-521-64244-6 Hardback

CONTENTS

PREFACE

The present volume again contains a mixture of national and international decisions. The latter include the first award, given in October 1998, of the arbitration tribunal established by the Governments of Eritrea and Yemen, two ICSID arbitration awards and five indications of views given by the United Nations Human Rights Committee. The jurisprudence of national tribunals is represented by cases from Australia, England, Germany, Italy, New Zealand and the United States of America. These include decisions from courts in Australia (p. 383), England (p. 402) and the United States (p. 606) regarding extradition to Hong Kong at the time of the reversion of Hong Kong to the People's Republic of China.

Many people have made possible the publication of this volume. Sir Robert Jennings, QC, President of the Eritrea–Yemen Arbitration Tribunal, kindly provided a copy of the award of that Tribunal and Mr P. J. H. Jonkman, Secretary-General of the Permanent Court of Arbitration, gave much valuable assistance regarding its publication. Professor James Crawford, SC and Professor John Dugard contributed decisions on the Hong Kong extradition issue. Mr Andrew Oppenheimer, Associate Editor for Civil Law Jurisdictions, prepared the summaries of the decisions of the German and Italian courts. Ms Rosemary Rayfuse, LLM, Lecturer in Law at the University of New South Wales, prepared the summary of the *Kaiser Bauxite* case and, together with Dr A. V. Lowe, Reader in International Law at the University of Cambridge, the summary in the *Klöckner* case. Ms Fiona Mucklow, LLM, prepared the summaries of four of the United Nations Human Rights Committee cases, as well as the New Zealand decision and the *Willoughby* decision from the United States. Ms Karen Lee, MA, prepared the summaries of the *Cox, Tse Chu-Fai, Launder* and *Lui* cases, as well as compiling the Tables of Cases and the Digest and seeing the volume through the press.

The German decisions were translated by Mr Tim Johnston, Solicitor, and Mrs Jane Martens, MA and the Italian decisions by Mr Tim Johnston and the law firm Verusio e Cosmelli in Rome. HE Miss Maureen MacGlashan, CMG, compiled the Index and Table of Treaties. Mrs Diane Ilott performed much valuable sub-editorial work. Mr Adrian Lee corrected the proofs. Mrs Anne Skinner gave valuable secretarial assistance.

We are also indebted to the following publishers for their kindness in allowing us to reproduce decisions from the reports which they publish: Cambridge University Press (*ICSID Reports*), Butterworths (Australia) Limited (*Australian Law Reports*), the Incorporated Council of Law Reporting for England and Wales (*Weekly Law Reports*),

Butterworths Law Publishers Limited (*All England Law Reports*), Jordan Publishing (*Family Law Reports*) and the West Publishing Company (*Federal Reporter, Pacific Reporter* and *Federal Supplement*).

Finally, we extend our thanks to our publishers, Cambridge University Press, and, in particular, to Ms Finola O'Sullivan and Ms Jayne Matthews, and to our printers, the Gomer Press, for the trouble which they have taken with this volume.

E. LAUTERPACHT

LAUTERPACHT RESEARCH CENTRE
    FOR INTERNATIONAL LAW,
UNIVERSITY OF CAMBRIDGE

C. J. GREENWOOD

LAW DEPARTMENT,
LONDON SCHOOL OF ECONOMICS
    AND POLITICAL SCIENCE

February 1999

EDITORIAL NOTE

The *International Law Reports* endeavour to provide within a single series of volumes comprehensive access in English to judicial materials bearing on public international law. On certain topics it is not always easy to draw a clear line between cases which are essentially ones of public international law interest and those which are primarily applications of special domestic rules. For example, in relation to extradition, the *Reports* will include cases which bear on the exception of "political offences" or the rule of double criminality, but will restrict the number of cases dealing with purely procedural aspects of extradition. Similarly, while the general rules relating to the admission and exclusion of aliens, especially of refugees, are of international legal interest, cases on the procedure of admission usually are not. In such borderline areas, and sometimes also where there is a series of domestic decisions all dealing with a single point in essentially the same manner, only one illustrative decision will be printed and references to the remainder will be given in an accompanying note.

DECISIONS OF INTERNATIONAL TRIBUNALS
The *Reports* seek to include so far as possible the available decisions of every international tribunal, e.g. the International Court of Justice, or *ad hoc* arbitrations between States. There are, however, some jurisdictions to which full coverage cannot be given, either because of the large number of decisions (e.g. the Administrative Tribunal of the United Nations) or because not all the decisions bear on questions of public international law (e.g. the Court of the European Communities). In these instances, those decisions are selected which appear to have the greatest long-term value.

Human rights cases. The number of decisions on questions of international protection of human rights has increased considerably in recent years and it is now impossible for the *Reports* to cover them all. As far as decisions of international jurisdictions are concerned, the *Reports* will continue to publish decisions of the European Court of Human Rights and of the Inter-American Court of Human Rights, as well as "views" of the United Nations Committee on Human Rights. Selected decisions of the European Commission of Human Rights will be printed, chosen by reference to the importance of the points at issue and their interest to public international lawyers generally. (All reports of decisions of the European Commission of Human Rights are published in an official series, the *Official Collection of Decisions of the European Commission of Human Rights,* as well as in the *European Human Rights Reports*). Decisions of national courts on the application of conventions on human rights will not be published unless they deal with a major point of substantive human rights law or a matter of wider interest to public international lawyers such as the relationship of international law and national law, the extent of the right of derogation or the principles of the interpretation of treaties.

International arbitrations. The *Reports* of course include arbitral awards rendered in cases between States which involve an application of public international law. Beyond this, however, the selection of arbitral decisions is more open to debate. As these *Reports* are principally concerned with matters of public international law, they will not include purely private law commercial arbitrations even if they are international in the sense that they arise between parties of different nationality and even if one of them is a State. (For reports of a number of such awards, see *Yearbook Commercial Arbitration* (ed. Pieter Sanders, under the auspices of the International Council for Commercial Arbitration)). But where there is a sufficient point of contact with public international law then the relevant parts of the award will be reported. Examples of such points of contact are cases in which the character of a State as a party has some relevance (e.g. State immunity, stabilization clauses, *force majeure*) or where there is a choice of law problem involving discussion of international law or general principles of law as possible applicable laws. The same criteria will determine the selection of decisions of national courts regarding the enforcement of arbitral awards.

DECISIONS OF NATIONAL TRIBUNALS
A systematic effort is made to collect from all national jurisdictions those judicial decisions which have some bearing on international law.

EDITORIAL TREATMENT OF MATERIALS
The basic policy of the Editors is, so far as possible, to present the material in its original form. It is no part of the editorial function to impose on the decisions printed in these volumes a uniformity of approach or style which they do not possess. Editorial intervention is limited to the introduction of the summary and of the bold-letter rubric at the head of each case. This is followed by the full text of the original decision or of its translation. Normally, the only passages which will be omitted are those which contain either statements of fact having no bearing on the points of international law involved in the case or discussion of matters of domestic law unrelated to the points of international legal interest. The omission of material is usually indicated either by a series of dots or by the insertion of a sentence in square brackets noting the passages which have been left out.

PRESENTATION OF MATERIALS

The material in this volume is of two kinds, material reproduced photographically and material which has been freshly set for this volume.

Material photographically reproduced.   This consists exclusively of reports originally printed in the English language. The material can usually be recognized by the differences between its type-style and the Baskerville type otherwise used in these *Reports*. The source of the material is identified by the reference to the "Report" in square brackets at the end of the case. Where more than one citation is given, the report used is the one first listed. The bold type figures in square brackets in the inner margin of each page refer to the pagination of the original report. The smaller figures in square brackets in the margins of these cases are the indicators of footnotes which have been editorially introduced.

Other material.   The remaining material in the volume has been typeset for this volume. This includes all material specially translated into English for these *Reports* as well as some material in English which in its original form was not suitable for photo-reproduction. The source of all such material is indicated by the reference to the "Report" in square brackets at the end of the case. The language of the original decision is also mentioned there. The bold figures in square brackets in the body of the text indicate the pagination of the original report. Small figures in square brackets within the text are indicators of footnotes which have been editorially introduced.

NOTES

Footnotes.   Footnotes enclosed in square brackets are editorial insertions. All other footnotes are part of the original report.

Other notes.   References to cases deemed not to be sufficiently substantial to warrant reporting will occasionally be found in editorial notes either at the end of a report of a case on a similar point or under an independent heading.

DIGEST OF CASES

With effect from Volume 75 the decisions contained in the *Reports* are no longer arranged according to the traditional classification scheme. Instead a Digest of Cases is published at the beginning of each volume. The main headings of the Digest are arranged alphabetically. Under each heading brief details are given of those cases reported in that volume which contain points covered by that heading. Each entry in the Digest gives the name of the case concerned and the page reference, the name of the tribunal which gave the decision and an indication of the main points raised in the case which relate to that particular heading of the Digest. Where a case raises points which concern several different areas of international law, entries relating to that case will appear under each of the relevant headings in the Digest. A list of the main headings used in the Digest is set out at page xvii.

CONSOLIDATED INDEX AND TABLES

A Consolidated Index and Consolidated Tables of Cases and Treaties for volumes 1-80 was published in two volumes in 1990 and 1991. A further volume containing the Consolidated Index and Consolidated Tables of Cases and Treaties for volumes 81-100 was published in 1996.

TABLE OF CASES REPORTED

ALPHABETICAL

(Cases which are reported only in a note are distinguished from cases which are reported in full by the insertion of the word "note" in parentheses after the page number of the report.)

TABLE OF CASES REPORTED

ARRANGED ACCORDING TO COURTS
AND TRIBUNALS (INTERNATIONAL CASES)
AND COUNTRIES (MUNICIPAL CASES)

(Cases which are reported only in a note are distinguished from cases which are reported in full by the insertion of the word "note" in parentheses after the page number of the report.)

I. DECISIONS OF INTERNATIONAL TRIBUNALS

II. DECISIONS OF MUNICIPAL COURTS

DIGEST OF CASES

List of Main Headings

(Those headings for which there are entries in the present volume are printed in italics. For a guide to the Digest, see the Editorial Note at p. xi.)

DIGEST OF CASES
REPORTED IN VOLUME 114

Claims

Consular Relations

Extradition

Governments

United Kingdom Government and new regime — Extent of international recognition of regime — Board of directors of company appointed by government of foreign State—Company possessing bank account with London bank—Directors appointed as signatories for bank account—New regime purporting to dismiss directors and appoint replacements — New directors giving fresh instructions to bank — Whether bank obliged to honour instructions from original board of directors or newly appointed board of directors—England, High Court, Queen's Bench Division

Human Rights

Detention—Arbitrary detention—International Covenant on Civil and Political Rights, 1966, Article 9 — Conditions of detention—Duty to treat detainees with dignity—International Covenant on Civil and Political Rights, 1966, Article 10—United Nations Human Rights Committee

Discrimination—Prohibited grounds of discrimination—Discrimination on grounds of status—Different treatment by France of soldiers of Senegalese origin — Whether justifiable — Whether discrimination regarding pension rights within the scope of the International Covenant on Civil and Political Rights, 1966—United Nations Human Rights Committee

Freedom from arrest—Arbitrary arrest and detention—International Covenant on Civil and Political Rights, 1966—United Nations Human Rights Committee

Freedom of expression—Author of complaint persecuted for membership of opposition political party—Violation of International Covenant on Civil and Political Rights, 1966, Article 19—United Nations Human Rights Committee

Freedom of expression — Freedom of movement — Right to participate in public affairs — One-party State — Zambia — Persecution of opposition politician contrary to International Covenant on Civil and Political Rights, 1966—United Nations Human Rights Committee

degrading treatment or punishment—United Nations Human Rights Committee

Scope of human rights treaty—International Covenant on Civil and Political Rights, 1966—Extradition proceedings—Threat of death sentence in requesting State—Relevance of Article 3 of the Convention against Torture and Other Cruel, Inhuman or Degrading Treatment or Punishment—United Nations Human Rights Committee

International Organizations

Immunity—Jurisdictional immunity—National of receiving State employed by international organization in managerial role— Whether integrated into organizational structure—Contract of employment—Termination—Claim for unlawful dismissal and reinstatement — Whether international organization entitled to jurisdictional immunity — Whether examination of legality of dismissal of employee involving interference with public functions of international organization — Bari Institute of International Centre for Advanced Mediterranean Agronomic Studies—Legal status—Whether engaged in ordinary commercial or public-law activities—Whether entitled to jurisdictional immunity—Paris Agreement establishing the International Centre, 1962 — Additional Protocol—Italian reservation—Whether recognition of jurisdictional immunity by municipal courts may violate guarantee of judicial protection for individuals under Italian Constitution, Article 24—Requirement for international organiz-ations to make adequate provision for settlement of employment disputes—Whether independent internal appeals procedure acceptable—Italy, Court of Cassation (Plenary Session)

International Tribunals

United Nations Human Rights Committee — Competence — Domestic remedies rule—Adequacy of domestic remedies— Ability to invoke International Covenant on Civil and Political Rights before domestic courts—Procedure—Reconsideration of earlier admissibility decision—United Nations Human Rights Committee

Sources of International Law

State Immunity

Jurisdictional immunity—Immunity of State officials for official acts—Extent—Diplomat returning to sending State with children —Whether an official act—Whether official immune in action in courts of receiving State—Relationship between State immunity and diplomatic immunity—England, High Court, Family Division and Court of Appeal, Civil Division

Jurisdictional immunity—National of receiving State employed as assistant in embassy of foreign State—Contract of employment—Claim against embassy for non-payment of social security contributions required by Italian law—Whether foreign State entitled to jurisdictional immunity—Whether claim relating to purely financial matters—Italy, Court of Cassation (Plenary Session)

Jurisdictional immunity—National of receiving State employed by commercial office of foreign State as secretary and administrative officer—Dismissal—Claim for reinstatement and unpaid allowances —Whether foreign State entitled to jurisdictional immunity—Restrictive theory of immunity—Scope of application to disputes concerning employment contracts—Limitation to cases where there is actual likelihood of interference with performance of sovereign functions—Types of claims involving such interference—Distinction between claims for reinstatement or damages and claims for unpaid allowances—Italy, Court of Cassation (Plenary Session)

Jurisdictional immunity—National of receiving State employed by information agency of foreign State as secretary and telephonist—Contract of employment—Claim for arrears of salary following termination of contract—Whether foreign State entitled to jurisdictional immunity—Whether employee integrated into the organizational structure of foreign State—Nature of work done by information agency—Whether inquiry by court into nature of employment tasks violating jurisdictional immunity—Italy, Court of Cassation (Plenary Session)

Jurisdictional immunity—National of sending State employed as member of technical and administrative staff of consulate of foreign State — Dismissal — Claim for damages for unlawful dismissal — Whether foreign State entitled to jurisdictional immunity—Restrictive theory of immunity—Scope of application to disputes concerning employment contracts—Employment involving performance of subordinate consular functions — Whether exercise of jurisdiction would constitute interference with performance of sovereign functions—Federal Republic of Germany, Federal Labour Court *(BAG)*

State Succession

States

Declaration") — Reversion of sovereignty of Hong Kong to People's Republic of China ("PRC") on 1 July 1997—Legal consequences of transfer of sovereignty—Extradition request—British Colony of Hong Kong requesting extradition of applicant from United Kingdom—Trial and sentence of applicant after transfer of sovereignty—"China point"—Effect of treaty—Basic Law of the Hong Kong Special Administrative Region of the PRC ("Basic Law") implementing treaty obligations owed by the PRC to the United Kingdom under the Joint Declaration—Whether rule of law and legal safeguards existing in requesting State likely to survive handover—Whether successor State likely to comply with treaty obligations—England, Divisional Court, Queen's Bench Division and House of Lords

Territory

Sovereignty—Historic claims—Whether international law contains doctrine of reversion of ancient title—Territory under sovereignty of Ottoman Empire—Whether title capable of reverting to State which existed prior to Ottoman period—Yemen—Evidence of prior sovereignty over Red Sea islands—Arbitration Tribunal

Sovereignty—Historical consolidation—Prescription—*Effectivités*—Nature and effect—Requirements of international law—Display of authority—Exercise of State functions—Peaceful possession—Petroleum agreements—Construction and maintenance of lighthouses—Acts of possession performed by military forces during civil war—Evidence of acts of third States—Arbitration Tribunal

Sovereignty—Islands—Contiguity—Principle that islands within territorial sea of State presumed to be part of that State — Circumstances in which presumption rebutted—Portico doctrine —Arbitration Tribunal

Sovereignty—Treaties—Treaty creating objective legal status for territory—Treaty of Lausanne, 1923—Peace Treaty with Italy, 1947—Red Sea islands—Arbitration Tribunal

Page

Treaties

War and Armed Conflict

TABLE OF TREATIES

This table contains a list, in chronological order according to the date of signature, of the treaties referred to in the decisions printed in the present volume. It has not been possible to draw a helpful distinction between treaties judicially considered and treaties which are merely cited.

In the case of bilateral treaties, the names of the parties are given in alphabetical order. Multilateral treaties are referred to by the name by which they are believed commonly to be known. References to the texts of treaties have been supplied, including wherever possible at least one reference to a text in the English language. The full titles of the abbreviated references will be found in the list of Abbreviations printed in the volume containing the Consolidated Tables to Vols 1–80.

[1] Including the amendments introduced by the Treaty on European Union (Maastricht Treaty) (7 February 1992).

Arbitration—*Compromis*—Interpretation—Parties concluding two consecutive agreements—Agreement on Principles and Arbitration Agreement—Latter agreement taking priority—Parties unable to agree on definition of scope of dispute—Scope of dispute left to Tribunal to decide on the basis of the respective positions of the Parties — Critical date — Whether dispute confined to issues raised by Parties by a particular date — *Compromis* providing for arbitration proceedings in two stages — Effect on first stage of proceedings

Arbitration — *Compromis* — Territorial dispute — Tribunal required to decide on territorial sovereignty — Whether required to do more than determine relative merits of competing claims

Arbitration—Evidence—Admissibility—Territorial dispute —Whether evidence of acts occurring after a particular date inadmissible—Maps—Historical evidence—Evidence submitted in response to question from Tribunal member

Arbitration — Procedure — *Ad hoc* tribunal created by agreement between two States—Tribunal using services of Permanent Court of Arbitration — Submissions by Parties

Territory — Sovereignty — Historic claims — Whether international law contains doctrine of reversion of ancient title—Territory under sovereignty of Ottoman Empire—Whether title capable of reverting to State which existed prior to Ottoman period — Yemen — Evidence of prior sovereignty over Red Sea islands

Territory—Sovereignty—Historical consolidation—Prescription — *Effectivités* — Nature and effect — Requirements of international law—Display of authority—Exercise of State functions—Peaceful possession—Petroleum agreements—Construction and maintenance of lighthouses — Acts of possession performed by military forces during civil war—Evidence of acts of third States

Territory — Sovereignty — Islands — Contiguity — Principle that islands within territorial sea of State presumed to be part of that State—Circumstances in which presumption rebutted — Portico doctrine

Territory—Sovereignty—Treaties—Treaty creating objective legal status for territory—Treaty of Lausanne, 1923—Peace Treaty with Italy, 1947 — Red Sea islands

Treaties—Effect—Doctrine of *res inter alios acta*—Interpretation—Treaties creating objective legal status for territory—Treaty of Lausanne, 1923—Peace Treaty with Italy, 1947

War and armed conflict — Peace Treaties — Treaty of Lausanne, 1923 — Peace Treaty with Italy, 1947 — Eritrea–Yemen hostilities 1995—Agreements ending conflict

GOVERNMENT OF THE STATE OF ERITREA AND
GOVERNMENT OF THE REPUBLIC OF YEMEN
(PHASE ONE: TERRITORIAL SOVEREIGNTY AND SCOPE OF THE DISPUTE)[1]

Arbitration Tribunal.   9 *October* 1998

(Sir Robert Jennings, *President;* Judge Schwebel, Dr El-Kosheri, Mr Highet and Judge Higgins, *Members)*[2]

SUMMARY:[3] *The facts:*—The State of Eritrea ("Eritrea") and the Republic of Yemen ("Yemen") were in dispute regarding sovereignty over islands in the Red Sea between their respective coastlines and the delimitation of the maritime boundary between the two States. Following hostilities in 1995, Eritrea and Yemen concluded an Agreement on Principles on 21 May 1996, by which they agreed to renounce force against each other and undertook to "settle their dispute on questions of territorial sovereignty and maritime boundaries peacefully". To that end, they agreed to conclude an agreement on arbitration establishing an arbitration tribunal. The Agreement on Principles provided that:

> . . . concerning questions of territorial sovereignty, the Tribunal shall decide in accordance with the principles, rules and practices of international law applicable to the matter, and on the basis, in particular, of historic titles.

---

[1] The State of Eritrea was represented by HE Mr Haile Weldensae, Agent, and Professor Lea Brilmayer and Mr Gary Born, Co-Agents. The Republic of Yemen was represented by HE Dr Abdulkarim Al-Eryani, Agent, HE Mr Abdullah Ahmad Ghanim, Mr Hussein Al-Hubaishi, Mr Abdulwahid Al-Zandani and Mr Rodman Bundy, Co-Agents, Professor Ian Brownlie, QC, as counsel.
 The map of the Award can be found at pp. 140-1.
[2] For details of the appointment of the President and Members of the Tribunal, see paragraph 4 of the Award. The Tribunal was established *ad hoc* under the terms of the Arbitration Agreement of 3 October 1996 between the two States. The Registrar was Mr P. J. H. Jonkman, Secretary-General of the Permanent Court of Arbitration. The arbitration was held in London but the location of the Tribunal's registry was the International Bureau of the Permanent Court of Arbitration in the Hague.
[3] Prepared by Professor Christopher Greenwood.

Eritrea and Yemen did not agree on which islands were the subject of the dispute. The Agreement on Principles therefore provided that the arbitration tribunal which was to be created should first determine the scope of the dispute and then, in a second phase of the arbitration proceedings, deal with both the dispute over territorial sovereignty and the dispute regarding maritime delimitation.

The Arbitration Agreement was concluded on 3 October 1996 and provided for the creation of a five-member Tribunal, consisting of two arbitrators nominated by each Party and a President appointed by the four arbitrators on the recommendation of the two Parties. Article 2 of the Arbitration Agreement provided that the Tribunal was to "provide rulings in accordance with international law" in two stages; the first stage concerning the dispute regarding territorial sovereignty and the scope of the dispute, the second regarding the delimitation of the maritime boundaries between the Parties.[4] Article 2(2) of the Arbitration Agreement provided that the Tribunal should decide "on the definition of the scope of the dispute on the basis of the respective positions of the two Parties".

Eritrea maintained that the scope of the dispute was to be determined by reference to the respective positions of the Parties as advanced before the Tribunal. Eritrea claimed sovereignty over the Mohabbakahs (principally Sayal Islet, Harbi Islet, Flat Islet and High Islet), the Haycocks (principally South West Haycock, Middle Haycock and North East Haycock), the South West Rocks, the Zuqar-Hanish Group (including the islands of Jabal Zuqar, Greater and Lesser Hanish), all of which were located in the southern Red Sea, and the Zubayr Group and Jabal al-Tayr, which were located further north.[5] Yemen, however, maintained that the critical date for determination of the scope of the dispute was the date of conclusion of the Agreement on Principles and submitted that, at that date, there was no dispute regarding the Zubayr Group or Jabal al-Tayr.

Both Eritrea and Yemen claimed title to the various islands on the basis of historic title and more recent acts which they submitted were manifestations of effective occupation of the islands. It was common ground that, prior to the colonization of Eritrea by Italy at the end of the nineteenth century, sovereignty over both shores of the Red Sea and over the islands had rested with the Ottoman Empire. During the Ottoman period, jurisdiction over the islands had been divided, with those islands off the African coast being subject to the jurisdiction of the Khedive of Egypt, while those off the Arabian coast were subject to the jurisdiction of the Ottoman authorities in the Arabian peninsula.

Eritrea asserted that, during the period of Italian rule in Eritrea, the Italian authorities had patrolled the islands in order to combat piracy and slave trading and had manifested control over the islands in other ways. By Article 16 of the Treaty of Lausanne, 1923,[6] the Ottoman Empire had relinquished any claim which it had once possessed and, according to Eritrea, Article 6 of that treaty did not operate to vest title in Yemen. Eritrea submitted that, by the 1920s, Italy had exercised such a degree of effective control over the

---

[4] The text of Article 2 is set out in paragraph 7 of the Award.

[5] See map at pp. 140-1 below. The names of some of the islands are not spelt the same way in the map and all of the documents to which the Award refers. The spellings used in the summary are those used in the operative part of the Award.

[6] See p. 49 below.

islands that it had acquired sovereignty. That sovereignty had then passed to Ethiopia when Eritrea became part of Ethiopia after World War Two. Ethiopia had performed numerous administrative and other acts which demonstrated sovereignty over the islands. Eritrea had succeeded to Ethiopia's title when it became independent in the early 1990s. Eritrea also maintained that its title to the islands had been acknowledged, or at least not disputed, by Yemen and pointed to the use of the islands by Eritrean fishermen who were dependent upon the islands for their livelihood.

Yemen advanced a claim based on ancient title which it asserted could be traced back to the sixth century and which reverted to Yemen after the end of Ottoman rule. It also argued that the principle of natural or geographical unity, taken together with evidence of the exercise of acts of jurisdiction and other manifestations of sovereignty, led to the conclusion that the islands were part of Yemen. Yemen relied upon the actual exercise of jurisdiction by Yemeni authorities in the islands and submitted that there were important economic and social links between the islands and the mainland of Yemen.

Both States submitted maps which, each claimed, provided evidence in support of its claim. Yemen, in particular, relied heavily upon cartographic evidence. In addition, both States made reference to the construction and operation of lighthouses in the islands. Although not raised by either State in the initial pleadings, in response to a question from a member of the Tribunal, both States submitted evidence regarding the grant of petroleum concessions by their respective governments and contended that this evidence supported their claims.

Held (unanimously):—(1) The somewhat technical critical date argument advanced by Yemen regarding the determination of the scope of the dispute had to be rejected. Whatever may have been the case at the time the Agreement on Principles was concluded, the Arbitration Agreement departed from the earlier Agreement by providing that the Tribunal should determine the scope of the dispute only after having heard the entire substantive contentions of both Parties on the question of sovereignty. The Arbitration Agreement did not qualify the phrase "the respective positions of the two Parties" and the ordinary meaning of that phrase in its context and in the light of the object and purpose of the Arbitration Agreement was that it was the positions of the Parties as at the date of the Arbitration Agreement, not some earlier date, that was intended. This interpretation was consistent with the way in which the Parties had developed their respective cases. The scope of the dispute thus concerned all the islands to which Eritrea had laid claim (pp. 26-30).

(2) Except in relation to the date at which the scope of the dispute was to be determined, the Parties had not submitted argument regarding the critical date. The Tribunal had therefore examined all the evidence submitted to it, irrespective of the date of the acts to which that evidence related (p. 32).

(3) The function of the Tribunal in the first stage of the proceedings was to render an award "on" territorial sovereignty, not to allocate sovereignty to one or other of the Parties. It was, therefore, within the competence of the Tribunal to find a common or divided sovereignty. Article 2 of the Arbitration Agreement required the Tribunal to decide territorial sovereignty

"in accordance with the principles, rules and practices of international law applicable to the matter, and on the basis, in particular, of historic titles". The notion of an historic title was well established in international law but had two different meanings: that of an ancient title long established by common repute, and that of a title created or consolidated by a process of prescription, acquiescence or long possession. The injunction to have particular regard to historic titles could not have been intended to mean that historic title was to be given some priority it might not otherwise possess. While the Tribunal was not called upon, at this stage of the proceedings, to consider the delimitation of the maritime boundary, it could not accept that the international law governing land territory and the international law governing maritime boundaries bore no juridical relevance to one another. The Tribunal was, therefore, entitled to take account of principles and rules derived from maritime law if they formed part of the international law applicable to title to territory (pp. 34-7).

(4) Yemen's claim to possess an ancient title to the islands which reverted to it upon the end of Ottoman sovereignty in the region could not be accepted. There was no basis for maintaining that a doctrine of reversion of title existed in international law. Even if such a doctrine did exist, it would not be applicable in the present case, because there had been a lack of continuity. To have accepted Yemen's claim would have been tantamount to a rejection of the Ottoman title to full sovereignty over the islands, a sovereignty which, in accordance with the principle of intertemporal law, had been lawful and had carried with it the right to dispose of the territory. That right had been exercised in the Treaty of Lausanne, by which Turkey had renounced her claims in favour of the Allied Powers. While the Treaty of Lausanne had been *res inter alios acta* as far as Yemen was concerned, it had created for the islands an objective legal status of indeterminacy pending a further decision of the interested parties. Moreover, the extent of pre-Ottoman Yemen was far from clear and it would be anachronistic to attempt to attribute to such a tribal, mountainous and Muslim medieval society the modern Western concept of sovereign title, particularly with respect to barren, uninhabited islands (pp. 38-60 and 115-16).

(5) Eritrea's claim to historic title over all the islands was also unfounded. Although Italy had entertained serious territorial ambitions with regard to the islands, the contention that Italy had possessed sovereignty over those islands during the period when it ruled Eritrea was undermined by several factors. First, such claims were incompatible with the status attributed to the islands by Article 16 of the Treaty of Lausanne. Secondly, during the inter-war period, the Italian Government had constantly and consistently given specific assurances to the British Government that Italy fully accepted and recognized the indeterminate legal position of the islands as established by the Treaty. Finally, the provisions of the Italian Peace Treaty, 1947, reaffirmed the legal position created by Article 16 of the Treaty of Lausanne, except that Italy renounced any rights which it might possess under that provision (pp. 37-60 and 116-17).

(6) The evidence of the display of functions of State and governmental authority over the islands was not sufficient to justify upholding either Party's claim to all of the islands in dispute.

(a) The modern international law of the acquisition (or attribution) of territory generally required that there be: an intentional display of power and authority over the territory, by the exercise of jurisdiction and State functions, on a continuous and peaceful basis (p. 69).

(b) While the standard of activity required to establish title might be subject to modification when dealing, as in the present case, with difficult or inhospitable territory, the establishment of territorial sovereignty was no light matter and it might be supposed that there was some absolute minimum requirement for the acquisition of such a right. In contrast to the position in the *Island of Palmas* case,[7] in which the *compromis* had required the arbitrator only to decide the relative strength of two competing claims, in the present case the Arbitration Agreement required that the Tribunal make an award on territorial sovereignty (pp. 117-18).

(c) The factual evidence of *effectivités* presented to the Tribunal was voluminous in quantity but sparse in useful content. In particular, the evidence of the assertion of sovereignty was frequently equivocal and no consistent pattern emerged from the evidence of actual acts of jurisdiction. In addition, many of the acts relied upon by Eritrea were acts of its predecessor, Ethiopia, which were not "peaceful", unless that term might be understood to include acts in prosecution of a civil war (pp. 69-94).

(d) The maps presented by the Parties did not point to any clear conclusion as regards title to the islands after the Ottoman period (pp. 94-100).

(e) The evidence of offshore petroleum contracts entered into by Yemen and by Ethiopia and Eritrea failed to establish or significantly strengthen the claims of either Party to sovereignty but they did lend a measure of support to a median line between the opposite coasts of Eritrea and Yemen, drawn without regard to the islands, dividing the respective jurisdiction of the Parties (pp. 100-14).

(f) Since the activities relied upon by the Parties did not lead to a clear conclusion, it was appropriate for the Tribunal to consider other factors which might strengthen the basis of decision. In particular, the geographical situation of the islands was relevant. There was some presumption that any islands off the coast of one of the Parties belonged to that Party because of their appurtenance to the coast unless the Party on the opposite coast was able to demonstrate a clearly better title ("the portico doctrine") (pp. 119-22).

(7) Since the legal history did not support either State's claim to sovereignty over all the islands, it was necessary to give separate consideration to each of the different groups of islands.

(a) The islands, islets, rocks and low-tide elevations forming *the Mohabbakahs* were subject to the territorial sovereignty of Eritrea. With the exception of one High Islet, the islands of this group lay within twelve miles of the Eritrean coast. Whatever the history, in the absence of any clear title being shown by Yemen, the fact that these islands lay within Eritrean territorial waters was sufficient for them to be regarded as Eritrean. This approach was confirmed by the principle in Article 6 of the Treaty of Lausanne that islands within the territorial sea of a State were to belong to that State, notwithstanding that the territorial sea then extended only three miles from the coast. Since the Mohabbakahs had always been regarded as one group, High Islet, although located just outside the Eritrean territorial sea, also belonged to Eritrea (pp. 122-4 and 139).

(b) The islands, islets, rocks and low-tide elevations forming *the Haycocks* were subject to the territorial sovereignty of Eritrea. These islands seem to have fallen under the jurisdiction of the Khedive of Egypt and their proximity to the African coast meant that the portico doctrine suggested that they formed part of Eritrea. In addition, the evidence of the construction and operation of the lighthouse here and the conclusion by Eritrea of petroleum agreements relating to the area around the Haycocks supported the Eritrean claim to sovereignty (pp. 60-9, 124-6 and 139).

(c) *The South West Rocks* were subject to the territorial sovereignty of Eritrea on the basis of historical evidence and proximity to the Eritrean coast (pp. 126 and 139).

(d) The islands, islets, rocks and low-tide elevations of *the Zuqar-Hanish Group* were subject to the territorial sovereignty of Yemen. The appurtenance factor was less significant here as the islands were positioned in the central part of the Red Sea. The legal history did not provide a clear answer. The maps submitted were marginally in Yemen's favour, suggesting a certain widespread repute that these islands belonged to Yemen. Of greater relevance was the evidence of activity in recent times, especially during the decade preceding the conclusion of the Arbitration Agreement. Yemen had constructed and maintained lighthouses in these islands, and had shown evidence of the exercise of sovereignty over the island of Zuqar. The position was less clear cut with regard to Hanish, although even here Yemen had shown evidence of more governmental activity than had Eritrea (pp. 127-34 and 139).

(e) The island of *Jabal al-Tayr* and the islands, islets, rocks and low-tide elevations forming part of *the Zubayr Group* were subject to the territorial sovereignty of Yemen. These islands were a considerable distance from the other islands in dispute and from the coasts of the Parties. The lighthouse history, particularly in recent years, and the petroleum agreements concluded by Yemen together with other relevant factors pointed to the conclusion that, whatever the uncertainties regarding these islands in the past, they were now regarded as part of Yemen (pp. 60-9, 100-14, 134-7 and 139).

(8) Western ideas of territorial sovereignty were strange to peoples brought up in the Islamic tradition and familiar with notions of territory very different from those recognized in contemporary international law. It was also necessary to take account of regional traditions and to render an Award which, in the terms of the Agreement on Principles, would allow the re-establishment and development of trustful and lasting cooperation. The findings of sovereignty were not inimical to, but rather entailed the perpetuation of, the traditional fishing regime in the region. In the exercise of its sovereignty over the islands, Yemen should ensure that the traditional fishing regime, including the free access and enjoyment for fishermen from both Parties, was maintained (pp. 137-9).

(9) The Award should be executed within ninety days (p. 139).

The text of the Award commences on the following page.

AWARD

CONTENTS

CHAPTER I   The Setting up of the Arbitration and the Arguments of the Parties

Introduction

1. This Award is rendered pursuant to an Arbitration Agreement dated 3 October 1996 (the "Arbitration Agreement"), between the Government of the State of Eritrea ("Eritrea") and the Government of the Republic of Yemen ("Yemen") (hereinafter "the Parties").

2. The Arbitration Agreement was preceded by an "Agreement on Principles" done at Paris on 21 May 1996, which was signed by Eritrea and Yemen and witnessed by the Governments of the French Republic, the Federal Democratic Republic of Ethiopia, and the Arab

Republic of Egypt. The Parties renounced recourse to force against each other, and undertook to "settle their dispute on questions of territorial sovereignty and of delimitation of maritime boundaries peacefully". They agreed, to that end, to establish an agreement instituting an arbitral tribunal. The Agreement on Principles further provided that

. . . concerning questions of territorial sovereignty, the Tribunal shall decide in accordance with the principles, rules and practices of international law applicable to the matter, and on the basis, in particular, of historic titles.

3. Concurrently with the Agreement on Principles, the Parties issued a brief Joint Statement, emphasizing their desire to settle the dispute, and "to allow the re-establishment and development of a trustful and lasting cooperation between the two countries", contributing to the stability and peace of the region.

4. In conformity with Article 1.1 of the Arbitration Agreement, Eritrea appointed as arbitrators Judge Stephen M. Schwebel and Judge Rosalyn Higgins, and Yemen appointed Dr Ahmed Sadek El-Kosheri and Mr Keith Highet. By an exchange of letters dated 30 and 31 December 1996, the Parties agreed to recommend the appointment of Professor Sir Robert Y. Jennings as President of the Arbitral Tribunal (hereinafter the "Tribunal"). The four arbitrators met in London on 14 January 1997, and appointed Sir Robert Y. Jennings President of the Tribunal.

5. Having been duly constituted, the Tribunal held its first meeting on 14 January 1997, at Essex Court Chambers, 24 Lincoln's Inn Fields, London WC1, UK. The Tribunal took note of the meeting of the four arbitrators, and ratified and approved the actions authorized and undertaken thereat. Pursuant to Article 7.2 of the Arbitration Agreement, the Tribunal appointed as Registrar Mr P. J. H. Jonkman, Secretary-General of the Permanent Court of Arbitration (the "PCA") at the Hague, and, as Secretary to the Tribunal, Ms Bette E. Shifman, First Secretary of the PCA, and fixed the location of the Tribunal's registry at the International Bureau of the PCA.

6. The Tribunal then held a meeting with Mr Gary Born, Co-Agent of Eritrea, and Mr Rodman Bundy, Co-Agent of Yemen, at which it notified them of the formation of the Tribunal and discussed with them certain practical matters relating to the arbitration proceedings.

7. Article 2 of the Arbitration Agreement provides that:

1. The Tribunal is requested to provide rulings in accordance with international law, in two stages.

2. The first stage shall result in an award on territorial sovereignty and on the definition of the scope of the dispute between Eritrea and Yemen. The Tribunal shall decide territorial sovereignty in accordance with the principles,

rules and practices of international law applicable to the matter, and on the basis, in particular, of historic titles. The Tribunal shall decide on the definition of the scope of the dispute on the basis of the respective positions of the two Parties.

3. The second stage shall result in an award delimiting maritime boundaries. The Tribunal shall decide taking into account the opinion that it will have formed on questions of territorial sovereignty, the United Nations Convention on the Law of the Sea, and any other pertinent factor.

8. Pursuant to the timetable set forth in the Arbitration Agreement for the various stages of the arbitration, the Parties submitted their written Memorials concerning territorial sovereignty and the scope of the dispute simultaneously on 1 September 1997 and their Counter-Memorials on 1 December 1997. In accordance with the requirement of Article 7.1 of the Arbitration Agreement that "the Tribunal shall sit in London", the oral proceedings in the first stage of the arbitration were held in London, in the Durbar Conference Room of the Foreign and Commonwealth Office, from 26 January through 6 February 1998, within the time limits for oral proceedings set forth in the Arbitration Agreement. The order of the Parties' presentations was determined by drawing lots, with Eritrea beginning the oral proceedings.

9. At the end of its session of 6 February 1998, the Tribunal, in accordance with Article 8.3 of the Arbitration Agreement, closed the oral phase of the first stage of the arbitration proceedings between Eritrea and Yemen. The closing of the oral proceedings was subject to the undertaking of both Parties to answer in writing, by 23 February 1998, certain questions put to them by the Tribunal at the end of the hearings, including a question concerning the existence of agreements for petroleum exploration and exploitation. It was also subject to the proviso in Article 8.3 of the Arbitration Agreement authorizing the Tribunal to request the Parties' written views on the elucidation of any aspect of the matters before the Tribunal.

10. In its Communication and Order No 3 of 10 May 1998, the Tribunal invoked this provision, requesting the Parties to provide, by 8 June 1998, written observations on the legal considerations raised by their responses to the Tribunal's earlier questions concerning concessions for petroleum exploration and exploitation and, in particular, on how the petroleum agreements and activities authorized by them might be relevant to the award on territorial sovereignty. The Tribunal further invited the Parties to agree to hold a short oral hearing for the elucidation of these issues.

11. Following the exchange of the Parties' written observations, the Tribunal held oral hearings on this matter at the Foreign and Commonwealth Office in London on 6, 7 and 8 July 1998. By agreement of the Parties, Yemen presented its arguments first. In the course of these hearings, the Tribunal posed a series of questions

concerning the interpretation of concession evidence, and the Parties were requested to respond thereto in writing within seven days of the end of the oral hearings. On 17 July 1998, both Parties submitted their written responses to the Tribunal's questions. Eritrea indicated at that time that it anticipated a brief delay in submission of the documentary appendix accompanying its submission; this documentary appendix was received by the International Bureau of the PCA on 22 July 1998. On 30 July 1998, the International Bureau received from Yemen a submission entitled "Yemen's Comments on the Documents Introduced by Eritrea after the Final Oral Argument". Eritrea objected to this late filing by Yemen.

12. In the course of the supplementary hearings in July 1998, the Tribunal informed the Parties of its intention to contact the Secretary-General of the Arab League, in order to ascertain the existence, and obtain copies, of any official Arab League reports of visits to any of the islands in dispute, particularly in the 1970s. A letter on behalf of the Tribunal was sent by fax to the Secretary-General of the Arab League on 20 July. His response, dated 28 July, was transmitted by the registry to the Co-Agents and the Members of the Tribunal.

Arguments of the Parties on Territorial Sovereignty

13. Eritrea bases its claim to territorial sovereignty over these "Red Sea Islands" (hereinafter the "Islands")[1] on a chain of title extending over more than 100 years, and on international law principles of "effective occupation". Eritrea asserts that it inherited title to the Islands in 1993, when the State of Eritrea became legally independent from the State of Ethiopia. Ethiopia had in turn inherited its title from Italy, despite a period of British military occupation of Eritrea as a whole during the Second World War. The Italian title is claimed then to have vested in the State of Ethiopia in 1952-3, as a consequence of Eritrea's federation with, and subsequent annexation by, Ethiopia.

14. Eritrea traces this chain of title through the relevant historical periods, beginning with the Italian colonization of the Eritrean mainland in the latter part of the nineteenth century. The Parties do not dispute that, prior to Italian colonization, the Ottoman Empire was the unchallenged sovereign over both coasts of the Red Sea and over the Islands. Bypassing the Ottomans and dealing directly with local rulers, Italy established outposts in furtherance of its maritime, colonial and commercial interests. Despite Ottoman objections, it proclaimed the Italian colony of Eritrea in 1890. Eritrea contends that

---

[1] The identification of the specific islands or island groups in dispute between the Parties has been entrusted to the Tribunal by Article 2 of the Arbitration Agreement (see para. 7, above), and is dealt with in the part of this Award dealing with the scope of the dispute. References to "the Islands" in this Award are to those Islands that the Tribunal finds are subject to conflicting claims by the Parties. The geographic area in which these islands are found is indicated on the map which can be found at pp. 140-1.

in 1892 Great Britain recognized Italian title to the Mohabbakah islands, a group of islands proximate to the Eritrean coast.

15. Eritrea asserts that, without challenging Ottoman sovereignty, Italy also maintained an active presence in other southern Red Sea islands at that time. Italian naval vessels patrolled the surrounding waters in search of pirates, slave traders and arms smugglers, and the colonial administration allegedly issued concessions for commercial exploitation on the Islands. According to Eritrea, there was no Yemeni claim to or presence on or around the Islands during this time. The Imam Yahya, who ultimately founded modern Yemen, occupied a highland region known as the *Gebel*, and, according to Eritrea, openly acknowledged his lack of sovereignty over the coastal lowlands known as the *Tihama*. This territorial arrangement was confirmed by the 1911 "Treaty of Da'an", an understanding between the Imam and the Ottoman Empire.

16. Eritrea asserts that the weakening of the Ottoman Empire in the years immediately preceding the First World War fuelled Italian plans to occupy an island group known as the "Zuqar-Hanish islands". These plans were preempted by a brief period of British military occupation in 1915, which was short-lived and, according to Eritrea, without legal consequences. At the end of the War, Italy purportedly renewed and expanded its commercial and regulatory activities with respect to what Eritrea refers to as the "Zuqar-Hanish and lighthouse islands". These activities are cited by Eritrea as evidence of Italy's intent to acquire sovereignty over the Islands.

17. The question of sovereignty over the Islands formed part of the post-First World War peace process that culminated in the signature of the Treaty of Lausanne in 1923. While certain former territory of the defeated Ottoman Empire was divided among local rulers who had supported the victorious Allies, Eritrea contends that none of the Arabian Peninsula leaders who had supported the Allies was in sufficient geographical proximity to the Islands to be considered a plausible recipient. The Imam of Sanaa was not a plausible recipient of the Islands, both because of his alliance with the Ottoman Turks, and because his sovereignty did not extend to the Red Sea coast. Eritrea cites Great Britain's rejection of claims made by the Imam in 1917-18 to parts of the Tihama, and relies on the Imam's character-ization of these territories as having been "under the sway of his predecessors" as acknowledging that the Imam indeed lacked possession and control at that time.

18. Eritrea traces Great Britain's failure to persuade the remaining Allies to transfer the Islands to Arab rulers selected by Great Britain, or to Great Britain itself, through the unratified 1920 Treaty of Sèvres and the negotiations leading up to the conclusion of the Treaty of Lausanne in 1923. Eritrea relies on Articles 6 and 16 of the Treaty of

Lausanne as having left the islands open for Italian occupation. Article 6 established the general rule that, in terms of the Treaty, "islands and islets lying within three miles of the coast are included within the frontier of the coastal State". Eritrea interprets this provision, and subsequent State practice under the Treaty of Lausanne, as withholding the islands in question from *any* Arabian Peninsula leader, because none of the Islands are within three miles of the Arabian coast. Eritrea further argues that the Imam could not have been given the disputed islands pursuant to Article 6, because his realm was neither a "State" nor "coastal" at the time the Treaty of Lausanne was signed.

19. Article 16 of the Treaty of Lausanne contained an express Turkish renunciation of all rights and title to former Ottoman territories and islands, and provided that their future was to be "settled by the parties concerned". Eritrea argues that because Article 16 did not transfer the Islands to any particular State, and did not specify any particular procedure for conveying ownership of the Islands, their ultimate disposition was left to general international law standards for territorial acquisition—conquest, effective occupation, and location within the territorial sea. Eritrea claims to find further support for this in subsequent State practice interpreting Article 16.

20. Eritrea asserts that by the end of the 1920s, Italy had acquired sovereignty over the disputed islands by effective occupation, and that neither the 1927 conversations between Great Britain and Italy, which came to be known as the "Rome Conversations", nor the aborted 1929 Lighthouse Convention were contra-indications. This effective occupation consisted, *inter alia*, of the construction in 1929 of a lighthouse on South West Haycock Island, which Eritrea claims led Great Britain to repeat acknowledgments of Italian sovereignty over the Mohabbakahs, previously made in 1892 and 1917. Eritrea finds further support for effective Italian occupation during this period in the dispatch of an expedition to the Zuqar-Hanish islands and their subsequent occupation by Italian troops. Eritrea asserts that in the period 1930-40 Italy exercised sovereign rights over the Islands through the colonial government in Eritrea. Eritrea cites, *inter alia*, the granting of fishing licences with respect to the surrounding waters, the granting of a licence for the construction of a fish processing plant on Greater Hanish, and the reconstruction and maintenance of an abandoned British lighthouse on Centre Peak Island. These satisfy, in Eritrea's view, the *corpus occupandi* requirement of effective occupation and, accompanied as they were by the requisite sovereign intent (*animus occupandi*), constitute the acquisition of sovereignty by effective occupation.

21. Eritrea further asserts that Yemen did not protest or question Italy's activities on the Islands during this time. Great Britain, however, sought assurances that Italian activities did not constitute a claim of

sovereignty. Eritrea characterizes Italy's responses that the question of sovereignty was "in abeyance" or "in reserve" as a refusal to give such assurances. According to Eritrea, this formula was understood by both Italy and Great Britain as preserving Italy's legal rights while allowing Great Britain to withhold diplomatic recognition of those rights. Tensions between the two States on this and other matters led to conclusion of the 1938 Anglo-Italian Agreement, which Eritrea claims is probative of Italian and British views at that time. It is said to reflect, among other things, the Parties' understanding that the Islands were not appurtenant to the Arabian Peninsula, and that Italy and Great Britain were the only two powers with a cognizable interest in them.

22. The 1938 Anglo-Italian Agreement also contained an express undertaking on the part of both Italy and Great Britain with respect to the former Ottoman Red Sea islands, that neither would "establish its sovereignty" or "erect fortifications or defences". This constituted, in Eritrea's view, not a relinquishment of existing rights, but simply a covenant regarding future conduct. Eritrea argues that, at the time of the Anglo-Italian Agreement, Italy's sovereignty over the Islands had already been established as a matter of law, and it remained unaffected by the agreement. Eritrea further asserts that in December of 1938, Italy formally confirmed its existing territorial sovereignty over the Islands by promulgating decree number 1446 of 1938, specifically confirming that the Islands had been, and continued to be, part of the territory of the Eritrean *Commissariato* of Dankalia.

23. Eritrea characterizes the eleven-year British occupation of Eritrea that commenced in 1941 in the wake of the Second World War as congruent with the law of belligerent occupation. Eritrea's territorial boundaries remained unchanged, and the territory of "all Italian colonies and dependencies" surrendered to the Allies in the 1943 Armistice "indisputably included", in Eritrea's view, the Islands. The 1947 Treaty of Peace provided for disposition of Italy's African territories by the Allied Powers, which was accomplished in 1952 by the transfer to Ethiopia, with which Eritrea was then federated, of "all former Italian territorial possessions in Eritrea". This marked, in Eritrea's view, the passing to Ethiopia of sovereign title to the Islands.

24. Eritrea claims that the drafting history of the 1952 Eritrean Constitution confirms the inclusion of the disputed islands within the definition of Eritrean territory. This is, according to Eritrea, the only plausible interpretation of the phrase "Eritrea, including the islands" in the definition of the territory of Eritrea, and it is said to be supported by advice given to Ethiopia at the time by its legal adviser, John Spencer. Eritrea claims that this was further reinforced by similar language in subsequent constitutional and legislative provisions, in particular, the 1952 Imperial Decree federating Eritrea into the Ethiopian Empire, and the 1955 Ethiopian Constitution.

25. Another basis for Ethiopian sovereignty put forward by Eritrea is the inclusion of the Islands within Ethiopia's territorial sea. Eritrea relies on the rule of international customary and conventional law that every island is entitled to its own territorial sea, measured in accordance with the same principles as those applicable to the mainland. In Eritrea's view, a chain of islands linked to the mainland with gaps no wider than twelve miles falls entirely within the coastal State's territorial sea and therefore under its territorial sovereignty. Thus, measuring from the Mohabbakah islands, which Eritrea asserts were indisputably Ethiopian, Ethiopia's 1953 declaration of a 12-mile territorial sea encompassed the Zuqar-Hanish islands.

26. The 35-year period between 1953 and Eritrean independence in 1991 is characterized by Eritrea as one of extensive exercise of Ethiopian sovereignty over the Islands. This allegedly included continuous, unchallenged naval patrols, which became increasingly systematic as the Eritrean Liberation Movement gathered strength. In addition, following transfer of the administration of the lighthouses to Asmara by the British Board of Trade in 1967, Ethiopia is said to have further consolidated its sovereignty by requiring foreign workers on the lighthouse islands to carry passports and similar documents, overseeing and regulating the dispatch of all provisions to the lighthouse islands, being involved in all employment decisions affecting lighthouse workers, approving all inspection and repair visits to the lighthouse islands, and tightly controlling radio transmissions to and from the lighthouse islands. Other alleged acts of Ethiopian sovereignty put forward by Eritrea include the exercise of criminal jurisdiction over acts committed on the Islands, regulation of oil exploration activities on and around the Islands, and an inspection by then President Mengistu and a group of high-ranking Ethiopian military and naval personnel during the late 1980s, for which Eritrea has submitted videotape evidence.

27. Eritrea claims that throughout the 1970s the two Yemeni States and their regional allies acknowledged Ethiopian control over the Islands by their statements and actions. It alleges that, until the early 1970s, neither North Yemen nor South Yemen had displayed any interest in the Islands. Regional interest in the Islands is said to have been sparked by false reports of an Israeli presence there in 1973. According to Eritrea, the presumption on the part of Yemen, its neighbouring States and the Arab media that Ethiopia had leased the Islands to Israel constituted an acknowledgment of Ethiopian sovereignty. In support, Eritrea claims that the Arab States not only condemned Ethiopia for having made Ethiopian islands available to Israel, but also looked ultimately to Ethiopia for permission to visit the Islands in order to investigate the allegations of Israeli military activity.

28. Eritrea contends that the final years before Eritrean independence

were marked by aerial surveillance and continuous naval patrols by Ethiopian forces.

29. Eritrea claims that, after winning its independence in 1991, it acquired sovereign title to the Islands and exercised sovereign authority over them. Eritrea asserts that, as they have been throughout recent history, Eritrean fishermen are dependent upon the Islands for their livelihood. Eritrean administrative regulations are said strictly to control fishing around the Islands, prescribing licensing and other requirements for fishing in the surrounding waters. Eritrea further contends that its vessels police foreign fishing vessels in Eritrean territorial waters, and routinely patrol the waters around the Islands in order to enforce fishing regulations, seizing vessels that fail to comply. It asserts that Yemen did not maintain any official presence in the Islands, and that it was only in 1995 that Eritrean naval patrols discovered a small Yemeni military and civilian contingent purportedly engaged in work on a tourist resort on Greater Hanish Island. This led, in December 1995, to hostilities that ended with Eritrean forces occupying Greater Hanish Island, and Yemeni forces occupying Zuqar.

30. With respect to territorial sovereignty, Eritrea seeks from the Tribunal an award declaring that Eritrea possesses territorial sovereignty over each of the "islands, rocks and low-tide elevations" specified by Eritrea in its written pleadings, "as to which Yemen claims sovereignty".

* * *

31. Yemen, in turn, bases its claim to the Islands on "original, historic, or traditional Yemeni title". Yemen puts particular emphasis on the stipulation in Article 2.2 of the Arbitration Agreement, that "[t]he Tribunal shall decide territorial sovereignty in accordance with the principles, rules and practices of international law applicable to the matter, and on the basis, in particular, of historic titles". This title can, according to Yemen, be traced to the *Bilad el-Yemen*, or realm of Yemen, which is said to have existed as early as the sixth century AD. Yemen advances, in support of this claim, map evidence,[2] declarations by the Imam of Yemen, and what it refers to as "the attitude of third States over a long period".

32. Yemen contends that its incorporation into the Ottoman Empire, from 1538 to *circa* 1635, and again from 1872 to the Ottoman defeat in 1918, did not deprive it of historic title to its territory. Yemen

---

[2] Although Eritrea has also submitted cartographic evidence showing the Islands to be Ethiopian, Eritrean or, in any event, not Yemeni, it places relatively little weight on this type of evidence. Eritrea takes the position that maps do not constitute direct evidence of sovereignty or of a chain of title, thereby relegating them to a limited role in resolving these types of disputes.

asserts that the creation of the Ottoman *vilayet* of Yemen as a separate territorial and administrative unit constituted Ottoman recognition of Yemen's separate identity. It relies on the work of seventeenth-, eighteenth- and nineteenth-century cartographers who allegedly depicted Yemen as a separate, identifiable territorial entity. Further map evidence is adduced in support of Yemen's contention that the Islands form part of that territory.

33. In further support of its assertions that Yemen maintained historic title to the Islands, Yemen retraces the drafting history of its 1934 Treaty with Great Britain, citing several exchanges of correspondence in which the Imam insisted, in one form or another, on his rights to the "Islands of the Yemen". Yemen cites Great Britain's rejection of the Imam's proposal to attach to the Treaty a secret appendix concerning the Islands, on the grounds that the Islands, as former Ottoman possessions, were to be dealt with pursuant to Article 16 of the Treaty of Lausanne.

34. Yemen argues that this did not constitute a denial of traditional Yemeni title, and puts forward documents that it claims support the characterization of British official opinion in the period 1933 to 1937 as being reluctant to challenge Yemeni title. Yemen further contends that the Treaty of Lausanne had no effect on Yemeni title, because Yemen was not a party to the Treaty, and because Turkey's renunciation of rights could not prejudice the interests of third parties. Yemen takes the view that the effect of Article 16 was not to make the Islands *terra nullius*, but rather, territory "the title to which was undetermined". Yemen argues in addition that Article 16 has, in any event, ceased to have effect between "the parties concerned", because of their own conduct, and that of third States, in recognizing, or failing to make reservations concerning, Yemen's sovereignty in respect of the Islands.

35. Another ground put forward in support of Yemen's claim that its original title extends to the Islands is "the principle of natural or geographical unity". Yemen argues that this doctrine is a corollary of the concept of traditional title, and that it operates in conjunction with evidence of the exercise of acts of jurisdiction or manifestations of State sovereignty. Yemen cites case-law of the International Court of Justice and arbitral decisions in support of the premise that once the sovereignty of an entity or natural unity as a whole has been shown to exist, it may be deemed, in the absence of any evidence to the contrary, to extend to all parts of that entity or unity. According to Yemen, there is a "concordance of expert opinion evidence on the character of the islands as an entity or natural unity", including British admiralty charts, the *Red Sea and Gulf of Aden Pilot*, produced by the United Kingdom Hydrographic Office, and the *Encyclopedia Britannica*.

36. Yemen relies on various categories of evidence of sovereignty,

which it asserts may serve to confirm and supplement the evidence of traditional or historic title, as well as constituting independent sources of title. These include economic and social links between the Islands and the Yemeni mainland, the exercise of sovereignty in the form of acts of jurisdiction, recognition of Yemen's title by third States, and confirmation of Yemeni title by expert opinion evidence.

37. Yemen cites case-law and commentary in support of its contention that, within the appropriate geographical context, the private activities of individual persons constitute relevant evidence of historic title to territory. Yemen's analysis of these facts and activities begins with the names "Hanish" and "Zuqar", which, it asserts, have Arabic roots. Yemen also notes the presence on the Yemeni coast of inhabitants with names derived from the word "Hanish", and a family history, as fishermen, intertwined with that of the Islands. Yemen points out that, during the disturbances of 1995, two members of such a family were taken prisoner by Eritrean forces while fishing near Greater Hanish Island. Yemen also alleges the existence of anchorages and settlements on the Islands bearing distinctly Yemeni Arabic names. Yemen claims that, for generations, Yemeni fishermen have enjoyed virtually exclusive use of the Islands, even establishing, in contrast to Eritrean fishermen, permanent and semi-permanent residence there.

38. Yemen further asserts that the Islands are home to a number of Yemeni holy sites and shrines, including the tombs of several venerated holy men. It points to a shrine used primarily by fishermen, who have developed a tradition of leaving unused provisions in the tomb to sustain their fellow fishermen.

39. In addition, Yemen points out that the Islands fall within the jurisdiction of a traditional system of resolving disputes between fishermen, in which a kind of arbitrator may "ride the circuit" along the coast and among the Islands, in order to insure access to justice for those fishermen who are unable to travel.

40. Yemen emphasizes the economic links between the Islands and the Yemeni fishermen who rely for their livelihood on them and their surrounding waters, and who sell their catch almost exclusively on the Yemeni mainland. Yemen contrasts this with the situation of the Eritrean fishermen, pointing out that, because of the difficulty of hygienic transport of fish to the interior of Eritrea (including the capital of Asmara), Eritrea lacks a fish-eating tradition. According to Yemen, most Eritrean fishermen find a better market for their wares on the Yemeni coast. Yemen asserts that for centuries, the long-standing, intensive and virtually exclusive use of the Islands by Yemeni fishermen did not meet with interference from other States.

41. Yemen provides an historical review of alleged Yemeni acts of administration and control, which are said to supplement and confirm

Yemen's historic title to the Islands, as well as forming independent, mutually reinforcing sources of that title. The earliest of these acts, a mission sent to Jabal Zuqar by the King of Yemen in 1429 to investigate smuggling, predates Ottoman rule. In the Ottoman period, Yemen asserts that the Islands were considered part of the *vilayet* of Yemen, and that the Ottoman administration handled, *inter alia*, tax, security, and maritime matters relating to the Islands. Yemen cites an 1881 lighthouse concession by the Ottoman authorities to a private French company, for the construction of lighthouses throughout the Empire, which included some of the islands in the *vilayet* of Yemen. Yemen also cites nineteenth-century Ottoman maps and annual reports, which place the Islands within the *vilayet* of Yemen.

42. Yemen emphasizes that the post-Ottoman British presence on the Islands was intermittent, and that Great Britain never claimed sovereignty over them. Following establishment of the Yemen Arab Republic in 1962, its Government allegedly asserted legislative jurisdiction over the Islands on at least two occasions. Yemen claims that its navy conducted exercises on and around the Islands, and that its armed forces played a key role in confirming the absence of Israeli troops on the Islands in 1973. In Yemen's rendition of the events surrounding the 1973 incident, the Islands are consistently characterized as Yemeni, rather than Ethiopian.

43. Yemen cites a number of examples of the issuance of licences to foreign entities wishing to engage in scientific, tourist and commercial activities in and around the Islands, and of the granting of permits for anchorage. Yemen presents evidence concerning the authorization given to a German company by the Yemeni Ministry of Culture and Tourism and the Yemen General Investment Authority in 1995 for the construction of a luxury hotel and diving centre on Greater Hanish Island. Yemen further asserts that it exercised jurisdiction over the Islands in respect of fishing, environmental protection, the installation and maintenance of geodetic stations, and the construction and administration of lighthouses, including the publication of relevant Notices to Mariners. Yemen has placed in evidence elaborate chronological surveys, covering a variety of time periods, of alleged Yemeni activities "in and around the Hanish Group".

44. Yemen contends that from 1887 to 1989, at least six States confirmed, by their conduct or otherwise, Yemen's title to the Islands. Yemen points out that upon conclusion of the Anglo-Italian Agreement of 1938, which Eritrea characterizes as being limited to future conduct, the Italian Government informed the Imam of Yemen that, pursuant to the agreement, Italy had undertaken not to extend its sovereignty on or to fortify the "Hanish Island group", and that it had, in the negotiations, "kept in mind . . . above all Yemen's interests". Yemen claims to find further acknowledgment of Yemeni rights in

British practice and "internal thinking", as reflected in Foreign Office and Colonial Office documents of the 1930s and 1940s. French recognition of Yemeni title is said to include a request for permission to conduct military manoeuvres in the Southern Red Sea in 1975, and for a French oceanographic vessel to conduct activities near the Islands in 1976.

45. Yemen attributes similar evidentiary value to German conduct and publications, and to official maps published by the United States Army and Central Intelligence Agency, as recently as 1993. Yemen offers evidence of what it terms "revealing changes in Ethiopian cartography" in support of its contention that Ethiopia did not claim title to the Islands. It relies particularly on Ethiopian maps from 1978, 1982, 1984 and 1985, on which all or some of the Islands appear, by their colouring, to be allocated to Yemen.

46. Yemen also puts forward cartographic evidence on which it relies as official and unofficial expert evidence of Yemeni title to the Islands. Such evidence serves, according to Yemen, as proof of geographical facts and the state of geographical knowledge at a particular period. Yemen supplements this cartographic evidence with the published works of historians and other professionals.

47. Yemen gives an historical review of this evidence, beginning with seventeenth- and eighteenth-century maps depicting the independent *Bilad el-Yemen*. Yemen asserts that while some eighteenth-century maps fail to depict the Islands accurately, the more accurate of these attribute them to Yemen. Yemen places great emphasis on writings and maps reflecting the first-hand impressions of Carsten Niebuhr, a Danish scientist and explorer who visited the Red Sea coast from 1761 to 1764. Niebuhr's works suggest political affiliation and other links between the Islands and the Yemeni mainland.

48. Yemen further submits in evidence a large number of nineteenth and twentieth-century maps, of varied origin, the colouring of which appears to attribute all or some of the Islands to Yemen. At the same time, it did not deny that certain Yemeni maps attribute the Islands to Ethiopia or Eritrea; or at least not to Yemen.

49. In addition to proffering cartographic and other evidence in support of its assertions of historic title to the Islands, Yemen argues that, until the events of December 1995, Ethiopian and Eritrean conduct was consistent with Yemeni sovereignty. Yemen alleges that as recently as November 1995, Eritrea acknowledged in an official communiqué to the President of Yemen that the Islands had ". . . been ignored and abandoned for many years since colonial times, including the eras of Haile Selassie and Mengistu, and during the long war of liberation".

50. Yemen insists that, during the Ottoman period, the Islands were consistently administered as part of the *vilayet* of Yemen, and that title

never passed to Italy during the period of Italian colonization of the Eritrean mainland. Yemen cites several occasions on which, in its view, Italy had declined to claim sovereignty. These include exchanges between the British and Italian Governments in the late 1920s and 1930s and culminated in the 1938 Anglo-Italian Agreement which amounts, in Yemen's view, to a definitive agreement by both Parties not to establish sovereignty over islands with respect to which Turkey had renounced sovereignty by Article 16 of the Treaty of Lausanne. Yemen interprets Italian decree number 1446 of 20 December 1938 not as a confirmation of existing territorial sovereignty but rather as a mere "internal decree providing for the administration of the islands to be undertaken from the Assab department of Eritrea".

51. Yemen argues further that the phrase "the territory of Eritrea including the islands" in the 1952 UN-drafted Eritrean Constitution does not refer to the disputed islands, because the official Report of the United Nations Commission for Eritrea, prepared in 1950, indicates Yemeni title to the Islands, by depicting them in the same colour as the Yemeni mainland on UN maps accompanying the Report. Yemen contests all Eritrean allegations of Ethiopian acts of sovereignty or administration, and asserts that Ethiopian conduct, particularly its publication of official maps on which the Islands were the same colour as the Yemeni mainland, constituted recognition of Yemeni sovereignty over the Islands.

52. According to Yemen, while Yemeni fishermen historically fished around the Islands and used them for temporary residence, Yemen exercised a wide array of State activities on and around them. These activities are alleged to have included, during the 1970s, the consideration of requests by foreign nationals to carry out marine and scientific research on the islands, periodic visits of Yemeni military officials to Greater Hanish and Jabal Zuqar, and related patrols on and around these islands. Yemen also claims to have protested the conduct of low-level military flights by France over the Hanish islands, as well as Ethiopia's arrest of Yemeni fishermen in the vicinity of the Islands, and further asserts that it investigated a number of lost or damaged foreign vessels around Greater Hanish and Jabal Zuqar.

53. With respect to the 1980s and 1990s, Yemen alleges that various Yemeni air force and naval reconnaissance missions were conducted over and around the Islands. Yemen also asserts that it granted licences allowing nationals of third States to visit the certain islands for scientific purposes and tourism, and that some of these visitors were accompanied by Yemeni officials. In 1988, Yemen is said to have embarked on a project to upgrade and build a series of lighthouses, accompanied by Notices to Mariners, on Centre Peak Island, Jabal al-Tayr, Lesser Hanish Island, Abu Ali, Jabal Zuqar and Greater Hanish Island. Yemen also claims to have erected geodetic stations on

Greater Hanish and Jabal Zuqar and authorized construction of a landing strip on Greater Hanish, which was used frequently in the early 1990s. Yemen also contends that, during this period, it continued its patrols of the islands, arresting foreign fishermen and confiscating vessels found operating in waters around the islands without a Yemeni licence.

54. With respect to territorial sovereignty, Yemen seeks from the Tribunal an award declaring "that the Republic of Yemen possesses territorial sovereignty over all of the islands comprising the Hanish Group of islands . . . as defined in chapters 2 and 5 of Yemen's Memorial".

Arguments of the Parties on the Relevance of Petroleum Agreements and Activities

55. In response to specific questions from the Tribunal, which were dealt with in supplemental written pleadings, at resumed oral hearings in July 1998, and in post-hearing written submissions, both Parties have presented evidence of offshore concession activity in the Red Sea. Yemen contends that its record of granting offshore concessions over the last fifty years reinforces and complements a consistent pattern of evidence indicating Yemeni title to the islands. As the granting of oil concessions serves to confirm and maintain an existing Yemeni title, rather than furnishing evidence of effective occupation, it need not, in Yemen's view, be supported by evidence of express claims. This is said to be congruent with Yemen's assertions of historic title.

56. In evidence of what it terms "longstanding and peaceful administration of its petroleum resources" on and around the Islands, Yemen has submitted agreements and maps concerning concession blocks granted or offered since 1974. One of these concession blocks (Tomen) encompasses some of the Islands, in this case, the "Hanish Group", while another (Adair) is bounded by a line that cuts through Greater Hanish. Yemen further relies on a 1991 hydrocarbon study of the Red Sea and Gulf of Eden regions carried out by the United Nations Development Program (UNDP) and the World Bank. As this study enjoyed the participation of the governments concerned, particularly Ethiopia and successive Yemeni governments, Yemen relies on it as a useful overview of petroleum activities undertaken by the two States from the early 1950s.

57. Yemen relies on both case-law (in particular the *Eastern Greenland* case[3]) and scholarly writing in support of its assertion that the granting of exploration permits and concessions constitutes evidence of title, addressing such evidentiary categories as: the attitude of the grantor State, its grant and regulation of the operation of the concession, ancillary government-approved operations, and the attitude of the

---

[3] *Legal Status of Eastern Greenland (Denmark v. Norway)*, 1933 PCIJ (Ser. A/B) No 53 [6 *Ann Dig* 95].

concessionaire and of international agencies. In addition, Yemen derives from the absence of protests evidence of Ethiopian and Eritrean acquiescence.

58. Yemen invokes the presumption that a State granting an oil concession does so in respect of areas over which it has title or sovereign rights. The activity of offering and granting concessions with respect to blocks that encompass or approach the Islands constitutes, in Yemen's view, a clear manifestation of Yemeni sovereignty over the Islands. Yemen cites, in addition, express reservations, in the relevant agreements, of Yemeni title to the concession areas. In addition to demonstrating Yemen's attitude regarding title, the granting of these economic concessions to private companies is said to constitute evidence of the exercise of sovereignty in respect of the territory concerned. Yemen finds additional evidence of the exercise of sovereignty in Yemen's monitoring and regulation of the operations undertaken by the various concessionaires and the granting of permits for ancillary operations such as seismic reconnaissance.

59. Yemen further argues that a company will not enter into a concession with a State for the development of petroleum resources unless it is persuaded that the area covered by the concession, and the underlying resources, in fact belong to that State. Furthermore, the reservations of Yemeni title in the concession agreements submitted by Yemen are said to constitute express recognition by the concessionaires of Yemeni title to the blocks concerned. The UNDP/World Bank study constitutes, in Yemen's view, recognition of Yemeni title by these international agencies, as well as expert evidence to the same effect.

60. Yemen also proffers the UNDP/World Bank study as evidence of Ethiopian acquiescence. Because the study was prepared in collaboration with, and ultimately distributed to, all concerned governments, Ethiopia can, in Yemen's view, be held to have had notice of the existence and scope of Yemeni concessions implicating the Islands, without issuing any protests. Yemen relies further on other maps and reports published in the professional petroleum literature, of which it asserts Ethiopia and Eritrea should have been aware.

61. Finally, Yemen asserts that Ethiopian and Eritrean petroleum activities did not encompass or touch upon the Islands, and therefore provide no support for a claim of sovereignty. Despite this, Yemen alleges that it consistently made timely protests with respect to those Ethiopian concessions that, in Yemen's view, encroached in any manner upon its territorial sea, continental shelf and exclusive economic zone.

62. Eritrea, in turn, proffers evidence of offshore petroleum activities, conducted primarily by Ethiopia, at a time at which, it alleges, "Ethiopia's title was already established". Eritrea cites oil-exploration related activities "on the islands" as confirming Ethiopia's

pre-existing claim to sovereignty, which could not, in its view, be divested by Yemen's unilateral grants of offshore mineral concessions. Eritrea also argues that, in the absence of any physical manifestation of control either on islands or in their territorial waters, the mere granting of concessions by Yemen would not suffice to establish title through effective occupation, "even if the islands had been previously unowned".

63. According to Eritrea, the concession evidence put forward by Yemen is irrelevant, because it represents unilateral attempts by Yemen to establish permanent rights to the seabed, in violation of customary international law and the United Nations Convention on the Law of the Sea (the "Law of the Sea Convention"). Yemen's concession agreements are further said to be irrelevant because they were entered into only after the present dispute arose, were not accompanied by Yemeni government activities, and did not pertain to the territory in dispute. Eritrea also questions the factual accuracy of Yemen's allegations concerning concession agreements, pointing to Yemen's failure to submit in evidence copies of certain of these agreements.

64. Eritrea argues that, under both the Law of the Sea Convention and customary international law, mineral rights to the seabed can neither be acquired nor lost through the unilateral appropriation of one competing claimant. Pending agreement with the opposite coastal State, Yemen was, in Eritrea's view, entitled only to issue concessions on a provisional basis. If the alleged concessions could not effectively confer the very mineral rights with which they purported to deal, they could not indirectly settle the question of sovereignty over the Islands. According to Eritrea, petroleum concessions are relevant only where they demonstrate the existence of a mutually recognized de facto boundary line. There had, in this case, been no attempt by Yemen to reach mutual agreement with Ethiopia or Eritrea.

65. Eritrea contends that the provisional character of any concessions issued by Yemen is derived not only from Article 87(3) of the Law of the Sea Convention, which permits the provisional granting of concessions, provided this does not prejudice a final delimitation, but also from Yemen's own continental shelf legislation, adopted in 1977, which provides that "pending agreement on the demarcation of the marine boundaries, the limits of territorial sea, the contiguous zone, the exclusive economic zone . . . shall not be extended to more than the median or equidistance line".

66. Eritrea further asserts that Yemen's offshore concessions were issued after 1973, with full knowledge of Ethiopia's sovereignty claims to the Islands. This is claimed not only to have implications for the delimitation of the surrounding seabed, but to limit as well the evidentiary value of Yemen's concession evidence in resolving the question of sovereignty.

67. Thus Eritrea argues that the post-1973 grant of concessions by Yemen reflects attempts to manufacture contacts with the disputed islands. This is further supported, in Eritrea's view, by the lack of any related Yemeni State activity pertaining specifically to the territory in dispute. According to Eritrea, concessions can be brought to bear on the question of territorial acquisition in two ways. The first is exemplified by the deep-sea fishing concession granted by Italy to the *Cannata* company in the 1930s, which led *inter alia* to construction of a commercial fishing station on Greater Hanish Island. According to Eritrea, the *Cannata* concession was accompanied by the direct involvement of State officials, including Italian troops stationed on the island.

68. Another way in which concessions may be relevant to territorial acquisition is that reflected in the *Eastern Greenland* case. *Eastern Greenland* does not, in Eritrea's reading, necessarily require the physical presence of a particular State official, but rather activities by individuals who, while not themselves employees of the State, act under colour of State law. Eritrea cites doctrine in support of its position that the concession activity of private individuals is relevant only when it involves some kind of real assertion of authority, since "the exercise or display must be genuine and not a mere paper claim dressed up as an act of sovereignty". Eritrea argues that the scope of Yemeni and private activity with respect to petroleum concessions "does not approach the quality and significance of Ethiopia's long-standing pattern of governmental activities on and around the disputed islands". Eritrea further asserts that the few concession agreements actually placed in evidence by Yemen ultimately bear little or no relationship to the islands in dispute.

69. In addition, Eritrea characterizes much of Yemen's petroleum activity as pertaining to "marine scientific research", rather than economic exploitation. Article 241 of the Law of the Sea Convention expressly precludes marine scientific research activities from constituting the legal basis for any claim to any part of the marine environment or its resources.

70. Eritrea argues that its failure to protest Yemeni concessions does not amount to acquiescence, particularly in light of military and political upheaval in Ethiopia during the relevant period. Eritrea has submitted evidence aimed at demonstrating that the 1991 UNDP/World Bank report relied on by Yemen as evidence of notice to Ethiopia may never have been received by Ethiopia, embroiled as it then was in the fall of the Mengistu regime and the end of the civil war. And even if it had been ultimately received, Eritrea posits that in 1991, knowing it would soon lose its entire coastline to the soon-to-be independent Eritrea, Ethiopia would have had no reason to protest Yemeni concessions.

71. Even if it had had actual notice of some or all of Yemen's

concessions, Eritrea contends that it was entitled to rely on their being provisional under Article 87(3) of the Law of the Sea Convention and under Yemen's own 1977 continental shelf legislation.

72. Finally, at the oral hearings in London in July 1998, Eritrea produced evidence of a 1989 Ethiopian concession agreement which, in its view, included at least some of the Islands, notably Greater Hanish, on which Eritrea relies as evidence of related activities which are said to have taken place on Greater Hanish Island, including the placement of beacons. Moreover, it has introduced evidence of publication in 1985 of a series of maps, one of which is entitled "Petroleum Potential of Ethiopia" and purports to encompass a block of the Red Sea that includes the Hanish islands.

CHAPTER II   The Scope of the Dispute

73. The Arbitration Agreement seeks from the Tribunal an award "on the definition of the scope of the dispute between Eritrea and Yemen". It further instructs the Tribunal to decide on the definition of the scope of the dispute "on the basis of the respective positions of the two Parties".

74. The Parties agree that this provision was included in the Arbitration Agreement as a result of the Parties' inability to reach agreement on the definition of the scope of the dispute. According to Eritrea, at the time of the military confrontation in late 1995, which resulted in an Eritrean military occupation of Greater Hanish and some of the small surrounding islands and the Republic of Yemen's military occupation of Zuqar Island, Eritrea wished to seek a determination of all respective Eritrean and Yemeni claims, either by international arbitration or adjudication. Yemen would not agree to such a submission, insisting instead, as Eritrea relates it, on limiting the scope of the dispute to Eritrea's alleged illegal occupation of Hanish Island. Because neither Party wanted this disagreement on scope to prevent the conclusion of the Agreement on Principles and subsequent Arbitration Agreement, they agreed to leave the determination of scope to the Tribunal.

75. In Eritrea's interpretation of the phrase "the respective positions of the Parties", both Parties are free to put forth and elaborate on their positions concerning the scope of the dispute at any point in the proceedings. Eritrea purports to have done so by including in its Memorial, submitted on 1 September 1997, a non-exhaustive list of "islands, rocks and low-tide elevations" with respect to which it asserts territorial sovereignty, and requesting the Tribunal to rule that the scope of the dispute includes each of these specified "islands, rocks and low-tide elevations". Eritrea insists that as its position with regard to scope has not altered over time, the time at which it was determined is

irrelevant. While indicating that it had not expected Yemen to claim the Mohabbakah islands, Eritrea has expressed willingness to defend its claim to the Mohabbakahs: i.e., to consider them encompassed by the scope of the dispute. Eritrea further asserts that Yemen was, in fact, aware of Eritrean claims to Jabal Al-Tayr and the Zubayr group.

76. Yemen, however, puts forward the view that "the respective positions of the Parties" are to be determined at the date of the Agreement on Principles (21 May 1996). Yemen submits that "the task of the Tribunal is to determine the extent to which there was a dispute between the Parties over certain islands in the Red Sea and their maritime limitation as of that date". According to Yemen, the respective positions of the Parties at that date reflected their mutual understanding that Jabal Al-Tayr and the Zubayr group of islands were not considered to fall within the scope of the dispute. Yemen characterizes the scope of the dispute as involving "the Hanish Group of Islands", comprising—in its view—Abu Ali island, Jabal Zuqar, Greater and Lesser Hanish, Suyul Hanish, the various small islets and rocks that surround them, the South West Rocks, the Haycocks and the Mohabbakahs. It asserts that the "Northern Islands" of Jabal Al-Tayr and the Zubayr group were never in dispute between the Parties, and were not reflected in Eritrea's "position" until 1 September 1997, the date of filing of the Parties' Memorials, and thus fell outside the scope of the dispute.

77. The Parties' divergent positions on the substance of the dispute are reflected in a document dated 29 February 1996, entitled "French Memorandum for Yemen and Eritrea". In the aftermath of the December 1995 hostilities, Eritrea and Yemen had, on advice from the UN Secretary-General, invited the French Government to "contribute to the seeking of a peaceful settlement of the dispute between them in the Red Sea". This memorandum was the result of three diplomatic missions to the region, consisting of in-depth talks with the representatives of the two Governments, and it led to the subsequent conclusion between the Parties of the Agreement on Principles, in May 1996, and the Arbitration Agreement, in October 1997.

78. As described in the French memorandum, "[t]he problem raised is as follows. According to Eritrea the dispute concerns at present not only the island of Great Hanish which underwent the events we know about in autumn 1995, but also all of the Hanish-Zucur archipelagoes, particularly the island of Djebel Zucur, since Yemen has stationed troops there whereas these archipelagoes come under Eritrean sovereignty". With respect to the Yemeni position, the French memorandum continues: "According to Yemen this dispute concerns the island of Greater Hanish, where Eritrea has sent troops, but cannot concern the Hanish-Zucur archipelagoes in their totality,

particularly the island of Djebel Zucur, since they come under Yemeni sovereignty."

79. The French mediator therefore proposed that the arbitral tribunal be asked "to provide rulings on the questions of territorial sovereignty, as well as delimitation of maritime boundaries, in a zone defined for example by geographical coordinates". This definition would, according to a French Draft Agreement on Principles dated 29 February 1996, take into account "the undisputed sovereignty of either Party on islands and rocks, such as, for example, the Dahlak Islands for Eritrea, or the Zubair Islands for Yemen". This proposal was rejected by the Parties, in favour of leaving the determination of the scope of the dispute to the arbitral tribunal.

80. Article 1 of the Agreement on Principles of 21 May 1996 provides:

. . .

1.2 They shall request the Tribunal to provide rulings in accordance with international law in two stages:
   a) in the first stage, on the definition of the scope of the dispute between Eritrea and Yemen, on the basis of the respective positions of the two parties;
   b) in the second stage, and after having decided on the point mentioned in letter a) above, on:
      i) questions of territorial sovereignty,
      ii) questions of delimitation of maritime boundaries.
2. They commit themselves to abide by the decision of the Tribunal.

81. Article 2 of the Arbitration Agreement, however, provides as follows:

1. The Tribunal is requested to provide rulings in accordance with international law, in two stages.
2. The first stage shall result in an award on territorial sovereignty and on the definition of the scope of the dispute between Eritrea and Yemen. The Tribunal shall decide territorial sovereignty in accordance with the principles, rules and practices of international law applicable to the matter, and on the basis, in particular, of historic titles. The Tribunal shall decide on the definition of the scope of the dispute on the basis of the respective positions of the two Parties.
3. The second stage shall result in an award delimiting maritime boundaries. The Tribunal shall decide taking into account the opinion that it will have formed on questions of territorial sovereignty, the United Nations Convention on the Law of the Sea, and any other pertinent factor.

82. Article 15 of the same Arbitration Agreement also provides:

1. Nothing in this Arbitration Agreement can be interpreted as being detrimental to the legal positions or to the rights of each Party with respect to

the questions submitted to the Tribunal, nor can affect or prejudice the decision of the Arbitral Tribunal or the considerations and grounds on which those decisions are based.

2. In the event of any inconsistency between the Agreement on Principles and this Arbitration Agreement implementing the procedural aspects of that Agreement on Principles, this Arbitration Agreement shall control. Except with respect to such inconsistency, the Agreement on Principles shall continue in force.

83. Since there is indeed in this respect an inconsistency between the Agreement on Principles and the Arbitration Agreement, under Article 15(2) of the Arbitration Agreement the provisions of the latter prevail to the extent of the inconsistency. The Tribunal must therefore decide the question of scope, as well as the resulting questions of sovereignty, in the present first stage of the proceedings.

84. This decision on scope has to be made "on the basis of the respective positions of the two Parties", and on this point the provisions of the two agreements are identical. It is apparent, however, from the submissions of the Parties in their written pleadings and in their oral presentations for the first stage that the positions of the two Parties differ with respect to the scope of the arbitration. Eritrea's position is that the scope includes all the islands of the Zuqar-Hanish chain, the Haycocks and the Mohabbakahs, and also the northern islands of Jabal al-Tayr and the Zubayr group. Yemen, however, though claiming all the islands of the Zuqar-Hanish chain, including, in their view, the Haycocks and the Mohabbakahs, does not concede that the northern islands are in dispute in this arbitration.

85. The contention of Yemen, as mentioned above, is that the respective positions of the two Parties at the time of the Agreement on Principles (21 May 1996) were different from what they became at the time of the subsequent Arbitration Agreement (3 October 1996). According to Yemen, at the time of the Agreement on Principles, Eritrea was apparently not seeking to claim the northern islands or to bring them within the scope of the arbitration, although it may be noted that there was already an existing dispute over the northern islands.[4] It seems clear, moreover, that Yemen, at the time of the Agreement on Principles, was not claiming the Mohabbakahs.

86. But, according to Yemen, the date of the Agreement on Principles is "the critical date" for the determination by the Tribunal of the "respective positions of the two Parties" on which the scope of the Arbitration is to be decided, because it was the date of the

[4] In a letter dated 4 January 1996, Yemen formally protested an Eritrean oil concession to the Andarko Company which, according to Yemen, constituted "a blatant violation of Yemeni sovereignty over its territorial waters in so far as it extends to the exclusive territorial waters of the Yemeni Jabal al-Tayr and al-Zubayr islands, in addition to the violation of the rights of the Republic of Yemen in the Exclusive Economic Zone".

definitive agreement of the Parties to submit the matter to this Arbitration. From this proposition Yemen concludes that the northern islands do not come within the scope of the present arbitration.

87. This somewhat technical "critical date" argument, fails, in the opinion of the Tribunal, to take sufficient account of the crucial change brought about in the Arbitration Agreement in the specification of the first stage of the Arbitration as being that in which this question of scope was to be determined by the Tribunal. Whereas, in the Agreement on Principles, the decision on scope was to be the whole matter of the first stage, the later Arbitration Agreement joined within that stage both the award on sovereignty and the decision on scope. This now meant that the Tribunal was to decide the issue of scope "on the basis of the respective positions of the two Parties" only after having heard the entire substantive contentions of both Parties on the question of sovereignty. This later provision must throw doubt upon the proposition that the Parties nevertheless intended the earlier date of the Agreement on Principles still to be the critical date for the determination of scope.

88. In addition, the later Arbitration Agreement did not, in its Article 2(2), qualify in any way its use of the phrase "on the basis of the respective positions of the two Parties". If not qualified, the ordinary meaning of that phrase in its context, and in the light of the object and purpose of the Arbitration Agreement, would seem to be that it is "the respective position of the two Parties" as at the date of the Arbitration Agreement, and not at some unspecified date, that should form the basis for the determination by the Tribunal of the scope of the dispute under the Arbitration Agreement.

89. Moreover, and by implication consistent with this analysis, Yemen, although taking some care in various ways to reserve its position on scope, has in fact provided a full argument in support of its claim to sovereignty over Jabal al-Tayr and the Zubayr group, and in the July 1998 supplementary hearings on petroleum agreements, considerably elaborated on that argument.

90. The Tribunal therefore, on the question of the scope of the dispute, prefers the view of Eritrea and accordingly makes an Award on sovereignty in respect of all the islands and islets with respect to which the Parties have put forward conflicting claims, which include Jabal al-Tayr and the Zubayr group, as well as the Haycocks and the Mohabbakahs.

CHAPTER III   Some Particular Features of This Case

In General

91. It is convenient at the outset to call attention to some features of this case. There is one striking difference between the Parties themselves. Yemen traces its existence back to medieval times and even before the

establishment of the Ottoman Empire; Eritrea on the other hand became a fully independent State, separate from Ethiopia, in the early 1990s. Nevertheless, Eritrea traces what it regards as its own title to the disputed islands through an historical succession from the Italian colonial period as well as through the post-Second World War period of its federation as part of the ancient country of Ethiopia. Accordingly the Tribunal has been presented by both Parties with great quantities of material put forward as evidence of the establishment of a legal title through the accumulated examples of claims, possession or use or, in the case of Yemen, through consolidation, continuity and confirmation of an "ancient title". All these materials of quite varying character and weight have had to be sifted, analysed and assessed by the Tribunal.

92. Since much of these materials relates to the actions and reactions or conduct of the Parties or of their predecessors, it is well to have in mind that both have experienced periods in which they were preoccupied by civil wars on either side of the Red Sea: Yemen from 1962-70, and Ethiopia with the severe and bloody conflict with Eritrean rebels which resulted in the independence of Eritrea in 1993.

93. The disputed islands and islets range from small to tiny, are uniformly unattractive, waterless, and habitable only with great difficulty. And yet it is also the fact that they straddle what has been, since the opening of the Suez Canal in 1869, one of the most important and busiest seaways in the world. These contradictory aspects of the disputed islands are reflected in the materials presented to the Tribunal. During the earlier periods the islands seem often hardly to have been noticed by coastal countries other than by local traditional fishermen who used them for shelter and their waters for anchorage; but did receive considerable attention, amounting even to temporary occupation, from rival colonial powers, notably Great Britain and Italy. This was no doubt because, after the opening of the Canal, this sea, narrowing in its southern part where the islands are situated, was the principal route from Europe to India, the East Indies and the Far East.

94. The former interest in these islands of Great Britain, Italy and to a lesser extent of France and the Netherlands, is an important element of the historical materials presented to the Court by the Parties, not least because they have had access to the archives of the time, and especially to early papers of the British Governments of the time. Much of this material is interesting and helpful. One general caveat needs, however, to be made. Some of this material is in the form of internal memoranda, from within the archives of the British Foreign Office, as it then was, and also sometimes of the Italian Foreign Office. The Tribunal has been mindful that these internal memoranda do not necessarily represent the view or policy of any government, and may be no more than the personal view that one civil servant felt moved to

express to another particular civil servant at that moment: it is not always easy to disentangle the personality elements from what were, after all, internal, private and confidential memoranda at the time they were made.

Critical Date

95. Faced with such a mass of legal and political history, the Tribunal has felt it right to consider whether the notion of the "critical date" or "critical period" might assist in the organization or the interpretation of this voluminous material. It has noted, however, that the Parties themselves have spoken of a critical date only in relation to the question discussed above: whether, in deciding on the scope of the Arbitration, the critical date is that of the Agreement on Principles or the Agreement on Arbitration. Neither of them has sought to employ a critical date argument in relation to any of the questions involving the substance of the dispute. In this situation the Tribunal has thought it best to follow the example of the 1966 award in the arbitration between Argentina and Chile presided over by Lord McNair, and has accordingly "examined all the evidence submitted to it, irrespective of the date of the acts to which such evidence relates".[5]

Uti Possidetis

96. Yemen in its Counter Memorial introduced the doctrine of *uti possidetis* to explain what it holds to have been the legal position of these islands after the dissolution of the Ottoman Empire following the end of the First World War. The position is said to have been, in the words used by Yemen, that "[o]n the dismemberment of an empire like the Ottoman Empire, there is a presumption, both legal and political in character, that the boundaries of the independent states which replace the Empire will correspond to the boundaries of the administrative units of which the dismembered Empire was constituted". The principle of *uti possidetis* presumably provides the legal aspect of this presumption on which Yemen relies. Eritrea strongly contests this.

97. There is, however, a prior problem regarding the facts on which a legal presumption of *uti possidetis* would purport to be based. For such a legal presumption to operate it is necessary to know what were indeed "the boundaries of the administrative units of which the dismembered Empire was constituted". It is known that by *firmans* issued in 1841, 1866 and 1873, the Sublime Porte granted to the Khedive of Egypt the right to exercise jurisdiction over the African coast of the Red Sea. Presumably this right of jurisdiction over the African coast might naturally have extended to the islands which were in the neighbourhood of the coast and geographically at least seemed to belong to that coast. But how far this jurisdiction extended over the

---

[5] *Argentina v. Chile* (9 Dec. 1966), 16 RIAA 111, 115; 38 *ILR* 16, 20 (1969).

archipelago which is the principal element in the present dispute is to some extent a matter for conjecture. It seems that, unsurprisingly, the *firman* did not mention the archipelago. The sources provided by the Parties in relation to this question are primarily British Foreign Office internal papers and memoranda. And the answers there given were, it is made quite clear, based upon informed speculation. It is known that there were from time to time small Ottoman garrisons upon Zuqar and upon Hanish, and there are suggestions that they came from the Arabian side, and probably had their supplies from that coast.

98. There is particularly the September 1880 memorandum of Sir Edward Hertslet (author of the celebrated and influential *Map of Africa by Treaty*, and Librarian of the Foreign Office) compiled in the Foreign Office for the use of the Board of Trade, which was responsible for lighthouses in the Red Sea and which had sought Foreign Office help with the question of jurisdiction over lighthouse islands. In this memorandum Hertslet carefully distinguished between sovereignty, which the Ottoman Empire possessed over all these possessions, and a right of jurisdiction over the African side, which had been conferred on the Khedive. He drew up three long lists of the islands in the Red Sea. The first list was of the islands which in his opinion could be said to be "in close proximity" to the African coast, and the second list was of those in close proximity to the Arabian coast. The first list includes the Mohabbakahs and the Haycocks; the second list contains the islands in the "Jabel Zukar Group", those in the "Little Harnish Group", and those in the "Great Harnish Group". This memorandum appears to have been accepted as a working paper by both the Foreign Office and the Board of Trade, notwithstanding the fact that the perception of the second group as being "in close proximity" to the Arabian coast might be regarded as questionable in terms of physical geography. The third list was a relatively short one of islands near "the Centre of the Red Sea" including Jabal Al-Tayr and the Zubayr group, the jurisdiction over which was thought by Hertslet to be "doubtful", although the sovereignty remained Ottoman.

99. It is doubtful how far it would be right to base a legal presumption of the *uti possidetis* kind upon these speculations of a concerned but not disinterested third-government department; and this quite apart from the legal difficulties of creating a presumption which would be plainly at odds with the specific provision made for at least some of these islands by Article 16 of the Treaty of Lausanne of 1923.[6] Yemen of course pleads that this was *res inter alios acta*. But Turkey having been in a position to refuse to accept the Treaty of Sèvres, the sovereignty over these islands must have remained with Turkey until the Treaty of Lausanne was signed, and presumably until

---

[6] Throughout this award, the date used for the Treaty of Lausanne is its date of signature, in 1923, rather than that of its entry into force (1926).

1926 when it was ratified. Added to these difficulties is the question of the intertemporal law and the question whether this doctrine of *uti possidetis*, at that time thought of as being essentially one applicable to Latin America, could properly be applied to interpret a juridical question arising in the Middle East shortly after the close of the First World War.

100. Nevertheless, all this material about the position of the Islands during and shortly after the period of the Ottoman Empire remains an instructive element of the legal history of the dispute. It is especially interesting that even when the whole region was under Ottoman rule it was assumed that the powers of jurisdiction and administration over the islands should be divided between the two opposite coasts.

Article 15, Paragraph 1 of the Arbitration Agreement
  101. This paragraph provides as follows:

Nothing in this Arbitration Agreement can be interpreted as being detrimental to the legal positions or to the rights of each Party with respect to the questions submitted to the Tribunal, nor can affect or prejudice the decision of the Arbitral Tribunal or the considerations and grounds on which those decisions are based.

The Tribunal finds this provision less than perspicuous. A question to the Parties about it evoked different answers; both were to the general effect that this clause was meant as a "without prejudice" clause concerning the arguments and points of view they might wish to present to the Tribunal. As both Parties have fully argued their cases without either of them having occasion to invoke this provision, it seems to the Tribunal best to leave the matter there.

The Task of the Tribunal in the First Stage
  102. The Agreement for Arbitration provides in the second paragraph of its Article 2:

2. The first stage shall result in an award on territorial sovereignty and on the definition of the scope of the dispute between Eritrea and Yemen. The Tribunal shall decide territorial sovereignty in accordance with the principles, rules and practices of international law applicable to the matter, and on the basis, in particular, of historic titles. The Tribunal shall decide on the definition of the scope of the dispute on the basis of the respective positions of the two Parties.

Several of the clauses of this paragraph call for consideration. First there is the requirement that this stage shall "result in an award on territorial sovereignty". Thus, the Agreement does not require the Tribunal, as is often the case in agreements for arbitration, to make an allocation of territorial sovereignty to the one Party or the other. The result furthermore is to be an award "on" territorial sovereignty not an award "of" territorial sovereignty. The Tribunal would therefore be within its competence to find a common or a divided sovereignty. This follows from the language of the clause freely chosen by the Parties. It seems right [. . .] to call attention to the broader possibilities admitted by this unusual arbitration clause. The Tribunal has indeed considered all possibilities.

103. Further consideration must be given to the clause that requires the Tribunal to "decide territorial sovereignty in accordance with the principles, rules and practices of international law applicable in the matter, and on the basis, in particular, of historic titles".

104. As already mentioned, both Parties rely on various elements of evidence of possession and use as creative of title, and this is itself an appeal to what is a familiar kind of historic claim. As Judge Huber said in the *Palmas* case, "[i]t is quite natural that the establishment of sovereignty may be the outcome of a slow evolution, of a progressive intensification of State control".[7]

105. But Yemen also relies primarily upon what it calls specifically an "historic title". This calls for reflection upon the meaning of "title". It refers not to a developing claim but to a clearly established right, or to quote Pollock, "the absolutely or relatively best right to a thing which may be in dispute".[8] It is a matter of law, not of possession, though it would normally indicate a right in law to have possession even if the factual possession is elsewhere.

106. The notion of an historic title is well known in international law, not least in respect of "historic bays", which are governed by rules exceptional to the normal rules about bays. Historic bays again rely upon a kind of "ancient title": a title that has so long been established by common repute that this common knowledge is itself a sufficient title. But an historic title has also another and different meaning in international law as a title that has been created, or consolidated, by a process of prescription, or acquiescence, or by possession so long continued as to have become accepted by the law as a title. These titles too are historic in the sense that continuity and the lapse of a period of time is of the essence. Eritrea pleads various forms of this kind of title, and so also does Yemen, which relies upon this latter kind of title as "confirmation" of its "ancient title".

107. The injunction to have regard to historic title "in particular" can hardly be intended to mean that historic title is to be given some

---

[7] *Island of Palmas (Netherlands v. US)* 2 RIAA 829 at 867 (4 Apr. 1928). Professor Max Huber, at the time President of the Permanent Court of International Justice, acted as sole arbitrator in proceedings conducted under the auspices of the Permanent Court of Arbitration, pursuant to the 1907 Convention for the Pacific Settlement of International Disputes [4 *Ann Dig* 3].

[8] Sir Frederick Pollock, *A First Book of Jurisprudence* 177 (6th edn, 1929).

priority it might not otherwise possess; for if there is indeed an established title—the best right to possession—then it is by definition a prior right. So perhaps the phrase "in particular" is put in out of abundant caution, lest the Tribunal, faced with a welter of other interests and uses, were to forget that there can be a separate category of title that does not depend upon use and possession, but is itself a right to possession whether or not possession is enjoyed in fact. At any rate, as will appear below, the Tribunal has not failed to examine historic titles of all kinds in its consideration of this case.

108. There have been different points of view between the Parties about the effects of this twofold division of a first stage award on territorial sovereignty and a second stage award on maritime boundaries. It was in the course of the supplementary proceedings on the Parties' petroleum agreements that Yemen became strenuously exercised over the possibility that the Tribunal might be tempted to "prefigure" (a nicely chosen expression) an eventual stage two maritime solution as an element of its thinking about stage one. Thus paragraph 20 of Yemen's written pleadings in the supplementary petroleum agreements phase states as follows:

This last element [prefiguring] is of particular concern to the Government of Yemen. It is always attractive to seek to discover a basis for dividing a group of islands, not least in an arbitration. The attraction must be the greater when the task of the Tribunal extends to the process of maritime delimitation, and no doubt caution will be needed to avoid a prefiguring of equitable principles and concepts, which are in law only relevant in the second phase of these proceedings.

This paragraph was repeated word for word in Yemen's oral argument in the July 1998 supplementary hearings.

109. A novel feature of Yemen's arguments, introduced at a late stage of the proceedings but clearly and strongly felt, concerned an apparently unacceptable supposition that an equitable solution was being contemplated for the first stage. This was curious, if only because it seems to have been the first and only reference to equity or equitable principles by either Party in course of the pleadings. Furthermore, no member of the Tribunal had mentioned equity or equitable principles.

110. This matter arose again in a somewhat different form in Yemen's answers to four questions put to both Parties at the close of Yemen's oral argument in the supplementary proceedings, and which questions both Parties answered later in writing. The purpose of these questions was simply to ask both Parties how it was that some of their petroleum agreements, particularly those of Yemen, appeared to be drawn to extend to some sort of coastal median line. In response,

Yemen felt obliged to "express the strongest possible reservation against the 'prefiguring' of a median line".

111. Eritrea replied, in the Tribunal's view rightly, that Article 2.2 of the Arbitration Agreement requires the Tribunal to "decide territorial sovereignty in accordance with the principles, rules and practices of international law applicable to the matter, and on the basis, in particular, of historic titles". That formula must include any principles, rules or practices of international law that are found to be applicable to these matters of sovereignty, even if those principles, rules or practices are part of maritime law. Certainly the Tribunal is not in this first stage to delimit any maritime boundaries or to prefigure any such delimitation. But that is an entirely different matter from applying all international law that may [be] relevant for the purpose of determining sovereignty, which is the province of this first stage.

112. In general, the Tribunal is unable to accept the proposition that the international law governing land territory and the international law governing maritime boundaries are not only different but also discrete, and bear no juridical relevance to each other. Such a theory is indeed disproved by Yemen's own request to the British Government to be allowed to attend the 1989 Lighthouses Conference on the ground that the northern islands were within Yemen's Exclusive Economic Zone.

113. It is well to have the considered view of the Tribunal on these questions stated at the outset of this Award. At the same time, it may be said that the Tribunal has no difficulty in agreeing with Yemen, and indeed also with Eritrea, that there can be no question of even "prefiguring", much less drawing, any maritime boundary line, whether median or indeed a line based on equitable principles, in this first stage of the arbitration.

CHAPTER IV   Historic Title and Other Historical Considerations

114. Article 2 of the Agreement for Arbitration enjoins the Tribunal to decide territorial sovereignty in accordance with applicable international law "and on the basis, in particular, of historic title". The Tribunal has thus paid particular attention both to the arguments relating to ancient titles and reversion thereof proposed by Yemen and arguments relating to longstanding attribution of the Mohabbakahs to the colony of Eritrea and to early establishment of titles by Italy pronounced by Eritrea. An important element of Yemen's case is that of an asserted "historic title" to the Islands, and this is indeed reflected in the very language of both the Agreement on Principles and the Arbitration Agreement. Thus the Tribunal fully recognizes that the intention of Article 2 is that, among all the relevant international law,

particular attention should be accorded to such elements. Notwith-standing its analysis of how the principles, rules and practices of international law generally bear on its decision on territorial sovereignty, the Tribunal has had the most careful regard to historic titles as they bear on this case.

115. For its part, Eritrea makes no argument for sovereignty based on ancient title, in spite of the undeniable antiquity of Ethiopia. Rather, Eritrea in part asserts an historic consolidation of title on the part of Italy during the inter-war period that resulted in a title to the Islands that became effectively transferred to Ethiopia as a result of the territorial dispositions after the defeat of Italy in the Second World War. This argument will naturally fall to be dealt with in the chapters below dealing with the inter-war periods and the armistice and related proceedings at the end of the Second World War.

116. Yemen has asserted an historic or "ancient title" running back in time to the middle ages, under which the islands are asserted to have formed part of the *Bilad el-Yemen*. This ancient title predated the several occupations by the Ottoman Empire, asserts Yemen, and reverted to modern Yemen after the collapse of the Ottoman Empire at the end of the First World War.

117. It is thus only Yemen that has raised substantial questions of an "historic" or "ancient" title that existed before the second Ottoman occupation of the nineteenth century; it is therefore to an appreciation of the historical background necessary for an understanding of that claim to an early title that the Tribunal now turns. This chapter will consider the ways in which the overall history of the Arabian Peninsula must be understood in then contemporary legal terms, as a preface to the Tribunal's ultimate conclusion on the legal questions concerning "historic titles". In addition, this chapter will address Yemen's theory of "reversion", which is critical to any decision as to the legal effect of an "historic title".

118. Yemen's arguments on historic and ancient title touch upon several important historical considerations. One relates to the identity of historic Yemen and whether it comprised the islands in dispute. A second questions the existence of a doctrine of reversion recognized in international law, and a third relates to the place of continuity within a concept of reversion of ancient title. Those claims advanced by Eritrea that are based on both history and international law are addressed elsewhere. This chapter further addresses such important historical matters as the tradition of joint use of the Islands' waters by fishermen from both sides of the Red Sea, and the Ottoman allocation of administrative jurisdiction between the two coasts.

119. Yemen's claim is based essentially on an "ancient" or "historical" title pursuant to which the Imam's inherent and inalienable sovereignty extended over the entirety of what historically has been known as *Bilad*

el-Yemen, which existed for several centuries and is alleged by Yemen to have included the southern Red Sea islands. This sovereignty is further characterized by Yemen as having remained unaffected by and having survived the Ottoman annexation of Yemen, in spite of the Sublime Porte's having declared Yemen to be one of the *vilayets* falling under Ottoman rule.

120. The arguments advanced by Yemen in this respect must be evaluated within the historical and legal context that prevailed during the relevant period, extending from the end of the nineteenth century until the dissolution of the Ottoman Empire.

121. The particularity of the relationship between the Ottoman Empire and Yemen should be taken into account as an important historical factor. In spite of the Treaty of Da'an, concluded in 1911, which granted the Imam of Yemen a greater degree of internal autonomy, he remained a suzerain acting within Ottoman sovereignty until the total disintegration of the Ottoman Empire and the loss of all its Arabian possessions, including the *vilayet* of Yemen.[9] It was only in 1923, by virtue of Article 16 of the Treaty of Lausanne, that the Ottoman Empire not only recognized the renunciation of all its sovereignty rights over Yemen, but explicitly renounced its sovereign title over the islands that had previously fallen under the jurisdiction of the Ottoman *wali* in Hodeidah.

122. The territorial extent of Imamic Yemen as an autonomous entity must be distinguished from that of the Ottoman *vilayet* of Yemen. During the entire period from the second half of the nineteenth century until 1925, the Imam of Yemen had neither sovereignty nor jurisdiction over the Tihama and the Red Sea coasts. Under his agreements with the Ottoman sultan, the Imam administered an exclusively land-locked territory, limited to the high mountains. The Ottoman *wali* exercised exclusive jurisdiction over the coasts until 1917. Thereafter, the coasts came under the control of the Idrisi, a local tribal ruler supported first by the Italians, and later by the British Government. The coast came under the Imam's rule only in 1926. As will be seen later, this fact has negative legal implications for the "reversion" argument advanced by Yemen, as well as for the application of certain other rules of international law, including the concept of ancient "historic title" in its full classical sense.

123. There can be no doubt that the concept of historic title has special resonance in situations that may exist even in the contemporary world, such as determining the sovereignty over nomadic lands occupied during time immemorial by given tribes who owed their allegiance to the ruler who extended his socio-political power over that

---

[9] See, in particular, John Baldry, "One Hundred Years of Yemeni History: 1849-1948", in L'Arabie du Sud, Vol. II at 85 (J. Chelhod *et al.*, eds, 1984); Roger Joint Daguenet, *Histoire de la Mer Rouge: de Lesseps à nos jours*, 113-16, 186-90, 240-1 (1997).

geographic area. A different situation exists with regard to uninhabited islands which are not claimed to be falling within the limits of historic waters.

124. In the present case, neither party has formulated any claim to the effect that the disputed islands are located within historic waters. Moreover, none of the Islands is inhabited on other than a seasonal or temporary basis, or even has the natural and physical conditions that would permit sustaining continual human presence. Whatever may have been the links between the coastal lands and the islands in question, the relinquishment by the Ottoman Empire of its sovereignty over the islands by virtue of Article 16 of the 1923 Treaty of Lausanne (discussed in greater detail in Chapter V) logically and legally adversely affects any pre-existing title.

125. It was recognized in the course of the oral hearings that, by the law in force at the time, Ottoman sovereignty over the regions in question was lawful. The fact that Yemen was not a party to the Treaty of Lausanne, and that it perceived both the British and the Italians as having been usurpers in the Red Sea, does not negate that legal consequence. It has not been established in these proceedings to the satisfaction of the Tribunal that the doctrine of reversion is part of international law. In any event, the Tribunal concludes that on the facts of this case it has no application. No "reversion" could possibly operate, since the chain of titles was necessarily interrupted and whatever previous merits may have existed to sustain such claim could hardly be invoked. During several decades, the predominant role was exercised by the western naval powers in the Red Sea after its opening to international maritime traffic through the Suez Canal, as well as through the colonization of the southern part of the Red Sea on both coasts. An important result of that hegemony was the maintenance of the status quo imposed after the First World War, in particular that the sovereignty over the islands covered by Article 16 of the Lausanne Treaty of 1923 remained indeterminate at least as long as the interested western powers were still in the region. As long as that colonial situation prevailed, neither Ethiopia nor Yemen was in a position to demonstrate any kind of historic title that could serve as a sufficient basis to confirm sovereignty over any of the disputed islands. Only after the departure of the colonial powers did the possibility of a change in the status quo arise. A change in the status quo does not, however, necessarily imply a reversion.

126. This should not, however, be construed as depriving historical considerations of all legal significance. In the first place, the conditions that prevailed during many centuries with regard to the traditional openness of southern Red Sea marine resources for fishing, its role as means for unrestricted traffic from one side to the other, together with the common use of the islands by the populations of both coasts, are

all important elements capable of creating certain "historic rights" which accrued in favour of both Parties through a process of historical consolidation as a sort of *"servitude internationale"* falling short of territorial sovereignty.[10] Such historic rights provide a sufficient legal basis for maintaining certain aspects of a *res communis* that has existed for centuries for the benefit of the populations on both sides of the Red Sea. In the second place, the distinction in terms of jurisdiction which existed under the Ottoman Empire between those islands administered from the African coast and the other islands administered from the Arabian coast constitutes a historic fact to be taken into consideration.

127. According to the most reliable historical and geographical sources, both ancient and modern, the reported data clearly indicate that the population living around the southern part of the Red Sea on the two opposite coasts have always been inter-linked culturally and engaged in the same type of socio-economic activities. Since times immemorial, they were not only conducting exchanges of a human and commercial nature, but they were freely fishing and navigating throughout the maritime space using the existing islands as way stations *(des îles relais)* and occasionally as refuge from the strong northern winds. These activities were carried out for centuries without any need to obtain any authorizations from the rulers on either the Asian or the African side of the Red Sea and in the absence of restrictions or regulations exercised by public authorities.

128. This traditionally prevailing situation reflected deeply rooted cultural patterns leading to the existence of what could be characterized from a juridical point of view as *res communis* permitting the African as well as the Yemeni fishermen to operate with no limitation throughout the entire area and to sell their catch at the local markets on either side of the Red Sea. Equally, the persons sailing for fishing or trading purposes from one coast to the other used to take temporary refuge from the strong winds on any of the uninhabited islands scattered in that maritime zone without encountering difficulties of a political or administrative nature.[11]

129. These historical facts are witnessed through a variety of sources submitted in evidence during the arbitral proceedings. A comprehensive evaluation of the evidence submitted by both Parties reveals the presence of deeply rooted common patterns of behaviour as well as the continuation, even in recent years, of cross-relationships which are marked by eventual recourse to professional fishermen's

---

[10] See in this respect, Yehuda Z. Blum, "Historic Rights", in 7 *Encyclopedia of Public International Law* 120 *et seq.;* and *Historic Titles in International Law* 126-9 (1965).

[11] See in particular, Charles Forster, *The Historical Geography of Arabia*, vol. I at 113, vol. II at 337 (1984) (first published in 1844); Joseph Chelhod *et al., L'Arabie du Sud—Histoire et Civilisation,* vol. I, at 63, 67-9, 252-5 (1984); Roger Joint Daguenet, *Histoire de la Mer Rouge: De Moïse à Bonaparte* 20-4, 86-7 (1995); and Yves Thoraval *et al., Le Yemen et la Mer Rouge* 14-16, 17-20, 35-7, 43-7, 51-4 (1995).

arbitrators (aq'il) in charge of settling disputes in accordance with the local customary law. Such understanding finds support in the statements attributed to fishermen from both coasts of the Red Sea, taken as a whole, which have been submitted by both Parties.

130. The socio-economic and cultural patterns described above were perfectly in harmony with classical Islamic law concepts, which practically ignored the principle of "territorial sovereignty" as it developed among the European powers and became a basic feature of nineteenth-century western international law.[12]

131. However, it must be noted that the Ottoman Empire, which directly or through its suzerains governed the quasi-totality of the countries around the Red Sea during the first half of the nineteenth century including *Bilad el-Yemen* and what became known thereafter as Eritrea, started after the end of the Crimean War in 1856 to abandon the communal aspects of the Islamic system of international law and to adopt the modern rules prevailing among the European concert of nations to which the Sublime Porte became a fully-integrated party during the Berlin Congress of 1875. According to this new modern international law, the legal concept of "territorial sovereignty" became a cornerstone for most of the State powers, and the situation in the Red Sea could no longer escape the juridical consequences of that new reality.

132. Hence, it is understandable that both Parties are in agreement that the islands in dispute initially all fell under the territorial sovereignty of the Ottoman Empire. Within the exercise of the Ottoman's sovereignty over these islands, it has to be noted that the Sublime Porte granted to the Khedive of Egypt the right to administer the Ottoman possessions (*vilayet*) on the African coast which at present form "the State of Eritrea", and this delegation of power included jurisdiction over islands off the African coast, including the Dahlaks and eventually the Mohabbakahs.

133. The sovereignty of the Ottoman Empire over both coasts of the Red Sea is undisputed up to 1880 and this remained the case with regard to the eastern, or Arabian, coast until the First World War. Among the various documents introduced in support of this historical fact, Eritrea has submitted the French-language version of a memorandum dated 6 December 1881, issued by the Egyptian Khedival Ministry of Foreign Affairs, which indicates that in May 1871, Italy recognized that the Ottoman flag had been flying since 1862 over the African coast at a point going beyond the south of Assab. The Egyptian memorandum added that until 1880 the Egyptian Government believed the affirmation of the Italian Government that the

---

[12] See in particular, A. Sanhoury, *Le Califat*, 22, 37, 119, 163, 273, 320-1 (1926); Majid Kadouri, "Islamic Law", 6 *Encyclopedia of Public International Law*, 227 *et seq.*; and Ahmed S. El Kosheri, "History of Islamic Law", 7 *Encyclopedia of Public International Law*, 222 *et seq.*

Italian presence had been essentially of private and commercial character. Consequently, the entire African coast and the islands off that coast remained until then under the Khedive's jurisdiction. At the same time, all other islands were, and continued to be, under the jurisdiction of the Ottoman *wali* stationed in Hodeidah and appointed by the Sublime Porte.

134. Hence, a clear distinction has to be made between the Red Sea islands which were under jurisdiction of the Khedive of Egypt acting on behalf of the Ottoman Empire until 1882 and the other Red Sea islands which remained under the Ottoman *vilayet* of Yemen until the dissolution of the Empire after the First World War.

135. A British Foreign Office Memorandum dated 10 June 1930, relying expressly on the Hertslet memorandum of 1880, indicates that the Khedive of Egypt exercised jurisdiction off the African coast over the "Mohabakah Islands, Harbi and Sayal". With regard to the other category, the British Memorandum describes "the Great Hanish group as being off the Arabic Coast and consequently under the sovereignty and within the exclusive jurisdiction of the Sultan".

Paragraph 16 of the same Memorandum emphasized that:

Great Hanish, Suyal Hanish, Little Hanish, Jebal Zukur, Abu Ail, being nearer to the Arabian Coast, appear before the war to have been considered as under both the jurisdiction and sovereignty of Turkey.

136. Furthermore, Eritrea has submitted Italian Colonial Ministry documents, including a note dated 11 October 1916, entitled "The Red Sea Islands", reflecting the findings of an inquiry conducted on the islands themselves. After devoting Part I to "Farsan" and Part II to "Kameran", Part III of the note deals with "the other islands", which included what is referred to as "Gebel Zucur". This heading included not only the "group of 12 sizeable rocks", but also "the two great and small Hanish islands". With regard to these islands, it was noted that "[t]he Ottoman authorities kept a small garrison of 40 there under the command of a Mulazim to monitor the movement of importation vessels to the Yemen Coast from Gibut", and further that, "faced with the difficulties of supplying water and victuals on account of a shortage of resources, the Ottoman authorities withdrew the garrison". After the bombardment of Midi by Italian warships, the Ottoman authorities are said to have "restored the garrison in 1909 and increased the number of askaris to 100".

137. These Italian colonial documents, which confirm Ottoman sovereignty over the Hanish-Zuqar islands and assert that they continued in 1916 to be administered by the *vilayet* of Yemen, are consistent with the views expressed in a telegram addressed by the Governor of the Eritrean Colony to the Italian Minister of the

Colonies and transmitted on 18 October 1916 to the Italian Minister of Foreign Affairs. A Foreign Ministry note entitled: "The Red Sea Islands", dating back to 31 July 1901, is attached thereto as "Appendix II". The 1901 Note bases the division of the islands into three groups:

The most northerly islands, which are of little or almost no relation to the Colony of Eritrea on account of the distance, those facing Massaua and the most southerly islands which are opposite the Eritrean Coasts of Beilul and Assab. Almost all are found on the eastern coast of the Red Sea, except the Dahalac islands, which are under our rule, and a few others of much less importance.

With regard to the second group, the Italian note indicates:

Leaving aside the archipelago of the Dahalac islands—which is under the sovereignty of Italy and which include the biggest islands in the Red Sea—Cotuma, Diebel Tair and Camaran are notable in this second group of the archipelago; all of which under Turkish rule.

The note explicitly characterizes as "Turkish": "Cotuma", "Djebel . . . called Gebel Sebair" and "Camaran".
Turning to the third group, the 1901 Italian note refers to a:

. . . group of islands known as Hanish or Harnish (Turkish). It comprises the island of Gebel Zucar, large and small Hanish islands and the other minor islands of Abu-ail, Syul-Hanish, Haycoc and Mohabbach, and a few islets amounting to large rocks.

138. Contemporary British documents also reflect the view that the islands in question, with the exception of Mohabbakahs, formed part of the *vilayet* of Yemen, and appear to link their future disposition to this historical attachment to the Arabian coast.

139. A Foreign Office Memorandum dated 15 January 1917 and entitled "Italy and the Partition of the Turkish Empire" provides in paragraph 38:

Lastly, everyone seems to be agreed that the islands in the Red Sea which were previously under Turkish sovereignty pass naturally to the Arab State, though some special regime will be necessary in Kamaran Island in view of the pilgrim traffic.

140. Lord Balfour, in a 13 March 1919 letter to Lord Curzon, indicated that the solution envisaged for "Abu Ail, Zabayir and Jebel Teir" as well as "Kamaran, Zukur and the Hanish Islands (Great Hanish, Little Hanish and Suyul Hanish group)" was either "to annex them" to the British Empire or "to claim that they should be handed

over to some independent Arab rulers on the mainland other than the Imam of Sanaa or the Idrisi".

141. Lord Curzon's letter addressed to Lord Balfour on 27 May 1919 linked the subject of any handover to Arab rulers with the essentially political question of the area's future, "the whole question of the future of the Red Sea Islands" was to be considered "ultimately bound with that of the future status of Arabia". Therefore, Lord Curzon indicated that:

[t]he policy of his Majesty's Government should in the first place be directed towards the recognition by the High Contracting Parties of the fact that the islands form a part of the mainland and will accordingly become the property of the Arabian rulers concerned; and that these rulers are to be in special relation with His Majesty's Government.

142. As will be expanded upon later, the allocation of administrative powers over the Red Sea islands, whether by the Ottoman Empire acting as sovereign power on both coasts or only as exercising jurisdiction from the Arabian coast alone, represents an historic fact that should be taken into consideration and given a certain legal weight.

143. Before leaving this study of the historical considerations, it is necessary to recall the question of ancient or historic Yemeni title, to which Yemen gave such crucial importance in the presentation of its case. It has been explained in this chapter that there are certain historical problems about this argument. First, there is the historical fact that medieval Yemen was mainly a mountain entity with little sway over the coastal areas, which were essentially dedicated to serving the flow of maritime trade between, on the one hand, India and the East Indies, and on the other, Egypt and the other Mediterranean ports. Second, the concept of territorial sovereignty was entirely strange to an entity such as medieval Yemen. Indeed, the concept of territorial sovereignty in the terms of modern international law came late (not until the nineteenth century) to the Ottoman Empire, which claimed, and was recognized as having, territorial sovereignty over the entire region.

144. But there are other problems with the Yemeni claim to an ancient title, in particular the effect of Article 16 of the Treaty of Lausanne and the necessity of establishing some doctrine of continuity of ancient title and of reversion at the end of the Ottoman Empire. This subject is explored in detail in the following chapter, and the final view of the Tribunal on this question of ancient title is expressed in Chapter X.

CHAPTER V   The Legal History and Principal Treaties and Other
Legal Instruments Involved; Questions of State Succession

145. The series of major instruments engaging, in various combin-
ations, the maritime users of the Red Sea form an important backdrop
to the legal claims of the Parties in this arbitration. Their binding
nature or otherwise, their status as directly legally significant or as *res
inter alios acta*, and the meaning of their terms, have all engaged the
attention of the Parties.

146. The so-called Treaty of Da'an of 1911 was in fact an internal
instrument by which the Imam of Yemen obtained for himself greater
internal powers of autonomy within the Ottoman Empire. However,
sovereignty over all the Ottoman possessions, including the islands in
dispute, remained vested in the Empire itself until it was legally divested
of its Arabian possessions after the First World War.

147. The Principal Allied Powers (the British Empire, France, Italy
and Japan) agreed at Mudros an armistice with Turkey on 30 October
1918. The 1918 Armistice of Mudros was a vehicle for ending
hostilities and indeed for permitting belligerent occupation. It was not
an instrument for the transfer of territory. It is not disputed that
immediately before the signing of the Armistice of Mudros title to all
the islands was Ottoman. It was further agreed in these proceedings
that Ottoman title had been secured by military occupation, which
was lawful by reference to the international law of the day. An
essential component of sovereign title is the right to alienate. Just as
the Ottoman Empire would have been free to cede title to the islands
to a third State at any time during the period 1872 to 1918, so it still
had the legal right itself to determine where title should go after 1918.
Its freedom in this regard was curtailed not by the operation of a
doctrine of reversion which would spring into operation upon any
divesting of title by Turkey, but by the realities of power at the end of
the War.

148. It cannot be the case therefore that title passed in 1918 to the
Imam. Accordingly the Tribunal is not able to accept that sovereignty
over the islands in dispute reverted to Yemen.

149. It was intended that a treaty of peace, containing the future
settlement of Turkish territory in Europe and elsewhere, should follow
the 1918 Armistice of Mudros. To that end, the Principal Allied
Powers (forming together with Armenia, Belgium, Greece, the Hedjaz,
Poland, Portugal, Roumania, the Serb-Croat-Slovene State and
Czechoslovakia the "Allied Powers") on the one hand, and Turkey on
the other, signed a Treaty of Peace at Sèvres on 10 August 1920. The
long and detailed provisions contained but a single clause that might
have had application to the islands in the Red Sea in dispute in the
present case. Article 132 provided:

Outside her frontiers as fixed by the present Treaty Turkey hereby renounces in favour of the Principal Allied Powers all rights and title which she could claim on any ground over or concerning any territories outside Europe which are not otherwise disposed of by the present Treaty.

Turkey undertakes to recognize and conform to the measures which may be taken now or in the future by the Principal Allied Powers, in agreement where necessary with third Powers, in order to carry the above stipulation into effect.

150. In the event, the Treaty of Sèvres was not ratified by Turkey and did not enter into effect. Accordingly, title to the Red Sea islands in dispute must thus have remained with Turkey—even though it knew that it would in due course be required to divest itself of such title. Indeed, Great Britain had been occupying certain islands since 1915 to forestall Italian activity, and had been displaying the flag but without claiming title.

151. The initial position of Great Britain at the peace talks at Sèvres was that the islands lying east of the South West Rocks off Greater Hanish Island should be placed under the sovereignty of the independent chiefs of the Arabian mainland. The British appreciated that reasons of history and geography would make the Arab mainland rulers strong claimants when Turkey finally relinquished title and future sovereignty had to be determined, and indeed that their desire to exclude any European Power from establishing themselves on the east coast would make the passing of title to a "friendly Arab ruler" a desirable outcome.[13] But that is a different matter from title passing automatically by reversion from Turkey to Yemen. In the event, a different proposal was agreed in Article 132 of the Treaty of Sèvres.

152. Much has been made by Yemen of the fact that throughout the years that ensued, the Imam protested to Great Britain that "the islands" had not been returned. These "islands" were not specified. While this may indeed support allegations of the existence of a Yemeni claim, there is no evidence that it was either intended, or interpreted, to include the islands in dispute in the present case. Furthermore, a State's protests about the refusal of others to allow it to exercise effective control over what it maintains in its own territory have little legal significance if the protesting State does not, in fact, have title. More relevant is the fact that Turkey undoubtedly had title in 1918 and failed to divest itself in 1920. The instrument by which it did finally divest itself was the Treaty of Lausanne in 1923.

---

[13] Compare the policy objective that was explored by the Foreign Office for the islands of Sheikh Saal, Kamaran and Farsan, and for Hodeidah, namely occupation. In the event, a 1915 telegram from the Viceroy of India indicates that the British flag had been hoisted on Jabal Zuqar and the Hanish islands. These events were characterized, in a message to the Foreign Office from the British Resident in Aden, as a "temporary annexation". By 1926 Britain did not regard itself as holding sovereign title.

153. The Imam was not a party to the Treaty of Lausanne and in that technical sense the Treaty was *res inter alios acta* as to Yemen. If title had lain with Yemen at that time, the parties to the Treaty of Lausanne could not have transferred title elsewhere without the consent of Yemen. But, as indicated above, title still remained with Turkey. Boundary and territorial treaties made between two parties are *res inter alios acta* vis-à-vis third parties. But this special category of treaties also represents a legal reality which necessarily impinges upon third States, because they have effect *erga omnes*. If State A has title to territory and passes it to State B, then it is legally without purpose for State C to invoke the principle of *res inter alios acta*, unless its title is better than that of A (rather than of B). In the absence of such better title, a claim of *res inter alios acta* is without legal import.

154. These are the legal realities with which an analysis of the Treaty of Lausanne must be approached. Two further realities are, as stated just above, that the Imam had asserted claims during this period though without specificity as to which particular islands his claims attached, and that Italy, by its conduct, had also revealed its aspirations for the islands. The formulation of the Treaty of Lausanne was undoubtedly agreed upon in full knowledge both of the position of the Imam and the ambitions of Italy.

155. Great Britain (which had briefly in 1915 sent troops to Jabal Zuqar and the Hanish islands) had been interested at one stage in an amendment to Article 132 of the Treaty of Sèvres which would have added to the rather general Turkish renunciation of all "rights and title" a specific clause which referred to "any islands in the Red Sea". As the first paragraph of this proposal referred to rights and title in the Arabian Peninsula, it may be assumed that Great Britain thought the islands were not encompassed in that reference, but that some particular provision was needed if they too were to pass out of Turkish title. The Treaty of Lausanne, signed in 1923, did make reference to islands as well as to territories though by now the earlier proposal that underlay the abortive Treaty of Sèvres (that Turkish title should pass to the Allied Powers,[14] whether as a condominium or otherwise) was dropped.

156. Article 6 provided that, in the absence of provisions to the contrary, islands and islets lying within three miles of the coast are included within the frontier of the coastal State. While some of the Dahlaks and some of the Assab islands would have fallen outside the three-mile limit, they were generally regarded as appurtenant to the African littoral and thus belonging to Italy. The Mohabbakahs (the nearest being almost six miles away) and the Haycocks did not fall

---

[14] The Treaty of Lausanne, entered into five years after the end of hostilities, in fact uses the term "High Contracting Parties" rather than Allied Powers. Those High Contracting Parties were the British Empire, France, Italy, Japan, Greece, Roumania and the Serb-Croat-Slovene State on the one hand, and Turkey on the other.

within the provisions, though, as will be shown below, Italian *jurisdiction* over them had been acknowledged. Whether or not the Mohabbakahs are islets rather than islands, and notwithstanding that Article 6 refers to islets, whereas Article 16 did not, the Mohabbakahs were not islets transferred to Italian title by virtue of Article 6.

157. Article 15 provided for the renunciation, in favour of Italy, of certain specified and named islands in the Aegean. Article 16 provided as follows:

Turkey hereby renounces all rights and title whatsoever over or respecting the territories situated outside the frontiers laid down in the present Treaty and the islands other than those over which her sovereignty is recognized by the said Treaty, the future of those territories and islands being settled or to be settled by the parties concerned . . .

158. Although "territories" and "islands" are separately mentioned, their treatment under Article 16 is identical. These phrases presumably covered also those islets not transferred by operation of Article 6. What was intended by "the parties concerned" is not wholly clear, but, given the knowledge of the claims of the Imam, as well as the hopes of Italy, and given further that the phrase used elsewhere in the Treaty is "The High Contracting Parties", it is not unreasonable to conclude that what was envisaged was a settlement of the matter in the future by all those having legal claims or high political interest in the islands, whether Treaty of Lausanne High Contracting Parties or not. A 1923 British Foreign Office document acknowledges, for example, the likelihood of France, Italy and Yemen being "interested parties". This interpretation accords with the assurances that Italy gave the Imam, at the time of the signature of the 1938 Anglo-Italian Agreement, that Yemen's "interests" had been "kept in mind", and with the working assumptions of the British Board of Trade with respect to the 1923 Treaty of Lausanne, that the "local Arab rulers on the mainland might put in their claim to be 'interested' parties".

159. It is not certain whether in 1923 either Great Britain or Italy would have regarded the reference to islands in the Red Sea over which Turkey had title as including the Haycocks. This was because Italian jurisdiction in those islands had already been acknowledged. Until the very end of the nineteenth century the Ottomans treated those living in Eritrea as being of Turkish nationality and subject to Ottoman jurisdiction. But certain accommodations were being reached. Italy had in 1883, 1887 and 1888 entered into a series of agreements with local Eritrean leaders. The Treaty of 1888 with the King of Shoa provided that "Italy will protect on the sea coast the safety of the Danakil littoral" (Art. VIII) and that "Italy will watch over the security of the sea and the Colony" (Art. IX). By Article V,

the Sultan Mohamed Hanfari ceded to Italy "the use of the territory of Ablis". In 1887 a further treaty, which seems to have no special relevance for the matters at issue, was signed. In 1888 a Treaty of Friendship and Commerce between Italy and the Head of the Danakils provided that Italy would guarantee the security of the Danakil coast. Further "The Sultan Mohamed Anfari recognises the whole of the Danakil coast from Afila to Ras Dumeira as an Italian possession" (Article 111). As a British Foreign Office Memorandum in 1930 was later to put it ". . . the Italian rights of surveillance drifted into what was tantamount to territorial rights to the littoral" and Great Britain, having made no protest, "could not now fall back upon the terms of the Agreement of May, 1887".

160. Exploring the possibility of a new shipping route on the African side of the Red Sea, and the need to light it, the British Government wrote to the Italian Government in 1892 referring to the proposed sites: North East Quoin (or alternatively Rahamet, on the coast), South West Rocks, "one of the Haycocks" and Harbi—and suggested that under Article 111 of the 1888 Treaty they appeared to be within the jurisdiction of Italy (though doubt was expressed internally about South West Rocks). It seems likely that this reading of Article 111 of the 1888 Treaty—which is not on its face self-evident— was influenced by the Hertslet memorandum of 1880 and its attached list. That Memorandum spoke of the western coast of the Red Sea as being under the jurisdiction of the Khedive of Egypt and the east coast as under the jurisdiction of the Sultan. Hertslet suggested that "the various islands and reefs in close proximity to the coast, and which are enumerated in List 1, would appear to be under" the Khedive's jurisdiction. List 1 includes "Harbi", White Quoin Hill, and "Mah-hab-bakah". The "Jibbel Zukur", "Little Harnish" and "Great Harnish" groups are attributed to the Eastern coast. "Haycock" appears twice within the list of islands appurtenant and in proximity to the east coast. As to the islands "near the centre" (listed by Hertslet as "Jibbel Teer" and the "Zebayar Group"), including a further Haycock, Hertslet in 1880 thought that "jurisdiction over the islands . . . would appear to be doubtful; but the sovereignty over them no doubt belongs to the Sultan".

161. It must also be noted that others within the British diplomatic service placed less weight on proximity.[15] Italy was asked whether it did indeed claim jurisdiction. Italy confirmed that "the places mentioned" were subject to its own jurisdiction. British recognition of Italian jurisdiction over the Haycocks (and presumably *a fortiori* of the Mohabbakahs) occurred in 1892. In 1930, internal British memoranda speak of Italian sovereignty over South West Haycock (or sometimes,

---

[15] See Reilly, *Aden and Yemen*, Colonial Office 1960, 69-70.

simply "the Haycocks") as having occurred in June 1892. But it was added "[e]xcept *as against ourselves*, the Italian claim to sovereignty over these islands does not appear to be very strong" (emphasis added).

162. Later evidence indicates that Great Britain regarded the issue of sovereignty as unsettled, even if Italian jurisdiction was acknowledged. Both the Mohabbakahs and the Haycocks would thus in 1923 be regarded by the Lausanne Treaty parties as Turkish territory falling, as to sovereignty, within the reach of Article 16, notwithstanding intermittent acceptance that they were under the jurisdiction of Italy.

163. The situation is clearer as regards Abu Ali, Jabal al-Tayr and the Zubayr group. They were envisaged at the time as having belonged to the Ottomans (but as never having previously been claimed by the Imam). These three islands fell under the terms of Article 16 of the Treaty of Lausanne.

164. There are three key points at issue in respect of Article 16. The first is the legal implications of it being *res inter alios acta* in respect of Yemen. The second is what islands in fact fell under this provision, i.e., were still under Ottoman sovereignty up to the date of the Treaty. The Tribunal has addressed these points above (see paras. 153-9). And the third is whether Article 16 either permitted acquisitive prescription by a single State of some or all of these islands and, if not, whether such acquisitive prescription could and did nonetheless occur (even if in violation of a treaty obligation).

165. The correct analysis of Article 16 is, in the Tribunal's view, the following: in 1923 Turkey renounced title to those islands over which it had sovereignty until then. They did not become *res nullius*—that is to say, open to acquisitive prescription—by any State, including any of the High Contracting Parties (including Italy). Nor did they automatically revert (in so far as they had ever belonged) to the Imam. Sovereign title over them remained indeterminate *pro tempore*. Great Britain certainly regarded it as likely that some undefined islands which "pertained to the Yemen" were covered by Article 16. Indeterminacy could be resolved by "the parties concerned" at some stage in the future—which must mean by present (or future) claimants *inter se*. That phrase is incompatible with the possibility that a single party could unilaterally resolve the matter by means of acquisitive prescription.

166. Given the Great Power politics in the region, the application of these legal principles was inevitably sometimes less than clear. Great Britain in fact secured jurisdiction over Kamaran island in this fashion; the records show that British civil servants and ministers over the years continued to entertain notions of appropriation of particular islands; but Great Britain was at pains to ensure the continued efficacy of Article 16 so far as Italian acts were concerned, through frequent enquiries to the Italian Government.

167. The islands to which the Article 16 proviso applied at the

outset were therefore the Mohabbakahs, the Haycocks, South West Rocks, and certainly the Zuqar-Hanish group, Abu Ali, Jabal al-Tayr and the Zubayr group.

168. Far from the Treaty of Lausanne "paving the way" for Italian sovereignty, as has been suggested by Eritrea, it presented a formidable obstacle. It is arguable that acquisitive prescription might nonetheless have been effected by Italy in the face of its obligations should the other parties to the Treaty of Lausanne have so allowed. Italy would have tried to secure the most favourable position, both on the ground and in diplomacy, for that day in the future when title would be determined. In terms of political aspiration, *animus occupandi* undoubtedly existed. But whether claims to sovereignty were made and acknowledged, so that certain islands would be effectively *au dehors* the reach of Article 16 of the Treaty of Lausanne, must be doubtful. Still less plausible is the contention that the High Contracting Parties (and Great Britain in particular) would have allowed, or acquiesced in, an incremental assumption of sovereignty by Italy.

The 1927 Rome Conversations

169. This conclusion is confirmed by the history following the Treaty of Lausanne. In 1927, conversations took place in Rome between the Italian Government and the British Government relating to British and Italian interests in Southern Arabia and the Red Sea ("the Rome Conversations"). In the signed record they agreed to cooperate in seeking to secure the pacification of Ibn Saud, the Imam Yahya and the Idrisi of Asir; and noted that Great Britain regarded it as "a vital imperial interest that no European Power should establish itself on the Arabian shore of the Red Sea, and more particularly on Kamaran or the Farsan islands, and that neither . . . shall fall into the hands of an unfriendly Arab Ruler". This proviso was repeated, *pari passu*, in respect of the west coast and Kamaran and the Farsan islands.

170. No such specific reference was made to the other islands now in dispute. Whereas Articles 4 and 6 apply to Kamaran and Farsan, Article 5 must, in the view of the Tribunal, be taken to apply to the other islands in dispute. Article 5 provided:

That there should be economic and commercial freedom on the Arabian coast and the islands of the Red Sea for citizens and subjects of the two countries and that the protection which such citizens and subjects may legitimately expect from their respective governments should not assume a political character or complexion.

171. This Article can only be understood to mean that acts which might otherwise be construed as providing an incremental acquisition of sovereignty were by the agreement of the parties not to be so

construed. To seek to identify acts "having a sovereign character" thus became without legal purpose.

172. Eritrea has argued that no legal weight is to be given to these provisions, in the first place because this record was not registered under Article 18 of the Covenant of the League of Nations and in the second place because it cannot be invoked by Yemen, either for that reason or because it was *res inter alios acta*. That this was not registered was undoubtedly because it was not regarded as a treaty between States. But it was nonetheless an accurate account of what both parties had agreed and was signed by them as such. It is simply evidence of the thinking of the time—this time by both parties—in much the same way as the Tribunal has been presented with a myriad of other evidence in non-treaty form. In so far as Yemen wishes to draw it to the attention of the Tribunal, it is not relying on a treaty that is *res inter alios acta*, nor indeed resting its own claim on it. It is diplomatic evidence, like any other, but of an undoubted interest because it reflects what was recorded by both parties as that which they had agreed to.

173. The provisions of Article 5 of the Rome Conversations were, of course, fully consistent with Article 16 of the Treaty of Lausanne, and indeed reinforced it. The former did not replace the latter but rather provided a further mechanism for assuring that fishing, commercial and navigation-related activities could continue without the indeterminate status of the islands being jeopardized.

174. Italy and Great Britain each now sought to ensure that sovereignty was indeed reserved. When Great Britain proposed to France certain arrangements concerning the management of the old Ottoman lighthouses at Abu Ail, Jabal al-Tayr, Centre Peak and Mocha, Italy asked for acknowledgment that the last belonged to Yemen and that sovereignty was reserved as to the first three islands. Great Britain was able to provide this. And when it was learned in London that Italy was preparing to build a lighthouse on South West Haycock (which it thought of as part of the Mohabbakahs) Great Britain sought assurance that the Haycocks as well as the Hanish islands were indeed viewed by Italy as falling under Article 5 of the Rome Conversations. Italy in 1930 informed Great Britain that it had sovereignty over South West Haycock, regarding which it made a specific reservation, that it lay in the Mohabbakahs, that it was prepared for South West Haycock and the rest of the Hanish islands to be treated in accordance with Article 5 of the Rome Conversations. The British reaction was not to take up the offer of talks from Italy, lest Italy should seek to have its sovereignty over South West Haycock "settled" within Article 16 of the Treaty of Lausanne, but rather tacit acceptance that everything should be treated under the framework of Article 5 of the Rome Conversations.

175. In 1931, further assurances were received from Italy over its establishment of armed posts on Greater Hanish and Jabal Zuqar. Italy assured Great Britain that these posts were for the protection of concessionaires and that sovereignty over the Hanish islands remained in abeyance. The juridical status of these islands was said to be the same as that of Farsan and Kamaran in the Rome Conversations of 1927. Further, Italy recalled that it had in 1926, during the negotiation of the abortive Lighthouse Convention of 1930, confirmed that sovereignty over Abu Ali, Zubayr and Jabal al-Tayr was equally to remain in abeyance, falling also under Article 5 of the Rome Conversations.

176. These assurances were also to be sufficient for the British authorities in the face of a 1933 incident in which *HMS Penzance* visited Jabal Zuqar and Hanish, noting, *inter alia*, the presence of Italian soldiers and the flying of the Italian flag. Great Britain, in the meantime, was providing comparable assurances regarding Kamaran.

177. The Italian Royal Legislative Decree No 1019 of 1 June 1936 made arrangements for the administration of Italian East Africa. It provided, *inter alia*, in its Article 4, that the territory of Dankalia was constituted by reference to a line from the lowlands to the east of Lake Ascianghi at the southern limit of Aussa and was part of Eritrea. Although no islands were named in terms, the specifying of the lines which constituted these administrative boundaries brought the Hanish-Zuqar group within the commissaryship of Dankalia. None of the line-drawing provided for by Decree 1019 covered Abu Ali, Zubayr or Jabal al-Tayr.

178. This was affirmed in terms by General Government Decree No 446 of 20 December 1938: "the Hanisc-Sucur Islands are deemed to be included within the bounds of the Commissaryship of the Government of Dancalia and Aussa (Assab)". In the view of the Tribunal these administrative arrangements cannot, in the light of the Rome Conversations and subsequent assurances, be regarded as international claims to sovereignty, rather than as to jurisdiction. Nor would they have been regarded as such by Great Britain. And only eight months beforehand Italy had assured the Imam that it had undertaken with Great Britain not to extend its sovereignty to the Hanish islands (and that it had been able to secure the dispatch of an Italian doctor to Kamaran on that basis).

179. At the same time, Italy unsuccessfully asked Great Britain to revoke its own Decree regarding Kamaran, which Italy regarded as upsetting the status quo agreement reached in 1927. At the same time, Great Britain did continue to regard the sovereignty over Kamaran as reserved.

180. Italy, which had recognized independent Yemen in 1926, entered into a treaty of Amity and Economic Relations with that

country in September 1937. While Italy confirmed unconditionally its "recognition of the full and absolute independence, without restrictions" of the King of Yemen and his Kingdom, the Tribunal cannot view this as illuminating the current problems.

181. Developments in Yemen and Saudi Arabia, including their relations with each other, made Italy and the United Kingdom believe that matters should be clarified further. After several months of negotiation there was signed on 16 April 1938 an Agreement and Protocols which entered into effect on 16 November 1938. Annex 3 of the Agreement included detailed dispositions of relevance to the Red Sea islands:

Article 1

Neither Party will conclude any agreement or take any action which might in any way impair the independence or integrity of Saudi Arabia or of the Yemen.

Article 2

Neither Party will obtain or seek to obtain a privileged position of a political character in any territory which at present belongs to Saudi Arabia or to the Yemen or in any territory which either of those States may hereafter acquire.

Article 3

The two Parties recognise that, in addition to the obligations incumbent on each of them in virtue of Articles 1 and 2 hereof, it is in the common interest of both of them that no other Power should acquire or seek to acquire sovereignty or any privileged position of a political character in any territory which at present belongs to Saudi Arabia or to the Yemen or which either of those States may hereafter acquire, including any islands in the Red Sea belonging to either of those States, or in any other islands in the Red Sea to which Turkey renounced her rights by Article 16 of the Treaty of Peace signed at Lausanne on the 24th July, 1923. In particular they regard it as an essential interest of each of them that no other Power should acquire sovereignty or any privileged position on any part of the coast of the Red Sea which at present belongs to Saudi Arabia or to the Yemen or in any of the aforesaid islands.

Article 4

(1) As regards those islands in the Red Sea to which Turkey renounced her rights by Article 16 of the Treaty of Peace signed at Lausanne on the 24th July, 1923, and which are not comprised in the territory of Saudi Arabia or of the Yemen, neither Party will, in or in regard to any such island:

(a) Establish its sovereignty, or

(b) Erect fortifications or defences.

(2) It is agreed that neither Party will object to:

(a) The presence of British officials at Kamaran for the purpose of securing the sanitary service of the pilgrimage to Mecca in accordance with the provisions of the Agreement concluded at Paris on the 19th June, 1926, between the Governments of Great Britain and Northern Ireland and of India, on the one part, and the Government of the Netherlands, on the other part; it is also understood that the Italian Government may appoint an Italian Medical Officer to be stationed there on the same conditions as the Netherlands Medical Officer under the said Agreement;

(b) The presence of Italian officials at Great Hanish, Little Hanish and Jebel Zukur for the purpose of protecting the fishermen who resort to those islands;

(c) The presence at Abu Ail, Centre Peak and Jebel Teir of such persons as are required for the maintenance of the lights on those islands.

182. The Ministry of Foreign Affairs of Italy had, in an internal Note of 31 March, made clear that the formula being negotiated would confirm that the Red Sea islands formerly under Turkish sovereignty "belong neither to Great Britain, Italy or the two Arab States, but remain of reserved sovereignty". An accompanying list of islands "of reserved sovereignty" indicated that Kamaran, Abu Ali and Jabal al-Tayr were at the time under British occupation, and described as occupied by Italy: Greater Hanish, Jabal Zuqar, Centre Peak, and Lesser Hanish. South West Haycock is not listed in the Italian Foreign Ministry Note as coming within this arrangement, notwithstanding the assurances on this point given to Great Britain in 1930 regarding understandings reached during the 1927 Rome Conversations. In the Treaty of 1938 itself, however, the islands agreed to fall within its provisions are not specified. Nor is there any reflection of an internal British proposal that the termination of the 1927 Rome Conversations be made clear.

183. It would seem that the 1938 Treaty is to be seen not as replacing but as supplementing and expanding the 1927 undertakings (always less than a formal treaty), the "political character and complex formula of the latter having been found unsatisfactory". The Rome Treaty was never registered with the League of Nations and by virtue of Article 18 of the Covenant could not be invoked by either party against the other. More relevant to Yemen is the fact that it is a third party to the treaty. There is no evidence, however, that either Italy or the United Kingdom failed to proceed with registration for any reason other than the approaching war clouds. The text of the treaty still has significance, which the Tribunal may properly take account of, as to the understanding of the parties in the autumn of 1938 regarding the current position of the islands and their intention at that moment as to how they should continue to be treated. No change is to be discerned from the essential thrust of what had gone before: claims were to remain inactive. The islands were not *res nullius* to be acquired by Italy or Great Britain.

184. The wording of Article 3 is not without its ambiguities. What it

does show is that, on the one hand, there *were* some islands in the Red Sea regarded in 1938 as belonging to Saudi Arabia and to Yemen. It also shows, on the other hand, that there were other Red Sea islands regarded as belonging to neither, and whose title was still indeterminate.

185. As Article 4 clearly and specifically refers to Kamaran, Greater Hanish, Little Hanish, Jabal Zuqar, Abu Ali, Centre Peak and Jabal al-Tayr as not being under the sovereignty of Saudi Arabia or Yemen, it is uncertain what islands were regarded as "at present belong[ing] to Yemen". In any event, Italy and the United Kingdom did not in 1938 regard title to any of the named islands as belonging to Yemen or as having been settled within the terms of Article 16 of the Treaty of Lausanne; and they each undertook not to establish sovereignty thereon. There is nothing in the record to show that the term "establish" in Article 4 was intended to mean other than "acquire" or "seek to acquire" sovereignty, as used in Article 3, through the various acts referred to in the Treaty, especially fortifications. It may be concluded that the 1938 Treaty evidences no recognition by Italy or Great Britain of any Yemeni title to the disputed islands. But at the same time the Treaty expressly excluded any Italian claims of sovereignty thereto.

186. The consequence of this series of international instruments and engagements was that from 1923 to 1938 Italy could make no claim that it already had a title that must be recognized. The only clear claim to sovereign title was to South West Haycock—but even that claim to an existing title was to be treated, at Italy's own suggestion, as "in abeyance" until title to the islands generally should later be settled by the parties concerned under Article 16 of the Treaty of Lausanne.

* * *

187. As for Yemen, it in turn made sporadic claims to Red Sea islands during this period, in general and unspecified terms. While Great Britain had assured Yemen that Italy's lighthouse activities did not prejudice Yemen's position, neither it nor Italy regarded the islands as being within Yemen's ownership up to 1938. As the Treaty of Lausanne provisions had been the mechanism by which the Ottoman Empire divested itself of ownership of these islands, that fact is not wholly without significance for Yemen, which, even putting the argument in its own terms, has to show not only a right of reversion but also that such a right overrode the decision that the previous sovereign had been obliged to make as to the future of the islands.

188. In 1933 Great Britain was in fact negotiating a Treaty with the Imam. The view was expressed within the Foreign Office that Yemen had legally been part of the Ottoman Empire and "any islands pertaining to it" were "fully covered by Article 16 of the Treaty of

Lausanne and the disposal was therefore a matter for international agreement". Contrary to the submissions of Yemen, this does not clearly assume Yemeni title—it assumes that what had been sovereign had now become indeterminate, until title was attributed by the "interested Parties".

189. The islands claimed by the Imam during the negotiation with the United Kingdom for the Treaty of Friendship and Mutual Cooperation of Sanaa of 1934 were without specific identification, but they were clearly later understood by the British to have meant Kamaran and the various unoccupied islands, the largest of which are Zuqar and Greater Hanish. The assertion of that claim was acknowledged although it was not reflected in the text of the Treaty and the refusal of the British Government to do more was made clear to the Imam.

* * *

190. As neither Italy nor Yemen held sovereign title at the outbreak of the Second World War, all the islands (save perhaps South West Haycock and the Mohabbakahs) may be assumed to have fallen within the relinquishment provisions that Italy was obliged to accept. This conclusion is also supported by an examination of the documents relating to the years 1941-50.

191. The 1941 Proclamation of British Military Jurisdiction brought under the command of Lieutenant-General Platt "[a]ll territories in Eritrea and Ethiopia". This wording seems to the Tribunal neither "broad" nor indeed "narrow", but merely general and uninformative geographically and legally. The Armistice did speak of the "[i]mmediate surrender of Corsica and of all the Italian territory, both islands and mainland, to the Allies . . ." (para. 6). But what islands are there referred to is wholly uncertain; the explanation in Article 41 of the "Additional Conditions of Armistice" with Italy that "the term 'Italian Territory' includes all Italian colonies and dependencies . . . (but without prejudice to the question of sovereignty) . . ." carries things no further. The phrase remains question-begging and in addition carries a specific caveat. Armistice agreements are instruments directed to stopping or containing hostilities and not to acknowledging or denying sovereign title.

192. In 1944 the British Colonial Office conducted an internal assessment on the status of Kamaran, the Great Hanish group, the Little Hanish group, the Jabal Zuqar group (including Abu Ali), the Zubayr group (including Centre Peak), and Jabal al-Tayr. In correspondence the history was briefly recounted, and it was recalled that under Article 16 of the Treaty of Lausanne "their future was to be settled by the 'parties concerned'. It never has been. They are in fact international waifs." The letter continued: "Once upon a time the Italians were interested in all these islands." It was thought that the

Dutch now had some interest.[16] "Apart from the British, however, the most serious claimant seems to be the Yemen, off whose coast all the islands lie." The claims of the Imam in 1934 were recalled.

193. The author of the letter (a civil servant within the Colonial Office) suggested that matters could be left as they were; or tidied up "in the same way"; or the UK could annex the islands.

194. Leaving aside the assessment of all the islands as "off Yemen's coast" or the assumption, without legal analysis, that they were free for annexation, the letter evidences what seemed to be a widely held view within the British Government that sovereignty over these islands remained unsettled within the terms of Article 16 of the Treaty of Lausanne.

195. By 1947 the question of title had, of course, to be faced in the Treaty of Peace with Italy. Under Article 23 Italy renounced "all right and title to the Italian territorial possessions in Africa, i.e., Libya, Eritrea and Italian Somaliland". The third paragraph of that provision then provided:

The final disposition of these possessions shall be determined jointly by the Governments of the Soviet Union, of the United Kingdom, of the United States of America, and of France within one year from the coming into force of the present Treaty . . .

That this did not refer to the islands here in issue is made fully clear by Article 43, which provides:

Italy hereby renounces any rights and interests she may possess by virtue of Article 16 of the Treaty of Lausanne signed on July 24, 1923.

Both the placement of this Article (at a point distant from Article 2) and the very need for such a provision made it clear that the disputed Red Sea islands did not fall to be disposed of under Article 23(3). This provision was not meant to operate as a revision or renunciation, by parties other than Italy, of Article 16 of the Treaty of Lausanne.

196. Instead, Article 16 of the Treaty of Lausanne remained intact. Italy was now obliged to renounce "any rights and interests" under it. This refers not merely, as has been submitted by Yemen, to Italy's right to protest at a purported acquisition by another or to be party eventually to a settlement of title. It refers also to a renunciation of any claims Italy might have made and any legal interests she might have asserted regarding the islands.

197. A United Nations working paper drawn up in December 1949 in connection with the preparation of the draft Eritrean Constitution

---

[16] The Dutch had not been signatories to the 1923 Treaty of Lausanne and had in fact remained neutral in the First World War.

supports the view that the Hanish, Zuqar and more northerly islands were not among those to be settled (and eventually affirmed as passing to independent Eritrea). The section on the Geography and History of Eritrea says that the Italian colony "includes the Dahlak archipelago off Massawa, and the islands further south off the coast of the Danakil country". This would seem to refer to those Mohabbakahs in proximity to Assab. The section that recalls the "attempts to colonize the highlands of Eritrea" makes no reference to any colonization of the islands.

198. The Ministry of Foreign Affairs of Ethiopia did protest when it commented on the draft Constitution. It pointed out that the language used in Article 2 of the draft Constitution "would impliedly exclude all archipelagoes and islands off the coast. Surely, this exclusion was not intended." But that language—namely that "the territory of Eritrea, including the islands, is that of the former Italian colony of Eritrea"—remained intact in the final text of the Constitution.

199. The Italian Government had also been invited to express its opinions on the future of Eritrea to the UN Commission on Eritrea. Italy urged independence for Eritrea, emphasizing that its renunciation of all title did not make Eritrea a *res nullius*. It spoke of the regions that had been occupied by Italy to establish Eritrea. In that context, reference was made to the Dahlak islands. In urging the continued unity of Eritrea no mention was made of any other islands. None of the rapidly ensuing instruments—the British Military Authority (BMA) Termination of Powers Proclamation of 1952, or the revised Constitution of Eritrea of 1955—changed matters.

CHAPTER VI   Red Sea Lighthouses

200. The Red Sea lights bear on this arbitration in three main ways. First, each of the Parties has at various moments suggested that its establishment or maintenance of lighthouses on the various islands constitute acts of sovereignty. Second, the diplomatic correspondence relating to the lighthouses might throw some light on the underlying claims to the islands where they are located, not least because the lighthouse islands were necessarily named. So much of the other material relates to islands without specification. Third, the relationship between the several lighthouse conventions and the provisions of Article 16 of the Treaty of Lausanne might have some legal significance.

201. From the late nineteenth century the Red Sea lights have had an historical importance in this region, although this is now somewhat reduced with the advent of radar. But radar may not be available to many of those fishing in the Zuqar-Hanish islands. The Ottoman authorities, and later the various coastal States, along with the major shipping users, have all played a role in the story of the Red Sea lights. In 1930, a proposed treaty regime for the lights was drawn up, but

never came into force. From 1962 until 1989, a treaty regime did indeed govern the lights.

202. In 1881, the Ottoman Empire granted a forty-year concession to the *Société des Phares de l'Empire Ottoman*, owned by Messieurs Michel and Collas, to build a series of lighthouses in the Red Sea and the Persian Gulf. Almost endless disputes were to arise regarding the concession for the Red Sea lighthouses.

203. The British Government had proposed to the Sublime Porte that four lights should be erected at Jabal al-Tayr, Abu Ail, Jabal Zubayr and at Mocha, to assist navigation. Anxious at the difficulties encountered with the concessionaires, it began in 1891 to revive an earlier idea to explore the possibility of a western navigation route through the Red Sea. As the envisaged route was to be "abreast of the Italian possessions at Assab", Italy was asked to facilitate the technical mission and to allow supplies to be taken on at Assab—a request to which Italy readily agreed.

204. Once a western route was recommended by the Board of Trade, the British Government had to concern itself with questions of title. The so-called "Western Hanish" route would have entailed lights on North East Quoin (or at Rakmat), South West Rocks, one of the Haycock islets and Harbi islet. In 1891 the Board of Trade, relying on the Hertslet Memorandum of 1880, suggested that North East Quoin and Harbi were within Egyptian jurisdiction and South West Rocks and the Haycocks within Ottoman jurisdiction—with the Sublime Porte claiming sovereignty to all four islands. The Marquis of Salisbury, in writing to the British Ambassador to Rome in January 1892, stated "The islands and rocks recommended by the Board of Trade . . ., with the exception of South-west Rocks, seems [sic] to be in effect within the jurisdiction of Italy. That over the South-west Rocks would appear to be doubtful." From 1881 to 1892 there was an extended international correspondence on this subject.

205. A Note of 3 February 1892 was addressed to the Italian Government to seek clarification. The Note included the statement that "according to Article 3 of the Treaty between Italy and Sultan Ahfari of Aussa of the 9th December 1888", the jurisdiction over the new sites, "with the exception perhaps of South-West Rocks, appears to belong to Italy". Italy was asked whether it claimed jurisdiction over these sites, and if so whether it would itself be prepared to erect lights there, or alternatively if it would be willing for Great Britain to do so.

206. The Italian Government replied in June of that year that "the King's Government consider these points as a maritime appendage of the territory over which they exercise their sovereignty" but urged the British Government to erect and maintain the lighthouses and to fix the method of reimbursement.

207. In the event, the western route was not proceeded with and the

Ottomans arranged for the building of four lighthouses at Mocha on the Arabian coast, and on Jabal al-Tayr, on Abu Ali and in the Zubayr group (on Centre Peak). This was maintained by the French concessionaires for the Ottomans until 1915. Great Britain occupied the three lighthouse islands in 1915.

208. When the Ottoman Empire was required to renounce its possessions, sovereignty over the lighthouse islands fell, under Article 16 of the Treaty of Lausanne, "to be settled by the parties concerned". The light at Mocha was recognized by Great Britain as being within the territory succeeded to by the Imam. Great Britain had on occasion contemplated trying to acquire sovereignty over the islands it occupied but on balance thought they did not have enough strategic value. It is significant that Great Britain did not regard itself as precluded from attempting to acquire sovereignty by the terms of Article 16 of the Treaty of Lausanne. It was not until 1927 that Great Britain formally stated (to France) that it had definitely renounced this idea. And in certain quarters the idea of annexing Hanish and Zuqar, as well as Jabal al-Tayr and Abu Ali, was not totally dead even in 1944.

209. It is also striking that, throughout the series of enquiries that Great Britain was to make after 1923 to Italy about the status of certain other islands, it never once put to Italy that a claim would be contrary to the terms of Article 16 of the Treaty of Lausanne. Rather, Great Britain was content to satisfy itself that Italy's position was consistent with the bilateral understandings of the Rome Conversations of 1927.

210. Notwithstanding this, the Tribunal has already indicated that in its view the history, text and purpose of Article 16 argues against the unilateral acquisition of title over the islands whose status was left undetermined in 1923. Nor is it necessary to consider whether Italy was seeking to establish title contrary to the agreement in hand and entered into in the Treaty of Lausanne, because Italy's posture was in fact much more cautious.

211. In 1927 Great Britain negotiated an agreement with France for the maintenance of all four lighthouses by the French company and approached the main users of the route—Germany, the Netherlands, Japan and Italy—to regulate the matter by a convention. Italy, expressing the wish that it had been consulted earlier, made two points. First, Mocha was claimed by the Imam and he should be a party. Second, Italy wished to know whether sovereignty of the islands was to be attributed to the neighbourhood coast or whether the point would be reserved. No Italian claim to any of the islands was presented. The British Government conceded that Mocha was under the rule of the Imam and affirmed that the status of the islands was to be reserved. These reassurances led to the conclusion of the Convention concerning the Maintenance of Certain Lights of 1930.

212. Although this Convention did not enter into force, and thus cannot be said to bind the parties as a treaty, it is useful evidence of their thinking at that date. The preamble and the annex refer to the renunciation by Turkey of both the islands and of Mocha, the occupation of the islands by Great Britain, and the provision in Article 16 of the Treaty of Lausanne that "the future of these islands, and of that territory [is] a matter for settlement by the Parties concerned". The annex continued: "(e) . . . no agreement on this subject has been come to among the parties concerned and it is desirable in the interests of shipping to ensure that the lighthouses on the said islands shall be maintained". It then proceeded to determine that a lighthouse company should take possession of and manage the lighthouses on Abu Ali, Zubayr and Jabal al-Tayr. Italy was prepared to put its signature to this and to Article 13, which clearly affirmed the continued operation of Article 16 of the Treaty of Lausanne:

Art. 13. In the event of the arrangement contemplated in article 16 of the Treaty of Lausanne being concluded between the parties concerned, the High Contracting Parties will meet in conference in order to decide whether it is desirable to terminate the present Convention, or to modify its terms with a view to making it conform to the aforesaid arrangement.

213. Although the 1930 Convention was ratified by Italy and the Netherlands, it did not come into force, because the French Government was locked in disagreement with the British Government as to whether the lighthouse company, Michel et Collas, should be paid on the basis of gold. France refused to ratify.

214. In the meantime, in the very same year, Italy was preparing to erect a lighthouse on South West Haycock. The Haycocks had not been specifically mentioned in the 1927 Rome Conversations and the British were anxious to establish that Article 5 thereof should nonetheless apply, the more so as "the erection of a lighthouse . . . may be regarded as implying some definite claim to sovereignty". Great Britain was concerned as to whether indeed South West Haycock did fall within the Rome Conversations—there were internal divisions on the question of title—and it noted that the islet was only twenty miles from the "Italian" coast. It was decided to seek assurances. These were sought in an *aide-mémoire* of 18 February 1930, in which Italy was reminded of the earlier exchanges in 1927. In that document Great Britain referred to South West Haycock as being "in the Hanish group of Islands".

215. In its Pro-Memoria of 11 April 1930, Italy observed that the lighthouse was being built for navigational reasons. It asserted that South West Haycock was not part of the Hanish islands, but rather belonged to the Mohabbakah archipelago over which it alleged that

the Ottomans had never claimed sovereignty.[17] Italy therefore made "a special reserve regarding Italian sovereignty over this island" and then consented to "the question being considered on the same lines as that of the sovereignty of all the islands of the Hanish group, in accordance with the spirit of the conversations of Rome of 1927".

216. The Pro-Memoria can only be read as a claim to sovereignty over South West Haycock by Italy (while at the same time agreeing that the erection of the lighthouse was to be treated as a commercial rather than a sovereign act) and a failure to advance a comparable claim to title over the Hanish group. The internal evidence shows that this was an assessment that Great Britain was at the time inclined to accept, and with which it was satisfied; although in other documents Great Britain treats South West Haycock as part of the Hanish group, and as having been Ottoman. In the event, all fell to be treated as provided by Article 16 of the Treaty of Lausanne, which was reinforced by the understandings reached in the Rome Conversations.

217. The South West Haycock lighthouse was extinguished in 1940. It was abandoned after 1945. When the 1930 Convention failed to come into effect the British authorities were left with the sole financial burden of the existing lights. It decided to abandon the Centre Peak light (in the Zubayr group) from September 1932 and Italy (which had been notified, along with France) reactivated the Centre Peak light in 1933. The decision was taken in Italy to inform the "interested powers" that this was being done for reasons of navigational necessity, and that the Imam "who lays claim to rights over the islands" should be "informed of the provisional nature of the occupation and the usefulness to himself in having the lighthouse reactivated". It was apparently originally intended to ask for contributions, but in the event this was not done.

218. The British authorities were notified by Note Verbale on 4 October 1933 of the anxieties of the Captain of the Port at Massawa as to safety on the Massawa–Hodeidah route, in the absence of the Centre Peak light, and of Italy's decision to take over the lighthouse. The Note Verbale expressly stated:

... the Royal Ministry for Foreign Affairs need hardly add that the presence of an Italian staff on the Island of Zebair (Centre Peak), which will ensure the operation of the light, implies no modification of the international judicial status of the island itself, which, together with the islands of Abu Ail and Gebel Taiz [sic], was considered by the Italian and British governments in 1928 during the negotiations for the Red Sea Lights Convention, when the conclusion was reached that the question of sovereignty of those islands should remain in suspense.

[17] The Tribunal notes, however, that prior to Italian occupation, the islands off the African coast were administered by the Khedive of Egypt on behalf of the Ottoman Empire.

219. Thus in the northern islands, too, Italy had established a navigational interest but affirmed that it had no implications for sovereignty. The British decided this was a sufficient comfort not to have to pursue this matter further with the Italians.

220. The situation remained essentially unchanged by the 1938 agreement. Article 4(2) of Annex 3 again affirmed that neither Great Britain nor Italy would establish sovereignty over the renounced islands, following Article 16 of the Treaty of Lausanne, and that no objections would be raised to lighthouse personnel.

221. By the outbreak of the Second World War it may be said that the maintenance of the lights is seen as a non-sovereign act and there is agreement that the underlying title to the islands concerned was left in abeyance—though Italy had asserted title (even if choosing not to press it) to South West Haycock. But this turned upon a perception of South West Haycock as being part of the Mohabbakahs, rather than upon any suggestion that the erection of a lighthouse thereon itself had a role in establishing sovereignty. In the course of the Second World War, the South West Haycock and the Centre Peak lights were extinguished.

222. In June 1948 the British Military Authority (BMA) in Eritrea sought legal advice as to whether it was liable under any international conventions for the re-establishment of various lights previously operated by the Government of Italy. These included those at South West Haycock and at Centre Peak. The advice (which eventually came from the Ministry of Transport) was that there was no obligation under any convention.

223. The decision by the BMA that it had no responsibility for the lights at South West Haycock and Centre Peak was not because it thought those islands were not Italian. No particular attention seems to have been given to that aspect. Rather, it was decided that as long as the Abu Ali light was maintained there was no real danger to shipping. Further, the Admiralty advised that a State was under no obligation to light its coasts. Thus even if South West Haycock and Centre Peak had been Italian (and neither was addressed in the 1948 correspondence nor is there any evidence that Zubayr was ever regarded by the British as Italian), no obligation was passed to the BMA as the occupying power.

224. After the Second World War, the British did continue to take responsibility for the lighthouses at Abu Ali and Jabal al-Tayr, and from 1945 received financial contribution from the Netherlands. These arrangements were in 1962 brought within an agreement made between Denmark, Federal Republic of Germany, Italy, the Netherlands, Norway, Sweden, the United Kingdom and the United States, and formally accepted also by Pakistan, the Soviet Union and the United Arab Republic. Yemen was not a party. Nor was Ethiopia.

The criterion for invitation was clearly that of navigational importance and not of title to the coast or islands. The opening recitals to the 1962 agreement rehearse the history of the Abu Ail and Jabal al-Tayr lights, recall the abortive 1930 Convention, refer to Article 16 of the Treaty of Lausanne, and add: "No agreement on the subject of the future of the above-mentioned islands has been come to among the Parties concerned."

225. Further, Article 8 was to make crystal clear that nothing in the text following was to be regarded either as a settlement of the future of the islands referred to in Article 16 of the Treaty of Lausanne, "or as prejudicing the conclusion of any such settlement". This Article reproduces the provisions of Article 15A of the 1930 Lighthouses Convention. The United Kingdom was affirmed as the "Managing Government" for these two lights and was entitled to appoint an agent for this purpose (Article 2). Article 6 provided for discontinuance of this role upon notice to the other parties, and indicated the procedures to be followed in that eventuality.

226. As in 1930, the managerial role of the United Kingdom had nothing to do with the issue of title to the islands; nor did management even place the United Kingdom in a favourable position for when the title issue came to be resolved. This clearly followed the pattern of the Rome Understandings (as they bear on the management of lights) and of the abortive 1930 Convention—even though the 1962 Convention concerned two lights only.

227. The United Kingdom managed the lighthouses at Jabal al-Tayr and Abu Ali from Aden, but realized that arrangements would have to be made when the British would leave Aden upon the independence of the People's Democratic Republic of Yemen in 1967. The Savon and Ries Company was accordingly appointed agent under Article 2 of the 1962 agreement, for management duties. It so happened that Savon and Ries were operating out of Massawa, and the staff engaged in lighthouse functions at the Board's request came increasingly from Ethiopia, but in the view of the Tribunal this was simply a matter of practical convenience. The various Ethiopian authorizations for inspection and repair visits to the islands and the control exercised over radio transmissions were immaterial as to sovereignty. Everything remained as it had been so far as title to the islands was concerned—that is to say, Article 8 of the 1962 Convention continued to govern.

228. In 1971 the British Government decided to replace the lights by automatic lights, dispensing with the services of lighthouse-keepers. The United Kingdom notified Yemen of this intention, assured that Government that "the action of the Board of Trade in accordance with [the 1962 Convention] does not infringe upon rights of sovereignty" and asked whether Yemen had any objection. The fact that the

communication was addressed to Yemen, a non-signatory of the 1962 Convention, would seem to indicate that, while the islands remained unattributed in accordance with the terms of the 1962 Treaty, Yemen was regarded by the United Kingdom as a "party concerned" within the terms of Article 16 of the Treaty of Lausanne and as having claims to Abu Ali and Jabal al-Tayr that should not be prejudiced. It may also be noted that by this time Italy had lost its possessions on the Red Sea coast and was not, therefore, any longer a "party concerned" within the meaning of Article 16 of the Treaty of Lausanne.[18]

229. Although at an earlier era the legal advice within the British Government was that Abu Ali and Jabal al-Tayr (as well as Centre Peak) were islands that were *res nullius* and various candidates had been suggested at different moments of time as "parties concerned", it would seem that by the early 1970s Yemen was regarded as the leading "party concerned" for purposes of Article 16 of the Treaty of Lausanne, at least so far as Abu Ali and Jabal al-Tayr were concerned.

230. In 1975 the management of these two lights was transferred from Savon and Ries' offices in Ethiopia to its offices in Djibouti. Five years later, the agency for management was passed by the British authorities to a new company it had formed, the Red Sea Lights Company.

231. In 1987 Yemen relit the lighthouse on Centre Peak, issued pertinent Notices to Mariners and, in 1988, upgraded it. This appears to have occasioned no protest by Ethiopia, which could not have assumed that such acts were rendered without significance by virtue of Article 16 of the Treaty of Lausanne (to which Yemen was not a party), or by the various bilateral Italian–UK agreements, or by the 1962 Lighthouse Convention—none of which were opposable to Yemen.

232. On 20 June 1989, Yemen contacted the United Kingdom regarding "the matter of the Lighthouses installed on Abu Ali (Ail) and Jabal al Tair Islands which is to be discussed on Tuesday 20 June 1989". Yemen formally stated that:

1. The two Islands mentioned above lie within the exclusive economic zone of the Yemen Arab Republic.

2. In the light of this fact the Yemen Arab Republic is willing to take the responsibility of managing and operating the said two lighthouses for the benefit of National and International Navigation. As you may be aware, the Ports and Marine Affairs Corporation in the Yemen Arab Republic is already running and operating several lighthouses some of which lie within the area of these two Islands.

---

[18] Nor has Italy or, for that matter, any State asserted that it considers itself to be "a party concerned" for this purpose. The Tribunal therefore concludes that, with respect to the islands in dispute, the only present-day "parties concerned" are the Parties to this arbitration.

233. Unless positive action was taken to extend the 1962 Convention, it would expire in March 1990. In 1988 and 1989 it became clear that many parties had denounced the 1962 Treaty or indicated their intention to do so. The United Kingdom, the managing authority of the lights, was among these. Egypt offered to take over that role, but it was clear that there were not sufficient votes for extending the Convention beyond 1990.

234. A meeting of the parties was held in London in June 1989. Having established its credentials and interest, Yemen was invited as an observer to the 1989 Conference on the future of the two northern lights, notwithstanding the fact that (like Ethiopia) it had not been a party to the 1962 agreement. The Report to the Government of Yemen of the Yemeni technicians attending the 1989 meeting refers to the fact that the British had confirmed the installation and operation by Yemen of new lighthouses on Jabal Zubayr and Jabal Zuqar. Manifested interest and professional competence appear to be the motivating factors for Yemen's presence. Ethiopia was not invited to attend and had not requested this.

235. Yemen supported the Egyptian proposal that Yemen would manage the lighthouses on Jabal al-Tayr and Abu Ali and did so without reserve as to title. The minutes show that they also indicated their willingness to operate lights on the two islands at their own expense with almost immediate effect should the agreement lapse. The minutes contain no reference by Yemen to the islands being in its Exclusive Economic Zone—though that point had been included in the pre-meeting exchanges with the United Kingdom.

236. The reference to Yemen's Exclusive Economic Zone rather than to title to the islands themselves does not appear to have been casual. It is mentioned twice again in the internal report sent after the 1989 conference from the Yemeni Director-General of the Ports and Maritime Affairs to the Government of Yemen. Yemen's offer—which was accepted—was in language other than claim of a right of sovereign title. Yemen did not say that it had title to Abu Ali or Jabal al-Tayr, nor to the nearby islands, and thus it would be for it alone to provide any lights. The 1961 agreement had no chance of survival and Egypt's offer to become managing authority could not provide the answer. The international treaty regime for the Red Sea lights was coming to an end.

237. The erection and maintenance of lights, outside of any treaty arrangements and for the indefinite future, had certain implications. The acceptance of Yemen's offer did not constitute recognition of Yemen sovereignty over islands. But it did accept the reality that Yemen was best placed, and was willing, to take on the role of providing and managing lights in that part of the Red Sea; and that when the time came finally to determine the status of those islands

Yemen would certainly be a "party concerned". (Yemen, of course, was not bound by Article 8 of the 1962 Convention and indeed appears not to have known at the time of the arrangements made under it.)

238. Eritrea has contended that there was no need for Ethiopia to have protested the relighting by Yemen of lights on Abu Ali and Jabal al-Tayr, as its "activities were merely a continuation of the historic activities of Great Britain on Jabal A'Tair and Abu Ali". But Yemen was not in the same legal relationship with Ethiopia over the matter of lights as had been Great Britain and, if such was the reasoning for a failure to reserve claimed Ethiopian sovereignty, it was misplaced.

CHAPTER VII   Evidences of the Display of Functions of State and Governmental Authority

Analysis of the Evidence

239. The factual evidence of "*effectivités*" presented to the Tribunal by both Parties is voluminous in quantity but is sparse in useful content. This is doubtless owing to the inhospitability of the Islands themselves and the relative meagreness of their human history. The modern international law of the acquisition (or attribution) of territory generally requires that there be: an intentional display of power and authority over the territory, by the exercise of jurisdiction and State functions, on a continuous and peaceful basis. The latter two criteria are tempered to suit the nature of the territory and the size of its population, if any. The facts alleged by Eritrea and Yemen in the present case must be measured against these tests, with the following qualification. Not only were these islands for long uninhabited and ungoverned or, if at all, governed in the most attenuated sense, but the facts on which Eritrea relies were acts by its predecessor, Ethiopia, which were not "peaceful", unless that term may here be understood to include acts in prosecution of a civil war. Nevertheless, the Tribunal cannot discount these facts, given the singular circumstances of this case.

240. The Tribunal has found it useful to classify the wide variety of factual evidence advanced by the Parties in relation to this subject, and will now examine these categories of evidence in turn.

Assertion of Intention to Claim the Islands

241. Evidence of intention to claim the Islands *à titre de souverain* is an essential element of the process of consolidation of title. That intention can be evidenced by showing a public claim of right or assertion of sovereignty to the Islands as well as legislative acts openly seeking to regulate activity on the Islands. The Tribunal notes that the evidence submitted by both Parties is replete with assertions of sovereignty and

jurisdiction that fail to mention any islands whatsoever, and with general references to "the islands" with no further specificity.

Public Claims to Sovereignty over the Islands

242. Eritrea's claim that these islands were included as part of "the former Italian colony of Eritrea" by the Italian Military Armistice of 1943, the 1947 Treaty of Peace, and the 1952 Constitution is barely supported by evidence. It is true that Italy wished to claim the islands and indeed established a presence on some of them; but these facts were always subject to repeated assurances that the islands' legal position was indeterminate in accordance with Article 16 of the Treaty of Lausanne and with the Rome Conversations (see Chapter V, above). The 1952 Eritrean Constitution defined the extent of Eritrean territory as "including the islands", but failed to specify which islands were intended. The same uncertainty existed in the language of Article 2 of the United Nations Resolution approving the 1952 Constitution, the 1955 Ethiopian Constitution, the 1987 revision of the Ethiopian Constitution, and the 1997 Constitution of the newly independent State of Eritrea.

243. The scant evidence of Ethiopian legislation before the Tribunal suffers from the same uncertainty as do the constitutional provisions. The 1953 Ethiopian Federal Crimes Proclamation and a 1953 Maritime Order put in evidence by Eritrea were not explicit about the Islands. The former was content merely to specify "any island which may be considered as appertaining to Ethiopia", and the latter simply republished the phrase "including the islands". A Maritime Proclamation of 1953 referred merely to "the coasts of the Ethiopian islands".

244. Seventeen years later, in 1970, Ethiopia promulgated an order for a state of emergency. This Order did not specify the Islands; nor did the implementing regulations promulgated by the Minister of National Defence. Three 1971 operations orders are cited by Eritrea to demonstrate that "the islands in dispute here fell within the ambit of Ethiopia's concern". They identify Greater Hanish and Jabal Zuqar as being "areas" to be visited or as reference points for patrol routes. In 1987, the Ethiopian Ministry of National Defence was given responsibility "for the defence of the country's territorial waters and islands" but, again, those "islands" remained unidentified.

245. In 1973, the Ministry of Foreign Affairs of the Yemen Arab Republic informed the Imperial Ethiopian Embassy in Sanaa of the YAR's plans to conduct a full aerial survey of its territory that would cover certain "Yemeni islands". These were identified as: "Great Hanish", "Little Hanish", "Jabal Zuqur", "Jabal al Zair", "Jabal Zal Tair", and "Humar". The reason given for the notification was that the photographs, which were to be taken from a height of 30,000 feet, might show "parts of the Ethiopian coasts". Ethiopia responded that

"some of the islands listed in the afore-mentioned note could not be identified under the nomenclature used, while others are Ethiopian islands". This exchange of correspondence is cited in a January 1977 "Top Secret" memorandum of the Ministry of Foreign Affairs of the Provisional Military Government of Socialist Ethiopia, which details the measures Ethiopia considered taking to protect its interests. The memorandum refers to islands in the southern part of the Red Sea that "have had no recognized owner", with respect to which Ethiopia "claims jurisdiction"[19] and "both North and South Yemen have started to make claims". It names the Hanish islands, Jabal Zuqar, Jabal al-Tayr and Jabal Zubayr, and points out that the 1973 response to the YAR had deliberately been left vague, because there was insufficient time to collect evidence in support of Ethiopia's "claim over the islands" and for fear of provoking a military response from Yemen and its Arab allies, particularly in the wake of false reports, in 1973, of an Israeli presence on certain Red Sea islands. The memorandum urges that "Ethiopia . . . take a clear stand in this respect in order to protect its ownership".

246. Yemen relies on a claim of historic title, asserted to stem from time immemorial. It was allegedly most early evidenced in 1429, when King al-Zahir of Yemen sent a mission to Jabal Zuqar to investigate two vessels engaged in smuggling that had run aground on the island. The relevance of this happening is vigorously contested by Eritrea on various grounds which were not responded to in substance by Yemen. It appears to be unique, and isolated. The Tribunal does not consider it important in relation to the determination of title to Zuqar. Its only significance (which has been substantially weakened by Eritrea's rebuttal of its relevance, not replied to by Yemen) might be that it could support an interpretation of the Imam's aspirations so as to include at least Jabal Zuqar, but that in turn fails since there is no evidence that when he advanced his claim of historic rights in 1918, the Imam knew of the 1429 expedition. Moreover, the source for that information was only published in 1976, long after the claim of historic rights had allegedly been advanced by the Imam.

247. In his reply to a British proposal for a treaty of friendship, the Imam is recorded as having requested, *inter alia*, "(2) Establishment of his rule and independence over all the Yemen, i.e., over that part which was once under the sway of his predecessors . . .". This claim could not have been more general. Indeed, the word "that part", being expressed in the singular, would not seem naturally applicable to islands. This generalized claim was apparently manifested on several occasions in bilateral diplomatic conversations during the inter-War period, but no constitutional or legislative act of Yemen or of the

---

[19] Eritrea has submitted two translations of this document, one of which refers to "jurisdiction" and the other to "sovereignty".

Imam claimed any of the Islands specifically or described them specifically as Yemeni territory.

248. Yemen asserted in the oral hearings that in 1933: ". . . certain British representatives expressed puzzlement as to why the Imam was so adamant about his claim to the islands of Al-Yemen, including the islands of the Hanish Group". The Yemeni Foreign Minister allegedly "made the Imam's claim to the Hanish Islands well known to German officials in 1930, France in 1936 and, of course, England, in connection with the 1934 treaty and on many other occasions". Yemen added that "the Imam stated and restated his historic claims to the British, to the French and to the Italians whenever this was practically possible", and this appears to be borne out by contemporaneous evidence from 1930 to 1936.

249. Other evidence of communications between the Imam and British diplomats, including the records of the Clayton mission of 1926, and Colonel Reilly's communications to the Foreign Office are too vague to serve as evidence of a specific claim by the Imam to the Islands at that time.

250. Although Yemen asserted in the oral hearings that Yemen's response to the granting of an oil concession by the United Kingdom in the area of Kamaran Island in 1956 "restated the claim to the Red Sea Islands", the language actually used in the official statement merely stated that "[t]he Yemeni Government considers Kamaran island and the other Yemeni islands to be a[n] inseparable part of Yemen". It also added that "[t]he Yemeni Government continues to insist upon its rights to the Yemeni islands and their liberation". A likely inference to be drawn from this is that the "islands" referred to could not have been the islands now in question since those were not islands that required "liberation".

251. In 1973 there were press reports that Israel had occupied Jabal Zuqar with the permission of Ethiopia. Substantial effort was devoted by both sides in the proceedings to seeking to demonstrate that the respective reactions to the matter were relevant to sovereignty over the Islands. A 1973 press statement issued by the Embassy of the Yemen Arab Republic in Mogadishu reported that Yemeni investigations had found "Lesser Hanash, Greater Hanash, Zukar, Alzubair, Alswabe and several other islands at the Yemeni coast" to be free of foreign infiltration, and further stated that:

[. . .]
The YAR always controls and maintains its sovereignty over its islands at the Red Sea, with the exception of the islands of Gabal Abu Ali and Gabal Attair which were given to Ethiopia by Britain when the latter left Aden and surrendered power in our Southern Yemen.

This supports an inference that the phrase "its islands in the Red Sea" included the disputed Islands; moreover, the press statement emphasized that the Yemen Arab Republic maintained its claim of sovereignty over those islands "given by Britain to Ethiopia", and urged Ethiopia to surrender those islands.

252. Yemen's "historic claim" was initially expressed in vague and general terms following the end of World War I, and reiterated in bilateral diplomatic contexts in the inter-War period. After World War II it was reasserted in 1956, even though largely in doubtful and indirect terms. In 1973, however, it was expressly revived in a public statement (which, although it said that Jabal al-Tayr and the Zubayr group had been "given to Ethiopia", also reasserted Yemen's "rights and possession" to them and was specific about the other, "mentioned", islands). The statement therefore left little room for doubt that Yemen had sustained or renewed its claim over all of the larger Islands, including the northern islands—or, at any rate, as of 1973. There is no evidence that Yemen subsequently abandoned or relinquished this claim. The evidence does, however, also suggest that Yemen had no presence on and little knowledge about Jabal al-Tayr and the Zubayr group at that time, and supposed that they were in the possession of Ethiopia. The fact was that, for many years, the northern lighthouses were administered from Ethiopia by employees of the lighthouse company.

Legislative Acts Seeking to Regulate Activity on the Islands

253. There is no evidence of post-war Ethiopian legislation seeking expressly to regulate activity on the Islands. As discussed above, no Ethiopian legislation between 1953 and 1992 specifically purported to exercise jurisdiction and State functions over the Islands. From 1992 to the inception of the dispute in 1995, no Eritrean legislation explicitly treated the Islands as being subject to the jurisdiction and control of Eritrea.

254. The Ethiopian Federal Crimes Proclamation and the 1953 Maritime Order put in evidence by Eritrea were not explicit. They applied to "any island which may be considered as appertaining to Ethiopia" and "the islands". A related Maritime Proclamation of 1953 referred merely to "the coasts of the Ethiopian islands". These instruments would of course have applied to the Dahlak group and to the islands in the Bay of Assab; but those islands are not disputed.

255. As to Yemen, the evidence of administrative and legislative decrees advanced to support a claim of the exercise of State functions follows substantially the same pattern as the evidence introduced by Ethiopia: there is silence as to whether the Islands are intended to be included in the ambit of the decrees. There is no evidence of Yemeni

legislation openly seeking to regulate activity on the Islands. From 1923 to the inception of the dispute in 1995, no Yemeni legislation specifically treated the Islands as being subject to the jurisdiction and control of Yemen.

256. In 1967, two decrees were issued by the President of the Yemen Arab Republic concerning territorial waters and continental shelf. However these did not mention the Islands by name. Yemen contends that the subsequent Yemeni licensing in 1987 of a research programme in waters off the Islands by the German research vessel, the *F. S. Meteor*, demonstrated their applicability to the Islands. While that is unclear, it is arguable that this incident can be viewed as crystallizing Yemeni intent as to the scope of the 1967 legislation.

257. In conclusion, the evidence on behalf of both Parties shows legislative and constitutional acts without any specific reference to the Islands by name. It should be borne in mind that during most of these years both Ethiopia and Yemen were distracted by civil war or strife, and serious internal instability. Yemen did not resile from the broad and loose claims made before World War II—which might or might not have embraced the islands in dispute—but did not pursue or articulate them until 1973.

Activities Relating to the Water

Licensing of Activities in the Waters Off the Islands

258. There is much evidence that Ethiopian naval units had for many years conducted surveillance in the Red Sea and in particular around the Zuqar/Hanish archipelago. As pointed out below, it is not clear whether those actions were evidence of fisheries control and administration or whether they primarily related to security measures, or both, particularly in light of the fierce struggle by the Eritrean freedom fighters in the two decades prior to Eritrean independence. In any event, there is little evidence that the Ethiopian activity was based on fisheries regulations or laws as such.

259. As to Eritrea, the evidence only dates from early 1992. In January of that year the Eritrean provisional government issued a notice prohibiting in general terms unlicensed fishing activity in "Eritrean territorial waters". Eritrea has asserted that its Ministry of Marine Resources "has regulated fishing in Eritrean waters since shortly after Eritrean independence". On 1 April 1995, the Ministry of Marine Resources issued a "Manual and Guidelines for the Administration of Foreing [*sic*] Vessel Licensing and Operations".

260. In September 1995, Trawler Regulation I was issued by the Ministry of Marine Resources. The statement is made by Eritrea that the handout appended to Trawler Regulation I "includes the Zuqar-

Hanish islands within Areas No 11 and 12 (Beilul and Berá isole)".[20] The areas are separated laterally by dotted lines. These lines do not however extend to, or surround, the Zuqar/Hanish archipelago. (Comparison with Maps 1 and 2 shows, in the case of Map 2's depiction of the Dahlak ("Dehalak") archipelago, a carefully drawn lateral boundary around the Dahlaks.)

261. As far as Yemen is concerned, there is no evidence of any regulation or order as such regulating fisheries as such in Yemeni waters. The evidentiary record is devoid of any assertion of a formal legal basis for fisheries jurisdiction assumed by the Yemeni Government over the waters surrounding the Zuqar/Hanish archipelago. A witness statement cited in support of the proposition that Yemeni Government "launches are vigilant in controlling illegal fishing" merely details that the witness (a Navy Captain) "was assigned by [his] . . . command to arrest foreign fishermen pirates . . . who were looting our maritime wealth in a random and illegal manner", but indicates no further detail.[21]

262. Yet Yemen has asserted that it has "tightly regulated fishing activities on and around the Hanish Islands" and that "the Government has actively controlled illegal fishing". There is a substantial record of fishing vessel arrests by Yemeni authorities between 1987 and 1990. It should be noted however that they are recent in time, and appear to have been primarily directed in recent years against large Egyptian industrial fishing vessels.

263. In conclusion, the Tribunal is of the view that the activities of the Parties in relation to the regulation of fishing allows no clear legal conclusion to be drawn. The record of these activities under Ethiopian administration is, as will be seen below, open to conjecture. Since Eritrean independence, the record is less than clear. Since 1987, Yemen appears to have been engaged in some regulation of fishing, primarily directed toward larger vessels. The balance of this evidence does not appear to tilt in one direction or another.

Fishing Vessel Arrests

264. Although there is evidence before the Tribunal that a substantial number of arrests of fishing vessels for violation of the respective fishing regulations and orders have occurred, the period of time comprised in that evidence is brief. It is difficult therefore to characterize those actions as the "continuous and peaceful display of state authority".

---

[20] Map 3 (dated November 1993) shows Area 10 ("Bera'isole") and Area 11 ("Beilul"), but Area 12 is actually "Assab-Dumeira".
[21] The samples of fishing and boat licences supplied by Yemen are not helpful; when they specify fishing areas, they only state "Red Sea".

265. The evidence before the Tribunal concerning Ethiopian regulation of fishing or fishing violation arrests is almost wholly derived from former Ethiopian naval officers. There are many detailed witness statements that recount service in the Ethiopian patrolling forces during the Eritrean war of independence. In most instances the whereabouts of particular incidents are rendered in general terms, albeit with frequent reference in particular to islands of the Zuqar/Hanish archipelago. Although there are few dates given for the various vessel arrests referred to in the witness statements, the majority of activities reported appear to have taken place during the two decades preceding Eritrean independence in 1991.

266. A fair reading of the witness statements shows that by far the principal concern of the Ethiopian military during this period was to combat the EPLF activities on and around the Islands and to deny the use of the Islands to rebel forces either as a staging area for strikes on to the Eritrean coast of Ethiopia or as supply depots and strategic bases. The Ethiopian naval officers concerned did also exercise police powers when they would stop and check fishing boats.

267. The primary purpose of such an exercise was suppression of the insurgency. In most of these cases the witnesses stated that part of their duties was to stop all fishing boats and check their papers and cargo. Thus, "[t]he Dankali fishermen were suspected of cooperating with the rebels in smuggling arms, ammunition and other supplies across the Red Sea". However the duties of these naval patrols also extended to keeping foreign fishermen out of what Ethiopia considered to be her territorial waters. Vessels that were not licensed to fish in the waters or that were of non-Ethiopian registration were arrested or requested to leave.

268. The Eritrean pleadings state that the evidence shows "the inspection of fishing and/or commercial vessels as a primary function of their routine patrols around the islands". Having regard to the fierce fighting that was going on over the years in question in and around the area in question, it is not clear that enforcing fishing regulations was the primary purpose of these Ethiopian naval patrols.

269. At the same time, the Tribunal is not disposed to discount the evidence introduced by Eritrea on the grounds that the acts were not "peaceful". Military action taken in a civil war is in any event not normally regarded as a belligerent act that would have no legal relevance for the question of title. Accordingly, even though the Tribunal does not accept Eritrea's contention that most activity was directed at fishing regulation, the Tribunal finds nonetheless that they are not without legal significance.

270. In 1976, an Ethiopian naval patrol boat arrested three Yemeni fishermen on Greater Hanish Island. Yemen protested to the United

Nations Security Council this "flagrant act of aggression and . . . distinct violation of the sovereignty of the Yemen Arab Republic". Ethiopia responded, in a formal letter from its UN Permanent Representative to the President of the Security Council, that "[t]he Ethiopian patrol boats were carrying out their responsibilities within Ethiopian jurisdiction".

271. Following independence, the record shows that much attention became devoted to control of Eritrean fisheries affairs, entailing *inter alia* a number of vessel arrests, some of which involved Yemeni fishermen. Although a substantial number of witness statements speak of supervisory authority and activity by Ministry of Marine Resources authorities in conjunction with the Eritrean Navy, the evidence dates from the time of Eritrean independence and in almost all instances relates to matters occurring after 1995. Without precise fixing of coordinates and distances, it is unfortunately difficult to see whether the activities and vessel arrests in question actually occurred with respect to the waters around the Zuqar/Hanish archipelago or Jabal al-Tayr and the Zubayr group. Many witness statements and reports are not clear as to how close to the contested islands the incidents were.

272. As to Yemen, a number of incidents between 1987 and 1995 are also in evidence. There is documentary evidence of an arrest in 1989 of an Egyptian trawler "next to Zuqar island . . . in the territorial waters of Yemen". There is also testimony from a Navy Captain that in May 1995 he was assigned "to arrest foreign fishermen pirates" and that he arrested "several launches" of "Gulf ownership" with Egyptian crews after a gun battle "in Yemeni territorial waters", "in an area between al-Jah and Zuqar". Although Yemen asserted that in 1990 four Egyptian fishing vessels were arrested "in the area of the Hanish Group", and the owners required to pay an indemnity to Yemen and undertake not to repeat their actions, the supporting document does not specify the location of the arrests.

273. However, a 1990 report addressed to the Yemeni Defence Ministry describes twenty separate incidents between 1987 and 1990 in which a total of more than sixty vessels are reported to have been arrested, accosted, "escorted to" a naval base, or "warned to leave"— a good number of these incidents appear to have related to Egyptian commercial fishing vessels. While some of these are described as having been in the vicinity of the Zuqar/Hanish archipelago or Jabal al-Tayr, Zubayr and Abu Ali, the report refers to the "area of" a named island or islands; one exception is a report of unlicensed fishing by two Egyptian trawlers "at Zuqar". In most instances, when vessels were ordered to leave, the report states that the warnings specified that they should depart "from territorial waters" or "from Yemeni waters".

Other Licensing Activity

274. Apart from fishing, there have been no attempts on the part of Eritrea to demonstrate any licensing activities in respect of the waters off the Islands. For its part, Yemen asserts the official approval in 1993 of plans for a tourist boat operation between al-Khawkha and Greater Hanish. There was also a licence granted by Yemen to a German company for the building of a diving centre on the north end of Greater Hanish in 1995. As will be discussed below, between 1972 and 1993 the Yemeni Government recorded eight instances of requests for approval for activities relating to the use of the waters around the Islands, and in several cases approval was given for research and diving expeditions and the like.

Granting of Permission to Cruise Around or to Land on the Islands

275. As discussed, there is an abundance of evidence before the Tribunal relating to the manifold activities of the Ethiopian Navy in the twenty-year period before Eritrean independence. That evidence largely indicates that the Ethiopian naval patrols operated intensive patrolling in and around the Islands during the Ethiopian war against the Eritrean insurgents. In that role, the naval vessels stopped ships, boats and dhows in those waters, requested identification and inspected equipment and cargo. Tourist vessels anchored near the Zuqar-Hanish islands were arrested and brought into Ethiopian ports for investigation and the film from their cameras was destroyed.

276. There is evidence that informal requests from third parties for permission to cruise around, anchor at or land on the Islands were sometimes made to naval patrols. For example, one witness statement indicates that radio requests made to Ethiopian patrol craft to anchor "at the north western cove off Hanish", received from "large foreign commercial vessels" (including ones of Greek, Japanese, Yugoslavian and Italian nationality), were granted for reasons such as "repairs, shelter or rest".

277. As to Yemen, there is evidence that in 1978 three Kuwaiti fishing trawlers requested and received shelter from a storm at Jabal Zuqar, and that on two occasions in 1991 foreign flag vessels sought and received permission to anchor at Zuqar and Hanish for repairs.

278. In addition, between 1972 and 1995 Yemen received at least eight formal requests from third parties, including one from a foreign government, for permission to cruise around, anchor at, or land on the Islands: A request from an Italian organization to conduct research on Jabal Zuqar was declined by the Government of the Yemen Arab Republic in 1972; the French Government in 1975 requested permission to conduct naval exercises in the vicinity of the Hanish Islands; in 1983 a request from a French organization to film submarine life was approved; in 1987, a German request for scientific research studies to

be conducted by the *F. S. Meteor* around the Hanish Islands was approved by an official governmental decree and the project was completed without incident; for indeed *The Meteor* seemingly carefully avoided the territorial waters of both Ethiopia and Yemen. In 1992 approval was given for a diving trip by a British yacht, the *Lady Jenny V*, around the Islands; in 1993 the Yemen Government approved a research expedition to the Zuqar/Hanish archipelago to be conducted with the Royal Geographical Society; in 1993, the Government approved the French research expedition of the Ardoukoba Society to Greater Hanish, and also approved a German diving expedition on the yacht *Cormoran*. There is also an unsupported statement that a Polish request for diving in the area was rejected in late 1995.

279. It should be noted however that there is no specification of the islands in the application or report of the cruise of the *Meteor* though the Report mentions the Hanish Islands and states that "maximum values were noted at the Hanish Islands . . .". Moreover, the terms of the licence specified that the "research operation must be conducted in waters at a depth of 100 meters or more", thus excluding research in any close proximity to the Islands.

280. What can be concluded is that there was somewhat greater Yemeni activity than Ethiopian/Eritrean activity in the granting of permission relating to the Islands in the periods stated.

Publication of Notices to Mariners or Pilotage Instructions Relating to the Waters of the Islands

281. Other than Eritrea's fishing regulations, Eritrea has produced no evidence of publication, by Ethiopia or by Eritrea, of general information concerning pilotage or maritime safety.

282. In the five years between 1987 and 1991 Yemen published six Notices to Mariners in connection with its installation of new lighthouses in the Islands. These were: Centre Peak (1987 and 1988); and Jabal Zuqar (1989). Following the 1989 London Conference on Red Sea Lights, Yemen issued a Notice to Mariners concerning a new solar lighthouse on Jabal al-Tayr, and one concerning a new system on Abu Ali. In 1991 the Yemen Ports Authority constructed a new lighthouse on Low Island, and an official telex notification was sent to the Hydrographer of the Royal Navy in Taunton (referring to it as "Hanish as Saghir" Island). In 1992 a similar telex was sent indicating a "beaconpipe" at "Jabal-at-Tair", a lighthouse at "Sawabey" (al-Zubayr), a lighthouse at Abu Ali, a beacon at Zuqar, and beacons at Hanish Sashir and Hanish Kabir.

283. The Tribunal notes that such notices form a natural adjunct to the operation and maintenance of lighthouses, but that latter function, in the particular circumstances of the Red Sea, does not generally have legal significance. The issuance of such notices, while not

dispositive of the title, nevertheless supposes a presence and knowledge of location. Moreover, it is to be noted that in relation to these indications, accuracy in identifying the navigational aid and its location is of the prime importance, rather than the provenance of the information.

Search and Rescue Operations

284. Eritrea has produced evidence maintaining that in 1974, the *MV Star of Shaddia* was stranded off Zubayr. There is no evidence as to her nationality. *HMS Ethiopia* attempted a rescue, but was unable to approach the ship because of severe weather and mechanical difficulties, and departed without being able to assist.

285. In 1990, the Yemeni Ports Authority rescued an Iraqi vessel, the *Basra Sun*, from the rocky coast of Jabal Zuqar after it had requested assistance.

286. Since there is under the law of the sea a generalized duty incumbent on any person or vessel in a position to render assistance to vessels in distress, no legal conclusions can be drawn from these events.

The Maintenance of Naval and Coast Guard Patrols in the Waters Around the Islands

287. Eritrea has produced a large amount of evidence relating to naval patrolling activity in and around the Islands. The activities alleged are for the most part not referred to in documentary evidence, but rather in affidavits prepared in connection with these proceedings. However, the Tribunal takes note of statements by Eritrea that a large amount of Ethiopian naval records were destroyed in the course of hostilities.

288. *1953-1973*: For the first twenty-year period (1953-73), Eritrea has introduced two types of evidence: naval logbooks from 1959 to 1967 and naval operations reports primarily from the 1970s.

289. *Naval logbooks*: The Eritrean Memorial states that "there are numerous records that the Islands were 'visited and/or observed'" (Eritrean Memorial, p. 427), implying that most of the logs indicate this. It also states that they "demonstrate in painstaking detail the continuous Ethiopian presence in the disputed islands" and characterizes them as "record[ing] visits" to the Islands.

290. However, the logs themselves—in contrast with the operations reports—relating to the years 1959, 1961, 1962, 1963, and 1967, do not use the word "visit". Moreover, it is not clear to the Tribunal what that term entailed. The "observations" are largely contained in Column (13) of the standard printed logbook form, labelled "Soundings Fixes Bearings Observations", and a study of the entries in that column shows that they are almost uniformly position "fixes" of azimuth bearings on land points and islands, sometimes from as far as fifteen

miles offshore.[22] The Tribunal cannot therefore draw many useful conclusions about Ethiopian exercise of governmental functions with respect to the Islands on the basis of these logs alone.

291. *Operations reports and orders*: Eritrea has placed in evidence three operations reports—two cruises in April 1970 and one in July 1971. However, the language in which the missions are recorded in the operations reports is too vague to be relied upon as establishing State functions with respect to the Islands in this case, e.g., patrolling the "area south" of Greater Hanish and the Haycocks, sailing "to Grand Hanish and back", and investigating vessels "south of Zuqar" and "vicinity Jebel Attair". The only relevant precision accorded by this evidence is in the operation report of *HMS Ethiopia* for July 20/21 and 25/26, where she "[a]nchored Zuqar" overnight in order to remedy mechanical difficulties. Episodes of that nature can hardly give rise to a legal claim of occupation and control.

292. Furthermore, although the Eritrean Memorial captions its description of the reports with a statement that they demonstrate the "continuous Ethiopian naval presence around the disputed islands", for the twenty years in question they cover only two cruises in April 1970 and one cruise in July 1971. In consequence, these documents hardly support the assertion that the Ethiopian Navy maintained a "continuous presence" around the Islands for the entire period of 1953-73.

293. There are also in evidence four operations orders of the Ethiopian Navy, from January, July, September and October of 1971. They instructed the preparation of "a Schedule" for visiting the different areas, including "Kebir Hanish" and "Zukar", and patrols "around Hanish I[s]lands", "within the route: Dumeira is—Fatmah Lt.—Rs Darma—Kabir Hanish—Zuqar—Edd and Ras Darma", and another with a similar routing. They cover less than one year out of twenty, though this may be explained by the asserted destruction of Ethiopian naval records during the civil war. In warfare continuing over several decades, it does not seem likely that Ethiopian activity in controlling insurgency would be limited to a single year.

294. *1974-1980*: Eritrea has also put forward documentary evidence of a similar nature relating to activities from 1974 up until the end of 1980, but this is just as sparse as that for the preceding twenty years. Again, it takes the form of log-books and orders which, being contemporaneous, have a special interest, as well as correspondence. The log-book entries for 1974, 1977 and 1980 reveal the same kind of imprecision as the earlier log-book records, one of which, for example, while purporting to "record . . . [a] visit . . . to Hanish (on August 16)

---

[22] In one example, it appears that the officer of the watch has helpfully added estimated radar ranges of distance, e.g.: "Ø Jabal at Tair Isl. 045° 6.0 by radar", and "Ø Haycock Isl. 106° 15 by radar", showing that the vessel (*HIMS PC-12*) was far offshore on both occasions.

[1977]", merely shows "Hanish" in the Column (13) of the Log under "Soundings Fixes Bearings Observations" as having been sighted by P-203 at 0400 on 16 August, at a bearing of 325° and at a *distance of 20 n.m.* This is not evidence of a "visit", nor of passage through the territorial sea of that island.

295. Additional evidence has been presented describing the Ethiopian/Eritrean sea battle off the island of Zuqar after the capture of the merchant ship *Salvatore* by the ELF on the way to Assab in June 1979, but it is not clear what evidentiary relevance can be ascribed to this incident. Finally, P-203's Log-Book in May 1980 records warning shots at a Canadian and a West German boat; the precise location is not indicated in the log but the incident is noted in an entry which begins "slipped out for patrolling Hanish to Zuqar". The 1980 capture of five wooden boats referred to in the pleadings is not particularized further than occurring "near the islands of Lesser Hanish". In April 1980 some Yemeni fishermen were captured "near Zuqar Island", and others were also captured "in the vicinity of the Zuqar/Hanish islands". This incident was in fact protested by North Yemen.

296. Eritrea states that the "most critical Ethiopian naval event of 1980" was "Operation Julia"; and that it "resulted in twenty four hour surveillance and a blockade of the entire area for the entire three month period of the operation". When the map submitted in evidence is consulted, it shows what appear to be four areas of patrolling off the Ethiopian/Eritrean coast: two close on shore, one half-way to Greater Hanish from the coast, and one lying approximately 3-4 n.m. west of Near Island and Shark Island on the west side of Jabal Zuqar, and running south across Tongue Island to just north of Marescaux Rock. The context of Operation Julia shows quite clearly that this was a series of grave incidents at sea between the Ethiopian naval forces and the rebel forces, and that the Ethiopian naval forces patrolled their own coastlines, and the sea mainly west of the Islands facing the Eritrean coast; a main purpose of the operation having been to stop rebels "infiltrating into Assab District".

297. *1973-1993*: For the second twenty-year period, Eritrea has also placed substantial evidence before the Tribunal, largely in the form of seven witness statements specially obtained from seven former Ethiopian navy officers and two witness statements obtained from two former EPLF naval fighters. With one exception, the testimony relates only to activities from 1968 on. The testimony, summarized in the written pleadings, largely concerns activities at sea extending over substantial periods between 1964 and 1991.

298. It is however possible only to rely on this testimony for the most general of indications. In ten out of the thirty incidents described by Eritrea the identity of the Ethiopian or Eritrean vessel is not given. The dates of the incidents are given in only nine cases. Their locations

are specified in only three, but in those three instances the time frame extends over indeterminate periods of eight months, five years, and one month respectively. There is therefore no evidence of an arrest or stopping by Ethiopian or Eritrean naval forces with *both* a precise location *and* a precise date, for the entire period from 1970 to 1995.

299. In a close reading of the witness statements provided by Eritrea, three other interesting points emerge with clarity which should assist in evaluating the context and scope of this evidence. These points have not been controverted in the proceedings.

300. The first point is that out of the seven witness statements of former Ethiopian naval officers, three record no landings on the Islands. The remaining four are imprecise with respect to either date or location. There are two witness statements that mention more than isolated landings during the entire period from 1973 to 1993.

301. The second point relates to the nature of the patrols which, as well as being fast, appear to have taken place at night, and sometimes in conditions of darken ship. These factors bear upon the absence of protest by Yemen.

302. Third, although some of the evidence does recite that the "purpose of these patrols was primarily to apprehend vessels carrying contraband and to keep foreign fishermen, who were generally from Yemen, out of our territorial waters", it is not clear that a major twenty-year military operation increasing in intensity can be viewed as primarily related to fishing. There is certainly some validity to the argument that checking fishing boats on a regular basis was an essential part of checking for insurgents and contraband weapons. Just as checking ELF dhows for small arms and ammunition was essential to defeating the rebels ("[t]he dhows could carry hundreds of sheep and goats, so they would hide the supplies underneath the livestock where it was impossible [f]or us to search") so was checking fishermen (". . . we would often see Dankali fishermen further east, in the area of the islands . . . We would check the identification papers for the boat, captain and crew and look for contraband and armaments.") However, normal fisheries surveillance does not require checking for "contraband and armaments".

303. There also appears to be, in this evidence, a discrepancy in Eritrean witness statements as to the presence of Yemeni fishermen. While some witnesses state that "Yemeni fishermen were almost never reported to be in the area of Zuqar and Hanish at this time" (the late 1980s) and "I never encountered a Yemeni fishermen [*sic*] in the waters around Zuqar and Hanish", others state: "[w]e patrolled east of the Dahlaks as well as the Hanish islands" and "[s]ometimes, our patrols would find Yemeni fishermen fishing in Ethiopian waters, including around Zuqar/Hanish".

304. *1983-1991*: These witness statements were also intended to

supplement the documentary evidence put in by Eritrea as to activities from 1983 through 1991 but this evidence is imprecise. Speaking almost consistently in terms such as "around Hanish and Zuqar", "the environs of Hanish", "in the vicinity of Jabal A'Tair", these operations and reports and sailing orders are sparse chronologically: May 1983, October 1984, September 1984, May 1986, July 1984, and August 1987. Even if this evidence were precise as to location and relevance to the Islands, it could still hardly provide a demonstration of a "continuous Ethiopian naval presence around the disputed islands" as it covers only six months out of ninety-six and leaves out four years entirely of that continuous naval presence.

305. Nevertheless, the extent of this evidence and its homogeneity do suggest the conclusion that the Ethiopian Navy, during the period in question, did in fact conduct widespread surveillance and military reconnaissance activities in the waters around the islands. It is uncontroverted that these patrols were frequent and, in the course of the Ethiopian war against the ELF and the EPLF, of steadily increasing intensity. Elements of the Ethiopian Navy anchored frequently off the Islands, sent details ashore for reconnaissance missions, and even bombarded suspected rebel facilities on the Islands.

306. With the exception of the 1976 incident discussed above (which was protested to the Security Council of the United Nations), North Yemen (and, later, the Republic of Yemen) did not protest any of these Ethiopian naval activities. Although such a lack of protest would normally appear to suggest a degree of acquiescence, four elements need to be weighed by the Tribunal in considering the evidence: the location of the Islands, the fact that they were not settled, and the fact that there was no normal line of communication from persons on or near the Islands to the mainland; the fact that many of the Ethiopian patrols appear to have been conducted at night under conditions of darken ship; the fact that many of those patrols were conducted at high speed; and the fact that civil hostilities were in progress.

307. At the same time, the failure of Yemen to protest the considerable presence of Ethiopian naval forces around and sporadically on the Islands over a period of years is capable of other interpretations. If Yemen did not know of that presence, that belies Yemeni claims that there were Yemeni settlements of fishermen on the Islands and that Yemen patrolled the waters of the Islands and indeed maintained garrisons on them. If Yemen did know of this Ethiopian presence, and if, as the record shows, did not protest it, that could be interpreted as an indication that Yemen did not regard itself as having sovereignty over the Islands, or, at any rate, as an acknowledgment by Yemen that it lacked effective control over them.

308. Yemen could take the view that belligerent acts by Ethiopia against insurgents using the Islands were not elements of continuous

and peaceful occupation by Ethiopia, or that Ethiopian regulation of Yemeni fishing vessels found within the waters of the Islands was incidental to Ethiopian belligerency. But such acts, belligerent or otherwise, could not normally be reconciled with Yemeni sovereignty over the Islands. Thus, if Ethiopia's naval presence in the Islands over the years does not establish Ethiopia's (and hence Eritrea's) title, it may nonetheless be seen as throwing into question the title of Yemen.

309. The Tribunal has found it necessary to address at some length the Eritrean evidence relating to naval patrolling over a substantial period of time. At the same time it must be noted that Yemen has not suggested to the Tribunal that it conducted more than a very few activities during this entire period of naval operations by Ethiopia. Yemen has not explained its lack of protest.

310. Essentially Yemen relies on two witness statements. In one statement, Yemen asserts that patrols of the Islands were "carried out on a regular basis"—weekly in the summer and "once every month or two" in the winter but the dates are unspecified. A specific date, but a very recent one, is given by this statement for an assignment "to arrest foreign fishermen pirates" (May 1995). This statement also tells of intercepting foreign warships (American, French and Russian) "in these islands" and requesting them to leave, but no dates are supplied except for an incident with a Russian merchant vessel "on the western side of Zuqar off of Shaykh Ghuthayyan about 1977-78". Interception of an ELF dhow between Zuqar and al-Jah was recorded "about 1974-75".

311. In the other statement, evidence is given that "during the years of 1965 to 1977" the Yemeni naval forces carried out regular patrols around the Islands, saying that "[t]hey always anchored at the anchorages of these islands and patrolled around them" (specifying the anchorages by name), and that "[o]ur soldiers and officers would land onto their shores". The statement adds, without specifying dates, that "[m]any times our officers and naval enlisted personnel would land on the shores of those islands (Zuqar, Greater Hanish, Lesser Hanish, and al-Zubayr) on dismounted reconnaissance missions (on foot), as well as to swim and relax". The period is not specified other than generally from 1965 to 1977.

Environmental Protection

312. Yemen reports having investigated an oil spill reported by a Russian freighter about 10 miles from Lesser Hanish in 1990.

Fishing Activities by Private Persons

313. There was substantial debate between the Parties as to whose fishing community was more important, and as to how important a part fishing and fish played in the economic life of each State. The Tribunal does not find these arguments pertinent, since in any event it

may be expected that population, and economic realities, will change inevitably over time. What may be very important today in terms of fishing may be unimportant tomorrow, and the reverse is also true.

314. For Eritrea, the evidence before the Tribunal includes the statement that "[t]here are more than 2,500 Eritrean fishermen, many of whom are artisanal fishermen engaged in small-scale fishing using traditional methods and equipment" and that "[t]he waters around the Zuqar-Hanish islands supply a significant portion of Eritrea's annual catch". For Yemen, the statement has been made that: "[f]ishing communities along the Yemeni Red Sea coast have historically depended on the neighbouring islands of the Hanish Group for their economic livelihood".

315. Numerous witness statements were submitted by both sides as to the longevity and importance of their respective fishing practices and the significance of fishing in the lives of their people. Yet, although substantial evidence of individual fishing practices in the record may be taken as a different form of "*effectivité*"—i.e., one expressive of the generally effective attitude and practice of individual citizens of Eritrea or of Yemen—it is not indicative as such of State activity supporting a claim for administration and control of the Islands. This varied and interesting evidence, on both sides, speaks eloquently concerning the apparent long attachment of the populations of each coast to the fisheries in and around the Islands, and in particular that around the Zuqar-Hanish islands. However it does not constitute evidence of *effectivités* for the simple reason that none of these functions are acts *à titre de souverain*. For State activity capable of establishing a claim for sovereignty, the Tribunal must look to the State licensing and enforcement activities concerning fishing described above.

316. Yemen has put into evidence a substantial number of arrests of commercial fishing vessels in the past few years in the waters around the Islands. These arrests have been accompanied by legal proceedings, expulsion of the vessels from the waters, and substantial fines. The arrested vessels appear to have borne foreign registries other than Ethiopian or Eritrean and in most cases seem to have been Egyptian. No protests of these activities have been recorded from Ethiopia or Eritrea. Eritrea also produced a witness who related that "between 1992 and 1993" while a commercial captain in the Zuqar-Hanish waters he reported about twenty Egyptian trawlers. "Some of these trawlers were confiscated . . ." He further stated that in his job at the Department of Marine Transport it is his current responsibility "to determine what should be done with them".

Other Jurisdictional Acts Concerning Incidents at Sea

317. A lost dhow was searched for off the Islands, and an investigation conducted by Yemeni authorities in 1976; a drowning at sea at Greater Hanish was investigated by Yemeni authorities in 1992.

Activities on the Islands

318. In order to examine the performance of jurisdictional acts on the Islands, the Tribunal must consider evidence of activities on the land territory of the Islands as well as acts in the water surrounding the Islands. This evidence includes: landing parties on the Islands; the establishment of military posts on the Islands; the construction and maintenance of facilities on the Islands; the licensing of activities on the land of the Islands; the exercise of criminal or civil jurisdiction in respect of happenings on the Islands; the construction or maintenance of lighthouses; the granting of oil concessions; and limited life and settlement on the Islands.

Landing Parties on the Islands

319. The direct evidence presented shows little or no landing activities on the Islands by either side.

320. Eritrea's evidence shows that during the twenty years of the emergency there was substantial activity onshore and off the Islands by elements of the Ethiopian navy engaged in suppressing the secessionist movements. The record indicates clearly that the Islands were used heavily by rebel forces in connection with their war of independence. As discussed above, in the context of naval operations around the Islands, two substantial patrols and a number of unspecified landing parties by Ethiopian military forces are in evidence for the period between 1970 and 1988.

321. On the part of Yemen, there was an official visit to Jabal Zuqar and the Abu Ali Islands in 1973 following the publicity about possible Israeli presence on those islands. In response to the Tribunal's request for specific information, the Secretary-General wrote to the President of the Tribunal on 28 July 1998, informing him that there had never been "any visit to any of the islands in the Red Sea by any official delegation of the League of Arab States headed by the Secretary-General". The letter reported a 1973 meeting between the Secretary-General of the Arab League and the Ethiopian Foreign Minister, to discuss Arab concern about reports of Israeli use of the Dahlak islands and other islands in the bay of Assab. The Ethiopians invited an Arab League delegation to visit the islands in order to confirm that there was no Israeli presence, "but no such visit was ever made". Finally, the Arab League letter states that "in 1971 and 1973, members of the League of Arab States' military committee, including Yemeni officers, visited the islands of the Hanish group including Zuqar as well as the Zubair islands with the sole cooperation and assistance of the Governments of the People's Republic of Yemen and the Yemen Arab Republic". According to the Secretary-General, no report of these visits had been found in the League's archives.

322. Other Yemeni assertions of military presence on the Islands rely heavily on one witness statement describing unspecified landings over a period of time with unspecified dates, other than generally from 1965 to 1977.

323. Yemen has also placed into evidence information concerning field trips by faculty and students of the Staff and Command College in 1987 and 1990. It does not appear that the trips were for more than a very brief period of time, or left any lasting effects.

Establishment of Military Posts on the Islands

324. The evidence presented shows no permanent military posts on the Islands before 1995. Although Eritrea's statements include the mention of landing parties, it was explained that no garrison had been established and the relevance of such garrisons was denied. Rather, Eritrea emphasized that what was legally relevant were sovereign acts tailored to the character of the territory in question, namely military surveillance and fishing regulation.

325. As to Yemen, although the written pleadings state that "a temporary military garrison" was "established . . . on Jabal Zuqar at the time of" the 1973 visit, and that "[d]uring the 1970s, the Government placed guard posts on other islands in the Group, including on Greater Hanish", no evidence was submitted to substantiate that statement. Photographs introduced into the record of groups of military personnel standing on the Island do not give the impression of permanence. It is also to be noted that no structure or building is shown in the photographs; one would have expected that, had there been any structure or building available, it would have been captured on film.

326. The Tribunal concludes that it cannot accept that a permanent garrison or military post was established on the Islands until following the outbreak of the dispute in 1995.

Construction and Maintenance of Facilities on the Islands

327. There is no evidence of the construction or maintenance of any type of facilities on the Islands by Eritrea. Eritrea nevertheless claims, as an indication of Ethiopia's "consolidation of sovereign control over the disputed islands", that following the hand-over of Aden in 1967 the lighthouses on Abu Ali and Jabal al-Tayr were managed by a private company then based on Asmara, and that Ethiopian regulations applied to transactions by that company in connection with its management and maintenance of those lighthouses. The Tribunal does not consider this to be persuasive.

328. Yemen has however constructed some lighthouses and has maintained others. The operation or maintenance of lighthouses and navigational aids is normally connected to the preservation of safe navigation, and not normally taken as a test of sovereignty.

Maintenance on these islands of lighthouses by British and Italian companies and authorities gave rise to no sovereign claims or conclusions. The relevance of these activities and of Yemen's presence at the 1989 Red Sea Lights Conference are examined in Chapter VI.

329. Yemen also points to the siting and installation of two geodetic stations by French companies in 1992 on behalf of the Yemeni Government on Jabal Zuqar and Greater Hanish as examples of State action. Eritrea's response is that these markers were placed secretly and are in any event modest. The Tribunal cannot give too much weight to such small monuments of this nature, and yet must also note that in fact the markers were installed before the exchange of correspondence between the two Heads of State in 1995; that they do exist; and that they are reflected on a map of geodetic stations in the Yemen.

330. The maintenance of shrines and holy places that was also presented in Yemen's materials appears to be of a private nature; no governmental activity is suggested. There is unsubstantiated testimony before the Tribunal that "[o]ur government built an airfield between al-Shura and al-Habal [on Greater Hanish] for helicopters". The airstrip constructed by Total on Greater Hanish with Yemen's authorization in relation to the 1985 Total concession and subsequently dedicated to rest and recreational visits by Total employees is discussed in Chapter IX.

331. Although evidence concerning the intentions in May 1995 of the Yemeni General Investment Authority is recent, and although such indications are only of State action without specific object, it nevertheless demonstrates that on a high governmental level the Yemeni authorities were seriously considering that investment should be encouraged for tourism on Greater Hanish, Lesser Hanish, Abu Ali, Jabal al-Tayr and al-Zubayr; thus official government policy implicitly relied on Yemeni sovereignty over these Islands at that time.

Licensing of Activities on the Land of the Islands

332. Eritrea has suggested that the fact that authorization was required for the private firm Savon & Ries to ship radio transmitters to Abu Ali and Jabal al-Tayr, the islands on which that firm maintained lighthouses, was indicative of the exercise of State control. However the regulation of electronic equipment used by a private firm whose personnel were operating in a zone in which military activities were conducted cannot be viewed as an exercise of sovereign authority with respect to the land territory of the islands concerned.

333. Eritrea has produced evidence of the grant of a licence for the operation of a radio transmitting station on Greater Hanish in connection with petroleum activities to be conducted in the vicinity.

334. As to Yemen, discussion follows concerning its construction and maintenance of lighthouses on the Islands. To the extent that

most of the useful economic activity and interest in the Islands is generated by their position in the Red Sea and by their relationship to their surrounding waters (whether for purposes of smuggling, fishing, or tourism), most of the licensing activities that have taken place have all been water-related. One brief but not insignificant use of the land resources on the Islands that was also water-related was the recent amphibious scientific research expedition of the Ardoukoba Society to Greater Hanish, authorized by Yemen.

Exercise of Criminal or Civil Jurisdiction in Respect of Happenings on the Islands
335. In 1976, a military court of the Ethiopian Government conducted a trial of employees of Savon & Ries, the lighthouse maintenance company servicing the lights on Abu Ali and Jabal al-Tayr, on accusations of leading and training a subversive group on those islands. The resulting execution of the finance officer and expulsion or imprisonment of a head lighthouse keeper and others caused the company to move its offices from Asmara to Djibouti.

336. The examples of contemporary exercises of criminal jurisdiction over matters occurring in the Islands by Yemeni authorities include a 1976 investigation of a missing dhow and, in 1992, the investigation of the loss at sea of a fisherman off Greater Hanish.

337. In addition, Yemen asserts that for many years the local fishermen have used their own customary law system of arbitration of local disputes under the authority of an *aq'il*—"a person known for wisdom and intelligence". There is a senior *"Aq'il* of the Sea" the most noted of whom is said to have "resided part of the year on the Yemeni mainland and part of the year at his settlement ('Izbat al-Sayyid 'Ali) on Greater Hanish". The final authority above village *aq'ils* or the *Aq'il* of the Sea is the *"Aq'il* of the Fishermen", who is a dignitary officially recognized by the Government of Yemen.

338. The *aq'ils* apply what is asserted by Yemen to be a "well-established Yemeni body of customary law, known as the *urf*", to resolve the fishermen's disputes. There is evidence before the Tribunal that the judgments or decisions of *aq'ils* are binding.[23] Indeed, in the man overboard case just referred to, the evidence before the Tribunal is that "[t]he owner and crew members both informed the local official, who is known as the *Aq'il* Sheikh of the Fishermen, and the Department was notified by the *Aq'il*".

339. The existence of this customary law system of arbitration of small disputes does not appear to be contested by Eritrea. There is evidence that the *urf* and the *aq'il* system appear to be applicable to

---

[23] According to a witness statement submitted by Yemen, ". . . any disputant who seeks to avoid an unfavorable decision of the Council may find himself subject to action by the State, including, under certain circumstances, prison".

Yemenis and non-Yemenis within Yemeni territory, and to be regularly applied to problems occurring on the Islands.

340. In the Tribunal's understanding, the rules applied in the *aq'il* system do not find their origin in Yemeni law, but are elements of private justice derived from and applicable to the conduct of the trade of fishing. They are a *lex pescatoria* maintained on a regional basis by those participating in fishing. This reflects the reality also that the principal market for fish is in Hodeidah, on the Yemeni side, and that the fishing activities in the area of the Islands have long been conducted indiscriminately by fishermen on each side of the Red Sea on a regional basis. The fact that this system is recognized or supported by Yemen does not alter its essentially private character.

Construction or Maintenance of Lighthouses

341. The question of lighthouses has already been discussed above in Chapter VI. The present section examines this material only for the purposes of the present chapter on *effectivités*. The lighthouses at Abu Ali and Jabal al-Tayr were administered by the lighthouse management company, Savon & Ries. This company maintained its operation in Asmara until 1976, when it moved its office to Somalia because of prosecution of its staff by the Ethiopian Government for allegedly subversive operations (see para. 335, above). There is however no legal basis for concluding that the location within a State of the office of a private firm, operating under a management agreement for the maintenance of lighthouse facilities on islands, constitutes an intentional display of power and authority by that State.

342. As to Yemen, starting in 1987 a programme of installation of new lighthouses in the Islands was undertaken, beginning with Centre Peak in 1987 and 1988, and Jabal Zuqar in 1989.

343. Following the 1989 London Conference on Red Sea Lights, Yemen installed new solar lighthouses on Jabal al-Tayr and Quoin (Abu Ali islands). In 1991, a new lighthouse was constructed on Low Island. Finally, a lighthouse was erected on Greater Hanish in 1991.

344. Yemeni Governmental authorities communicated the construction and identification of each of these lighthouses to the public by means of public notices or Notices to Mariners, as described more fully in paragraph 282 above.

345. The legal effect to be given to the construction and maintenance of lighthouses in this particular case has been dealt with in Chapter VI, above.

Granting of Oil Concessions

346. Because of the significant attention devoted to the legal implications of petroleum agreements and activities in supplemental written and oral pleadings, this topic is treated separately in Chapter IX.

Limited Life on the Islands

347. There is also evidence that some of the Yemeni fishermen have maintained "dwellings" on Greater Hanish, Lesser Hanish, and Zuqar, and have traditionally maintained those structures for a long time; or have "settled" on Greater Hanish for the summer, or on Addar Ail Islets or Lesser Hanish for the summer.

348. Eritrea has advanced some evidence that Eritrean fishermen would stay for brief periods on the Islands during the fishing season, but the assertions of "settlements" do not appear to be as prominent in the evidentiary record as those made on behalf of Yemen. There is evidence by one fisherman however that "the longest that I know of anyone staying on the islands is 7 to 8 months".

349. In the pleadings Yemen states that "some Yemeni fishing families have for generations maintained a permanent presence in the Hanish Group", and refers to "fishing families resident in the Hanish Group" in the same context as its discussion of "temporary dwellings" and other temporary residence by fishermen. No specific evidence has been produced about families living on the Islands.

350. One Yemeni witness statement records that naval landing parties "would meet many Yemeni fishermen . . . who were settled on some of these islands, salting and drying fish, and staying there for several months".

351. During the fishing seasons the fishermen from each side could be expected to spend days and nights on end fishing in and around the Islands, since returning to port—whether in Ethiopia/Eritrea or in Yemen—would cost a full day's sailing even if the winds were right. Eritrean evidence is that the Yemeni fishermen "would stay around the islands for only three or four days and then go home". Another old Eritrean fisherman recounts that "[w]e would go to the islands twice a year for three months at a time. Some of us preferred to sleep on the islands, and others would sleep on the boats. Since the islands were not inhabited, no one told us we could not sleep there."

352. A Yemeni witness declared in his statement that "[a]t Greater Hanish I would settle at the al-Shura anchorage . . . There were trees there under which we would seek the shade. We would not have to make dwellings." The statement continues to describe the anchorages on Greater Hanish, saying that "[n]ear the Jafir anchorage is the dwelling of Capt. Ibrahim Salim and his crew . . . At the other end of the island many others have settled, such as the anchorage where I am at al-Shura, then the al-Habal dwelling, and beyond is the Ibn 'Alwan anchorage. In the summer many people settle at the Ibn 'Alwan anchorage. From al-Qataba alone there are over 40 *huris* [small boats]."

353. The first conclusion must be that settled life on the Islands does not exist, but that episodic or seasonal habitation occurs, and that it

appears to have taken place for many years. Eritrea asserts that its fishermen have been predominant, and Yemen asserts the reverse. There is no evident manner in which the Tribunal can, on the basis of the sparse and conflicting evidence before it, decide the matter one way or another. The likelihood is not that one nationality prevailed and the other was absent, but that both were present on the Islands in varying numbers and at various times—and that any precise calculation of relative use would, over time, reveal what may be perceived as a genuinely common use of the waters and their resources.

354. The second conclusion appears to be that the manner of living on the Islands is equally indiscriminate: some fishermen stay on their boats; others sleep on the beach; some construct small shelters; other use larger shelters; some consider their structures "settlements". The one thing that is clear from the record is that there is no significant and permanent dwelling structure, or in fact any significant and permanent structure of any other kind, that has been built and that has been used to live in.

355. The third conclusion is that it is not clear from the evidence, in spite of occasional references to "families" staying on the Islands, whether any family life is in fact present on the Islands. Inasmuch as the use of the islands is necessarily seasonal, this would seem to be *a priori* inconsistent with family life in the sense of family units migrating to a location where normal community activities continue, as for example with nomadic herdsmen.

356. The final conclusion must be that life on the Islands, such as it is, is limited to the seasonal and temporary shelter for fishermen. The evidence shows that many of them, of both Eritrean and Yemen nationality, appear to stay on the islands during the fishing season and in order to dry and salt their catch, but that residence, although seasonal and regular, is also temporary and impermanent.

357. For the time being however it would appear that there is little question but that this type of activity on the part of nationals of both Yemen and of Eritrea (and Ethiopia) is activity which, in the words of the Court in the *Anglo-Norwegian Fisheries* case of 1951, represents a "consideration not to be overlooked, the scope of which extends beyond purely geographical factors: that of certain economic interests peculiar to a region, the reality and importance of which are clearly evidenced by a long usage".[24]

General Activities

358. Finally, evidence of more general activities has been presented to the Tribunal by the Parties. This evidence includes assertions of conduct relating to overflight and miscellaneous activities.

---

[24] *Fisheries Case (UK v. Norway)* 1951 ICJ 116 (18 Dec.) at 133 [18 *ILR* 86].

Overflight

359. The act of overflying a substantially deserted group of islands is not one that would appear to constitute with any cogency an intentional display of power and authority over them. However it may be noted that in its Attachment 2 to the response given by Yemen to Question 18 ("Chronology of Selected Yemeni Acts Manifesting Sovereignty . . .") a number of overflights are recorded, commencing in April 1982 and proceeding through 1988. Doubtless they were important incidents of watching the unfolding of the Eritrean liberation struggle during that decade, but in any event the Tribunal can accord no substantial weight to these activities.

Miscellaneous Activities

360. Yemen has listed a broad variety of actions and acts in a sixteen-page attachment to its response to the Tribunal's Question 18. A variety of actions of many different categories have been advanced as supporting the respective contentions for consolidation of title over the Islands. The Tribunal has noted the most legally significant acts and positions in its earlier analysis.

361. Considerable emphasis, however, has been placed by Eritrea on an inspection tour conducted by President Mengistu and his staff in 1988. A videocassette of this tour around the Islands was also provided to the Tribunal. The Tribunal is unable to draw any conclusions from this episode, however, as the presidential party passed the Islands at speed and at some distance offshore, and did not stop or go ashore. No question of an intentional display of power and authority over a territory would seem to be raised by such a passage.

CHAPTER VIII   Maps

362. Finally, maps must be considered. It appears to the Tribunal that maps are used by the Parties at different times for different purposes, and that they have relevance to the dispute in several different ways.

Use of Maps by the Parties

363. Older maps, from the eighteenth and early nineteenth centuries, are adduced by Yemen in support of its thesis that the Islands once belonged to Yemen and that Yemen therefore possesses an ancient title which should cause sovereignty in the Islands to revert to it following termination of the Article 16 suspension under the Treaty of Lausanne. Similarly, maps subsequent to 1872 and earlier than 1918 are adduced by Yemen to show that the Islands fell under Ottoman sovereignty during the period in question and fell within the *vilayet* of Yemen. Eritrea then asserts that maps from the early twentieth

century through the late 1930s show that Italy claimed to be, or was received as being, the sovereign over the Islands.

364. Both Eritrea and Yemen have introduced maps produced by third parties in order to demonstrate that informed opinion recognized the Islands as respectively forming part of Ethiopia, or of Yemen, during the period from the early 1950s to the early 1990s.

365. Yemen has introduced maps from the period of the early 1950s to demonstrate that the United Nations considered the Islands not to be part of the Province of Eritrea (within Ethiopia). Both Parties have introduced maps from the period of the 1960s onwards, from a variety of sources, respectively indicating that Yemen treated the Islands as non-Yemeni and that Ethiopia treated them as non-Ethiopian—and that third parties and authoritative sources considered them respectively to be one or the other.

366. Finally, Yemen has introduced evidence showing that Ethiopia, the Eritrean liberation movement before independence, and the Eritrean Government after independence have not considered the Islands to be Ethiopian or Eritrean—but rather Yemeni. Eritrea has introduced evidence to show that Yemen has attributed the Islands to Ethiopia or to Eritrea. Each side has also accused the other of waging a deliberate "maps" campaign—from the early 1970s on the part of Yemen to the early 1990s on the part of Eritrea—to alter the designations, labels, and colours on maps so as to "claim" the Islands as a part of the other's territory.

367. In general however the positions of the Parties emerged as quite different overall in the usefulness they attributed to maps. Even whilst seeking to make the points just enumerated, Eritrea's essential position was that map evidence in general (and the evidence in this case in particular) was contradictory and unreliable and could not be used to establish serious legal positions.

368. Yemen's position was diametrically different; it sought to justify its use of maps in the case for at least four reasons: as "important evidence of general opinion or repute" (in the words of Sir Gerald Fitzmaurice, cited in the oral hearings); as evidence of the attitudes of governments; to reveal the intention of the Parties in respect of State actions; and as evidence of acquiescence or admissions against interest.

The Purposes Claimed to be Served by Maps in the Case
Pre-1872

369. Older maps, from the eighteenth and early nineteenth centuries, are adduced by Yemen in support of its thesis of an ancient or historic title. Most of the maps clearly show the Zuqar-Hanish group and the northern islands as identifiable with the Arabian rather than with the African side of the Red Sea. The Tribunal is not able to judge the extent of the precise territory of the Kingdom of Yemen (*Bilad el-*

Yemen). Moreover, in these older maps there is no attribution of the territory of the Islands to Yemen, as such.

370. It appears not unreasonable to infer from the map evidence that rulers (including in particular the Imam of Yemen) of Southern Arabia before the 1872 Ottoman conquest probably did perceive that the Islands fell within their territorial claim as part of Yemen or of the Arabian coast. However this impression must be qualified by the fact that it is not possible to evaluate the *colour* of maps produced during periods when hand-colouring had to be applied to maps at a second stage. These factors are therefore not determinative with regard to the issue of reversionary historic title. Moreover, there is no evidence that Southern Arabian rulers themselves ever saw or authorized these maps. Conclusions based on this material would be tenuous at best.

1872-1918 period

371. Similarly, maps subsequent to 1872 and earlier than 1918 are adduced by Yemen to show that the Islands fell under Ottoman sovereignty during the period in question and fell within the *vilayet* of Yemen and were administered as part of that *vilayet*. The map evidence appears to confirm the fact that the Ottoman Empire was sovereign over the Islands, upon which fact the Parties are in agreement.

Period between 1924 and 1939

372. Yemen has introduced a number of maps that appear to prove that Italy in the inter-war period did not officially consider itself as sovereign over the Islands. These maps were produced by the Ministry of Colonies in 1933, 1935, and 1937 and by the Ministry of Italian Africa in 1939, and they show that the Italian colonial authorities did not consider at the time that the Islands formed part of the Italian Colony of Eritrea. Yemen has also submitted other official Italian maps from the Ministry of Colonies (*c.* 1925 and 1933) and the Ministry of Italian Africa (1939) of which the first two attribute the Islands clearly to *Yemen* as opposed to the Province of Eritrea, and the third merely omits them from territory of Italian East Africa.

373. Eritrea has introduced an official Italian map of the 1920s to a contrary purpose. It is however hard to discern and appears to be done by hand. Weighed against the evidence submitted by Yemen in terms of official Italian maps of the period, it is not as clear as the Ministry of Colonies' 1933 and 1935 Maps. Nor is its date specified.

374. To the extent that these may be viewed as admissions against interest from official Italian sources, which are not controverted by Eritrean evidence, they have relevance to the Eritrean claim that Italy considered herself sovereign over the Islands at the outbreak of the Second World War. The best interpretation of this evidence appears

to be that official Italian cartography did not wish formally to portray the Islands as being under Italian sovereignty in the inter-war period—and even went so far as to assign the Islands to Yemen. On balance, the evidence seems to establish that Italy, in the interbellum period, did not consider the Islands to be under Italian sovereignty or at least does not establish that Italy in that period did consider the Islands to be under Italian sovereignty.

375. However, since the Tribunal has arrived at its legal conclusions about the status of the Islands on the basis of the diplomatic record and agreements entered into between 1923 and 1939, the map evidence —whilst supportive of and consistent with the conclusions reached—is not itself determinative. Were there no other evidence in the record concerning the attitude or intentions of Italy, this evidence would be of greater importance.

United Nations Treatment in 1950

376. Yemen has introduced maps from the period of the early 1950s to demonstrate that the United Nations considered the Islands not to be part of the Province of Eritrea (within Ethiopia). The key evidence here is a United Nations Map of 1950. Eritrea has vigorously contested the accuracy of this map, its provenance, authenticity and effect, saying that "[n]o official map was adopted by the United Nations".

377. It is well accepted that, in the United Nations practice, its publication of a map does not constitute a recognition of sovereign title to territory by the United Nations.

378. Whether the map was attached to the report of the United Nations Commission for Eritrea as an official commission map, or as a compromise—or even as a merely illustrative map—seems to be beside the point. What it bears witness to is that it was used and circulated—and received no objection. No protest was recorded in 1950 or at any later time, and Ethiopia itself voted in favour of the report with full knowledge of the map.

379. The map however cannot affirmatively prove that the Islands were Yemeni, even if they bear the same colour as Yemen. In this instance, the United Nations was not concerned with Yemen. The map did not in fact concern Yemen as such. What it shows is that the United Nations when it acted on the future of Ethiopia and Eritrea did *not* consider the Islands to be Ethiopian or Eritrean. As already mentioned in connection with the Italian map evidence of the 1920s and 1930s, since the Tribunal has reached the conclusion that Italy had not acquired sovereignty over the Islands by 1940, it could not then reach the conclusion that Ethiopia (and thus Eritrea by derivation) could have acquired title ten years later by inheritance from Italy.

Informed Opinion

380. Both Eritrea and Yemen have introduced a number of maps produced by third parties (such as independent or commercial cartographic sources, or the intelligence, mapping and navigational authorities of third States) in order to demonstrate that informed opinion recognized the Islands as respectively forming part of Ethiopia, or of Yemen, during the period from the early 1950s to the early 1990s.

381. Although the Tribunal must be wary of this evidence in the sense that it cannot be used as indicative of legal title, it is nonetheless "important evidence of general opinion or repute" in the sense advanced by Yemen. But while a considerable number of the maps submitted appear in general to confirm an impression that the Islands, from and after 1952 to the present day, are mainly attributed to Yemen, and not to Ethiopia or Eritrea, there are noteworthy exceptions.

382. Although Eritrea, on its part, has introduced some respectable independent cartographic evidence, this evidence appears to be somewhat outweighed by the contrary evidence from the other side. In some instances the Tribunal cannot agree with the characterization of the maps sought by the Party introducing it. Moreover, the Tribunal is unwilling, without specific direction from the map itself, to attribute meaning to dotted lines rather than to colouration or to labelling. The conclusions on this basis urged by Eritrea in relation to a number of its maps are not accepted.

383. There are also Central Intelligence Agency maps introduced by Yemen and the corroborative labelling in the US Defence Department Mapping Agency charts of 1994.

Admissions Against Interest

384. In 1967, the United States Department of State distributed a press package on the occasion of a State visit by Emperor Haile Selassie to Washington together with "Background Notes" that included a map that very clearly showed the Islands as not being Ethiopian. They are clearly shown in black, just as are Kamaran and the Farasan islands; the Dahlaks are also clearly shown in white, as part of Ethiopia.

385. Yemen has introduced evidence showing that Ethiopia, the Eritrean liberation movement before independence, and the Eritrean Government after independence have not considered the Islands to be Ethiopian or Eritrean—but rather Yemeni. Eritrea has also introduced evidence to show that Yemen has itself attributed the Islands to Ethiopia or to Eritrea. The Tribunal is of the view that most of this evidence tends to cancel itself out, except possibly for the Eritrean maps published after 1992.

386. Yemen further contended that a particular map, asserted by Eritrea to have been produced for the Eritrean Ministry of Tourism by a private firm and to contain a number of inaccuracies, had in fact

been distributed to foreign missions, including those of Yemen and the United States, and that it also "hung in Eritrean Government offices in Asmara". This statement was not controverted. The Tribunal notes that an early map produced by Eritrea after it became independent did not attribute to Eritrea all of the islands that it now claims.

387. On its part, Eritrea asserts as well that Yemen has authorized the production of maps that can be interpreted against its interest, including a map published in 1975 which clearly appears to ascribe the Islands to Ethiopia.

Conclusions as to Maps
388. On balance, the Tribunal has reached the following conclusions:

As to the period prior to 1872
Although Yemen has shown in general that most ancient and nineteenth-century maps attributed the Islands to the Arabian sphere of influence rather than to the African coast, the precise attribution of the Islands to "Yemen" has not been demonstrated.

For the period from 1872 to 1918
The maps produced by each side demonstrate without difficulty that the Islands were under Ottoman domination during the last years of the Empire's existence. There is no evidence in the record, nor was there any discussion in the case, about the effect of this widespread recognition on the validity *vel non* of the asserted Yemeni claim to a reversionary interest.

For the period between the Wars
The map evidence is to some extent contradictory, but by and large the official Italian maps of the time demonstrate that even if Italy harboured a desire to annex the Islands after the Treaty of Lausanne, it certainly did not accompany this desire with any outward manifestation of State authority in its official cartography.

For the post-war period
It is not possible to conclude from the history of the 1950 United Nations maps that Ethiopia acquired the Islands after the Second World War, from Italy or otherwise.

For the period between 1950 and 1992
The evidence for this period is beset with contradictions and uncertainties. Each Party has demonstrated inconsistency in its official maps. The general trend is, however, that Yemeni map evidence is superior in scope and volume to that of Eritrea. However, such weight as can be attached to map evidence in favour of one Party is balanced

by the fact that each Party has published maps that appear to run counter to its assertions in these proceedings.

For the period from 1992 to 1995

Finally, evidence is in the record showing broadly publicized official and semi-official Eritrean cartography shortly after independence which shows the Islands as non-Eritrean if not Yemeni. The evidence is, as in all cases of maps, to be handled with great delicacy.

CHAPTER IX   Petroleum Agreements and Activities

389. It is a singular fact of the proceedings that neither Party on its own motion pleaded, described, or relied upon oil contracts and concessions relating to the Red Sea and the disputed Islands. The pleadings of the Parties in respect of oil contracts and concessions came in response to questions posed by a Member of the Tribunal at the close of its hearings in February 1998; in the absence of those questions, it appears that those pleadings would not have been made in this phase of the proceedings.

390. Nevertheless, in response to questions put to them, both Parties submitted considerable data and argument. In the view of the Tribunal, that data and argument left some questions unanswered. It accordingly called for renewed hearings to be devoted solely to Red Sea petroleum contracts and concessions. Those hearings took place in London from 6 to 8 July, with the benefit of substantial further written pleadings as well as oral argument, in the course of which, and after which, still further material data was introduced. In those hearings, Eritrea largely maintained that these contracts and concessions were probative of little that was relevant to the issues before the Tribunal, whereas Yemen maintained that they were of major significance in support of its position. Yemen contended that the pattern of Yemen's offshore concessions, unprotested by Ethiopia and Eritrea, taken together with the pattern of Ethiopian concessions, confirmed Yemen's sovereign claims to the disputed Islands, acceptance of and investment on the basis of that sovereignty by oil companies, and acquiescence by Ethiopia and Eritrea. Yemen stated that lack of time had been the reason for its not having pleaded the contracts and concessions on its own initiative.

The Provisions of the Pertinent Contracts and Concessions

391. Both Yemen and Eritrea have concluded contracts and concession agreements for oil exploration, development, production, and sale of commercial quantities of petroleum that might be found under the Red Sea. While in the event no such quantities have so far been found, those contracts and concessions merit the Tribunal's consideration for what they show and do not show. Of particular

significance for the issues before the Tribunal may be any *effectivités* arising out of or associated with those contracts and concessions.

Contracts and Concessions entered into by Yemen

392. Yemen has submitted information on Red Sea contracts and concession agreements as follows.

Shell Seismic Survey, 1972

393. Yemen states that, in 1972, its predecessor, the Yemen Arab Republic, entered into a contract with Shell International Petroleum Company for "a major geophysical scouting survey in the Red Sea". It maintains that the survey, carried out on Shell's behalf by Western Geophysical Company of America in March 1972, involved the shooting of seismic reconnaissance lines in the area of the Red Sea that encompassed the islands of the Zuqar-Hanish group, the Zubayr group and Jabal al-Tayr, and from that fact argues that the survey is supportive of Yemeni sovereignty over those Islands. It states that, as a result of the survey, Shell decided that the southern third of the area surveyed, a substantial zone that encompassed the Zuqar-Hanish group, was not promising, but that it would take up a concession contract for a more northerly block which included Zubayr Island.

394. Yemen has not been in a position to provide a text of the survey contract, whose existence Eritrea questions. It does provide a report of Shell International Petroleum Maatschappij NV of January 1977, which refers to an offshore scouting survey whose results were used to select the area of the agreement discussed below. It introduced as well in the course of the hearings on 7 July 1998 the *Final Operations Report, Marine Seismic Survey, Offshore Yemen (Red Sea)* by Western Geophysical Company of March 1972. That report states that the objective of the survey was to provide a preliminary seismic coverage of "the concession area" (though at that stage there was no concession), and notes that the field office and base of operations for the seismic survey were in Massawa, Ethiopia. The report attaches a map of the "approximate area covered by seismic program" (Plate I), which extends right up to the Ethiopian coast.

395. That map indicates that the survey area is irrelevant to questions of title; Yemen hardly is claiming jurisdiction over the territorial waters of Eritrea, and could not have meant to do so by the authorization or performance of the seismic survey in question. The fact that the survey area embraced Islands in dispute accordingly is not probative.

Shell Petroleum Agreement, 1974

396. The Yemen Arab Republic and Deutsche Shell Aktiengesellschaft concluded a Petroleum Agreement on 16 January 1974. The

contract area was defined as meaning the specified area and its subsoil and seabed "under the jurisdiction of the Yemen Arab Republic". It comprised a Red Sea block north of the Zuqar and Hanish islands, which islands it names but does not encompass. It does not encompass Jabal al-Tayr, which is to the west of the contract area, nor does it name it. It names none of the islands it does encompass. It includes the Zubayr group among the unnamed islands within the contract area.

397. A reconnaissance survey was contracted for by Shell that entailed seismic, gravity and magnetic data acquisition in the contract area; the survey report does not state that the survey was carried out within the territorial waters of the Zubayr group. A well was drilled by Shell at a point far from the islands in dispute; oil was not found in commercial quantities; and the agreement was terminated.

398. In a *Final Report on the Exploration Venture of Yemen Shell Explorations GMBH Yemen Arab Republic* of May 1981, it is stated that: "The concession area granted to Deutsche Shell . . . under the terms of the Petroleum Agreement of 16 January 1974 extended from . . . the Yemen mainland in the east to approximately the median line of the Red Sea in the west."

399. In view of that statement and the fact that the concession contract speaks not of an area and its subsoil and seabed under the sovereignty but under the jurisdiction of Yemen, the Tribunal concludes that the 1974 Shell concession was granted and implemented in exercise not of Yemen's claims to sovereignty over the islands and their waters within the contract area but in exercise of its rights to the continental shelf as they then were. It further is of the view, in the light of the foregoing factors, that, since the contract does not name the Zubayr group and since Shell conducted no activities on the islands of the Zubayr group or within their territorial waters, the 1974 Shell Petroleum Agreement was entered into without particular regard to the Zubayr group. Those islands appear to have been included within the contract area because the Zubayr group fell on the Yemeni side of the median line, on a continental shelf over which Yemen could exercise jurisdiction.

400. At the same time, the Petroleum Agreement between Yemen and Shell was known to the industry, was published, and its existence and, with sufficient diligence, its terms, could have been known to Ethiopia had it followed the pertinent publications (such as Barrow's *Basic Oil Laws and Concession Contracts*). Ethiopia may be argued to have had notice, at any rate, constructive notice, of its existence and provisions. It made no protest about the agreement, despite its contract area including the Zubayr group to which Eritrea now lays claim. Eritrea maintains that Ethiopia in fact was unaware of the terms of the agreement; that, as a poor country locked in civil war, Ethiopia cannot be charged with gaining knowledge of it, and that, in any event, since

conclusion and publication of a concession contract is not a title-generating act, there was nothing to protest in the absence of concrete and visible activities of Shell or the Yemeni Government on the Zubayr group. Yemen, for its part, attaches significance to the failure of Ethiopia to protest. Such absence of protest by Ethiopia, and later Eritrea, characterizes all the concessions granted by Yemen in the Red Sea, and will be evaluated below.

401. The area of the 1974 Petroleum Agreement between Yemen and Shell is further reproduced in a map dated December 1976. That map was prepared by Shell, and is found in a Shell Report of January 1977 marked "Confidential". It is not contended that it has been published or could or should have been known to Ethiopia. It shows the area of the agreement and the areas of detailed survey within it (which are not near the Zubayr group). To the west of the area of the agreement, there runs a line which is described as the "Approximate tentative international boundary". That boundary runs west of the Zubayr group and west of Zuqar and the Hanish islands as well. No evidence was offered about the considerations that in the view of the drawer of the line gave rise to it, nor did Eritrea specifically comment upon it. In *Yemen's Comments on the Documents introduced by Eritrea after the Final Oral Argument, 29 July 1998,* maps 5 and 6 prepared by Yemen are described as reproducing the line.

402. It appears to the Tribunal that the author of the Shell map was of the view that the "approximate tentative international boundary" was to be drawn on the basis of Yemeni sovereignty over most of the disputed islands and all of the larger ones. That impression is supported not only by the fact that the "approximate tentative international boundary" runs west of those islands. It is strengthened by the author's having accorded the major disputed islands, including Zuqar and the Hanish islands, an influence on the course of the boundary as drawn.

Tomen–Santa Fe Seismic Permit, 1974

403. A Seismic Permit Agreement was concluded between the Yemen Arab Republic and Toyo Menka Kaisha Ltd ("Tomen") in 1974, which was extended to include Santa Fe International Corp. The agreement was initially characterized by Yemen in these proceedings as a "concession", which was contested by Eritrea; when its text was later introduced, it was found to be entitled, "Seismic Permit", and to provide for Tomen's conducting a marine seismic survey in the contract area. The contract area is specified by the contract to be outlined in "Exhibit A"; however, Yemen has not placed "Exhibit A" in evidence and has not offered an explanation for its absence from the text of a contract otherwise provided in full. The contract itself gives the coordinates of the contract area and Yemen has placed in evidence maps which it states were prepared for these proceedings on the basis of those coordinates.

404. Yemen affirms on the basis of those coordinates and maps that the contract area embraced the whole of Zuqar and the Hanish islands. However, in an "Exploration History Map" prepared by the United Nations Development Programme (UNDP) and the World Bank, undated but apparently prepared late in 1991, on whose probative force Yemen repeatedly has relied, the western line differs. The western line appears to run through, rather than to the west of, the southern extremity of Greater Hanish Island (the explanatory block on the map reads, "Tomen & Santa Fe, started 1974, ended 1975, seismic, 2150 km."). It may be that the line on the UNDP map runs through Greater Hanish along a median line, as two other concessions, one concluded by Yemen and another by Eritrea, appear to do.

405. The Tomen–Santa Fe Seismic Permit Agreement recites that Yemen has "exclusive authority to mine for Petroleum in and throughout" the contract area, and that the contract area "means the offshore area within the statutory mining territory of Yemen" described in the permit. The term of the contract is six months (and appears to have been extended to a year). The contract specifies that, "The execution of the work program shall not conflict with obligations imposed on the Government of Yemen by International Law." It provides that the contractor shall have the right of ingress to and egress from the contract area and adjacent areas. It further provides that Tomen shall, within the contract term, have the right to apply for a Petroleum Licence for all or part of the contract area for the exploration, development and production of petroleum, the terms of which are to be agreed upon guided by the terms of similar licences in OPEC countries.

406. The Seismic Permit Agreement, while not a concession agreement, accordingly is a petroleum-related contract that looks towards the conclusion of such an agreement in certain circumstances. Its assertion of an exclusive authority of Yemen to mine for petroleum within the contract area, and its reference to the statutory mining territory of Yemen, is consistent with conclusion of a contract for exercise of Yemen's rights on its continental shelf. Decree No 16 concerning the Continental Shelf of the Yemen Arab Republic of 30 April 1967, in proclaiming Yemeni sovereign rights over the seabed and subsoil of its continental shelf and the continental shelf of its islands, asserts the exclusive right to prospect for natural mineral resources of the shelf. The contractual reference to obligations imposed upon Yemen by international law is also of interest, and may be a reference to limited continental shelf rights. In the view of the Tribunal, the Seismic Permit Agreement of itself does not constitute a claim by Yemen to sovereignty over the islands within its contract area, nor does Eritrea's failure to protest the agreement indicate

acquiescence in any such claim. However to some extent it presupposes some measure of title to any islands contained within the contract area. The contract area included the land territory and territorial waters of the islands within its extent; this would have included the land territory and also the territorial waters of some or all of Greater Hanish and all of Zuqar and Lesser Hanish.

407. Eritrea argues that in any event seismic surveys are not indicative of sovereign claims. It relies on the Law of the Sea Convention, Part XIII on "Marine Scientific Research". Article 241 provides: "Marine scientific research shall not constitute the legal basis for any claim to any part of the marine environment and its resources." Article 246 provides for the regulation by coastal States of marine scientific research in the exclusive economic zone and on the continental shelf; research which shall be conducted with the consent of the coastal State. States shall in normal circumstances grant their consent for marine scientific research projects by other States or competent international organizations "in order to increase scientific knowledge of the marine environment for the benefit of mankind". In the view of the Tribunal, these provisions do not relate to the seismic and other explorations for petroleum for commercial purposes carried out by licensees of the Parties in the circumstances of these proceedings.

408. Accordingly, activities undertaken in pursuance of the Tomen–Santa Fe Seismic Permit and other like authorizations by licensees of the Parties have a certain importance, and must be weighed by the Tribunal. In the period between 23 July 1974, when the vessel *Western Geophysical I* departed from Hodeidah, and the completion of its voyage on 9 September 1974, a period of some six weeks, "Of the originally scheduled 1500 miles of program, only 1336 miles were recorded due to . . . dangerous shoaling in the offshore islands area." That suggests that there were difficulties in working close to the islands; there are a number of references in the report to the Zuqar and Hanish islands, but no indication is given that suggests any activity on the islands. It is not easy to deduce from the text and maps provided whether seismic work was performed within the territorial waters of the islands. One, for example, speaks of an aerial survey 2 square miles in extent "East of Little Hanish Island". But how far east—and whether within or without the territorial waters of Little Hanish Island—is not shown, nor was the question precisely pursued by counsel for Yemen, who confined himself to stating that operations were conducted "very close" to the islands. Figure 1 of the Santa Fe Report, "Location map & geophysical map", indicates that the areas of detailed survey avoided the immediate waters of the islands, but the map of itself does not show at what proximity to the islands seismic work was conducted. However, if, for example, the geographic position stated "West side Zuqar Island; southwest intersection Lines

50 and 8" is matched against the survey grid found in Figure 1—each of the bigger blocks being 10 square kilometres—it appears that seismic activities did extend well into Zuqar's territorial waters. As far as can be determined from a review of the report, it is uncertain whether the same can be said for the waters of the Hanish islands.

409. The Santa Fe Report continues: "During the seismic survey, the Zuqar and Hanish islands were observed from aboard ship by the writer, appearing to be made entirely of volcanic rocks . . . Later, Mr Hazem Baker, a geologist with the Yemeni government, went ashore on Zuqar Island and collected samples . . . all basaltic." It seems reasonable to presume that he believed that he was landing on an island at least under Yemeni jurisdiction.

Hunt Oil Company Offshore Production Sharing Agreement, 1984

410. Yemen and Offshore Yemen Hunt Oil Company on 10 March 1984 concluded an Offshore Area Production Sharing Agreement. It recites, "Whereas, all Petroleum in its natural habitat in strata lying within the boundaries of YEMEN is the property of the STATE; and Whereas the STATE wishes to promote the development of potential oil resources in the Area and the CONTRACTOR wishes to join and assist the State in the exploration, development and production of the potential Petroleum resources in the Area . . .". Hunt is appointed Contractor "exclusively to conduct Petroleum Operations in the Area described . . . the STATE shall in its name retain title to the area covered . . .". The agreement provides that Yemeni laws shall apply to the Contractor provided that they are consistent with the agreement, and that the rights and obligations of the parties shall be governed by the agreement and can be altered only with their mutual agreement. The agreement was approved by Government Decree. The coordinates of the area covered by the agreement are set out in Annex A, to which is attached a map at Annex B showing those coordinates but not naming or showing any of the disputed islands. Yemen has prepared and submitted a map to the Tribunal which shows the Hunt concession as running in the west very close to the edge of, but not including, Jabal al-Tayr, and, at the southern end of the contract boundary, just including the Zubayr group.

411. In fulfilment of its exploration obligations under the agreement, Hunt contracted with Western Geophysical to conduct a seismic survey of the concession area. It did so in 1985, "infilling" Shell data collected a decade earlier. That operation included the area of the Zubayr islands and, it is claimed, Jabal al-Tayr even though the latter did not fall within the concession area. Seismic soundings were taken "around the Zubayr islands and Jabal al-Tayr" but it is not claimed or shown that seismic activities were conducted within their territorial waters. No activities on the Islands are alleged or shown. Aeromagnetic

surveys in the contract area were conducted by an aircraft flying from Yemen, and consequently permission to fly through Yemeni airspace was sought and accorded; that fact neither supports nor detracts from Yemen's claims about the status of the contract area. Equally neutral is the fact that, in connection with well drilling, permission was sought "to enter YAR territorial waters and conduct offshore drilling operations", which were nowhere near the Islands. Two wells were drilled far from the Islands; neither produced oil in commercial quantities, and the concession was relinquished.

412. The Production Sharing Agreement does not in terms state a claim of sovereignty of Yemen over the concession area, and, as noted, it takes no notice of the Islands within it, verbally or in the annexed map. It could be interpreted as a concession issued within the area demarcated by a median line in implementation of Yemen's rights on its continental shelf, a concession which includes the Zubayr group but stops just short of including Jabal al-Tayr. It may be said that if it was the intention of Yemen in issuing the concession to assert sovereignty over the disputed islands, the concession would have included Jabal al-Tayr. What seems likelier is that this concession, as others, was issued with commercial considerations in mind and without particular regard to the existence of the Islands. The fact that title to the contract area is stated to remain in the State of Yemen is not determinative; Yemen holds title to resources on and under its continental shelf; but since the agreement specifies that Yemen retains title "to the area covered" that may be read as a reservation of sovereign title. The reference to the "boundaries of Yemen" is also suggestive of a claim of sovereignty, though "boundaries" does not exclude continental shelf boundaries. The Hunt Production Sharing Agreement was reported in the petroleum literature and gave rise to no protest on the part of Eritrea.

BP Production Sharing Agreement, 1990

413. Yemen and British Petroleum concluded a Production Sharing Agreement on 20 October 1990, whose terms are very similar and in pertinent respects identical to the foregoing Hunt Agreement. It covers the same Antufash Block offshore Yemen that Hunt operated in earlier, and thus embraces the Zubayr islands but not Jabal al-Tayr. However, and this may reflect the policy of Yemen in respect of potential petroleum blocks offered by it in the 1990s, the BP Agreement's description of the block is more specific than that found in the Hunt Agreement, providing: "Whereas, the State wishes to promote the development of potential Petroleum Resources in the Agreement Area block 8, As-Sakir, Shabwa Province, ROY . . .". The text of the agreement was published in *Barrow's*. It elicited no protest from Eritrea.

414. BP conducted extensive aeromagnetic surveys of the agreement area. Low-level flights, conducted with the permission of the Govern-

ment of Yemen, covered the Area, including the Zubayr islands, and Jabal al-Tayr though it was outside the Area. A Yemeni military officer accompanied the aircraft during its survey. Survey results were unpromising and BP relinquished its rights in the Area in 1993.

415. The Tribunal does not attach much importance to overflights by either of the Parties of the islands in dispute. In the circumstances of the case, it is not clear that overflights of these uninhabited islands are tantamount to a claim of jurisdiction, still less sovereignty, over the Islands. However the agreement's characterization of the Antufash block as comprising or being within a province of the Republic of Yemen is a factor of significance in favour of Yemen; it indicates a sovereign rather than a jurisdictional claim. At the same time, the fact that the agreement was entered into in 1990 and published about that time is noteworthy. Ethiopia was then locked in its final struggle with the Eritrean liberation movement, the Mengistu regime was close to collapse, and to suggest that Eritrea today should be taxed with Ethiopia's failure during that period to find and protest the terms of the agreement may be unreasonable.

Total Production Sharing Agreement, 1985

416. Yemen and Total-Compagnie Française des Pétroles concluded a Production Sharing Agreement in 1985, to which Texaco later became party. Its terms appear close to those of the Hunt Agreement concluded the year before, summarized in pertinent passages above. It however recites, "Whereas, all Petroleum in its natural habitat in strata lying within the boundaries of Yemen and in the seabed subject to its jurisdiction is the property of the State; . . .". Since the area of the agreement is onshore as well as offshore, this could be read as an indication of an offshore claim only to jurisdiction and not sovereignty, and could be taken as an indication of such a Yemeni assumption in other petroleum agreements. The Area is stated to be described in Annex A and shown on the map labelled Annex B, but neither Annex is attached to the text submitted by Yemen to the Tribunal. However, it is common ground between the Parties that the Total Agreement's western line runs to the east of Zuqar and the Hanish islands. There is no ground for concluding that this fact suggests a lack of entitlement of Yemen to enter into agreements embracing the disputed islands. It rather again suggests that the petroleum agreements entered into by Yemen were concluded without regard to the Islands.

417. Since the agreement area does not include any of the islands in dispute, it is of limited interest for these proceedings, except in the following respects. Total commissioned seismic studies, which were concentrated between the agreement's western line (which fell short of the Hanish islands) and the coastline of Yemen. The single well drilled—which proved unproductive and led to the agreement's

termination in 1989—was distant from the Hanish islands and towards the coast. However, less detailed seismic surveys were conducted to the west of the Hanish islands, outside the contract area, which entered territorial waters of those islands. Yemen acted as if it were entitled to authorize, and Total's agent acted as if it were entitled to conduct, those surveys in Hanish territorial waters.

418. Having come to know the Hanish islands through its offshore concession, Total in 1993 decided to become a sponsor of the French Ardoukoba scientific mission to the islands to study marine life in the reefs. Total requested and received Yemeni Government permission to establish a landing strip on Greater Hanish so that a Total aeroplane could transport equipment to it. It is also claimed that Total sought and received permission to establish a radio station on Greater Hanish and to permit visiting scientists to use its frequency; evidence in support of this claim has not been provided. Evidence has been provided showing that access to the Hanish islands, described by Total as uninhabited, was subject to authorization delivered by the "Central Operation of the Army". After the conclusion of the Ardoukoba mission, Total produced a report that referred to "les îles Hanish en république du Yemen". Thereafter it sought and received governmental authorization to improve the landing strip and fly Total personnel to Greater Hanish for rest and recreation. For a time, a Total aircraft flew frequently to Greater Hanish, carrying passengers for these purposes.

419. Incidental as it may have been to Total's Petroleum Agreement, the building and use of an airstrip on Greater Hanish is in the view of the Tribunal a material *effectivité*. It demonstrates the exercise by Yemen of jurisdiction over Greater Hanish, a recognition of that jurisdiction by Total, and the conduct of visible indicia of that jurisdiction—an airstrip in active use—over a period of time. Eritrea appears to have been unaware of it and in any event made no protest. However, Eritrea has introduced evidence showing that a report of activities of a French company in the waters around Greater Hanish was received in May 1986, the period when Total was operating in that area; that an Ethiopian patrol vessel was dispatched to the area to investigate, and that nothing was found. This evidence suggests that, in the perspective of Eritrea, sovereignty over Greater Hanish lay with it.

Adair International Production Sharing Agreement, 1993

420. Yemen and Adair International entered into a Production Sharing Agreement in 1993. The text of the agreement has not been offered in evidence and accordingly the Tribunal is not in a position to analyse it. The agreement was not ratified by Yemen and did not come into force. Yemen has, however, provided maps of the agreement area which show it as falling within Block 24 or the Al Kathib block in

which the Tomen–Santa Fe area fell. It maintains that Yemen had on offer an offshore block that included the whole of the Hanish islands, and that Adair chose to take a contract area slightly less than the total block on offer. The maps of the Adair area provided by Yemen show the western line to cut through the southern portion of Greater Hanish Island, leaving the larger part, but not all, of Greater Hanish within the area of the agreement. It explains that Adair drew that western line for commercial reasons. As far as the Tribunal can judge, the Adair Agreement's western line roughly runs along a median line between the coasts of Yemen and Eritrea, drawn without regard to the islands in dispute.

Blocks Offered by Yemen

421. Beginning in 1990, Yemen no longer responded to proposals by prospective concessionaires for rights in areas drawn by them, but began offering concession blocks, dividing most of Yemen and its offshore into blocks. It states that the blocks include the Zubayr islands and the Hanish islands—it offers no explanation for not including Jabal al-Tayr—and maintains that this is further evidence of Yemen holding itself out as the sovereign of disputed islands.

422. Such weight as the Tribunal might be disposed to give to that contention may be qualified by the evidence about the western lines of the offshore blocks provided by Yemen. Yemen has submitted not only its depiction of the blocks. It has also submitted and relied upon, as "expert opinion evidence confirming Yemen's exercise of State authority over the Hanish islands and other islands", a number of maps prepared by Petroconsultants SA of Geneva, illustrations of Petroconsultants' series, "Foreign Scouting Service, Current Status". The maps are dated from 1989 until November 1997. Three of these maps show a western line of Yemen's relevant block running not to the west of Greater Hanish Island but through it, as the Adair Area line does. The map for 1994 is linked to the Adair Agreement but the maps for 1996 and 1997 are not.

Petroleum Agreements and Activities of Ethiopia and Eritrea

423. Ethiopia in the 1970s entered into a number of offshore concession agreements, which stop short of the deep trough that runs through the middle of the Red Sea. At that time, oil technology was unable to support drilling in so deep a trough. While Yemen maintains that these agreements—which it rather than Eritrea introduced in these proceedings—showed a recognition by Ethiopia and the companies concerned that Ethiopia was not entitled to issue concessions embracing the disputed islands, in the view of the Tribunal these agreements simply reflect technological and commercial realities and carry no implication for the rights of the parties at issue in these

proceedings. It is reinforced in this conclusion by the fact that Ethiopian concessions typically contain a formula such as the following (as, *mutatis mutandis*, do maps attached to Yemeni concessions): "The description of the eastern boundary of the contract area does NOT necessarily conform to the international boundaries of Ethiopia and accordingly nothing said herein above is to be deemed to affect or prejudice in any way whatsoever the rights of the Government in respect of its sovereign rights over any of the islands or the seabed and subsoil of the submarine area beneath the high seas contiguous to its territorial waters or areas within its economic zone." The Tribunal also finds unenlightening two Red Sea offshore petroleum contracts concluded by Eritrea as late as 1995 and 1996, which were promptly protested by Yemen as overlapping its waters. But Ethiopia's contract with International Petroleum/Amoco is important.

International Petroleum/Amoco Production Sharing Agreement, 1988

424. Ethiopia concluded a Production Sharing Agreement with International Petroleum Ltd of Bermuda on 28 May 1988. The concession covered "the onshore–offshore area known as the Danakil Concession in the PDRE" (People's Democratic Republic of Ethiopia). It recites that, "WHEREAS, the title to all Petroleum existing in its natural condition on, or under the Territory of Ethiopia is vested in the State and people of Ethiopia . . . and the Government wishes to promote the exploration, development and production on, in or under the Contract Area . . .", the Government grants to the Contractor "the sole right to explore, develop and produce Petroleum in the Contract Area . . .". On 1 November 1989, 60 per cent of the contract was assigned to Amoco Ethiopia Petroleum Company. Amoco assumed operative responsibility under the assignment.

425. The map attached to the 1988 Production Sharing Agreement shows "Ethiopia–Red Sea Acreage", onshore and offshore, the latter's eastern line running through the southwest extremity of Greater Hanish Island. The description of the Contract Area runs "To the Offshore point 13 at the intersection of LAT 14 DEG 30 with the international median line between North Yemen and Ethiopia, then along the Offshore median line". The agreement contained a *force majeure* clause, including wars, insurrections, rebellions and terrorist acts, during which the life of the contract would be prolonged. Apparently in view of the fighting between Ethiopian and Eritrean units, *force majeure* was declared on 9 February 1990 and as of June 1992 was stated to be still in effect.

426. However there is ambiguity about the extent of the Contract Area, at any rate in depictions of it on maps. Amoco Ethiopia Petroleum Company filed four Annual Reports with the People's Democratic Republic of Ethiopia which are in point.

427. The Annual Report for 1989 recounts that geologic activities were undertaken in 1989, that Delft Geophysical Company was awarded a contract to acquire marine seismic, gravity and magnetic data, and that a scout trip by Delft was completed in December. Preliminary seismic interpretation and mapping was initiated. The map attached to the 1989 Report shows virtually all of Greater and Lesser Hanish within the area of the contract, i.e., considerably more than does the map attached to the Production Sharing Agreement.

428. The Annual Report for 1990 observes that activities were suspended with the advent of *force majeure* on 9 February 1990; as of the end of 1990, the security situation within the Danakil area was considered to remain unsafe for normal seismic operations. It reports on considerable geologic and geophysical activity before that time, and lists some $2,000,000 in expenditures under the agreement. While the description of the Contract Area matches that in the 1989 report, two maps are attached to the 1990 Annual Report. The first map of the Danakil Contract Area shows the eastern line as running not through but rather west of the Hanish islands. The second map of that Contract Area shows virtually all of Greater and Lesser Hanish within the Contract Area, duplicating the map attached to the 1989 Annual Report.

429. The 1991 Annual Report notes that *force majeure* has effectively extended the initial period of the contract. While normal seismic operations were unsafe in 1991, substantial technical evaluation of existing data continued. The map of the Contract Area in the 1991 Annual Report shows virtually all of the Hanish islands within the Contract Area, duplicating the maps to that effect in the 1989 and 1990 Reports.

430. The 1992 Annual Report reports limited reprocessing work. It states that Amoco and International Petroleum representatives met with officials of newly independent Eritrea in Asmara on 24 June 1993, when assurances were received that the Danakil Production Sharing Agreement would be recognized by Eritrea. It attaches a contract summary entitled, "Eritrea Danakil Block" and gives an expiration date of 9 February 1997, "to be delayed because of *force majeure*". The governing law is now described as Eritrean. The Danakil Block map attached to the 1993 Annual Report shows virtually all of the Hanish islands within the Contract Area, as does a "composite magnetic map of the Danakil concession".

431. A map prepared by Petroconsultants, on whose maps Yemen has repeatedly relied, also shows the Amoco Contract Area as embracing the greater part of Greater Hanish.

432. Yemen, while not denying that it never protested the terms or geographical extent of the International Petroleum–Amoco Production Sharing Agreement, argues that it could not be charged with doing so.

It observes that an article in the *Petroleum Economist* of October 1991 presents a map which shows an Amoco concession that does not include the Hanish islands. (The UNDP map, which is an "Exploration History Map", does not name the Amoco concession.) Yemen also maintains that the Amoco contract lasted only some three months and that, by the time it might have come to its attention, *force majeure* prevailed, which might have induced Yemen to take no action.

433. The Tribunal does not find Yemen's position entirely persuasive. As the Annual Reports summarized above demonstrate, the IPC/Amoco contract was extended well beyond three months and into the days of Eritrean independence; its life compares with that of the contracts on which Yemen relies. If Yemen had secured and read Amoco's Annual Reports—annual reports of American oil companies are generally publicly available for the asking—and if Yemen had evinced the alertness it did in respect of Eritrea's contracts of 1995 and 1996, it would have seen that Ethiopia claimed the right to contract for the exploration, development and production of oil in an area claimed as its territory that included some or virtually all of Greater Hanish islands. Amoco is a major player on the international petroleum scene, and in the immediate area; indeed, one of the maps introduced into evidence by Yemen, shows Amoco together with BP in the Antufash block and shows the Danakil Amoco concession angling into the Adair area in the Al Kathib block.

434. Yemen in its argument has made a great deal about what it alleges is the failure of Ethiopia or Eritrea to grant any concession contract that included disputed islands, and their failure to protest grants of Yemen that did include those islands. But it has been demonstrated that, in the lately pleaded International Petroleum–Amoco Production Sharing Agreement, Ethiopia did grant a concession including much or virtually all of the Hanish islands, and that Yemen failed to protest that agreement. It is of further interest that the map attached to the Production Sharing Agreement speaks of drawing the boundary along the international median line between Yemen and Ethiopia.

435. Eritrea also claims certain pertinent *effectivités*. It has submitted a copy of an Ethiopian radio transmitting licence granted *circa* 1988-9 (the earlier date on the contract is apparently of the Ethiopian calendar) to Delft Geophysical Co. for the establishment of a station on Greater Hanish Island, presumably in connection with the seismic work which Amoco had contracted with Delft to perform. It has provided the text of a detailed order to the most senior military commanders to provide protection to a petroleum exploration expedition of the Ethiopian Ministry of Mines and Energy to be deployed to areas "including Greater Hanish Island". It has provided an Ethiopian memorandum on oil exploration in the Red Sea carrying the Ethiopian

date of 13 April 1982 (which is *circa* 1989 AD), stating that Amoco–Ethiopia Petroleum Company "has installed navigation beacons to enable it to conduct seismic study . . . including on Greater Hanish Island". The memorandum continues:

An Amoco professional team of contractors will be available starting 3rd week of December to select areas for the installation as follows:

> For two weeks installation of navigation beacons on the 8 selected locations;
> At the end of the two-week period, conduct 6 week-long seismic tests . . .

and it calls for ensuring the protection of the contractors and their equipment during beacon installation and for the protection of the installed beacons. It further requests protection for the Delft Geophysical ship while it is conducting seismic tests. Another memorandum states that an Amoco contracting team will conduct helicopter patrols to select locations for the installation of navigation beacons, including locations "on Greater Hanish". It is not entirely clear whether these activities were in fact completed, although the Amoco Annual Report for 1989 does corroborate that Delft Geophysical did conduct a scout trip in December of 1989 (see para. 427, above).

* * *

436. In the light of this complex concession history, the Tribunal has reached the following conclusions:

437. The offshore petroleum contracts entered into by Yemen, and by Ethiopia and Eritrea, fail to establish or significantly strengthen the claims of either Party to sovereignty over the disputed islands.

438. Those contracts however lend a measure of support to a median line between the opposite coasts of Eritrea and Yemen, drawn without regard to the islands, dividing the respective jurisdiction of the Parties.

439. In the course of the implementation of the petroleum contracts, significant acts occurred under State authority which require further weighing and evaluation by the Tribunal.

CHAPTER X   Conclusions

440. Having examined and analysed in great detail the extensive materials and evidence presented by the Parties,[25] the Tribunal may now draw the appropriate conclusions.

---

[25] The Tribunal wishes to note the sheer volume of written pleadings and evidence received from the Parties in this first phase of the arbitral proceedings. Each Party submitted over twenty volumes of documentary annexes, as well as extensive map atlases. In addition, the Tribunal has carefully reviewed the verbatim transcripts of the oral hearings, which together far exceed 1,000 pages. The Tribunal further notes that the majority of documents were submitted in their original language, and the Tribunal has relied on translations provided by the Parties.

Ancient Title
441. First there is the question of an "ancient title" to which Yemen attaches great importance; moreover the Agreement for Arbitration requires the Tribunal to decide the question of sovereignty "on the basis in particular of historic titles". Yemen contends that it enjoys an ancient title to "the islands", which title existed before the hegemony of the Ottoman Empire and indeed emanates from medieval Yemen. It contends, moreover, that this title still subsisted in international law at the time when the Turks were defeated at the end of the First World War, and that therefore, when the Ottoman Empire renounced their generally acknowledged sway over the islands by the Treaty of Lausanne in 1923, the right to enjoy that title in possession "reverted" to Yemen.

442. This is an interesting argument and one that raises a number of questions concerning the international law governing territorial sovereignty. No one doubts that during the period of the Ottoman Empire—certainly in the second Ottoman period 1872-1918—the Ottomans enjoyed possession of, and full sovereignty over, all the islands now in dispute, and thus not only factual possession but also a sovereign title to possession. When this regime ceased in 1923, was there a "reversion" to an even older title to fill a resulting vacuum?

443. It is doubted by Eritrea whether there is such a doctrine of reversion in international law. This doubt seems justified in view of the fact that very little support for such a doctrine was cited by Yemen, nor is the Tribunal aware of any basis for maintaining that reversion is an accepted principle or rule of general international law. Moreover, even if the doctrine were valid, it could not apply in this case. That is because there is a lack of continuity. It has been argued by Yemen that in the case of historic title no continuity need be shown, but the Tribunal finds no support for this argument.

444. Yemen's argument is difficult to reconcile with centuries of Ottoman rule over the entire area, ending only with the Treaty of Lausanne (see Chapter V, above). This is the more so because, under the principle of intertemporal law, the Ottoman sovereignty was lawful and carried with it the entitlement to dispose of the territory. Accepting Yemen's argument that an ancient title could have remained in effect over an extended period of another sovereignty would be tantamount to a rejection of the legality of Ottoman title to full sovereignty.

445. The Treaty of Lausanne did not expressly provide, as the Treaty of Sèvres would have done, that Turkey renounced her territorial titles in favour of the Allied Powers; which provision would certainly have excluded any possibility of the operation of a doctrine of reversion. Yemen was not a party to the Treaty of Lausanne, which was therefore *res inter alios acta*. Nevertheless, none of the authorities

doubts that the formerly Turkish islands were in 1923 at the disposal of the parties to the Lausanne Treaty, just as they had formerly been wholly at the disposal of the Ottoman Empire, which was indeed party to the treaty and in it renounced its sovereignty over them. Article 16 of the Treaty created for the islands an objective legal status of indeterminacy pending a further decision of the interested parties; and this legal position was generally recognized, as the considerable documentation presented by the Parties to the Tribunal amply demonstrates. So, it is difficult so see what could have been left of such a title after the interventions of the Ottoman sovereignty which was generally regarded as unqualified; and its replacement by the Article 16 regime which put the islands completely at the disposal of the "interested parties".

446. There is a further difficulty. Yemen certainly existed before the region came to be under the domination of the Ottomans. But there must be some question whether the Imam, who at that period dwelt in and governed a mountain fortress, had had sway over "the islands". Further, there is the problem of the sheer anachronism of attempting to attribute to such a tribal, mountain and Muslim medieval society the modern Western concept of a sovereignty title, particularly with respect to uninhabited and barren islands used only occasionally by local, traditional fishermen.

447. In keeping with the dictates of the Arbitration Agreement, both Parties, and Yemen especially, have placed "particular" emphasis on historic titles as a source of territorial sovereignty. They have, however, failed to persuade the Tribunal of the actual existence of such titles, particularly in regard to these islands.

448. Eritrea's claims too, in so far as they are said to be derived by succession from Italy through Ethiopia, if hardly based upon an "ancient" title, are clearly based upon the assertion of an historic title. There is no doubt, as has been shown in Chapters V, VI and VII above, that Italy in the inter-war period did entertain serious territorial ambitions in respect of the Red Sea islands; and did seek to further these ambitions by actual possession of some of them at various periods. Major difficulties for the Eritrean claims through succession are, as has been shown above in some detail, first the effect of Article 16 of the Treaty of Lausanne of 1923, and later the effects of the provisions of the Italian Peace Treaty of 1947. But there is also the fact that the Italian Government, in the inter-war period, constantly and consistently gave specific assurances to the British Government that Italy fully accepted and recognized the indeterminate legal position of these islands as established by treaty in 1923. No doubt Italy was hoping that the effect of her active expansionist policies might eventually be that "the parties concerned" would be persuaded to acquiesce in a *fait accompli*. But that never happened.

449. So there are considerable problems for both Parties with these versions of historic title. But the Tribunal has made great efforts to investigate both claims to historic titles. The difficulties, however, arise largely from the facts revealed in that history. In the end neither Party has been able to persuade the Tribunal that the history of the matter reveals the juridical existence of an historic title, or of historic titles, of such long-established, continuous and definitive lineage to these particular islands, islets and rocks as would be a sufficient basis for the Tribunal's decision. And it must be said that, given the waterless and uninhabitable nature of these islands and islets and rocks, and the intermittent and kaleidoscopically changing political situations and interests, this conclusion is hardly surprising.

450. Both Parties, however, also rely upon what is a form of historic claim but of a rather different kind; namely, upon the demonstration of use, presence, display of governmental authority, and other ways of showing a possession which may gradually consolidate into a title; a process well illustrated in the *Eastern Greenland* case, the *Palmas* case, and very many other well-known cases. Besides historic titles strictly so-called the Tribunal is required by the Agreement for Arbitration to apply the "principles, rules and practices of international law"; which rubric clearly covers this kind of argument very familiar in territorial disputes. The Parties clearly anticipated the possible need to resort to this kind of basis of decision—though it should be said that Yemen expressly introduces this kind of claim in confirmation of its ancient title, and Eritrea introduces this kind of claim in confirmation of an existing title acquired by succession—and the great quantity of materials and evidences of use and of possession provided by both Parties have been set out and analysed in Chapter VII above, together with Chapter VIII on maps and Chapter IX on the history of the petroleum agreements. It may be said at once that one result of the analysis of the constantly changing situation of all these different aspects of governmental activities is that, as indeed was so in the *Minquiers and Ecrehos*[26] case where there had also been much argument about claims to very ancient titles, it is the relatively recent history of use and possession that ultimately proved to be a main basis of the Tribunal decisions. And to the consideration of these materials and arguments this Award now turns.

Evidences of the Display of Functions of State and Governmental Authority

451. These materials have been put before the Tribunal by the Parties with the intention of showing the establishment of territorial sovereignty over the islands, in Judge Huber's words in the *Palmas* case,[27] "by the continuous and peaceful display of the functions of state

---

[26] *Minquiers and Ecrehos (UK v. France)*, 1953 ICJ 47 [20 *ILR* 94].
[27] *Island of Palmas (US v. Netherlands)*, 2 RIAA 829 (1929) [4 *Ann Dig* 3].

within a given region". But the kind of actions that may be deployed for this purpose has inevitably expanded in the endeavour to show what Charles de Visscher named a gradual "consolidation" of title. Accordingly, the Tribunal is faced in this case with an assortment of factors and events from many different periods, intended to show not only physical activity and conduct, but also repute, and the opinions and attitudes of other governments (the different classes of materials are set out above in Chapter VII).

452. It is well known that the standard of the requirements of such activity may have to be modified when one is dealing, as in the present case, with difficult or inhospitable territory. As the Permanent Court of International Justice said in the *Legal Status of Eastern Greenland* case, "[I]t is impossible to read the records of the decisions in cases as to territorial sovereignty without observing that in many cases the tribunal has been satisfied with very little in the way of the actual exercise of sovereign rights, provided that the other state could not make a superior claim."[28]

453. This raises, however, a further important question of principle. The problem involved is the establishment of territorial sovereignty, and this is no light matter. One might suppose that for so important a question there must be some absolute minimum requirement for the acquisition of such a right, and that in principle it ought not normally to be merely a relative question.

454. It may be recalled that this question of principle did arise in the *Palmas* case, but there Huber was able to meet it by appealing to the particular terms of the *compromis*, which, said Huber, "presupposes for the present case that the Island of Palmas (or Miangas) can belong only to the United States or to the Netherlands and must form in its entirety part of the territory either of the one or of the other of these two Powers, parties to the dispute", and "[t]he possibility for the arbitrator to found his decision on the relative strength of the titles invoked on either side must have been envisaged by the parties to the Special Agreement".

455. The Arbitration Agreement in the present case, however, is in different and even unusual terms. The Tribunal is required only to make "an award on territorial sovereignty" and "to decide the sovereignty". The compromissory provision which led Huber to the possibility of deciding only on the basis of a marginal difference in weight of evidence cannot be said to apply in the present case.

456. There is certainly no lack of materials, evidence, or of arguments in the present case. The materials, on the contrary, are voluminous and the result of skilled research by the teams of both

---

[28] *Legal Status of Eastern Greenland (Denmark v. Norway)*, 1933 PCIJ (Ser. A/B) No 53 [6 *Ann Dig* 95].

Parties, and of the excellent presentations by their counsel. But what these materials have in fact revealed is a chequered and frequently changing situation in which the fortunes and interests of the Parties constantly ebb and flow with the passage of the years. Moreover, it has to be remembered that neither Ethiopia nor Yemen had much opportunity of actively and openly demonstrating ambitions to sovereignty over the islands, or of displaying governmental activities upon them, until after 1967, when the British left the region. For, as shown above, the British were constantly vigilant to maintain the position effected by the Treaty of Lausanne that the legal position of "the islands" was indeterminate.

457. In these circumstances where for all the reasons just described the activities relied upon by the Parties, though many, sometimes speak with an uncertain voice, it is surely right for the Tribunal to consider whether there are in the instant case other factors which might help to resolve some of these uncertainties. There is no virtue in relying upon "very little" when looking at other possible factors might strengthen the basis of decision.

458. An obvious such factor in the present case is the geographical situation that the majority of the islands and islets and rocks in issue form an archipelago extending across a relatively narrow sea between the two opposite coasts of the sea. So there is some presumption that any islands off one of the coasts may be thought to belong by appurtenance to that coast unless the State on the opposite coast has been able to demonstrate a clearly better title. This possible further factor looks even more attractive when it is realized that its influence can be seen very much at work in the legal history of these islands; beginning indeed with the days of Ottoman rule when even under the common sovereignty of the whole region it was found convenient to divide the jurisdiction between the two coastal local authorities (see paras. 132-6, above). Moreover, in the present case, the examination of the activities material itself shows very clearly that there was no common legal history for the whole of this Zuqar-Hanish archipelago; some of the evidence not surprisingly refers to particular islands or to sub-groups of islands.

459. Thus the Tribunal has found it necessary, in order to decide the question of sovereignty, to consider the several subgroups of the islands separately, if only for the reason that the different subgroups have, at least to an important extent, separate legal histories; which is only to be expected in islands that span the area between two opposite coasts. This may seem only a natural or even manifest truth, but Yemen in particular has emphasized the importance it attaches to what it calls a principle of natural unity of the islands, and some comment on this theory is therefore required.

Natural and Physical Unity

460. Yemen's pleadings insist strongly on what it calls "the principle of natural or geophysical unity" in relation to the Hanish group of islands; Yemen uses the name of the "Hanish Group" both in its texts and in its illustrative maps to encompass the entire island chain, including the Haycocks and the Mohabbakahs (the present comments do not refer of course to the northern islands of Jabal al-Tayr and the Zubayr group, which will be considered separately later on).

461. This "principle" is described in Chapter 5 of the Yemen Memorial, where impressive authority is cited in support of it, including Fitzmaurice, Waldock and Charles de Visscher. That there is indeed some such concept cannot be doubted. But it is not an absolute principle. All these authorities speak of it in terms of raising a presumption. And Fitzmaurice is, in the passage cited, clearly dealing with the presumption that may be raised by proximity where a State is exercising or displaying sovereignty over a parcel of territory and there is some question whether this is presumed to extend also to outlying territory over which there is little or no factual impact of its authority. The Tribunal has no difficulty in accepting these statements of high authority; but what they are saying is in fact rather more than a simple principle of unity. It will be useful to cite Fitzmaurice again:

The question of "entity" or "natural unity"
This question can have far-reaching consequences. Not only may it powerfully affect the play of probabilities and presumptions, but also, if it can be shown that the disputed areas (whether by reason of actual contiguity or of proximity) are part of an entity or unity over which as a whole the claimant State has sovereignty, this may (under certain conditions and within certain limits) render it unnecessary—or modify the extent to which it will be necessary—to adduce specific evidence of State activity in relation to the disputed areas as such—provided that such activity, amounting to effective occupation and possession, can be shown in the principle established by the *Island of Palmas* case that "sovereignty cannot be exercised in fact at every moment on every point of a territory".[29]

462. Thus, the authorities speak of "entity" or "natural unity" in terms of a presumption or of probability and moreover couple it with proximity, contiguity, continuity, and such notions, well known in international law as not in themselves creative of title, but rather of a possibility or presumption for extending to the area in question an existing title already established in another, but proximate or contiguous, part of the same "unity".

463. These ideas, however, have a twofold possible application in the present case. They may indeed, as Yemen would have it, be

---

[29] 32 BYIL (1955-6) 73-4.

applied to cause governmental display on one island of a group to extend in its juridical effect to another island or islands in the same group. But by the same rationale a complementary question also arises of how far the sway established on one of the mainland coasts should be considered to continue to some islands or islets off that coast which are naturally "proximate" to the coast or "appurtenant" to it. This idea was so well established during the last century that it was given the name of the "portico doctrine" and recognized "as a means of attributing sovereignty over off-shore features which fell within the attraction of the mainland".[30] The relevance of these notions of international law to the legal history of the present case is not far to seek.

464. Thus the principle of natural and physical unity is a two-edged sword, for if it is indeed to be applied then the question arises whether the unity is to be seen as originating from the one coast or the other. Moreover, as the cases and authorities cited by Yemen clearly show, these notions of unity and the like are never in themselves roots of title, but rather may in certain circumstances raise a presumption about the extent and scope of a title otherwise established.

465. In spite of unity theories, the fact is that both Parties have tacitly conceded that, for the purposes at any rate of the exposition of their pleadings, it may be accepted that there can be sub-groups within the main group. The nomenclature within common use indicates at least three of the sub-groups: the Mohabbakahs; the Haycocks; and what it will be convenient at least for the moment to call the Zuqar-Hanish group and its many satellite islands, islets, and rocks. These names will all be found in the *British Pilot and Sailing Directions for the Southern Red Sea* (Yemen has cited this publication as authority for regarding all these islands as one group, but of course if one is concerned with them as sailing hazards or landmarks when traversing the Red Sea there is really no other way to do it). There are also the two northern islands: Jabal al-Tayr, and the group of which the biggest island is Jabal Zubayr. The Tribunal will now consider its conclusions in respect of each of the three sub-groups and then, finally, the northern islands.

466. Thus, in order to make decisions on territorial sovereignty, the Tribunal has hardly surprisingly found no alternative but to depart from the terms in which both Parties have pleaded their cases, namely by each of them presenting a claim to every one of the islands involved in the case. The legal history simply does not support either such claim.[31] For, as has been explained above, much of the material is found on examination to apply either to a particular island or to a

---

[30] D. O'Connell, *The International Law of the Sea* 185 (1982).

[31] In this connection it is interesting to see the statements made in the 1977 "Top Secret" memorandum of the Ministry of Foreign Affairs of the Provisional Military Government of Socialist Ethiopia, discussed above in para. 245. This memorandum refers to islands in the

sub-group of islands. The Tribunal has accordingly had to reach a conclusion which neither Party was willing to contemplate, namely that the islands might have to be divided; not indeed by the Tribunal but by the weight of the evidence and argument presented by the Parties, which does not fall evenly over the whole of the islands but leads to different results for certain sub-groups, and for certain islands.

The Mohabbakahs

467. The Mohabbakah Islands are four rocky islets which amount to little more than navigational hazards. They are Sayal Islet, which is no more than 6 nautical miles from the nearest point on the Eritrean mainland coast, Harbi Islet and Flat Islet; all three of these are within 12 nautical miles of the mainland coast. Finally, there is High Islet, which is less than 1 nautical mile outside the twelve-mile limit from the mainland coast, and about 5 nautical miles from the nearest Haycock island, namely South West Haycock.

468. Eritrea has sought to show that Italy obtained title to the Mohabbakahs along with the various local agreements Italy made with local rulers (see para. 159, above), which led to its securing title over the Danakil coast; this was not protested by Turkey and came to be recognized by Great Britain. The diplomatic history has some interest for this case, especially in highlighting the question of whether South West Haycock is a Mohabbakah island, or part of a separate group of Haycocks, or part of a larger "Zuqar-Hanish group" (see para. 215, above, for the 1930 Italian claim to sovereignty over South West Haycock).

469. Eritrea thus contends that the Mohabbakahs were comprised within what was passed to Ethiopia and so to Eritrea after the Second World War and that this is affirmed by the reference in Article 2 of the 1947 Peace Treaty to the islands "off the coast" and by the constitutional arrangements.

470. Yemen claims that the only islands Ethiopia secured jurisdiction over through local rulers were the islands in Assab Bay; and that, because formerly both coasts of the Red Sea fell under Ottoman rule; and because after the end of the First World War Yemen reverted to its "historic title"; and also because the Mohabbakahs are

---

southern part of the Red Sea that "have had no recognized owner", with respect to which Ethiopia "claims jurisdiction" and "both North and South Yemen have started to make claims". South Yemen's position is that the islands were illegally handed over to Ethiopia by the British when Britain was giving up its rights in the protectorate of Aden. It adds "the North Yemen government has now raised the question of jurisdiction over the islands". It goes on to recommend bilateral negotiations which seem in fact to have been entered into before the time of this memorandum for it goes on to say that "[b]oth states . . . have informally mentioned the possibility of dividing the islands between the two of them. The proposal is to use the median line, which divides the Red Sea equally from both countries' coastal borders, as the dividing line . . . Ethiopia rejected this proposal as disadvantageous."

properly to be perceived as a unity with the Haycocks and the Zuqar-Hanish group, title to all these islands lies with Yemen. The Tribunal rejects this argument.

471. The Tribunal has already noted that there is no evidence that the Mohabbakah islands were part of an original historic title held by Yemen, even were such a title to have existed and to have reverted to Yemen after the First World War. And, even if it were the case that only the Assab Bay islands passed to Eritrea by Italy in 1947, no serious claims to the Mohabbakahs have been advanced by Yemen since that time, until the events leading up to the present arbitration.

472. The Tribunal need not, however, decide whether Italian title to the Mohabbakahs survived the Treaty of Lausanne, and passed thereafter to Ethiopia and then to Eritrea. It is sufficient for the Tribunal to note that all the Mohabbakahs, other than High Islet, lie within 12 miles of the Eritrean coast. Whatever the history, in the absence of any clear title to them being shown by Yemen, the Mohabbakahs must for that reason today be regarded as Eritrean.[32] No such convincing alternative title has been shown by Yemen. It will be remembered indeed that Article 6 of the 1923 Treaty of Lausanne already enshrined this principle of the territorial sea by providing expressly that islands within the territorial sea of a State were to belong to that State. In those days the territorial sea was generally limited by international law and custom to 3 nautical miles, but it has now long been twelve, and the Ethiopian territorial sea was extended to 12 miles in a 1953 decree.

473. At this point it will be convenient to look at the ingenious theory enunciated by Eritrea, based on the undoubted rule that the territorial sea extends to 12 miles not just from the coast but may also extend from a baseline drawn to include any territorial islands within a twelve-mile belt of territorial sea. Thus the baseline can lawfully be extended to include an entire chain, or group of islands, where there is no gap between the islands of more than 12 miles; the so-called leapfrogging method of determining the baseline of the territorial sea. As already mentioned, the entire chain or group of these islands consists of islands, islets, or rocks proud of the sea and therefore technically islands, with no gap between them of more than 12 miles. The only such gap is the one between the easternmost island (the Abu Ali islands) and the Yemen mainland coast.

474. The difficulty with leapfrogging in the instant case is that it

---

[32] See D. Bowett, *The Legal Regime of Islands in International Law* 48 (1978), where he says of islands lying within the territorial sea of a State, "Here the presumption is that the island is under the same sovereignty as the mainland nearby"; and he also interestingly quotes Lindley, *The Acquisition and Government of Backward Territory in International Law* 7 (1926), writing, it may be noted, in the mid-1920s that "An uninhabited island within territorial waters is under the dominion of the Sovereign of the adjoining mainland."

begs the very question at issue before this Tribunal: to which coastal State do these islands belong? There is a strong presumption that islands within the twelve-mile coastal belt will belong to the coastal State, unless there is a fully-established case to the contrary (as, for example, in the case of the Channel Islands). But there is no like presumption outside the coastal belt, where the ownership of the islands is plainly at issue. The ownership over adjacent islands undoubtedly generates a right to a corresponding territorial sea, but merely extending the territorial sea beyond the permitted coastal belt, cannot of itself generate sovereignty over islands so encompassed. And even if there were a presumption of coastal-State sovereignty over islands falling within the twelve-mile territorial sea of a coastal-belt island, it would be no more than a presumption, capable of being rebutted by evidence of a superior title.

* * *

475. Therefore, after examination of all relevant historical, factual and legal considerations, the Tribunal unanimously finds in the present case that the islands, islet, rocks, and low-tide elevations forming the Mohabbakah islands, including but not limited to Sayal Islet, Harbi Islet, Flat Islet and High Islet are subject to the territorial sovereignty of Eritrea. It is true that High Islet is a small but prominent rocky islet barely more than 12 miles (12.72 n.m.) from the territorial sea baseline. But here the unity theory might find a modest and suitable place, for the Mohabbakahs have always been considered as one group, sharing the same legal destiny. High Islet is certainly also appurtenant to the African coast.

The Haycocks

476. The Haycocks are three small islands situated along a roughly southwest-to-northeast line. They are, from south to north, South West Haycock, Middle Haycock and North East Haycock. South West Haycock is some 6 nautical miles from the nearest point of Suyul Hanish, though there is the very small Three Foot Rock about midway between them.

477. As already mentioned above, the Haycocks do have a peculiar legal history and it is for this reason mainly that they need to be discussed separately here. That legal history is very much bound up with the story of the Red Sea lighthouses. But one might begin the salient points of this legal history by recalling the 1841, 1866 and 1873 *firmans* of the Ottoman Sultan (see para. 97, above), by which the African coast of the Red Sea and the islands off it were placed under the jurisdiction and administration of Egypt, though of course the whole of this part of the world was then under the sovereignty of the

Ottoman Empire. There seems little doubt that this African-coast administration would have extended to the Mohabbakahs and the Haycocks. At this time the territorial sea was limited to 3 miles, and there were still grave doubts about the nature and extent of the territorial waters regime. Nevertheless there was a feeling, based upon considerations of security as well as of convenience, that islands off a particular coast would, failing a clearly established title to the contrary, be under the jurisdiction of the nearest coastal authority. As mentioned above, this was sometimes called the "portico doctrine".

478. Another stage in this legal history is at the end of the nineteenth century, when the British Government was interested in the possibility of establishing an alternative western shipping channel through the Red Sea, which needed lighting if it was to be used at night. Various islands were considered as sites for a light (see paras. 203, 204, above), including South West Haycock, which in the end proved to be the successful candidate. This involved inquiries about the "jurisdiction" under which the island would come, and the British Board of Trade satisfied itself that South West Haycock was subject to Italian jurisdiction and at any rate probably not Ottoman.

479. In 1930, when the Italians were constructing a lighthouse on South West Haycock, there was an instructive correspondence between the Italian and British Governments. An internal Foreign Office memorandum reveals the opinion that "the establishment of the Italian colony of Eritrea makes it difficult, therefore, to resist the claim that the islands off the coast of Eritrea are to be considered as an appendage of that colony".[33] This was the official reaction to a letter from the Royal Italian Government of 11 April, claiming South West Haycock, *inter alia* for reasons of its "immediate vicinity" to the Eritrean Red Sea coast.

480. Eritrea employs these arguments to support its claim to the Haycocks, but puts it in the form of a succession derived from the Italian colony of Eritrea, and by way of the subsequent federation of Ethiopia and Eritrea, through to Eritrean independence in 1993. There are difficult juridical problems with this theory of succession, not least the terms of the Italian armistice of 1943 and the peace treaty of 1947, whereby Italy surrendered her colonial territories for disposition by the Allies and in default of agreement amongst them, to disposition by the United Nations, which of course is what actually happened to Eritrea. However this may be, the geographical arguments of proximity to the Eritrean coast remain persuasive and accord with the general opinion that islands off a coast will belong to the coastal State, unless another, superior title can be established. Yemen has failed, in this case, to establish any such superior claim.

[33] Foreign Office Memorandum dated 10 June 1930, prepared by Mr Orchard.

481. The Eritrean claim to the Haycocks also finds some support in the material provided by both Parties for the supplementary hearing on the implications of petroleum agreements. None of the Yemen agreements extends as far to the south-west as the Haycocks; the 1974 Tomen–Santa Fe agreement appears to encompass the Hanish group, but stops short of the Haycocks. On the other hand, the fully documented agreements of the Eritrean Government and Shell, Amoco and BP do cover the areas of the Haycocks, and of course the Mohabbakahs. There was no protest from Yemen, though Yemen did protest when an agreement with Shell appeared to it to trespass upon its claim to the northern islands.

482. Therefore, after examination of all relevant historical, factual and legal considerations, the Tribunal unanimously finds in the present case that the islands, islet, rocks, and low-tide elevations forming the Haycock Islands, including, but not limited to, North East Haycock, Middle Haycock, and South West Haycock, are subject to the territorial sovereignty of Eritrea. It follows that the like decision will, apart from other good reasons noted above, apply to High Islet, the one island of the Mohabbakah sub-group that is outside the Eritrean territorial sea.

483. There remains a question whether the South West Rocks should for these purposes be regarded as going along with the Haycocks. No doubt South West Rocks are so called because they lie south-west of Greater Hanish and there is no other feature between them and that island. There is some evidence that South West Rocks were, at various times, considered to form the easternmost limit of African-coast jurisdiction. While the British Foreign Office documentation relied on by both Parties reflects divergent views (referring in at least one case to Italian jurisdiction over South West Rocks as "doubtful"), the Parties agree that in the early 1890s, Italy responded to direct British inquiries concerning potential lighthouse sites with assertions of jurisdiction over all of the proposed sites, including South West Rocks. Furthermore, Italy did not object to the subsequent British suggestion that the Sublime Porte be informed of the Italian position. This thinking surfaced again in 1914, in Great Britain's initial proposal for a post-war distribution of relinquished Ottoman territory, which would have placed everything east of South West Rocks under the sovereignty of "the independent chiefs of the Arabian mainland".

484. In light of this, it seems reasonable that South West Rocks should be treated in the same manner as the other islands adminis-tered from the African coast: the Mohabbakahs and the Haycocks. South West Rocks are therefore unanimously determined by the Tribunal to be subject to the territorial sovereignty of Eritrea.

The Zuqar-Hanish Group

485. There remains to be determined the sovereignty over Zuqar and over the Hanish islands, and their respective satellite islets and rocks, including the island of Abu Ali, to the east of the northern end of Zuqar, which was for long a principal site for a lighthouse.

486. This has not been an easy group of islands to decide on, one reason for this being that, positioned as they are in the central part of the Red Sea, the appurtenance factor is bound to be relatively less helpful. A coastal median line would in fact divide the island of Greater Hanish, the slightly greater part of the island being on the Eritrean side of the line. Zuqar would be well on the Yemen side of a coastal median line.

487. The Parties have put before the Tribunal many aspects of the local legal history which are said to point the decision one way or the other. These have all been examined in detail in the chapters above. It is however already apparent from that examination that any expectation of a clear and definite answer from that earlier legal history is bound to be disappointed. The Yemeni idea of a reversionary ancient title has been discussed earlier in this chapter and found unhelpful in regard to these islands. More helpful perhaps is the material which suggests that, when the Ottomans decided in the later nineteenth century to grant to Egypt the jurisdiction over the African coast, this possibly included islands appurtenant to that coast, and according to some respectable authorities this did not include this central group of islands, both Zuqar and Hanish being regarded as still within the jurisdiction of the *vilayet* of Yemen. If this was so, though that position can hardly have been carried over to the present time in spite of Article 16 of the Treaty of Lausanne, it would constitute an impressive historical precedent. Hertslet's opinion about the proper distribution of jurisdiction over the islands of the Red Sea clearly impressed the British Foreign Office, but it seems to be Hertslet's view of what should be done about all the islands in the Red Sea rather than evidence of existing titles.

488. There are some echoes of the idea of Yemeni title to be found in the earlier part of the present century in for example the record of the negotiations between the Imam and a British envoy, Colonel Reilly, in which talk the Imam is said to have referred to the need to return to him certain Yemeni islands. But there is no doubt that the main grievance the Imam had in mind was the island of Kamaran and its surrounding islets, which was then occupied by the British. There was also a claim which an internal Foreign Office memorandum referred to as the Imam's claim to "unspecified islands". The British civil servants were quite prepared themselves to speculate that these islands might have included Zuqar and Hanish, which had been

temporarily occupied by the British in 1915. But it is in the end difficult to attach decisive importance to a claim which could not be specified with any certainty.

489. Eritrea seeks to derive an historical title by succession, through Ethiopia, from Italy. There is no doubt that Italy had serious ambitions in respect of these central islands in the 1930s and did establish a presence there. But as has been seen above that position was constantly neutralized by assurances to the British Government that Italy fully accepted that the legal status of the islands was still governed by Article 16 of the Treaty of Lausanne. And then there is also the difficulty of deriving a title from Italy in view of the provisions of the Italian Peace Treaty of 1947.

490. Then of course there are the maps. These islands are large enough to find a place quite often—though by no means always—on even relatively small-scale maps of the region. It is fair to assert that, thanks to the efforts of counsel and especially those of Yemen, the Tribunal will have seen more maps of every conceivable period and provenance than probably have ever been seen before, and certainly a very much larger collection than will have been seen at any time by any of the principal actors in the Red Sea scene. In fact, the difficulty is not so much the interpretation of a plethora of maps of every kind and provenance, as it is the absence of any kind of evidence that these actors took very much notice of, or attached very much importance to, any of them. The Tribunal is of the opinion that in quite general terms Yemen has a marginally better case in terms of favourable maps discovered, and looked at in their totality the maps do suggest a certain widespread repute that these islands appertain to Yemen.

491. As to the other aspects of the legal history of this central group, it does inevitably reflect the ebb and flow of the interest, or the neglect, as the case may be, of both sides, varying from time to time, and qualified always by the unattractive nature of these islands, relieved from time to time by occasional usefulness, as for siting navigational lights, or by their sometimes perceived or imagined strategic importance; for they have never been considered "remote" in the sense of Greenland or the Island of Palmas. Accordingly, in the Tribunal's opinion, although some of this older historical material is important and generally helpful and indeed essential to an understanding of the claims of both Parties, neither of them has been able on the basis of the historical materials alone to make out a case that actually compels a decision one way or the other. Accordingly the Tribunal has looked at events in the last decade or so before the Agreement of Arbitration for additional materials and factors which might complete the picture of both Parties' cases and enable the Tribunal to make a firm decision about these two islands and their satellite rocks and islets. The Tribunal is confirmed in this approach by the fact that both Parties

have anticipated the need for such material by providing supplementary data in connection with the hearings held in July 1998. It should be added, however, that the more recent legal history of these islands shows in some respects differences between Zuqar and Hanish. Because this is so, the islands should be, and will be, considered separately. It would be wrong to assume that they must together go to one Party or the other. In this extent the Tribunal rejects the Yemen theory that all the islands in the group must in principle share a common destiny of sovereignty.

492. Of the recent events perhaps the first heading to look at is that of the Red Sea lighthouses which have featured in the arguments of both Parties. It is evident from the lighthouse history, again dealt with in detail in Chapter VI above, that the undertaking by a government of the maintenance of one of these lights has generally been regarded as neutral for the purpose of the acquisition of territorial sovereignty, although it should also be remembered that, when Great Britain wished in 1892 to secure the building of a light for the proposed western shipping channel, the British Government was anxious to know which government had "jurisdiction" over the chosen site on South West Haycock, and Italy not only made a claim but had its claim to jurisdiction recognized by the British Government. Four lights have been constructed by and appear to be maintained by Yemen in the area now being dealt with (though it should be added that such lights are of course no longer manned). These are sited as follows: on the island of Abu Ali, which is some 3 nautical miles west of the northern tip of Zuqar, on the south-eastern tip of Zuqar itself; on Low Island which is off the north-eastern tip of Lesser Hanish; and on the north-eastern tip of Greater Hanish. The latter was constructed in July 1991 by Yemen and there is in evidence a picture of it with an inscription giving the name of the Republic of Yemen. It can hardly be denied that these lights, clearly intended to be permanent installations, are cogent evidence of some form of Yemen presence in all these islands.

493. Of relatively recent events, Eritrea attaches much importance to the history of Ethiopian naval patrols and the log books which evidence their occurrence, and which involved in particular the islands of Zuqar and Hanish; and this is indeed a possible factor where the islands must be taken as a group; for these were patrols in these waters generally rather than voyages to particular islands. There is no doubt that these patrols occurred on a large scale, and they are fully examined in Chapter VII and it is well known that these islands were used by the rebels, probably mainly as staging posts and relatively safe anchorages for vessels attempting to convey supplies to the rebel armies fighting on the mainland of Ethiopia, some of them possibly from Yemen, which is known to have sympathized with the rebel cause.

494. A strange aspect of these naval patrols possibly over a matter of several years—though the actual evidence Eritrea has been able to provide leaves a number of blank periods—is the lack of protest from Yemen. If Ethiopia had been patrolling the islands on the assumption that it was merely patrolling its own territory, then the lack of Yemen protest is all the more remarkable and calls for some explanation which Yemen has not altogether provided. Yemen was of course preoccupied with its own civil war between 1962 and 1970; and a good deal of this naval patrolling must have been on the high seas rather than in the territorial seas of the islands. Eritrea claims that the Ethiopian naval patrols were also enforcing fishing regulations. This seems credible for it would have provided cover for inspecting the papers of vessels even on the high seas and the rebels would hardly have confined their supply operations to ships flying the Ethiopian flag.

495. And yet these logbooks of naval patrols give relatively little evidence of activity on or even near to the islands. It is interesting to consider in this context the press statement issued by the Yemen Embassy in Mogadishu on 3 July 1973 stating "the YAR always maintains its sovereignty over its islands in the Red Sea, with the exception of the islands of Gabal Abu Ali and Gabal Attair which were given to Ethiopia by Britain when the latter left Aden and surrendered power in our Southern Yemen". This surmise was of course mistaken. But it does amount to a statement that Yemen at this time had no presence in either of these two mentioned islands and had little idea what was happening there. This, however, was the time of the Arab press rumours of Ethiopia having allowed Israel the use of certain Red Sea islands. This same press release stated that Yemen had, accompanied by journalists and press correspondents, investigated the position on "Lesser Hanish, Greater Hanish, Zuqar, Alzubair' Alswabe', and several other islands at the Yemeni coast". These were found to be "free from any foreign infiltration whatsoever". Presumably this was also the inspection by the military committee of the Arab League (see para. 321, above). This statement has the ring of truth. It most probably was the position that these islands, including Zuqar and both Hanish islands, were then normally empty of people or activity other than that of small coastal fishermen plying their traditional way of life and calling at the islands when their work took them there. But it is significant that Yemen could apparently take the above inspection party without any repercussions from Ethiopia.

496. There is much that is ambiguous and unexplained on both sides in this evidence of naval patrols. On balance the episode appears to the Tribunal to lend some weight to the Eritrean case. But again it is a matter of relative weight. There is no compelling case here for either Party. And again it is very difficult on the basis of this material to give it great weight in claims to land territory.

497. The petroleum agreements made by Yemen and by Ethiopia (and then by Eritrea) from 1972 onwards do surprisingly little to resolve the problem, for these agreements, in so far as they extended to offshore areas, were not really concerned with the islands at all, but with either the outer boundary formed by the extent of the then exploitable depths of seabed, or by the coastal median line, which was the temporary boundary actually contemplated for such agreements by the 1977 Yemeni continental shelf legislation. As was reflected by the questions put to the Parties in the closing moments of the July 1998 hearings, the agreements seemed almost to ignore the islands; not surprisingly, considering that the volcanic geological nature of the islands meant that they were totally uninteresting to the oil companies.

498. As already stated above, the Tribunal attaches little importance to the agreements by both Parties with Shell for geological investigations. The area covered by the contract activities likely traversed these islands. But the Tribunal has little doubt that Shell was operating with the permission of both Parties, and was getting information primarily for its own use, in order to decide about which areas of the continental shelf it might be worth making production agreements.

499. When it comes to actual agreements for exploitation, whether in the form of full petroleum production-sharing agreements or less than that, two of the agreements made by Yemen encompassed the Zuqar-Hanish Islands totally (one with Adair, which was very short-lived and never went into effect, and one with Tomen–Santa Fe), while the agreements made by Ethiopia (Ethiopia/Shell) avoided extending to these islands or, in the instance of the Ethiopia–IPC/Amoco agreement of 1989, cuts across Greater Hanish, the division apparently depending on precisely how one plots the coastal median line.

500. After the careful examination of the contract areas of the oil agreements of both Parties, the conclusions to be drawn from this material seem to be reasonably clear. Eritrea can and does point to the IPC/Amoco agreement with Ethiopia which cuts the Island of Hanish. There are various versions. In some versions of the attempts to draw the contract area on a map, only the tip of Hanish is within the Eritrean side of the line; in others the line appears to portray most of the island as Eritrean, leaving only a relatively small portion of it to Yemen. It is surely apparent that the contract area was defined simply in terms appropriate for the essentially maritime interests of the contracting party, and that this, in conformity with normal practice where there is no agreed and settled maritime boundary, was made the coastal median line, ignoring the possible effect of islands. It seems in effect to have been agreed and drawn on the illustrative map of the contract simply ignoring the islands. If Ethiopia had had it in mind to use the agreement for the purpose of illustrating a claim to the island of Hanish, Ethiopia would surely not have given itself only two-thirds

of the island; it would have had the line make an excursion round and embrace the whole island. As it is, it seems to the Tribunal that the Ethiopian and Eritrean agreements are in effect neutral as far as the present task of the Tribunal is concerned; as indeed Eritrea argued. This does not mean that the Eritrean claim to these islands is unfounded; but it does mean that the oil agreements do little to assist that claim, except in so far as the IPC/Amoco Agreement tends to neutralize the Yemeni argument that petroleum agreements as such provide confirmation of sovereignty.

501. Yemen, besides the unconvincing suggestion that the Shell Company's seismic investigation of a large area right across the southern Red Sea somehow confirms the Yemeni claims to the Zuqar and Hanish islands, has in the Tomen–Santa Fe seismic agreement of 1974-5 referred to an agreement in which the contract does apparently embrace both Zuqar and Hanish, or most of Greater Hanish Island. This also resulted in certain activities by the company, including a collection of samples from Zuqar (see para. 409, above). This again does not establish that Yemen has validated its claim to both these islands. But as concluded above, the agreements produced by both parties fail to establish evidence of sovereignty. Perhaps it helps to see these petroleum agreements of the seventies in perspective to remember that in 1973 there was a Yemeni inspection of the islands, with journalists and representatives of the Arab League military committee, that found all these islands empty.

502. It was later that there was more activity; notably the construction in 1993 by the Total Oil Company of an air landing strip on Hanish, for the recreational visits of their employees, and as a by-product of their concession agreement with Yemen. That agreement did not encompass either Zuqar or Hanish. Nevertheless, the fact that there were regular excursion flights constitutes evidence of governmental authority and the exercise of it. Nor did it apparently attract any kind of protest from Eritrea; though of course by this time the civil war was over and Eritrea was established as an independent State.

503. As neither Party has in the opinion of the Tribunal made a convincing case to these islands on the basis of an ancient title in the case of Yemen, or, of a succession title in the case of Eritrea, the Tribunal's decision on sovereignty must be based to an important extent upon what seems to have been the position in Zuqar and Hanish and their adjoining islets and rocks in the last decade or so leading up to the present arbitration. Anything approaching what might be called a settlement, or the continuous display of govern- mental authority and presence, of the kind found in some of the classical cases even for inhospitable territory, is hardly to be expected. For very few people would wish to visit these waterless, volcanic islands except for a special reason and probably a temporary one.

Nevertheless, it is clear from the documents mentioned earlier in this Award that both Yemen and Ethiopia had formulated claims to both islands at least by the late eighties and had indeed it would seem held secret negotiations on the claims; which negotiations, at least according to the Eritrean "Top Secret" internal report, had at first promised a compromise solution on the basis of a median line which would presumably have given Zuqar and Little Hanish to Yemen and Greater Hanish to Ethiopia. But this came to nothing. So now one must look at the *effectivités* for the solution.

504. Yemen has been able to present the Tribunal with a list of some forty-eight alleged Yemeni happenings or incidents in respect of "the islands", which occurred in the period between early 1989 and mid-1991. This list is not confined to the central group, for there is included for example the decisions of the 1989 London Conference on the lighthouses, and the building of a lighthouse on al-Tayr in July 1989. It is evident though that Zuqar features very prominently in the list. It is also evident that Eritrea has relatively very little to show in respect of Zuqar. The Tribunal has no doubt that the island of Zuqar is under the sovereignty of Yemen.

505. In respect of Hanish the matter is not so clear cut. The Eritrean claim is well established as a claim and is clearly of great importance to that very newly independent country. The refusal to agree to a Yemeni aerial survey of the Islands and Ethiopia's responsive claim of title to some of them is significant. So also is its arrest of Yemeni fishermen on Greater Hanish and its assertion, in response to Yemen's protest to the Security Council, that the area was within Ethiopian jurisdiction.

506. There was some emphasis by Eritrea on a scheme to put beacons on Hanish to assist Amoco's seismic testing; there is no clear evidence that they were actually installed. Any such installation of beacons covered several locations, of which Greater Hanish Island was only one, and would have been short-lived: the evidence provided by Eritrea mentions two weeks, and provides for removal of the beacons on completion of the seismic work. Moreover, the beacons were placed by the oil company, Amoco, with only a limited role for the Ethiopian Government in protecting the oil company personnel and the temporary beacons from the attentions of "random individuals". Finally, there is evidence of the issuance, in 1980, of an Ethiopian radio transmitting licence to Delft Geophysical Company, which provided for a station to be located at "Greater Hanish Island, Port of Assab vicinity".

507. Yemen has more to show by way of presence and display of authority. Putting aside the lighthouse in the north of the island, there was the Ardoukoba expedition and campsite which was made under the aegis of the Yemeni Government. There is the air landing site, as well as the production of what appears to be evidence of frequent

scheduled flights, no doubt mainly for the off-days of Total employees; and there is the May 1995 licence to a Yemeni company (seemingly with certain German nationals associated in a joint venture scheme) to develop a tourist project (recreational diving is apparently the possible attraction to tourism) on Greater Hanish.

* * *

508. Therefore, after examination of all relevant historical, factual and legal considerations, the Tribunal finds in the present case that, on balance, and with the greatest respect for the sincerity and foundations of the claims of both Parties, the weight of the evidence supports Yemen's assertions of the exercise of the functions of State authority with respect to the Zuqar-Hanish group. The Tribunal is further fortified in finding in favour of Yemen by the evidence that these islands fell under the jurisdiction of the Arabian coast during the Ottoman Empire; and that there was later a persistent expectation reflected in the British Foreign Office papers submitted in evidence by the Parties that these islands would ultimately return to Arab rule. The Tribunal therefore unanimously finds that the islands, islet, rocks, and low-tide elevations of the Zuqar-Hanish group, including, but not limited to, Three Foot Rock, Parkin Rock, Rocky Islets, Pin Rock, Suyul Hanish, Mid Islet, Double Peak Island, Round Island, North Round Island, Quoin Island (13°43′N, 42°48′E), Chor Rock, Greater Hanish, Peaky Islet, Mushajirah, Addar Ail Islets, Haycock Island (13°47′N, 42°47′E; not to be confused with the Haycock Islands to the south-west of Greater Hanish), Low Island (13°52′N, 42°49′E) including the unnamed islets and rocks close north, east and south, Lesser Hanish including the unnamed islets and rocks close north-east, Tongue Island and the unnamed islet close south, Near Island and the unnamed islet close south-east, Shark Island, Jabal Zuquar Island, High Island, and the Abu Ali Islands (including Quoin Island (14°05′N, 42°49′E) and Pile Island) are subject to the territorial sovereignty of Yemen.

Jabal al-Tayr and the Zubayr Group of Islands

509. Both the lone island of Jabal al-Tayr, and the Zubayr group of islands and islets, call for separate treatment, as they are a considerable distance from the other islands as well as from each other. They are not only relatively isolated, but also are both well out to sea, and so not proximate to either coast, though they are slightly nearer to the Yemeni coastal islands than they are to the coast and coastal islands of Eritrea. Both are well eastward of a coastal median line. Here again, the Tribunal has had to weigh the relative merits of the Parties' evidence, which has been sparse on both sides, of the exercise of functions of State and governmental authority.

510. The traditional importance of both groups has been that they have been lighthouse islands (the Zubayr light was on Centre Peak, the southernmost islet of the group). It will be clear from the history of the Red Sea lighthouses (see Chapter VI, above) that, although, or perhaps even because, lighthouses were so important for nineteenth- and early-twentieth-century navigation, a government could be asked to take responsibility or even volunteer to be responsible for them, without necessarily either seeming to claim sovereignty over the site or acquiring it. The practical question was not one of ownership, but rather of which government was willing, or might be persuaded, to take on the responsibility, and sometimes the cost, if not permanently then at least for a season.

511. It will be recollected that Centre Peak in the Zubayr group was an island in which Italy, in its 1930s period of colonial expansion, had taken a great interest; the Centre Peak light was abandoned by the British in 1932, but reactivated by Italy the following year. The British sought and obtained the usual assurances about the Treaty of Lausanne status of the island (see paras. 216-18 above). So for a time at least this group fell under the jurisdiction of the authority on the African coast.

512. Yet during the Second World War and the subsequent British occupation of Eritrea, it was decided that Great Britain was under no obligation to maintain the Centre Point light or indeed the Haycock light.

513. An important turning point in the history of the northern islands of Jabal al-Tayr and the Zubayr group was the 1989 London Conference about lighthouses. This was rather different from previous conferences. This conference was to be the last of its kind, because its main purpose was to liquidate the former international arrangements for administration of the lights and the sharing of costs. The final arrangements made for the lights (which were then still of the greatest importance for navigation) were therefore intended to be permanent. No further conference was envisaged.

514. It will be remembered that Yemen was invited to the conference as an observer on the plea to the British Government that the two lighthouse islands of Abu Ali and Jabal al-Tayr, "lie within the exclusive economic zone of the Yemen Arab Republic", and that because of this Yemen was willing to take on the responsibility of managing and operating the lights. It was also the fact that Yemen had already installed new lights on both of these sites. The offer from Yemen was gratefully accepted by the conference. There had been hopes that Egypt might take on the work but Egypt was not willing to do so.

515. The matter of sovereignty was not on the agenda of the conference, nor was it discussed. Yemen's own request to be invited to

the conference had wisely avoided raising the matter. Moreover, there were at the conference the usual references to the Treaty of Lausanne formula concerning indeterminate sovereignty.

516. Nevertheless, the decision of the conference to accept the Yemeni offer over the lights does reflect a confidence and expectation of the member governments of the conference of a continued Yemeni presence on these lighthouse islands for, at any rate, the foreseeable future. Repute is also an important ingredient for the consolidation of title.

517. There is also another matter where Yemen is able to show what amounts to important support for its case over these northern islands, and that is the substantially new information on petroleum agreements that was made available to the Tribunal at the supplementary hearings held for this purpose in July 1998. There are two such agreements which appear to be relevant for the islands presently under discussion.

518. First, there is the agreement made by the Yemeni Government with the Shell company on 20 November 1973. The western boundary of the contract area in this agreement is drawn so as to include within it the Zubayr group. It does not include Jabal al-Tayr, but passes at a distance which might encompass the territorial sea of that island, depending on the breadth of the territorial sea allowed to it for the purposes of a maritime delimitation.

519. The second is the Hunt Oil production sharing agreement ratified on 10 March 1985. The western contract area boundary of this agreement again includes the Zubayr group, but also appears from the illustrative map to brush the island of Jabal al-Tayr, and of course plainly includes a part of its territorial sea.

520. These agreements were not protested by Ethiopia (though it should be remembered that the Hunt agreement was made at a time when the Ethiopian civil war was still raging).

521. Neither Ethiopia nor Eritrea has made any petroleum agreements encompassing these islands. Eritrea did, however, make agreements in 1995 and 1997 with the Anadarko Oil Company, which extended in the direction of these islands and towards what appears to be an approximate median line between coasts. Yemen protested this line on 4 January 1997 as a "blatant" violation of the territorial waters of both groups and of her economic rights "in the region". This was, of course, some time after the signature of the Agreement on Principles and indeed the Arbitration Agreement initiating these proceedings.

522. The legal history of these northern and isolated islands has been mixed and varied. It has been seen that even as late as 1989 it was assumed that their sovereign status was still indeterminate in accordance with the status impressed upon them, until it should be

changed in a lawful way, by the Treaty of Lausanne. Nevertheless, by 1995 it was doubtful whether any dispute over Yemen's claim to them would be agreed to be submitted to this Tribunal. Even Eritrea at one point made a proposal for an agreement in which these islands were not mentioned.

523. The Tribunal has not found this particular question an easy one. There is little evidence on either side of actual or persistent activities on and around these islands. But in view of their isolated location and inhospitable character, probably little evidence will suffice.

524. Therefore, after examination of all relevant historical, factual and legal considerations, the Tribunal unanimously finds in the present case that, on the basis of the foregoing, the weight of the evidence supports the conclusion that the island of Jabal al-Tayr, and the islands, islets, rocks and low-tide elevations forming the Zubayr group, including, but not limited to, Quoin Island (15°12'N, 42°03'E), Haycock Island (15°10'N, 42°07'E; not to be confused with the Haycock Islands to the south-west of Greater Hanish), Rugged Island, Table Peak Island, Saddle Island and the unnamed islet close north-west, Low Island (15°06'N, 42°06'E) and the unnamed rock close east, Middle Reef, Saba Island, Connected Island, East Rocks, Shoe Rock, Jabal Zubayr Island, and Centre Peak Island are subject to the territorial sovereignty of Yemen.

The Traditional Fishing Regime

525. In making this award on sovereignty, the Tribunal has been aware that Western ideas of territorial sovereignty are strange to peoples brought up in the Islamic tradition and familiar with notions of territory very different from those recognized in contemporary international law. Moreover, appreciation of regional legal traditions is necessary to render an Award which, in the words of the Joint Statement signed by the Parties on 21 May 1996, will "allow the re-establishment and the development of a trustful and lasting cooperation between the two countries".

526. In finding that the Parties each have sovereignty over various of the Islands the Tribunal stresses to them that such sovereignty is not inimical to, but rather entails, the perpetuation of the traditional fishing regime in the region. This existing regime has operated, as the evidence presented to the Tribunal amply testifies, around the Hanish and Zuqar islands and the islands of Jebel al-Tayr and the Zubayr group. In the exercise of its sovereignty over these islands, Yemen shall ensure that the traditional fishing regime of free access and enjoyment for the fishermen of both Eritrea and Yemen shall be preserved for the benefit of the lives and livelihoods of this poor and industrious order of men.

CHAPTER XI   Dispositif

527. Accordingly, the Tribunal,

taking into account the foregoing considerations and reasons,

Unanimously finds in the present case that

i. the islands, islet, rocks, and low-tide elevations forming the Mohabbakah islands, including but not limited to Sayal Islet, Harbi Islet, Flat Islet and High Islet, are subject to the territorial sovereignty of Eritrea;

ii. the islands, islet, rocks, and low-tide elevations forming the Haycock Islands, including, but not limited to, North East Haycock, Middle Haycock, and South West Haycock, are subject to the territorial sovereignty of Eritrea;

iii. the South West Rocks are subject to the territorial sovereignty of Eritrea;

iv. the islands, islet, rocks, and low-tide elevations of the Zuqar-Hanish group, including, but not limited to, Three Foot Rock, Parkin Rock, Rocky Islets, Pin Rock, Suyul Hanish, Mid Islet, Double Peak Island, Round Island, North Round Island, Quoin Island (13°43′N, 42°48′E), Chor Rock, Greater Hanish, Peaky Islet, Mushajirah, Addar Ail Islets, Haycock Island (13°47′N, 42°47′E; not to be confused with the Haycock Islands to the south-west of Greater Hanish), Low Island (13°52′N, 42°49′E) including the unnamed islets and rocks close north, east and south, Lesser Hanish including the unnamed islets and rocks close north-east, Tongue Island and the unnamed islet close south, Near Island and the unnamed islet close south-east, Shark Island, Jabal Zuquar Island, High Island, and the Abu Ali Islands (including Quoin Island (14°05′N, 42°49′E) and Pile Island) are subject to the territorial sovereignty of Yemen;

v. the island of Jabal al-Tayr, and the islands, islets, rocks and low-tide elevations forming the Zubayr group, including, but not limited to, Quoin Island (15°12′N, 42°03′E), Haycock Island (15°10′N, 42°07′E; not to be confused with the Haycock Islands to the south-west of Greater Hanish), Rugged Island, Table Peak Island, Saddle Island and the unnamed islet close north-west, Low Island (15°06′N, 42°06′E) and the unnamed rock close east, Middle Reef, Saba Island, Connected Island, East Rocks, Shoe Rock, Jabal Zubayr Island, and

Centre Peak Island are subject to the territorial sovereignty of Yemen; and

vi. the sovereignty found to lie with Yemen entails the perpetuation of the traditional fishing regime in the region, including free access and enjoyment for the fishermen of both Eritrea and Yemen.

528. Further, whereas Article 12.1(b) of the Arbitration Agreement provides that the Awards shall include the time period for their execution, the Tribunal directs that this Award should be executed within ninety days from the date hereunder.

* * *

Done at London this 9th day of October, 1998.

[Report: Unreported]

[The map of the Award in the Arbitration between the Government of the State of Eritrea and the Government of the Republic of Yemen (Phase One: Territorial Sovereignty and Scope of the Dispute) can be found on the following pages.]

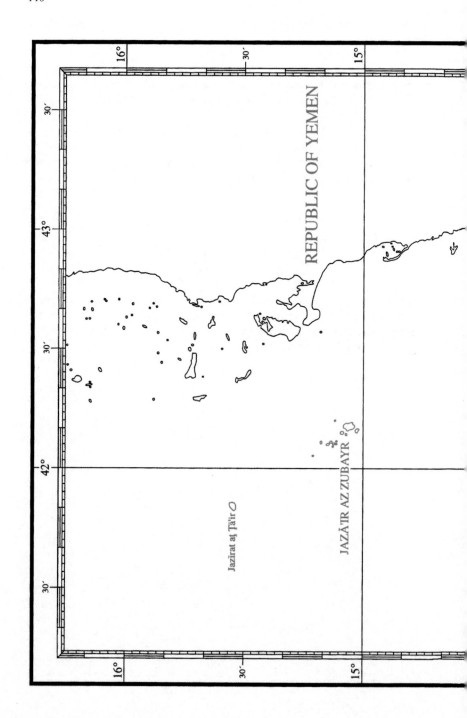

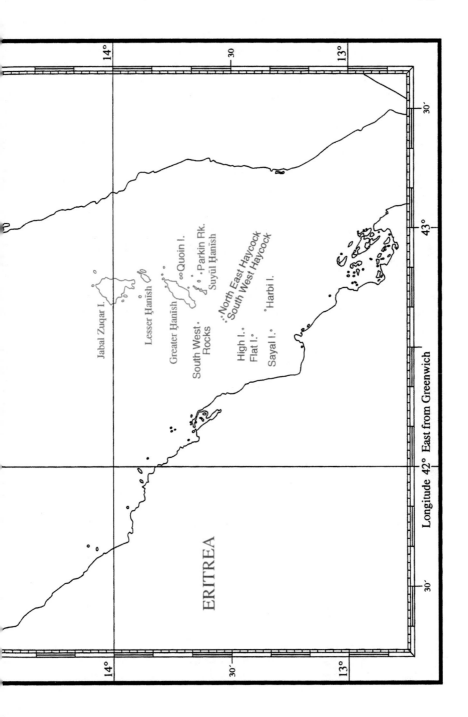

Arbitration—Arbitrators—Appointment—Arbitration clause submitting disputes to International Centre for the Settlement of Investment Disputes ("ICSID") contained in investment agreements—Arbitrators to be appointed by parties—State refusing to appoint arbitrator—Procedure in default of party appointment

Arbitration—Jurisdiction—Agreement to arbitrate—Requirement of written consent—Arbitration clause submitting disputes to ICSID contained in agreements—Whether sufficient written consent—Dispute regarding jurisdiction — Competence of tribunal to determine jurisdiction — Unilateral notification by State of intention to exclude type of dispute from ICSID jurisdiction—Whether notification effective in relation to prior agreement—Jurisdiction of tribunal in respect of legal disputes arising from investment—Meaning of "investment"

Arbitration—Procedure—Procedure to be followed in default of appearance by party—Jurisdictional issue—Determination as preliminary question

KAISER BAUXITE COMPANY *v.* GOVERNMENT OF JAMAICA[1]

International Centre for the Settlement of Investment Disputes, Arbitration Tribunal

(Dr Jørgen Trolle, *President*; Sir Michael Kerr and Dr Fuad Rouhani, *Members*)

6 *July* 1975

SUMMARY: *The facts:*—In 1952 Kaiser Bauxite Company ("Kaiser"), a company incorporated in the United States, commenced operations in Jamaica. In 1957 Kaiser entered into an agreement with the Government of Jamaica ("the Principal Agreement") relating to the ownership and operation of its bauxite mining facilities in Jamaica. The Principal Agreement contained

---

[1] The *Kaiser* case was one of three proceedings brought against Jamaica by aluminium and bauxite producers. *Alcoa Minerals of Jamaica Inc.* v. *Jamaica* (Case No ARB/74/2) and *Reynolds Jamaica Mines Limited and Reynolds Metals Company* v. *Jamaica* (Case No ARB/74/4) were registered at the same time as the *Kaiser* case on 21 June 1974. Although the proceedings were not joined, the same tribunal heard all three cases, Sir Michael Kerr being appointed to the Tribunal in February 1975 on the resignation of Mr Elihu Lauterpacht QC, who had become Legal Adviser of the Department of Foreign Affairs, Australia. The decisions in the *Alcoa* and *Reynolds* cases are not available for publication. They are, however, in all material respects identical to the decision in the *Kaiser* case. Chronologies for the three cases are published in 1 *ICSID Reports* xxi. The summary of the *Kaiser* case was prepared by Ms R. Rayfuse.

a "no further tax" clause pursuant to which Jamaica undertook not to impose any additional royalties or taxes which had not been specifically provided for and referred to in the Principal Agreement. The Principal Agreement was amended by further agreements in 1969 ("the 1969 Agreement") and in 1972 ("the 1972 Agreement"), both of which provided for the submission of disputes arising under any of the agreements to ICSID.

In 1974 Jamaica enacted the Bauxite (Production Levy) Act ("the Act") which provided for an additional tax to be paid on all bauxite extracted in Jamaica on or after 1 January 1974. On 8 May 1974, Jamaica, which had ratified the ICSID Convention in 1968 without reservation, filed a notification with ICSID pursuant to Article 25(4) of the Convention purporting to remove from the jurisdiction of ICSID all disputes arising directly out of investments relating to minerals or other natural resources.

In June 1974 Kaiser initiated ICSID arbitration proceedings seeking a declaration that the Act did not apply to it and seeking the return of monies paid to Jamaica pursuant to the Act. Jamaica refused to appoint an arbitrator and the Tribunal was eventually established by the Chairman of the Administrative Council pursuant to Article 38 of the Convention and Arbitration Rule 4. The first meeting of the Tribunal took place on 2 April 1975 and Jamaica failed to appear. In view of the non-appearance of Jamaica and its failure to appoint an arbitrator the Tribunal decided to deal with its own jurisdiction and competence as a preliminary issue in order to determine whether the dispute fell within the subject-matter jurisdiction of ICSID and whether Jamaica's notification of 8 May 1974 had had the effect of withdrawing the dispute from the scope of its prior agreement to arbitrate.

Held:—(1) The dispute was within the jurisdiction of ICSID. Article 25(1) of the Convention provided that the jurisdiction of the Centre extended "to any dispute arising out of an investment". The dispute concerned the alleged rights and obligations stemming from particular provisions in the agreements between Kaiser and Jamaica and was therefore a legal dispute. Likewise, where a mining company had invested substantial amounts in a foreign State in reliance upon an agreement with that State, the "investment" must be among those contemplated by the Convention. The Convention had entered into force for both the United States and Jamaica at the time of the 1969 and 1972 Agreements and, accordingly, Jamaica was a Contracting State and Kaiser a national of another Contracting State for the purposes of the application of the Convention. The arbitration clauses contained in the 1969 and 1972 Agreements constituted the parties' written consent to ICSID arbitration (pp. 149-50).

(2) The Jamaican notification did not affect the prior agreement to arbitrate which was contained in the 1969 and 1972 Agreements. This agreement could not be unilaterally withdrawn by either party. The notification given by Jamaica could only operate in respect of potential future investors. To find otherwise would be to deprive the Convention of any practical value for Contracting States and investors alike (pp. 150-1).

The text of the decision of the Tribunal commences on the following page.

I   **[298]**

1. By letter of June 17, 1974, Kaiser Bauxite Company (hereafter called "Kaiser") addressed a request for arbitration against the Government of Jamaica to the Secretary-General of the International Centre for Settlement of Investment Disputes (hereafter called "Centre") pursuant to Article 36(1) of the Convention on the Settlement of Investment Disputes between States and Nationals of Other States (hereafter called "Convention") and Rule 1 of the Centre's Institution Rules. In order to found the jurisdiction of the Centre the request relied on provisions expressing the consent of the parties to arbitration proceedings pursuant to the Convention contained in agreements dated December 30, 1969 and February 24, 1972, respectively, between the Government of Jamaica, and Kaiser and Kaiser Aluminum and Chemical Corporation, of which certified copies had been duly deposited with the Centre.

2. The Secretary-General registered the request on June 21, 1974 and promptly notified the parties thereof, pursuant to Article 36(3) of the Convention and Institution Rule 6(1).

3. The records of the Centre show the following relevant facts with respect to the constitution of the Tribunal. On June 27, 1974 Kaiser made proposals to the Government of Jamaica with respect to the constitution of an Arbitral Tribunal. On September 19, 1974 Kaiser, not having received a reply to its proposals, chose that the Tribunal be constituted in accordance with Article 37(2)(b) of the Convention, that is to say, that the Tribunal was to consist of three arbitrators, one arbitrator to be appointed by each party and the third, to be the President of the Tribunal, to be appointed by agreement of the parties. Kaiser appointed Elihu Lauterpacht (British) to be an arbitrator. The Government of Jamaica did not appoint an arbitrator. The Tribunal not having been constituted within 90 days after notice of registration by the Secretary-General of the request for arbitration, Kaiser on November 8, 1974 requested the Chairman of the Administrative Council, pursuant to Article 38 of the Convention and Arbitration Rule 4, to appoint two arbitrators and to designate one of them as the President of the Tribunal. The Chairman, after consultations in accordance with Arbitration Rule 2, on December 9, 1974 appointed Mr Jørgen Trolle (Danish) and Mr Fuad Rouhani (Iranian) as arbitrators and designated Mr Trolle as the President of the Tribunal. As required by Article 40(1) of the Convention, both Mr Trolle and Mr Rouhani were appointed from the Panel of Arbitration, Mr Trolle having been designated to the Panel by the Kingdom of Denmark pursuant to Article 13(1) of the Convention on August 20, 1973 and Mr Rouhani having been designated by the Chairman pursuant to Article 13(2) of the Convention on November 19, 1974. All three arbitrators having accepted their appointment, the Tribunal was constituted on December 16, 1974. Prior to the first session of the Tribunal, Mr Lauterpacht on January 20, 1975 submitted his resignation upon assuming

[299] his duties as Legal Adviser of the Department of Foreign Affairs of the Government of Australia. On February 3, 1975 the remaining members of the Tribunal consented to Mr Lauterpacht's resignation as required by Arbitration Rule 8. Kaiser thereupon duly appointed Sir Michael Kerr (British) as arbitrator and upon the latter's acceptance of his appointment the Tribunal in its present composition was reconstituted on March 10, 1975.

4. On the same day the parties were convened for a first meeting with the Tribunal to be held at the seat of the Centre at Washington, DC on April 2, 1975, i.e. within the time limit fixed by Arbitration Rule 13.

5. At this session Kaiser appeared while the Government of Jamaica did not appear and was not represented. The President announced that the Tribunal had determined that it was properly constituted under the Convention and the Arbitration Rules.

II

6. Although no formal objection to the jurisdiction of the Centre and the competence of the Tribunal had been received from either side in this case, in view of the failure of the Government of Jamaica to appear and the notice, dated May 8, 1974, referring to Article 25 of the Convention, filed by it with the Centre, the Tribunal decided that it was appropriate that the question of the jurisdiction of the Centre and the competence of the Tribunal should be dealt with as a preliminary issue. Furthermore, there was at this stage nothing before the Tribunal except a request for registration of these proceedings filed by the claimant, but it was pointed out by the Tribunal that it was necessary to consider the question of jurisdiction and competence on the basis of the nature of the claimant's claim and the relief sought by it in these proceedings.

7. Having regard to this the Tribunal made the following order:

> I. Kaiser to file with the Centre by May 4, 1975, a Memorial dealing with the following:
> (i) a full statement of the nature of Kaiser's claim and the relief sought in these proceedings (but without at this stage adducing evidence or argument in support); and
> (ii) full argument on any issue as to the jurisdiction of the Centre and the competence of the Tribunal having regard to the notice, dated May 8, 1974, referring to Article 25 of the Convention for the Settlement of Investment Disputes between States and Nationals of Other States, filed by the Government of Jamaica with the Centre, and *on any issue that might arise*[2] from the wording of the arbitration clause on which Kaiser founds jurisdiction and competence or in any other connection.
>
> II. The Government of Jamaica to file a Counter-Memorial by June 11, 1975, in reply to the aforesaid Memorial.

---

[2] Secretary-General's note: the underscored [italicized] words had been inadvertently omitted from the text signed by the arbitrators:

III. All further matters in the proceedings to be stood over for the time **[300]**
being.

8. Kaiser filed a Memorial within the fixed time limit.
9. No Counter-Memorial has been filed by Jamaica.

III

10. The Tribunal regrets that Jamaica has failed to appear and to bring
forward any objections to the jurisdiction of the Centre and the competence
of the Tribunal which it might entertain. The Tribunal nevertheless, decided
to examine its own jurisdiction *proprio motu* and in doing so to consider any
objections which might be raised against its jurisdiction.

11. At the present stage and by virtue of Article 41 of the Convention and
Arbitration Rules the Tribunal is concerned to pronounce upon this issue.
The issue being thus limited, the Tribunal will avoid not only all expressions
of opinion on matters of substance, but also any pronouncement which
might prejudge or appear to prejudice any eventual decision on the merits.

12. The facts relevant to the question of competence and jurisdiction are,
as alleged by Kaiser:

> (a) Kaiser owns and operates bauxite mining facilities on the north coast of
> Jamaica, and has invested over $63 million in its Jamaican facilities. It has been
> conducting operations in Jamaica since 1952, and in 1973 it was the largest
> single taxpayer in the country, having paid $9,869,471 in royalties and income
> taxes to the Government of Jamaica (the 'Government'). Kaiser decided to
> invest its capital and to conduct operations in Jamaica in reliance upon
> particular contractual arrangements with the Government. These investment
> agreements with the Government are set forth in three documents. They are:
>> (1) the Principal Agreement, executed on March 15, 1957 ('Principal
>> Agreement');
>> (2) an amendment to the Principal Agreement, executed on December 30,
>> 1969 ('1969 Agreement'); and
>> (3) a further amendment to the Principal Agreement, executed on
>> February 24, 1972 ('1972 Agreement').
> These agreements specifically define Kaiser's obligations to the
> Government concerning taxes and royalties. The particular contractual
> provisions are complex, and are set out at paragraphs 2-5 and 7-9 of the
> Principal Agreement; paragraphs 1-5 of the 1969 Agreement; and paragraphs
> 1-6 of the 1972 Agreement.
> Paragraph 5 of the Principal Agreement was drafted to prevent the
> imposition of additional royalties and taxes that were not specifically provided
> for and referred to in the Agreement. This provision states:
>> 5. *FURTHER TAXES*: No further taxes will be imposed on bauxite, bauxite
>> reserves or bauxite operations or any assets used in bauxite operations or
>> dividends on bauxite operations.

'Further Taxes' shall include all taxes, burdens, levies, excises and imposts on bauxite operations and all assets used in connection therewith in Jamaica or its territorial waters (including but not limited to any additional royalty under the Mining Law and any other royalty, and any tax, burden or impost on severance, transportation, storage, handling, exportation, employment, sales, shipping, capital and reserves).

[301]

It is understood that taxes dealt with elsewhere in this agreement and normal license duties of general application, such as licenses on motor vehicles and harbour and light dues of general application and flat local service rates on land and import duties of general application (but not any duty which would be a tax, burden or impost of the nature of any of those enumerated in the above definition of 'further taxes') are excluded from this clause.

Kaiser's claim is that this provision has been contravened by the Government's enactment of legislation which does impose such a 'further tax' on bauxite mined by Kaiser in Jamaica. This legislation, called the Bauxite (Production Levy) Act, 1974 (the 'Act') provides in relevant part that:

'notwithstanding anything in any law, enactment or agreement, a tax to be known as a Production Levy shall be paid on all bauxite ... extracted ... in Jamaica on or after the 1st January, 1974 ...' Act, Paragraph 3(1).

(Memorial, pp. 1-3)

(b) Para. 6 of the 1969 Agreement referred to above provides as follows:

6. (1) Each of the parties hereto hereby Agrees and Consents to any legal dispute arising under the Principal Agreement or this Agreement being submitted to the International Centre for Settlement of Investment Disputes established by the Convention set out in the Schedule to the Investment Disputes Awards (Enforcement) Act, 1966 of Jamaica.

(2) The foregoing constitutes a consent both to conciliation proceedings and to arbitration proceedings under the said Convention but the consent to arbitration proceedings shall not be to the exclusion of any other remedy which may be open to either party.

(3) In determining any dispute submitted to arbitration as aforesaid, the Arbitration Tribunal shall apply the law of Jamaica and such rules of international law as may be applicable excluding however any enactments passed or brought into force in Jamaica subsequent to the date of this agreement which may modify or affect the rights of the parties under the Principal Agreement or this Agreement and excluding also any law or rule which could throw doubt upon the authority or ability of the Government to enter into the Principal Agreement and this Agreement.

(c) Para. 7 of the 1972 Agreement referred to above provides as follows:

7. (1) Each of the Parties hereto hereby Agrees and Consents to any legal dispute arising under the Principal Agreement, the 1969 Agreement or this Agreement being submitted to the International Centre for Settlement of Investment Disputes established by the Convention set out in the Schedule to the Investment Disputes Awards (Enforcement) Act, 1966 of Jamaica. 6/

6/ Subparagraphs 7(2) and 7(3) of the 1972 Agreement are identical to
subparagraphs 6(2) and 6(3) of the 1969 Agreement.

(Memorial, p. 8)

(d) The relief sought by Kaiser in this arbitration is that the Tribunal:

A. *State* that the Government is legally bound to respect its undertaking, as
set forth in Paragraph 5 of the Principal Agreement, not to impose
'further taxes' on Kaiser, including imposition of the Bauxite   **[302]**
(Production Levy) Act.

B. *Declare* that Kaiser is not legally obliged to pay any further monies to the
Government pursuant to the requirements of the Bauxite (Production
Levy) Act, and

C. *Award* Kaiser an amount equal to all monies paid by Kaiser pursuant to
the Bauxite (Production Levy) Act up to and including the date of the
Tribunal's award, together with interest thereon computed at the rate of
six per cent per annum.

(Memorial, p. 5)

V[3]

13. The jurisdiction of the Centre is established under the Convention in
accordance with Article 25 which in its material parts provides as follows:

(1) The jurisdiction of the Centre shall extend to any legal dispute arising
directly out of an investment, between a Contracting State (or any constituent
subdivision or agency of a Contracting State designated to the Centre by that
State) and a national of another Contracting State, which the parties to the
dispute consent in writing to submit to the Centre. When the parties have given
their consent, no party may withdraw its consent unilaterally.

(2) 'National of another Contracting State' means:

(a) . . . .

(b) any juridical person which had the nationality of a Contracting State
other than the State party to the dispute on the date on which the
parties consented to submit such dispute to conciliation or
arbitration and any juridical person which had the nationality of the
Contracting State party to the dispute on that date and which,
because of foreign control, the parties have agreed should be
treated as a national of another Contracting State for the purposes
of this Convention.

(3) . . . . .

(4) Any Contracting State may, at the time of ratification, acceptance or
approval of this Convention or at any time thereafter, notify the Centre of the
class or classes of disputes which it would or would not consider submitting to
the jurisdiction of the Centre. The Secretary-General shall forthwith transmit
such notification to all Contracting States. Such notification shall not
constitute the consent required by paragraph (1).

[³ There appears to be no Section IV in the decision.]

14. On May 8, 1974 the Government of Jamaica sent the following notification to the Centre:

> In accordance with Article 25 of the Convention establishing the International Centre for the Settlement of Investment Disputes, the Government of Jamaica hereby notifies the Centre that the following class of dispute at any time arising shall not be subject to the jurisdiction of the Centre.

[303]   *Class of Dispute*

> Legal Dispute arising directly out of an investment relating to minerals or other natural resources.

VI

15. The Tribunal therefore has to consider:
— whether there is a legal dispute between the parties;
— whether such dispute arises directly out of an investment,
— whether Jamaica is a Contracting State under the Convention;
— whether Kaiser is a national of another Contracting State;
— whether Kaiser and Jamaica each consented in writing to submit the dispute to the Centre; and
— whether Jamaica's notification, dated May 8, 1974, submitted under Article 25 to the effect that disputes regarding minerals or other natural resources shall not be subject to the jurisdiction of the Centre, operates to deprive the Centre of jurisdiction.

16. The Tribunal finds that the dispute concerning the alleged legal rights and obligations stemming from particular provisions in Kaiser's agreements with the Government is a legal dispute.

17. The Tribunal finds that the dispute arises directly out of an investment. It is said in the Report of the Executive Directors of the International Bank for Reconstruction and Development accompanying the Convention when submitted to Governments (hereafter called ED Report), para. 27, that no attempt was made to define the term "investment" given the essential requirement of consent by the parties. It follows that the intention of the Convention was that the consent of the parties should be entitled to great weight in any determination of the Centre's jurisdiction. Moreover, it seems clear to the Tribunal that a case like the present, in which a mining company has invested substantial amounts in a foreign State in reliance upon an agreement with that State, is among those contemplated by the Convention.

18. Jamaica signed the Convention on June 21, 1965, and deposited its Instrument of Ratification on September 9, 1966. Pursuant to Article 68(2) of the Convention, it entered into force with respect to Jamaica on October 14, 1966.

19. Kaiser is a private corporation organized under the laws of the State of Nevada in the United States of America. The United States signed the Convention on August 27, 1965, and deposited its Instrument of Ratification on June 10, 1966. Pursuant to Article 68(2) of the Convention it entered into force with respect to the United States on October 14, 1966.

20. Accordingly, at the time of the 1969 and 1972 Agreements, Jamaica was a Contracting State and Kaiser was a national of another Contracting State.

21. The Tribunal considers that paras 6 and 7, respectively, of the 1969 and 1972 Agreements constitute written consent by the parties as required by Article 25(1) of the Convention to submit to the Centre disputes such as the present dispute. In this connection the Tribunal agrees with the view **[304]** expressed in para. 24 of the ED Report that consent may be given in a clause included in an investment agreement providing for the submission to the Centre of future disputes arising out of that agreement. It follows from the foregoing and from Article 25(1) of the Convention that, written consent to the jurisdiction of the Centre having been given in this case by both parties, neither party could unilaterally withdraw such consent and deprive the Centre or the Tribunal of jurisdiction.

22. The Government of Jamaica appears to contend that its notification to the Centre on May 8, 1974 deprives the Centre and consequently the Tribunal of jurisdiction. The Tribunal cannot accept this view.

23. In the present case the written consent was contained in the arbitration clauses between the Government and Kaiser which have already been quoted. This consent having been given could not be withdrawn. The notification under Article 25 only operates for the future by way of information to the Centre and potential future investors in undertakings concerning minerals and other natural resources of Jamaica. This view of Article 25 is shared by the ED Report which states the following:

31. While no conciliation or arbitration proceedings could be brought against a Contracting State without its consent and while no Contracting State is under any obligation to give its consent to such proceedings, it was nevertheless felt that adherence to the Convention might be interpreted as holding out an expectation that Contracting States would give favorable consideration to requests by investors for the submission of a dispute to the Centre. It was pointed out in that connection that there might be classes of investment disputes which governments would consider unsuitable for submission to the Centre or which, under their own law, they were not permitted to submit to the Centre. In order to avoid any risk of misunderstanding on this score, Article 25(4) expressly permits Contracting States to make known to the Centre in advance, if they so desire, the classes of disputes which they would or would not consider submitting to the Centre. The provision makes clear that a statement by a Contracting State that it would consider submitting a certain class of dispute to the Centre would serve for purposes of information only and would not constitute the consent required to

give the Centre jurisdiction. Of course, a statement excluding certain classes of disputes from consideration would not constitute a reservation to the Convention.

24. The Tribunal accordingly finds that the Government could not withdraw, and did not by its notification of May 8, 1974 validly withdraw its consent to arbitration given in the 1969 and 1972 Agreements. In addition to the reasons already given, the Tribunal considers that any other interpretation would very largely, if not wholly, deprive the Convention of any practical value for Contracting States and investors and this cannot have been intended.

[305]   VII

25. For the foregoing reasons the Tribunal concludes that the present dispute is within the jurisdiction of the Centre and the competence of the Tribunal. The Tribunal has, accordingly, made the necessary Order for the continuation of the procedure pursuant to Arbitration Rule 41(4).

[Report: 1 *ICSID Reports* 298][4]

NOTE.—A settlement was eventually reached by the parties and the proceedings were discontinued at the request of Kaiser. An Order taking note of the discontinuance was issued by the Tribunal on 27 February 1977 pursuant to Arbitration Rule 44.

---

[4] The text of the decision was originally supplied by, and is reproduced with the permission of, Kaiser Bauxite Company.

Arbitration — Jurisdiction — ICSID arbitration clauses in agreements between government and company — Whether superseded by later agreement—Jurisdiction *ratione materiae* — Doctrine of *forum prorogatum* — Written submissions — Whether sufficient evidence of acceptance of tribunals' jurisdiction

Arbitration—Annulment—Grounds for annulment—Excess of jurisdiction—Requirement that excess must be manifest —Uncertainty to be resolved *in favorem validitatis sententiae* —Distinction between non-application of applicable law and mistaken application of applicable law — Alleged absence of deliberation and other irregularities—Alleged lack of impartiality — Whether constituting failure of tribunal to adhere to fundamental rules of procedure — Contradiction of reasons—Dubious or hypothetical reasons —Sufficiently relevant reasons—Alleged failure of tribunal to deal with questions submitted to it — Challenge to award of arbitral tribunal—ICSID—Reference to *ad hoc* Committee—Powers of Committee—Whether limited to annulment for manifest excess of jurisdiction—Whether error of law constituting manifest excess of jurisdiction— Consequences of annulment — Whether award to be annulled in whole or in part

Arbitration—Applicable law—ICSID arbitration—Absence of express choice of law—Law of Contracting State to apply—Inclusion of Contracting State's rules on conflict of laws—Part of Contracting State applying common law while other part applying civil law—Geographical location of project—Applicability of civil law

Claims—For breach of contract—Effect of non-disclosure of circumstances adversely affecting profitability of project— Deductions from claim as result of failure adequately to perform contractual obligations—*Exceptio non adimpleti contractus*—Release of one party from obligations by virtue of non-performance by other party—Whether principle of international law

Claims—Counterclaim—For damages—Claim by State for losses attributable to participation in failed joint venture project—Capital contribution to joint venture company— Government-guaranteed loans—Non-financial damages— Alleged failure of company to perform duty of disclosure—

Effect of denial of company's claim for contract price on government's counterclaim

Treaties—Interpretation—Annulment provisions of ICSID Convention — Interpretation of provisions relating to applicable law—Whether interpreted in accordance with general principles of treaty interpretation

KLÖCKNER INDUSTRIE-ANLAGEN GMBH AND OTHERS v. REPUBLIC
OF CAMEROON

International Centre for the Settlement of Investment Disputes

Award on the Merits.   21 *October* 1983

(*Arbitration Tribunal*: Dr Eduardo Jiménez de Aréchaga, *President*;
Mr William Rogers and Professor Dominique Schmidt, *Members*)

Decision on Annulment.   3 *May* 1985

(*Ad hoc Committee*: Professor Pierre Lalive, *President*; Professor Ahmed
El-Kosheri and Professor Ignaz Seidl-Hohenveldern, *Members*)

SUMMARY:[1] *The facts:*—On 4 December 1971 a multinational European company, Klöckner Industrie-Anlagen GmbH ("Klöckner"), and the United Republic of Cameroon ("Cameroon") signed a Protocol of Agreement under which Klöckner undertook to supply, erect and manage for a period of at least five years a fertilizer factory in Cameroon ready for use and with a production capacity of 157,000 tons per year. Klöckner and its European partners were to own 51 per cent of the shares in the joint venture company, the Société Camerounaise des Engrais (SOCAME), established for the project; the remaining 49 per cent of the shares were to be held by the Cameroonian Government. The Government undertook to provide a site for the factory and to guarantee a loan arranged by Klöckner to cover the price of the factory. The contract contained an ICSID arbitration clause. A Supply Contract containing more detailed provisions concerning the project was concluded by the Government and Klöckner on 4 March 1972. All of the Government's rights and obligations under this contract, which also contained an ICSID arbitration clause, were transferred to SOCAME on its establishment in 1973. However, the Government remained liable as guarantor of the price payable to Klöckner in the event of SOCAME's default. An Establishment Agreement was signed by the Government and SOCAME in 1973, and it, too, contained an ICSID arbitration clause. In 1977, two years after Klöckner began managing the operation, SOCAME and Klöckner signed a Management Agreement intended to ensure Klöckner's responsibility for the company's

[1] Prepared by Dr A. V. Lowe and Ms R. Rayfuse.

technical and commercial management. This agreement provided for the arbitration of disputes arising therefrom in Switzerland under International Chamber of Commerce (ICC) Rules. In 1978 Klöckner and its European partners refused to subscribe to a capital increase, and lost majority control of SOCAME.

After a period of unprofitable operation, the factory was shut down by the Cameroonian Government, first in December 1977 and finally, after an unsuccessful attempt to restart it, in 1980. In April 1981 Klöckner filed with ICSID a request for arbitration against the United Republic of Cameroon and SOCAME. Klöckner claimed CFA francs 10,350 million, being the balance of the price of the fertilizer factory supplied by it to Cameroon. The Cameroonian Government counterclaimed for CFA francs 12,156 million in damages for all losses it had incurred in the abandoned SOCAME fertilizer project.

Held (Professor Schmidt dissenting):—The Tribunal had jurisdiction over the proceedings. Both the claim and the counterclaim were rejected.

(1)(a) The Tribunal had jurisdiction over the parties and the subject-matter of the dispute. Jurisdiction over the proceedings was based on the ICSID clauses in the 1971 Protocol of Agreement, and the 1972 Supply Contract. The provision for ICC arbitration in the 1977 Management Agreement related to disputes arising exclusively from that agreement and could not be interpreted as an implicit waiver of the undertaking to submit to ICSID disputes arising from the 1971 Protocol of Agreement (pp. 161-2).

(b) Once the Tribunal had been validly seized of a case, consent to the extent of the Tribunal's jurisdiction *ratione materiae* could be expressed at any time, including the stage of written submissions to the Tribunal (*forum prorogatum*). The Tribunal's jurisdiction over the subject-matter of the dispute including the counterclaim, had been expressly acknowledged in the pleadings. The parties could not subsequently alter their position on this (pp. 162-6).

(c) SOCAME was an appropriate party to the proceedings. The inclusion of the ICSID arbitration clause in the 1973 Establishment Agreement presupposed and implied an agreement to consider SOCAME to be a company under foreign control which had capacity to act in ICSID proceedings. Klöckner had benefited from the jurisdiction flowing from SOCAME's treatment in the 1973 Establishment Agreement as a company under foreign control during the period 1973-8 in which Klöckner held the majority of shares in SOCAME. It would therefore be inequitable to allow Klöckner now to contest ICSID jurisdiction on the grounds of its loss of majority control of SOCAME, at least in respect of matters arising during the period 1973-8 (p. 165).

(2) The law applicable to the substance of the dispute was to be determined by the application of Article 42 of the ICSID Convention which, in the absence of an agreed choice of law, referred the matter to the law of the Contracting State Party, including its rules on the conflict of laws. Since the agreements were finalized and the factory located in the eastern part of Cameroon that part of Cameroonian law based on French civil law, and not that part based on English common law, would be applied (p. 208).

(3)(a) Klöckner was not entitled to recover the whole of the contract price. Klöckner had failed fully to disclose changed economic circumstances adversely affecting the profitability of the project. Had it done so the Government might have terminated the project at an early stage. This lack of frankness constituted a breach of the duty of confidence and loyalty which existed in relation to international joint venture contracts such as those in issue here. Accordingly, deductions from the contract price claimed by Klöckner would be made for departures from the original contractual specification for the factory; periodical payments of principal and interest made by Cameroon which were not due under the contract because Klöckner had not fulfilled its contractual obligation to deliver a factory "ready for use"; the cost of repairs, borne by Cameroon; and a part of the operating losses during the period 1977-9 (pp. 208-10).

(b) The civil law principle *exceptio non adimpleti contractus*, according to which one party would be completely or partially released from its contractual undertakings by virtue of the other's total or partial failure to fulfil its own contractual undertakings, was reflected in both English and international law, and could be invoked at any stage, even if no prior notice of default had been given to the non-performing party. Obligations in the international investment context were not to be determined by examining each constituent contract in isolation from the others but on the basis of the single legal relationship which they established. Klöckner's obligations under the contracts had been performed in an imperfect and partial manner such that Cameroon was relieved from any further performance of its contractual obligations (pp. 210-21).

(c) Cameroon had paid Klöckner almost 30 per cent of the total price for the factory, which was approximately the proportion of the planned production capacity achieved by the plant and the approximate value of the components supplied by Klöckner. In the light of this equilibrium Klöckner was entitled to the payment it had already received and to no more (pp. 219-21).

(4) There was no justification for charging Klöckner with losses incurred by the joint venture, and Cameroon's counterclaim would accordingly be rejected (p. 226).

Dissenting opinion of Professor Schmidt: (1) As had been recognized by the Tribunal in passages in its Award contradicting any such finding, Klöckner had not failed in its duty of full disclosure to its partner. SOCAME had accepted delivery of the factory from Klöckner, and any production shortfalls were attributable to SOCAME's lack of funds to acquire raw materials and spare parts. Klöckner had, in fact, done all that was contractually required of it in relation to the management of the plant (pp. 227-9).

(2) Cameroon should have given formal notice to Klöckner demanding performance but had not done so and, indeed, had made payments to Klöckner in a manner indicating an acknowledgement that it was the debtor of the amounts owed by it to Klöckner under the contracts (pp. 233-4).

(3) The Tribunal had failed to give reasons for the deduction of specific amounts from the sums due to Klöckner and it had been inconsistent in its calculations of amounts owing (pp. 237-8).

(4) The Tribunal lacked jurisdiction over the Management Contract and over the question of Klöckner's possible responsibility arising from its alleged failure to perform that contract. Consent to submit to ICSID jurisdiction could not be given after ICSID had been seized of a case. Accordingly, the Tribunal's Award was vitiated (pp. 238-42).

Annulment Decision: 3 May 1985

In February 1984 Klöckner applied for the annulment of the Award of 21 October 1983. Klöckner argued that the Tribunal had manifestly exceeded its powers due to its lack of jurisdiction over disputes arising from the Management Contract; that the Tribunal had manifestly exceeded its powers by incorrectly applying the choice of law provisions of Article 42(1) of the ICSID Convention; that the Tribunal had departed seriously from fundamental rules of procedure, in particular by holding no true deliberation, failing to respect due process, and obviously lacking impartiality; and that the Tribunal had failed to give an adequate statement of reasons and to deal with all the questions submitted to it.

Held (unanimously):—The Award was annulled.

(1)(a) In applications of this sort an *ad hoc* Committee must first decide whether the Tribunal had exceeded its jurisdiction in any way whatsoever and, if it had, the Committee must then determine the extent to which such an excess of jurisdiction might be characterized as a manifest excess of powers within the meaning of Article 52(1)(b) of the Convention. An ICSID award would be subject to annulment for excess of jurisdiction only whether the excess was sufficiently well established and recognized as manifest (pp. 245-6).

(b) Although two interpretations of the agreement were possible it did not follow that the one adopted by the Tribunal was untenable and constituted an excess of powers. Any doubt or uncertainty with respect to the validity of the Tribunal's interpretation should be resolved *in favorem validitatis sententiae* as long as the right of each party to be heard had been respected and so long as the Tribunal's construction had remained within the legal framework provided by the parties (pp. 246-65).

(2) The Tribunal had failed to apply correctly the law of the Contracting State to the dispute. Although the Tribunal had correctly identified Franco-Cameroonian law as the applicable law it had failed to apply that law by limiting its reasoning to postulating and not demonstrating the existence of relevant principles or exploring rules by which such principles could take concrete form. In applying concepts and principles which it undoubtedly considered equitable but which were outside the framework of the law of the Contracting State Party, the Tribunal manifestly exceeded its powers. It was impossible to dissociate the operative parts of the Tribunal's reasons relating to the breach of the alleged duty of full disclosure from the rest of the Tribunal's reasoning such that a partial annulment could be awarded. Accordingly, the whole of the Tribunal's award was annulled (pp. 265-74).

(3) Although not necessary for the purposes of deciding this application, as this was the first annulment application to be considered under the ICSID system, it was appropriate for the Committee to examine the allegations relating to a serious departure from a fundamental rule of procedure and the failure to state reasons. Given the tenor of the Award, the Claimant's challenge to the impartiality of the Tribunal and to other aspects of its proceedings was understandable. However, the arguments were unfounded. Likewise, an absence of sufficiently relevant reasons could constitute a failure

to state reasons. While some issues had been adequately dealt with the Tribunal had not dealt with a number of questions submitted to it by Klöckner. There had therefore been a failure to state reasons with respect to those issues (pp. 274-310).

The texts of the Award and Annulment Decision are set out as follows:

The following is the text of excerpts of the Award of 21 October 1983:

[9]   AWARD, 21 OCTOBER 1983

(Translation)

Table of Contents

I. THE ARBITRAL PROCEDURE   **[10]**

A. *The Request*

On 10 April 1981, Klöckner Industrie-Anlagen GmbH, a German
company whose principal office is in Duisburg, acting on its own behalf as
well as on behalf of Klöckner Belge SA, a Belgian company whose principal
office is in Brussels, and Klöckner Handelsmaatschappij BV, a Netherlands
company whose principal office is in The Hague, (hereafter "Claimant")
delivered to the Secretary General of the International Centre for the
Settlement of Investment Disputes (hereafter "the Centre") in Washington,
DC, a request for arbitration against the United Republic of Cameroon
("the Government") and the Société Camerounaise des Engraise (SOCAME)
SA (hereafter "the Company"), (hereafter "Defendant") accompanied by a
Supply Contract for a fertilizer factory (hereafter "the Contract"), dated 4
March 1972, between the federal Republic of Cameroon and Klöckner
Industrie-Anlagen GmbH, containing an arbitration clause referring to the
Convention on the Settlement of Investment Disputes between States and
Nationals of Other States (hereafter "the Convention"), all in conformity
with the provisions of Article 36 of the Convention, Articles 1, 2, and 4 of
the Rules for the Institution of Proceedings, and Article 15(1) of the
Administrative and Financial Regulations.

The Secretary-General of the Centre registered the Request on 14 April
1981.

B. *The Constitution of the Tribunal*

On 3 July 1981, Claimant designated Me Dominique Schmidt, a French national, as arbitrator. Me Schmidt notified the Centre of his acceptance on 17 September 1981. On 10 September 1981, Defendant designated William D. Rogers, Esq., a US national, as arbitrator. Mr Rogers notified the Centre of his acceptance on 22 September 1981. On 9 October 1981 the two arbitrators, by mutual agreement in accordance with the parties' chosen method of constituting the tribunal, designated Dr Eduardo Jiménez de Aréchaga, a national of Uruguay, as arbitrator and Chairman of the Arbitral Tribunal (hereafter "the Tribunal"). Dr Jiménez de Aréchaga notified the Centre of his acceptance on 15 October 1981. The Tribunal deemed to be constituted, the proceedings were commenced on 26 October 1981 in conformity with the provisions of Article 6(1) of the Rules of Arbitration.

C. *Representatives of the Parties*

During the proceedings, Claimant was represented by Philippe Nouel, Esq., and Defendant was represented by the Minister of Industrial and [11] Commercial Development, the Minister of Finance, and Jan Paulsson, Esq., of the firm Coudert Frères, Paris.

D. *Preliminary Consultations*

[The following italicized summaries are supplied by the translator who omitted the text of these sections from the translation:]

The arbitrators met in New York on 22 November 1981 in order to discuss procedural matters. One of the questions they dealt with was that of SOCAME's participation in the arbitration in light of Article 20 of the ICSID Arbitration Rules; they decided that this question was one relating to the Tribunal's jurisdiction.

E. *First Session*

The arbitrators met with the parties in New York on 23 November 1981 to decide certain procedural questions. With the agreement of the parties, a certain number of rules were established, notably:
— *the language of the arbitration would be French;*
— *the seat of the Tribunal would be the World Bank offices in Paris;*
— *deadlines were set for Klöckner's Memorial and Cameroon's Counter-Memorial;*
— *deadlines for the Reply Memorial and the Rejoinder Memorial would be established later;*

— *a decision whether there would be oral proceedings would be taken in due course;*

— *the Cameroonian Government would take a position by 15 December 1981 as to whether it would voluntarily make an* ad hoc *designation of* SOCAME *as a party to the proceedings, as required with respect to state or parastatal entities under Article 25 of the Convention.*

F. *The Written Phase*

The principal stages of the written phase of the arbitration were the following:

7 December 1981: The Government designated SOCAME *as a constituent subdivision of the State of Cameroon as understood by Article 25(1) of the Convention, and approved its participation in the arbitration.*

11 December 1981: Klöckner submitted its Memorial.

25 June 1982: Cameroon submitted its Counter-Memorial.

30 October 1982: Klöckner submitted its Reply Memorial.

23 March 1983: Cameroon submitted its Rejoinder Memorial.

25 April 1983: The arbitrators met with the parties in Paris to establish rules for oral proceedings. In particular, it was decided that lists of witnesses **[12]** *would be communicated in advance, that counsel would present oral arguments after hearing of the witnesses, and that no further written submissions would be allowed during the hearings or thereafter.*

G. *The Oral Phase*

Hearings were held during the week of 18 July 1983. Klöckner presented two German witnesses and an English technical expert. Cameroon presented five Cameroonian witnesses, one French witness, and an English technical expert. The witnesses were heard on 18, 19, 20, and 21 July.

Philippe Nouel, Esq., presented Klöckner's oral argument on 22 July 1983.

Jan Paulsson, Esq., presented the Government of Cameroon's oral argument on 23 July 1983.

The same day, the parties submitted updated computations of the claimed amounts as well as French legal texts. The Chairman of the Tribunal thereupon declared the proceedings to be at an end pursuant to Article 38(1) of the ICSID *Arbitration Rules.*

On 25 July 1983, the arbitrators met in Paris. They decided under Article 38(2) of the ICSID *Arbitration Rules to ask the parties to respond in writing by 10 August 1983 to the following question of fact:*

Was Mr van der Ploeg or another qualified representative of Ferticonsult personally present during the test runs of the sulphuric acid unit from 11–14 July 1976 and of the NPK unit from 28–31 July 1976?

After the parties had submitted responses to this question, the arbitrators met in London on 22–23 August 1983.

II. THE PARTIES' RESPECTIVE PRAYERS

Klöckner requested the Tribunal to order Cameroon to make payment of the outstanding balance, expressed in German marks, Belgian francs, and Dutch florins, of the price of the fertilizer factory supplied by Klöckner. By the end of the arbitration, the amount of this balance, as updated by Klöckner with interest, at the then rates of exchange, was 10,350 million CFA francs. (CFA francs are linked to the French franc at an invariable rate of 50 CFA francs to 1 French franc.).

Cameroon requested the Tribunal to dismiss Klöckner's claim, and, by way of counterclaim, to order Klöckner to compensate Cameroon for all losses it had incurred in the abandoned SOCAME fertilizer project, to wit 12,156 million CFA francs.

[13]   III. THE JURISDICTION OF THE ARBITRAL TRIBUNAL

Claimant has seized the Arbitral Tribunal on the basis of Article 18 of the Supply Contract for the fertilizer factory signed on 4 March 1972 by the Federal Republic of Cameroon and Klöckner. This Article of the Contract provides that:

> Disputes relating to the validity, the interpretation, or the application of the clauses of the present protocol shall be settled by the parties' agreement, failing which they shall be resolved in conformity with the arbitral procedure
>
> established by the International Convention on the Settlement of Investment Disputes of the International Bank for Reconstruction and Development (IBRD).

For its part, while accepting the jurisdiction of the Tribunal on the basis of Article 18 of the Supply Contract, Defendant has broadened the jurisdictional foundation of this case by also invoking Article 22 of the Protocol of Agreement previously signed by the same parties on 4 December 1971. Said Article 22 is identical to Article 18 of the Supply Contract. Claimant does not contest this extension of the Tribunal's jurisdiction.

It is important to note that Claimant sets forth, on p. 11 of its Reply Memorial, that it acknowledges that "ICSID has jurisdiction with respect to the Protocol of Agreement." Claimant thus accepts that the ICSID clause, contained in the Protocol of Agreement, applies to all of the undertakings agreed by the parties in said Protocol, including Claimant's undertaking in

Article 9 to "be responsible for the technical and commercial management
of the Company, ensured by a Management Contract."

A submission has been made within the Arbitral Tribunal that the
International Chamber of Commerce arbitration clause contained in Article
8 of the Management Contract had the effect of removing disputes relating
to the Article 9 undertaking from the jurisdiction of this Tribunal, and to
subject them to the jurisdiction of an arbitral tribunal that might be set up by
the International Chamber of Commerce, and which would apply Swiss law.

The Tribunal cannot share this view, under which ICSID jurisdiction would
have existed from the date of the Protocol, 4 December 1971, but would
have evaporated by a kind of implicit derogation on 7 April 1977, the date
the Management Contract was signed. There might doubtless be disputes
arising exclusively from the Management Contract – relating for example to
payment of fees established in said Contract – and such disputes would
naturally fall beyond the jurisdiction of this Tribunal, and be subject to the
ICC clause. Article 8 of the Management Contract provides for ICC
jurisdiction only for "all disputes arising from the present contract." But
disputes flowing from Klöckner's performance, non-performance, or flawed
performance of the technical and commercial management of SOCAME were
subject to the ICSID clause from the start-up of the factory and remain subject
to this clause by virtue of the combined effect of Articles 9 and 22 of the **[14]**
Protocol of Agreement, which establishes ICSID jurisdiction for the
settlement of "disputes relating to the validity, the interpretation, or the
application of the clauses of the present protocol".

The Management Contract, intended according to Article 9 of the
Protocol of Agreement to ensure Klöckner's responsibility for the
Company's technical and commercial management, cannot be interpreted
as an implicit waiver of a fundamental undertaking of the Protocol of
Agreement, either in its substance, or with respect to its jurisdictional
guarantees. In effect, Klöckner's undertaking to carry out the technical and
commercial management of the factory was the essential precondition of the
investment, acknowledged in the Preamble of the Protocol as well as in the
"discussions that preceded the drafting of this Protocol" to which Article 4
refers. This technical and commercial management was in fact performed by
Klöckner, which alone ran SOCAME, before as well as after the signature of
the Management Contract. One proof of this fact is the decision made in
December 1977, after the signature of the Management Contract, to shut
down the factory. This decision was adopted by SOCAME's management,
comprised (with one single exception) of expatriates recommended by
Klöckner, and without any evidence in the file that SOCAME's Board of
Directors had given its prior approval, or even been consulted.

If the least doubt remained with respect to this Tribunal as far as Article 9
of the Protocol of Agreement is concerned, there is another decisive
consideration: the consent expressed by Claimant in its Reply Memorial (p.
11). In this document, Claimant maintained that the Management Contract

in and of itself falls outside the scope of this Tribunal's jurisdiction, which is exact. But it expressly acknowledged the Tribunal's jurisdiction "with respect to the Protocol of Agreement" without making an exception as to its Article 9. It was only within the Arbitral Tribunal that an objection was raised to the effect that the Management Contract had the consequence of excluding Article 9 of the Protocol of Agreement from the ambit of the ICSID clause.

But according to the Convention, the jurisdiction of an ICSID tribunal is based on the parties' consent, the "cornerstone of the Centre's jurisdiction." Once the Centre has been validly seized (as it was in this case by Klöckner's Request), consent as to the "*ratione materiae*" extent of the Tribunal's jurisdiction may be expressed at any time, even in written submissions to the Tribunal ("*forum prorogatum*"). On this score, the Report of the Executive Directors of the World Bank indicates at paragraph 24 that "the Convention does not ... specify the time at which consent should be given."

Defendant invoked a third jurisdictional foundation for the Tribunal: Article 21 of the Establishment Agreement signed on 23 June 1973 between the United Republic of Cameroon and the Société Camerounaise des Engrais (SOCAME), which is almost identical to Article 18 of the Supply Contract and to Article 22 of the Protocol of Agreement.

Claimant does not accept this jurisdictional basis, maintaining that

[15]   there is first of all a lack of consent by the parties. In the meaning of Article 46 (of the ICSID Convention), the parties are the Claimant and the Defendant. The Establishment Agreement is, after all, an agreement between the two defendants ... Likewise, the second condition of Article 46 is not fulfilled, because SOCAME is not 'a national of another Contracting State' but a Cameroonese company listed in the Registry of Commerce in Douala. (Reply Memorial, pp. 11–12.)

If the jurisdiction of the Centre may not, in principle, be extended to "any juridical person which (has) the nationality of the Contracting State" (Article 25(2)(b) of the Convention), this principle is subject to a significant exception in the case of a legal entity created in the host country of the investment,

which, because of foreign control, the parties have agreed should be treated as a national of another Contracting State for the purposes of this Convention. (Article 25(2)(b) *in fine*.)

Consequently, as the Report of the Executive Directors on the ICSID Convention explains clearly, at para. 30:

A juridical person which had the nationality of the State party to the dispute would be eligible to be a party to proceedings under the auspices of the Centre if that State had agreed to treat it as a national of another Contracting State because of foreign control.

This acceptance "confers on the legal entity a kind of subsidiary, functional nationality for the jurisdictional purposes of the Centre only," M. Amadio, *Le contentieux international de l'investissement privé et la Convention de la Banque Mondiale du 18 mars 1965*, p. 115.

The reason for this exception has been explained by Mr Broches as follows:

> there was a compelling reason for this last provision. It is quite usual for host States to require that foreign investors carry on their business within their territories through a company organized under the laws of the host country. If we admit ... that this makes the company technically a national of the host country, it becomes readily apparent that there is need for an exception... If no exception were made for foreign-owned but locally incorporated companies, a large and important sector of foreign investment would be outside the scope of the Convention. A. Broches, "The Convention on the Settlement of Investment Disputes between States and Nationals of Other States", 136 *Recueil des Cours de l'Académie de Droit International*, pp. 358–9.

On 23 June 1973, when the parties to the Establishment Agreement consented to submit any disputes to ICSID arbitration, SOCAME was a Cameroonian company, but subject to the majority control of foreign interests. This is clear from Article 2 of the Protocol of Agreement of 4 December 1971, in which it is stipulated that "Klöckner and its European **[16]** partners" would subscribe to 51% of SOCAME's capital.

The ICSID Convention does not specify the manner in which the parties may express their agreement as to the existence of the conditions giving rise to the exception defined in Article 25(2)(b) *in fine*. In practice, this agreement may be manifest in the explicit acknowledgment of foreign control, contained in Article 2 of the Protocol, in conjunction with the simple inclusion of an ICSID clause, as was done by Article 21 of the Establishment Agreement. As it has been noted in commentary on the Convention, "a consent clause may be simple, recording no more than an agreement to submit certain matters to conciliation and/or arbitration under the auspices of the Centre," Szasz, "A Practical Guide to the Convention on the Settlement of Investment Disputes," 1 *Cornell International Law Journal*, p. 23.

The insertion of an ICSID arbitration clause by itself presupposes and implies that the parties were agreed to consider SOCAME at the time to be a company under foreign control, thus having the capacity to act in ICSID arbitration. This is an acknowledgment which completely excludes a different interpretation of the parties' intent. Inserting this clause in the Establishment Agreement would be nonsense if the parties had not agreed that, by reason of the control then exercised by foreign interests over SOCAME, said Agreement could be made subject to ICSID jurisdiction.

It is true that in 1978 a change occurred when the foreign interests lost majority control over the Company because they refused to subscribe to a capital increase decided upon at that time. Knowledgeable writers are divided on the issue of the effects on the ICSID arbitration clause of a subsequent change of nationality or control. On the one hand, Mr Amerasinghe has maintained that this change affects neither the validity nor the effect of the forum clause because, in his view,

> the ICSID Convention implies that the relevant time for the fulfilment of the nationality requirement is that date when the consent to jurisdiction is effective for both parties. It also means that any change in the nationality of the juridical person after that date is immaterial for purposes of ICSID's jurisdiction. C. F. Amerasinghe, "The International Centre for the Settlement of Investment Disputes and Development through the Multinational Corporation", 9 *Vanderbilt Journal of Transnational Law*, p. 809–810 (1976).

This opinion finds support in a phrase contained in Article 25(2): "on the date on which the parties consented." On the other hand, Mr Delaume seems to be of a different view; in analysing the hypothesis of an assignment to a third party of the investment agreement during its performance, he maintains that if the assignee is a "national of the State party to the agreement or of a non-contracting State," the Centre's jurisdiction would disappear, G. Delaume, "Le Centre International pour le Règlement des Différends Relatifs aux Investissements (CIRDI)," 109 *Journal du droit international* 797 (1982).

[17]   Even if one accepts the second view, it must be noted that the question arising in this case is not whether the Tribunal has "*ratione personae*" jurisdiction as regards SOCAME. This question, which was posed in the *Holiday Inns v. Morocco*[1] case and decided negatively, is here resolved affirmatively in view of Defendant's letter of 7 December 1981 to the Arbitral Tribunal.

The question before the present Tribunal is thus different: to determine whether it has jurisdiction "*ratione materiae*" to rule on the application and interpretation of the Establishment Agreement. This Agreement, although formally signed by the Government and SOCAME, was in fact negotiated between the Government and Klöckner, as is shown by (*minutes of a negotiating session submitted as an annex to the Rejoinder Memorial* [translator's note]). Moreover, it is undeniable that it was manifestly concluded in the interest of Klöckner, at a time when Klöckner was SOCAME's majority shareholder. The Establishment Agreement reflected the contractual relationship between a foreign investor, acting through a local company, and the host country of this foreign investment.

In these conditions, it would be inequitable to accept that Klöckner, having benefited from 1973 to 1978 from the existence of the ICSID arbitral clause, underlying the legal, economic, financial, and fiscal advantages and guarantees granted in the Establishment Agreement, be allowed today to contest ICSID jurisdiction with respect to questions relating to the application

---

[[1] The decision in the *Holiday Inns* case has not been made available to the public. A description of the case is found in the article reproduced at Annex 1 of Volume 1 of the *ICSID Reports*.]

of the same Agreement, at least during the 1973–1978 period, when the arbitration clause is invoked by the Government which consented to it.

The preceding factors lead to the conclusion that the Arbitral Tribunal has jurisdiction to rule both on the claim and the counterclaim, while taking into account the Establishment Agreement which, together with the Protocol of Agreement and the Supply Contract, constitutes an indivisible whole.

As for the Management Contract of 7 April 1977 between Klöckner and SOCAME, also invoked by Defendant, Claimant is right in denying the jurisdiction of the Arbitral Tribunal to rule on disputes arising from this contract. According to Article 8 of this contract: "All disputes arising from the present contract shall be finally settled in accordance with the Rules of Conciliation and Arbitration of the International Chamber of Commerce by one or more arbitrators named in conformity with said Rules. The Arbitral Court shall have its seat in Bern, Switzerland, and shall apply Swiss substantive law".

Nevertheless, on the basis of Article 9 of the Protocol of Agreement, the Tribunal has jurisdiction to rule on the performance of the parties' obligations with respect to Klöckner's responsibility for "the technical and commercial management" of SOCAME, which was to be ensured by means of a Management Contract.

The three contracts establish the jurisdiction of the tribunal with respect **[18]** to the counterclaim, given the direct connection between the three instruments and the parties' claims.

IV. THE AGREEMENTS GOVERNING THE INVESTMENT

At this point, it is necessary to examine the parties' obligations arising from the three closely connected agreements that govern the investment and with respect to which this Tribunal has jurisdiction to pronounce itself.

The first of these agreements, not only in time but also from the perspective of its fundamental importance, is the Protocol of Agreement of 4 December 1971.

In effect, this Protocol was the cornerstone of the parties' contractual structure. The two other agreements – the Supply Contract and the Establishment Agreement – were concluded only in application of the Protocol. One may therefore consider the Protocol to be the *accord cadre* governing all aspects of the investment involved in the present case.

A. *The Protocol of Agreement of 4 December 1971*

The Protocol of Agreement refers expressly in Articles 3, 6, and 21 to a future contract to be concluded between the two parties relating to the supply of a fertilizer factory, but it clearly results from the Protocol that the Government was not satisfied with the mere supply of a fertilizer plant.

According to the Protocol, much more was expected and demanded of the supplier of the plant.

First, the Preamble of the Protocol, after having noted that the Government had foreseen, "in its IIIrd Plan for Economic and Social Development, the construction of a fertilizer factory," adds "that Klöckner accepts to contribute to the realization of this factory by giving its financial and technical assistance to the Cameroonian Government."

Next, and with the same perspective of technical assistance the key obligation assumed by Klöckner is set forth in Article 9 of the Protocol:

> Klöckner shall be responsible for the technical and commercial management of the Company (SOCAME), ensured by a management agreement for at least 5 years from startup, with an option to renew.

Thus, as has already been noted, the Protocol requires that the foreign investment be channeled through a Cameroonian legal entity. This decision was based on a suggestion made by Klöckner in the technical and commercial report it presented in September 1971. According to Article 1 defining the object of the Protocol:

> the Government and Klöckner agree to create as soon as possible a Cameroonian limited liability company whose purpose shall be to construct and operate a Fertilizer Factory in the Federal Republic of Cameroon, market and distribute all of the fertilizer products, and carry out programs to introduce fertilizer products in rural areas.

[19]

The Protocol does not content itself with Klöckner's undertaking in Article 9 to carry out "the technical and commercial management of the Company". Klöckner is also required (once again at its own suggestion) to become, with its European partners, majority shareholders controlling 51% of the Cameroonian company to be set up (Article 2).

By Article 3, the "Program to be Accomplished":

> The Government accepts to entrust Klöckner with the realization of a fertilizer factory having a production capacity of:
>
> | | |
> |---|---|
> | Sulphuric acid | — 60,000 t/yr (98% H_2SO_4) |
> | Ammonium sulphate | — 50,000 t/yr (21% N) |
> | Single superphosphate | — 20,000 t/yr (20% P_2O_5) |
> | Complex fertilizers | — 27,000 t/yr (6750 t/yr of each of the formulae: 20-10-10; 15.5-12.25-12.25; 12-6-24; 14-14-14). |

The factory's total production capacity is thus stated very precisely as 157,000 tons per year of products of stated qualities and characteristics. In the technical and economic report presented by Klöckner in September 1971, which was the source of the Protocol, it is stated that the production of the various units should be that defined in Article 3, and the profitability

studies for the plant were prepared on the assumption of production in the
first year of 99,550 tons of marketable fertilizer, and 102,500 tons the second
year, broken down as follows:

	1st year	2nd year
Ammonium sulphate	38,000	35,600
SSP	19,730	19,680
NPK	27,000	32,400
Sulphuric acid	14,820	14,820
Total tons/year	99,550	102,500

Article 4 of the Protocol provides that:

On the basis of the study presented by Klöckner in September 1971 and the
discussions that preceded the drafting of this Protocol, the investments
necessary to accomplish the program defined in Article 3 above have been
estimated at CFA francs 4,822,400 or DM 60,280,000 broken down as
follows...
(*The turnkey factory cost was given as CFA francs 3,984,000,000 or DM
49,800,000. The total investment was to be financed 30% by equity
contributions; 70% by loans* [translator's note]).

Chapter III of the Protocol is entitled "Klöckner's Undertakings."

In Article 5, Klöckner undertakes to "take all steps necessary to create the [20]
Company and to assist it in presenting in due form an application for
approval under the Investment Code." Thus was envisaged, and defined as
one of Klöckner's undertakings, the conclusions by the new Company of an
Establishment Agreement "under Law No. 60/64 of 27 June 1960
promulgating the Investment Code, modified by laws 64/LF/6 of 6 April
1964 and 66/LF/5 of 10 June 1966" (preamble to the Establishment
Agreement).
Article 6 provides that "a contract for supply and financing shall be
concluded between Klöckner and the Company to be created, on the basis of
supplier's financing of DM 39,840,000 (CFA francs 3,187,200,000) over 10
years at 8.5% interest, the first repayment to be scheduled 6 months after the
mechanical completion of the factory". Klöckner undertakes by Article 7
"within 24 months from the date of entry into force of the contract for supply
and financing, to perform the engineering, supply, erection, and startup of
the factory" and by Article 8 "to supply the Company with raw materials for
the first six months of production in the form of suppliers' financing over 180
days, free of interest."
Article 9, establishing Klöckner's fundamental obligation to take
"responsibility for the technical and commercial management of the
Company" for at least 5 years, has already been mentioned. By Article 10,
Klöckner undertakes "to train the Cameroonian personnel indispensable to
the proper functioning of the factory, and to start doing so as of the
incorporation of the Company."

According to Article 11, "Klöckner shall endeavor to explore for and to make use of local raw materials necessary for the factory's output, at the express request, and with the assistance, of the Government."
Article 12 provides that:

> With a view to popularizing use of fertilizer products in rural areas, Klöckner shall take necessary measures, as of incorporation of the Company, to assist it in conceiving and carrying out a fertilizer distribution program in Cameroon with the help of the concerned technical departments of the state, in particular the agricultural departments.

Finally, Article 13 sets forth that

> In the factory design, Klöckner provides for a flexible plant capable of adjusting to a possible increase of future consumption. The plant should also be adaptable to a method for producing products having other characteristics, including the range of complex fertilizers. Klöckner also undertakes in such a case to market abroad any excess output that may result from such an extension.

Chapter IV of the Protocol enumerates "the Government's Undertakings."
The first of these undertakings is that provided in Article 14:

[21] The Government shall give to the Company to be created a site of approximately 40,000 m² within the Bonaberi Industrial Zone, Douala, where the necessary infrastructure for the functioning of the factory exists. This site should comply with the technical norms for the construction of this factory. The Government shall as soon as possible provide Klöckner with the detailed specifications of the site and the results of test boring. Within 4 weeks of receiving this technical information, Klöckner shall inform the Government if it can maintain the price of the factory at DM 49,800,000 (CFA francs 3,984,000,000).

Article 16 establishes the guarantee of the Cameroonian Government: "The Government guarantees the repayment of the long-term loan defined in Article 4, the payment of interest, as well as the remittance to Germany of the amounts of principal and interest."
By Article 17, "the Government undertakes to authorize the Company, as of its incorporation, to import and distribute fertilizer products, in order to allow the Company to execute its program of initiating and popularizing fertilizer use in rural areas."
In Article 18, "the Government assures Klöckner that there will be a receptive examination of the application to be filed in view of obtaining benefits indispensable to the functioning of the Company, under Law No. 64/LF/6 of 6 April 1964 and the Treaty of Brazzaville." Once again one perceives in this assurance Klöckner's interest in obtaining the benefits deriving from the Establishment Agreement.

Finally, in Article 19, "the Government undertakes to do everything within the scope of its authority in order that the schedule of works mentioned above may be kept."

After these two chapters enumerating the two parties' undertakings, which thus demonstrate the bilateral nature of the Protocol, Chapter V contains "Miscellaneous Provisions."

By Article 20:

> each of the parties undertakes not to assign the shares they will hold in the Company without first offering them to the other party. The Government, however, reserves the right to assign its shares to any public or parapublic organ that it may designate.

Article 21 refers once again to the Supply Contract, providing that:

> the two parties shall do everything necessary to accelerate the conclusion and entry into force of the Supply Contract before 31 January 1972, after which date Klöckner shall no longer be able to maintain its prices.

Article 22 is the one that established ICSID jurisdiction. The final Article 23 provides that "the present Protocol enters into effect as of its signature," 4 December 1971.

B. *The Supply Contract of 4 March 1972*   [22]

Three months after having signed the Protocol of Agreement, the same parties – the Cameroonian Government and Klöckner – concluded the Supply Contract envisaged in Articles 3, 6, and 21 of the Protocol of Agreement.

The first Article of this Contract contains a very precise definition of what the document itself calls "the object" of the contract.

This object is thus defined:

> The Government has decided to conclude a contract for the construction of a fertilizer factory for the production of: 50,000 t/yr of Ammonium Sulphate, 20,000 t/yr of Single Super Phosphate, 27,000 t/yr of Complex Fertilizers, 60,000 t/yr of Sulphuric Acid.
>
> The Government has accepted Klöckner's specifications for the design, supply, erection, and startup of said factory.
>
> These specifications, comporting the following annexes, are an integral part of the present Contract: I – Description of processes, II – Performance guarantees and test runs, III – Civil engineering and construction, IV – List of installations, V – Documentation, VI – Mechanical erection, VII – Supervision of startup, VIII – Training of Cameroonian manpower.
>
> The Government orders from Klöckner the factory which is the object of the present Contract, and Klöckner accepts this order.

Both Article 3 of the Protocol and Article 1 of the Supply Contract clearly specify what the Protocol calls the "production capacity" of the factory "which is the object of the present Contract," and the same numbers are used in the two documents to define this "production capacity."

Klöckner undertakes in Article 7 of the Protocol and in Article 1 of the Contract to supply a factory "for the production" of the volumes of fertilizer products specified in the two documents.

Article 2 of the Contract defines the consideration for Klöckner's undertaking, establishing "the price of the factory, ready for use, erected in Cameroon and conforming to the description contained in the Annexes." This price is the same as that defined in Article 4 of the Protocol, the only difference being that the Contract defines it only in DM.

Article 2 of the Contract also makes clear that "this price includes the engineering, knowhow, licenses, supply of installations free-at-site including freight insurance, civil engineering including buildings, erection, supervision of startup."

Article 3 of the Contract defines the "conditions of payment" as follows:

a) 10% within 30 days following entry into force of the Contract

b) another 10%, half of which shall be payable *pro rata* according to delivery of material F.O.B. on presentation of documents, and the other half after completion of erection of the plant, but at the latest 24 months after the first payment under (a) (i.e., 11 April 1975); and

[23]   c) the remaining 80% in 20 successive and equal biannual payments, the first due six months after completion of erection, but at the latest 30 months after the first payment under (a), (i.e., 11 October 1975).

It is also stipulated that the Government shall pay interest at an annual rate of 8.5% on the amount outstanding, computed from the date on which 50% of the material has been shipped.

It is set forth that the 80% as well as interest shall be guaranteed by promissory notes of equal amounts, endorsed by the Minister of Finance of Cameroon as State guarantees.

According to a subsequent contractual document (Amendment No. 3), the 10% down payment was made by SOCAME to Klöckner on 11 April 1973, that is to say even before the entry into force of the Contract on 24 September 1973 (Amendment No. 2).

C. *The Amendments to the Supply Contract Concerning Price and Conditions of Payment*

The first Amendment to Article 3 of the Supply Contract was adopted on 25 July 1973, reducing the 20 biannual payments to 16 successive equal biannual payments and fixing a deadline for the payment of interests "at the latest 21 months after" payments of the 10% down payment, to wit 11

January 1975. Amendment No. 1 was signed by Klöckner and SOCAME because the Supply Contract had been assigned by the Government to SOCAME, as of 25 March 1983.

One year later, on 5 July 1974, the same parties agreed to Amendment No. 2 in which a date (24 September 1973) is fixed for the "entry into execution" of the Contract and an extension is given for the payment of the second 10%: 29 months instead of 24, to wit 11 September 1975.

Amendment No. 3 of 5 October 1975 provides that the 80% of the price of the factory is to be expressed not in DM alone but in three currencies: one part in DM, another in Belgian francs, and a third in florins (Dutch guilders).

It also makes clear that SOCAME made "the first and second payment of interest" on 11 January 1975 and 11 July 1975.

Amendment No. 4 of 2 April 1976, "in view of SOCAME's financial condition during the factory's startup period," sets forth the parties' agreement "to extend the deadline for the second principal payment initially fixed at 11 April 1976" and provides that "the principal payment to the German, Belgian, and Dutch party shall be effected in four successive equal biannual payments, of which the first on 11 October 1978."

Amendment No. 5 of 11 April 1977, "considering the fact that the fertilizer factory project has been delayed two years," sets forth that "the partners have agreed to adjust the price of the fertilizer factory to take into account the increase of supplemental investment costs resulting from this two-year delay."

The price increase is in the amount of DM 7,040,000, or more than 14% of **[24]** the initial price.

It is established that 20% of the price increase shall be paid immediately upon signature of this Amendment, the remaining 80% in successive biannual payments commencing 11 October 1978.

A payment of interest is also set for 11 October 1977, and the remaining payments at six months intervals.

Amendment No. 6, also dated 11 April 1977, contains the parties' agreement to extend the fourth, fifth, and sixth due dates, i.e., 11 April 1977, 11 October 1977, and 11 April 1978, to 11 October 1983, 11 April 1984, and 11 October 1984.

D. *Other Provisions of the Supply Contract*

The Contract is concluded between Klöckner and the Government but Article 17 provides that it may be assigned "to the new Company that shall be incorporated for the operation of the plant which is the object of this Contract." Said Article 17 stipulates that:

the new Company would thus become Klöckner's cocontractant in the Government's place. At this time, all rights and obligations resulting from the present Contract shall be assigned unaltered by the Government to the new Company. By this assignment, the Government is not freed from its obligations to Klöckner. The Government in particular guarantees the payment of the price in the event its contractual successor fails to pay.

By a letter of assignment to SOCAME dated 23 March 1973, the Government assigns:

> all rights and obligations resulting from the Contract. You thus become, as of now, Klöckner's cocontractant in place of the Government. However, this assignment does not alter the provisions of Article 17, nor those of the other articles of the above mentioned Supply Contract, which remain in force unaltered.

One should thus read "SOCAME" each time the Government is mentioned, for example in Article 4, paras. 5 and 6 concerning delays and penalties for delay; in Article 9, para. 6 concerning the guarantee of material; in Article 10 concerning the guarantee test runs (to be analysed in detail subsequently), in Article 14 concerning the performance of the Government, and in Article 15 concerning secrecy.

E. *The Establishment Agreement of 23 June 1973*

On 23 June 1973, the Government and SOCAME signed the Establishment Agreement "pursuant to Law No. 60/64 of 27 June 1960 promulgating the Investment Code, modified by the Laws 64/LF/6 of April 1964 and 66/LF/5 **[25]** of 10 June 1966." By the first Article, SOCAME "is granted the advantages of Category C established by Law 60/64 of 27 June 1960." By Articles 2 and 3, the "United Republic of Cameroon assures SOCAME of the stability of general legal, economic, and financial conditions" as enumerated in Articles 9 to 16, the Government undertaking to this effect "that no legislative or regulatory disposition entering into force at a date subsequent to that of the signature of the present Agreement shall have the effect of restricting its provisions."

Articles 4 and 5 reiterate the obligations of the Company resulting from the protocol and the Supply Contract. By Articles 6, 7, and 8, SOCAME "undertakes to carry out exploration and use of local raw materials" at the Government's request; to give priority to employment of Cameroonian workers; to provide professional training and technical expertise; to construct an infirmary, housing, etc. for the personnel.

By Article 9 *et seq.*, the Government undertakes to grant SOCAME certain legal, economic, financial, and fiscal guarantees, for example:

> to place no obstacle on the import of goods and raw materials to be used by SOCAME... to grant the Company the most favorable treatment if, in order to safeguard its economy, the Government were led to take restrictive measures

affecting trade, provided that the products were competitive in quality and price with normal prices of imported goods (and) ... to take appropriate measures, if needed, to protect SOCAME's output from international competition (Article 12)... exempting SOCAME from corporate income tax during its first 5 years of operation (Article 16).

By Article 18, SOCAME:

> formally undertakes not to make any claims on the Government resulting from the technical risks of its operations or from the evolution of general economic conditions, such developments not being considered events of *force majeure*.

Finally, the Establishment Agreement provides in Article 19 that "the Protocol Agreement signed on 4 December 1971 and the Supply Contract for the factory shall be annexed to the present Agreement as integral parts hereof," thus confirming the unity and the close reciprocal relationship existing between these three documents governing Klöckner's investment in Cameroon, all three referring to ICSID jurisdiction.

V. THE FACTS

Let us now examine the facts. The evidence before the Tribunal demonstrates, as we shall explain, that Klöckner is not entitled to recover the entire price defined in the Contract. First of all, we have established that during the critical period before and during the construction of the factory, Klöckner failed to meet its obligations to deal frankly with its Cameroonian partner. Secondly, although Klöckner had undertaken to deliver a factory "ready for use", the procedure of acceptance of the factory was not carried **[26]** out in conformity with the agreements, and the factory never functioned as Klöckner had said that it would, and as the agreements envisaged it would, during the entire period of the agreement of association between Klöckner and SOCAME. The facts that justify these conclusions are the following:

A. *Klöckner's Conduct Vis-à-vis its Partner*

Defendant has argued that it is entitled to refuse to pay the price fixed in the Supply Contract because Klöckner had acted in bad faith, manoeuvring with an intent to defraud and to manipulate. Defendant especially attacked the original feasibility study submitted by Klöckner in 1971, which forecasted that the factory would be profitable once it was built. This forecast was characterized during hearings in Paris as so erroneous that one must ask whether there was not a deliberate intent to lead the Government into error. When all is said and done, however, we have not found the evidence to be sufficient to conclude that Klöckner acted with an intent to harm, either in the 1971 study or thereafter. Nevertheless, we believe, for reasons which we will specify below, that Klöckner did not act with requisite frankness in these circumstances.

This was a joint venture between Klöckner, a multinational European corporation, and a developing country. The plant to be built was an example of imported modern technology and engineering. Cameroon had no experience in manufacturing fertilizer products. The factory was to be acquired with the Government's guarantee of payment; its output being of major importance for the country's agriculture, and agriculture being in turn the very foundation of Cameroon's economic ambitions. Cameroon counted on Klöckner to supply all that was necessary to ensure the success of the project. Klöckner had carried out the initial feasibility study. It had designed the plant and carried out the technical studies. Klöckner had undertaken to organize the long-term financing, over ten years, of the project. It built or bought from others all the machinery and all the material. It coordinated the work of suppliers and sub-contractors. It was to execute, operate, and manage the project, procure necessary raw materials, and organize the marketing of output. By accepting – and indeed seeking out – these responsibilities, Klöckner had taken on a serious obligation. Klöckner claimed to be capable of supplying all the knowhow, all the material, and all the management skills necessary to ensure the project's success, the Government's only role being to supply a site and to guarantee payment of the contract price.

In this operation, the Government trusted Klöckner. Klöckner expected that its conduct would be judged by high standards. It promised its partner, if not an unconditional guarantee of the factory's profitability at all times, at least very pronounced frankness and loyalty. Klöckner had a particularly strong obligation to keep Cameroon informed of any facts that might have a

[27] crucial influence upon the Government's decision to assume, and to continue assuming, the very onerous financial engagements upon which Klöckner now seeks to rely.

Klöckner failed to live up to these obligations. We do not hold that this failure was due to a fraudulent intent. But we conclude that Klöckner demonstrated less than a full measure of frankness, of candor, *vis-à-vis* its partner, and that what it did not disclose to its partner may have been decisive in the Government's decision whether or not to pursue the project. We thus hold that Klöckner did not respect its duty of confidence and loyalty *vis-à-vis* its partner in this joint venture. We base these conclusions on the following facts:

a) In pushing for the project in 1971, Klöckner submitted a voluminous technical and economic report. This study predicted that the project would be profitable (without subsidies). While the study was criticized during the hearings on the grounds that it was incompetent under professional standards, we do not hold that it was so intentionally false and likely to lead into error that the price established in the Contract should not be paid in 1983. This study did, however, reflect hypotheses as to the cost of raw materials – all of which had to be imported for the factory – and as to the price of final products, that were based on 1971 economic conditions. The economic prospects of the fertilizer industry changed radically in the following years. The explosion of the price of petroleum in 1973–74 led to price spirals on the raw-material market as well as on that for finished products. The result was that the price relationships between raw materials and finished products were fundamentally modified during the 1973–1976 period and this inevitably rendered the 1971 forecasts invalid.

b) Yet at no moment prior to the construction of the plant did Klöckner modify its original representation that the project would be profitable.

To the contrary, on 12 April 1973 Klöckner wrote to Mr Ntang, Chairman of the Board, to inform SOCAME of the fact that the Common Market governments had decided to restrict their financing of foreign projects such as this to seven-year terms rather than ten years as envisaged by the Supply Contract and the 1971 feasibility study. This was a matter of considerable legal significance. The Protocol of Agreement, in Article 6, and the Supply Contract, in Article 3(c), both provided that SOCAME would have a ten-year period in which to make the 8 last payments of the contract price. Thus, the fact that Klöckner did not provide financing with a 10 year term constituted a failure of a condition precedent. SOCAME could have declared the Contract to be at an end and to abandon the project with entirely minor penalties. The factory had not yet been constructed. To repay the cost of the plant over a 7-year period rather than a 10-year period constituted a significant increase of the venture's annual debt-service charge. In spite of that, Klöckner pushed Cameroon to go ahead with the project. Mr J. van de Weert informed Mr Ntang of the fact that there had been general price increases during the period following the signature of the Protocol of Agreement. He did not, however, indicate that this would make necessary an increase of the contractual price. Rather, his letter of 12 April 1973 stressed the fact that **[28]** any further delay would have the result of increasing the costs of the factory "if the Supply Contract does not enter into force within the shortest time possible." The only thing that was missing for the Contract to enter into force was SOCAME's acceptance of the new 7-year financing schedule. Klöckner therefore pushed SOCAME to accept the new 7-year financing immediately.

This, Klöckner said, would not affect the profitability of the factory, but meant only that "the management of this venture, which is our responsibility, must be more dynamic." In short, although the terms of financing the project were less favourable than had been anticipated initially, Klöckner affirmed, on the one hand, that this would not modify the original profitability studies and, on the other hand, warned the Government that if it did not accept the new conditions rapidly, it would have to face an increase in the cost of the factory. On this basis, and with the assurance that profitability would not be affected, SOCAME waived the possibility of halting the project and accepted 7-year financing.

In all this, Klöckner failed to make adequate efforts to deal frankly with its partner. Klöckner could have said that the economic circumstances had changed since the initial agreement. The conditions of financing had become tougher, and prices had changed. It is impossible to determine whether the Government would have decided to halt the project if Klöckner had revealed clearly and fully to the Government that the economic hypotheses of 1971, with respect to the relative prices of raw materials and finished products as well as to the definitive price of the factory, were no longer valid. But it is clear that Klöckner did nothing to propose an alternative to its partner; its letter of 12 April 1973 lacked frankness and honesty. We deem that this was not appropriate conduct for a party to a contract such as this.

c) A second occasion arose the following year: an occasion for Klöckner to make quite clear to the Government that the economic analysis of the factory in 1974 was not what it had seemed to be in 1971, and, in consequence, an occasion for Cameroon to abandon the project without great loss. On 27 and 29 March, Klöckner met in Amsterdam with its subcontractor, Kellogg Continental. No Cameroonian representative was present. The minutes of this meeting became known to the Government only recently. These minutes make clear that Klöckner knew it would end up invoking a letter dated 5 February 1972 signed by Klöckner and the Minister of Industrial and Commercial Development, which provided for a variable price clause. Klöckner had realized before March 1974 that economic circumstances had changed sufficiently radically to justify an increase of the cost of the factory. As we have remarked, on 12 April 1973 Klöckner had told SOCAME that it would have to increase the price "unless" SOCAME accepted the 7-year financing, and SOCAME quickly accepted on the assumption that thus no increase would be necessary. Now, a year later, Klöckner told Kellogg Continental that a price increase was inevitable, but Klöckner was not disposed to say as much to its partner, SOCAME. Klöckner:

[29]   alerted Kellogg Continental to the fact that the time was not yet ripe to ask the Cameroonian Government for the additional amount foreseen in the amendment. Kellogg Continental should not, in any event, ask for this money until a propitious moment. (Klöckner) will say when this is the case.

d) Three months later, on 12 June 1974, Kellogg Continental and Klöckner signed a protocol in which they agreed that they would request an increase in the project price, in conformity with the amendment. They recited that the price increase had become necessary due to the radical changes that had occurred in the international economy – the "additional costs caused by the oil crisis," as the protocol calls them. But they agreed that the time was not yet right to take up the matter with Klöckner's partner. According to this protocol, the request would be presented in December. (In fact, it was not communicated to SOCAME until September the following year.)

At this moment in time, the investment in the factory itself had not yet begun. The site was cleared and almost ready, but the large outlays for the acquisition and the erection of the installations were yet to come. This was the right time for Cameroon to reconsider the venture and to cut losses if this is what it wanted to do. A request by Klöckner for an increase in the cost of the factory, especially if it were justified (as was the case one year later) on the grounds of the "oil crisis," could well have forced Cameroon to rethink the whole project. SOCAME would have been particularly impressed if Klöckner had simultaneously submitted an overall reassessment of the economic analysis it had prepared in 1971 as to the profitability of the production of fertilizer in Cameroon from imported raw materials, whose costs had increased in such a dramatic fashion, and if it had told SOCAME that it was no longer clear that the factory would be profitable. But Klöckner did not do so. Klöckner remained silent. It thus allowed the construction of the factory to commence without any indication to its partner that an increase in the costs of the factory was in the offing, nor that the "oil crisis" had modified the costs and the economics of the project. The evidence before us does not explain the delay that occurred. On the basis of the facts of this case, we cannot conclude that Klöckner acted as a contractual partner should.

e) The file also includes a memorandum dated 14 October 1974 from Klöckner's headquarters to M von Einem in Douala, incorporating a new analysis of the profitability of the project. The results of this new study were very different from those of the original analysis of 1971. Even under the hypothesis of 100% utilization in the second year, the forecast was that the factory would not be able to produce dividends before 1979. These strikingly different results stemmed from the fact that the new study was based on costs of production that had been considerably readjusted – certain items to the extent of 250% – and also on new readjusted world prices for finished products. There was a handwritten note on the memorandum indicating that is should not be passed on to SNI, the Cameroonian governmental agency responsible for investment projects. It would be difficult to claim that this is the kind of frank and loyal conduct between partners that the law requires, **[30]** especially since the construction work had barely commenced at the end of 1974, and there was still time to avoid the heavy outlays required to erect the factory.

In fact, Klöckner did not present its request for an increase in the cost of the factory until 3 September 1975, almost one year and a half after Klöckner had acknowledged the need for an adjustment. And still, even at the end of 1975, Klöckner did not hesitate to affirm that the factory would be profitable. The request for a price increase was in effect presented with a new profitability forecast which, even after the price spirals on the markets for petroleum and fertilizer products in 1973 and 1974, concluded with the declaration to Cameroon that "the profitability study demonstrates that in spite of the increase in the original investment, the profitability of the factory is ensured".

These failures of disclosure by Klöckner are of a capital importance. We do not hold that these failures were intentional; nor do we conclude that Klöckner intended to deceive. But in each case, Klöckner's silence may have led Cameroon into error. Klöckner's lack of frankness may have caused SOCAME to proceed with the project at a point in time when, if it had been appropriately informed by its partner, it could have used its juridical prerogative of halting further investment even before erection of the factory. Surely, if in 1973 and in June 1974, and perhaps even in mid-1975, Klöckner had taken back its initial representations concerning the profitability of the factory to take account of the new realities of the international fertilizer market, Cameroon could have reconsidered and avoided the costly investment which everybody now agrees was unwise.

During the hearings, Klöckner suggested that the factory's problem was financial rather than technical. The factory's economic difficulties emerged to a large extent as a result of Klöckner's very failure of disclosure. Klöckner cannot now complain that the Government did not ensure the profitability of the factory in the face of the precise economic problems that Klöckner had recognized but had diligently avoided calling to the attention of the Government at a time when construction of the plant could have been stopped. In our opinion, this is not compatible with the obligations of a partner in an international joint venture of this importance.

B. *Acceptance of the Factory*

a) *Claimant's Allegations*

In the Request for Arbitration, Claimant affirms that the factory "was definitively accepted by Defendant" and attaches "four Certificates of Final Acceptances in Annex 5." In the Memorial, Claimant adds that "the factory was accepted finally and without reservation in 1976."

[31]   b) *Defendant's Allegations*

In its Counter-Memorial, Defendant maintains that:

under Article 10 of the Supply Contract, the production units were to be deemed accepted only when the guaranteed standards had been attained or when compensatory penalties had been paid. No one can affirm that these conditions were fulfilled, given the one-sided character of the procedures of acceptance.

The abusively indulgent acceptance procedure, by which Klöckner made itself judge of its own cause, creates a strong presumption that Klöckner did not meet its obligations.

After having called attention to the fact that the Certificates of Acceptance were signed on behalf of SOCAME by Mr Von Einem or Mr Petersen, two officers designated and sent out by Klöckner, the Defendant writes:

> Klöckner organized the acceptance of the factory to be effected not by a veritable representative of the Cameroonian party but by an expatriate technician seconded by Klöckner to SOCAME. This procedure is highly unusual in projects of this type, where the *bona fides* of the method of acceptance (and thus its binding nature *vis-à-vis* the purchaser) is generally ensured by every possible precaution.

Defendant recalls the remark by the British Sulphur Corporation (*a firm of consultants on fertilizer economics which prepared two reports submitted by Cameroon as annexes to its memorials* [translator's note]) that it was "uneasy about the notion that persons recruited or seconded by Klöckner or its subordinates would sign all certificates and confirmations of test runs."

Defendant adds that no acceptance procedure was effected in the presence of a Cameroonian representative in spite of Article 10(2) of the Supply Contract. As for the Partial Certificates of Reception invoked today by Klöckner, none is binding on Cameroon. A presumption should apply against a supplier who (having also the role of manager) puts itself in a position to avoid a bilateral acceptance procedure.

c) *Claimant's Reply*

In its Reply Memorial, Claimant indicates that the reception procedures:

> were memorialized in Protocols of Final Acceptance signed by representatives of both parties... To assist it in controlling the procedures of acceptance, SOCAME engaged a consultant, the Ferticonsult company of the Netherlands. Its representative, Mr Van der Ploeg, was present during the acceptance procedures and prepared two reports. The Protocols of Acceptance for each of the units, comforted by the reports of Ferticonsult, establish beyond cavil that the parameters defined in Annex 2 of the Contract were attained.

d) *The Agreement with Ferticonsult*   [32]

This agreement in English between SOCAME, represented by the General Manager Von Einem, and the Netherlands company Ferticonsult was signed on 4 August 1976 in Douala.

It begins with a "whereas clause" in which it is written:

> Whereas: in the contract (de livraison) under art. 10.2 SOCAME has to be represented permanently by a delegate during the entire period of the tests of guarantee of operation;

SOCAME desires to appoint for this purpose an independent technical consultant acceptable to both parties to the contract;

Both SOCAME and Klöckner have indicated their agreement to appoint said Ferticonsult as independent consultant;

The relevant dispositions of the agreement provide:

2.1. The consultants undertake to make the regular services of Mr Van der Ploeg available to perform the duties mentioned under this article.

2.2 The consultants may be required to be present at the performance test run or runs which may be held as set out in the contract to demonstrate that the different parts of the plant attain the capacities indicated in the specifications of the contract.

3.3 The consultants shall act as independent consultants and neither consultants nor their employees shall be deemed to be representatives of SOCAME and/or INA and/or Kellogg Continental.

e) *The Van der Ploeg Report of 28 August 1976*

In his report, Mr Van der Ploeg affirms that:

a survey was carried out from 6-8-1976 until 26-8-76 in the plant in Bonaberi. During this period the various units of the plant were operating under test-run conditions to verify the production and consumption figures guaranteed by the supplier in the Agreement between Klöckner and SOCAME of 5 February 1972. The results of these test-runs have been laid down in the annexes to the Protocol of Acceptance. Ferticonsult witnessed the above test-runs and checked the figures obtained during the test-runs against the guaranteed values and came to the following conclusion:

1. The performance of the sulphuric acid plant is in accordance with the stipulations of the Agreement. The guaranteed production figures were attained at the guaranteed consumption figures... Therefore, the conditions of the Agreement have been duly fulfilled upon which this unit is acceptable and has been accepted without restrictions.

Protocols of acceptance have been signed by parties concerned.

2. The performance of NPK unit is in accordance with the stipulations of the Agreement. A 72-hours test-run was made for NPK 15.5-12.25-12.25 (the formula chosen by SOCAME) during which all the guaranteed values were **[33]** verified. For two other formulas NPK 6.24.6 and NPK 20.10.10 capacity tests during 24 hours were made... It was further observed during the test run that on various places the steam-line was not properly insulated and various steam flanges were leaking. The latter points will be repaired by the supplier as part of the reservation list. Therefore, the conditions of the Agreement have been duly fulfilled upon which this unit is acceptable and is accepted without restrictions. Protocols of acceptance are signed by parties concerned.

3. The performance of the SSP-unit is in accordance with the stipulations of the Agreements. The guaranteed production capacity was attained at the

guaranteed consumption figures which are the most important figures for this unit. The figures for the quality of the SSP cannot be measured during the test-run, as a curing time of some weeks is part of the SSP process. Therefore, during a number of days the contents of moisture, free of acid and P_2O_5 must be analysed from samples taken from the curing pile.

This was done from August 12 till August 26; the results were well within the limits that can be expected for the phosphate rock used.

Therefore, the conditions of the Agreements have been duly fulfilled upon which this unit is acceptable and is accepted without restrictions. Protocols of acceptance have been signed by parties concerned.

4. Ammonium Sulphate Unit

During the initial runs of this unit a number of technical and technological problems were encountered which are of such a nature, that it can be said that this unit is not ready for test-run.

Main problems are corrosion in one of the reactors and vibrations in both reactors. Furthermore, various operational problems have occurred.

To remedy these shortcomings, a number of actions have to be taken. To this effect a letter of Agreement is signed between Kellogg-Continental and Klöckner-INA to the contents of which we agree (see copy).

After finalization of above measures a test-run can be agreed upon.

f) *Observations on the Van der Ploeg Report*

Defendant has questioned Mr Van der Ploeg's impartiality, noting that the same man was introduced by Klöckner to SOCAME's Board of Directors as Klöckner's technical adviser, and that he was present in this capacity at the Board meeting of 31 October 1978. Moreover, Defendant submitted documents in annex to its Rejoinder Memorial which show that before the signature of the contract with Ferticonsult it was Klöckner that advised "SOCAME with insistence to engage" Mr Van der Ploeg to supervise the guarantee test runs since "it states that difficult decisions may have to be made here on the acceptance or the refusal of the production results obtained." It also appears from the documents that Klöckner suggested to Mr Von Einem "that you forward the signed contract to Ferticonsult and that you name it SOCAME's representative in accordance with paragraph 1.5."

Defendant also submitted a letter from SOCAME's General Manager Mr Von Einem to Mr Van der Ploeg indicating that "SOCAME would be interested in obtaining, at its expense, your assistance during the operating test runs for its fertilizer factory. Klöckner-INA has been authorized by [34] SOCAME to negotiate the details with you on its behalf." One of the witnesses presented by Defendant observed that Mr Van der Ploeg had been requested to negotiate the conditions of his intervention directly with Klöckner and that "this is in contradiction with the essential condition of his expert evaluation: his independence *vis-à-vis* the supplier."

The Tribunal is not in a position to question or to rule on the independence or the impartiality of the consultant. His report does, however, deserve some comments on its content *per se.*

The report creates the impression that Mr Van der Ploeg personally "witnessed the above test-runs and checked the figures obtained during the test-runs against the guaranteed values" and also that "above test-runs" were those that "have been laid down in the annexes to the Protocols of acceptance."

But a simple reference to the dates on which the "test-runs laid down in the annexes" were carried out, and a comparison with the dates on which Mr Van der Ploeg was present in Douala (according to his report, from 6 August 1976 to 26 August 1976) show that this was not the case.

For example, the Certificate of Guarantee test-run and Final Acceptance of the Sulphuric Acid units shows that this test-run was carried out from 1800 hours on 11 July 1976 to 14 July 1976, when Mr Van der Ploeg was not there. This means that Mr Van der Ploeg simply accepted the Certificate of Acceptance dated 5 August, one day before his arrival, signed by Klöckner and by Mr Petersen for SOCAME. Klöckner acknowledged that "at the time of acceptance of the sulphuric acid unit which has already been accepted (sic), his presence would not be absolutely indispensable, Ferticonsult should however prepare a post facto certificate here." (*Citation to a document submitted by Cameroon.* [translator's note])

The same situation arose with respect to the NPK unit. The Van der Ploeg report gives the impression that in his presence "a 72 hour test-run was made for NPK 15.5.12.25.12.25 (the formula chosen by SOCAME) during which all the guaranteed values were verified."

But again the certificate signed by Mr Petersen for SOCAME demonstrates that the 72 hour guarantee test run required by the Supply Contract and its annexes was effected from 28 to 31 July 1976, that is to say before the arrival of Mr Van der Ploeg (p. 3 of the annex to the Certificate of Acceptance).

The only accepted production unit test runs at which Mr Van der Ploeg was present were those of the single super phosphate unit, which took place 8–11 August 1976. And according to the documents submitted, there were many shutdowns and difficulties during this test run: "the product is of poor quality, lumpy and quite sticky" (p. 6); "the plant running in bad condition" (p. 7); "a belt was clogged at the discharge and the entire belt conveyor system tupped [sic]" (p. 8); "another belt was going overside during the shift" (p. 9); "a conveyor stopped due to electric failure" (p. 14); "the bucket elevator stopped" (p. 15); "the payloader lifting system is out of order" (p. 18) and "was not working" (p. 19).

[35] This acceptance was thus accompanied by a rather significant "protocol of reservations," as Klöckner promised to deliver "a replacement belt for belt conveyor", "cleaning devices for belt conveyors," "a heating element for filter," and to effect, among other things, the following modifications or repairs: "repair of roof over grinding mill," "modification on inlet chute bucker elevator," "improvement of ventilation on runway belt conveyor,"

"installation of belt conveyor," "improvement on spillage problems on belt conveyors," etc. It was finally set forth that "Klöckner-INA will demonstrate the proper functioning of the automatic control equipment after repair and/ or replacement of the relevant equipment items."

In the Rejoinder Memorial it is affirmed that "Klöckner never supplied the parts identified at paragraphs 1.1.1 and 1.1.3 of the reservations." This observation was never answered.

g) *Significance of the Preceding Observations*

The absence of Mr Van der Ploeg during the test runs on which the acceptance of the sulphuric acid and NPK production units was based has important consequences with respect to the contractual stipulations. In effect, Article 10 of the Supply Contract concerning the "operating guarantee test runs" set forth in paragraph 10.2 that:

> Klöckner shall advise the Government in writing of the date fixed for the first sequence of test runs at least 3 days in advance:... the Government and Klöckner shall sign a joint protocol memorializing the results of said test runs. It is well understood that the Government shall be permanently represented by its Delegate during all of these test runs... Klöckner shall ask the Government to have its Delegate present 10 days before the date set for the commencement of startup.

Paragraph 10.5 adds: "If the Government does not ensure that it is represented during the test runs, Klöckner shall note the results obtained in a Protocol in the presence of a bailiff (*huissier* [translator's note])"

Even if one should in these clauses read "SOCAME" every time the Contract speaks of the "Government", it is clear that the contractual requirements were not respected, at least with respect to the sulphuric acid and NPK units. According to the contract with Ferticonsult, SOCAME had designated Mr Van der Ploeg as its representative in conformity with Article 10.2 of the Contract. This representative was to be present permanently; during all of these test runs. Moreover, the Government's (SOCAME's) representative and Klöckner were to sign "a joint protocol memorializing the results of said test runs." It appears from the documents submitted, and it has been admitted by Claimant, that Mr Van der Ploeg was not present when the test runs of the sulphuric acid and NPK units were carried out, and that he signed no Certificates of Acceptance. These are not purely technical observations, because on the dates when the test runs were carried out, there were difficulties, electrical and mechanical failures, and shutdowns for adjustments. This is the reason why "a protocol of reservations" was signed **[36]** on 12 August by Klöckner and Kellogg Continental concerning important defects in the NPK unit. One of these defects, concerning the weighting scale, was not repaired and was, according to a letter dated 27 October 1977, a constant cause of shutdowns.

Furthermore, if the different production units were operating well and could attain sustained production at the capacity guaranteed by the Contract after the startup of the plant, one has the right to ask why the presence of Mr Van der Ploeg between 5 and 26 August 1976, while he was waiting out the "curing time" for the SSP process, was not used to repeat the test runs of the two other units, instead of having him endorse *post facto* test runs carried out in his absence.

One must thus conclude that the procedures of acceptance for the sulphuric acid and NPK units, and even that for the SSP unit (certificate not signed by Mr Van der Ploeg) were not carried out in accordance with the provisions of the Supply Contract.

h) *The Ammonium Sulphate Unit*

As already noted, in August 1976 this production unit was rejected and the following letter was signed between the subcontractor Kellogg Continental and Klöckner, approved by Mr Van der Ploeg as well:

> The AS Unit cannot be accepted by Klöckner-INA/SOCAME due to various failures. SOCAME however welcomes the possibility to produce AS in limited quantities. Therefore the responsibility for the Unit will be split between KC and SOCAME as from 26/8/76 until further notice. SOCAME will be responsible for the consequences of normal wear and tear and provide the usual maintenance. KC will remain responsible for all other consequences especially for those of the failures already known and will check the operation of SOCAME and be continuously available for consultation.

It must be noted that this type of agreement was not provided for in the Supply Contract.

i) *Report of the Institute for Building Material and Building Structures (TNO/IBBC) (October 1976)*

This Institute prepared a report on "Investigations on the vibrational behavior of the two saturators in the SOCAME fertilizer plant," submitted by Defendant. This report concerns the ammonium sulphate unit.

In its report, the Institute describes the problem as follows:

> Essential in this process are the reaction vessels-saturators. After starting up of the plants these vessels, containing a boiling liquid, showed a vibration, sometimes becoming very heavy. After some time it was established that some of the welds between vertical supports and doubling plates, fig. 2, were partly **[37]** cracked, starting from the lower side. These welds were repaired and the support stiffening as mentioned in 3.3 were constructed [sic]. Since this stiffening did not improve the situation TNO/IBBC was asked to investigate the matter.

The Institute, after observing that the measured stress ranges quite frequently exceed the upper bound limit of 200 Kfg/cm² the maximum value measured reaching 1250 Kfg/cm², concluded that the present situation especially with relation to the vessels is unsafe as far as the influence of fatigue can be established with the available knowledge and recommended that certain improvements should be carried in order to reduce the stress fluctuations [sic].

... Kellogg Continental BV required TNN/IBBC to inspect visually the status of the steel structure and also to measure the wall thickness of saturator DB since locally corrosion on the inside has been found.

... the corrosion protection (of the steel structure) is in a bad to very bad shape, specially in the ammonium sulphate part of the plant. In our opinion the present situation is unacceptable.

... on the inside of saturator DB a corroded area had been detected below the SA inlet.

j) *Acceptance of the Ammonium Sulphate Unit*

On 22 December 1976, Mr Van der Ploeg visited Douala a second time and presented the following report "on the test-run of the Ammonium Sulphate Unit."

From 16th till 19th Dec. 1976, a test-run was held witnessed by us – after the majority of the measures to overcome the shortcomings discovered in August have been executed. The reason for the corrosion has been discovered and remedied. The cause for the vibration of the reactors lies apparently in their boiling pattern, which could as yet not be changed. The effect of the vibration on the reactors has been reduced considerably by stiffening of shells and supports. Various other parts of the unit have been improved or modified. For details about the various actions taken see separate Report. The performance of the AS unit is in accordance with the stipulations of the Agreement. The guaranteed production capacity was attained at the guaranteed consumption figures. Therefore, the conditions of the agreement have been duly fulfilled and a protocol of acceptance has been signed. Some modifications still outstanding are laid down in the list of reservations as Annex II which forms an integral part of the protocol.

Once again, the Certificate of Acceptance was not signed by SOCAME's representative, Mr Van der Ploeg.

Defendant has submitted documents which would lead to the conclusion that the acceptance procedures were not satisfactory, and the foreman noted that "the production figures must be considered with some scepticism" because, in his opinion, the person who conducted the tests "did not care about how the plant runs but only wants to get the highest production possible". According to Annex 53, "the drier was not working satisfactorily," "the crystals and the outlet were not always dry," "the [38] instrument to measure the vibrations of the saturators was useless as Kellogg people took the precaution to make the plant run at low concentration, where the vibrations are the smallest." It is also noted that "we must pump the water to the NH3 evaporator to make the temperature increase," which would create personnel problems once the plant was in operation.

There was a protocol of reservations. In this protocol, Klöckner requests SOCAME to carry out, among others, the following modifications and reparations:

> a proper vibrating conveyor is to be installed for the cyclone dust into the elevator; occasionally the product is too wet as a consequence of uneven flow of the crystals either or the too low capacity of the drier [sic]; the type of painting of the structural steel is not adequate, especially not for the corrosive conditions in the AS plant; the damages to the sewer system resulting from AS leakage will be repaired; various leaking pipes will be repaired for which materials will be provided; various pipes, valves and instruments will be supported more rigidly; fumes from B-reactor must be stopped; the damaged floor plates around the reactors will be restored; supply and modifications on the corroded area of reactor B.

It is also provided that "the materials and labour costs for the execution of these modifications and repairs as listed above amounts to DM 50,000 which amount will be paid by Klöckner-INA within one month".

Finally, reference is made to "a second visit of TNO people to be arranged before the 1st March 1977, for additional measurements on the repaired reactors. The recommendations of TNO will be discussed between both parties and finally settled".

Defendant affirms in its Rejoinder Memorial that "this visit never took place." Claimant has not responded to this comment and there is no document in the file indicating that this second visit took place.

This kind of acceptance procedure with such reservations and conditions was neither provided for nor envisaged in the Supply Contract.

k) *Discussions in Meetings of the Board of Directors*

The questions raised by the procedures of acceptance of the various production units were discussed during the meeting of SOCAME's Board of Directors on 12 January 1977. The minutes of this meeting state that:

> with respect to technical difficulties having appeared during the weeks immediately following startup, the Chairman of the Board (who represented Cameroon as minority shareholder) inquired whether these technical difficulties had finally been dealt with and whether the current functioning of the plant could be considered to be in conformity with the norms prescribed in the Supply Contract.
>
> ... The General Manager answered him that acceptance both with respect to the plant (acceptance of mechanical completion) and the production process (guarantee test runs) had taken place and were entirely satisfactory as compared with the stated criteria of the Supply Contract. The documents related thereto were prepared and signed jointly by Klöckner and by SOCAME.

[39]

We have seen that this answer was not entirely exact.

At the express request of the Chairman of the Board, who asked if the Government had been fully associated with the formalities of acceptance of the factory,... (the General Manager answered) the Government was represented in this procedure by Mr Moudio, director of Mining and Energy, acting by authorization, from SNI (Société Nationale d'Investissement, the Cameroonian Government's holding company and shareholder of SOCAME).

Claimant has submitted a letter from Mr Moudio dated 7 October 1976 concerning "the procedure of acceptance of the SOCAME factory."
In this letter, Mr Moudio makes the following observations:

... apparently in agreement with SNI, SOCAME asked me to be present during the procedures of technical acceptance of the various production units of the fertilizer factory.
My visit took place on 24 September 1976, from 9.00 hours to 17.30 hours... The transfer of title, after technical control of each production unit, had already been carried out between the builders and the operator, and the corresponding Protocols duly signed by all the parties. My task was for this reason reduced to taking note, from the Protocols, of the essential observations and reservations expressed by SOCAME on the occasion of each acceptance procedure, and to check the various relevant units of the factory in their current state.
... on each occasion, a Protocol was signed comporting the appropriate reservations, either with respect to operating anomalies in some of the machinery or with respect to defects of certain components of the production units.
... repairing and replacing machinery and defective components identified during the acceptance procedure ... remain the obligation of the companies responsible for erecting the factory...
Thus, three of the four units of the factory have proved satisfactory and now operate normally.
Only the ammonium sulphate unit is a troubling failure, as currently its output does not exceed 25% of its optimal capacity. And in these circumstances, SOCAME had to refuse acceptance of this part of the factory, questioning not only its functioning, but also the conformity of certain of its components with the specifications of the ... supply contract.
... No one on the Cameroonian side can pronounce himself with certitude as to the exact condition of the industrial material as delivered and erected, nor to their quality, their resistance, and their durability. It is likewise difficult to say, given the absence of data for comparison, that the factory defined in the contracts in reality corresponds to the factory that has been built.

It is clear from the introduction of Mr Moudio's report that his visit took place at a date on which no operating test run was carried out. His role was limited to studying the reports and protocols in existence on 24 September [40] 1976. In consequence, this visit may not be considered to constitute active participation by the Cameroonian Government in the contractual procedure of acceptance of the factory, nor as any correction whatsoever of the failures to follow the contract already noted with respect to the involvement of Mr Van der Ploeg.

C. The Functioning of the Factory

After startup, the factory's output suffered from significant shortfalls.

Defendant has presented statistical studies showing that the plant's total output during the 18 months of production attained with difficulty a level of less than 30% of the promised total capacity.

Even without taking into consideration these statistics, a great inadequacy was revealed in reports to SOCAME's Board of Directors, and in Minutes of the Board, submitted by Klöckner.

a) The Board Meeting of 11 June 1977

In the meeting of the Board held on 11 June 1977, General Manager Von Einem declared that "at the present time, orders from SOCAME's customers exceed its capacity to perform. There is a production problem which should be solved in the coming months." Administrative Director Ekani specified "that production of ammonium sulphate has recommenced, as well as that of complex fertilizer. Stocks are at the lowest level as a result of a temporary shutdown of the plant." Chairman Nyassa observed that with effort "the plant could approach its production capacity." He thus recommended "that shutdowns of the factory be avoided in order to improve production and allow the loan to be repaid."

During this meeting, it is noted that "losses as of 30 June 1977 are estimated at CFA francs 940 million. According to the General Manager, these losses are to be explained by production shortfalls and by low market prices, these two factors having approximately equal impact."

The written report of the General Manager, presented at the same meeting, begins as follows:

> whether one considers sales, production, or the financial picture, the overall situation of the Company seems worrisome for several reasons. While the "Sales" and "Production" departments necessarily suffer from the permanent impecuniosity of our finances, one should however note that certain difficulties with respect to each of these sectors, which had merely been perceived in the beginning of the year, have become amplified to such a degree that they now constitute veritable bottlenecks.
>
> As of 31 May 1977, that is to say after eleven months of activity we have had firm orders for 66,130 tons of all types of products ... during the same period, we have delivered 18,112 tons of our products.

This means that the factory produced less than 20% of the output **[41]**
promised for the first year, and thus far less than the contractually
guaranteed capacity of production.

Under the heading "Production," the general Manager's report continues
as follows:

> During the first five months of 1977, we recorded a level of production of 7,343
> tons of fertilizer products and 2,825 tons of sulphuric acid. Given the quantities
> ordered by customers as well as the plant's capacity, this is not very much, in
> any event not more than 30% of what would have been a normal level of
> production during the same period. the reasons for this state of things are
> several: our storage capacity, supplies of raw materials, and spare parts. We
> have had to improvise a system for storing finished products in the open air,
> with all attendant risks in a climate such as that of Douala. This problem
> remains unsolved and will become extremely pressing the day the plant
> produces at full capacity. As for spare parts, the construction of an operational
> warehouse of sufficient size continues at the same time as we put into effect a
> system for planning, managing, and controlling our stocks of spare parts, so as
> to protect us from long shutdowns due to an absence of parts.

This report is accompanied by a production table covering January to May
1977 which shows, for example, that the sulphuric acid unit had functioned
only two months of the five analysed, and the single superphosphate unit
only one month.

b) *Board Meeting of 21 July 1977*

During the meeting of the Board of 21 July 1977, the General Manager, at
the request of the Chairman "indicates that sales have reached 30,000 tons,
of which 22,197 tons come from SOCAME's own production." Intervening in
the discussions, the Chairman observed that "output has reached one-third
of the capacity of the plant."

Dr Remy, Klöckner's representative on the Board, proposed "that a
Committee of Experts, including representatives of Klöckner, SNI, and even
the Government, be constituted to seek medium-term and long-term
solutions. This Committee's proposed measures would be examined at the
next meeting of the Board on 30 September 1977."

c) *Report of the Study Committee*

The report of the Study Committee is annexed to the Minutes of the
meeting of 30 September 1977 and it contains conclusive information of a
comprehensive character as to the plant's production shortfalls.

The report begins by indicating that the first of the important problems is
the "insufficiency of the present rate of utilization of the capacity of the
plant, which results in a cost of production (ex-factory) which remains high
when compared to current market prices." The report proposes with respect

[42] to production "to use all of the production units in an optimal manner" and to "carry out necessary adjustments and restructuring of the production units with a view to improving their output."

The report summarizes the situation with respect to production as follows:

> Since startup of the plant in 1976, SOCAME has produced: 12,087 tons of sulphuric acid as compared to a capacity of 60,000 tons; 12,480 tons of ammonium sulphate as compared to a capacity of 40,000 tons; 1,643 tons of single superphosphate as compared to a capacity of 20,000 tons; 11,491 tons of NPK as compared to a capacity of 27,000 tons.
>
> During the past year, there have been many problems related to the startup of an industrial complex of the size of SOCAME, but also related to overall structures:
>
> ... the factory has frequently been shut down for the following principal reasons: mechanical breakdowns, inexperience of the work force, lack of spare parts, inability to maintain stocks of raw materials, congestion of the storage areas for final products.
>
> ... the storage areas for raw materials, intermediary and final products, and auxiliary installations (utilities) have been shown to be inadequate for current operating conditions: a slower circulation of raw materials and finished products, and an imperfect scheduling of production, sales, distribution, and supplies.

The report also notes "the disequilibrium between the financial structure of the balance sheet and the continual lack of funds, with its consequences with respect to supplies and production."

It is interesting to note the recommendations of the Study Committee, because they reveal some of the causes of the production shortfalls.

The recommendations related to "output levels and the transformations and adaptations that appear necessary for a better functioning of the four production units":

1. Sulphuric acid unit
1.1. Current situation: Daily capacity of 180 t/day. In 1976/77, this unit produced only 20% of its capacity. Given the fact that the unit still does not function continuously at 80%, it does not yet produce enough steam to drive the plant, requiring recourse to an auxiliary heating system which currently consumes fuel at a monthly cost of approximately 10 million CFA francs.
1.2. Recommendations: Operate the sulphuric acid unit continuously at 80% of capacity. To do so, it is necessary to dispose of sufficient storage capacity. Taking into account the consumption of sulphuric acid by the ammonium sulphate unit, two storage tanks do not suffice to avoid numerous shutdowns of the sulphuric acid unit, which explains the need for a third storage tank which, by increasing the storage capacity, would diminish the frequency of shutdowns...

2. Ammonium sulphate unit
2.1. Current situation: Daily capacity of 150 t/day. 1976–77 production at 25% of its capacity.

2.2. Recommendations: Increase output to a high level in order to utilize a   **[43]**
maximum of sulphuric acid.

3. Single superphosphate unit (SSP)
3.1. Current situation: Daily capacity of 60 t/day. This unit had an output of
only 8% of its capacity.
   3.2. Recommendations: a) increase output of this unit to a high level; b)
produce large quantities of complex fertilizer products, which require much
SSP.

4. NPK unit
4.1. Current situation: Daily capacity of 80 t/day. 1976–77 production at 42%
of its capacity. In the present operating conditions of the factory, the NPK unit
must be stopped each time the sulphuric acid unit is to be started up... There
are moreover a rather high number of mechanical breakdowns.
4.2. Recommendations: a) Immediately purchase a ventilator to coordinate
the operation of the NPK unit with the startup of the sulphuric acid unit...
...
c) Continue the efforts to adapt and simplify the equipment in order to reduce
the number of breakdowns.
d) Improve personnel supervision in the NPK unit and study the effects of a
performance bonus to increase the output of this production unit.

5. Organization of production
These technical problems are coupled with other problems relating to storage,
supplies, and the administration of personnel.
5.1. Storage. SOCAME has an acute problem of storage of raw materials and
finished products, as well as of intermediary products and spare parts.
5.2. Recommendations: a) An initial measure envisaged would be the use of
SSP purification tanks for raw materials, adding an additional simple tank
beside the SSP unit. b) Increase the storage areas by immediately requesting
MAGZI (*the State authority for industrial zones* [translator's note]) to reserve a
lot of approximately 2000 m² beside the current site of SOCAME. c) Ensure
regular shipments of final products... d) Increase the spare parts warehouse.
5.3. Supplies
a) Raw materials. There have been numerous production shutdowns due to a
lack of raw materials. Even though these shutdowns were essentially caused by
a lack of funds, there must be a better coordination between the commercial,
production, and service departments.
b) Spare parts. It is necessary to put in place a system that permits planning for
the replacement of parts in order to avoid serious production shutdowns.
Moreover, the spare parts warehouse should be better organized and
supervised in order to avoid losses of and damage to stored parts.
5.4. Personnel administration. The Committee notes that the number and the
costs of personnel are very high. Personnel costs currently represents 34% of
fixed costs.

d) *Discussion of the Report in the Board Meeting of 30 September 1977*

The recommendation to make the sulphuric acid unit function at 80% was
examined first, and it was noted that "this measure is aimed especially at

[44] reducing the rather frequent number of breakdowns and to increase the onstream time of this unit." Mr Ishani, the representative of SICA, one of the Klöckner's European partners, raised "the problem of the utilization of the surplus production that will result." Mr Von Einem, the General Manager, answered that "we must indeed look for a market for an additional 20,000 tons of sulphuric acid; exports to the neighbouring countries are possible." In conclusion, "the Board decides to have a study made of the purchase of this third tank and ask the General Manager to explore export markets for sales of surplus production, in particular Congo, Gabon, Nigeria, Zaire, and Chad."

As for the recommendation to try to adapt and simplify the equipment in order to reduce the number of breakdowns, the Chairman noted that "the problem of breakdowns is mentioned throughout the Report and raises the question whether and how these breakdowns can be avoided." The General Manager answered that "the frequency of breakdowns is caused especially by shortages of spare parts and raw materials due to a lack of funds and thus a lack of bank credit."

Dr Remy remarked that:

> ... apart from the questions of the availability of funds and the maintenance of stocks of spare parts, there is a problem of personnel and of organization. Until now, Mr Petersen, whose area is that of production, has dealt with this problem under the terms of a contract signed with Klöckner. Klöckner has also sent Mr Mula to be an on-site adviser for the organization of the stocks of spare parts. (I) propose that the Board appoint Mr Mula Technical Director, and to appoint Mr Petersen, who has a wider vision of things, Director of Production.

Finally, it was agreed that a decision with respect to this proposal would be made at the January 1978 Board meeting, but it was recalled that Klöckner had seconded Mr Mula to SOCAME in order to study the problems of maintenance and operations. Ultimately, "all the recommendations of the committee with respect to the organization of production were adopted by the Board. Mr Mula, the proposed Technical Director, will begin to examine these recommendations closely."

D. *The Shutdown of the Factory in December 1977*

a) *Reports Submitted to the Board Meeting of 6 January 1978*

The first of the documents and reports submitted to the meeting of the Board of Directors on 6 January 1978 was a summary of a meeting chaired by the General Manager with the participation of Messrs Mula, Von Dietze, Goutier, Simen, and Ekani Nkodo, on the subject of SOCAME's situation as of 15 December 1977. The first sentence of this summary is: "The detailed examination of the situation has led the Steering Committee to decide to shut down totally production in the factory as of 23 December 1977."

After announcing the intent to recommence production on 1 March 1978, **[45]** the report adds:

> During this period, the following steps will be taken: repairs of the production units, replenishment of stocks of raw materials, and the purchase final products intended to make up for production shortfalls [sic]; finally, customers will continue to be supplied normally.

Next were examined the reparations necessary "with a view to repairing all the units," involving the import of spare parts at a total cost of approximately CFA francs 400 million.

The report on corporate activities during 1977/78 presented by the General Manager to the Board of Directors and to the General Assembly bears the date of 21 December 1977. It begins as follows:

> This Report is addressed to the Board of Directors and to the General Assembly at a time when the financial structure and the market situation of the Company demands that fundamental decisions of principle be made.

The Report notes an improvement of the factory's output, since

> ... we have supplied 25,398 tons of all types of fertilizer products during the 6 first months of the current accounting year, as against 29,664 tons during the preceding year.

But, it is added:

> ... we have been forced to put an end to our sales campaign on 15 November and to halt sales to all customers without exception, given sales prices which do not ensure profitability.

This Report refers to the purchase and warehousing of spare parts and notes that "most of the orders are made via Klöckner or directly in accordance with the instructions of the person initiating the orders. Klöckner role is that of an agent and Klöckner is paid 15% to 20% of the price of the order." It is also stated that: "There is practically no forecasting for purchases. Given the shortages of stocks at the factory, when our personnel require parts they demand that unscheduled purchases be made as the need arises, threatening shutdown of the factory. And then, there is a scramble to get to the Supply Department."

Under the heading "Situation as of 5 January 1978," the General Manager Writes:

> Production in the factory was in essence stopped on 23 December 1977. This situation is the direct consequence of several facts that should be listed:
> 1st, the Company's lack of funds, resulting in
> 2nd, irregular supplies of spare parts, resulting in
> 3rd, rapid deterioration of the mechanical state of the installations,

[46]   4th, the need for a long shutdown for reparations,
5th, heavy indebtedness to the bank and main suppliers, with the result of
6th, making it almost impossible to purchase raw materials.
The production shutdown itself has the following immediate consequences:
1st, inability to meet a significant portion of customers' orders,
2nd, layoff of part of the personnel, and
3rd, inability to pay the continuing fixed costs.

The General Manager concludes this summary of the situation as of 5 January 1978 by stating that:

> ... the problem is thus whether or not the factory should be started up again. If it is to be started up, it would be indispensable to establish a salvage program like the one proposed herewith. If the factory were to be shut down definitively, a certain number of measures should be taken in order to dissolve SOCAME and to liquidate its assets.

In the programme for curtailing corporate activity, it is noted that there is a technical problem of "cleaning and protecting the installations," and, to this effect, despite the layoff of personnel, it is necessary to keep a "maintenance team."
Finally, the report of the statutory auditors of 27 December 1977 contains the following passage:

> We note a large disproportion between the amount of expenses incurred and the volume of corporate activity. Even if we allow for the fact that the factory operated at approximately 22% of its normal capacity, the amount of expenses is so high that even at full capacity your company will hardly attain its profitability threshold.

b) *The Board Meeting of 6 January 1978*

The General Manager Von Einem summarized the documents presented and stated that to recommence operations, CFA francs 2,000 million would be required.
Chairman Nyassa then stated that:

> It is clear that the situation is extremely serious, but for the last year our discussions have been futile... In January 1977, an initial set of measures were recommended, and in April 1977, a Chairman's report was submitted to the Board comporting a number of measures, some of which to be taken by the Shareholders. They did nothing ... Do the Board members want the Company's activities to be continued or not?

The Board member representing the majority shareholder, Dr Remy, stated he:

wished to make some remarks concerning the capital increase and the problem **[47]** of mutual confidence. Klöckner does not accept that the problem of the capital increase be tied to that of confidence in the venture. We are confident that SOCAME can be profitable, subject to certain reservations that we have explained to the Cameroonian partner, in particular at Duisburg. Klöckner does not accept that its refusal of the capital increase be taken as proof of our lack of confidence. As for the capital increase itself, Klöckner's means are limited with respect to investments, as the Group's situation is difficult worldwide. We have already stated that we are prepared to become the minority shareholder; until now the Cameroonian partner has always refused it. We should try to find solutions without resorting to an overly large capital increase because we cannot contribute 51% of an increase on the order of 1,3000 million CFA francs.

Chairman Nyassa declared that he:

had noted that everyone is prepared to accept the measures recommended by the Board, but this positive attitude disappears when the subject arises of injecting new funds into the Company. It was the technically competent partner who prepared all the studies that preceded the creation of the Company, and who asked for and obtained the roles of manager and majority shareholder until the loans were repaid. Moreover, this partner also turns out to be the supplier of the factory. It is inappropriate at the very time when difficulties have arisen to propose to the Cameroonian partner that it assume the position of majority shareholder. If the company were profitable, would Klöckner and SICA accept to give up their majority position? Faced with this attitude, it is justified to conclude that what Klöckner was interested in was only the sale of material.

... the Government proposes to assist SOCAME by granting a significant loan at an interest rate and with a repayment schedule that are particularly favorable. However, the shareholders should increase the Company's capital from 2,500 to 3,500 million CFA francs, which would represent fresh funds of 1,300 million CFA francs, since capital contributions have only been effected up to the amount of 2,200 million CFA francs.

Mr Remy declared that "Klöckner cannot meet the demand for a capital increase of such an amount."

Mr Nyassa called attention to the fact that "as for the Government, the repayment of the loan for the purchase of the factory remains linked to the satisfactory functioning of the plant and to the respect for its undertakings by the 'technical partner', which supplied the factory".

Mr Remy requested "that it be noted in the Minutes that SOCAME's activities are halted because Klöckner/SICA declares itself unable to contribute 51% of the recommended capital increase."

c) *Documents Submitted at the Board Meeting of 16 February 1978*

In a document on "the Company's situation," under the heading "Finances," the following sentences may be cited: "It will subsequently be

[48] necessary to repair the factory, which is badly corroded. The amount of 400 million CFA francs, envisaged for this purpose four months ago, will likely be insufficient." Under the heading "Technical Department," the following is set forth:

> While the overall situation of the factory has hardly evolved over the past two months, the state of the equipment, on the other hand, is becoming increasingly worrisome. Accelerated very likely by the rain and humidity, corrosion has set in at such a rate that it will be necessary, in due time, to clean all metal equipment by sand blasting.
>
> All of the maintenance personnel having been present since April, we will try as best as possible to halt the corrosion process, but it is certain that if the material and the spare parts necessary for maintenance are not available in the near future, the overdue repairs of the installations would require expenditures of such magnitude that one might as well scrap them.

d) *Board Meeting of 16 February 1978*

At this meeting there was discussion of a telex sent by the Cameroonian Government to Klöckner on 26 January 1978, in which the Government's conditions for the improvement of SOCAME's situation were confirmed as follows:

> 1. Capital increase of 1000 million CFA francs of which at least 500 million to be subscribed by Klöckner/INA and SICA.
> 2. Agreement to control SOCAME's fertilizer imports.
> 3. Agreement to reschedule payments to SOCAME for fertilizer product by Fonader (*the Cameroonian public institute for rural development* [translator's note])
> 4. Agreement to restructure SOCAME's management.
> 5. Agreement for long-term loan of 1500 million CFA francs to SOCAME at rate of 5%, repayable over 15 years with initial moratorium of 5 years. Government to contact German Government for loan of same amount to be extended to SOCAME by KFW.
>
> 6. Agreement for 5% annual increase of prices as proposed by Technical Committee.
> In event of acceptance of subscription of capital increase of 5000 million by Klöckner-INA and SICA, all above conditions would be accomplished before 1 March 1978.
> Kindly advise whether accepted.
> Minister of the Economy and Planning (signed: Youssoufa Daouda).

Mr Remy acknowledged:

> ... that the Government's telex indeed expresses its will to save the Company and that Klöckner ... has decided to contribute 400 million CFA francs under certain conditions to be discussed among shareholders. But as the Government demands that Klöckner and SICA subscribe in the amount of 500

million, they are ready to consolidate the 100 million loan on current account **[49]**
as a capital increase.

The Chairman pointed out that:

according to the Government, it is indeed 1,000 million CFA francs that are
required by way of capital increase, in view of the indebtedness of the
Company. To consolidate the shareholder loan – which for that matter has
already been spent – is likely to reduce to 800 million CFA francs the real
capital increase in spite of the fact that the increase is intended precisely to give
the Company 1000 million in fresh funds in order to allow it to pay back a
significant portion of debts owed as of today, which amount to almost 1200
million CFA francs. In so doing, the Company would utilize the Government
loan to order the raw materials and the spare parts required for a production
schedule of at least six months and also to be able to meet the large payments
(notes for the price of the factory) due in October 1978.

Mr Remy stated that:

on the basis of the Technical Committee's report, Klöckner's Board of
Directors has met and, not without difficulty, accepted under certain
conditions to contribute to the capital increase to the extent of 400 million
CFA francs. To ask it today to increase this amount to 500 million would seem
unacceptable. Moreover, the telex which was sent to Klöckner-INA and SICA
did not bear a signature name, although it came from the Ministry of the
Economy and Planning.

The Chairman recalled that:

the Government has made a considerable effort in granting a special loan at
particularly favorable conditions. It is now up to the shareholders to show that
they are disposed to continue to support the Company ... it is in the interest of
the shareholders and of the Company to accept the Government's proposal,
since it is the first time that assistance to such an extent and with such benefits is
accorded by the Government to a private company.

The Minutes end as follows:

a long and pointed discussion ensues on the question of the capital increase,
following which the Board suspends deliberation at 1130 hours in order for
Messrs Remy and Ishani to meet with the Minister of the Economy and
Planning to obtain the Government's agreement to the 400 million CFA franc
level of Klöckner and SICA's contribution to the capital increase. The Board
was to reconvene after this meeting with the Minister. As it did not take place,
Messrs Remy and Ishani immediately departed for Europe. The Board was
thus unable to reconvene and the meeting was broken up without any decisions
by the Board on the issues of the capital increase.

[50]   e) *Board Meeting of 8 April 1978*

At this meeting, the General Manager explained that:

> The situation of the Company is practically unchanged since the last meeting of the Board. Production has been halted since December 1977 ... On the technical side, the state of equipment is becoming an increasingly troubling subject and its corrosion is accelerating. Nothing has been done to remedy this, given the lack of funds. Minor maintenance work has, however, been carried out, such as repairs to the roof of the main building.

The Chairman "stresses particularly the seriousness of the continued corrosion; the expenditures required for repairs will not be known until operations recommence."

Dr Remy intervened to call attention to the fact that:

> one of the most important measures is in (my) view to obtain an import monopoly for SOCAME to try to cover the fixed costs that continue to increase and presently amount to 90 million CFA francs without any corresponding source of revenue ... as for Klöckner and SICA, the private shareholders, the 400 million CFA francs proposed for the capital increase are the last limits of their resources ... Continuation of operations is possible, because the Cameroonian demand for fertilizer products is high and the prices now accepted by the Government would make the Company profitable.

Finally, the Board decided to adopt the measures proposed by the Government:

> These measures will be carried out with respect to the capital increase, as follows:
> 1st   600 million CFA francs will be subscribed and paid in with fresh funds.
> 2nd   500 million CFA francs will be subscribed by Klöckner and SICA, of which 400 million shall represent fresh funds and 100 million the consolidation into capital of the shareholder's current-account loan already made.

Dr Remy "informed the Board of Mr Von Einem's resignation as General Manager" and proposed that "given the decisions made as to the change of majority shareholders, the post of General Manager should be filled by Cameroon. Klöckner of course remains bound by its obligations under the Management Contract."

E. *The State of the Plant After the Shutdown*

a) *Board Meeting of 10 July 1978*

At the meeting of 10 July 1978, a programme for production startup was presented in which it is stated that:

The sulphuric acid and ammonium sulphate plants may be restarted about two **[51]** months after the delivery and installation of machinery ... The NPK unit requires a longer period for repairs since much of the equipment is unusable because it is irreparable, and we anticipate it will take eight months to get parts. When the NPK unit starts up, it will be only for NPK mixtures that do not require a urea additive. All formulas calling for a urea additive will require a great modification of the production process. The SPP plant may be started up as soon as the spare parts arrive. They have been ordered and are under way. The construction of the intermediary SPP products storage lot behind the manufacturing building will take about four weeks after concluding a contract with a local builder.

A memorandum was also presented concerning SOCAME's situation as of 1 July 1978. Regarding technical conditions, it is stated that:

Following contacts made in Paris by the Chairman of the Board of Directors and the General Management of SOCAME, three teams of experts came to Bonaberi between 19 June and 5 July. These teams, from Lebanon Chemicals Co., the Metha Group of London, and the French company Potasses d'Alsace, inspected our physical plant and are to inform us of their findings and perhaps their recommendations in the next few weeks. But their first impressions were, on the whole, pessimistic as to the time necessary to restart the factory and as to the cost of these reparations.

The Chairman cited some measures "taken to allow the General Management to recommence the Company's operations progressively," among others "recruiting 3 expatriates to deal essentially with maintenance of the factory, which presently is not performed carefully despite the corrosion."

He mentioned three firms specialized in the production of fertilizer that had:

already inspected on site the physical state of the SOCAME plant. According to the first summary report of these firms, it is confirmed that: the corrosion is significant; the sulphuric acid unit is almost intact; the ammonium sulphate and especially the NPK units are in a very damaged condition. As for the NPK unit in particular, significant transformations would have to be effected like, for example, the system for elevating products.

Mr Remy remarked that "as to the experts that were contacted, Potasses d'Alsace are our competitors and (I) fear their report may not be very objective." He proposed:

... to restart the units that are not very damaged as quickly as possible and at the same time to engage an expert or a specialized firm to come and prepare a detailed medium- and long-term analysis of the other units ... all the units are not in the same condition. If we engage an expert who is to prepare a diagnosis of the plant before any works are commenced, the startup of the sulphuric acid and SSP units may be delayed. Specific measures have in fact already been

[52]   taken with respect to the ammonium sulphate unit. A Klöckner expert will be
on site with the necessary spare parts to ensure the startup of this unit. It also
seems that the sulphuric acid plant will not present much difficulty. The Board
should therefore decide to allow the works that have been commenced by
SOCAME's maintenance team to be continued. As for an expert who might be
called in, he would be charged with preparing a general report.

Mr Mbayen of SNI insisted:

on the need to call on specialists to prepare an estimate of costs for the
installations and assist in restarting the factory. It would be best to have a
complete report on this factory ... all the more so as management doubts the
ability of the present Technical Director and the entire maintenance team to
restart the plant.

Mr Ekani maintained that there must be "an expert evaluation of amounts
so that the overall design of each unit is reviewed for improved utilization
and capacity. This goes beyond mere repairs, given the present state of the
factory and its initial design."
The Minutes indicate that there was a discussion on the issue whether the
operation of the production units is individualized or not, which would
determine whether it is possible to repair individual units without further
delay."
The Chairman suggested:

... that repairs of the sulphuric acid and SSP units be continued and that there
be an evaluation of the cost of potential improvements of the other units
considering the need to modify the methods of weighing, mixing, and
granulating, and to resolve the problems of the electrical plant. All this must
be done with the assistance of specialists.

Mr Remy stated that "with respect to the problems raised in connection
with the design changes that are to be envisaged: the factory was not shut
down because of technical design defects ... everything can be repaired ...
Klöckner is ready to provide technicians to effect the necessary startup
quickly."
Mr Mbayen recalled the fact that "Klöckner is responsible for SOCAME's
technical installations. What is needed is thus on the one hand an expert to
prepare a kind of new feasibility study and, on the other hand, a specialized
firm to supervise and assist the work to be performed by Klöckner and
SOCAME's Technical Direction [sic] in restarting all the installations."
Finally, the Board asked the management "quickly to consult a
specialized firm that will carry out and supervise all of the work to start up
the factory."

b) *Board Meeting of 31 October 1978*   **[53]**

At this meeting, a report from management was presented, which contained the following passage under the heading "Technical":

> The corrosion continues to cause serious damage to the various units and equipment. This situation is due to the very long shutdown of the factory and especially to the fact that there have not been funds sufficient to recover the windward facade. The AS unit's building has been entirely renovated after sand-blasting and rust-resistant painting.
>
> The AS plant is 50% redone for startup. We have had to hold repairs for lack of spare parts.
>
> The sulphuric acid unit has been 75% renovated and we have also had to halt repairs.
>
> The vapour turbine must be repaired by specialists, as the wheel has been attacked by corrosion and the machine is therefore dangerously unbalanced. A part of the factory using Polish components has been modified so as to allow utilization of spare parts from Europe (*sic*). This was decided to avoid overly long waits whenever spare parts are ordered from Poland.
>
> The corrosion of the NPK building and machinery can be dealt with only partially because the windward facade is still exposed. The old protection with non sand-blasted painting was quickly attacked again and requires protection by intensive sand-blasting and painting.
>
> Part of the NPK system has been modified and repaired so as to allow KCl bagging. We have had to slow down production due to the low capacity for storing finished products ... As for security, at least 90% of the fire-fighting equipment is unusable due to the corrosion ... We have mainly sought to halt corrosion and to maintain the existing material in good condition, while awaiting a visit by experts and an evaluation of the costs of the repairs to be effected.

A report concerning the evaluation of the costs of repairing the factory was also presented. It indicated that:

> of the various contacts that have been made by the Chairman of the Board of Directors and the Management, only one has led to concrete results. The team sent to Douala in early July by the Société Commerciale des Potasses et de l'Azote (SCPA) prepared a report which was transmitted to us at the end of July, at the same time as a proposal for a longer-term SCPA mission. In spite of the Chairman's immediate approval of this second mission, the two experts did not arrive in Douala until 11 September. They stayed for three weeks. We present annexed hereto their conclusions as well as the detailed inventory, including amounts, of the repairs, indeed transformations, to be carried out.

At this meeting of the Board, "Mr Remy in turn introduced Mr Van der Ploeg, Klöckner's Technical Adviser, who had been invited to participate in the discussions related to the expert report prepared by the French SCPA Group."

The Chairman presented the report stating that he:

[54] ... asked that the major repairs be halted ... The report of the mission that took place between 11 to 29 September 1978 was received on 30 October 1978 and 4 conclusions may be derived from it:

1st   The damage to the factory is not complete.

2nd Major repairs are to be carried out in the sulphuric acid, ammonium sulphate, SSP and NPK units.

3rd The cost of repairs necessary to make the factory as operational as before is 600 million CFA francs, including 240 million for spare parts. On the other hand, if it is necessary to make modifications in the techniques of production, the cost reaches approximately 1,300 million CFA francs, including 245 million CFA francs for engineering.

4th It would require 3 months to start up the sulphuric acid and ammonium sulphate units and 9 months for the other units.

Mr Remy expressed his "satisfaction that the report confirmed what had been said a few months previously with respect to the general state of the factory and the estimate of CFA francs 400 million for repairing the existing units."

c) *Mr Boucherat's Affidavit and* SCPA'*s First Report*

Defendant has submitted an affidavit of Mr Boucherat, one of the experts who prepared the SCPA reports.

It suffices to consider only those passages of this affidavit that confirm the report submitted to and discussed by the Board of Directors on 31 October 1978 (not challenged by Messrs Remy and Van der Ploeg), as well as Mr Mula's letter of 5 October 1978, in order to determine the state of the factory after the shutdown in December 1977. We shall also refer to other contemporaneous documents.

Storage of raw materials

1) The raw materials warehouses were entirely or partially in the open air. The humidity due to the tropical climate manifested itself in the form of mud on the floor. This humidity resulted in significant losses of products and in corrosion of handling and weighing systems.

2) The storage capacity was insufficient considering the long waits for supplies from abroad.

3) Sulphur was stored in the open air and was completely exposed to rainfall; the resulting buildup of acid generated corrosion.

4) The cooling compressors worked poorly or not at all. The only condenser installed was of insufficient power.

5) The pumps supposed to transport ammonium to the sulphate ammonium plant had broken down; consequently, the insufficiency of the flow of ammonium prevented the ammonium sulphate unit from functioning at its nominal capacity.

Auxiliary installations   **[55]**

6) The flow of air produced by the compressed air unit remained too humid due to deficient functioning of two aluminum dryers, and too high in oil content due to the poor functioning of the oil filter.

7) The ordinary steel pipe from the water wells was very rusty; the conditions of use require a flexible cast-steel pipe.

8) The output of the water treatment unit was insufficient, given the higher quantity of ferrous oxide and impurities than that foreseen when the factory was designed.

9) The maintenance system required basic machinery to allow more effective interventions.

10) The quantity of spare parts in storage was largely insufficient, not to say ridiculous, which prevented fully safe operation of the factory: "the spare parts delivered at initial startup have mostly disappeared from the warehouse, and the few that remain are unusable due to the completely careless manner in which they have been handled."

The sulphuric acid production unit

11) The conveyor belt for sulphur was heavily corroded and required reparation.

12) The steel smelter was very corroded because sulphuric acid and sulphurous acid dissolved with water, resulting in much corrosion.

13) The pumps that transported sulphur to the furnace and pulverized the sulphur were not entirely satisfactory, particularly in the event of frequent shutdowns.

14) The heater was in very bad condition, corroded by the mineral salts present in the insufficiently purified water.

15) The turbo blower could no longer guarantee operations. While the factory was onstream, several failures were noted, in particular vibrations due to the machine's imbalance, which worsened with time. The situation was the result of corrosion of the wheel of the machinery, due in turn to the numerous prolonged shutdowns of the factory, the last, during approximately ten months, having almost destroyed the wheel.

The SSP production unit

16) Very significant difficulties in the technical functioning were encountered with respect to the mixer whose blades had been put down beside the machine and were quite worn down.

17) Attacked by the sulphuric acid, natural phosphate frees fluor [sic] in the form of a very corrosive gas. These fumes have caused the destruction of the machinery's control units as well as the degradation of all of the plant's water and acid pipes and valves.

[56]   *The ammonium sulphate production unit*

18) The problem of vibrations in the saturator had not disappeared, because the report notes that it would not be advisable to exceed the capacity of 90 to 95 T/d per unit since, beyond that point, the vibrations are too great and the manufactured products become too finely grained.

The complex fertilizer production unit

19) Weighing was done manually by an operator; this archaic system caused a significant lack of precision in the composition of the products.

20) Machines such as the sieves and the grinders were completely destroyed.

21) It was necessary to modify the raw materials in the flow system for the granulator, which was inoperative, imprecise, and dangerous. The intake of water was very imprecise, with the consequence that products were either not wet enough and therefore could not be granulated, or too wet, blocking the circuits and causing sudden shutdowns of the production unit.

22) The drying system was insufficient and not adapted to local conditions. This was one of the causes of the extreme corrosion of the installation and waste of final products. The affidavit adds that the complex fertilizer products, especially those with a urea base, absorb the water vapour of the ambient atmosphere. In a tropical atmosphere, with a high level of humidity, the fertilizer loses its consistency and becomes pasty. Moreover, the unit was equipped with slatted shutters and was thus not protected from inflow of humid air. In consequence, the complex fertilizers were of mediocre quality, which gave rise to many complaints. These conclusions are corroborated by what was revealed under V.E.a. above.

The bagging unit and the interdependence of the production units

23) In the unit where final products were bagged, the phenomena of corrosion and destruction were repeated as a consequence of the humid ambient atmosphere. The essential problem was to fight humidity because, since the unit was no longer enclosed, the humid air entered constantly and the fertilizer dust absorbed water to the point of deliquescence, which resulted in mud on the floor and humidity buildup on the machinery giving rise to uncontrollable corrosion.

24) The storage capacity for bagged final products was insufficient, particularly if one took into consideration the very seasonal nature of purchases by farmers. The warehouses were full on several occasions and products had to be stored in the yard. NPK and sulphate products were stored directly in two silos having a capacity of only 30 m³ each. They allowed no more than two-hour autonomy for the production units. This means that if for any reasons whatever one of the bagging machines were stopped for

more than two hours, the corresponding production unit had to be shut [57] down in turn.

25) There was a close operational interdependence among the production units, so that the shutdown of one unit had repercussions on the others, because sulphuric acid is used in manufacturing ammonium sulphate, which itself is an element of SSP and NPK. Consequently, when the bagging unit broke down, the complex fertilizer unit quickly had to shut down, which caused a shutdown of the ammonium sulphate plant, which in turn caused the shutdown of the sulphuric acid plant. Similarly, the functioning of the NPK plant was disturbed whenever, for one reason or another, there was not enough steam, in particular when the sulphuric acid plant was started up. (See also Annex 50M to the Rejoinder Memorial, in which Mr Von Einem states "without a continuous AS production the rest of the plant cannot run either.")

26) As for the sulphuric acid unit, the production halts were also caused by the fact that two of the uses Klöckner had provided for this product (raw material for the production of single superphosphate and direct sales to local industries) proved to be almost nil. The disproportion between production and consumption of sulphuric acid caused frequent shutdowns that harmed the machinery, designed for continuous operation. As the need for sulphuric acid did not exceed 32,000 t/year, this unit could function at no more than 53% of its capacity, which according to those who operated it, is practically impossible.

d) *The Mechim Report and the Bureau Veritas Reports on the Sulphuric Acid Plant*

In its first report, SCPA noted with respect to the sulphuric acid plant that "an inspection of the brickwork of the furnace should be envisaged." It was also pointed out with respect to the absorber and the drying tower that "numerous cakes of rust have loosened from the inner surface and the domes." Consequently, an expert evaluation was requested from the firm Mechim, whose report noted:

27) The nearly complete destruction of the brickwork of the catalysis cistern: the isolating bricks have been loosened from the wall due to the effects of strong dilatation which, since it was thwarted vertically, had the result of splitting the wall.

   On level 5 may be identified an entire zone in which the bricks were obviously badly laid ... in front of the wall instead of right in the center of the wall!!! ... there appears to have been no understanding of the problem of dilatation ... The difficulties of this masonry work may not have been studied by sufficiently competent specialists.

28) It was also noted that there were manholes in the absorber and drying tower. The Mechim report states that:

[58]   ... in all our experience with sulphuric acid, we have never come across towers containing acid having such openings for access ... In the drawings, the tubulatures of these manholes are specified as being made of cast iron; in point of fact, the corrosion which has affected this tubulature shows without any possible mistake that they were made of steel and not of cast iron. The tubulature constituting the lower manhole is comprised of two points placed end-to-end without being welded. As this manhole is submerged under the acid, one can understand very readily that the acid could have infiltrated the interior metal face of the tower and perforated it.

This was confirmed by Bureau Veritas in a report that established that the exterior metal walls of the absorber and drying tower were performated [sic] in various places and that their nominal thickness of 8 mm had been reduced to 4 mm at several spots around the manholes.

29) Bureau Veritas also measured the thickness of the pump tank casings of the absorber and drying tower, and found "areas of weakness and decay of very significant diameter and depth, so advanced as to perforate the lower section."

F. *The Repair of the Factory and its Functioning in 1980*

In 1978, the Government decided to make yet another effort to make the factory work. It requested the views of scpa which, after a detailed study, concluded that the factory should be redesigned in order to modify the processes, and that it could thus be ready to function again. Cameroon offered Klöckner the possibility to participate. Klöckner refused to make any additional capital contribution to socame and instead yielded its majority shareholding in socame to the Government. It was expected that once these repairs had been carried out the factory would function in a satisfactory manner and thereafter the problem would only be of an economic rather than a technical nature. And, in fact, the evidence submitted indicates that, after this considerable expenditure, the factory functioned well during several months, with a new design and with new output forecasts. The Government's decision finally to shut down the factory in 1980 was, according to the evidence before us, founded entirely on profitability considerations.

VI. THE LAW

Article 42 of the icsid Convention stipulates that:

The Tribunal shall decide a dispute in accordance with such rules of law as may be agreed by the parties. In the absence of such agreement, the Tribunal shall apply the law of the Contracting State party to the dispute (including its rules on the conflict of laws) and such rules of international law as may be applicable.

In addition to the rules adopted by the parties in the three contracts on which the jurisdiction of the Tribunal is founded, it is necessary to determine the legal system or the contractual law governing those three instruments. It [59] is naturally the civil and commercial law applicable in Cameroon.

A. *Applicable Law*

Defendant maintains that in Cameroon both French civil law and British "common law" are applied. The first affidavit presented on this subject, in which it is stated that "Cameroonian law is defined by reference to two legal systems (Common Law and Napoleonic Codes) inherited from the colonial period," adds however that "whenever two residents of the same city are involved, it is logical and customary to apply to them the particular legal system of the region, whether it be Francophone or Anglophone." And the second affidavit indicates with greater precision that "there have been two systems of law in the territory, viz, the former Republic of Cameroon retains the French Civil Code and the former British Cameroon retains the common law of England." According to Article 42 of the Convention, one should apply "the law of the Contracting State party ... including its rules on the conflict of laws."

One must therefore acknowledge the correctness of Claimant's position when it says that "since the SOCAME factory project was located in the eastern part of the country, only that part of Cameroonian law that is based on French law should be applied in the dispute." Furthermore, the three agreements were finalized in Yaoundé, that is to say in the eastern part of the country.

Among the different arguments of French civil law invoked should be cited the following: wrongful inducement to contract (*défaut de consentement*), wrongful conduct by a contracting party (*dol*), and hidden defects (*vices cachés*). The two grounds which we deem applicable are: (i) the fact that Klöckner did not manifest *vis-à-vis* its Cameroonian partner the frankness and loyalty required in international contractual relations of this complexity and (ii) the *exceptio non adimpleti contractus*.

B. *The Duty of Full Disclosure to a Partner*

We take for granted that the principle according to which a person who engages in close contractual relations, based on confidence, must deal with its partner in a frank, loyal and candid manner is a basic principle of French civil law, as is indeed the case under the other national codes which we know of. This is the criterion that applies to relations between partners in simple forms of association anywhere. The rule is particularly appropriate in more complex international ventures, such as the present one.

We have not established that there is a law applicable to such contracts. We do not intend to apply new or exceptional legal principles to turn-key operations only because they concern projects affecting the economic and social development of a given country. But we are convinced that it is

[60] particularly important that universal requirements of frankness and loyalty in dealings between partners be applied in cases such as this one, where a multinational company seeks and freely undertakes the obligation to supply an overall package of feasibility, analysis, design, management, bidding, construction and marketing for an industrial plant, and obtains in return the agreement of the Government to pay for the factory, whether or not it is profitable.

In the present case, as we have suggested, we do not feel that Klöckner has dealt frankly with Cameroon. At critical stages of the project, Klöckner hid from its partner information of vital importance. On several occasions it failed to disclose facts which, if they had been known to the Government, could have caused it to put an end to the venture and to cancel the contract before the expenditure of the funds whose payment Klöckner now seeks to obtain by means of an award. When a partner in a financially complex international venture learns of certain facts which could influence the attitudes and the actions of the other partner with respect to the project; when the first partner fails to disclose this information to the other; and the second thereupon continues with the project and incurs additional costs, the first partner has not acted frankly and loyally *vis-à-vis* his partner, and he cannot rightly present a claim to funds whose expenditure would perhaps never have been necessary if he had been frank and candid in his dealings. In a very significant sense, the fault is his. The fact that the funds were spent becomes his responsibility and not that of his partner. In this respect, we decide that Klöckner violated its fundamental contractual obligations and may not insist upon payment of the entire price of the Supply Contract.

But if Klöckner may not insist on the entirety of the contract price, it nevertheless supplied certain factory components which were later used by Cameroon. As has been demonstrated elsewhere, Klöckner never delivered a factory "ready for use". At no moment prior to the reparations carried out by Potasses d'Alsace in 1979–80 did the factory function in a satisfactory manner. Nevertheless, elements of the factory built by Klöckner were used in the 1980 reconstruction, and the factory functioned well until its definitive shutdown by the Government at the end of that year. The decision to repair and restart the factory was made entirely by the Government; Klöckner, as noted, had by then given up its majority share of SOCAME. The Cameroonian Government thus accepted and used certain components of the factory supplied by Klöckner. Klöckner has the right to be paid for them.

It is our duty to determine the appropriate amount of the payment, which should be inferior to the contract price. If the factory as designed, built, and operated by Klöckner had functioned as promised, the price which Cameroon should have paid would have been DM 56,840,000 – the original price of DM 49,800,000 plus the DM 7,040,000 increase provided for in the Contract.

We think however, that to determine the value in 1980 of the Klöckner components, it is appropriate to deduct the following elements from the contract price:

1) First, the 1980 factory was not the same as that designed and built by **[61]** Klöckner. Potasses d'Alsace had implemented significant design modifications. In particular, they had modified all production capacities, doubled the NPK capacity and abandoned the use of urea, which had caused serious corrosion and resulted in significant shutdowns. An entire production line was eliminated. Klöckner thus does not have the right to claim on the basis of the entire factory which it had delivered in 1975–76, because all of the factory was not used in the 1980 project.

2) Furthermore, Defendant has already made payments in principal of about DM 16,719,000.

3) Cameroon has also made interest payments to Klöckner. These interest payments were made at a time when Klöckner still had not delivered the promised factory. The factory was never "ready for use" until the redesign and the reparation of 1979-80 had been completed. As we have said, we can therefore not hold that Klöckner had fulfilled its contractual obligations, and the contract price was thus not due at the times when the periodic payments of principal and interest were effected by Cameroon. We thus believe that Defendant has the right to be credited with the amounts of interest paid, and we accordingly deduct these payments as well.

4) The cost of reparations, as we have said, was paid by Cameroon. Klöckner refused to participate. Cameroon thus has the right to be credited with the total cost of these expenditures as well.

5) Finally, there were considerable operating losses during the 1977–79 period when the factory was not producing, especially by reason of the operating difficulties which we have described above. The Minutes of the meeting of the Board of Directors of 30 June 1980 indicates that the losses suffered during this period were on the order of CFA francs 3,500 million. Klöckner should at any rate assume part of the responsibility for these losses, thus offsetting its claims with respect to the components used by the Government in 1980.

Taking into account these factors, we reach the conclusion that Klöckner violated its contractual obligations of full disclosure, that it does not have a right to the contract price, that it has a right to be paid for the value of what it delivered and Cameroon used, and that Cameroon has already made sufficient payments for the components of the factory it received from Klöckner in 1974–75 and which it used in the factory as redesigned in 1980.

C. *The Exceptio Non Adimpleti Contractus*

a) *French, English and International Law*

It would appear difficult to deny that the Cameroonian Government, in answering the request for arbitration, invoked *eo nomine*, and thus in timely

[62] fashion, the *exceptio non adimpleti contractus*. Indeed, on page 91 of the Counter-Memorial, which was defendant's first written submission, one reads the following:

> As guarantor, the Cameroonian Government undertook to substitute itself for SOCAME for the repayment of the loan and the payment of interest. Its undertaking was not, however, unlimited. Like any obligation, its performance may, according to general principles of contract law, be suspended by virtue of the *exceptio non adimpleti contractus*, that is to say in the event Klöckner failed to fulfil its own contractual undertakings. Klöckner's faulty performance of its contractual obligations thus had the effect of liberating the Cameroonian Government from its financial undertaking.

And it is added on page 145 of the Counter-Memorial:

> It is important to note that even in the event the Tribunal were to deem the Cameroonian party obliged to pay the price of the factory, it would be justified in not paying the entirety of the price, taking into account the Cameroonian claim arising from Klöckner's failure to perform its obligations as promoter, manager and/or shareholder, and this on the grounds of the *exceptio non adimpleti contractus* and of judicial setoff, both of which are commonly accepted in international arbitration.

The *exceptio non adimpleti contractus* may be invoked at any time, even during judicial or arbitral proceedings, without giving prior notice of default to the non-performing party. See Esmein, in Planiol and Ripert, *Traité pratique de droit civil français*, vol. VI (1930), No. 455, p. 626; Cassin, *De l'exception tirée de l'inexécution dans les rapports synallagmatiques, op. cit.*, pp. 583–584.

The first-mentioned author writes: "the exception based on non-performance may be invoked without either authorization by the judge or prior notice of default." And A. Weil, basing himself on case law, adds that the *exceptio non adimpleti contractus* "requires neither a claim in court, nor even a notice of default. It is sufficient that the *excipiens* invokes the exception against his protagonist at such time as the latter demands satisfaction of his right," A. Weil, *Droit civil, Les obligations*, 3rd ed., p. 547, No. 475.

It is true, as Cassin puts it in a treatise that has become classic (*De l'exception tirée de l'inexécution dans les rapports synallagmatiques*), that the French Civil Code nowhere "mentions the *exceptio non adimpleti contractus* among the means by which a party may protect itself when faced with its cocontractant's failure to respect undertakings," (p. III). But French case law, practice, and commentary "refuse to believe that by its silence alone the Civil Code would put aside an elementary rule of equity" (*op. cit.*, p. IV). To the contrary, case law and commentary have "erected a clear system of rules that allow this exception to be effective", J. Voulet, comment in 74 *Jurisclasseur périodique* II, p. 17707.

In particular, the views of President Cassin on the *exceptio non adimpleti* [63] *contractus* have been followed and adopted in French case law. It has been written recently that his work "remains solid and has victoriously survived an evolution of the law whose path it has illuminated," P. Reynaud, Preface to J. F. Pillebout, *Recherches sur l'exception d'inexécution*, Paris, 1971.

Planiol, in his *Traité élémentaire de droit civil*, p. 2, No. 994, 2520, put forth the decisive argument in favour of the *exceptio non adimpleti contractus* in French civil law: "if I have the right to reclaim what I have already delivered in the event the other party does not fulfil its promise, I have *a fortiori* the right to refuse to perform my obligation."

In view of the parties' divergence of views as to applicable law under Article 42 of the ICSID Convention, it is appropriate to remark that English law and international law reach similar conclusions.

In English law, as Lord Devlin has written ...:[2]

> it is of the essence of every contract that there should be mutuality. A contract is an exchange of one promise for another ... A contract can consist of an exchange of promises on one subject, e.g. payment against delivery; then if the seller does not deliver on the due date, the buyer may release himself from his obligation to pay.

As for the principles of international law, to which Article 42 of the ICSID Convention refers, the *exceptio non adimpleti contractus* also applies. There is no doubt:

> that the principle underlying this conclusion (*in adimplenti non est adimplendum*) is so just, so equitable, so universally recognized, that it should also be applied to international relations. In any event, this is one of those 'general principles of law recognized by civilized nations' which the Court applies by virtue of Article 38 of its Statute. (Opinion of Judge Anzilotti, case on *Diversion of Water from the Meuse*, Permanent Court of International Justice, 28 June 1937, Ser. A/B, No. 70, p. 50.[3])

b) *Partial or Imperfect Performance*

Writers have examined the question whether the *exceptio non adimpleti contractus* is available to a defendant even if the failure of performance is not total but only partial or imperfect. French commentary and case law take the view that failure of performance triggering the *exceptio* may be total or partial. See Cassin, *op. cit.*, p. 514 *et seq.*; Capitant, *De la cause des obligations*, No. 131; Saleilles, *Théorie générale de l'obligation d'après le projet de Code Civil allemand*, 3rd ed., 1914, No. 12; and Mazaeud, *Leçons de droit civil*, T.II, No. 1129.

---

[2] Reference to *Fertilizer Corporation of India* Award (Annex II hereof), paras 98 and 115.
[[3] 8 *Ann. Dig.* 411]

[64] As Cassin puts it, "performance is either perfect or not, and if it is not, the obligee retains the right to make a claim on that basis, by court action or by invoking the exception," p. 525.

And Capitant adds: "what the contracting party wants is to obtain full performance of all of its adversary's undertakings, and it is only by disregarding his intention that one could hold him bound to perform his own obligation if he has received only part of what he has been promised," *op. cit.*, No. 131.

The only divergence among the authors relates to whether one should in this situation speak of the *exceptio non adimpleti contractus* or whether the argument invoked by the defendant "changes in its nature because the failure of performance is not total, and the plaintiff has rendered partial or imperfect performance," Cassin, *op. cit.*, p. 504. For this writer, "there is no *exceptio non rite adimpleti contractus* fundamentally distinct from the *exceptio non adimpleti contractus*," *ibid.* But this discussion of terminology does not alter the substance of the question; the defendant retains in principle the right to refuse to perform in the face of non-performance of any degree. It would, however, be a violation of good faith "if the defect or insufficiency of performance is of slight importance in view of the whole picture," Cassin, p. 572. Accordingly, the *exceptio non adimpleti contractus* is barred whenever "the significance of the contractual non-performance attributable to the other party is minimal," p. 405.

The formulation adopted by French case law has become classic: "in bilateral contracts, failure of performance by one of the parties of some of its undertakings does not necessarily liberate the other party of all of its obligations; it behooves the judge to decide, in view of the circumstances of the case, if this non-performance was of sufficient moment to give rise to such a result," *Cour de cassation, Sect. Soc.*, decision of 1 June 1950; *Sirey* 51.89; comment by Brunet; *Cass. Soc.*, decision of 21 October 1954, *Jurisclasseur périodique* 55.II.8565, comment by Oubliac and Juglart; see comment by A. Huet, *Jurisclasseur périodique* 70.II.16554, under the decision of the *Cour de cassation* of 27 January 1970.

Case law also establishes that "judges charged with deciding the merits of a dispute have full authority to evaluate whether one party's failure of performance of its obligations under a bilateral contract is such that it frees the other party from its corresponding obligations," *Cour de cassation*, 1ère, decision of 5 March 1974; 74 *Jurisclasseur périodique* II. No. 17707, comment by J. Voulet, who also cites the decision of the *Cour de cassation*, 3ème, of 12 March 1969; *Bulletin Civil* III, p. 168, and *Cass. Civ.* 3ème, decision of 6 May 1979, *Bulletin Civil* III, p. 235.

c) *Extent of Failure of Performance in this Case*

In the present case, Klöckner's shortcomings in the performance of its undertakings are very far from being minimal.

By the Supply Contract, Klöckner had assumed a fundamental obligation: **[65]** that of supplying a factory capable of producing fertilizer products conforming to specific descriptions and in guaranteed quantities.

Article 2 of the Supply Contract stipulates that Cameroon should pay Klöckner the agreed price for a factory, "ready for use, erected in Cameroon, and conforming to the description made of it in the annexes" – thus, a factory capable of producing finished products of specified quantity and quality. Article 2 accordingly defines the substance of the relationship between the price and the nature of the thing for which payment was to be effected; Defendant did not purchase merely a group of machines, pipes and a building. What it wanted, and what it agreed to pay for, was an integrated total system of production capable of producing the products defined in the agreements during a continuous period.

In our opinion, this meant a factory that could produce these specified quantities at a practical rate of utilization of the plant. An undertaking to build and manage a manufacturing plant whose objective would be to deliver 50,000 tons of ammonium sulphate to Cameroonian farmers is, for example, an undertaking to supply a factory whose theoretical capacity at a 100% rate of efficiency might be significantly in excess of 50,000 tons, if the practical rate of utilization of the factory happened to be inferior to 100%. Klöckner had thus assumed the risk that the factory might reveal itself incapable of functioning at 100% of its estimated capacity.

In the present case, the factory did not function at the level of production foreseen in the agreements. Klöckner thus did not deliver to Cameroon what it had promised.

And by the Protocol of Agreement Klöckner had assumed another obligation just as fundamental as the first: that of assuming "responsibility for the technical and commercial management" of SOCAME "beginning with the start-up of the factory".

This case involves one and the same bilateral relationship, because the three instruments are bound together by a close connecting factor: agreement was reached for the supply of a fertilizer factory, and its technical and commercial management, in return for payment of a price and for certain investment guarantees. The reciprocal obligations had a common origin, identical sources, and an operational unity. They were assumed for the accomplishment of a single goal, and are thus interdependent. The ICSID Arbitral Tribunal in the *Holiday Inns v. Morocco* case stated:

> It is well known, and it is being particularly shown in the present case, that investment is accomplished by a number of juridical acts of all sorts. It would not be consonant either with economic reality or with the intention of the parties to consider each of these acts in complete isolation from the others. It is particularly important to ascertain which is the act which is the basis of the investment and which entails as measures of execution the other acts which

[66]   have been concluded in order to carry it out. P. Lalive, "The First World Bank
Arbitration", 51 *British Yearbook of International Law* 1980, p. 159.[4]

There is consequently a single legal relationship, even if three successive
instruments were concluded. This is so because the first, the Protocol of
Agreement, encompasses and contains all three. As Professor Kahn notes in
his opinion, "the mutuality of the parties' obligations should therefore be
established on an overall basis, and not contract by contract." (*Reference is
made to a consultation by Professor Philippe Kahn, submitted by Cameroon.*
[translator's note])

The facts recited in Chapter V demonstrate that Klöckner's two
fundamental obligations were performed in an imperfect and partial
manner.

First of all, one cannot affirm that the contractual clauses of the contract
concerning the procedures of acceptance of the factory were respected. Test
runs of two production units were carried out in the absence of the
representative named by SOCAME in conformity with Article 10(2) of the
Contract, that is to say Mr Van der Ploeg (see V.B. above); the signature of
said representative was omitted from all Certificates of Acceptance; and
reservations, objections and observations made with respect to the other
production units remained unclarified. The least one could say is that for the
purposes of the payment of the price of the factory there was no Acceptance
acknowledging the conformity of delivery, even by silence or failure to
object. In consequence, this "Acceptance" does not prevent the *exceptio
non adimpleti contractus* from being invoked.

Next, the production capacities defined in the Supply Contract and the
Protocol of Agreement were never attained after startup of the factory. This
is a failure of performance of the greatest importance because, as the Report
of British Sulphur Corporation notes, "to be interesting, this marginal
project depended on a 100% rate of use of capacity". And Claimant's Reply
Memorial admits that "profitability was calculated on the basis of factory
output at full capacity." The factory's production shortfall was
demonstrated by the reports of operators of the plant (see V.C.), for causes
that without doubt included ones attributable to Klöckner. This capital
point was admitted by the General Manager Von Einem (see V.C., *passim*).

In order to perform the relevant contracts correctly, it was not sufficient to
supply a fertilizer factory; the factory had to have the required capacity and
had to be managed in the manner necessary to attain the proposed goals.

It is always difficult for a judge or an arbitrator to determine if a failure of
performance is of a sufficient degree of gravity. For this reason, certain
criteria for such a determination have been suggested. Thus it has been
proposed that "the court shall establish the failure and its gravity; but it
should allow the exception if it finds that the failure is such that the obligee, if
he had foreseen it, would not have contracted." Mazeaud, *Leçons de droit*

[⁴ 1 *ICSID Reports* 645 at 680.]

civil, vol. II(1), p. 1127, par. 1130. And Professor Capitant proposed a **[67]** criterion leading to a similar result: "It is possible to draw this line with some certainty only by being guided by the intent of the contracting parties, that is to say the objective pursued. One must therefore ask if the fact of non-performance that has been invoked is of such importance that it prevents or could prevent the achievement of the result sought by the other party," *op. cit.*, No. 131.

The answer to this question was supplied by Lord Devlin in the award reproduced in the Annex 29 to the Counter-Memorial,[5] where he says, at p. 2, in words fully applicable to the present case, that the supplier "was in breach of contract by supplying a plant which was incapable of producing the guaranteed quantity of fertilizer products."

The supplier, adds Lord Devlin, at para. 112:

> failed to supply a plant of the nature contracted for. The thing tendered, in this case the plant, is commercially different from that which was promised... The plant was producing rather less than half of the designed figures and was operating at a loss. A plant that can only be operated at a loss is not a commercial proposition; it is the equivalent of a constructive total loss ... The buyer would not have got the thing he contracted for or anything like it.

One must recall again that Claimant's responsibility was not extinguished upon delivery of the factory and satisfactory test runs over three days. Klöckner had undertaken to ensure continuous functioning and maintenance of the factory (technical management) as well as to perform its commercial management.

In the discussion of 23 October 1972 with officials of the German Federal Ministry for Economic Cooperation, Klöckner's representatives indicated how they expected to perform their obligations in this respect: "Klöckner will recruit competent European experts so that during the first five years all key posts may be occupied by German or foreign experts."

In this regard, it is also interesting to recall a letter of 12 April 1973, submitted by Defendant, in which Klöckner explains to the Chairman of the Board of Directors of SOCAME how it interprets Article 9 of the Protocol with respect to commercial management:

> According to our studies, even in the improbable event the financing schedule should remain at 7 years, the profitability of the factory will not be affected; only the management of this venture, which is our responsibility, must be more dynamic. As a shareholder who is also responsible for the management of the factory, we can assure you that even with 7-year financing, the plans for accomplishing a well-running factory will be duly fulfilled.

And it was through the absolute control exercised by the General Manager Von Einem, Klöckner's man, that Klöckner became SOCAME's

---

[5] The *Fertilizer Corporation of India* Award, Annex II hereto.

[68] manager, at least from 1973 to 1978. For example, in Klöckner's letter of 26 October 1976 to Mr Von Einem, Klöckner told him:

> Given the fact that at the present time SOCAME finds itself in the critical phase of the beginning of its industrial life, and that during this phase SOCAME will have to overcome difficult problems with respect to the areas of production, marketing, purchasing, and financing, we propose to entrust the General Manager with the duty of following and supervising the aforementioned areas more closely. According to our proposal, from now on a greater part of the decisions in these areas will be made by the General Manager. The authority which the General Manager shall take in the future will be clarified by himself with the assistance of Klöckner-INA in its contractual capacity as management adviser. The liaison between SOCAME's General Manager and the management adviser will be carried out by Mr Dietrich, Klöckner-INA's General representative. We would ask you kindly to confirm the agreement you gave to our proposal during our discussions.

And this management authority was exercised by Klöckner, for example with respect to the purchase of raw materials, in forbidding Mr Von Einem to have direct contacts with other suppliers.

The most conclusive proof of Klöckner's failure to perform its duty of technical and commercial management results simply from the fact of the shutdown of the factory in December 1977, by decision of Klöckner personnel sent to Cameroon, after 18 months of underproduction and operating losses.

e) *Responsibility for Factory Maintenance*

Regarding this aspect of responsibility for the maintenance of the factory, the Reply Memorial maintains that "Klöckner's responsibility may in no way be at issue" with respect to "problems having to do with corrosion of the plant, resulting from defective maintenance during the period while the factory was shut down."

In our opinion, this conclusion merits particular attention, because it is one of the key questions of the present case.

According to Article 9 of the Protocol of Agreement, Klöckner was responsible for and undertook the technical management of SOCAME, and this responsibility existed from the beginning of operations; it was exercised when Klöckner's representatives within SOCAME decided (without a prior meeting of the Board of Directors) to shut down the plant in December 1977. This responsibility for the technical management of the factory did not cease when Klöckner became a minority shareholder in April 1978. The responsibility created by Article 9 of the Protocol did not depend on Klöckner's being a majority shareholder; in other words, Article 9 was separate from and independent of Article 2 of the Protocol. That this responsibility was maintained even after Klöckner became a minority shareholder was admitted on two occasions by Dr Remy to the Board of Directors. On 8 April 1978, after having announced that Klöckner was disposed to become a minority shareholder, he added: "Klöckner obviously **[69]** retains all of its obligations under the Management Contract." On 30 April 1977, he had said: "Even if Klöckner loses its majority position ... that would not discharge its responsibilities."

In examining the counterclaim, the Reply Memorial affirms, at p. 85, that "Klöckner's responsibility in the management of SOCAME results only from the Management Contract concluded between the companies."

This affirmation does not take into account Article 9 of the Protocol of Agreement, from which three consequences flow: 1) first, that Klöckner "shall have responsibility for the technical and commercial management of the Company"; 2) that this responsibility shall "be carried out under a Management Contract"; and 3) that this responsibility shall last "for at least 5 years after start-up with an option for its extension."

The Tribunal does not have jurisdiction to evaluate the Management Contract or to interpret it. It must however proceed from the following presumption: that this Contract, intended to assign to Claimant "responsibility for the technical and commercial management of the Company," could neither qualify nor diminish Klöckner's undertaking by virtue of the basic agreement: the Protocol of Agreement. Even if the Tribunal does not have jurisdiction to interpret the Management Contract, it should presume that there is perfect compatibility between the two instruments, the Protocol of Agreement constituting the charter (*accord-cadre*) of the investment and the Management Contract simply being intended to ensure performance of the basic agreement. A declaration made to the Board of Directors on 12 January 1977 confirms this conclusion. The Minutes of this meeting set forth, at p. 6:

> Since it would appear that the management structure of the Company does not function to everyone's satisfaction, Mr Mazur informs the Board of Directors that Klöckner, within the framework of the Management Contract to be signed, will proceed after studying the matter to make such improvements that are likely to render the Company's management more efficient.

Klöckner thus admits being the manager of the factory.

The proof that Article 9 of the Protocol was not a mere promise of future agreement, nor an inoperative stipulation requiring a subsequent contract defining performance in order to become applicable, but an essential, firm, and "self-executing" undertaking, lies in the fact that the Management Contract was not signed until 7 April 1977. Consequently, the technical and commercial management of the factory during the entire critical period in 1976, and the first three months of 1977, was carried out by Klöckner on the basis of Article 9 of the Protocol alone. This Article was the single source of all the authority Klöckner exercised during this period, and consequently of all of its responsibility for the management of the factory.

Once this point is established, it suffices to recall that Mr Mula's memorandum of 30 March 1978, barely three months after the shutdown, already calls attention to fact that:

[70]   the corrosion in the production department is increasing since the early beginning of the rainy season ... the corrosion has increased to such thickness that it will be absolutely necessary to clean the metallic items by sand-blasting; ... unless immediate measures are taken most items can be scrapped.

And the SCPA report of September 1978 met with no objection from either Mr Remy or his assessor Mr Van der Ploeg, when it was submitted to the Board of Directors (see V.E.c.). It demonstrates the importance of the corrosion observed at the factory, which the manager should have foreseen and prevented (see items 3, 7, 11, 12, 14, 15, 16, 17, 20, 22 and 23, section V.E.c.). And this corrosion had begun previously, even before the shutdown of the plant (four citations to various descriptions of corrosion in Chapter V). Moreover, the subsequent reports of Mechim and Bureau Veritas revealed the extent of the corrosion of the sulphuric acid unit, resulting from serious defects of the plant's original design (see V.E.d.).

The SCPA report also reveals serious technical design defects in the plan from an engineering viewpoint (see items 8, 9, 19, 22, 24, 25, 26 and 28 of V.E.c.); flaws in planning with respect to climate and other local conditions (items 1, 2, 3, 23); significant defects of installation or construction (items 4, 5, 6, 7, 13, 18 and 27) or simply of administrative and commercial management (items 10 and 21).

It is obvious that Defendant would have assumed such onerous obligations only in order to obtain a factory capable of producing that which one might reasonably and legitimately have hoped to obtain from the contracts, and a plant free from these defects of corrosion and other flaws in design and construction. The equality of the parties would be clearly disturbed if Klöckner could now claim payment from SOCAME or from the Government of the contested promissory notes.

This would be an evident rupture of the contractual equilibrium of obligation. The Republic of Cameroon has not received the promised counter-performance; its undertaking thus lacks consideration (*cause*).

As Capitant says, *La cause dans les obligations, op. cit.*, No. 124:

the voluntary action of the parties is not only their acceptance of an obligation, that is to say in expressing consent, but also consists of the intention to attain a given legal goal, that is to say to obtain execution of the performance promised in exchange for the contracted obligation. It would therefore be inconsistent with the intent of a contracting party to force him to deliver the thing he has promised if he does not receive the counterpart he expected.

The rejection of Klöckner's claim for payment of the remainder of the price of the factory serves only to maintain the equilibrium of reciprocal contractual undertakings as defined by the parties themselves. Taking into account the unity of the bilateral relationships established by the three instruments, as explained in VI.3.c above, it may be affirmed that the supply and management of the factory, and the total payment of the agreed price, are obligations of which each constitutes the legal consideration (*cause*) of the other; as Saleilles put it, *op. cit.* No. 171, "a bilateral relationship is a [71] whole which neither party may arbitrarily divide."

Even in one considers that the DM 49,800,000 price fixed in the Protocol was the precise counterpart of the plant, it must be remembered that the Protocol gave Klöckner much more than this price; nothing less than the guarantee of the Government, established in Article 16. This guarantee, which is the foundation of the present claim, may be considered to be the counterpart of Klöckner's undertaking to be responsible for SOCAME's technical and commercial management.

It is true that Claimant did make partial delivery, however defective. But there was also partial performance by Defendant, because it repaid the initial 10% of the loan; the additional 20% of the price agreed on the occasion of the adjustment of the price for the factory; and the interest on several occasions, these payments amounting to DM 16,719,000 on account and repayment of principal, and DM 11,852,974 as repayment of interest. The first of these amounts represents almost 30% of the total price for the factory.

This is in fact the percentage of the overall production of the plant during the eighteen months of operation, according to the statistical studies presented by Defendant (see V.C.). Mr Von Einem informed SOCAME's Board of Directors on 11 June 1977 that after eleven months of activity "the factory produced less than 20% of the production capacity promised for the first year, that is to say much less than the contractually guaranteed production capacity" (see V.C.). Finally, on 27 December 1977, on the eve of shutdown of the factory, SOCAME's statutory auditor stated that the "plant has only functioned at approximately 22% of its normal capacity".

Moreover, the total sum repaid in principal and interest was almost 50% of the total modified cost of the factory, Cameroon having paid Klöckner a total amount of DM 28,215,699.

One may, in this equitable evaluation, take into account the interest payments since, when the *exceptio non adimpleti contractus* is applicable, no notice of default to the obligor is required either with respect to the price or to interest on account of delay, Esmein, *op. cit.*, p. 625, No. 457. As for contractually defined interests paid by the Cameroonian party, such payment had no objective correlative in the faulty performance of Klöckner, such interests, as Cassin puts it, "being nothing but the equivalent of the benefit of use," *op. cit.*, p. 530.

And in the present case, there was no benefit of productive use of the factory; on the contrary, there were considerable losses from startup onwards, see Section V.C. Cassin concludes that when the *exceptio non adimpleti contractus* is validly invoked, the "obligation to pay interest will evaporate", p. 659.

French case law and commentary maintains that one must make a quantative comparison of the respective failures of performance; that it is necessary "to measure the relative effect of the refusal to perform against the seriousness of the faulty performance," Capitant, *op. cit.*, No. 131,

[72] because there must be a "certain correspondence between the degree of gravity of the failure of performance alleged by the *excipiens* as compared with that of the refusal of performance to which he claims to be entitled," J.F. Pillebout, *Recherches sur l'exception d'inexécution*, p. 213 (1971).

In the present case, taking into account, on the one hand, the significant payments effected by Defendant, and, on the other hand, the significance of Claimant's failures to live up to contractual undertakings, it is appropriate to conclude that the amount paid corresponds equitably to the value of Klöckner's defective performance. There is a certain equilibrium, a certain relationship, as we have suggested above, between that which was paid and the approximate value of the components supplied by Klöckner in 1974–1975 and used by Defendant in the redesigned factory, which was restarted successfully in 1980. The two methods of analysis lead to results approximately equivalent, and we have thus concluded that Klöckner is entitled to what it has already received, but to nothing more.

D. *The Reasons for the Failure According to the Claimant*

In its response, Claimant gives its opinion with respect to the causes of the failure of the investment, to wit the great disruption of prices of imported raw materials, dumping of fertilizer products, and a failure of Cameroon's political will in refusing to take the measures necessary for the success of the project.

Before analysing these explanations, it must be remarked that, even if they were justified, they would in no manner diminish the significance of the facts described above insofar as they show the seriousness of the Claimant's failure of contractual performance. The question before the Tribunal is not that of responsibility for the economic failure of the joint venture, which could be a shared responsibility, but the simpler and objective question whether Claimant's failure of performance was sufficiently serious to justify the refusal to pay the unpaid notes.

At any rate, the great disruption of the price of raw materials and finished products caused by the petroleum crisis began in 1973 and, in consequence, Klöckner could have foreseen and updated its financial calculations before construction of the factory even began in 1975. Annex 9 of the Counter-Memorial contains an agreement dated 14 June 1974 between Klöckner and a supplier, Kellogg Continental, in which reference is made to "additional costs due to the oil crisis". Claimant could have made similar corrections in its profitability and engineering analyses to take account of this disruption, of which it complains today. Even if one disregards Defendant's charge that Klöckner and Ritter's studies were distorted by the motive of selling the plant, it is undisputable that Klöckner cannot invoke the inexplicable fact that it did not revise its profitability calculations.

Moreover, Annex 5.5 of the Reply Memorial shows that the increase in price of raw materials took place in 1974. These prices fell in 1975 and 1976, the years during which construction and operation commenced.

Claimant also refers to dumping by producers as one of the causes of [73] failure. On this score, by Article 12 of the Establishment Agreement, Cameroon had undertaken to "take necessary measures in order to ensure if needed that SOCAME's production be protected from international competition." But this article does not create a concrete obligation of the Government, and therefore does not accord an absolute protection, as Claimant acknowledged during the hearings.

Moreover, Annex 5.9 of the Reply Memorial shows that "in 1970–71 export sales were being made at under half of the domestic prices. By the end of December 1974 the situation had reversed with international sales commanding very much more than domestic prices." The documents submitted also demonstrate that this problem of the difference between local and international prices already existed in 1970–71 and that it thus should have been taken into account in the profitability calculations. Annex 31 of the Rejoinder Memorial thus confirms that Klöckner had been made aware of such a potential development with respect to ammonium sulphate as early as 1972. It was also known, at least since 1974, that the FAO contributed free fertilizer products in Cameroon. It is not justified to attribute to this donor programme the high costs of fertilizer produced by the factory, which could not satisfy all the market demand. The high production costs were the consequence of under-production due to technical (frequent shutdowns) and financial (cash shortage) reasons. It would be totally unjustified to claim that the Government should pass on these high costs to farmers.

The Reply Memorial also refers to financial difficulties due to delays in payment for fertilizer products, and deems these difficulties to be the principal reason for the shutdown of the factory.

But the cause of these difficulties was not only belated payments for the products. The shortage of funds had also to a considerable extent been caused by Klöckner itself, since it received payment on 11 April 1973 of 10% of the initial price, the first payment of interest on 11 January 1975 and, on 11 July 1975 the second payment of interest – all before the plant had begun to produce.

SOCAME's corporate report on its activities dated 16 May 1975 states:

> this schedule of payments is in accordance with the agreements reached at the time the Supply Contract was concluded. An initial delay of 21 months preceding the first payment had appeared to be sufficient for the construction of the factory as well as for its startup. This would have permitted the financing of all payments of loan, principal, and interest thanks to the revenues derived from the marketing of SOCAME's fertilizer products. This hope was not realized, due to unforeseen and unexpected delays in site preparation. As a result of these delays, we are obliged to make the payments covered by a Government guarantee but whose amounts exceed the Company's income.

SOCAME had been called upon "by Klöckner to open letters of credit at a time when our finances did not allow it", Annex 42 to the Rejoinder Memorial.

[74] And even Mr Von Einem wrote to Klöckner on 9 June 1976: "at this time, our expenses are equal to the costs of a fully producing factory. However, we are unable to attain marketable production".

Finally, the Reply Memorial criticizes the Government for having failed to subsidize either SOCAME or farmers, as is done in other African or Asian countries. But none of the contractual documents contains any Governmental undertaking in this respect; nor was the subject broached during discussions with Governmental authorities. To the contrary, in Article 18 of the Establishment Agreement, SOCAME:

> formally undertakes not to make any claim on the Government of the United Republic of Cameroon resulting from the technical risks of operating the plant or from the evolution of the general economic situation, such developments not being considered to be events of *force majeure*.

Furthermore, certain documents submitted by Defendant show that SOCAME had obtained the customs protection to which it was entitled.

Klöckner maintains that Cameroon did not provide economic protection of the plant, that a subsidy or a prohibition of imports would have ensured sufficient cashflow to finance raw materials purchases as well as spare parts necessary for optimal functioning of the factory, and that the failure to protect the factory constituted a violation of the agreement with Cameroon. The argument is based on Article 12 of the Establishment Agreement.

It is true, as Klöckner points out, that the Establishment Agreement contained a general stabilization clause (Article 2) as well as a more precise undertaking to "take restrictive measures with respect to trade in this area, provided that the production is competitive in quality and in price with normal import prices" (Article 12, para. 4). We do not think, however, that this is tantamount to an unlimited undertaking to establish a permanent policy of price protection for the plant, irrespective of its inefficiency, and without regard to the relationship between import costs and the price of fertilizer on the market. If Cameroon had wanted a national fertilizer industry at any cost, it would have been easy for the country to have one by subsidizing it. (Import bans would have isolated the domestic market from competing imports, but the price to the farmer would have been high.) Experience during the periods when the plant was operational showed that if the venture was to survive, it would have required nearly permanent subsidies.

We are told (Nyassa affidavit) that an undertaking to make unlimited subsidies in favour of a new industry is contrary to the general policy of Cameroon. Moreover, no submissions in the course of oral testimony suggested that Cameroon was disposed to adopt a different policy in this particular case; no subsidy was suggested for the plant in any of the feasibility studies submitted by Klöckner nor in the Protocol of Agreement, the Supply Contract, or the Establishment Agreement. In fact, each of these studies concluded that the project would be perfectly feasible with revenues derived only from sales on the open market. The affirmation in the basic feasibility study of 1971 that the factory would be profitable was based only [75] on the purchase of raw materials on the international market and on the sale of finished products on the free domestic market.

There is strong proof that Klöckner presented the studies with the intent that they would be accepted as trustworthy analysis of SOCAME's prospects. In fact, the testimony of witnesses presented by Defendant indicates that Cameroon based itself on these studies when it decided to approve the project and to undertake to make the investment. In these circumstances, we cannot conclude that Cameroon is responsible for the failure of the project because it refused to subsidize it.

The failure of this project is due to an ensemble of technical and financial difficulties. A subsidy or another programme of protection would of course have ensured the profitability of the factory. And a sufficiently high level of profits could probably have resolved all difficulties of a technical order. But it would require a much stretching [sic] to conclude from this that Cameroon's failure to subsidize was a violation of the agreements of such importance that Klöckner should thereby find itself excused from having failed to deliver functionable installations.

The negotiating history of Article 12 of the Establishment Agreement supports this point of view. The minutes of the drafting session demonstrate that the parties were initially unable to agree. Klöckner proposed that the Government promise to take "restrictive measures" unconditionally and without limits. Cameroon insisted upon the condition that the products should be competitive with imported products in quality and in price. Klöckner opposed this idea, affirming that SOCAME had the responsibility to produce at the lowest possible cost, apparently without any reference to imported competitive products, and envisaging that import prices could drop as a result of European over-production; this "would make harder SOCAME's task of following (import) prices in such an event." The Government replied that its experience did not lead it to favour industrial protection. It favoured a liberal commercial policy. Certain factories built in Cameroon had produced products of inferior quality and at higher prices than those of imported products, "and when they could not succeed on the domestic market, they requested the Government to forbid imports." The Government reminded Klöckner that Klöckner had affirmed that the plant would be profitable thanks to Klöckner's technical know-how and management, and not because there would be a captive market. This led to a deadlock until Klöckner's representatives accepted the condition that SOCAME's products should be competitive, in quality as well as price, to normally priced imported products.

We thus reach the conclusion that Article 12 of the Establishment Agreement did not oblige Cameroon to launch an indefinite programme of subsidies and protection and that the Government's failure to aid SOCAME in this manner does not excuse the prior failure of Klöckner to supply the operational fertilizer factory it had promised.

[76] E. *The Allegation of Waiver*

It has also been suggested that the Cameroonian Government waived any right it may have had to refuse to make payment in 1983, having ratified and accepted Klöckner's defective performance.

Klöckner bases its argument on the letter dated 12 November 1980 in which the Cameroonian Government informed the Government of the Federal Republic of Germany that CFA francs 2,000 million had been disbursed by the Minister of Finance for the satisfaction of overdue payments. We do not, however, deem this to constitute a waiver of Defendant's claims and defenses in these arbitral proceedings. The declaration was not made to Klöckner but in communications between two governments; none of Klöckner's actions was based on this letter. No concessions were made on the grounds of this letter.

Moreover, the payment was conditional. Annex 45 of the Rejoinder Memorial contains minutes of a meeting held 1 December 1980 in Yaoundé with the Ambassadors of Germany, Belgium and the Netherlands and Klöckner's representatives, on the one hand, and the representatives of Cameroon, on the other hand. The meeting had manifestly been agreed in order to discuss the failure of payment of the CFA francs 2,000 million. The hosts informed the Ambassadors of the allocation of the 2,000 million to the overdue payments and of the fact that in general Cameroon would not refuse to honour its debts, "but it would be desirable to negotiate." The Cameroonian party indicated that Klöckner had prepared the feasibility study, had sold the installations, had managed the plant, and had been a 51% shareholder. In these circumstances, Cameroon "felt that Klöckner was responsible for the shutdown ..." Klöckner replied that the problem was that of the domestic price of fertilizer products; the Ambassadors warned that a failure to pay "would have very serious consequences on the assistance programmes between the concerned countries and Cameroon." But Cameroon's representatives, "reaffirming that Cameroon did not refuse to pay, repeated that the Government wished to renegotiate with Klöckner, which was responsible in the matter."

We conclude from this that the letter of 12 November 1980 did not constitute a waiver. The Cameroonian spokesman carefully explained that Cameroon deemed Klöckner to be at least partially responsible for the failure of the factory. In these circumstances, the letter was conditional, and subject to all of Cameroon's rights to claim that Klöckner was not entitled to the whole contract price. Such partial payment, or promise to pay, did not constitute a waiver of the right to invoke Klöckner's failure to deliver a factory ready for use, as promised.

F. *The Counterclaim*

In invoking ᵗhe *exceptio non adimpleti contractus*, Defendant does not seek to procure a special benefit apart from the rejection of Claimant's request, because the *exceptio* "remains a guarantee of a passive nature", [77] Cassin, *op. cit.,* p. 411.

But the Defendant Government has added a counterclaim for damages on the principal grounds of reparation of all losses attributable to its participation in the project (initial capital contribution to SOCAME and to capital increases, loans guaranteed by the Government, loans granted to SOCAME, and subsidies to SOCAME), *lucrum cessans,* and non-financial damages (*préjudice moral*). It also prays in the alternative for compensation for SOCAME's losses until the month of July 1978.

There is no justification for charging Claimant with the losses incurred by the Government in a joint venture where the two parties participated, or should have participated, with open eyes and full understanding of their actions. One could hardly accept that a State, having access to many sources of technical assistance, could be entitled to compensation for the fact that it was misled by a private company proposing a particular contract. If this had been the case, the Government would also have had a concurrent responsibility, excluding the counterclaim. There is even less justification for charging Klöckner with loans or capital increases in 1979 and 1980, intended to be used for the transformation of the factory or for its operation by one of Klöckner's competitors. Klöckner's responsibility for the defects in the supply of the factory and in its technical and commercial management have been sufficiently sanctioned by the rejection of its claim under the unpaid promissory notes. For the same reasons there is no reasons in this case to allocate *lucrum cessans* or compensation for any non-financial damages.

VII. THE AWARD

The Tribunal decides by the majority:
1. to reject the claim;
2. to reject the counterclaim; and
3. that each party is to bear half of the costs of arbitration, including the costs and fees of the Tribunal, and all of its own expenses and fees of counsel and advisers.

The following is a translation from the French of excerpts from the dissenting opinion of Professor D. Schmidt:

The undersigned is under a duty to give a dissenting opinion. He feels that the Award relies on a mistaken assessment of the facts and documents submitted to the Arbitral Tribunal.

The Award rejects the submissions of the Claimant (hereinafter termed "Klöckner") on three grounds:

[78] 1. Failure of Klöckner in its "duty of full disclosure to a partner" (pp. 105–107 and 44–53);[1]
2. Non-performance by Klöckner of its obligation to deliver a factory ready to operate, in accordance with the contractual provisions (pp. 114–118);
3. Failure of Klöckner to ensure the good commercial and technical management of SOCAME (pp. 118–120).

The undersigned is in a position to demonstrate that these three complaints are baseless and that the Award cannot be approved.

I. FAILURE IN THE "DUTY OF FULL DISCLOSURE TO A PARTNER"

On p. 106, the Award sets forth this failure in the following terms:

At critical stages of the project, Klöckner hid from its partner information of vital importance. On several occasions, it failed to disclose facts which, if they had been known to the Government, could have caused it to put an end to the venture and to cancel the contract before the expenditure of the funds whose payment Klöckner now seeks to obtain by means of an award.

The facts which Klöckner is alleged to have failed to disclose are mentioned on pp. 46–51 as follows:

— Klöckner submitted a technical and economic report in 1971 but did not inform the Cameroonian Government in 1973–74 that the economic prospects of the fertilizer industry had radically changed: "The explosion of the oil price in 1973–74 led to price spirals on the raw-material market as well as on that for finished products. The result was that the price relationships between raw materials and finished products were fundamentally modified during the 1973–1976 period and this inevitably rendered the 1971 forecasts invalid";
— "Klöckner could have said that the economic circumstances had changed since the initial agreement";
— "Klöckner (did not) reveal clearly and fully to the Government that the economic hypotheses of 1971, with respect to the relative prices of raw materials and finished products as well as to the definitive price of the factory, were no longer valid";
— In 1974, Klöckner agreed with the subcontractor Kellogg to request from the Cameroonian party an increase in the project price but Klöckner did not communicate to the latter party the revision in price until September 1975;
— Klöckner "thus allowed the construction of the factory to commence without any indication to its partner that an increase in the cost of the

[1 The dissenting opinion referred to "paragraphs" of the award which did not correspond with the paragraph numbers of the final version of the award. These references to the page numbers of the award were inserted by the editors of *Journal of International Arbitration* with whose permission these excerpts are reproduced.]

factory was in the offing, nor that the "oil crisis" had modified the costs **[79]**
and the economics of the project";
— The memorandum of 14 October 1974 was not communicated to the
 Cameroonian governmental agency responsible for investment
 projects.
The undersigned cannot agree in any way with this accusation of failure to
reveal these facts to the Cameroonian party:
— The memorandum of 14 October 1974 was in fact communicated to
 SOCAME and to SOCAME's banks;
— That memorandum expressly dwells (as indicated by the Award itself
 on p. 51) on the "costs of production that had been considerably
 readjusted – certain items to the extent of 250 per cent – and also on
 new readjusted world prices for finished products"; it is clear from the
 foregoing that, before the construction of the factory, Klöckner had
 informed very precisely the Cameroonian party of the change in
 "economic circumstances" since 1971;
— It is not reasonable to claim that the Government of Cameroon was not
 aware of "the relative prices of raw materials and finished products",
 when in fact that Government was in total control of the fertilizer
 market through its power to deliver import licences for fertilizers,
 through its calls for international tenders, through its control of the
 whole fertilizer distribution network in Cameroon, and through the
 fixing by administrative order of the sale price for fertilizers in
 Cameroon. One may well wonder what conceivable information
 Klöckner could have revealed to the Government of Cameroon which
 that Government did not know already, with regard to fertilizer prices;
— The Award itself confirms this full awareness on the part of the
 Government of Cameroon; *on the one hand*, the Award does not draw
 any conclusion from the alleged non-disclosure by Klöckner, since its
 rejection of the main claim is exclusively based on the "relationship...
 between that which was paid and the approximate value of the
 components supplied by Klöckner in 1974–75 and used by Defendant
 in the re-designed factory" (p. 127) and since it rejects the counterclaim which was precisely based on the alleged non-disclosure; *on the
 other hand, and more importantly*, the Award states on p. 136:

There is no justification for charging Claimant with the losses incurred by the
Government in a joint venture where the two parties participated, or should
have participated, *with open eyes and full understanding of their actions*. One
could hardly accept that a State, having access to many sources of technical
assistance, *could be entitled to compensation for the fact that it was misled by a
private company* proposing a particular contract. If this had been the case, the
Government would also have had a concurrent responsibility, excluding the
counterclaim.

Accordingly, the complaint based on alleged non-disclosure of information

[80] is not only unfounded but has been acknowledged as such by the Award itself, which thus suffers from an obvious self-contradiction in its reasons.

Moreover, it must be noted that the alleged "juridical prerogative of halting further investment even before erection of the factory" (p. 52) does not exist in French law, which rejects the *exceptio rebus sic stantibus* and which penalizes – by the award of damages – a contracting party which attempts to release itself unilaterally from the contract when economic circumstances subsequently change.

II. REGARDING THE NON-PERFORMANCE OF THE OBLIGATION TO DELIVER A FACTORY READY TO OPERATE, IN ACCORDANCE WITH THE PROVISIONS OF THE CONTRACT

● ● ●

[This portion of the dissenting opinion in which the dissenting arbitrator provides his analysis of the facts has not been released for publication. The dissenting opinion continues:]

● ● ●

In conclusion, after these extensive considerations, the undersigned cannot but note that Klöckner did in fact deliver what it had promised, namely a factory capable of functioning in conformity with the stipulations of the contract. Of course, there were "teething problems" as with any new factory starting its operation; of course, structural problems also arose, resulting from the necessity to adapt the factory to the conditions of a fluctuating demand (absence of orders for the SPP plant) and distribution (transport and storage); the solutions to those problems were known and had been adopted by the Board of Directors at its meeting of 30 September 1977; all that was lacking were the financial means for SOCAME to implement the solutions. This said, if the Award is to rely on the *exceptio non adimpleti contractus* as its legal basis, one must determine the extent and value of the performance by Klöckner, as compared to the deficiencies or inadequacies which may have been observed; since it is Utopian to demand perfection, and since a new factory can always be improved, it is perfectly admissible to claim that, in December 1977, the factory was perhaps not in a position to function at its optimum contractual capacity; but the difference between this optimum level and effective capacity is clearly brought out in the report of the Management Committee to the Board of Directors of 6 January 1978:

> With a view to refitting the plants as a whole, it appears essential to acquire two machine-tools at an estimated cost of 20 million CFA francs and to import spare parts in a total value of about 400 million CFA francs.

Even if one takes the figure (spare parts included) contained in the minutes of the Board of Directors' meeting of 30 September 1977, i.e. CFA francs

400 million, Klöckner's deficient performance appears *minute*, by [81] comparison with the revised contractual price of the factory, which was DM 56,840,000.

The undersigned cannot accept that a contracting partner who has performed his obligations to the extent of 95 per cent should be deprived, as the Award implies, of 80 per cent of the price, as well as of the delay-interest.

It is apparently for the purpose of compensating for this flagrant imbalance between the value of Klöckner's performance and the denial of payment of the price that the Award invokes also certain errors of technical and commercial management attributed to Klöckner.

III. KLÖCKNER'S RESPONSIBILITY FOR THE COMMERCIAL AND TECHNICAL MANAGEMENT

The opinion set forth hereunder is subject to an express reservation regarding the jurisdiction of the Arbitral Tribunal: see section VI below.

It cannot be denied that Klöckner had to ensure the commercial and technical management of SOCAME. It is likewise undeniable that Klöckner was actually in charge of the commercial and technical management of SOCAME until January 1978 (on which date the Cameroonian party terminated the Management Contract and entrusted the management to the Société Commerciale des Potasses d'Alsace). It follows from the foregoing that Klöckner has duly discharged its obligation to manage SOCAME at the commercial and technical plane.

The only remaining problem is to determine whether Klöckner has managed SOCAME well at the commercial and technical level.

The reply given on this point by the Award consists in the allegation that Klöckner did not fulfil its duty of good management. This allegation is stated as follows:

— on p. 117: "For the proper fulfilment of the contracts in question it was not enough to deliver a fertilizer factory; it was also necessary for that factory to possess the necessary capacity *and to be managed in such a manner as to achieve the desired objectives*".

— on p. 120: "The most conclusive proof of Klöckner's failure to perform its duty of technical and commercial management derives simply from the shutdown of the factory in December 1977, by decision of Klöckner personnel sent to Cameroon, after 18 months of underproduction and operating losses".

The undersigned cannot accept this reasoning at all. The reasoning is vitiated by an error of omission, in the form of the failure on part of the Award to investigate the actual content of the duty of management. An obligation of this kind can be construed in two manners: *on the one hand*, it may be viewed as a duty to achieve a result, in which case it is termed an obligation of result (*obligation de résultat*) and is only deemed fulfilled when the result is achieved; *on the other hand*, it may be regarded as a duty to

[82] provide the means and the diligence normally required in a given situation, in which case it is termed an obligation of means (*obligation de moyen*) and is deemed fulfilled when all the means which can reasonably be required have been applied, even if the result is not achieved.

The Award did not investigate the content of the duty of management, or the question whether it constituted an obligation of result or of means; the above citation (p. 120), however, indicates that the Award decided necessarily – but albeit implicitly – that it was an obligation of result.

This is unacceptable. For indeed, when a person undertakes to manage a company, there are no grounds for assuming that he thereby undertakes also to produce profitable results and to prevent every conceivable technical accident, breakdown or defect. On the contrary, the person who undertakes to manage a company only undertakes to apply all the means that can reasonably be required to ensure a management that is on a par with that of a prudent manager placed in a similar situation. *A contrario*, in the case – an extremely rare one in practice – where an obligation of result is imposed on a manager, this will be clearly stated and specified in clauses which set out very precisely the results to be achieved, the margins of tolerance and the penalties if any.

There is nothing of the kind in the present instance. Not only was there no obligation as to the result of the management provided for in the contractual agreements, but – a fact which is even more important – these agreements explicitly and formally exclude all responsibility on Klöckner's part. Thus, Article 13 (not cited in the Award) of the Turnkey Contract expressly provides as follows:

> In particular, Klöckner shall not be liable for compensation in respect of indirect damages inherent in the operation and functioning of the factory.

Of course, this provision does not in any way exonerate Klöckner from the obligation to deliver a factory conforming with the specifications of the contract; on the other hand, it rules out completely the contention that Klöckner could be bound by an obligation of result, merely because it undertook a duty of management.

Since it is thus apparent that Klöckner was bound solely by an obligation of means, the question which arises is whether Klöckner did in fact apply all the means that could be reasonably expected of it to manage SOCAME properly at the commercial and technical plane.

(a) With regard to commercial management, the Award does not raise any criticism against Klöckner. The mere existence of an operating deficit does not prove that a fault was committed. Actually, the operating deficit and the losses sustained by SOCAME were attributable to a long series of factors which have nothing to do with any fault on the part of Klöckner: the price fluctuations in world markets (with prices in 1976 much below those of domestic markets, as indicated in the minutes of many Board of Directors' meetings and in the report of 22 April 1977 by the President of SOCAME), the importation by Cameroonian governmental and para-governmental bodies of fertilizers bought at dumping prices in international markets, the **[83]** authoritarian fixing by the Government of sale prices for SOCAME at levels which did not cover production costs, the very heavy financial burdens shouldered by SOCAME, the high production costs attributable to SOCAME's low output, itself due to SOCAME's financial inability to obtain supplies of raw materials and spare parts. While on this issue of commercial management, it may be added that SOCAME's freedom in that matter had been reduced to nothing; the Cameroonian fertilizer market is anything except free, since it is entirely controlled by the Government in the following ways: by the delivery of import licences, by the system of subsidies paid through Fonader, a governmental entity, by the State's hold on the governmental and para-governmental bodies which buy fertilizers, by the free distribution of fertilizers by FAO, through the fixing of SOCAME sale prices and by the control by the State of the whole transport and distribution circuit.

Bearing in mind the constraints upon the commercial management of SOCAME, and the real causes of the operating deficit, the undersigned considers the following proposition as self-evident: if the Award does not note any failing on the part of Klöckner in the commercial management of SOCAME, it is simply because no such failing as to commercial management can be blamed on Klöckner.

(b) As regards technical management, the Award is equally silent with respect to the whole period up to the shutdown at the end of December 1977. No failing is attributed to Klöckner, bearing in mind that the shutdown of the factory in December 1977 does not itself constitute a failing, since moreover it was basically due to financial considerations peculiar to SOCAME. As for the period after 15 December 1977, the Award blames Klöckner for not ensuring the proper maintenance of the factory, but although stress is laid (on pages 120–127, 103 *et seq.*) on the problem of corrosion, no reference is made to any omission on Klöckner's part to take reasonable steps to avoid corrosion of a factory that was shut down. On the contrary, both the Board of Directors' minutes of the meetings held since January 1978 and the B report of October 1978 contain numerous references to all the maintenance work effected during the year 1978; undoubtedly, this maintenance work and these steps to prevent corrosion could have been even more effective but it is undeniable that SOCAME's financial situation, which had already prevented the restart of the factory on 1 March 1978, prevented also the carrying out of more extensive maintenance work and further steps to prevent corrosion.

Thus, in the absence of all positive proof of any failure by Klöckner to fulfil its obligation of diligence in the technical management of the factory, the abstract and imprecise accusations made in the Award must be rejected.

In any case, even supposing that Klöckner had – in very small part – failed in its obligations regarding commercial and technical management, this would not suffice to justify depriving Klöckner of 80 per cent of the price of the factory as well as of the interest thereon.

[84]   IV. THE RELATIONS BETWEEN THE CAMEROONIAN AND GERMAN PARTIES

The undersigned has expressed in sections I to III above his dissenting opinion to the effect that Klöckner did not fail in its duty of disclosure, that it supplied a factory conforming with the specifications of the contract, and that no reasonable blame can be attached to it for any faults in the technical and commercial management of the company.

The dissenting opinion thus expressed by the undersigned is supported not only by the arguments stated above and based on documents filed in the Arbitral Tribunal proceedings, but also by the actual conduct of the Cameroonian party.

(a) It must be pointed out in the first place that, at no time after the signing of the basic contracts and until the commencement of arbitration proceedings, did the Cameroonian party serve a *formal notice ("mise en demeure") upon Klöckner* demanding performance.

It cannot be claimed that such formal notice was unnecessary on the grounds that Klöckner was aware of the defective functioning of the factory and that it had the duty to ensure its proper functioning, or again that Klöckner was aware of its poor management and at the same time knew its duty of proper management. Any such claim would run counter to the very meaning of the concept of formal notice (*mise en demeure*).

Formal notice constitutes the expression of a creditor's intention to demand from his contracting partner the performance of the obligations undertaken by the latter; it accordingly embodies, in the first place, a statement that the obligation has not been performed and asserts, in the second place, the liability of the contracting partner for that non-performance; lastly, it purports to demand performance.

Now, no such formal notice was ever given to Klöckner by the Cameroonian party, neither at the time when Klöckner was the majority shareholder and manager nor during the period when Klöckner was a minority shareholder and had ceased to be responsible for management.

There is thus no indication from the Cameroonian party asserting Klöckner's responsibility regarding the functioning of the factory or the management of the company. Conversely, all the evidence forcefully indicates that if the Cameroonian party had felt that Klöckner was liable for the malfunctioning of the factory or the mismanagement of the company, it would have put Klöckner formally on notice to perform its contractual obligations.

This failure to put Klöckner formally on notice thus constitutes an essential element of the dispute, because it proves that the Cameroonian party at no time felt that the operation of the factory and the management of the company brought into play Klöckner's liability in any way.

Additionally in the second place, the Cameroonian party has never disputed its obligations and its debts towards Klöckner. This is of course in perfect consonance with its failure to put Klöckner on notice and, moreover, proves that, in the eyes of the Cameroonian party, Klöckner did not fail in its obligations as to delivery and as to management. In support of this [85] statement, in the first place, the essential facts concerning the operation of the factory have to be recalled:

— start-up of operation: second half of 1976;
— operation from July 1976 to December 1977;
— shutdown of operation: December 1977;
— refitting work: 1979 to mid-1980;
— satisfactory operation of the factory: second half of 1980;
— final shutdown: end of 1981.

We will show below that from the commencement of operations (July 1976) until the date on which the factory's operation was acknowledged to be satisfactory (July–August 1980), the Cameroonian party consistently expressed its willingness (and not its unwillingness) to pay.

•   •   •

[This portion of the dissenting opinion in which the dissenting arbitrator discusses and quotes from a number of documents drawn up by the parties between October 1976 and 1980 has not been released for publication. The dissenting opinion continues, citing from a document relating to a meeting of the Board held on 7 March 1980 in which the question was raised whether it would be possible for the Cameroonian party to claim damages from the supplier of the factory:]

•   •   •

Replying to the first question of Mr Bobbo, the General Manager admits that it is difficult for him to be very precise on this point. But on a whole, SOCAME does not possess the technical documents nor the statements of the acceptance of the plant. It is consequently difficult to know in which state the equipment was at the end of the erection and to confirm that certain materials did not correspond to the descriptions of the contract.

Coming back to the deficiencies found in the plant, the President thinks that it is a burden characterizing the processes of industrialization of the country for the simple reason that a contract of technical and management assistance is generally concluded with the foreign partners who construct the plant and accept it. Consequently, everything seems to go normally and if one has to deplore this state of the facts, it is more than imperative to use all efforts for the technical training of the Cameroonians... .

It is striking to observe that, at a time when Mr Bobbo expressly raised the question of Klöckner's possible liability, the Board of Directors took no decision, and made no complaints against Klöckner: no view was expressed by that Board on the subject, nor did the Board make any allegation regarding Klöckner's supposed liability, no step – even of a purely preventive nature – was taken, and no investigation decided or even contemplated. It would have been all the easier to invoke an alleged liability on Klöckner's part in that, on March 7 1980, Klöckner became a minority

[86] shareholder and ceased to be responsible for the management and to be in charge of the General Management. The conclusion to be reached, in all logic, is that there is a strong presumption that Klöckner's liability was not involved.

The factory restarted operations *in July 1980*. As will be shown later, it functioned to the full satisfaction of the Cameroonian party.

On 20 September 1980, the Ministry of Finance decided (Decision No. 001901/MIN FI/89) as follows:

> Authority is hereby given for the *payment* of an amount of CFA francs 2,000 million as an exceptional subsidy to SOCAME and *intended for the settlement of the bills of exchange which have matured on the Klöckner loan since October 11, 1978.* (reference to filed documents)

At a date which is not legible but which must certainly lie between 20 September and 12 November 1980, the Ministry of Finance issued a "payment order" for CFA francs 2,000 million:

> to the order of SOCAME and intended for the settlement of the bills of exchange which have matured on the Klöckner loan since 11 October 1978. (reference to filed documents)

On 12 November 1980, the Ministry for Foreign Affairs of the United Republic of Cameroon wrote to the Ambassador of the Federal Republic of Germany as follows:

> The Ministry for Foreign Affairs of the United Republic of Cameroon presents its compliments to the Embassy of the Federal Republic of Germany and has the honour to inform it that *payment* of the sum of CFA francs 2,000 million, *intended for the settlement of the bills of exchange which have matured on the Klöckner loan since 11 October 1978* has been effected by the Ministry of Finance, Budget Division, into Account No ... opened in the name of SOCAME in the books of the BIAO bank at Douala.

In the light of the foregoing, it is absolutely obvious and altogether indisputable that the Cameroonian party:

— not only never invoked Klöckner's alleged liability regarding the functioning of the factory or the management of the company;
— but also, and above all invariably and constantly acknowledged itself the debtor of the amounts owed by it to Klöckner under the contracts.

There can be no better proof of the fact that – as set forth by the undersigned in sections I, II and III above – the Cameroonian party never considered that Klöckner's liability could be invoked either because of a lack of information, under the Turnkey Contract or under the duty of management.

It was only after the final shutdown of the factory in December 1981 (due to economic and financial causes, as indicated in the Award), and during the actual arbitration proceedings, that the Cameroonian party refused to pay,

pretending for the first time that Klöckner had committed certain failings. **[87]**
This change of attitude can be explained by the desire to charge Klöckner
with the losses incurred by the Cameroonian party "in a joint venture where
the two parties participated, or should have participated, with open eyes and
full understanding of their actions" (page 136 of the Award). The
undersigned finds altogether inadmissible the attitude of the Cameroonian
party, after it had acknowledged that the other contracting party had
correctly performed its obligations, of trying to charge the latter with
financial losses which do not pertain to it. This is all the more inadmissible
since Klöckner too had incurred heavy losses in the same joint venture, and
in particular the loss of its share of capital in SOCAME (over DM 9 million)
and of the amounts standing to its credit on account.

Finally on this point, a comment is in order regarding the payment of CFA
francs 2,000 million by the Cameroonian Government in October 1980. As
stated above, the payment order for CFA francs 2,000 million in favour of
Klöckner was dated 20 September 1980 and signed by the Minister of
Finance. Actually, this amount was never received by Klöckner and was
purely and simply kept by SOCAME which thus deliberately violated the terms
of the Ministerial decision of 20 September 1980. The Award points out
(page 134) that this payment was "conditional" and that it did not involve a
waiver by the Cameroonian party of its claim to invoke Klöckner's liability.

The undersigned must point out that, on the one hand, the mere decision
to pay a sum of money, and its actual payment, do not constitute a waiver
of the right to invoke the other contracting party's liability; on the other
hand, the decision to pay, and the payment itself, constitute an admission
(once again) by the Cameroonian party that, in its view, Klöckner had
duly performed its obligations. It is moreover completely mistaken to claim
that the payment in question was "conditional". The payment was
unconditional.

●   ●   ●

[The dissenting arbitrator quotes from the minutes of the meeting of
SOCAME's Board of Directors following payment by the Government of the
sum referred to above. This portion of the dissenting opinion has not been
released for publication. The dissenting opinion continues:]

●   ●   ●

With regard to the conduct of SOCAME at the beginning of 1981, the
undersigned is struck not so much by the misappropriation to the detriment
of Klöckner as by the fact that no claim was made asserting Klöckner's
possible responsibility for the functioning of the factory and the
management of the Company. If at any time the Cameroonian party had
considered that Klöckner was not entitled to the CFA francs 2,000 million
paid by the Government, it would have been easy for it to state that this

[88] amount was going to be kept by SOCAME as compensation for the damage caused by Klöckner. That would have been all the easier to do since, at the time, Klöckner had no influence whatever over SOCAME, being very much in a minority position and no longer in charge of the management. Even after the wrongful misappropriation of funds, however, SOCAME felt that it had no basis for a claim of liability against Klöckner, which had properly performed its obligations under the contracts.

V. SUPPLEMENTARY REMARKS

As the undersigned sees it, there is a very serious contradiction in the grounds which the Award invokes in order to deprive Klöckner of the balance of the price of the factory, representing 80 per cent of the capital, apart from the interest.

The Award explains (p. 127) that "[t]here is a certain equilibrium, a certain relationship, as we have suggested above, between that which was paid and the approximate value of the components supplied by Klöckner in 1974–1975 and used by Defendant in the redesigned factory, which was restarted successfully in 1980."

This means that, according to the Award, the value of the components delivered by Klöckner, and used by the Cameroonian party, is equal to the amount received by Klöckner, i.e. DM 16,719,000 in capital and DM 11,852,974 in interest; thus, according to the Award, Klöckner had delivered a factory worth DM 28,215,699 but was not entitled to any further payment – whence the rejection of its claim.

The Award, however, states elsewhere (p. 107):

In order to determine the 1980 value of the Klöckner components, it is necessary to deduct the following elements from the contract price...

The Award accordingly proceeded to deduct certain amounts reflecting the modifications made to the factory since 1980, the payment in respect of principal, interests, cost of repairs, and operating losses.

Apart from the fact that no figures are given for the first, fourth and fifth of the elements thus deducted (a fact which constitutes a failure to state the reasons) it will be noted:

— that in order to determine the "1980 value of the components" delivered by Klöckner, deductions have been made that have no relation whatsoever with the components delivered;

— that the method used on page 107 of the Award is completely different from that used on page 127;

— that the deduction made on page 107 in respect of "operating losses" is in total contradiction with the grounds given in the Award in support of its decision to reject the counterclaim;

— that on page 107 the amount of interest is deducted from the components delivered by Klöckner whereas page 127, although it concludes that Klöckner is not entitled to the said interest, **[89]** nevertheless adds the accrued interest to the paid-up capital in order to maintain that Klöckner is not entitled to any supplement.

These contradictions in the grounds for the Award, aggravated by the absence of any grounds at all on some points, compel the undersigned to file his dissenting opinion, apart from the express reservations in sections I, II, III and IV above.

VI. JURISDICTION OF THE ICSID TRIBUNAL

The Arbitral Tribunal held that it had jurisdiction to evaluate Klöckner's commercial and technical management of SOCAME. The Tribunal's decision on this point is based on Article 9 of the Protocol which provides that Klöckner

shall be responsible for the technical and commercial management of the Company, to be carried out under a Management Contract, for at least 5 years from start-up, with an option for its extention.

As it is known, a Management Contract was in fact signed between the parties; it specified that:

All disputes arising from the present contract shall be finally settled in accordance with the Rules of Conciliation and Arbitration of the International Chamber of Commerce by one or more arbitrators named in conformity with said Rules. The Arbitral Court shall have its seat in Bern, Switzerland, and shall apply Swiss substantive law.

In support of the Arbitral Tribunal's contention that it had jurisdiction to evaluate Klöckner's technical and commercial management of SOCAME, the Award states (page 22):

The Tribunal cannot share this view, under which ICSID jurisdiction would have existed from the date of the Protocol, 4 December 1971, but would have disappeared by a kind of implicit derogation on 7 April 1977, the date the Management Contract was signed... Article 8 of the Management Contract provides for ICC jurisdiction only for 'all disputes arising from the present contract'. But disputes flowing from Klöckner's performance, non-performance, or flawed performance of the technical and commercial management of SOCAME were subject to the ICSID clause from the start-up of the factory and remain subject to this clause...

The Management Contract, intended according to Article 9 of the Protocol of Agreement to ensure Klöckner's responsibility for the Company's technical and commercial management, cannot be interpreted as an implicit waiver of a fundamental undertaking of the Protocol of Agreement, either in its substance, or with respect to its jurisdictional guarantee.

[90]   But it [the Claimant] expressly acknowledged the Tribunal's jurisdiction "with respect to the Protocol of Agreement" without making an exception as to its Article 9... On this score, the Report of the Executive Directors of the World Bank indicates at paragraph 24 that 'the Convention does not... specify the time at which consent should be given. (pp. 23–24)

On p. 122 the Award states:

> The Tribunal does not have jurisdiction to evaluate the Management Contract nor to interpret it. It must, however, proceed on the following presumption: That this contract, intended to impose on the Claimant "responsibility for the technical and commercial management of the Company", could neither qualify nor diminish Klöckner's undertaking by virtue of the basic agreement: the Protocol of Agreement. Even if the Tribunal does not have jurisdiction to interpret the Management Contract, it must presume that there is perfect compatibility between the two instruments, the Protocol of Agreement constituting the charter (*accord-cadre*) of the investment and the Management Contract simply being intended to ensure performance of the basic agreement... The best proof that Article 9 of the Protocol was not a mere promise of future agreement, nor an inoperative stipulation requiring a subsequent contract defining performance in order to became applicable, but an essential, firm and 'self-executing' undertaking, lies in the fact that the Management Contract was not signed until 7 April 1977. Consequently, the technical and commercial management of the factory during the entire critical period in 1976 and the first three months of 1977, was carried out by Klöckner on the basis of Article 9 of the Protocol alone. This Article was the single source of all the authority Klöckner exercised during this period and consequently of all of its responsibility for the management of the factory.

The complexity of these arguments, set forth in two separate parts of the Award (pp. 22–23 and 121–122) and the fact that they are unrelated to the realities of the problem, show clearly the Tribunal's embarrassment when trying to justify in the Award its jurisdiction over a matter where its lack of jurisdiction is manifest.

In the first place, attention must be drawn to certain obvious errors:

— It is a mistake to say that "the disputes flowing from Klöckner's performance, non-performance or flawed performance of the technical and commercial management of SOCAME were subject to the ICSID clause..." In fact, the technical and commercial management of SOCAME began, in accordance with Article 9, "from the start-up of the factory", but the management remained entirely governed by the Management Contract which, by virtue of its Article 9, *entered into force on 1 January 1975*. The parties had thus expressed their intention to make the technical and commercial management of SOCAME subject to the provisions of the Management Contract, even before the start-up of the factory;

— The Award makes another mistake when it relies, as grounds for the Tribunal's jurisdiction, on the consent allegedly expressed by the Claimant in its Reply Memorial; in fact, in that Memorial, the

Claimant pointed out that "Klöckner's obligations regarding the **[91]**
management of SOCAME flow only from the Management Contract
concluded between the parties" (Reference to the Memorial and p. 121
of the Award);

— A further mistake made in the Award was to consider that consent to
submit the dispute to ICSID arbitration could be given after the Centre
had been seized of the case; indeed, the "Report of the Executive
Directors of the World Bank", mentioned in paragraph 2 of the
Award, states on this point:

"The consent of the parties must be given *before the Centre is seized of the case*"
(para. 24 of the Report of the Executive Directors).[2]

Apart from these mistakes, the Award errs on its page 122 because it fails
to give any grounds for its conclusions, which rely on the totally baseless
assertion that even if "[t]he Tribunal does not have jurisdiction to evaluate
the Management Contract or to interpret it, it must, however, proceed from
the following presumption: That this Contract, intended to assign to
Claimant "responsibility for the technical and commercial management of
the Company", could neither qualify nor diminish Klöckner's undertaking
by virtue of the basic agreement: The Protocol of Agreement".

The question then arises of the grounds on which this presumption is
based: no such grounds are given in the Award. Moreover, a "presumption"
cannot have the effect of a postulate. Lastly, even if the presumption were
valid – something which remains to be proved – it would still be necessary to
show how the stipulation of an ICC arbitration clause (instead of the ICSID
arbitration clause) could have as its purpose, or as its effect, to "qualify" or
"diminish" Klöckner's undertaking by virtue of the basic agreement, i.e. the
Protocol of Agreement. The stipulation of an arbitration clause does not
detract from undertaking to manage SOCAME, nor does it diminish that
undertaking in any way.

The foregoing remarks are equally valid with regard to the next argument
put forward in the Award and according to which the Tribunal "should
presume that there is perfect compatibility between the two instruments".
Apart from the fact that no grounds exist on which to base this alleged
presumption, one fails to see how the management which Klöckner had to
carry out "under the Management Contract" could preclude the inclusion in
that same Management Contract of an arbitration clause different from that
in the Protocol of Agreement.

Lastly, the Award says that the undertaking stipulated in Article 9 was a
"self-executing" undertaking and that this Article "was the single source of
all the authority Klöckner exercised during this period, and consequently of
all of its responsibility for the management of the factory". Now, as pointed
out above, the Management Contract came into effect on 1 January 1975, a
fact which reflected the intention of the parties to rely on that Management

[² 1 *ICSID Reports* 23 at 28.]

[92] Contract as the single source of all the authority Klöckner exercised during the period in question, and consequently of all its responsibility for the management of the factory. The Award thus misrepresents the very clear and precise terms of the Management Contract.

Having thus exposed the above errors, failure to state the grounds and misrepresentation of the contract, we must now discuss the problem of the Arbitral Tribunal's jurisdiciton by placing it in its proper setting. This proper setting for the discussion was perceived by the Tribunal itself (on page 122) of the Award, but did not draw from it the necessary consequences. On page 122, it is stated that the Protocol of Agreement constituted "the charter (*accord-cadre*) of the investment" and that the Management Contract was "intended to ensure performance of the basic agreement".

Accordingly, the question arises of determining whether the Tribunal having jurisdiction to evaluate the charter (*accord-cadre*) equally had jurisdiction with respect to the implementing agreement.

This question evidently calls for a negative answer; since the parties had made a point, in the implementing agreement for the charter (*accord-cadre*), of departing from the arbitration clause of that charter and agreeing on a different arbitration clause for the implementing agreement itself, it was clearly their intention that the latter should not be subject to the ICSID clause of the charter.

This is all the more obvious in that the Management Contract signed by the parties after lengthy negotiations contained an ICC arbitration clause, *whereas* the earlier draft – drawn up but not signed – contained an ICSID arbitration clause. The parties thus *expressly agreed and intended* that all disputes relating to the technical and commercial management carried out under the Management Contract should be subject to ICC arbitration and not to ICSID arbitration.

The undersigned can see no valid argument which might contradict this self-evident proposition; there are, on the contrary, good arguments to support it.

In the first place, Article 9 does not state only that Klöckner "shall have responsibility for the technical and commercial management of the factory"; it adds that this responsibility "shall be carried out under a Management Contract". This means that a Management Contract had to be signed, relating to the technical and commercial management by Klöckner.

Why was it thus stipulated that the management in question would "be carried out under a Management Contract"? It was because the Protocol, being an *accord-cadre*, did no more than lay down a framework and had not the purpose – nor could it have the effect – of regulating the conditions of performance. These conditions, which related to Klöckner's rights, powers, remuneration, obligations and responsibility in respect of management, and to the arbitration clause, were the subject of a separate agreement, namely the Management Contract.

It follows that any attempt to identify Klöckner's powers and its responsibilities in respect of management *must of necessity* involve an analysis and evaluation of the Management Contract. What is more, any [93] attempt to do so without such analysis and evaluation would constitute a *violation* of the Protocol of Agreement, which specifies clearly that the responsibility in question "shall be carried out under a Management Contract".

The statement on page 122 that the Management Contract "could neither qualify nor diminish Klöckner's undertaking by virtue of the basic agreement" misses the real issue, because the Management Contract was not intended to qualify or diminish any undertaking; the purpose of the Management Contract was to *define the undertaking* subscribed by Klöckner in the charter (*accord-cadre*).

Moreover, it is incoherent to claim at one and the same time that the Protocol of Agreement is a framework agreement (*accord-cadre*) and also that it is an implementing agreement whose Article 9 defines Klöckner's powers, duties and responsibilities. Given this reasoning, it is illogical to rely on the Turnkey Contract as the basis for evaluating Klöckner's responsibility as the supplier of the factory. It would be enough to invoke Articles 3, 6 and 7 of the Protocol!

This is obviously of little weight: just as the Turnkey Contract was intended to describe Klöckner's responsibilities regarding the supply of the factory, the Management Contract purported to describe Klöckner's duties and responsibilities in the management of the factory. Moreover, just as it would be an absurdity to pass judgement on the supplier of the factory without examining the Turnkey Contract, it would be equally absurd to pass judgement on the manager without examining the Management Contract.

It is therefore the undersigned's considered opinion that the Arbitral Tribunal had no jurisdiction to evaluate Klöckner's possible responsibility resulting from the fact that it was in charge of technical and commercial management.

The important mistakes, the numerous contradictions and failures to state the grounds, and the misrepresentation of contract clauses, which vitiate the Award and which are exposed in the present dissenting opinion make it imperative for the undersigned to reject the Award, which is moreover in flat contradiction with the Cameroonian party's constant and repeated acknowledgement without reservation over many years of its debt towards Klöckner.

[*Source*: The full text of the award is unpublished. The exerpts from the [94] award produced here are an English translation of the French original. Extensive excerpts of the French original are published in 111 *Journal de Droit International* 409 (1984). Excerpts of the English translation of the award are published in 1 *Journal of International Arbitration* 145 (1984). The excerpts of the dissenting opinion are taken, with the permission of the *Journal of International Arbitration*, from an article by Dr Friedrich Niggeman: "The ICSID *Klöckner v. Cameroon* Award: The Dissenting Opinion" published in 1 *Journal of International Arbitration* 331.]

[The following is the text of the Annulment Decision of 3 May 1985:]

DECISION ON ANNULMENT, 3 MAY 1985

(Translation)

INTRODUCTION

1. On 10 February 1984, the Klöckner Company (hereafter referred to as the Claimant) lodged with the ICSID Secretariat an Application for the Annulment of an Award pursuant to Article 52 of the Convention on the

Settlement of Investment Disputes between States and Nationals of Other **[96]** States (Washington Convention) of 18 March 1965. The Award was rendered on 21 October by an Arbitral Tribunal constituted in 1981 following the registration on 14 April 1981 of a Request for Arbitration lodged on 10 April 1981 by Klöckner Industrie-Anlagen GmbH, a company incorporated under German law having its principal place of business (*siège social*) in Duisburg.

The Tribunal consisted of Messrs Dominique Schmidt, a French national, appointed by the Claimant; William D. Rogers, an American national, appointed by the United Republic of Cameroon and the Cameroon Fertilizer Company (SOCAME SA), the Respondent; and Eduardo Jiménez de Aréchaga, a Uruguayan national, appointed President by agreement of the two arbitrators.

The Application for Annulment was registered by the ICSID Secretariat on 16 February 1984. On 28 February the Chairman of the Administrative Council appointed Professors Ahmed El-Kosheri, an Egyptian national, Ignaz Seidl-Hohenveldern, an Austrian national, and Pierre Lalive, a Swiss national, as members of the *ad hoc* Committee provided for in Article 52(3) of the Washington Convention. Professor Pierre Lalive was elected President of the Committee.

Following a preliminary meeting of the *ad hoc* Committee in Geneva on 8 May 1984, in the presence of ICSID's representative, Mr G. R. Delaume, the parties and their counsel (for Klöckner, Maître Philippe Nouel of Gide, Loyrette and Nouel, Paris, and for Cameroon, Maître Jan Paulsson of Coudert Frères, Paris) held a first meeting with the *ad hoc* Committee on 23 May to discuss various procedural matters. As a result of this meeting, a procedural order was issued on 24 May setting the time limits for the exchange of memorials, the dates for the oral proceedings and miscellaneous questions of detail.

In accordance with this order and the ICSID Arbitration Rules, Cameroon's Counter-Memorial (in reply to Klöckner's Application for Annulment, which was considered as the First Memorial) was filed on 2 July 1984; Klöckner's Reply Memorial on 3 August 1984; and Cameroon's Rejoinder (entitled "Reply") on 31 August 1984. The oral pleadings then took place in Geneva on 24 and 25 September 1984.

On 27 September 1984 the Committee issued two procedural orders requesting the parties to provide various documents and authorizing them to file notes on their oral pleadings no later than 31 October 1984. Both parties complied with these orders.

During November and December 1984, various procedural questions were before the Committee. There was in particular a request from Klöckner for the transcription of oral pleadings before the arbitrators in July 1983. Cameroon objected to this request. On 20 December 1984 the Committee decided to reject the request but authorized the Claimant to submit a summary, not exceeding five pages, of its July 1983 oral pleading by 31 December 1984. The Respondent was authorized to submit a summary of

[97] its reply oral pleading by 10 January 1985. The Claimant submitted its summary on 29 December 1984. The Respondent decided that it would be useless to do so.

During the first months of 1985, the *ad hoc* Committee held several working sessions in Geneva, and requested that the ICSID Secretariat forward to it several documents relating to the arbitral proceeding. Documents requested on 14 January and 10 April 1985 were supplied on 15 January and 22 April respectively.

On 25 April 1985 the President of the Committee requested ICSID to inform the parties that the proceeding was closed.

2. In its Application for Annulment, the Claimant contested the Award on several grounds. These may be grouped as follows:

   I. Manifest excess of powers (Article 52(1)(b)) due to the Arbitral Tribunal's lack of jurisdiction;

   II. Manifest excess of powers (Article 52(1)(b)) due to a violation of Article 42(1) of the Convention;

   III. Serious departure from a fundamental rule of procedure (Article 52(1)(d)); and

   IV. Failure to state reasons (Article 52 (1)(e)).

3. Before proceeding to examine each complaint in the order listed above, the *ad hoc* Committee considers it necessary to note, by way of a preliminary observation, that the remedy provided by Article 52 of the Convention of 18 March 1965 is in no sense an *appeal* against arbitral awards. This provision permits each party in an ICSID arbitration to request the annulment of the award on one or more of the grounds listed exhaustively in the first paragraph of Article 52 of the Convention.

As will be shown later, application of the paragraph demands neither a narrow interpretation, nor a broad interpretation, but an appropriate interpretation, taking into account the legitimate concern to surround the exercise of the remedy to the maximum extent possible with guarantees in order to achieve a harmonious balance between the various objectives of the Convention. The very language of the provision demands a cautious approach: sub-paragraph (b) requires that the Tribunal's excess of powers be *"manifest."* Likewise, under sub-paragraph (d), only a *"serious* departure" from a *fundamental* rule of procedure can justify challenging an award. Finally, the Convention envisages in sub-paragraph (e) a "failure to state" reasons and not, for example, a mistake in stating reasons. With respect to each complaint, the *ad hoc* Committee will determine the meaning which must be given to the legal concepts involved.

I. EXCESS OF POWERS DUE TO THE ARBITRAL TRIBUNAL'S LACK OF JURISDICTION (ARTICLE 52(1)(b))

4. Starting from the foregoing preliminary observation, it must be noted that the term "excess of powers" (*excès de pouvoir*) used in sub-paragraph

(b)[1] is multi-faceted: it can cover a variety of complaints formulated against **[98]** the contested award.

Clearly, an aribral tribunal's lack of jurisdiction, whether said to be partial or total, necessarily comes within the scope of an "excess of powers" under Article 52(1)(b).

Consequently, an applicant for annulment may not only invoke lack of jurisdiction *ratione materiae* or *ratione personae* under Articles 25 and 26 of the Convention, but may also contend that the award exceeded the Tribunal's jurisdiction as it existed under the appropriate interpretation of the ICSID arbitration clause.

Confronted by an application of this nature, the *ad hoc* Committee should: *primo* decide whether the Tribunal has indeed exceeded its jurisdiction in any way whatsoever; and *secundo*, if it has, determine the extent to which such an excess might be characterized as a "manifest excess of powers."

An award would be subject to annulment only where the excess of jurisdiction is sufficiently well established and recognized as manifest.

5. In the present case, the question of jurisdiction was raised for the first time with regard to the counterclaim. The Claimant asked the Tribunal to declare itself incompetent with regard to that claim (Reply Memorial dated 30 October 1982, pp. 10–14), on the ground that the Management Contract concluded exclusively between Klöckner and SOCAME contains an arbitration clause conferring jurisdiction on the ICC Court of Arbitration and not on ICSID.

6. Examining its jurisdiction in general, the Tribunal first noted (p. 21) that it had been seized by the Claimant on the basis of Article 18 of the Fertilizer Factory Turnkey Contract of 4 March 1972; that this jurisdiction was accepted by the Respondent who "expanded" it by also invoking Article 22 of the Protocol of Agreement of 4 December 1971, which is identical to Article 18 of the Turnkey Contract; and that such expansion was not contested by the Claimant.

The Award continues (p. 21) by considering as "important" the Claimant's acceptance (Reply Memorial, p. 11) of ICSID's jurisdiction "with respect to the Protocol of Agreement" because it would "therefore" have accepted:

> that the ICSID clause, contained in the Protocol of Agreement, applies to all of the undertakings agreed by the parties in said Protocol, including the Claimant's undertaking in Article 9 to "be responsible for the technical and commercial management of the Company, to be carried out under a Management Contract."

The importance of this acceptance is further underscored on page 23 of the Award. Here the Tribunal considers what it calls "the consent expressed

---

[1] Translator's note: The French text of Article 52(1)(b) reads "excès de pouvoir manifeste du Tribunal." The English text reads "that the Tribunal has manifestly exceeded its powers."

[99] in this regard (i.e., the Arbitral Tribunal's jurisdiction under Article 9 of the Protocol of Agreement) by the Claimant on page 11 of its Reply Memorial" to be a "decisive consideration" capable of casting aside any doubt. The Award continues (p. 23):

> In this document, the Claimant maintained that the Management Contract in and of itself falls outside the scope of this Tribunal's jurisdiction, and that is correct. But it expressly accepted the Tribunal's jurisdiction "with respect to the Protocol of Agreement," without excepting its Article 9.

7. Challenging the award for excess of powers within the meaning of Article 52(1)(b) of the Washington Convention, the Claimant criticized this argument, particularly on pages 8 and 9 of its Application for Annulment. It repeats several of its previous statements (for example on pp. 12–13 of the same Memorial cited by the Tribunal) which show that it has indeed accepted ICSID's and the Tribunal's jurisdiction "with respect to the Protocol of Agreement" generally but while specifying simultaneously how, in its opinion, this acceptance should be interpreted.

Thus, for example, in its Memorial (pp. 12–13) it wrote:

> *Neither could jurisdiction result from the arbitration clause of the Protocol of Agreement providing in its Article 9 for the conclusion of a management contract.* Article 22 of the Protocol of Agreement confers jurisdiction on ICSID over disputes "regarding the validity, interpretation or application of the provisions of the present Protocol." The arbitration clause of the Management Contract (VI, 8) covers "all disputes arising from the present Contract." Article 22 of the Protocol of Agreement thus only applies to the question of whether KLÖCKNER fulfilled its obligation to *conclude* a management contract pursuant to Article 9.

8. Under these circumstances, it must be acknowledged that the Award at the very least suffers from a serious ambiguity when it states (p. 23) that the Claimant has "expressly accepted the Tribunal's jurisdiction with respect to the Protocol of Agreement, without excepting its Article 9."

This statement is only apparently correct. If the Claimant did not think it useful or even possible to make a formal "exception" regarding Article 9 of the Protocol, this was in reality because it expressly confined its scope solely to the obligation to conclude a management contract. Whether this interpretation is correct or not is of no importance here, since we need only determine whether, as the Award states, the Claimant "expressly consented" to the Tribunal's jurisdiction with respect to Article 9 of the Protocol of Agreement *as interpreted by the Tribunal*, not by the Claimant. If the latter did indeed "expressly accept the Tribunal's jurisdiction *with respect to the Protocol of Agreement*," it is because it interpreted the Protocol (correctly or incorrectly) in a specific way, not because it accepted in advance any different interpretation the Tribunal might give it.

9. Whatever the correct interpretation of Article 9, it was impossible to base the Tribunal's jurisdiction on the alleged "express consent" of the

Claimant regarding Article 9 of the Protocol of Agreement as interpreted by **[100]**
the Tribunal. On the contrary, it is obvious that the Claimant never in the
arbitral proceeding accepted such jurisdiction *"ratione materiae" in the sense
that the Award accepted it.* To this extent, the Claimant's criticism appears
well founded. It was therefore superfluous for the Award to add that consent
to ICSID's jurisdiction may be expressed at any time, under the principle of
"forum prorogatum".

10. However, it still does not follow that the Award is tainted by manifest
excess of powers as required by the Convention.

The central question in this regard is whether, as the Claimant maintains,
the Tribunal manifestly exceeded its powers by finding:

— *on the one hand*, that it had:

> jurisdiction to rule on the performance of the parties' obligations with respect
> to Klöckner's responsibility for the technical and commercial management of
> SOCAME, which was to be carried out under a Management Contract (Award,
> p. 29);

and:

— *on the other*, (p. 22) that it did:

> *not have jurisdiction* to rule on disputes "arising exclusively from the
> Management Contract," Article 8 of which, according to the Tribunal,
> established the ICC's jurisdiction only for "all disputes arising from the present
> Contract."

According to the Application for Annulment (p. 7, para. 2, Discussion):

> a) The Arbitral Tribunal has clearly exceeded its jurisdiction. Having noted
> the parties' will, free of any ambiguity or equivocation, to submit the
> Management Contract and its performance to the jurisdiction of the
> International Chamber of Commerce, the Tribunal could not without
> contradicting itself examine the allegedly deficient nature of KLÖCKNER's
> management of SOCAME since in order to do so the Tribunal should have
> necessarily applied the provisions of the Management Contract.

This criticism is at the heart of the Claimant's argument that the Tribunal
"manifestly exceeded its powers" in its decision on its jurisdiction. It is
therefore necessary that the Award's reasons in this regard be examined
more closely.

11. On page 29 therein there appears the following:

> *As for the Management Contract* of 7 April 1977 between KLÖCKNER and
> SOCAME, also invoked by Respondent, *the Claimant is right in denying the
> jurisdiction of the Arbitral Tribunal to rule on disputes arising from this
> contract.* According to Article 8 of this contract: "All disputes arising from the
> present Contract shall be finally settled in accordance with the Rules of
> Conciliation and Arbitration of the International Chamber of Commerce..."

[101]   One immediately notices the absence of any formal correspondence between the reference to "disputes" arising from the Management Contract on the one hand and the text of Article 8 itself on the other hand. The text, which is cited by the Award; speaks of "*All* disputes arising" from this contract. This difference seems to have escaped the Tribunal. The Tribunal seems to have attached no weight or meaning to the generality, devoid of all qualification, of the terms "*all* disputes arising from the present Contract..."

After quoting the text of the (ICC) arbitration clause of the Management Contract (Article 8), the Award adds:

> Nevertheless, on the basis of Article 9 of the Protocol of Agreement, the Tribunal has jurisdiction to rule on the performance of the parties' obligations with respect to KLÖCKNER's responsibility for "the technical and commercial management" of SOCAME, which was to be carried out under a Management Contract.

This statement must be understood in light of the Tribunal's interpretation of Article 9 of the Protocol of Agreement (Award, pp. 21–24) which can be summarized here as follows:

> The Protocol of Agreement contained, as "a basic obligation" (*cf.* also p. 34), "KLÖCKNER's obligation to ensure the technical and commercial management of the plant; this was the "essential condition of the investment" (by KLÖCKNER or by the Government?). In other words, the Protocol would not be limited to providing, as the Claimant held, for the conclusion by the parties of the Management Contract. It would be "self-executing," that is, it would contain "by its wording" a sufficiently clear and precise definition of the parties' obligations. (Application for Annulment, p. 7, para. 2(b))

12. The Tribunal saw a basis for, or confirmation of, its interpretation in the chronology of events, and especially in the following factor: the "technical and commercial management was in fact performed by Klöckner, which alone ran SOCAME, *before as well as after the signature of the Management Contract.*" One proof of "*this fact*," in the Tribunal's opinion (p. 23), results from a decision taken in December 1977, after the signing of the Management Contract, to shut down the factory. This was a decision "adopted by the management, comprising (with only one exception) expatriates recommended by Klöckner, and without any evidence in the file that the corporation's Board of Directors had given its prior approval, or had even been consulted."

This passage calls for two remarks:

(i)   By "proof of *this* fact," the Award was referring only to the fact of management *after* the signing, not before. At this point, the Award gives no indication of proof of the fact that *before* the signing Klöckner had "run SOCAME entirely by itself," *da facto* or *de jure*. Subsequently (p. 119), however, the Award refers to a letter from Klöckner dated 12 April 1973 in which Klöckner notes that it "is responsible for running the factory."

(ii) The Award does not explain why the composition of SOCAME's **[102]**
management in December 1977 (a majority of expatriates
"recommended" by Klöckner) would itself be relevant and decisive.

13. Be that as it may, the Claimant's criticism (p. 8) of the Award's
"chronology" reasoning essentially addresses the misreading of the

> text of the (Management) Contract, the provisions of which had been
> definitively set and applied about two years before it was signed and "which
> consequently stipulated that *it was retroactive to 1 January 1975*; the parties
> had thus clearly decided to submit SOCAME's management to the provisions of
> the Management Contract alone."

It is true that in its Chapter III ("Jurisdiction of the Arbitral Tribunal") the
Award does not discuss this argument, although it would have warranted
some remarks. It may however be assumed that the Tribunal in fact did not
accept it: such assumption appears justified when we consider the Tribunal's
opinion (p. 22) on what it calls, in rejecting it, the theory that there was an
"implicit derogation" of the (ICSID) arbitration clause of the Protocol of
Agreement by the (ICC) arbitration clause (Article 8) of the Management
Contract:

> The Tribunal cannot share this view, under, which ICSID jurisdiction would
> have existed from the date of the Protocol, 4 December 1971, but would have
> evaporated by a kind of implicit derogation on 7 April 1977, the date the
> Management Contract was signed. There might doubtless be disputes arising
> exclusively from the Management Contract – relating for example to the
> payment of fees established in said Contract – and such disputes would
> naturally fall beyond the jurisdiction of this Tribunal, and be subject to the ICC
> clause....

14. Consequently, *even if* the Tribunal had taken into account (which it
seems not to have done) the Management Contract's stipulation that "it was
retroactive to 1 January 1975," (Application, p. 8), it would not have
accepted – given its interpretation of Article 9 of the Protocol – that the (ICC)
arbitration clause of the Management Contract could modify in any way
whatsoever, i.e., "derogate" from, ICSID's jurisdiction established by the
Protocol of Agreement of 4 December 1971.

Clearly, diverse opinions are possible in this regard. It might, for
example, be held that nothing prevents contracting parties, *after* concluding
a contract containing (as the Protocol does) an ICSID clause, from modifying
this clause (like any other clause in the contract), or limiting its scope by
another mutually agreed clause, since if they agree, they could equally well
modify or even eliminate the entire first contract.

It might also be asked why, in a case where two clauses apply to the same
subject matter, the second, more recent, one, could not "implicitly
derogate" from the first, assuming that this is a case of "implicit" derogation.
In this regard, reference should be made to Article VI(5) of the
Management Contract, according to which *"this Contract comprises the*

[103] entire agreement between the parties and cancels all prior correspondence..." This provision does not seem to have attracted the Tribunal's attention, as it did not ask if it was compatible with an examination of Klöckner's management obligations solely on the basis of the Protocol of Agreement.

Finally, a question might be asked regarding the statement in the Award (p. 22) that:

> Article 8 of the Management Contract provides for ICC jurisdiction *only* for *"all* disputes arising from the present Contract" (Emphasis added.)

It could be added that the Award does not seem to give full effect to the terms *"all disputes arising...,"* since it refers (p. 22) to "disputes arising *exclusively* from the Management Contract" as being outside its jurisdiction.

15. But the essence of the controversy is not there: it is whether the two successive arbitration clauses indeed have *different* fields of application (the first broader, the second more restricted). This is what the Tribunal maintains, apparently as a necessary consequence of its interpretation of the Protocol of Agreement with respect to Klöckner's obligations.

In the final analysis, it is therefore this interpretation which is at issue in the Claimant's contention that the Tribunal "manifestly exceeded its powers", allegedly by assuming jurisdiction to judge Klöckner's technical and commercial management, while declining jurisdiction over disputes arising from the Management Contract (or, more precisely, arising "exclusively" from this contract, such as those relating to the payment of compensation thereunder, *cf.* p. 22).

16. It is therefore appropriate to recall the text of Article 9 of the Protocol of Agreement:

> KLÖCKNER will be responsible for the technical and commercial management of the Company, to be carried out under a Management Contract for at least five years from start-up, with an option to renew.

It has been seen that Klöckner interprets this clause as imposing on the parties an obligation to *conclude* such a management contract. The Tribunal gives it a broader interpretation, essentially on the basis of Klöckner's performance of that obligation *before* the conclusion of the Management Contract and even before the date set by the retroactive effect clause, i.e., 1 January, 1975).

In reading the text of Article 9, it must be admitted that *both* interpretations – the Tribunal's and Klöckner's – are possible. Either one could have corresponded to the parties' joint and genuine intention. But it obviously does not follow that the one adopted by the Award is untenable and that it constitutes an excess of powers.

17. It is neither contestable nor contested that the arbitrators have "the power to determine their own jurisdiction" (*la compétence de la compétence*), subject only to the check of the *ad hoc* Committee in the case

of annulment proceedings provided by the Washington Convention's **[104]** system. They have exercised this power by interpreting the Protocol of Agreement in itself and with respect to the Management Contract. Even if it is assumed that they thereby exceeded their powers, which remains to be proven, it would, as required by Article 52(1)(b) of the Convention, be necessary that this be "manifest" for the Application to be accepted.

18. We shall deal first with the Award's interpretation of the Management Contract and its arbitration clause (Article 8) which provides that "all disputes arising from the present Contract" shall be submitted to ICC arbitration.

The Tribunal did not ask itself why the parties to the Management Contract, Klöckner and SOCAME, chose an ICC arbitration clause rather than continue to provide for ICSID arbitration. The Tribunal does not seem to have considered the possibility or likelihood that the parties thereby might have wished or sought to avoid the problem posed under the Washington Convention by the Cameroonian nationality of SOCAME, juridically a distinct legal entity but at the same time simply a means of implementing the project.

We should point out in passing that Cameroon's method, followed in many other "development" contracts, was to set up an enterprise, SOCAME, under the laws of the host country, with the latter having at least initially a minority share, and the enterprise being responsible for exercising the country's rights under the contract. This is a formula likely to be the source of legal complications and of conflicts, especially for the enterprise's management, consisting partially of expatriates.

19. The Tribunal adopts an interpretation of the purpose and scope of the ICC arbitration clause which requires examination for its consistency with the Tribunal's power to determine its own jurisdiction. There is of course room for discussion. A question may be asked in particular on the distinction the Award makes, if not explicitly, between disputes arising "*exclusively*" from the Management Contract and, to use the Tribunal's words (p. 22), disputes that, "flowing from Klöckner's performance, non-performance, or deficient performance of the technical and commercial management of SOCAME were subject to the ICSID clause from the start-up of the factory and remain subject to this clause by virtue of the combined effect of Articles 9 and 22 of the Protocol of Agreement..."

20. According to the Application for Annulment (p. 6 *et seq.*), the Tribunal could not, as it had done, declare itself incompetent with regard to the Management Contract and *at the same time* assert its jurisdiction with respect to Klöckner's management of the factory "by virtue of the combined effect of Articles 9 and 22 of the Protocol of Agreement." (Award, p. 22)

21. Therefore, it should first be determined whether the Tribunal assumed jurisdiction to "hear and determine the rights and obligations of the parties which constituted the *raison d'être*" of the Management Contract (Application, p. 7), or whether it "examined the allegedly deficient nature of Klöckner's management of SOCAME" (Application, p. 7, para. 2) and, in so doing, "necessarily applied the provisions of the Management Contract."

[105] In Section "VI. The Law" of the Award (p. 104 *et seq.*), the Arbitral Tribunal, as part of its examination of the "*exceptio non adimpleti contractus,*" considers (under letter c, p. 114 *et seq.*) what it calls the "significance of failure of performance in this case," and finds that:

> In the present case, Klöckner's shortcomings in the performance of its undertakings are very far from being minimal.

Reviewing these various undertakings, the Tribunal (after considering the obligation to furnish a factory having the prescribed production capacity) reaches the management obligation (p. 117):

> In order to perform the relevant contracts correctly, it was not sufficient to supply a fertilizer factory, the factory had to have the required capacity *and had to be managed* in the way necessary to obtain the proposed goals.

We shall return later to this sentence, which *prima facie* seems to place upon Klöckner (as does the Tribunal's conclusion, p. 120, cited below) an obligation of result (*obligation de résultat*). It will suffice here to relate the sentence to two other assertions in the Award:
First (p. 118):

> Klöckner had undertaken to ensure continuous functioning and maintenance of the factory (technical management) and its commercial management.

In addition, the following conclusion of the Tribunal (p. 120, end of Section 3 (c), which it may be noted in passing is followed by a Section 3(e) and not (d)):

> The most conclusive proof of Klöckner's failure to perform its duty of technical and commercial management results simply from the shutdown of the factory in December 1977, by decision of Klöckner personnel sent to Cameroon, after 19 months of underproduction and operating losses.

This is not the place to discuss the content of this conclusion, which has been the subject of the Claimant's criticisms, and of a detailed rebuttal in the Dissenting Opinion (p. 26 *et seq.*)

22. The few quotations above in any case suffice to show that the Tribunal undeniably pronounced on Klöckner's management (which, as we have seen, it deemed itself to have jurisdiction to do on the basis of the Protocol of Agreement).

It therefore remains to examine whether in so doing the Tribunal "necessarily applied" the provisions of the Management Contract, as the Claimant alleges, or whether instead it was able to reach the conclusion that Klöckner failed to perform its management obligations *without* applying the provisions of the Management Contract.

In the first case, the Tribunal would have fallen into a patent contradiction and would have manifestly exceeded its powers by taking a decision on a contract over which it stated it had no jurisdiction. In the second case, it **[106]** would not have exceeded the limits of its jurisdiction at all.

23. The question is therefore decisive. It calls for close examination and, first, for a reference to the Tribunal's own words justifying its position (p. 121 *et seq.*):

> In examining the counterclaim, the Reply Memorial affirms that "Klöckner's responsibility in the management of SOCAME results only from the Management Contract concluded between the companies." (p. 85)
>
> This affirmation does not take into account Article 9 of the Protocol of Agreement, from which three consequences flow: (1) first, that Klöckner "will be responsible for the technical and commercial management of the Company", (ii) that this responsibility will "be carried out under a Management Contract"; and (iii) that this responsibility will last "for at least five years from start-up, with an option to renew."
>
> *The Tribunal does not have jurisdiction to pronounce on the Management Contract itself or on its interpretation.* It must, however, proceed from the following presumption: That this Contract, intended to make the Claimant "responsible for the technical and commercial management of the Company," could neither qualify nor diminish Klöckner's management undertaking by virtue of the basic agreement: the Protocol of Agreement. Even if the Tribunal does not have jurisdiction to interpret the Management Contract, it should proceed from the presumption of perfect compatibility between the two instruments, the Protocol of Agreement constituting the investment's framework agreement (*l'accord cadre*) and the Management Contract being simply intended to carry out the basic agreement. (p. 122)

24. This passage of the Award raises a number of issues which it will be useful to list in a preliminary manner, without prejudice to the discussion to be undertaken in the light of the Applicant for Annulment's criticisms (especially on the basis of the Dissenting Opinion to which it refers).

(a) The text of Article 9 (like that of Article 6, which provides for the conclusion of a delivery and financing contract), uses the future tense, not the present (as used for example in Articles 5, 7, 8: "Klöckner *undertakes...*"):

   (i) Klöckner "*will be* responsible..."; and

   (ii) this responsibility is "*to be* carried out under a Management Contract ...,", etc. The Award does not examine whether any significance can or should be attached to this use of the future tense.

(b) The Award states that the Tribunal "*should* proceed" from a "*presumption* of perfect compatibility" between the Protocol of Agreement and the Management Contract. It states but gives no reason why the Tribunal has or would have this obligation, any more than it explains this "presumption," except perhaps indirectly by saying that the first of these instruments (the Protocol) constitutes "the framework agreement" (*l'accord cadre*), while the second, the

[107]   Management Contract, is "simply intended to carry out the basic agreement." (p. 122)

(c) This interpretation confirms, or returns to, a previous observation in the Award (p. 116) which is clearly inspired by one of the decisions in the first dispute submitted to ICSID, the *Holiday Inns*[2] case:

> There is consequently a single legal relationship, even if three successive instruments were concluded. This is so because the first, the Protocol of Agreement, encompasses and contains (*sic*) all three.

25. Other passages in the Award may be cited to shed light on the Tribunal's reasoning. For example, the Award cites a statement to the Board of Directors on 12 January 1977 that "Klöckner, *under the Management Contract* to be signed, will proceed after study to introduce improvements which will make the Company's management more efficient," and on this basis emphasizes that Klöckner "therefore admits to being the manager of the factory." (p. 122)

Taken by itself, this statement or "admission" appears not only compatible with Cameroon's argument, but also with Klöckner's for whom it is the Management Contract – and it alone – which, once it takes effect (1 January 1975), is the only source of the management obligations. It should however be recalled that the Tribunal also cites in support of its argument the letter of 12 April 1973 in which Klöckner accepts responsibility for managing the factory even well before the retroactive entry into force of the Management Contract.

In addition, the Award explains (p. 122 *in fine*) that:

> Article 9 of the Protocol was not a mere promise of future agreement, nor an inoperative stipulation requiring a subsequent contract defining performance in order to become applicable, but an essential, firm, and "self-executing" undertaking.

26. This "self-executing" qualification (a term borrowed from public international law) was criticized by the Claimant as a mere assertion:

> ... the Arbitral Tribunal has not even taken the trouble to attempt to demonstrate in what way and why this text is "self-executing." This expression would necessarily assume that the parties' respective obligations were defined, which obviously is not the case.

A number of questions may be asked in this regard. Is this "self-executing" character ultimately inconsistent with the conclusion (provided for from the start by the parties in the Protocol) of a Management Contract, i.e., a performance agreement? Is the conclusion of a "framework

[[2] The text of this decision has never been made available for publication. For an account of this case see Annex 1 in Volume 1 of the *ICSID Reports*.]

agreement" to use the Award's own words, or a "programme agreement," **[108]** sufficient to define the parties' rights and obligations, whether in the areas of delivery, management, etc.?

The Tribunal finds "proof" of the "self-executing" (i.e., independent, autonomous and self-sufficient) character in the fact that the Management Contract was only signed on 7 April 1977. It concludes from this that:

> Consequently, the technical and commercial management of the factory during the entire critical period in 1976, and the first three months of 1977, was carried out by Klöckner on the basis of Article 9 of the Protocol alone. This Article was the single source of all the authority Klöckner exercised during this period, and consequently of all its responsibility for the management of the factory. (pp. 122–123)

27. This reasoning seems to raise the following questions or observations:

(a) The Tribunal does not take into account or even mention the stipulation in the Management Contract expressly giving it retroactive effect (to 1 January 1975). Would this be because it deemed itself incompetent to apply or interpret the contract? How then could it reach a decision on the basis of the signature date (treating it as a fact?) without taking into account at the same time the other "fact," namely the contract's "retroactive" effect? It is true that Cameroon contests this interpretation of Article 9 of the Management Contract. According to Cameroon, there is a simple explanation for the clause. It was in the 1973 draft which became the 1977 contract, without the parties having made the modifications they seem, however, to have considered during their negotiations from 1973 to 1976.

(b) The Tribunal appears to postulate that, since Klöckner began to manage before the signature of the Management Contract (and in fact even 1 January 1975, the date agreed for it to take retroactive effect), it *necessarily* follows that such management can *only* be based on the framework agreement, that is, on Article 9 of the Protocol, which the Tribunal considers to be the "single source" of Klöckner's management authority. This seems to dismiss or exclude any possibility that even *without* the Protocol of Agreement (or with this Protocol as Klöckner interprets its Article 9, as a simple "*pactum de contrahendo*"), parties can act (and one of them manage) on the basis of a tacit or oral agreement intended to be made more precise or concrete as soon as possible in a text, for example, on the basis of initial practical experience (several examples of this may be found in international practice).

28. The Tribunal's "proof" for its characterization of the management obligation it finds in Article 9 as "self-executing" therefore appears *prima facie* fragile. This does not, however, make the Tribunal's interpretation untenable, since it is not at all impossible that in this case the parties actually gave to Klöckner the power (and obligation) to manage under Article 9 of

[109] the Protocol, before concluding a management contract (orally or in writing).

29. It is therefore necessary to examine the Award's reasoning in other respects, particularly in the light of three criticisms made by the Dissenting Opinion on this topic.

30. According to that Opinion (p. 51):

> Article 9 of the Protocol of Agreement does not state only that "Klöckner will be responsible for the technical and commercial management,"

but the Article carefully adds:

> to be carried out under a Management Contract (*assurée par un Contract de Management*).

This observation is interesting in itself. It may be understood as implicitly reproaching the Award for considering, contrary to the usual principles of interpretation, only the first part of the sentence, that is, the words "Klöckner will be responsible for the technical and commercial management," *without* also taking into account the words which follow.

As the dissenting arbitrator notes, these words clearly mean "that a Management Contract *will have* to be signed on Klöckner's technical and commercial management." However, this does not seem to be helpful in resolving the present question.

31. What would warrant examination but does not seem to have attracted the attention either of the Tribunal or of the dissenting arbitrator is the precise meaning and scope of the term "carry out" (*assurer*). *Prima facie*, several interpretations of the term are possible which are more or less consistent with one or the other of the two arguments.

32. If we leave aside this question of literal interpretation, we must, like the dissenting arbitrator (p. 52), ask:

> Why provide that such management will be "carried out under a Management Contract"?

The Dissenting Opinion replies:

> It was because the Protocol, being a framework agreement, did no more than lay down a framework and did not have the purpose – nor could it have the effect – of regulating the conditions of performance. These conditions, which related to Klöckner's rights, powers, remuneration, obligations and responsibility in respect of management, and to the arbitration clause, were the subject of a separate agreement, namely the Management Contract.

It may be asked whether these views contradict or not those of the Tribunal. For the Tribunal (p. 122), the Protocol of Agreement is the investment's framework agreement, "the Management Contract *being simply intended to carry out the basic agreement.*"

33. This last formula again uses the rather equivocal term "carry out." **[110]**
Whatever its exact meaning may be in the Tribunal's mind, it does not
appear fundamentally different from the Dissenting Opinion's concept
(p. 52) of "regulating the conditions of performance"; indeed, it is difficult to
see how it would be possible to "carry out the basic agreement" (containing
for the Tribunal the principle of the right and obligation to manage) without
"regulating the conditions of performance" of the management obligation.

34. The Dissenting Opinion continues (p. 52):

> It follows that any attempt to identify Klöckner's powers and its
> responsibilities in respect of management *must of necessity* involve an analysis
> and evaluation of the Management Contract.

This statement is *prima facie* persuasive: as indicated above, the Award
undeniably pronounces on Klöckner's management responsibility and notes
"shortcomings in the performance" in this regard which "are very far from
being minimal." (p. 114) It further notes (p. 117) that for there to have been
"correct" performance of the contracts in question (which doubtless means
the "three successive instruments" mentioned on p. 116), it would have been
necessary for the factory "to be managed in the *way* necessary to obtain the
proposed goals" (p. 117). Finally, the Tribunal holds (p. 116) that the facts
conclusively demonstrate "that Klöckner's two basic obligations (i.e. the
delivery obligation and the technical and commercial management
obligation) were performed in an imperfect and partial *manner*."

35. If the Tribunal had found that the management obligation had *not
been performed at all*, or even partially, it would doubtless be easier to
accept that the Tribunal could reach the conclusion *solely* on the basis of the
Protocol of Agreement, without using the Management Contract, and
without interpreting or applying it.

On the other hand, once the Award, to use its own words, passed on the
manner ("imperfect and partial") (p. 116) in which the obligation was
performed, or on the "*way*" (p. 117) the management would have to be
conducted "to obtain the proposed goals," it seems more difficult to
understand how the Tribunal made such judgments (on the "manner" or
"way," or on the degree of perfection of the performance of the
management obligation) *without* bringing in the Management Contract,
which it recognized (p. 122) was "intended to carry out the basic agreement"
("*simply* intended" it is true, but this adverb, without further explanation,
seems to relegate the Management Contract to a very subsidiary position).

36. The difficulty no doubt did not escape the Arbitral Tribunal. It
attempted to get around the obstacle by using (as noted above) a
"presumption of perfect compatibility between the two instruments," the
Protocol of Agreement and the Management Contract. (p. 122) According
to the Tribunal, the latter contract "could neither qualify nor diminish
Klöckner's management undertaking by virtue of the basic agreement: the
Protocol of Agreement." (p. 122)

[111] 37. Both components of its reasoning seem to lack relevance: it in no way proves the "self-executing" character of Article 9 of the Protocol (which as we saw above is affirmed solely because of the de facto situation existing *before* the Management Contract took effect).

In addition, it is difficult to see why a subsequent agreement could not modify ("qualify" or "diminish") the same parties' undertaking in a previous agreement, even if the latter is a framework agreement (at least in the absence of an expressly established hierarchy of norms or agreements).

Finally, and above all, even if "the presumption of perfect compatibility between the two instruments" can be accepted, it does not directly answer the question posed here. The question is whether, while the *principle* of Klöckner's management was (in the Tribunal's view) established by Article 9 of the Protocol, a definition, even a hazy one, of the "*conditions of performance*" of this obligation, of the rights, powers and responsibilities of the manager, may be found in the Protocol alone, as the "single source," or must inevitably be sought (also?) in the Management Contract.

38. The "presumption" of perfect compatibility does not answer this question. It certainly states or implies, if we understand the Tribunal correctly, that the Management Contract may not contain anything contrary to Article 9. But it does not state that the Tribunal may by this presumption somehow "transfer" from the Management Contract to the Protocol the conditions of performance and the regulation of Klöckner's rights and duties if these were defined in the Management Contract alone!

39. "If", in the words of the Dissenting Opinion, "we wish to ascertain Klöckner's rights and responsibilities as manager," it would not be enough to consider only Article 9 of the Protocol, which (again in the Tribunal's view) establishes the principle and the "framework" of the obligation. To do this, "we cannot but analyse and evaluate the Management Contract." (p. 52) If there is to be an evaluation of the "*manner*" ("imperfect and partial," according to the Award (p. 116)) in which Klöckner performed its basic management obligation, the Award does not explain how the Tribunal could make this evaluation *without* "pronounc[ing] on the Management Contract itself or on its interpretation." (p. 122)

40. To avoid any misunderstanding, it should be made clear that it is *one thing* to consider (as did the Award, p. 122) that:

> Article 9 of the Protocol was not a mere promise of future agreement, nor an inoperative stipulation requiring a subsequent contract defining performance in order to become applicable...;

and it is *another thing* to say that it would be possible to pronounce on the "manner" in which the management obligation was performed, and to evaluate the manager's responsibilities, *without* interpreting or applying the Management Contract.

The fact that Article 9 of the Protocol contains a basic management obligation (and not merely one to conclude a management contract) is affirmed by the Tribunal, no doubt with reason. It sees therein "a firm,

essential undertaking," and a "self-executing" one in the sense (but perhaps **[112]**
in this sense only) that the obligation, in order to exist and to be binding on
Klöckner, requires no subsequent performance contract. It will be noted
that the Tribunal's view is apparently that this Article has already implicitly
provided the application of the basic principles for running a factory; these
principles subsist and are not contradicted by any specific provision in the
Management Contract (which contains no exceptional clause compared to
the average contents of management contracts in general).

However, the conclusion that Article 9 of the Protocol is not "an
inoperative stipulation requiring a subsequent contract defining
performance in order to become applicable" is ambiguous. It is correct if one
is speaking of the existence of the obligation. It seems incorrect if one is
speaking of judging as satisfactory or less than satisfactory the *manner* in
which the obligation was performed and judging, with any degree of
precision, the manager's responsibility. It also seems to underestimate the
fact that, however "operative" or even "self-executing" it may be, Article 9
of the Protocol was in fact followed, in accordance with its terms, by a
Management Contract which "carried it out."

41. At the very most it may be conceded that if no management contract
had in the end been concluded (which is not the case here), contrary to the
provisions of Article 9 itself, it would have been possible, though not
without great difficulty, for a Tribunal to pronounce *on the extent of the
manager's responsibility*. In this case, however, a Management Contract *was
concluded* regulating the parties' rights and duties and the terms and
conditions of the basic management obligation. It therefore seems
impossible that a Tribunal could pronounce on the manager's
responsibilities and avoid pronouncing – admittedly perhaps also on Article
9 of the Protocol, which established the basic obligation – on the
Management Contract and its interpretation, something the Tribunal here
declared itself incompetent to do.

42. While the Award carefully does not cite any of the Management
Contract's provisions, it obviously cannot avoid all reference to this
contract. It is curious to note in this regard that, after declaring itself
incompetent to interpret the Management Contract and laying down the
"presumption of perfect compatibility" between this contract and the
Protocol of Agreement (which, as we have seen, was the framework
agreement that the Management Contract was "simply intended to carry
out"), the Tribunal finds "confirmation" for this conclusion (p. 122) in a
statement by Klöckner "admitting on 12 January 1977 that it is the manager
of the factory *under the Management Contract to be signed*." The following
similar statement of 8 April 1978 on Klöckner's responsibility for technical
management is cited by the Tribunal at page 121:

Klöckner obviously retains all its obligations *under the Management Contract.*

43. Clearly the Tribunal did not imagine that these quotations, and these
statements by Klöckner, might weaken its argument that it would be

[113] possible for it to pronounce on Klöckner's management obligations *without* pronouncing on or interpreting the Management Contract.

44. The Dissenting Opinion (p. 152) contains another argument as to the impossibility of pronouncing on Klöckner's management responsibilities without interpreting the Management Contract:

> What is more, any attempt to do so without such analysis and evaluation would constitute a *violation* of the Protocol of Agreement, which specifies clearly that management is "to be carried out under a Management Contract."

45. It is not certain that this observation can be accepted, at least so absolutely (considering the impression of the term "carried out"). But it rightly brings up one aspect of the basic difficulty the Tribunal encountered once it held itself incompetent to deal with the Management Contract: if it is accepted that this contract was intended to define, i.e., to specify, Klöckner's management undertaking in the Protocol of Agreement, it is difficult to see how judgments could be made on management problems without also necessarily referring to the Management Contract (unless the issue was a matter only of basic principles, or of the *complete* failure to perform the management obligation). This is what the Dissenting Opinion means when it says (p. 52, para. 3) that "the Management Contract's very purpose is to *define the undertaking* made by Klöckner in the framework agreement," by which we should understand that it would spell out the undertaking and fix its modalities, performance conditions, sanctions, etc., in detail.

46. From this point of view, it must be pointed out that the Award provides only a very brief explanation of the Tribunal's idea of the purpose, role and significance of the Management Contract in relation to Article 9 of the Protocol of Agreement, the "framework agreement." It is said (p. 122) that the Management Contract is "*simply* intended to carry out the basic agreement," but no explanation is given of the exact meaning of these terms. It is reasonable to think that for the Tribunal this contract only occupies a subsidiary position in the hierarchy of contractual norms, especially as in another context (p. 116) it is stated that the first of the "three successive instruments," i.e., the Protocol of Agreement, "*encompasses* and *contains* all three.'"

47. Here one can see a first way the Tribunal could, in its opinion, avoid what may be called the obstacle of its lack of jurisdiction with respect to the Management Contract.

A second way, already mentioned, is the "presumption of perfect compatibility" between the Protocol of Agreement and the Management Contract. (p. 122)

Neither of these two ways or methods seems decisive: the first amounts to a fairly laconic assertion; the second, as has already been pointed out, in no way resolves the issue: to say that the Management Contract is "perfectly compatible" with the Protocol, it must be repeated, does not explain how the much more detailed regulation of the parties' rights and duties, and especially of the manager's responsibilities, could be transferred or inserted **[114]** into the Protocol in order to decide issues regarding the manager's responsibility by applying – the Protocol *without* applying the Management Contract!

48. The foregoing conclusion is in no way affected by the finding the Award makes in another context, following the *Holiday Inns* case. This concerns the "close connection" between the three contractual instruments (p. 115), their "interdependence," and the idea that the parties are bound by "a single legal relationship" for which the first, the Protocol of Agreement, "encompasses and contains" the three successive instruments. (p. 116) Such an idea could perhaps have led the Tribunal to uphold its jurisdiction also to deal with disputes arising from the Management Contract. However, the Award hardly explains here how this general conception may be reconciled with the finding the Tribunal made elsewhere that it lacked jurisdiction to interpret or pronounce upon the Management Contract.

49. Another objection, raised in the Dissenting Opinion to which the Applicant for Annulment refers, deserves examination:

> It is incoherent to claim at one and the same time that the Protocol of Agreement is a framework agreement and also that it is an implementing agreement whose Article 9 defines Klöckner's powers, duties and responsibilities. Given this reasoning, it is illogical to rely on the Turnkey Contract as the basis for evaluating Klöckner's responsibility as the supplier of the factory. It would be enough to invoke Articles, 3, 6 and 7 of the Protocol!

50. It is difficult to deny the weight of this argument, in view of the close parallel between these two implementing agreements of the framework agreement, namely the Turnkey Contract and the Management Contract. This leads the dissenting arbitrator to continue (p. 53):

> Just as the Turnkey Contract was intended to describe Klöckner's responsibilities regarding the supply of the factory, the Management Contract purported to describe Klöckner's duties and responsibilities in the management of the factory. Moreover, just as it would be an absurdity to pass judgment on the supplier of the factory without examining the Turnkey Contract, it would be equally absurd to pass judgment on the manager without examining the Management Contract.

It will be recalled in this regard that according to the very terms of the Award (p. 114 *et seq.*) Klöckner had assumed two "basic obligations": "by the *Turnkey Contract* ... that of supplying a factory ..." (p. 114) and "by the *Protocol of Agreement* ... that of carrying out the responsibility for technical and commercial management." (p. 115)

51. Considering the parallelism and connections among the various contractual instruments, it will be noted that the Tribunal considers that it is "by the Turnkey Contract" that Klöckner had assumed its basic obligation to supply the factory (p. 114), while it is (not by the Management Contract but) "by the Protocol of Agreement" that Klöckner had "assumed another

[115] obligation as basic as the first," that of carrying out the technical and commercial management (p. 115). This divergence seems to be explained by the Tribunal's concern to maintain consistency with the finding that it lacked jurisdiction over the Management Contract.

52. *To summarize,* the following conclusions may be drawn from the preceding examination:

(a) It is obviously not up to the *ad hoc* Committee constituted under Article 52 of the Washington Convention to say whether the contested Award's interpretation is or is not the best, or the most defensible, or even whether it is correct, but only whether the Award is tainted by manifest excess of powers.

(b) There may of course be differences on the correct interpretation of the Protocol of Agreement and its Article 9 and, for example, its relationship to a subsequent agreement like the Management Contract. The inclusion of an ICC arbitration clause in this latter contract may also be interpreted in opposing ways. In this case, the Tribunal refused to accept, in the absence of completely precise and unequivocal contractual provisions, that the parties to the Management Contract wanted to "derogate" from the Protocol's ICSID clause. The Tribunal may have implicitly accepted that the ICSID clause constituted for both parties an "essential jurisdictional guarantee," the relinquishment of which could neither be presumed nor accepted in the absence of clear evidence.

Such an interpretation of the agreements and especially of the two arbitration clauses, whether correct or not, is tenable and does not in any event constitute a manifest excess of powers. To this extent, the complaint, while admissible, is unfounded.

(c) Another complaint is that there was internal contradiction between the Tribunal's finding that it lacked jurisdiction with respect to the Management Contract and its decision to condemn Klöckner for what the Award on several occasions considers its shortcomings in its management obligations. On this subject, a distinction should be made between two processes: (a) the *application* (including the interpretation) of the Management Contract – which, in its own view, is beyond the Tribunal's jurisdiction; and (b) the *taking into consideration* of the same contract for the purposes of interpreting and applying the Protocol of Agreement and for understanding the general context between the parties to the arbitration. A constant practice of international arbitral tribunals shows that the second process is perfectly possible, standard and appropriate, and the Tribunal's lack of jurisdiction with respect to the Management Contract poses no obstacle to this. On the other hand, the first process is forbidden to a tribunal lacking jurisdiction, as the Award itself expressly recognized (e.g., p. 122):

The Tribunal does not have jurisdiction to pronounce on the **[116]**
Management Contract itself or on its interpretation.

(d) Now, in its rejection (pp. 136–137) of the claim for payment of
the unpaid promissory notes, particularly because of Klöckner's
"responsibility for failures in its technical and commercial
management," a rejection it declares a sufficient *"penalty"* (and also
in its interpretation of the Protocol), did not the Tribunal necessarily
pronounce on the Management Contract, for the reasons given
above? Could it, as it indisputably did, pronounce on the
performance of Klöckner's management obligation *solely* on the basis
of Article 9 of the Protocol *without* (also) pronouncing on the
Management Contract? Could it evaluate the existence and degree of
Klöckner's "failures" or shortcomings in performing its management
obligations, without interpreting the Management Contract? Could
it avoid this difficulty, as it tried to do, by holding that the Protocol
of Agreement "encompassed" and "contained" the Management
Contract (p. 116) so that, in short, it could not exceed its jurisdiction
so long as it decided on the questions encompassed or contained in the
Protocol of Agreement?

(e) It is possible to have different opinions on these delicate questions, or
even, as do the Applicant for Annulment or the Dissenting Opinion,
to consider the Tribunal's answers to them not very convincing, or
inadequate. But since the answers seem tenable and not arbitrary,
they do not constitute the manifest excess of powers which alone would
justify annulment under Article 52(1)(b). In any case, the doubt or
uncertainty that may have persisted in this regard throughout the long
preceding analysis should be resolved *"in favorem validitatis
sententiae"* and lead to rejection of the alleged complaint.

53. Before leaving the subject of jurisdiction, it may also be noted in
passing, and solely for the sake of completeness, that the Tribunal (in
Chapter III of the Award, p. 21 *et seq.*) bases its jurisdiction not only on the
Protocol of Agreement and on the Turnkey Contract but also on Article 21
of the Establishment Agreement of 23 of June 1973 (which it essentially
analyses on p. 42 *et seq.* of the Award) between Cameroon and the
Cameroon Fertilizer Company (SOCAME). This ground is invoked by the
Respondent, but contested by the Claimant (Award, p. 24) for the twofold
reason that (a) it is not an agreement between the parties but between the
two Respondents and (b) SOCAME, a Cameroonian company, does not meet
the condition imposed by Article 46 of the Washington Convention.

54. The Tribunal refuted (pp. 25–28) the second objection at some
length, observing that the question of the Tribunal's jurisdiction *"ratione
personae"* with regard to SOCAME did not arise in this case (p. 27). It
definitively rejected the objection on the basis that the Establishment
Agreement, the Protocol of Agreement and the Turnkey Contract formed

[117] an "inseparable whole". (pp. 28–29; *cf.* page 43; as for the Management Contract, however, see pp. 115–116)

It will suffice to observe that in its Application for Annulment, the Claimant did not think it necessary to repeat its objection in this regard, or criticize the Tribunal's reasoning as to its jurisdiction to rule on the counter-claim; and rightly so, as it is difficult to see what complaint the Claimant could have made in this regard.

55. On the other hand, the Claimant asserted that it never occurred to the parties to deal with Klöckner's management *independently* of the Management Contract (over which the Tribunal declared itself incompetent) and that this latter contract was necessary to show what the Protocol meant.

Likewise, the Claimant held that, while Article 9 of the Protocol was indeed the *source* of the management obligation, the *substance* of that obligation was determined by the Management Contract. Article 9 of the Protocol, according to the Claimant, was only a "stipulation for a third party" (*stipulation pour autrui*), requiring Klöckner to sign a Management Contract with a company to be formed, SOCAME, and also requiring Cameroon to have the said contract signed by the said company.

Moreover, the Claimant stressed that the problem in the present case was completely different from that before the Tribunal in the *Holiday Inns v. Morocco* case, where it was a matter of simultaneously applying several contracts and not, as here, a framework agreement, the Protocol of Agreement, *followed* by the conclusion of a Management Contract.

Finally, the Claimant noted that at no time during the arbitration proceeding did the respondent Government claim that the Tribunal could or should base itself solely on Article 9 of the Protocol as "self-executing," and examine Klöckner's management without interpreting or applying the Management Contract.

56. With the exception of the latter, these various arguments do not call for any particular comments, since, as we have seen, the question is not whether they are correct or plausible, or more plausible or more correct than the Tribunal's. The only issue is whether they prove a manifest excess of powers, which is not the case.

Regarding the last argument, it may be added that it is obviously not decisive, even if it is correct. It matters little in principle that the Tribunal's legal construction was different from that of one or the other of the parties, so long as the right of each to be heard was respected and, as will be seen below (*infra*, para. 91) so long as it remains within the "legal framework" provided by the parties. And this is indeed the case here.

II. EXCESS OF POWERS DUE TO A VIOLATION OF ARTICLE 42(1) OF THE
WASHINGTON CONVENTION

57. According to Klöckner's Application for Annulment (p. 11 *et seq.*),

the Award should be annulled for manifest excess of powers, as that term is **[118]**
used in Article 52(1)(b) of the Washington Convention, because of a
"violation of Article 42(1) of the Convention."

According to the Application, "this Article requires the Tribunal to
respect the rules set forth therein in rendering its award":

> The Tribunal shall decide a dispute *in accordance with such rules of law as may
> be agreed by the parties.* In the absence of such agreement, the Tribunal shall
> apply the law of the Contracting State party to the dispute (including its rules
> on the conflict of laws) and such rules [or principles[3]] of international law as
> may be applicable.

The Claimant maintains that the Tribunal must therefore "render its
award by applying Cameroonian law based on French law, since this, as the
Tribunal itself has held, is the law applicable to the present dispute."
According to the Claimant, the Tribunal "ignored this principle and went
beyond its powers."

58. Is this complaint admissible?

We shall not pause over the objection raised in Respondent's oral
pleadings against the alleged novelty or lateness of the complaint, which is in
no way established and runs counter to the fact that the Application for
Annulment itself raises this ground. We shall seek instead to determine
whether in its substance it is admissible within the framework of Article
52(1)(b), the one on excess of powers. This raises the question of the
interpretation of Article 42(1) of the Washington Convention and of the
consequences of a possible failure to observe it.

In the opinion of the *ad hoc* Committee, the provisions of Article 42 could
not be interpreted as stating simple advice or recommendations to the
arbitrators or an obligation without sanction. Obviously, and in accordance
with principles of interpretation that are recognized generally – for example,
by Article 31 of the Vienna Convention on the Law of Treaties – Article 52
on the annulment of awards must be interpreted in the context of the
Convention and in particular of Articles 42 and 48, and vice versa. It is
furthermore impossible to imagine that when they drafted Article 52, the
Convention's authors would have forgotten the existence of Articles 42 or
48(3), just as it is impossible to assume that the authors of provisions like
Articles 42(1) or 48(3) would have neglected to consider the sanction for
non-compliance.

59. The Washington Convention furthermore was not being innovative
when it recognized excess of powers with regard to the basic rules to be
applied by the arbitrators as a possible grounds for annulment. In the
famous *Orinoco Steamship Company* case, the Permanent Court of
Arbitration (Award of 25 October 1910, Scott, p. 226) held that

---

[3] Translator's note: The English text of Article 42(1) of the Convention, unlike the French text,
speaks of "rules" of international law, but the use of the word *"principes"* in the French version
appears relevant for the discussion in this part of the Committee's decision.

[119] excessive powers may consist, not only in deciding a question not submitted to the arbitrators, but also in misinterpreting the express provisions of the agreement in respect of the way in which they are to reach their decisions, notably with regard to the legislation or the principles of law to be applied.

Excess of powers may consist of the non-application by the arbitrator of the rules contained in the arbitration agreement (*compromis*) or in the application of other rules. Such may be the case if the arbitrator (like Umpire Barge in the *Orinoco* case) applies rules of local law while the arbitration agreement prescribes that he decide "on the basis of absolute equity, without regard ... to the provisions of local law," or if, conversely, he reaches a solution *in equity* while he is required to decide *in law (North Eastern Boundary between Canada and the United States* case, Award of 10 January 1831).

60. While the complaint based on failure to observe Article 42 is thus admissible in principle, it remains to be determined what exactly constitutes not deciding "in accordance with such rules of law as may be agreed by the parties," or not "applying the law of the Contracting State party to the dispute." This raises the fine distinction between "non-application" of the applicable law and mistaken application of such law.

61. It is clear that *"error in judicando"* could not in itself be accepted as a ground for annulment without indirectly reintroducing an appeal against the arbitral award, and the *ad hoc* Committee under Article 52 of the Convention does not, any more than the Permanent Court of Arbitration in the *Orinoco* case, have the "duty ... to say if the case has been well or ill judged, but whether the award must be annulled."

Whether theoretical or practical, the discussions which have taken place on the distinction between excess of powers as a ground for annulment and error in law or mistaken application of the law have drawn attention to the issue's uncertainty or obscurity. This is illustrated by the positions taken before the International Court of Justice by Honduras and Nicaragua regarding the *Arbitral Award Made by the King of Spain*[4]. Honduras maintained in substance that error in law had no independent place as a ground for annulment and should only be taken into consideration when it constituted excess of powers, for instance "if the arbitrator had manifestly misunderstood a clause in the arbitration agreement which should have shown him the principles or rules to be followed to reach his decision." (Reply, para. 55) Nicaragua argued that "the flagrant misinterpretation" of a certain document was an essential error for which the award should be annulled. (Counter-Memorial, paras. 87 and 143; *cf.* Court's Opinion, ICJ 1960 Reports, p. 216)

From the few known precedents, to which may be added that of the *Trail Smelter*[5] (with respect to the award's revision), it is at least possible to

[4 30 *ILR* 457.]
[5 9 *Ann. Dig.* 315.]

conclude that an error in law, even an essential one, does not generally **[120]** constitute an excess of powers, at least if it is not "manifest."

62. The attitude of reserve imposed in this regard on the *ad hoc* Committee established under Article 52 of the Washington Convention requires no particular justification. However, it does not mean, as has been alleged, that Article 52 must be interpreted *narrowly*, any more, of course, than it may be interpreted *broadly*. Of course, the system for settling disputes established by the Convention would be seriously jeopardized if there were any laxity in deciding whether the conditions listed in Article 52, taken in itself or in relation to Articles 42 and 48, are met. On the other hand, the rules in Section 5 of the Convention regarding the interpretation, revision, and annulment of the award (Articles 50 to 52) are part of the same system and must be interpreted according to the customary principles of interpretation, including the principle of effectiveness.

63. Is the complaint well founded?

With the admissibility of the complaint now established, we may now examine whether it is well founded in the light of these general considerations. According to the Application for Annulment (pp. 11–12), the Tribunal violated Article 42(1) of the Convention and exceeded its powers because it did not apply Cameroonian law, the "law of the Contracting State party to the dispute," which the Tribunal itself declared (p. 104 *in fine*) applicable in accordance with Article 42 of the Convention. The Award deals with this subject (p. 105) as follows:

> One must therefore acknowledge the correctness of the Claimant's position when it says that "since the SOCAME factory project was located in the eastern part of the country, *only that part of Cameroonian law that is based on French law should be applied in the dispute*."

The Award continues (p. 105):

> Among the different arguments of French civil law invoked by the Respondent the following should be cited: absence of consent (*défault de consentement*), wrongful inducement to contract (*dol*), and hidden defects (*vices cachés*). The two grounds which we deem applicable are (i) the fact that Klöckner did not manifest *vis-à-vis* its Cameroonian partner the frankness and loyalty required in such complex international contractual relations and (ii) the *exceptio non adimpleti contractus*.

64. The first of the Tribunal's "two grounds" is the subject of pages 105 to 109 of the Award, under the headings: "2. *The Duty of Full Disclosure to a Partner*." These words are repeated at the end of this Section 2, when the Tribunal (p. 109) reaches the "conclusion that Klöckner violated its duty of full disclosure," and therefore "that it is not entitled to the contract price, that it is entitled to payment for the value of what it delivered and which Klöckner [*sic* – the Award reads "Cameroon"] used, and that Cameroon has already paid enough...."

[121]   65. It is undeniable that this conclusion is presented by the Award as having been reached by applying the applicable law in accordance with Article 42 of the Convention, i.e., the law of the Contracting State, "Cameroonian law based on French law" or even "French civil law." (p. 105, paras. 2 and 3)

According to the Application for Annulment (p.12), however, the Tribunal actually based itself "not on a principle of French law, but on a sort of declaration, as general as it is imprecise, of principles which are allegedly universally recognized."

66. It is therefore necessary to examine the Award's text from this point of view. On "the duty of full disclosure to a partner," the Tribunal says the following (p. 105):

> We assume that the principle according to which a person who engages in close contractual relations, based on confidence, must deal with his partner in a frank, loyal and candid manner is a basic principle of French civil law, as is indeed the case under other national codes which we know of...

67. It may immediately be noticed that here the Tribunal does not claim to ascertain the existence (of a rule or a principle) but asserts or postulates the existence of such a "principle" which (after having postulated its existence) the Tribunal *assumes* or takes for granted that it "is a basic principle of French civil law."

This assumption appears to be based on the idea that the same is "indeed the case under other national codes which we know of." The Award states that "this is the criterion that applies to relations between partners in simple forms of association anywhere," and that "the rule (*sic*) is particularly appropriate in more complex international ventures, such as the present one."

We may also note that the arbitrators state a little later (p. 106) that they are "convinced that it is particularly important that *universal requirements* of frankness and loyalty in dealings between partners be applied in cases such as this one...."

The remainder of the Section (pp. 106–109) is devoted to applying this "basic principle" to the case. The statement of legal grounds is thus limited to the passages quoted above.

68. This reasoning calls for several observations:

First, it should be asked whether the arbitrator's duty under Article 42(1) to apply "the *law* of the Contracting State" is or can be fulfilled by reference to *one* "basic principle," and what is more, without making any more precise reference. This may be doubted if one considers the difference between "rule" and "principle" (and in particular "basic principle") and the classic definition of law in the objective sense as a *body of rules*. It will also be noted in this context that Article 42(1) itself distinguishes between the concepts of "rules of law" and "principles of law".

69. Furthermore, the reference to "other national codes which we know of," to the "particularly appropriate" character of the rule "in more complex

international ventures, such as the present one" (p. 105) and to the **[122]** particular importance that "universal requirements of frankness and loyalty ... be applied in cases such as this one" seem to indicate that the Tribunal may have wanted to base, or thought it was basing, its decision on the general principles of law recognized by civilized nations, as that term is used in Article 38(3) of the Statute of the International Court of Justice. It is not impossible that the Tribunal was prompted to do so by the reference in Article 42(1) *in fine* to the "principles of international law as may be applicable" although these are not to be confused with "general principles."

Such an interpretation is conjectural and cannot be accepted. Article 42 of the Washington Convention certainly provides that "in the absence of agreement between the parties, the Tribunal shall apply the law of the Contracting State party to the dispute ... and *such principles of international law as may be applicable*." This gives these principles (perhaps omitting cases in which it should be ascertained whether the domestic law conforms to international law) a dual role, that is, *complementary* (in the case of a "lacuna" in the law of the State), or *corrective*, should the State's law not conform on all points to the principles of international law. *In both cases*, the arbitrators may have recourse to the "principles of international law" only *after* having inquired into and established the content of the law of the State party to the dispute (which cannot be reduced to *one* principle, even a basic one) and *after* having applied the relevant rules of the State's law.

Article 42(1) therefore clearly does not allow the arbitrator to base his decision *solely* on the "rules" or "principles of international law."

70. It will also be noted that it is only in Section 3, on the *exceptio non adimpleti contractus*, that the Award mentions (p. 112) the "principles of international law to which Article 42 of the ICSID Conventions refers" and the "general principles of law recognized by civilized nations." One is tempted to conclude from this that in Section 2, on the duty of "full disclosure," the Award did *not* mean to refer to these principles of international law. In any event, one can hardly see on what basis the Tribunal could have done so, since this would correspond neither to the complementary function nor to the corrective function of the principles of international law in Article 42.

71. Does the "basic principle" referred to by the Award (p. 105) as one of "French civil law" come from positive law, i.e., from the law's body of rules? It is impossible to answer this question by reading the Award, which contains no reference whatsoever to legislative texts, to judgments, or to scholarly opinions. In this respect the contrast is striking between Section 2 (on the "duty of full disclosure") and Section 3 (on the *exceptio non adimpleti contractus*, pp. 109–114 and pp. 118, 124, 126, etc). Section 3 contains a great number of references to scholarly opinion (*doctrine*) as well as, directly or indirectly, to case law (*jurisprudence*). One could therefore assume that in the case of Section 2, regarding the duty of frankness, the arbitrators either began a similar search for authorities but found it

[123] unproductive or, more likely, thought that a search for positive law was unnecessary.

72. In the latter case, is it possible to hold that the Award has "applied the law of the Contracting State" as required in Article 42(1)?

It is true that the principle of good faith is "at the basis" of French civil law, as of other legal systems, but this elementary proposition does not by itself answer the question. In Cameroonian or Franco-Cameroonian law does the "principle" affirmed or postulated by the Award, the "duty of full disclosure," exist? If it does, no doubt flowing from the general principle of good faith, from the obligation of frankness and loyalty, then *how*, by what *rules* and under what *conditions* is it implemented and within what *limits*? Can a duty to make a *"full* disclosure," even to one's own prejudice, be accepted, especially without limits? Is there a single legal system which contains such a broad obligation? These are a few of the questions that naturally come to mind and that the Award provides no basis for answering.

73. It is not the responsibility of the *ad hoc* Committee under Article 52 to determine instead of the Tribunal what rules of French civil law might be applicable, to insert them in some a *posteriori* way into the Award, either in place of the reasoning found there and cited above, or in place of non-existent reasoning. The Committee can only take the Award *as it is*, interpreting it according to the customary principles of interpretation, and find that it indeed refers to general principles or "universal requirements," postulated rather than demonstrated, and which are affirmed as being "particularly appropriate" or "particulary important" in cases such as the present one.

Of course, one can only applaud the Award's emphasis on the importance of loyalty in dealings, especially in international contracts of the sort which gave rise to the present arbitration, but such approbation cannot exempt the Committee from ascertaining whether the conditions of Article 42 of the Washington Convention have been met.

74. Before concluding on this point it may be permissible, partly *"ex abundati cautela,"* to examine written pleadings filed during the arbitral proceeding for a possible explanation of the Tribunal's approach, even though the *ad hoc* Committee is not required to do this.

The examination, however, proves disappointing. Cameroon did invoke "the principle of good faith and loyalty," (*cf.* Counter-Memorial, p. 102 *et seq.*) "the obligation to advise and the contractual duty of disclosure." (p. 112 *et seq.* 5.2.3) However, Cameroon dwelt mainly on the *"precontractual* duty of disclosure," the non-observance of which, like wrongful inducement to contract (*dol*) (a ground not used by the Tribunal), "vitiates consent." Only rather summarily did Cameroon deal with the duties of advice and disclosure *after* conclusion of the contract. Curiously, the Claimant did not find it necessary to address this issue in writing and contented itself with answering (Reply of 30 October 1982, p. 25) that this was "only a matter of applying the general principles of responsibility." The Claimant may have discussed this point in its final oral pleading, but it did not find it necessary to

accept the ICSID Secretariat's offer of a transcript of this pleading. It is **[124]**
therefore not possible for the Committee to know what arguments the
Claimant made or would have made on the "obligation of frankness and
loyalty."

75. In any event, in the absence of any information, evidence or citation
in the Award, it would seem difficult to accept, and impossible to *presume*,
that there is a general duty, under French civil law, or for that matter other
systems of civil law, for a contracting party to make a "*full* disclosure" to its
partner. If we were to "presume" anything, it would instead be that such a
duty (the basic idea of which may, of course, be accepted as it follows from
the principle of good faith; *cf.* Article 1134, para. 3 of the French Civil Code)
must, to be given effect in positive law, have conditions for its application
and limits!

76. One of the Award's features is that it repeatedly censures Klöckner's
violation of "its contractual duty of full disclosure." (p. 109) According to
the Award, the Claimant did not "deal frankly with Cameroon," "hid from
its partner information of vital importance at critical stages of the project,"
"failed to disclose facts which, if they had been known to the Government,
could have caused it to put an end to the venture" and "did not act frankly
and loyally towards its partners" (p. 106), so that, "in a very significant
sense, it is its fault."

The repetition of these criticisms, and the harm to reputation (*préjudice
moral*) likely to result therefrom, regardless of the Award's material
consequences, would have justified, or better, required, special caution by
the arbitrators in ascertaining and formulating the rules of law of the State
party to the dispute, the applicable law under Article 42(1) of the
Washington Convention.

77. Now, the Award's reasoning and the legal grounds on this topic (to
the extent that they are not in any case mistaken because of the inadequate
description of the duty of "full disclosure") seem very much like a simple
reference to equity, to "universal" principles of justice and loyalty, such as
amiable compositeurs might invoke.

According to the Award itself, this is one of the decision's two grounds. It
may even be the main ground, for on page 109, paragraph 2, the *Tribunal
concludes that, because of this violation, Klöckner is not entitled to the
contract price*, and this even before the Award examines either the *exceptio
non adimpleti contractus* (Section 3, p. 109 *et seq.*) or Klöckner's arguments
on "The Reasons for the Failure." (Section 4, p. 127 *et seq.*)

78. Considering the question's fundamental importance and the
seriousness of the censure in this regard, it is impossible to explain how the
Award can base such censure on a simple postulate or a presumption that
there is a "basic principle," without any argumentation whatsoever, and
without touching on *rules* defining how this "principle" is to be applied, i.e.,
the respective rights and duties of the debtor and the creditor, the duty of
disclosure, of frankness and loyalty, in general and this particular case, as
well as the legal effects of a breach of this duty.

[125] The absence of any indication in the Award, however, imprecise, of the applicable rules of law is all the more regrettable since it was apt to create in one of the parties an impression of injustice. This is precisely what the ICSID system and rules, and in particular Articles 42, 48(3) and 52 of the Convention, are designed to prevent.

79. *In conclusion*, it must be acknowledged that in its reasoning, limited to postulating and not demonstrating the existence of a principle or exploring the rules by which it can only take concrete form, the Tribunal has not applied "the law of the Contracting State."

Strictly speaking, it could not be said that it made this decision without providing reasons, within the meaning of Articles 48(3) and 52(1)(e). It did, however, act outside the framework provided by Article 42(1), applying concepts or principles it probably considered equitable (acting as an amiable compositeur, which should not be confused with applying "equitable considerations" as the International Court of Justice did in the *Continental Shelf* case). However justified its award may be (a question on which the Committee has no opinion), the Tribunal thus "manifestly exceeded its powers" within the meaning of Article 52(1)(b) of the Washington Convention.

80. The finding that there is a ground for annulment of the Award under Article 52 of the Washington Convention immediately raises the question of the *consequences* of that finding. According to Article 52(3) *in fine*, the "Committee shall have the authority to annul the award *or any part thereof* on any of the grounds set forth in paragraph (1)."

In concrete terms, the question is whether, applying the principle of *favor validitatis* or "partial annulment of legal acts," *only a part* of the contested award should be annulled, or whether it should be annulled in its *entirety*.

Generally speaking, partial annulment would seem appropriate if the part of the Award affected by the excess of powers is identifiable and detachable from the rest, and if so, the remaining part of the Award has an independent basis.

81. Such is clearly not the case here. Indeed, the Award rejected Klöckner's claim for payment by a single decision. (pp. 136–137) What the Tribunal terms "this company's responsibility for shortcomings in delivering the factory and in its technical and commercial management" and in the alleged duty of "full disclosure" seem, insofar as one can understand in the Award, to be linked both to the delivery obligation and doubtless above all to the management obligation. It is because of the breach of this "contractual duty of full disclosure" that the Award concludes (p. 109) that Klöckner "is not entitled to the contract price" and that it has already been "paid enough." Since in the Tribunal's view the Award forms a whole, and since the Tribunal, in rejecting the counterclaim, as it were made parallel decisions based on the alleged illegality of Klöckner's lack of frankness, the Award's annulment should also extend to the part relating to the counterclaim.

That being the case, one does not see how, at least in the Award's operative parts, one can dissociate matters relating solely to a breach of the

alleged "duty of full disclosure," and to decide on only a partial annulment. **[126]**
This conclusion is moreover confirmed and reinforced, as will be seen
below, by the response to some of the other complaints of the Applicant for
Annulment.

82. Once the *ad hoc* Committee has concluded that the Award is to be
annulled because of a manifest excess of powers, it could dispense with
examining the other complaints of the Applicant for Annulment, who also
invoked Articles 52(1)(d) (serious departure from a fundamental rule of
procedure) and 52(1)(e) (failure to state reasons).

In view of this case's importance, the fact this is the first Application for
Annulment ever lodged against an ICSID award and, finally, because it may
be of interest to the parties and to the new Tribunal that may be constituted
under Article 52(6) of the Washington Convention to have additional
indications, it would nonetheless be appropriate to examine, albeit in less
depth, the main arguments raised and discussed in the course of the
annulment proceeding.

III. SERIOUS DEPARTURE FROM A FUNDAMENTAL RULE OF PROCEDURE (ARTICLE 52(1)(d))

82bis. Under a variety of headings, Klöckner refers to various violations
of basic rules of procedure in its Application for Annulment. (pp. 27–28; *cf.*
also its Reply to the Counter-Memorial, p. 53 *et seq.*) In particular, it alleges
that (A) there was no true deliberation, (B) there were various other
procedural irregularities, including failure to respect due process (*le
contradictoire*), and (C) there was an "obvious lack of impartiality on the
part of the Arbitral Tribunal." In addition, Klöckner makes complaints
based also or especially on the idea of absence, contradiction or inadequacy
of reasons, and perhaps even on the concept of manifest excess of powers
(to the extent that it is apparently claimed that the Tribunal rules "*ultra
petita*").

83. Apart from the precise characterization of the various complaints,
which are often overlapping to a certain extent, it should be recalled that as a
rule an application for annulment cannot serve as a substitute for an appeal
against an award and permit criticism of the merits of the judgments rightly
or wrongly formulated by the award. Nor can it be used by one party to
complete or develop an argument which it could and should have made
during the arbitral proceeding or help that party retrospectively to fill gaps in
its arguments.

A. *Absence of Deliberation*

84. The Claimant alleges (p. 2) that it was "impossible that there was
serious deliberation among the arbitrators." It seeks to demonstrate this by
comparing the text of the Award to that of the Dissenting Opinion.

[127]   While this ground is not expressly provided for in Article 52, it is possible to hold that the requirement of deliberation among the arbitrators is a "basic rule of procedure." It is also possible to hold that such deliberation must be real and not merely apparent. But the Claimant did not explain how the Committee could determine whether the condition is met. How, for example, could the Committee judge the degree of seriousness of the deliberation in view of its secrecy. (Rule 15 of the Arbitration Rules) Nor did the Claimant explain what it meant by a "normal" process of deliberation. (Application, p. 28)

85. In fact, the Annulment Application's very text shows that the complaint rests on a simple assertion, or on purely personal conceptions of deliberation and the function and content of a dissenting opinion. (Application, pp. 27–28) "A reading of the dissenting opinion," the Claimant explains, "shows that such a confrontation (i.e., between the arbitrators' opposing views, which 'must in any case have led them to agree on the facts of the case, the applicable principles of law ... and the arguments of the parties which should be answered') did not take place."

These assertions do not establish that there was no deliberation. On the contrary, the existence of deliberation is shown or made at least highly likely by the ICSID Secretariat's minutes, which were communicated to the Committee. Furthermore, the Award refers at least twice (pp. 22 and 23) to a minority opinion which was advanced "within the Tribunal." This shows that there was at least some deliberation.

The complaint is therefore not sustainable and can only be rejected.

86. Of course, it is understandable that the Claimant was struck by the total divergence between the Award and the Dissenting Opinion. However, the divergence, first, is not such as to establish the alleged absence of deliberation, and second, is probably largely attributable to the ICSID system. Since the minority arbitrator may only prepare his dissenting opinion within the same time limit as the Award, in practice the system hardly allows the majority to study the draft "dissent" and hence perhaps to benefit from it if it thinks this useful. More appropriate provisions for dissenting opinions, perhaps inspired by the practice of the International Court of Justice, would doubtless make it possible to avoid repeating this type of situation in the future, if the observations made below (see para. 113) on the time given to arbitrators are also taken into account.

B. *Other Irregularities in the Arbitral Procedure*

87. Subject to what will be said below regarding respect for due process and the arbitrator's power to base their decision on an argument other than that made by either party, it must be said that the Claimant's criticism regarding the irregularity of the arbitral procedure is totally lacking in precision and substance.

It is clear from the parties' explanations in the annulment proceeding and **[128]** from the documents they produced that the proceeding was conducted in a perfectly normal fashion. In particular, the Claimant had every opportunity to express itself and present its case. It is true that after Cameroon's Reply of March 1983 Klöckner made a "solemn protest against procedures which, because of the lateness and importance of the communication, constitute an attack on its rights as a party in this arbitration," and that it requested that the hearings of late April 1983 be devoted to questions of jurisdiction, the conduct of the proceeding, and the possible submission of new documents.

It also appears that while the Claimant protested against the volume of documents submitted by the Respondent, it did not make use of the opportunity it was given to do likewise, stating that it would reply through its witnesses and its oral pleading. Finally, it may be recalled that the Claimant did not avail itself of its right to reply other than orally to Cameroon's last instrument. Furthermore, it declined the ICSID Secretariat's offer to have the oral pleadings transcribed for the Tribunal.

88. To summarize, it suffices to note that the Claimant has not established that it made a timely protest against the serious procedural irregularities it now complains of. Subject to what will be said later, Rule 26 of the ICSID Rules of Procedure for Arbitration Proceedings would therefore rule out a good part of its complaints. This rule provides as follows:

> A party which knows or should have known that a provision of ... these Rules, of any other rules or agreement applicable to the proceeding, or of an order of the Tribunal has not been complied with and which fails to state promptly its objections thereto, shall be deemed – subject to Article 45 of the Convention – to have waived its right to object.

89. In fact, the "serious departure from a fundamental rule of procedure" complained of by Klöckner (leaving aside the alleged "absence of serious deliberation," commented on above, and the alleged "obvious lack of impartiality," which will be examined below) brings us back to the argument that the Tribunal failed to respect the principle of "*due process*" by basing its decision on arguments not advanced or at the very least not developed by either of the parties or at any rate not discussed by the parties. One is essentially speaking here of the Tribunal's interpretation of Article 9 of the Protocol of Agreement as "self-executing," which was discussed above. This complaint should apparently be distinguished from that made elsewhere on failure to state reasons (and especially on "failure to deal with every question submitted to the Tribunal").

90. As we saw above, the Award seems to have taken a somewhat intermediate position on the question of jurisdiction and Article 9 of the Protocol of Agreement between the parties' respective positions. It is of course possible that, if counsel had expressed themselves on this "intermediate" position of the ultimately "self-executing" nature of Article 9 of the Protocol, the Tribunal might perhaps have modified its views and the Award might perhaps have been different on one point or another. But the

[129] parties' counsel were not prevented from advancing other, subsidiary hypotheses or interpretations alongside their main arguments, even if only "*ex abundati cautela*" in case the Tribunal should adopt some other legal argument.

91. As for the Tribunal itself, when in the course of its deliberations it reached the provisional conclusion that the true legal basis for its decision could well be different from either of the parties' respective arguments, it was not, subject to what will be said below, in principle prohibited from choosing its own argument. Whether to reopen the proceeding before reaching a decision and allow the parties to put forward their views on the arbitrators' "new" thesis is rather a question of expedience.

The real question is whether, by formulating its own theory and argument, the Tribunal goes beyond the "legal framework" established by the Claimant and Respondent. This would for example be the case if an arbitral tribunal rendered its decision on the basis of tort while the pleas of the parties were based on contract.

Within the dispute's "legal framework," arbitrators must be free to rely on arguments which strike them as the best ones, even if those arguments were not developed by the parties (although they could have been). Even if it is generally desirable for arbitrators to avoid basing their decision on an argument that has not been discussed by the parties, it obviously does not follow that they therefore commit a "serious departure from a fundamental rule of procedure." Any other solution would expose arbitrators to having to do the work of the parties' counsel for them and would risk slowing down or even paralysing the arbitral solutions to disputes.

92. Bearing in mind what was said above regarding jurisdiction, it is impossible to hold that the Tribunal failed to respect the principle of "due process" or the equality of the parties in adopting its interpretation of Article 9 of the Protocol of Agreement and deciding that the Management Contract and its ICC arbitration clause did not prevent it from pronouncing on Klöckner's management obligations. A reading of Part III of the Award leaves no doubt on this score. And even if the parties regard the Tribunal's interpretation as incorrect or shaky, they will have difficulty challenging it on the ground that they never anticipated it, or analysed or developed it insufficiently, in their written or oral pleadings.

C. Obvious Lack of Impartiality

93. The Application for Annulment criticizes the Award as being systematically hostile to Klöckner and as revealing "the Tribunal's obvious lack of impartiality." (p. 2) In particular, it criticizes the Award for having violated fundamental rules of procedure (especially "the Tribunal's duty to maintain strict impartiality." (p. 27) It concludes (p. 28) that "the principle of due process was violated by the total failure to examine Klöckner's arguments in the oral pleadings ..." and that " such exceptionally grave facts

reveal the obvious lack of neutrality and impartiality on the part of the **[130]** Arbitral Tribunal."

94. Such accusations are certainly serious. Given the terms of the statement signed by each arbitrator pursuant to Article 6 of the Arbitration Rules, and the high reputation of the members of the Tribunal in this case, they are *prima facie* implausible. This implausibility does not exempt the Committee – quite the contrary – from the duty of carefully examining the complaints, if only for the sake of the reputation of the members of the Tribunal.

95. Is the complaint admissible?

There can be no doubt as to the admissibility of this complaint. Impartiality of an arbitrator is a fundamental and essential requirement. Any shortcoming in this regard, that is any sign of partiality, must be considered to constitute, within the meaning of Article 52(1)(d), a "serious departure from a fundamental rule of procedure" in the broad sense of the term "procedure," i.e., a serious departure from a fundamental rule of arbitration in general, and of ICSID arbitration in particular.

96. Is the complaint well founded?

As to whether this serious accusation is well or ill founded, it will first be noted that the Claimant attempts to substantiate its complaint by the Award's text, by what it does and does not contain, and apparently at the same time, by its wording and style. Here again we find complaints made elsewhere, in particular under the headings of "absence or inadequacy of reasons," "failure to deal with questions submitted to the Tribunal," "serious departure from a fundamental rule of procedure," and, in particular, "lack of due process."

While it is superfluous here to return to each criticism of the Award, it is incumbent upon the Committee, in the interest of the Tribunal itself and in the higher interest of the arbitration system set up by the Washington Convention, not to leave any of the Claimant's essential complaints unanswered.

97. The Claimant believes that there are signs of partiality and even hostility towards it particularly in the passages of the Award on "Klöckner's conduct with regard to its partner" (pp. 44–53) and "the duty of full disclosure to a partner." (pp. 105–109)

In Part "V. The Facts" of the Award, there is a section introduced by the heading: "A. Klöckner's Conduct with regard to its Partner." On each page (pp. 44–53) of this section, we find one and often several severe observations by the Arbitral Tribunal on the serious and "very pronounced" character of Klöckner's obligation of frankness and loyalty and particularly on the fact that "Klöckner failed to live up to these obligations," showed "less than a full measure of frankness, of candor," "did not respect its duty of confidence and loyalty," (p. 46) did not make "adequate efforts to deal frankly," (p. 48) did not have "appropriate conduct," (p. 49) wrongfully remained "silent," and "induced" Cameroon or SOCAME into maintaining the project or accepting new financing (pp. 47, 48, 50), did not "act as a contractual partner

[131] should" and did not have the "kind of frank and loyal conduct between partners that the law (sic) requires," (p. 51) committed "failures of disclosure" which "are of a capital importance," (p. 52) and that these failures, without being "intentional" or committed with "the intention to deceive" (pp. 52, 46) "may have" caused the Government to forge ahead, or "led Cameroon into error", (pp. 46, 52) and that Klöckner "diligently avoided calling the Government's attention" to specific economic problems (p. 52) – a conduct that "is not compatible with the obligations of a partner in an international joint venture of this importance." (p. 53)

The same expressions are again found in part "VI. The Law" under the heading "2. The Duty of Full Disclosure to a Partner." (pp. 105–109) It is often repeated here, in particular on pages 106–107, that the Claimant "failed to disclose facts" or "information of vital importance" and "did not act frankly and loyally vis-à-vis its partners" so that "in a very significant sense, it is its fault."

As we have seen, the Arbitral Tribunal concludes from this that Klöckner "may not insist on payment of the entire price of the Turnkey Contract." (p. 107) According to the Tribunal (p. 109): "we reach the conclusion that Klöckner violated its contractual duty of full disclosure, that it is not entitled to the contract price, that it is entitled to payment for the value of what it delivered, and which Klöckner (sic-apparently a slip for "Cameroon") used, and that Cameroon has already paid enough for the components of the factory it received from Klöckner in 1974–1975 which it used in the redesigned operation in 1980."

98. Such evaluations, however severe they are or may be, cannot in themselves justify the allegation or even the suspicion of partiality. Their wording and repetition simply show the high idea the Tribunal had of the duties of cooperation and mutual disclosure of parties to such a legal relationship and reflect a high moral conception.

99. Three additional factors seem – at least it may be assumed, from reading the Application for Annulment – to have aroused the Claimant's sharp reaction, leading it to make the serious accusation of lack of impartiality:

(A) The fact, already mentioned, that according to the Application (p.12) the Tribunal adopted as one of the two grounds for its decision "this obligation of frankness and loyalty, based not on a principle of French law, but on a sort of declaration, as general as it is imprecise, of principles which are allegedly universally recognized."

The present decision has already acknowledged the legitimacy of this complaint in another context, that of Article 52(1)(b) of the Convention. Given the Award's emphasis on the importance of both "the duty of full disclosure" and Klöckner's shortcomings, the absence of any reference to a precise legal basis is all the more regrettable in the present context in that the legal argument's incomplete character was such as to arouse the losing party's incomprehension and even suspicion.

100. (B) A second, additional factor doubtless relates to the Award's **[132]** very structure. Part "VI. The Law" is subdivided into six sections. Two of these (the first is on applicable law) concern the Claimant's duties and shortcomings, and cover a total of twenty-two pages. Two other, shorter, sections concern the Claimant's arguments. These are Section 4, the Claimant's Reasons for the Failure (pp. 127–134), and Section 5, Alleged Waiver (i.e., Cameroon's acknowledgment of the debt), pp. 134–135. The last Section (6) is on the counterclaim (about one page).

The fact that, in its Law part, the Award devotes much more space (about three times more) to the Claimant's duties and its shortcomings in carrying them out than to the respondent Government's duties obviously does not justify any suspicion of partiality. However, it may have contributed to creating the Claimant's impression that there was "no serious discussion of Klöckner's case" (p. 1) or a "complete failure to examine Klöckner's arguments." (p. 28)

101. Finally, a certain impression of imbalance may have been aroused or reinforced in the Claimant by another aspect of the Award's structure. The Arbitral Tribunal's decision rejecting Klöckner's claim for payment of the price seems already *given* at the very start of Part "VI. The Law," Section 2 ("The Duty of Full Disclosure to a Partner"), *before* any discussion of the other subjects dealt with in the following sections, and in particular before any discussion of the "Claimant's Reasons for the Failure," i.e., Klöckner's principal arguments concerning the Government's duties and responsibility. Indeed, there appears the following on page 109, at the end of Section 2.

> Taking these considerations into account, we reach the conclusion that Klöckner violated its contractual duty of full disclosure, *that it is not entitled to the contract price*, that it is entitled to payment for the value of what it delivered..., etc.
>
> The same conclusion was for that matter already formulated, more briefly, at page 107: We decide that Klöckner violated its fundamental contractual obligations and may not insist upon payment of the entire price of the Turnkey Contract.

102. In other words, among the "two legal bases" adopted by the Tribunal as the basis for its award (p. 105), the first ("the fact that Klöckner did not act *vis-à-vis* its Cameroonian partner with the required frankness and loyalty ...") seems to have been enough to justify the final decision. The conclusion is simply repeated at the end of Section 3 (on the *exceptio non adimpleti contractus*) where it is stated (p. 127):

> *We have thus concluded* that Klöckner is entitled to what it has already received, but to nothing more.

It is therefore *after* reaching this conclusion (and repeating it) on the basis of the Claimant's shortcomings that the Arbitral Award examines (in Section 4, "The Claimant's Reasons for the Failure") Klöckner's arguments

[133] on the causes of the investment's failure, among which are the Government's alleged failures to perform its obligations. But *"before* analysing these explanations,*"* the Award takes care to stress that "even if they were justified, they in no manner diminish the significance of the facts described above insofar as they show the seriousness of the Claimant's failure of contractual performance." The Tribunal adds that in its opinion (p. 127) "it is not responsibility for the economic failure of the joint venture" that is the question before it, "but the simpler and objective question whether the Claimant's failure of performance was sufficiently serious to justify the refusal to pay the unpaid notes."

103. (C) While it is likely that the structure thus given to the Award played a part in giving the Claimant the impression of imbalance or even bias, this impression was apparently reinforced by a third "additional factor." This was the comparatively brief examination of the Government's obligations, or even an apparent underestimation of the latter's responsibilities (for example, on pages 125, 129 to 132).

104. The Tribunal thus seems to attach little importance to the Claimant's argument giving "dumping by producers as one of the causes of failure." On this point, the Claimant referred to Article 12 of the Establishment Agreement under which Cameroon had undertaken to:

take necessary measures in order to ensure, if needed that SOCAME's production be protected from international competition.

The Tribunal limits itself to rejecting this argument in the following words: "but this Article does not create a *concrete* (*sic*) obligation of the Government and *therefore* does not accord an *absolute* (*sic*) protection ... "– which cannot possibly mean no protection at all if Article 12 of the said Agreement has any meaning (p. 128). Returning to the same subject, the Award notes (p. 131) that:

it is true, as Klöckner points out, that the Establishment Agreement contained a general stabilization clause, as well as a more precise undertaking to "take restrictive measures with respect to trade in this area ..." We do not think, however, that this is tantamount to an *unlimited* (*sic*) undertaking to establish' a permanent policy of price protection for the factory ...

105. Likewise, the Arbitral Award attributes only limited importance to the "late payment for the fertilizer" (p. 129) as a cause of the financial difficulties, while admitting that it was one of the causes of these difficulties. The Award concludes (p. 134):

... that Article 12 of the Establishment Contract did not oblige Cameroon to introduce an *indefinite* program of subsidies or of protection, and that the lack of such aid to SOCAME from the Government does not excuse the previous failure of Klöckner, which did not deliver the fertilizer factory in an operating condition as it had promised.

In this regard, we may cite the Award's indirect reference (p. 130) to **[134]** "unforeseen and unexpected delays in development of the site," which was the Government's responsibility (Article 14 of the Protocol of Agreement). But the Award seems to attach no importance to these delays and does not take them into account in assessing responsibilities.

106. In this same Section 4, on "The Claimant's Reasons for the Failure," the Claimant expected no doubt to see an analysis (as careful as that which had been made of its own obligations) of the obligations and responsibilities of the respondent Government. Yet, the Award begins here by stressing "the seriousness of the Claimant's failure of contractual performance" (p. 127; *cf.* also p. 126 *in fine*). In addition, the analysis of the Government's obligations under the Establishment Agreement may have seemed to the Claimant singularly summary and "assuaging": there is a refusal to recognize the "concrete" nature of the undertakings; no examination of the "limits" within which the Government perhaps could have and should have provided support to the Company; and rapid or summary reasoning, brushing aside the Government's responsibility on the grounds of the "previous failure of Klöckner" to perform its delivery obligation, without any reference to the management obligation and the role the Government's attitude may have played in the management difficulties.

107. To summarize, these various additional factors, and especially these particularities of structure and presentation of the Award, added to the severity and frequency of the censures of the Claimant's conduct, no doubt explain, without justifying, the latter's sharp reaction and its accusations of partiality and hostility.

108. It is clear from the Application for Annulment that the Claimant also had an impression of imbalance, inequality and even hostility because, in its opinion (Application, p. 25), the Tribunal

> ... ignored the contractual provisions and Klöckner's arguments regarding the *clauses limiting liability.*

A similar remark may be made regarding Part VI, Section 5 of the Award ("Alleged Waiver," pp. 134–135) in which the Award refuses to attribute any significance, at least as regards Klöckner, to a letter of 12 November 1980 in which the Government of Cameroon informed the Government of the Federal Republic of Germany that "a sum of CFA francs 2 billion had been paid by the Ministry of Finance, *in settlement of the overdue installments.*"

109. Klöckner's argument that Cameroon never held Klöckner responsible, even when it was decided to halt the factory's operation in December 1977, should also be mentioned. (Annulment Rejoinder, p. 14) Cameroon responded to this argument by urging that its requests (to have Klöckner increase SOCAME's capital) should be interpreted as an implicit attempt to bring this responsibility into play.

This point should be related to Klöckner's arguments that Cameroon acknowledged its debt in various ways, without ever invoking the Claimant's

[135] responsibility until the arbitration proceeding. Hence the Application for Annulment, after criticizing various aspects of the Arbitral Award and in particular serious errors of fact or law, "systematically to Klöckner's detriment," (p. 26) adds: "In addition the Tribunal could not have taken into account Cameroon's many acknowledgments of its debts to Klöckner." (p. 26) We shall return to these criticisms later, in another context.

110. Do these various elements and features of the Award, added to those already mentioned, in particular regarding the complaint that there was a failure to deal with questions submitted to the Tribunal, justify the accusation of partiality or hostility, whether systematic or otherwise?

The answer can only be negative. None of these elements would suffice to establish or even to cause one to assume partiality on the part of the arbitrators, who in all conscience and neutrality could perfectly well have arrived at the Award's interpretations and conclusions. The complaint must therefore be rejected, and there can be no question of annulling the Award on this ground.

111. Having regard also to the decision which must be taken on the costs of the present proceeding, it is important to state that the above conclusion does not mean that the Application was rash in this respect. This is true especially if we recall the severity of the Tribunal's moral evaluations of the Claimant and the harm to reputation likely to result therefrom (particularly as the Award was then published by the Respondent's counsel).

It is not up to the Committee to pass on the justice or equity of the Tribunal's solutions but rather to state whether, on the basis of Article 52(1)(d) or on the basis of the fundamental principles of international arbitration as reflected in the ICSID system, the Award is to be annulled for partiality of the arbitrators.

While the *ad hoc* Committee was able without hesitation to respond negatively, it had to note that certain appearances, due to the Award's wording and structure, may rightly or wrongly have aroused the Claimant's emotions and suspicions. This is to be regretted if we recall the English adage, from which every international arbitration could usefully take inspiration: "It is not enough that justice be done, it must be seen manifestly to be done." From this point of view, it is essential to note than an award has not fully attained its purpose if it leaves one of the parties with the feeling – no doubt mistaken but perhaps understandable in the circumstances of the case – of unequal treatment and injustice.

112. Given the importance of this issue, not only in this case, but for the development of international arbitration and especially for the future of the arbitration system established by the Washington Convention, the Committee believes that it should draw the attention here to the most probable cause of the situation which produced these serious accusations. The contested Arbitral Award was rendered on 21 October 1983, while the proceeding was closed the preceding July 23. According to Rule 46 of the ICSID Arbitration Rules:

The award shall be drawn up and signed within 60 days after the closure of the **[136]** proceeding. The Tribunal may, however, extend this period by a further 30 days if it would otherwise be unable to draw up the award.

It can be seen that the Arbitral Award was rendered two days before expiry of the maximum period allowed by Rule 46. Bearing in mind what was said above regarding the existence of deliberation, this explains why the Tribunal could not have taken material advantage, if it had so desired, of the Dissenting Opinion's arguments. Be that as it may, it is extremely probable that, had they had more time and had they not been threatened by the peremptory time limit of Rule 46, the Tribunal's members could have pursued their study of the case and their deliberations and drawn up the Award differently.

113. The complexity of most international investment disputes, the nature and variety of the many legal problems which arise, involving various branches of domestic law as well as international law, the volume of the parties' memorials and files, in which clarity of organization and coherence are not always the dominant characteristic, the breadth and difficulty of the work required of international arbitrators, and the time for reflection desirable for assimilating and judging important cases of this nature, are all factors which make the rule in Rule 46 of the Arbitration Rules – whose primary effect is no doubt to give potential users certain illusions regarding the speed of international arbitration – seem generally unrealistic and dangerous.

The constrains of such a peremptory time limit cannot always be reconciled with the higher exigencies of a healthy administration of justice, whether national or international. While of course being conscious of the need for speed, international arbitration rules should take inspiration from the following observation by a great judge, Justice Felix Frankfurter of the United States Supreme Court: "The judgments of this court ... presuppose ample time and freshness of mind for the private study and reflection ... indispensable to thoughtful, unhurried decision."

IV. FAILURE TO STATE REASONS (ARTICLE 52(1)(e)), INCLUDING FAILURE TO DEAL WITH QUESTIONS SUBMITTED TO THE TRIBUNAL

114. According to the Application for Annulment (p. 14 *et seq.*, in particular pp. 24–26), the Arbitral Award is tainted by a "failure to state reasons", which, for the Claimant,

... covers pure and simple failure to state reasons, but also the different forms which failure to state reasons assumes:
— contradiction of reasons,
— use of dubious or hypothetical reasons or reasons lacking relevance,
— absence or inadequacy of reasons because of misconstruction or distortion (*dénaturation*),

[137]   — failure to deal with questions submitted to the Tribunal (on this last point, the application refers to Article 48(3) of the Convention, according to which "the award shall deal with every question submitted to the Tribunal and shall state the reasons upon which it is based").

For the Claimant, this is a matter of rules of "public policy," respect for which is "imperative and non-observance sanctioned by annulment of the arbitral award." They are meant "to protect the parties against arbitrary decisions and to allow the Tribunal (*sic*) constituted under Article 52 to ensure the award's legality."

115. This presentation calls first for several *general comments*.

With regard to Article 48(3) of the Convention, and the obligation to "deal with every question submitted to the Tribunal," it may be noted that there is one sanction in Article 49(2). Article 49(2) provides that: "upon request by one of the parties, made within 45 days after the date on which the award was rendered" the Tribunal may, after notifying the other party, "decide on any question which it had omitted to decide in the award, and shall rectify any clerical arithmetical or similar error in the award." This is not relevant in the present case and the part of Article 48(3) imposing the obligation to give reasons is obviously enforced by Article 52(1)(e).

Prima facie, therefore, one does not see how a failure to deal with "every question submitted to the Tribunal" can have a sanction other than annulment for a failure to state reasons – unless, of course, the failure to deal with "every question submitted to the Tribunal" is considered to be a "serious departure from a fundamental rule of procedure" under Article 52(1)(d), a question which need not be examined here under the heading "failure to state reasons."

116. As for "contradiction of reasons," it is in principle appropriate to bring this notion under the category "failure to state reasons" for the very simple reasons that two *genuinely* contradictory reasons cancel each other out. Hence the failure to state reasons. The arbitrator's obligation to state reasons which are not contradictory must therefore be accepted.

Establishing the existence of such a contradiction may certainly give rise to difficulties, for example if one of the reasons involves a principal claim, while the other involves a counterclaim. This, however, cannot in itself warrant passing over the question of contradiction, at least in terms of admissibility.

It should also be noted that, in the event that contradictory reasons lead to the conclusion that there was a failure to state reasons, it may be asked whether this failure causes any harm to the party seeking annulment (*cf.* the principle "no annulment without grievance") and whether the award is not sufficiently well founded by other reasons stated in the award.

117. Another general question: is it possible to liken *inadequacy* of reasons to a failure to state reasons?

The question has been discussed in general international law. In the case of the expropriation of Norwegian shipbuilding contracts (American

Journal of International Law 1923, p. 287), the United States criticized the **[138]**
inadequacy of the Tribunal's reasons, but did not contend that the award was
therefore void. In the *Arbitral Award Made by the King of Spain*[6] case
before the international Court of Justice, Nicaragua claimed that there had
been both failure to state and contradiction of reasons. (Counter-Memorial,
paras. 88 and 91) The Court, however, disagreed, observing "that the
Award ... deals in logical order and in some detail with all relevant
considerations and that it contains ample reasoning and explanations in
support of the conclusions arrived at by the arbitrator." (1960 Reports,
p. 216)

118. It is worth noting that the "reasons" referred to in Article 52(1)(e)
are, as indicated more clearly[7] in the English and Spanish texts of the
Washington Convention, "the reasons upon *which it is based*" or "los
motivos *en que se funde.*" The reasons should therefore be the basis of the
Tribunal's decision, and in this sense "sufficient." The latter notion should
obviously be approached with special caution if the application for
annulment under Article 52 is not to serve as an appeal in disguise. One
illustration of this danger is found in the Application for Annulment where,
criticizing "the inadequacy of reasons because of misconstruction"
(*dénaturation*) (pp. 17, 24) (a concept known in French law but absent
from the Convention's text), the application puts forward a variety of
considerations, some of which belong to an appeal proceeding and are
consequently inadmissible.

Interpretation of the concept of "failure to state reasons" is therefore
decisive. It is especially delicate because of the absence of any previous
interpretation of the Washington Convention and the lack of sufficiently
clear or consistent indications from prior international practice.

119. The *ad hoc* Committee, which also has "the power to determine its
own jurisdiction," has the power and the duty to interpret Article 52(1)(e).
In so doing, it adopts neither a narrow interpretation nor a broad
interpretation, but bears in mind the customary principles of treaty
interpretation and, in particular, the objective of the Convention and of the
system it establishes.

The preparatory works of the Convention seem to indicate that the
intention was to limit the institution of annulment proceedings. This would
not, however, be enough. What is decisive, more than the "historic"
interpretation (assuming it can be established), is the "correct meaning" of
the interpreted provision, i.e., Article 52(1)(e).

The text of this Article requires a *statement* of reasons *on which the award
is based.* This does not mean just any reasons, purely formal or apparent, but
rather reasons having some substance, allowing the reader to follow the
arbitral tribunal's reasoning, on facts and on law.

The questions can be posed in the following terms: in order to rule out
annulment under Article 52(1)(e), is it enough that there be "apparently

[6 30 *ILR* 457.]
7 Translator's note: the French text of Article 52(1)(e) reads simply "*défaut de motifs.*"

[139] relevant" reasons, or is it necessary that there be "relevant" reasons? In the first case, control by the Committee will be reduced; in the second, it will be broader.

120. In the opinion of the Committee, one could hardly be satisfied simply by "apparently relevant" reasons. This would deprive of any substance the control of legality Article 52 of the Convention is meant to provide. On the other hand, interpreting this provision as (indirectly) requiring "relevant reasons" could make the annulment proceeding more like an appeal and lead the Committee to substitute its own appreciation of the relevance of the reasons for that of the Tribunal.

A middle and reasonable path is to be satisfied with reasons that are "sufficiently relevant," that is, reasonably capable of justifying the result reached by the Tribunal. In other words, there would be a "failure to state reasons" in the absence of a statement of reasons that are "sufficiently relevant," that is, reasonably sustainable and capable of providing a basis for the decision.

Of necessity, the interpretation here can only be based on general *standards* or criteria, which do not lend themselves to any abstract and rigorous delimitation.

A. *Contradiction of Reasons*

121. The Application for Annulment complains that the Award contains a contradiction of reasons (p. 15), which it holds to be equivalent to a failure to state reasons. It must first be asked whether this complaint is admissible.

On this subject, it will be noted that the Application refers in this respect to two observations in Part VI, The Law, of the Arbitral Award:

First observation: on page 106, the Tribunal holds that Klöckner:

> ... at critical stages of the project, hid from its partner information of vital importance. On several occasions it failed to disclose facts which, if they had been known to the Government, could have caused it to put an end to the venture and to cancel the contract before the expenditure of the funds whose payment Klöckner now seeks to obtain by means of an award ...

The Tribunal deduces from this that Klöckner, at "fault" and "in a very significant sense," bears responsibility for the "fact that the funds were spent" and that having violated its "duty of full disclosure" to its partner, it "may not insist upon payment of the entire price of the Turnkey Contract." (pp. 106–107).

Second observation: on page 136 of the Award, the Tribunal turns to Cameroon's counterclaim (which it distinguished from the *exceptio non adimpleti contractus*, invoked simply to procure the claim's dismissal). This "counterclaim for damages" requests compensation for all losses attributable to its participation in the project, and in the alternative, compensation for SOCAME's losses. Just as it rejected Klöckner's claim, the **[140]** Tribunal dismisses the counterclaim, for the following reasons:

> There is no justification for charging the Claimant with the losses incurred by the Government in a joint venture where the two parties participated, or should have participated, with open eyes and full understanding of their actions. One could hardly accept that a State, having access to many sources of technical assistance, could be entitled to claim compensation for the fact that it was misled by a private company proposing a particular contract. If this had been the case, the Government would also have had a concurrent responsibility, thereby excluding the counterclaim.

122. A comparison of these two observations elicits the following comment from the Applicant for Annulment (Application, p. 15):

> Hence, in order to dismiss Klöckner's claim, the Tribunal holds that it "could have deceived" the Cameroonian Government, while in dismissing the Cameroonian Government's claim, it emphasizes that the latter could not have been deceived.

In response, the Respondent claimed that the supposedly contradictory reasons do not support a single decision but *several* decisions: (i) one involving the principal claim, and (ii) the other regarding the counterclaim. Each decision is based on different reasons: (i) Klöckner has misled; (ii) Cameroon should not have allowed itself to be so misled; and each reason supports a different decision. Therefore there is no contradiction of reasons within the same award.

The argument that there were two different decisions does not stand up to examination. Neither in form nor in substance can the Award of 21 October 1983 be viewed as a number of separate awards. This would not, in any case, correspond to the intentions of the Tribunal, which evidently had an overall view of the dispute and sought to work out a sort of equitable setoff between the opposing claims.

The complaint is therefore admissible in principle, but it remains to be determined whether it is well founded.

123. Is the complaint well founded?

This does not seem to be the case. Indeed, unlike the Application for Annulment's presentation, the true reason for the Tribunal's award on the first point (p. 106) is not that there was or could have been deception, but that there was omission or dissimulation on the part of the Claimant (and in short, disregarding the result). The true reason is that not having "acted frankly and loyally," the Claimant "cannot rightly present a claim to funds ..." It is apparently on this ground, that of the claim or right to claim – which evokes "*préclusion*" or "estoppel" – that the Tribunal definitively held that the Claimant "*may not insist* upon payment of the entire price of the Turnkey Contract."

Similarly, on page 136, the Award denies that the Cameroonian State could be entitled to *claim* compensation for "the fact that it was misled by a

[141] private company"; whether it was deceived or not changes nothing: it acted with either full understanding or with open eye, and if it was "misled," it would have a "concurrent responsibility" which *excludes* the counterclaim. Therefore, we also seem to find ourselves here in the field of "equity," relying on the notions of "*préclusions*" or "estoppel."

In reality, the two reasons are not contradictory, despite certain ambiguities in language. In neither case is the decision based on the existence or non-existence of the result, a deception, or on its possibility or impossibility. The complaint must therefore be rejected.

B. *Dubious or Hypothetical Reasons*

124. The above analysis makes it possible to deal expeditiously with the Applicant's criticisms of what it calls the "*dubious or hypothetical nature of the reasons adopted*" in various passages of the Award on the consequences which Klöckner's omissions or reticence, or its various shortcomings in fulfilling the "duty of full disclosure to its partner," *could have had* on the Cameroonian Government's decision. (Application, p. 16)

125. For example, the Tribunal criticized the Claimant for not having revealed "facts which, if they had been known to the Government, *could have* caused it to put an end to the venture...." It also found that the "expenditure would *perhaps* never have been necessary" if the Claimant "had been frank and candid in its dealings." (p. 106) Prior to this, in the "Facts" part of the Award, the Tribunal observes that "it is *impossible to determine* whether the Government would have decided to put an end to the project if Klöckner had clearly and plainly revealed .... (p. 48), etc.

The Application for Annulment reproaches the Award for "systematically (using) the conditional, or purely hypothetical formulas." (p. 16) Even if it were admissible, such a vague and general criticism would have no relevance.

126. It was incumbent upon the Applicant for Annulment to show that the contested Award is *based*, on one point or another, on a simple hypothesis, instead of on facts or definite legal arguments. But in this regard the Claimant's analysis either is equivalent to an appellant's criticism of the first judge's evaluation of the facts or law, or makes no distinction or an inadequate distinction between the *ratio decidendi* and simple, overabundant considerations, or, finally, loses sight of the fact that an arbitrator or judge may be perfectly entitled to reason where necessary on the basis of hypotheses or to take into account, as a fact, that one party has been deprived of a certain "possibility" by the conduct or fault of the other party (as in the case of "loss of an opportunity" (*perte d'une chance*), well known to French civil law).

C. *Absence and Inadequacy of Reasons* [142]

127. We shall dwell no further on the complaint regarding the hypothetical or dubious character of the reasons and shall now examine the Applicant's main argument for annulment based on Article 52(1)(e): "absence and inadequacy of reasons." (Application, pp. 17–26) This, as the Claimant itself did (p. 22 *et seq.*), is also the place to examine the complaint that there was a *"failure to deal with questions submitted to the Tribunal."*

In this part of its Application for Annulment (the arguments for which are taken up again in the Reply of 31 July 1984 to the Republic of Cameroon's Counter-Memorial of 30 June 1984) the Claimant cites what it considers to be the main examples of absences and inadequacies of reasons in the Award, of which "several ... are combined with particularly serious misconstructions and distortions." (p. 17)

On this score, the Application successively examines various parts of the Award, comparing them either to its own documents or to those of its adversary, or to documents in the file relating to (1) acceptance of the factory; (2) Klöckner's responsibility for the production shortfall; (3) causes of the production shortfall; (4) the condition of the factory. At the same time, its comparative critique is complemented by various references to the Dissenting Opinion.

128. This presentation of the Application for Annulment calls for an initial general comment: the Committee under Article 52 of the Washington Convention is not an appeal tribunal, and in principle has no jurisdiction to review the arbitrators' findings of fact or law.

As we saw earlier in discussing the concept of excess of powers and Article 42(1)(b) of the Convention, the *ad hoc* Committee has no power to correct a mistaken application of law or *"error in judicando"* beyond the strict limits of Article 52.

While *inadequacy of reasons* may under certain conditions constitute a failure to state reasons within the meaning of Article 52(1)(e), there can be no question of expanding the concept so as to permit a sort of disguised appeal, even though, as we saw above (*supra* para. 120), Article 52(1)(e) should be interpreted as indirectly requiring that the Award generally give sufficiently or reasonably relevant reasons. It has been mentioned that the specific applications of this general standard turn on each particular case, and it should be recalled that it is up to the Applicant for Annulment to establish a "failure to state reasons" in the sense of an absence of "sufficiently relevant" or "reasonably sustainable" reasons under the circumstances of the case.

129. Having recalled this, it must be stated that the Claimant's contentions to a large extent comprise arguments and reasoning which by their nature are those of an appeal memorial, even though they ostensibly address "obvious misconstructions" or "distortions."

This is how the Claimant criticizes (p. 17 of the Application) the Tribunal's conclusion, inferred from Mr Van der Ploeg's absence, on the

[143] irregularity of the factory acceptance. The Tribunal's evaluation of evidence concerning a certain Mr Moudio, the Cameroonian Government's representative (p. 18), or again (p. 19) the Tribunal's conclusion on Klöckner's responsibility for the production shortfall, a conclusion based on the shutdown of the factory and contradicting the report of SOCAME's management committee, a document cited by the Award itself, are criticized in the same way. The Award is similarly criticized as being wrong on questions of fact or in its evaluation of evidence in the shape of certain experts' reports.

It may be that these various statements or evaluations of evidence in the Award are erroneous or contrary to the documents in the file, but the Committee has no power to make judgments in this regard. The question is not whether there was a misconstruction – obvious or otherwise – of the facts and arguments, but whether there is a "failure to state reasons." Now, it is clear from the Claimant's own exposition that to a large extent its criticisms of the Award are aimed not so much at the absence of reasons (or absence of "sufficiently relevant" reasons), but at the reasons themselves!

130. There would be a "failure to state reasons" if no reasoning or explanation whatsoever, or no "sufficiently relevant" or "reasonably acceptable" reasoning could be found for some conclusion or decision in the Award. Such would not be the case if the Tribunal, having justified its finding or a particular decision in a certain way, even if subject to criticism, did not address this or that particular argument (subject to what will be said below on failure to deal with questions submitted to the Tribunal). Yet it is enough to read, for example, the Award's analysis of the parties' respective arguments on the subject of the factory acceptance (pp. 53–54; *cf.* also p. 61 *et seq.*) to see that the Application for Annulment's criticism (pp. 17–18) can in no way be considered as relating to a "failure to state reasons" in the sense that this concept has been interpreted here.

D. *Failure to Deal with Questions Submitted to the Tribunal*

131. As for the failure to deal with questions submitted to the Tribunal, reference should be made both to Article 48(3), as we have been, and to Article 52(1)(e) (failure to state reasons) or (d) (serious departure from a fundamental rule of procedure).

According to a general principle, embodied in Article 48(3), the Award must deal with "every question submitted to the Tribunal" (*tous les chefs de conclusions soumises au Tribunal*). Given the relative ambiguity of the term "questions" (*conclusions*), it should first be noted that these may be formulated separately, at the end of an application or memorial, or constitute part of an argument. It may therefore be that certain "questions submitted to the Tribunal" are presented formally in the main text of the parties' documents rather than, for example, in the form of "final conclusions" or "submissions."

On the other hand, while some arguments may therefore really be **[144]** "questions submitted to the Tribunal," it is clear that the arbitrators do not have to deal with all of the parties' arguments.

132. In its Application for Annulment Klöckner lists (pp. 22–24) "Klöckner's essential arguments on which the Award undertook no study (*sic*)."

This approach is misleading; in order to judge the admissibility and then the validity of the complaints, it need only be determined whether these "essential arguments" constituted or involved "questions submitted to the Tribunal" and whether the Tribunal dealt with them in the Award, regardless of whether it undertook any "study" of them.

The *first complaint* listed is that "the Arbitral Award held that Klöckner had an obligation which is in fact an obligation of result" (*obligation de résultat*).

Second complaint: the Tribunal did not examine the conditions required by Article 1116 of the Civil Code for wrongful inducement to contract (*dol*), or consider Klöckner's arguments on the number and importance of the functions assumed by the Cameroonian Government in the performance of the contract.

Third complaint: the Award takes no account of Klöckner's pleas regarding contractual limitations of the Claimant's warranties and liability.

Fourth complaint: the Award takes no account of Cameroon's unconditional acknowledgement of its debt and of the arguments the Claimant based on this.

Fifth complaint: the Award did not respond to the Claimant's pleas regarding the rules of French law limiting a supplier's liability for hidden defects (*vices cachés*) and time barring claims.

(1) The First Complaint

133. According to the Application for Annulment (p. 22 *et seq.*), a first ground for annulment is that "Klöckner's pleas ... are never or almost never mentioned," that "the Award undertook no study" of various essential arguments (p. 22) which were "systematically ignored," and that therefore "this failure to deal with questions submitted to the Tribunal should necessarily lead to annulment of the Arbitral Award." (p. 24)

In particular, the Claimant maintains that the Award imposes on Klöckner an "*obligation of result*" even though the Claimant had only assumed a "best efforts obligation" (*obligation de moyen*). (p. 23) This complaint is furthermore apparently linked to a third complaint (p. 23, para. 3) to the effect that the Award "took no account" of the contractual limitations of liability and of the exclusion of any indirect damages.

134. This point of view is elaborated by the Claimant as follows (pp. 22–23):

[145]   The Award applied to Klöckner an obligation which is in fact an obligation of result. Indeed, as has been seen above, the mere fact, for the Tribunal, that actual production was below the guaranteed capacity puts Klöckner at fault. But Klöckner had established (pages 26, 30, 85, 96), and Cameroon had recognized (page 115, Counter-Memorial), that it had only a best efforts obligation, which meant therefore that the Cameroonian party had the burden of proof and had to demonstrate Klöckner's fault; these pleas by Klöckner are, completely ignored by the Tribunal, which does not attempt to establish the existence of a fault nor *a fortiori* to determine its seriousness and consequences.

These passages should be read together with the following ones from Chapter 2, "Excess of Powers and the Obligation of Result" of the Application, (p. 10):

... seeking however to judge Klöckner's management, the Arbitral Tribunal finds it defective, inferring from Article 9 of the Protocol of Agreement an obligation of result which was never provided for but violated merely because factory production was not equal to the contractual capacity.

This obligation of result had been expressly excluded in the Management Contract signed by the parties, as Cameroon itself recognized (page 115 of the Counter-Memorial).

It should be noted that a similar criticism is repeated in Klöckner's Rejoinder of 31 July 1984. (p. 7)

135. It is difficult to determine from the Claimant's none too clear explanations whether the complaint is based on Article 52(1)(b) (manifest excess of powers) or on Article 52(1)(e) (failure to state reasons) (and more precisely failure to deal with questions submitted to the Tribunal), or on both. Be that as it may, before determining whether there exists one of the grounds for annulment under Article 52, we should first determine whether, *prima facie* and on a reading of the Award, it may be said that the decision finds that Klöckner has an "obligation of result." If the answer is no, the complaint must be immediately rejected. If the answer is yes, it would remain to be seen whether the Tribunal "manifestly exceeded its powers" within the meaning of Article 52(1)(b) or whether its decision is tainted by a "failure to state reasons." (Article 52(1)(e))

136. Did the Award hold, as claimed, that Klöckner had an obligation of result?

It will be noted in this connection that the Application does not seem to distinguish clearly between the obligation to deliver the factory and the management obligation (although it seems to connect the idea of obligation of result mostly to the second obligation). But a similar comment may no doubt be made on the Award itself, which, especially in Chapter 2, on the *exceptio non adimpleti contractus*, shifts constantly from one to the other of these obligations or considers them together, in their somewhat cumulative effect. This may, of course, be explained from an industrial or economic perspective but does not always facilitate legal analysis.

In order to answer this first question, we should examine, in part "VI. The [146] Law" of the Award, Sections 3(b) "Partial or Imperfect Performance" (p. 112 *et seq.*) and 3(c) "Significance of Failure of Performance in this Case" (p. 114 *eq seq.*) to determine whether the Claimant's allegation is well founded.

137. The following passages of the Award will, for example, be noted in this regard:

> It is true that the Claimant did not make partial delivery, however defective ..., (p. 125)

which leads us to inquire whether the Tribunal reached this finding on the ground (whether it is one among others is of no importance) that the "result" was not achieved.

> It is obvious that the Claimant would have assumed such onerous obligations only in order to obtain a factory capable of producing that which one might reasonably and legitimately have hoped to obtain from the contracts ... (p. 124)

Analysing the *Turnkey Contract* (p. 114), the Tribunal stresses that "a fundamental obligation" of Klöckner was to supply "a factory *capable of producing* fertilizer products conforming to specific descriptions and in guaranteed quantities..." It adds that what Cameroon had agreed to pay for:

> was an integrated total system of production *capable* of producing the products defined in the agreements.... In our opinion, this meant a factory *that could produce* these specified quantities at a practical rate of utilization of the factory. (p. 115)

The Award concludes in the next paragraph with the following significant sentence:

> In the present case, the factory did not function at the level of production foreseen in the agreements. Klöckner *thus* (*sic*) did not deliver to Cameroon what it had promised. (p. 115)

It should be noted that the Award immediately goes on to analyse "another obligation just as fundamental as the first," the obligation of technical and commercial management. From this it may be thought that the above citations, to the extent that they establish an obligation of result, relate the obligation to the Turnkey Contract alone, and not to the management obligation. As shown below and already mentioned, the Award's reasoning actually most often relates the two. Thus, on page 116, there appears the following:

> The facts recited in Chapter III demonstrate that Klöckner's two fundamental obligations were performed in an imperfect and partial manner.

[147]   After having dealt with the factory acceptance (which, in its opinion, was not done according to the Contract), the Tribunal continues (p. 117):

> Next, the production capacities defined in the Turnkey Contract and the Protocol of Agreement were never attained after startup of the factory [N.B. For obvious reasons, the Award makes no mention of the Management Contract, over which the Tribunal held itself to have no jurisdiction.] This is a failure of performance of the greatest importance....
>
>   In order to perform the relevant contracts correctly, it was not sufficient to supply a fertilizer factory; the factory had to have the required capacity and had to be managed in the way necessary to *attain the proposed goals*.

138. It is difficult not to interpret these various quotes, taken from the Award's Law section, as expressing the Tribunal's opinion that the Claimant incurred liability because *the anticipated results were not achieved*, either in terms of delivery or management, or yet again in terms of both.

However, let us add that in Section "V. The Facts" the Tribunal (p. 45) did not seem so certain of the existence of an obligation of result. There we read that Klöckner "promised its partner *if not unconditional guarantee of the factory's profitability* at all times, at least very pronounced frankness and loyalty."

As Cameroon's alleged admission that Klöckner was bound only by a best efforts obligation, the Application for Annulment (p. 23) cites Cameroon's Counter-Memorial of 15 June 1982 (p. 115). But this refers only to Klöckner's obligation to advise, which is said to be a primary obligation under the Management Contract:

> Assumed by Klöckner as part of its consulting activities for SOCAME's technical and commercial management, this is a best efforts obligation, liability being incurred only in case of serious professional failing.

139. We will not, at least directly, consider for the purposes of the present question the detailed treatment of the facts, technical reports or discussions between the parties found in Part "V. The Facts" (pp. 44–103) of the Award. The Committee need not seek to determine and much less issue an opinion as to whether the Claimant company in fact bears responsibility for the failure to achieve the results hoped for by the contracting parties.

The issue is whether, as the Applicant for Annulment claims, the Award wrongly held the Claimant to have an "obligation of result" (a classic concept of French or Cameroonian civil law, applicable to this case) and in short, by presuming a failure, reversed the burden of proof to the Claimant's detriment. *And this without taking into account* either the legislative or contractual provisions, in particular the provisions of the Civil Code on the warranty against hidden defects and the period of such warranty's validity and the contractual provisions limiting liability (for example, Article 9 of the Turnkey Contract, on "the warranty for the equipment," and in particular Article 9(2)):

the warranty period for each shop shall be one year from the date of its entry **[148]** into service, but no more than 36 months from the start of performance of the Contract,

and, finally, without taking into account the consideration that no entrepreneur would warrant a result, and hence the success of the enterprise, if he does not have the right to determine the sale price of its product, a right which SOCAME did not possess.

140. This Committee's first task in this regard is to examine the Tribunal's reasons for so interpreting Klöckner's delivery and management obligations and concluding that these two obligations had not been performed largely, if not exclusively, *because the production goal was not reached*. It would only be *after* examining these reasons that it would be possible to determine whether the argument that there was a failure to state reasons (or perhaps that of manifest excess of powers) could possibly be upheld.

141. In this regard, it is essential to note that the Award's text gives no indication of the reasons why the Tribunal decided, in substance if not in so many words, that there was an "obligation of result." Above all, it did not take into consideration Klöckner's pleas on the best efforts obligation or the contractual or legislative provisions limiting seller/supplier liability. Despite many readings of the text, it is impossible to discern how and why the Tribunal could reach its decision on this point. For example, the following is a significant passage from the Award:

> The factory's production shortfall was demonstrated by reports of operators of the plant (see para. C, pp. 69 to 58 supra) to have causes (*sic*) that without doubt included ones for which Klöckner was responsible.... In order to perform the relevant contracts correctly, it was not sufficient to supply a fertilizer factory; the factory had to have the required capacity and had to be managed *in the way necessary to attain the proposed goals*.

That the "factory's production shortfall" was "demonstrated" is in fact of no interest here. What should be noticed is the rather cryptic observation: "... that without doubt *included* ones for which Klöckner was responsible." One may wonder whether this is "technical" responsibility, or "legal" responsibility. But it is especially interesting to note that the Tribunal here necessarily accepts that the "causes" of this "production shortfall" *also* "*included*" causes not attributable to Klöckner. Finally, more significant still is the statement that the factory "had to be managed in the way necessary to attain the proposed goals." Klöckner's responsibility for the results is later again affirmed (p. 118) when it is stated:

> One must recall again that the Claimant's responsibility was not extinguished upon delivery of the factory and satisfactory test runs over three days...

142. In the case of the obligation of result in the area of technical and commercial management, it is possible that the Tribunal thought it necessary to refrain from citing the provisions of the Management Contract

[149] because it had declared itself incompetent in this regard, and had tried to reason solely on the basis of Article 9 of the Protocol of Agreement (interpreted, as was seen above, as "encompassing" the Management Contract – a concept which need not be discussed here but which seems difficult to reconile *prima facie* with a refusal to take into account the contractual arrangements provided by the parties in the Management Contract). But the same does not hold for the Turnkey Contract. It is very surprising, and regrettable, that in accepting the theory of an obligation of result for Klöckner, the Tribunal considered it unnecessary to explain why it did not have to take into account Article 9 of the Turnkey Contract or why it did not feel it more necessary or appropriate to apply the provisions of Franco-Cameroonian law on the warranty against hidden defects.

143. The absence of any discussion by the Award of the contractual provisions on the warranty or limitation of liability is all the more astonishing as the basic reason given by the Tribunal for its decision is the desire "to maintain *the equilibrium of reciprocal contractual undertakings as defined by the parties themselves.*" (p. 124)

Now, it immediately springs to mind that provisions such as those in Article 9 of the Turnkey Contract, or the provisions of the Management Contract, or generally all clauses on the responsibility of the seller and buyer, are an integral part of the desired "equilibrium of reciprocal contractual undertakings as defined by the parties themselves."

144. *In conclusion*, it is superfluous to examine whether, as the Claimant alleges, the Arbitral Tribunal manifestly exceeded its powers on this point, since the Award in no way allows the *ad hoc* Committee or for that matter the parties to reconstitute the arbitrators' reasoning in reaching a conclusion that is perhaps ultimately perfectly justified and equitable (and the Committee has no opinion on this point) but is simply asserted or postulated instead of being reasoned.

The complaint must therefore be regarded as well founded, to the extent that it is based on Article 52(1)(e).

(2) The Second Complaint

145. The Claimant likewise considers that there is a failure to state reasons, due to a "failure to deal with questions submitted to the Tribunal" because "the Award undertook no study" of another of "Klöckner's essential arguments" (p. 22):

> Contrary to what Klöckner had requested, the Arbitral Tribunal in no way examines the conditions under which *Article 1116 of the Civil Code on wrongful inducement to contract (dol)* may be invoked. (Application for Annulment, p. 23)

It is difficult to grasp the exact meaning of this complaint, if one considers the fact that the Award neither accepted the Respondent's allegation of

wrongful inducement to contract nor declared on the nullity of the Contract. **[150]**
The counterclaim, primarily for compensation for all losses, *lucrum cessans*,
and non-financial damages (*préjudice moral*), was dismissed by the Award
because a State, "having access to many sources of technical assistance,"
could hardly be "entitled to claim compensation for the fact that it was
misled." (p. 136) Furthermore, regarding the Claimant's conduct and "the
duty of full disclosure to its partner," the Tribunal makes it clear that it did
not find there was fraudulent intent (p. 46) or an "intention to deceive."
(p. 52)

Having refused to accept that there was wrongful inducement to contract,
no doubt within the scope of its power to evaluate the facts and evidence, the
Tribunal could not be required to examine or discuss "the conditions under
which Article 1116 of the Civil Code on wrongful inducement to contract
may be invoked."

146. It could be surmised that the Claimant wished to argue, by analogy
to the second paragraph of Article 1116 of the Civil Code, that Klöckner's
"lack of frankness" could not be presumed either and should, like wrongful
inducement to contract, be proven by the Respondent. Be that as it may, the
Tribunal could hardly be blamed for not having pronounced on surmises of
this sort or on unelaborated arguments.

(3) The Third Complaint

147. Under the heading "Failure to Deal with Questions Submitted to the
Tribunal," (pp. 23 and 25) the Application for Annulment criticizes the
Award which, in its opinion, is tainted by a failure to state reasons on the
question of limitation of Klöckner's liability. According to the Claimant:

> In its Memorial (page 64) and its oral pleading, Klöckner recalled the existence
> of contractual provisions limiting the warranties given. In particular,
> Klöckner's liability could not exceed 3% of the contract price (Article 10.10 of
> the Turnkey Contract), whereas Articles 9 and 13 excluded any indirect
> damages. Any modification would in addition exempt Klöckner unless the
> latter agreed in writing (Article 9.5). (p. 23)

The Claimant continues (p. 25):

> The Tribunal then ignores the contractual provisions and Klöckner's
> arguments regarding the clauses limiting liability. It does likewise with
> Klöckner's pleas regarding the brief time allowed [in French law, limiting the
> period during which a claim may be made for hidden defects]. The absence of
> any response to these decisive arguments deprives the Award of all validity.

The same question of clauses limiting liability was discussed by the
Respondent in the arbitration in its Counter-Memorial of June 1982.
(pp. 116 *et seq.*)

148. Is this complaint admissible?

[151]   It will be noted first that the complaint is admissible, whether it be described as "failure to state reasons" or, more precisely, as a "failure to deal with questions submitted to the Tribunal."

It is clear that the argument Klöckner bases on the contractual clauses limiting liability can and should be considered a "question submitted to the Tribunal" and that this is an essential question for both parties. The Claimant has a major interest in seeing these contractual clauses deemed applicable and applied. The Respondent has a major interest in seeing them judged inapplicable or irrelevant to the present case. Both parties have for that matter addressed this subject.

149. Is the complaint well founded?

It must be noted that the Award says nothing on this essential question and contains no reason on this topic, or, more precisely, no *expressed* reason. Now, as we have seen, the English text of Article 52(1)(e) provides as a ground for annulment that "that award has failed *to state* the reasons on which it is based" and the Spanish text of the same provision permits an application for annulment on the ground: "que no se hubieren *expresado* en el laudo los motivos en que se funde."

It is thus *prima facie* undeniable that the Tribunal did not deal with one of the Claimant's essential questions. This provisional conclusion must however be tested.

150. The Respondent has submitted that it was not necessary for the Tribunal to deal with this point, as applying the contractual clauses limiting liability would presuppose that Klöckner had always acted honestly, while its lack of frankness and loyalty would make the provisions in question inapplicable. This position could be understood if the Tribunal had reached the conclusion that the Turnkey Contract had become void for wrongful inducement to contract or if, at the very least, the Tribunal had declared that the Claimant could not take advantage of these limiting clauses because of its failure – an argument it would furthermore have had to justify on the basis of the applicable law. Now, while the Tribunal may have *thought* that the Claimant's breaches of its obligations of delivery and management brought about a sort of forfeiture of the right to invoke the clauses limiting liability, nothing in the text of the Award makes it possible to say with certainty that the Tribunal actually considered the question and resolved it in this way.

151. The Tribunal could for example have referred to or adopted the Respondent's arguments in its Counter-Memorial of June 1982 (p. 116 *eq sea.*) (arguments on a "fundamental breach" and on the judge's power to increase or moderate (the penalty)) or could have used reasoning analogous to that which it employed on page 136 of the Award to reject the counterclaim.

Be that as it may, it is not for the Committee to imagine what might or should have been the arbitrators' reasons, any more than it should substitute "correct" reasons for possibly "incorrect" reasons, or deal "*ex post facto*" with questions submitted to the Tribunal which the Award left unanswered. The only role of the Committee here is to state whether there is one of the grounds for annulment set out in Article 52 of the Convention, and to draw [152] the consequences under the same Article. In this sense, the Committee defends the Convention's legal purity, it being understood that, when it has found that there is a ground for annulment, it will remain for it to decide, pursuant to Article 52(3), whether the Award should be annulled in whole or in part. This question, which was already mentioned (*supra*, para. 80) raises a problem, not expressly resolved by Article 52, namely, whether the finding of a ground for annulment leads "automatically" to annulment. This will be examined later.

To conclude on this point, the *ad hoc* Committee can only note that the complaint is not only admissible but well founded, given the failure to state reasons and to deal with the Claimant's pleas concerning the application of contractual clauses limiting liability.

(4) The Fourth Complaint

152. According to the Application for Annulment, there is also a failure to state reasons and to "deal with questions submitted to the Tribunal" (pp. 24 and 26) because the Tribunal took "no account of the very many *confirmations by Cameroon of its debts to Klöckner*," mentioned above in connection with the allegation of partiality (para. 93 *et seq.*).

This complaint being admissible *per se*, it should be determined whether it is well founded. The issue is therefore whether, on the one hand, the Claimant made pleas based on an alleged acknowledgement by Cameroon of its debt and whether, on the other hand, the Award was silent on them and gave no reason for the decision to dismiss the claim for payment, despite the Claimant's arguments based on the Respondent's alleged acknowledgment of the debt.

153. On this first point, it is correct that the Claimant (Application, p. 26) availed itself of the fact that Cameroon not only never called upon Klöckner to fulfill its contractual obligations, but moreover, never disputed its obligations and its debts to Klöckner.

In particular, Klöckner cited the Cameroonian Finance Minister's decision No. 001901 authorizing "payment of a sum of CFA francs 2,000,000,000 to SOCAME as an exceptional subsidy, intended for the settlement of the promissory notes due on the Klöckner loan since 11 October 1978." (Klöckner Annex 1.2) The decision was followed by a "payment order" of CFA francs 2 billion "in favour of SOCAME and *intended for the settlement of the promissory notes due on the Klöckner loan since 11 October 1978*." There was also a letter of 12 November 1980 from the Cameroonian Minister of Foreign Affairs to the FRG Ambassador stating "that payment of the sum of CFA francs 2 billion intended for the settlement of the promissory notes due on the Klöckner loan since 11 October 1978 has been effected by the Ministry of Finance, Budget Division ... to SOCAME." Following this and the final shutdown of the factory, SOCAME kept the

[153] payment, even though it had been made by the Government for Klöckner's benefit.

Clearly such an argument, based on the Respondent's alleged acknowledgment of the debt, must be considered to be a question submitted to the Tribunal, calling for a response.

154. It must be noted that the Award does tackle this question in Part "VI. The Law," Section 5. Under the heading "Alleged Waiver," the Tribunal observes that:

> It has also been suggested that the Government of Cameroon waived all rights it may have had to refuse to pay in 1983 and confirmed and accepted Klöckner's defective performance.

In this context, it is appropriate to point out that the Tribunal chose to qualify the Claimant's argument or plea as an "alleged waiver" of the right to refuse to pay, which is not necessarily the same as an alleged acknowledgment of the debt by the debtor. But it is unnecessary to wonder about this nuance, since it is clear that the arbitrators did not fail in their duty to provide reasons by characterizing, in the manner they deemed proper, the question submitted by the Claimant.

155. It is undoubtedly more significant that, according to the Arbitral Award (p. 134):

> Klöckner bases itself on the letter of 12 November 1980 (Annex 1.1 to the Memorial) by which the Government of Cameroon informed the Government of the Federal Republic of Germany that a sum of CFA francs 2 billion had been paid by the Ministry of Finance in settlement of the arrears.

The Tribunal considers (pp. 134–135) that "the statement was not made to Klöckner but between two governments ...," that "in addition, the payment was conditional" and that "the letter of 12 November 1980 consequently did not constitute a waiver."

156. Criticism of these reasons is not admissible in the present annulment proceeding. Certainly the Claimant may regret that, from the Claimant's pleading, the Tribunal chose only to rely on the letter of 12 November 1980 between two governments (Annex 1.1 to the Memorial), without mentioning or discussing Annex 1.2 of the Memorial on the Finance Minister's decision and his order for Klöckner's payment through SOCAME. The Award limits itself to mentioning that "Klöckner based none of its actions on this letter" (from Cameroon to the FRG), but it fails to mention that Klöckner did indeed base its action in part on the other documents already cited, and in particular on those contained in Annex 1.2 to its Memorial.

It would be impossible to conclude from this that there is really a failure to state reasons, since the Tribunal held that "in addition, the payment was conditional." The complaint must therefore be rejected.

157. The same is not true for the rest of Cameroon's debts, over and **[154]** above the CFA francs 2 billion paid to SOCAME, according to the Respondent, as an incentive to renegotiate. The Award does not mention this. To this extent, there is a failure to state reasons and the complaint is well founded.

(5) The Fifth Complaint

158. The same complaint regarding failure to deal with questions submitted by the Tribunal and to state reasons is again invoked by the Claimant (p. 24), who recalls:

> that it could only be held responsible for *hidden defects*. (pp. 28–30 and 64, and oral pleadings)

According to the Claimant, the brief time limit within which a claim may be made with respect to hidden defects under French law had long since expired and no evidence that there was a hidden defect had ever been advanced by Cameroon. Such evidence could in any case no longer have been adduced, since Cameroon had unilaterally made many modifications contrary to the contractual provisions (Article 9(5) of the Turnkey Contract).

This, too, would be one of "Klöckner's essential arguments on which the Award undertook no study" (p. 22), and an illustration of the fact that:

> the Arbitral Tribunal systemically ignored Klöckner's arguments, drawing up the Arbitral Award as if Klöckner had never submitted any questions. (p. 24)

159. The complaint is clearly admissible, for the reasons already given. Is it well founded?

It is true that during the arbitral proceeding (*cf.* especially Klöckner's Reply of 30 October 1982, p. 27 *et seq.*), the Claimant invoked Article 1641 (on the warranty against hidden defects) and Article 1648 (on the obligation of purchaser to act "within a brief time limit") of the Civil Code to show that the Cameroon's argument was "without any legal basis." (p. 28) The Claimant formally concluded that "this claim [the counterclaim filed on June 15, 1982] was inadmissible" because it ignored the obligation to act within a brief time limit, such inadmissibility being "all the more clear as the factory's condition as delivered by Klöckner can no longer be ascertained," for it had been "subjected to an overhaul decided on in 1978 after thorough technical studies carried out unilaterally by the purchaser." Moreover, the Claimant considered the plea of hidden defects to be unsound and expressly referred to Article 9 of the Turnkey Contract, regarding the equipment warranty, and to the contractual warranty period specified in Article 9(2) for each shop.

160. The Award does not discuss these arguments and questions. In Part "VI. The Law," Section 3, "The Exceptio Non Adimpleti Contractus,"

[155] under the heading (c) *"The Significance of Failure of Performance in this Case,"* the Award begins by stating that "Klöckner's shortcomings in the performance of its undertakings are very far from being minimal," and that:

> by the Turnkey Contract Klöckner had assumed a fundamental obligation: that of supplying a factory capable of producing fertilizer products conforming to specific descriptions and in guaranteed quantities.

The Award then comments on Article 2 of the Turnkey Contract, concluding (p. 115) that:

> Klöckner had thus assumed the risk that the factory might reveal itself incapable of functioning at 100 per cent of its estimated capacity. In the present case, the factory did not function at the level foreseen in the agreements. Klöckner thus (*sic*) did not deliver to Cameroon what it had promised.

The Award goes on to analyse the Claimant's other fundamental obligation, that of assuming "responsibility for technical and commercial management."

161. The Award then returns to these subjects, going in turn from the delivery obligation to the management obligation, to the finding that "the expected production capacities ... were never attained after start-up of the factory" and that in order for there to have been proper performance of the contracts in question,

> it was not sufficient to deliver a fertilizer factory; the factory had to have the required capacity and had to be managed *in the way necessary to obtain the proposed goals.* (p. 117)

Then, seeking to determine "if a failure of performance is of a sufficient degree of gravity," a task it believes is "always difficult," (p. 117) the Award cites French authors and an English judgment before returning to the technical and commercial management. According to the Award, failure to perform this obligation "results simply from the shutdown of the factory in December 1977." (p. 120) Then, under letter (e) "Responsibility for the maintenance of the Factory," there is another discussion of "one of the key questions of the present case," (p. 121) Klöckner's responsibility for management, which, as we have seen, the Tribunal bases not on the Management Contract but on the Protocol of Agreement. It refers, on the basis of an SCAP[8] report of September 1978 (p. 123), to "serious technical failings in the factory's design" and concludes (p. 124) that:

> the rejection of Klöckner's claim for payment of the remainder of the price of the factory *serves only to maintain the equilibrium of reciprocal contractual undertakings as defined by the parties themselves.*

---

[8] Translator's note: SCAP, Commercial Company for Potash and Azote.

This Section ends (pp. 124–127) with an attempt at an "equitable [156] evaluation" of the "quantitative comparison of the respective failure of performance," (p. 126) (of the two parties) concluding that the amount already paid "corresponds equitably to the value of Klöckner's defective performance." (p. 127)

162. In this entire analysis, one finds no discussion either of the conditions of the seller's warranty under Article 1641 *et seq.* of the Civil Code, or of the provisions of Article 9 of the Turnkey Contract on the equipment warranty, and in particular of the warranty period set forth in Article 9(2). These are conditions which, quite obviously, are also part of the "equilibrium of reciprocal contractual undertakings as defined by the parties themselves," to use the Award's formula. (p. 124)

163. It is difficult to follow the Tribunal's thinking where different considerations, of fact and of law, are mixed together, with the same topics treated in ways that are now similar, now different. Nevertheless, it is possible to discern quite clearly a dominant concern, inspired by equity, which will ultimately send the parties back to "square one" – each keeping what it already has, but each having its claim rejected, be it the principal claim for payment of the balance of the price or the counterclaim for damages. But it must also be recognized here that the Award is based more on a sort of general equity than on positive law (and in particular French civil law) or precise contractual provisions, such as Article 9 of the Turnkey Contract.

164. *In conclusion*, it must be accepted that the Tribunal did not deal, at least expressly, with the questions submitted to it by Klöckner. In order to be exhaustive, it might however be asked whether there is an *implicit* rejection of these questions elsewhere in the reasoning.

This thesis could hardly be accepted. On the one hand, the passages which have just been analysed appear in a chapter dealing with the "*Exceptio non adimpleti contractus.*" On the other hand, the general considerations which are stated under this heading can only with difficulty be interpreted as applying to questions as precise as those of a contractual warranty period or the "brief time limit" in Article 1648 of the Civil Code.

On a question as essential as the warranty against defects and the conditions, especially the time limit, for its enforcement, it is in any case difficult to conceive that an indirect and implicit response may be found in reasons given on another subject.

The complaint is therefore well founded.

V. OTHER COMPLAINTS OF THE APPLICANT FOR ANNULMENT

A. *The Exceptio Non Adimpleti Contractus*

165. On pages 25 and 26, the Application for Annulment challenges the Award for adopting two of the Respondent's arguments (Award, p. 105,

[157] para. 2) on the duty of "full disclosure to a partner" and on the "*exceptio non adimpleti contractus*," in order to dismiss Klöckner's claims. The Application considers (p. 26) that the Tribunal thought it could overcome the "diriment impediments" to its reasoning by:

> the concept of the *exceptio non adimpleti contractus*, the only one it thought could be invoked without prior notice and without respecting any deadline; *this is to forget the suspensive nature of such an exception* and to make a serious error in law.

Finally, in its Reply (pp. 16–7) of 31 July 1984 to the Respondent's Counter-Memorial, the Claimant states that:

> In order to allow the Government of Cameroon to retain nearly 80% of the price of the factory, the Tribunal applied the *exceptio non adempleti* (sic) *contractus* which in French law is normally intended to obtain the performance of a corresponding obligation, not to penalize failure of performance.
>
> It was thus led to establish in Cameroon's favour a claim for damages that could be offset by the balance of the price of the factory.

166. Is this complaint admissible?

It should first be noted that the complaint is not formally characterized by the Claimant. No reference is made in this regard to one of the precise grounds set forth in Article 52 of the Convention. The above-cited passages of the Application are found under the heading "Failure to State Reasons" (p. 24). This leads one to think that the Claimant intended to invoke Article 52(1)(e). On the other hand, the Reply of 31 July 1984 refers to the *exceptio* (p. 46) in Chapter 3 ("Grounds for the application for Annulment") under item "*A. Excess of Powers*" (p. 29) and not under item "*B. Failure to State Reasons*" (p. 49). Thus in its chapter on excess of powers (p. 46), the Applicant for Annulment states that:

> By adopting Article 9 of the Protocol as the only basis for its decision and by applying the *exceptio non adempleti* (sic) *contractus*, the Tribunal has created for Klöckner all sorts of obligations to which the parties had not agreed, thus substituting its own will for that of the parties ...

However incomplete and imprecise they may be, these arguments permit one to infer that the complaint is that the Tribunal manifestly exceeded its powers within the meaning of Article 52(1)(b) or, alternatively or subsidiarily, that the Tribunal failed to state why it thought the *exceptio* of French law could be applied as it was in the Award.

In any case, the complaint is admissible.

167. It remains to be seen whether it is well founded.

The Award devotes rather a lengthy discussion in Part "VI. The Law," Section 3 (p. 109 *et seq.*), to the question of the "exceptio non adimpleti contractus."

It begins by noting (p. 109, under the heading "French, English and [158] International Law") that the Cameroonian Government, "in responding to the request for arbitration, and thus in good time, advanced *eo nomine* the *exceptio non adimpleti contractus.*" Then it cites the Respondent's Counter-Memorial, according to which the performance of its undertakings towards Klöckner:

> may be suspended (*sic*) by virtue of the *exceptio non adimpleti*, that is to say, in the event Klöckner failed to fulfill its own contractual undertakings. Klöckner's faulty performance of its contractual obligations thus had the effect of liberating (*sic*) the Cameroonian Government from its financial undertaking.

The Award also observes that Cameroon expressly requested that, if it were found obliged to pay the price of the factory, it should not be required to pay the entirety of the price, "taking into account Cameroon's claim arising from Klöckner's failure to perform its obligations ... and this on the grounds of the *exceptio non adimpleti contractus* and of judicial setoff." (p. 110)

168. After citing several French authors on the exception based on non-performance (pp. 110 and 111), the Award continues:

> In view of the parties' divergence of views as to the applicable law under Article 42 of the ICSID Convention, it is appropriate to note that English law and international law reach similar conclusions. (p. 111)

This superfluous observation is rather difficult to reconcile with the Tribunal's previous decision (p. 105) that, as the Claimant argued, "*only* that part of Cameroonian law that is based on French law should be applied in the dispute."

In Section 3(b), "Partial or Imperfect Performance" the Award examines and quotes French scholarly opinion and case law. The quotations seem to establish that the exception is also available to a defendant where there is partial or imperfect performance and that judges "have full authority to evaluate whether one party's failure of performance of its obligations under a ... contract is such that it frees the other party from its corresponding obligations."

169. It would be impossible to ask whether there was a "manifest excess of powers" regarding this "exception" without examining the Award's *reasoning*. We must therefore first consider the complaint that there was a "failure to state reasons" within the meaning of Article 52(1)(e). Only if the Award's reasons reveal, as the Applicant for Annulment alleges (p. 26), a "serious error in law" would it then be necessary to decide whether this alleged error, assuming it is established, may be attributed to a simple "mistaken application of law" or "*error in judicando,*" or to an excess of powers, and finally to decide whether this excess of powers is "manifest."

170. As is already apparent from the above, the Award clearly gave reasons on the *exceptio non adimpleti contractus* under French civil law. For

[159] example, it points out, apparently correctly, that the exceptio may be invoked at any time without prior formal notice (*mise en demeure*), even during judicial or arbitral proceedings. Supported by references, it also explains that the exceptio may be invoked in case of partial non-performance, except where in a case of slight non-performance there would be a violation of good faith. (p. 113)

The Award then evaluates (in Section 3(c)) the "Significance of Failure of Performance in this Case" (p. 114 *et seq.*) on pages where there are also certain general considerations on the criteria to be applied by a judge or arbitrator to evaluate the degree of gravity of the failure to perform. (pp. 117–118, with references to French and English law)

171. Given the Claimant's complaints in this connection, it must be noted that the Award does not examine all of the conditions required under French law for a defendant to invoke the exception based on non-performance, for ' example the twofold condition of existence and exigibility of the debt relied on by the "*excipiens.*" It does not examine the detailed conditions for application of the rule, and especially whether the *excipiens* can itself have failed to perform, or whether the exception merely has a suspensive effect, as claimed by the Claimant, or again whether the burden of proof is reversed.

To summarize, while the Award contains *some* reasoning on the conditions for applying the exception based on non-performance, the question may be asked whether these reasons are sufficient or "sufficiently relevant." It is not necessary to answer this, since on the question of the *effects* of the exception based on non-performance, the Award does not state the legal grounds nor does it state the rules of civil law (reinforced by references to scholarly opinion and case law comparable to those which the Award cited on the general principle) which could justify its conclusion. In reality, everything occurs as if the Arbitral Tribunal had considered the *exceptio non adimpleti contractus* as a ground for *extinguishing* obligations under French law. On the basis of the Award's own citations, this conclusion does not necessarily follow, nor does it conform to the understanding the *ad hoc* Committee may have of this area of law, but in any case it should have been expressly justified.

The complaint that there was a failure to state reasons therefore appears to be not only admissible but well founded.

B. *The Calculation of the Respective Amounts Due*

172. Similar considerations apply to another criticism by the Applicant for Annulment, which concerns the Tribunal's evaluation of the parties' respective obligations. For example, in the Reply of 31 July 1984 to the Counter-Memorial, pp. 49 and 50, there are the following criticisms:

1. In order to decide that the Government of Cameroon no longer had to pay the balance of the factory price, the Tribunal attempted to establish an

equivalence between the price already paid by the Government of Cameroon [160] and the value of that part of the factory it kept....

... The Tribunal thus deducted, from precisely calculated payments in principal and interest, costs of repairs and operating losses which are not precisely calculated at all. This constitutes a failure to state reasons.

In addition to failure to state reasons, this curious determination of the amount of Klöckner's indemnification amounts to a contradiction in reasons, since the Tribunal assigns responsibility for operating losses to Klöckner and thus accepts the counterclaim, which it expressly rejected on the grounds that operating losses could not be charged to Klöckner. The same is true for the repair costs which were required for the factory to resume operation....

A similar criticism is made in the Dissenting Opinion, in particular on pages 44 and 45.

173. The complaint regarding failure to state reasons and contradiction of reasons is certainly admissible, for reasons already mentioned. It remains to be examined whether it is well founded.

On page 107 of the Award, the Tribunal decides that Klöckner, having violated its fundamental obligations, "may not insist on payment of the entire price," but "is entitled to be paid" for "certain components of the factory delivered by Klöckner." In order "to determine the 1980 value of the Klöckner components," the Tribunal believes it must "deduct from the contract price the following elements..." listed under numbers 1 through 5 on page 108. With one exception, these elements are not quantified; they include certain payments of principal, interest payments, cost of repairs, and "considerable operating losses." The Tribunal notes that:

> Klöckner should in any case assume part of the responsibility for these losses, thus setting off its claims regarding the components utilized by the Government in 1980. (p.109)

On pages 126–127, the Tribunal concludes "that the amount paid (by the Respondent) corresponds *equitably* to the value of Klöckner's defective performance. There is *a certain equilibrium, a certain relationship*, as we suggested above, between that which was paid and the *approximate* value of the components supplied by Klöckner... and used by the Respondent."

The Tribunal concludes this Section 3 with the following words:

> The two methods of analysis lead to *approximately equivalent* results, and we have thus concluded that Klöckner is entitled to what is has already received, but to nothing more.

174. It is true that the two methods used by the Tribunal seem to lead to "approximately equivalent" results, contrary to what the Dissenting Opinion states (pp. 44–45), but it is also true that the above passages show that the Tribunal's evaluation was "equitable," emphasizing that there is "a certain equilibrium," or "a certain relationship" between the amount already paid and the "value of the defective performance."

[161] 175. Finally, under the heading "6. The Counterclaim" (pp. 136 and 137), the Award again refers briefly, in rejecting the counterclaim, to the idea that "there is no justification for charging the Claimant with the losses incurred by the Government...." It concludes that the Claimant's "responsibility for defects in the supply of the factory and in its technical and commercial management have been sufficiently sanctioned by the rejection of its claim under the unpaid promissory notes."

176. In the Award's passages on the evaluation of the respective obligations or debts, the main ones of which have just been cited, it is difficult to find any legal reasoning as required by provisions of Articles 52(1)(e) or 48(3). Instead, there is really an "equitable estimate" (to use the Tribunal's own words, p. 126; *cf.* also p. 127) based on "approximately equivalent" estimates or approximations, which is in any case impossible to justify solely on the basis of the Award's explanations of the *exceptio non adimpleti contractus* or the counterclaim.

The complaint is therefore not only admissible but well founded.

C. *Other Criticisms*

177. Is is superfluous to examine the Claimant's other, more or less subsidiary or secondary, criticisms of the Award. These criticisms either partially overlap the complaints examined above or were not given any particular characterization and therefore leave uncertain which of the grounds for annulment listed in Article 52 of the Convention they refer to. This is the case for example with "the particularly serious misconstructions (*dénaturations*) and distortions" alleged by the Application. (p. 17, under the heading "Inadequacy of Reasons." In Klöckner's opinion such "misconstruction" affects "an essential element in the reasoning" of the arbitrators and "abundantly" demonstrates "the Award's defects.")

The Application for Annulment gives as examples of these "defects" the Award's explanations for the factory's acceptance, for Klöckner's responsibility for the production shortfall, for the causes of the production shortfall and for the condition of the factory. (pp. 17–22) It has already been mentioned that the concept of "misconstruction" (*dénaturation*) as such is unknown to Article 52 of the Convention, and that, furthermore, the criticism of the alleged errors in the Award's reasoning, which are more in the nature of an appeal than an application for annulment, could drag the Committee into an area which must remain foreign to it.

178. Once one or another of the grounds listed in Article 52(1) of the Washington Convention has been found to exist, what role and powers does the *ad hoc* Committee have?

It obviously cannot remit the case to the Tribunal for a decision, by analogy to Article 49(2), on "any question which it had omitted to decide in the award" or for a fresh decision. Nor can the *ad hoc* Committee decide on

the merits, as a court of appeal would do, or declare that it would have **[162]**
reached the same result on other grounds or for other reasons.

179. It will be noted that according to Article 52(1), taken literally, a
party may only "*request* annulment" ("demander ... l'annulation," "solicitar
la anulacion") of the award "on one or more of the following grounds."
Paragraph 1 of this Article does not therefore seem to confer a right to *obtain*
annulment. Article 52(3) *in fine* provides that:

> the Committee *shall have the authority to annul the award* ("Le Comité est
> habileté à annuler la sentence," "Esta Comision tendra facultad para resolver
> sobre la anulacion").

Considered as a whole, it seems that Article 52 of the Washington
Convention can be interpreted in two ways, at least if taken literally:
  (a) First, as triggering inevitable and "automatic" annulment on a finding
      that there is one of the grounds for annulment under Article 52(1), the
      committee lacking discretion and having no power to abstain from
      annulling an award tainted on one or other of the grounds listed in
      paragraph 1;
  (b) Second, as containing a sort of space or "no man's land" between the
      finding under Article 52(1) that there is a ground for annulment and
      the declaration of annulment under Articles 52(3) and 52(6). This
      would give the Committee a certain margin of appreciation. It could,
      for example, have the power to abstain from annulling if it believes
      that the ground for annulment either did not harm the Applicant (*cf.*
      the adage well-known in some legal systems, "no annulment without
      grievance") or did not substantially affect the arbitral award taken as
      a whole, which perhaps amounts to the same thing. In such a case
      even a purely partial annulment could seem excessive and contrary to
      the spirit of the Convention. Finally, the Committee could abstain
      from annulling because the Claimant abused its rights in invoking the
      said ground.

Save under exceptional circumstances, which in any case are not present
here, the Committee is inclined to consider that the finding that there is one
of the grounds for annulment in Article 52 (1) must in principle lead to total
or partial annulment of the award, without the Committee having any
discretion, the parties to the Washington Convention and the parties to an
arbitration under the ICSID system having an absolute right to compliance
with the Convention's provisions, and in particular with the provisions of
Article 52.

The contested arbitral Award must therefore be annulled and, for the
reasons given above, annulled in its entirety under Article 52(3) (*in fine*) of
the Convention.

180. It remains for the *ad hoc* Committee to decide on the costs of the
present annulment proceeding, pursuant to Rule 53 and 47(1)(j) of the
Arbitration Rules.

[163]   Taking into account the nature of the present proceeding, its outcome and all circumstances, it is justifiable to divide the costs equally and to leave each party responsible for its own expenses.

FOR THESE REASONS.

The *ad hoc* Committee constituted under Article 52 of the Washington Convention of March 18, 1965,
    Ruling unanimously,
    Decides:
(1) The Arbitral Award rendered on October 21, 1983 by the Arbitral Tribunal constituted by ICSID in Case ARB/81/2 is annulled;
(2) The costs of the present annulment procedure shall be borne equally by the two parties, each remaining responsible for its own expenses.

[*Source*: This English translation from the French original of this decision is published in 1 *ICSID Review – FILJ* No. 1 90 (1986). This translation was prepared by Mr Antonio R. Parra.]

[Report: 2 *ICSID Reports* 9]

NOTE.—In July 1985 the case was resubmitted to a new ICSID tribunal pursuant to Article 52(6) of the Convention. The Award on the Resubmitted Case was issued on 26 January 1988. On 1 July 1988 the parties filed applications for the annulment of the Resubmitted Award. On 17 May 1990 the Decision on the Annulment Application was rendered, rejecting the parties' applications for annulment of the Award of 26 January 1988. These decisions have not been made available for publication.

Human rights — Discrimination — Prohibited grounds of discrimination — Discrimination on grounds of status — Different treatment by France of soldiers of Senegalese origin — Whether justifiable — Whether discrimination regarding pension rights within the scope of the International Covenant on Civil and Political Rights, 1966

GUEYE *et al. v.* FRANCE

(Communication No 196/1985)

United Nations Human Rights Committee.[1]   3 *April* 1989

SUMMARY: *The facts:*—The authors of the communication, Ibrahima Gueye and 742 other retired soldiers of Senegalese nationality, had served in the French Army prior to the independence of Senegal in 1960. Under a French law of 1951 all retired members of the French Army enjoyed equal treatment regardless of their nationality. However, in 1974 a new French law was enacted which provided for different treatment of Senegalese soldiers regarding their pension rights. In 1979 another French law further extended the regime of "crystallization" of military pensions to the nationals of four States formerly part of the French Union, which included Senegal. In 1980 and 1982 other retired Senegalese soldiers sought to challenge the laws in question. However, a French Finance Law enacted in 1981, applied with retroactive effect to January 1975, frustrated further recourse before French tribunals. In October 1985 the authors submitted a communication to the Human Rights Committee claiming that the French legislation was racially discriminatory.

France submitted that the communication was inadmissible as it was incompatible with the provisions of the International Covenant on Civil and Political Rights, 1966. In addition, France argued that the communication was inadmissible *ratione temporis* as the 1979 legislation pre-dated May 1984, the date of the entry into force of the Optional Protocol to the Covenant in respect of France. France also argued that the communication was unfounded because pension rights fell outside the scope of the Covenant and because the contested legislation did not contain any discriminatory provisions.

In November 1987 the communication was declared admissible. The Committee had considered that although it had no competence to examine any alleged violations which had occurred prior to May 1984, it had

---

[1] The members of the Committee in 1989, with the country of nationality of each member placed in parentheses, were: Francisco José Aguilar Urbina (Costa Rica), Nisuke Ando (Japan), Christine Chanet (France), Joseph A. L. Cooray (Sri Lanka), Vojin Dimitrijević (Yugoslavia), Omran El Shafei (Egypt), János Fodor (Hungary), Rosalyn Higgins (United Kingdom), Rajsoomer Lallah (Mauritius), Andreas V. Mavrommatis (Cyprus), Joseph A. Mommersteeg (Netherlands), Rein A. Myullerson (USSR), Birame Ndiaye (Senegal), Fausto Pocar (Italy), Julio Prado Vallejo (Ecuador), Alejandro Serrano Caldera (Nicaragua), S. Amos Wako (Kenya) and Bertil Wennergren (Sweden).

Pursuant to the Committee's provisional rules of procedure, Christine Chanet (France) did not participate in the adoption of the views of the Committee. Mr Birame Ndiaye (Senegal) did not participate in the adoption of the views pursuant to Rule 85.

competence to determine whether there had been violations of the Covenant subsequent to that date, and which had occurred as a consequence of acts or omissions related to the continued application of French laws and decisions concerning the rights of the authors.

Held:—(1) France had not discriminated against the authors on racial grounds. Nationality did not figure among prohibited grounds of discrimination listed in Article 26 of the Covenant, nor did the Covenant protect the right to a pension. As there had been a differentiation by reference to nationality acquired upon independence, there had been discrimination on grounds of "other status" within the meaning of Article 26 of the Covenant (pp. 318-19).

(2) A subsequent change in nationality could not by itself be considered as a sufficient justification for different treatment and the basis for the grant of the pension had been the same service which both the authors and the soldiers who had remained French had provided. The differences in the economic, financial and social conditions between France and Senegal could not justify such unequal treatment, nor could mere administrative inconvenience or the possibility of some abuse of pension rights (p. 319).

(3) The difference in treatment of the authors was not, therefore, based on reasonable and objective criteria and thus constituted discrimination prohibited by Article 26 of the Covenant. Accordingly, France was obliged to remedy the violations suffered by the authors (p. 319).

The following is the text of the views of the Committee:

Views under Article 5, paragraph 4, of the Optional Protocol

1.1 The authors of the communication (initial letter of 12 October 1985 and subsequent letters of 22 December 1986, 6 June 1987 and 21 July 1988) are Ibrahima Gueye and 742 other retired Senegalese members of the French Army, residing in Senegal. They are represented by counsel.

1.2 The authors claim to be victims of a violation of Article 26 of the Covenant by France because of alleged racial discrimination in French legislation which provides for different treatment in the determination of pensions of retired soldiers of Senegalese nationality who served in the French Army prior to the independence of Senegal in 1960 and who receive pensions that are inferior to those enjoyed by retired French soldiers of French nationality.

1.3 It is stated that pursuant to Law No 51-561 of 18 May 1951 and Decree No 51-590 of 23 May 1951, retired members of the French Army, whether French or Senegalese, were treated equally. The acquired rights of Senegalese retired soldiers were respected after independence in 1960 until the Finance Act No 74.1129 of December 1974 provided for different treatment of the Senegalese. Article 63 of this Law stipulates that the pensions of Senegalese soldiers would no longer be subject to the general provisions of the Code of Military

Pensions of 1951. Subsequent French legislation froze the level of pensions for the Senegalese as of 1 January 1975.

1.4 The authors state that the laws in question have been challenged before the Administrative Tribunal of Poitiers, France, which rendered a decision on 22 December 1980 in favour of Dia Abdourahmane, a retired Senegalese soldier, ordering the case to be sent to the French Minister of Finance for purposes of full indemnification since 2 January 1975. The authors enclose a similar decision of the *Conseil d'Etat* of 22 June 1982 in the case of another Senegalese soldier. However, these decisions, it is alleged, were not implemented, in view of a new French Finance Law No 81.1179 of 31 December 1981, applied with retroactive effect to 1 January 1975, which is said to frustrate any further recourse before the French judicial or administrative tribunals.

1.5 As to the merits of the case, the authors reject the arguments of the French authorities that allegedly justify the different treatment of retired African (not only Senegalese) soldiers on the grounds of: (a) their loss of French nationality upon independence; (b) the difficulties for French authorities to establish the identity and the family situation of retired soldiers in African countries; and (c) the differences in the economic, financial and social conditions prevailing in France and in its former colonies.

1.6 The authors state that they have not submitted the same matter to any other procedure of international investigation or settlement.

2. By its decision of 26 March 1986, the Human Rights Committee transmitted the communication under Rule 91 of the Committee's provisional rules of procedure to the State Party requesting information and observations relevant to the question of the admissibility of the communication.

3.1 In its initial submission under Rule 91, dated 5 November 1986, the State Party describes the factual situation in detail and argues that the communication is "inadmissible as being incompatible with the provisions of the Covenant (Art. 3 of the Optional Protocol), additionally, unfounded", because it basically deals with rights that fall outside the scope of the Covenant (i.e. pension rights) and, at any rate, because the contested legislation does not contain any discriminatory provisions within the meaning of Article 26 of the Covenant.

3.2 In a further submission under Rule 91, dated 8 April 1987, the State Party invokes the declaration made by the French Government upon ratification of the Optional Protocol on 17 February 1984 and contends that the communication is inadmissible *ratione temporis*:

France interprets Article 1 [of the Optional Protocol] as giving the Committee the competence to receive communications alleging a violation of a right set forth in the Covenant "which results either from acts, omissions, developments or events occurring after the date on which the Protocol entered into force for the Republic, or from a decision relating to acts, omissions, developments or events after that date".

It is clear from this interpretative declaration that communications directed against France are admissible only if they are based on alleged violations which derive from acts or events occurring after 17 May 1984, the date on which the Protocol entered into force with respect to France under Article 9, paragraph 2, of the said Protocol.

However, the statement of the facts contained both in the communication itself and in the initial observations by the French Government indicates that the violation alleged by the authors of the communication derives from Law No 79.1102 of 21 December 1979, which extended to the nationals of four States formerly belonging to the French Union, including Senegal, the regime referred to as "crystallization" of military pensions that had already applied since 1 January 1961 to the nationals of the other States concerned.

Since this act occurred before ratification by France of the Optional Protocol, it cannot therefore provide grounds for a communication based on its alleged incompatibility with the Covenant unless such communication ignores the effect *ratione temporis* which France conferred on its recognition of the right of individual communication.

4.1 In their comments of 22 December 1986, the authors argue that the communication should not be declared inadmissible pursuant to Article 3 of the Optional Protocol as incompatible with the provisions of the Covenant, since a broad interpretation of Article 26 of the Covenant would permit the Committee to review questions of pension rights if there is discrimination, as claimed in this case.

4.2 In their further comments of 6 June 1987, the authors mention that although the relevant French legislation pre-dates the entry into force of the Optional Protocol for France, the authors had continued negotiations subsequent to 17 May 1984 and that the final word was spoken by the Minister for Economics, Finance and Budget in a letter addressed to the authors of 12 November 1984.

5.1 Before considering any claims contained in a communication, the Human Rights Committee must, in accordance with Rule 87 of its provisional rules of procedure, decide whether or not it is admissible under the Optional Protocol to the Covenant.

5.2 With regard to the State Party's contention that the communication was inadmissible under Article 3 of the Optional Protocol as incompatible with the Covenant, the Committee recalled that it had already decided with respect to prior communications (Nos 172/1984, 180/1984, 182/1984) that the scope of Article 26 of the Covenant permitted the examination of allegations of discrimination even with respect to pension rights.

5.3 The Committee took note of the State Party's argument that, as the alleged violations derived from a law enacted in 1979, the communication should be declared inadmissible on the grounds that the interpretative declaration made by France upon ratification of the Optional Protocol precluded the Committee from considering alleged violations that derived from acts or events occurring prior to 17 May 1984, the date on which the Optional Protocol entered into force with respect to France. The Committee observed in this connection that in a number of earlier cases (Nos 6/1977, 24/1977) it had declared that it could not consider an alleged violation of human rights said to have taken place prior to the entry into force of the Covenant for a State Party, unless it is a violation that continues after that date or has effects which themselves constitute a violation of the Covenant after that date. The interpretative declaration of France further purported to limit the Committee's competence *ratione temporis* to violations of a right set forth in the Covenant, which results from "acts, omissions, developments or events occurring after the date on which the Protocol entered into force" with respect to France. The Committee took the view that it had no competence to examine the question whether the authors were victims of discrimination at any time prior to 17 May 1984; however, it remained to be determined whether there had been violations of the Covenant subsequent to the said date, as a consequence of acts or omissions related to the continued application of laws and decisions concerning the rights of the applicants.

6. On 5 November 1987, the Human Rights Committee therefore decided that the communication was admissible.

7.1 In its submission under Article 4, paragraph 2, of the Optional Protocol, dated 4 June 1988, the State Party recalls its submission under Rule 91;[2] it adds that Senegalese nationals who acquired French nationality and kept it following Senegal's independence are entitled to the same pension scheme as all other French former members of the armed forces. Articles 97, paragraph 2, to 97, paragraph 6, of the Nationality Code offer any foreigner who at one point in time possessed French nationality the possibility of recovering it. The State Party argued that this possibility is not merely theoretical, since, in the past, approximately 2,000 individuals have recovered French nationality each year.

7.2 The State Party further explains that a Senegalese former member of the armed forces who lost his French nationality following Senegal's independence and then recovered his French nationality would *ipso facto* recover the rights to which French nationals are entitled under the Pension Code, Article L 58 of which provides that "the right to obtain and enjoy the pension and life disability annuity is suspended: . . . by circumstances which cause a person to lose the status of French national for as long as that loss of nationality shall last". This implies that once nationality is recovered, the right to a pension is re-established. The State Party concludes that nationality

[2] Submission dated 5 November 1986, paragraph 3.1 above.

remains the sole criterion on which the difference in treatment referred to by the authors is based.

8.1 In their comments on the State Party's submission, the authors, in a letter dated 21 July 1988, submit that the State Party has exceeded the deadline for submission of its submission under Article 4, paragraph 2, of the Optional Protocol by twelve days, and that for this reason it should be ruled inadmissible.[3] In this connection, they suspect that "(b) by stalling and making full use, even beyond the deadlines set under the Committee's rules of procedure, of procedural tactics so as to delay a final decision, the State Party hopes that the authors will die off one by one and that the amounts it will have to pay will drop considerably". Alternatively, the authors argue that the Committee should not further examine the State Party's observations as they repeat arguments discussed at length in earlier submissions and thus should be considered to be of a dilatory nature.

8.2 With respect to the merits of their case, the authors maintain that the State Party's argument concerning the question of nationality is a fallacious one. They submit that the State Party is only using the nationality argument as a pretext, so as to deprive the Senegalese of their acquired rights. They further refer to Article 71 of the 1951 Code of Military Pensions, which stipulates:

Serving or former military personnel of foreign nationality possess the same rights as serving or former military personnel of French nationality, except in the case where they have taken part in a hostile act against France.

In their view, they enjoy "inalienable and irreducible pension rights" under this legislation. Since none of them has ever been accused of having participated in a hostile act against France, they submit that the issue of nationality must be "completely and definitely" ruled out.

8.3 The authors argue that they have been the victims of racial discrimination based on the colour of their skin, on the purported grounds that:

(a) In Senegal, registry office records are not well kept and fraud is rife;

(b) As those to whom pensions are owed, i.e. the authors, are blacks who live in an underdeveloped country, they do not need as much money as pensioners who live in a developed country such as France.

The authors express consternation at the fact that the State Party is capable of arguing that, since the creditor is not rich and lives in a poor country, the debtor may reduce his debt in proportion to the degree of need and poverty of his creditor, an argument they consider to be contrary not only to fundamental principles of law but also to moral standards and to equity.

---

[3] The deadline for the State Party's submission under Article 4, paragraph 2, expired on 4 June 1988. Although the submission is dated 4 June 1988, it was transmitted under cover of a note dated 16 June 1988.

9.1 The Human Rights Committee, having considered the present communication in the light of all the information made available to it by the parties, as provided in Article 5, paragraph 1, of the Optional Protocol, bases its views on the following facts, which appear uncontested.

9.2 The authors are retired soldiers of Senegalese nationality who served in the French Army prior to the independence of Senegal in 1960. Pursuant to the Code of Military Pensions of 1951, retired members of the French Army, whether French or Senegalese, were treated equally. Pension rights of Senegalese soldiers were the same as those of French soldiers until a new law, enacted in December 1974, provided for different treatment of the Senegalese. Law No 79/1102 of 21 December 1979 further extended to the nationals of four States formerly belonging to the French Union, including Senegal, the regime referred to as "crystallization" of military pensions that had already applied since 1 January 1961 to the nationals of other States concerned. Other retired Senegalese soldiers have sought to challenge the laws in question, but French Finance Law No 81.1179 of 31 December 1981, applied with retroactive effect to 1 January 1975, has rendered further recourse before French tribunals futile.

9.3 The main question before the Committee is whether the authors are victims of discrimination within the meaning of Article 26 of the Covenant or whether the differences in pension treatment of former members of the French Army, based on whether they are French nationals or not, should be deemed compatible with the Covenant. In determining this question, the Committee has taken into account the following considerations.

9.4 The Committee has noted the authors' claim that they have been discriminated against on racial grounds, that is, one of the grounds specifically enumerated in Article 26. It finds that there is no evidence to support the allegation that the State Party has engaged in racially discriminatory practices vis-à-vis the authors. It remains, however, to be determined whether the situation encountered by the authors falls within the purview of Article 26. The Committee recalls that the authors are not generally subject to French jurisdiction, except that they rely on French legislation in relation to the amount of their pension rights. It notes that nationality as such does not figure among the prohibited grounds of discrimination listed in Article 26, and that the Covenant does not protect the right to a pension, as such. Under Article 26, discrimination in the equal protection of the law is prohibited on any grounds such as race, colour, sex, language, religion, political or other opinion, national or social origin, property, birth or other status. There has been a differentiation by reference to nationality acquired upon independence. In the Committee's opinion, this falls within the reference to "other status" in the second sentence of

Article 26. The Committee takes into account, as it did in communication No 182/1984, that "the right to equality before the law and to equal protection of the law without any discrimination does not make all differences of treatment discriminatory. A differentiation based on reasonable and objective criteria does not amount to prohibited discrimination within the meaning of Article 26."

9.5 In determining whether the treatment of the authors is based on reasonable and objective criteria, the Committee notes that it was not the question of nationality which determined the granting of pensions to the authors but the services rendered by them in the past. They had served in the French Armed Forces under the same conditions as French citizens; for fourteen years subsequent to the independence of Senegal they were treated in the same way as their French counterparts for the purpose of pension rights, although their nationality was not French but Senegalese. A subsequent change in nationality cannot by itself be considered as a sufficient justification for different treatment, since the basis for the grant of the pension was the same service which both they and the soldiers who remained French had provided. Nor can differences in the economic, financial and social conditions as between France and Senegal be invoked as a legitimate justification. If one compared the case of retired soldiers of Senegalese nationality living in Senegal with that of retired soldiers of French nationality in Senegal, it would appear that they enjoy the same economic and social conditions. Yet, their treatment for the purpose of pension entitlements would differ. Finally, the fact that the State Party claims that it can no longer carry out checks of identity and family situation, so as to prevent abuses in the administration of pension schemes, cannot justify a difference in treatment. In the Committee's opinion, mere administrative inconvenience or the possibility of some abuse of pension rights cannot be invoked to justify unequal treatment. The Committee concludes that the difference in treatment of the authors is not based on reasonable and objective criteria and constitutes discrimination prohibited by the Covenant.

10. The Human Rights Committee, acting under Article 5, paragraph 4, of the Optional Protocol to the International Covenant on Civil and Political Rights, is of the view that the events in this case, in so far as they produced effects after 17 May 1984 (the date of entry into force of the Optional Protocol for France), disclose a violation of Article 26 of the Covenant.

11. The Committee, accordingly, is of the view that the State Party is under an obligation, in accordance with the provisions of Article 2 of the Covenant, to take effective measures to remedy the violations suffered by the victims.

[Report: Doc. CCPR/C/35/D/196/1985]

Human rights — Freedom of expression — Freedom of movement—Right to participate in public affairs—One-party State—Zambia—Persecution of opposition politician contrary to International Covenant on Civil and Political Rights, 1966

Human rights—Freedom from arrest—Arbitrary arrest and detention—International Covenant on Civil and Political Rights, 1966

BWALYA v. ZAMBIA

(Communication No 314/1988)

United Nations Human Rights Committee.[1]   14 *July* 1993

SUMMARY: *The facts:*—The author of the communication was Zambian and a member of a political party called the People's Redemption Organization ("the Organization"). In 1983 he had stood for election to a parliamentary seat but he claimed that the Zambian authorities had prevented him from properly preparing his candidacy and from participating in the electoral campaign. In 1986 he had been dismissed from his employment and he and his family had been expelled from their home by Zambian authorities. The author maintained that he had emigrated to Namibia due to harassment and hardship to which he and his family were being subjected. At an unspecified date, the author had returned to Zambia and had been arrested and placed in custody. By September 1988 the author had been detained for thirty-one months on charges of belonging to the Organization, an association which was considered illegal under the constitution then in force in Zambia, and of having conspired to overthrow the then Zambian Government. At an unspecified date the author was released. In 1987 the author had instituted proceedings in the Zambian courts against the Zambian authorities. Although a Zambian district tribunal had confirmed in August 1987 that he had been no threat to national security, the author had remained in custody. A further approach to the Supreme Court had met with no success.

In March 1990 the author submitted a communication to the Human Rights Committee claiming that his arrests had been arbitrary and his detentions unlawful. As a political activist and as a former prisoner of conscience, the author contended that he had been placed under surveillance by the Zambian authorities, that he continued to be subjected to restrictions on his freedom of movement, and that he had been denied a passport. He

---

[1] The members of the Committee in 1993, with the country of nationality of each member placed in parentheses, were: Francisco José Aguilar Urbina (Costa Rica), Nisuke Ando (Japan), Tamás Bán (Hungary), Marco Tulio Bruni Celli (Venezuela), Christine Chanet (France), Vojin Dimitrijević (Yugoslavia), Omran El Shafei (Egypt), Elizabeth Evatt (Australia), Laurel Francis (Jamaica), Kurt Hendl (Austria), Rosalyn Higgins (United Kingdom), Rajsoomer Lallah (Mauritius), Andreas V. Mavrommatis (Cyprus), Birame Ndiaye (Senegal), Fausto Pocar (Italy), Julio Prado Vallejo (Ecuador), Waleed Sadi (Jordan) and Bertil Wennergren (Sweden).

also claimed that he had been denied the right to take part in the conduct of public affairs and had been discriminated against on account of his political opinion. In July 1990 the author had been re-arrested and had been transferred to a prison without information about the reason for his arrest and detention.

In March 1991 the Committee had declared the communication admissible in so far as it raised issues under Articles 9, 12, 19, 25 and 26 of the Covenant. Despite the author's release in January 1992, he requested the Committee to continue consideration of his case. Zambia had failed to provide any information of substance on the author's allegations.

Held:—The Committee found violations of Articles 9(1) and (3), 12, 19(1), 25(a) and 26 of the Covenant, and urged Zambia to compensate the author.

(1) There had been a violation of Article 19 of the Covenant due to the uncontested response of Zambian authorities to the attempts by the author to express his opinions freely and to disseminate the political tenets of the Organization (p. 324).

(2) There had been a violation of Article 9(3) of the Covenant. The author had been detained for thirty-one months solely on charges of belonging to a political party considered illegal. Furthermore, he had not been brought promptly before a judge or another officer authorized by law to determine the lawfulness of his detention (p. 324).

(3) As the right to liberty and security of the person under the Covenant could be invoked not only in the context of arrest and detention, and since the author had been subjected to continued harassment and intimidation after his release, Zambia had violated Article 9(1) of the Covenant (pp. 324-5).

(4) There had been a violation of Article 12(1) of the Covenant because the author continued to suffer restrictions on his freedom of movement and because the Zambian authorities had refused to issue him a passport (p. 325).

(5) There had been a violation of Article 25 of the Covenant as Zambian authorities had unreasonably restricted the author's right to take part in the conduct of public affairs. In this context, the Committee observed that restrictions on political activity outside the only recognized political party amounted to an unreasonable restriction of the right to participate in the conduct of public affairs (p. 325).

(6) There had been a violation of Article 26 of the Covenant because the author had been discriminated against in his employment due to his political opinions (p. 325).

The following is the text of the views of the Committee:

The facts as submitted by the author
1. The author of the communication is Peter Chiiko Bwalya, a Zambian citizen born in 1961 and currently chairman of the People's Redemption Organization, a political party in Zambia. He claims to be a victim of violations of the International Covenant on Civil and Political Rights by Zambia.

2.1 In 1983, at the age of twenty-two, the author ran for a parliamentary seat in the constituency of Chifubu, Zambia. He states that the authorities prevented him from properly preparing his candidacy and from participating in the electoral campaign. The authorities' action apparently helped to increase his popularity among the poorer strata of the local population, as the author was committed to changing the Government's policy towards, in particular, the homeless and the unemployed. He claims that in retaliation for the propagation of his opinions and his activism, the authorities subjected him to threats and intimidation, and that in January 1986 he was dismissed from his employment. The Ndola City Council subsequently expelled him and his family from their home, while the payment of his father's pension was suspended indefinitely.

2.2 Because of the harassment and hardship to which he and his family were being subjected, the author emigrated to Namibia, where other Zambian citizens had settled. Upon his return to Zambia, however, he was arrested and placed in custody; the author's account in this respect is unclear and the date of his return to Zambia remains unspecified.

2.3 The author notes that by September 1988 he had been detained for thirty-one months, on charges of belonging to the People's Redemption Organization—an association considered illegal under the terms of the country's one-party Constitution—and for having conspired to overthrow the Government of the then President Kenneth Kaunda. On an unspecified subsequent date, he was released; again, the circumstances of his release remain unknown. At an unspecified later date, Mr Bwalya returned to Zambia.

2.4 On 25 March 1990, the author sought the Committee's direct intercession in connection with alleged discrimination, denial of employment and refusal of a passport. By letter of 5 July 1990, the author's wife indicated that her husband had been rearrested on 1 July 1990 and taken to the Central Police Station in Ndola, where he was reportedly kept for two days. Subsequently, he was transferred to Kansenshi prison in Ndola; the author's wife claims that she was not informed of the reasons for her husband's arrest and detention.

2.5 With respect to the requirement of exhaustion of domestic remedies, the author notes that he instituted proceedings against the authorities after his initial arrest. He notes that the district tribunal reviewing his case confirmed, on 17 August 1987, that he was no danger to national security but that, notwithstanding the court's finding, he remained in custody. A further approach to the Supreme Court met with no success.

The complaint

3.1 In his initial submissions, the author invokes a large number of provisions of the Covenant, without substantiating his allegations. In subsequent letters, he confines his claims to alleged violations of Articles 1, 2, 3, 9, 10, 12, 25 and 26 of the Covenant.

3.2 The author contends that, since he never participated in any conspiracy to overthrow the Government of President Kaunda, his arrests were arbitrary and his detentions unlawful, and that he is entitled to adequate compensation from the State Party. He submits that following his release from the first period of detention he continued to be harassed and intimidated by the authorities; he claims that he denounced these practices.

3.3 The author states that, as a political activist and former prisoner of conscience, he has been placed under strict surveillance by the authorities, and that he continues to be subjected to restrictions on his freedom of movement. He claims that he has been denied a passport as well as any means of making a decent living.

Issues and proceedings before the Committee

4.1 Before considering any claims contained in a communication, the Human Rights Committee must, in accordance with Rule 87 of its rules of procedure, decide whether or not it is admissible under the Optional Protocol to the Covenant.

4.2 During its forty-first session, the Committee considered the admissibility of the communication. It noted with concern the absence of cooperation from the State Party which, in spite of four reminders addressed to it, had failed to comment on the admissibility of the communication. It further noted that the author's claim that the Supreme Court had dismissed his appeal had remained uncontested. In the circumstances, the Committee concluded that the requirements of Article 5, paragraph 2(b), of the Optional Protocol had been met.

4.3 As to the claims relating to Articles 7 and 10 of the Covenant, the Committee considered that the author had failed to substantiate his claim, for purposes of admissibility, that he had been subjected to treatment in violation of these provisions. Accordingly, the Committee found this part of the communication inadmissible under Article 2 of the Optional Protocol.

4.4 With respect to the author's claims that he: (a) had been subjected to arbitrary arrest and unlawful detention; (b) had been denied the right to liberty of movement and arbitrarily denied a passport; (c) had been denied the right to take part in the conduct of public affairs; and (d) had been discriminated against on account of political opinion, the Committee considered that they had been substantiated, for purposes of admissibility. Furthermore, the Committee was of the opinion that, although Articles 9, paragraph 2, and 19 had not been invoked, the facts as submitted might raise issues under these provisions.

4.5 On 21 March 1991, the Committee declared the communication admissible in so far as it appeared to raise issues under Articles 9, 12, 19, 25 and 26 of the Covenant.

5.1 In a submission dated 28 January 1992, the State Party indicates that "Mr Peter Chiiko Bwalya has been released from custody and is a free person now". No information on the substance of the author's allegations, nor copies of his indictment or any judicial orders concerning the author, have been provided by the State Party, in spite of reminders addressed to it on 9 January and 21 May 1992.

5.2 In a letter dated 3 March 1992, the author confirms that he was released from detention but requests the Committee to continue consideration of his case. He adds that the change in the Government has not changed the authorities' attitude towards him.

6.1 The Committee has considered the communication in the light of all the information provided by the parties. It notes with concern that, with the exception of a brief note informing the Committee of the author's release, the State Party has failed to cooperate on the matter under consideration. It further recalls that it is implicit in Article 4, paragraph 2, of the Optional Protocol that a State Party examine in good faith all the allegations brought against it, and that it provide the Committee with all the information at its disposal, including all available judicial orders and decisions. The State Party has not forwarded to the Committee any such information. In the circumstances, due weight must be given to the author's allegations, to the extent that they have been substantiated.

6.2 In respect of issues under Article 19, the Committee considers that the uncontested response of the authorities to the attempts of the author to express his opinions freely and to disseminate the political tenets of his party constitute a violation of his rights under Article 19.

6.3 The Committee has noted that when the communication was placed before it for consideration, Mr Bwalya had been detained for a total of thirty-one months, a claim that has not been contested by the State Party. It notes that the author was held solely on charges of belonging to a political party considered illegal under the country's (then) one-party constitution and that, on the basis of the information before the Committee, Mr Bwalya was not brought promptly before a judge or other officer authorized by law to exercise judicial power to determine the lawfulness of his detention. This, in the Committee's opinion, constitutes a violation of the author's right under Article 9, paragraph 3, of the Covenant.

6.4 With regard to the right to security of person, the Committee notes that Mr Bwalya, after being released from detention, has been subjected to continued harassment and intimidation. The State Party has not contested these allegations. The first sentence of Article 9, paragraph 1, guarantees to everyone the right to liberty and security of person. The Committee has already had the opportunity to explain that this right may be invoked not only in the context of arrest and detention, and that an interpretation of Article 9 which would allow a State Party to ignore threats to the personal security of non-detained persons within its jurisdiction would render ineffective the guarantees of the Covenant.[2] In the circumstances of the case, the Committee concludes that the State Party has violated Mr Bwalya's right to security of person under Article 9, paragraph 1.

6.5 The author has claimed, and the State Party has not denied, that he continues to suffer restrictions on his freedom of movement, and that the authorities have refused to issue a passport to him. This, in the Committee's opinion, amounts to a violation of Article 12, paragraph 1, of the Covenant.

6.6 As to the alleged violation of Article 25 of the Covenant, the Committee notes that the author, a leading figure of a political party in opposition to the former President, has been prevented from participating in a general election campaign as well as from preparing his candidacy for this party. This amounts to an unreasonable restriction on the author's right to "take part in the conduct of public affairs" which the State Party has failed to explain or justify. In particular, it has failed to explain the requisite conditions for participation in the elections. Accordingly, it must be assumed that Mr Bwalya was detained and denied the right to run for a parliamentary seat in the constituency of Chifubu merely on account of his membership in a political party other than that officially recognized; in this context, the Committee observes that restrictions on political activity outside the only recognized political party amount to an unreasonable restriction of the right to participate in the conduct of public affairs.

6.7 Finally, on the basis of the information before it, the Committee concludes that the author has been discriminated against in his employment because of his political opinions, contrary to Article 26 of the Covenant.

7. The Human Rights Committee, acting under Article 5, paragraph 4, of the Optional Protocol to the International Covenant on Civil and Political Rights, is of the view that the facts as found by the Committee disclose violations of Articles 9, paragraphs 1 and 3, 12, 19, paragraph 1, 25(a) and 26 of the Covenant.

8. Pursuant to Article 2 of the Covenant, the State Party is under an obligation to provide Mr Bwalya with an appropriate remedy. The Committee urges the State Party to grant appropriate compensation to the author. The State Party is under an obligation to ensure that similar violations do not occur in the future.

9. The Committee would wish to receive information, within ninety days, on any relevant measures taken by the State Party in respect of the Committee's Views.

Done in English, French and Spanish, the English text being the original version.

[Report: Doc. CCPR/C/48/D/314/1988]

[2] Views on Communication No 195/1985 (*Delgado Páez* v. *Colombia*), adopted on 12 July 1990, paragraphs 5.5 and 5.6.

Human rights—Freedom of expression—Author of complaint persecuted for membership of opposition political party— Violation of International Covenant on Civil and Political Rights, 1966, Article 19

Human rights — Freedom of movement — International Covenant on Civil and Political Rights, 1966, Article 12

Human rights—Detention—Arbitrary detention—International Covenant on Civil and Political Rights, 1966, Article 9— Conditions of detention—Duty to treat detainees with dignity — International Covenant on Civil and Political Rights, 1966, Article 10

KALENGA v. ZAMBIA

(Communication No 326/1988)

United Nations Human Rights Committee.[1]   27 *July* 1993

SUMMARY: *The facts:*—The author was a Zambian citizen who had been arrested in February 1986. In March 1986 he had been informed of the charges brought against him and had subsequently been held in detention. He had been charged with having been one of the founding members, and having sought to disseminate the views, of the People's Redemption Organization, which was a party considered illegal under the one-party constitution then in force in Zambia. He had also been charged with having prepared subversive activities aimed at overthrowing the regime of President Kaunda. During his detention the author had instituted proceedings against Zambia. The dismissal of his application for writ of habeas corpus in June 1986 was followed by the dismissal of another request for writ of habeas corpus in April 1989. In December 1988 a special tribunal had heard his petition and had recommended his immediate release which had not occurred until ten months later. After the author's release the Zambian authorities had placed him under surveillance and denied him a passport.

In November 1988 the author submitted a communication to the Human Rights Committee claiming that, as a prisoner of conscience, he had been subjected to unlawful detention. The author also contended that the charges against him had had no basis in fact at the time of his arrest and that they had been fabricated by the police in order to justify his detention. He further contended that throughout his detention he had not been brought before a judge or judicial officer to establish his guilt and he had been subjected to inhuman and degrading treatment during his detention.

In October 1991 the Committee had declared the communication admissible in as much as it raised issues under Articles 7, 9, 10, 12 and 19 of the Covenant. Despite his release in January 1992, the author requested the Committee to continue consideration of his case.

[1] For the composition of the Committee, *see* p. 320, note 1.

Held:—The author was entitled to compensation for the violation of his rights under Articles 9(2) and (3), 10(1), 12(1) and 19.

(1) The uncontested response of the Zambian authorities to the author's attempts to express his opinions freely and to disseminate the tenets of the People's Redemption Organization constituted a violation of Article 19 of the Covenant (p. 330).

(2) There had been a violation of Article 9(2) of the Covenant as Zambia had taken almost one month to inform the author about the reasons for his arrest and of charges against him. Similarly, as the author had not been brought promptly before a judge or other official authorized by law to exercise judicial power, the Committee found a violation of Article 9(3) of the Covenant (p. 330).

(3) The uncontested facts that the author continued to suffer restrictions on his freedom of movement and that the Zambian authorities had denied him his passport amounted to a violation of Article 12(1) of the Covenant (p. 330).

(4) Although the author had not shown that the treatment in detention had been cruel, inhuman and degrading within the meaning of Article 7 of the Covenant, the Committee considered that Zambia had violated the author's right under Article 10(1) of the Covenant to be treated with humanity and respect for the inherent dignity of his person (p. 330).

The following is the text of the views of the Committee:

The facts as presented by the author

1. The author of the communication is Henry Kalenga, a Zambian citizen currently residing in Kitwe, Zambia. He claims to be a victim of violations by Zambia of Articles 9, 14 and 19 of the International Covenant on Civil and Political Rights.

2.1 On 11 February 1986, the author was arrested by the police of the city of Masala; he was forced to spend the night in a police lock-up. On 12 February 1986, a statement was taken from him. The following day, a police detention order was issued against him pursuant to Regulation 33(6) of the Preservation of Public Security Act. This order was revoked on 27 February 1986 but immediately replaced by a Presidential detention order, issued under Regulation 33(1) of the said Act.

2.2 The author notes that the Preservation of Public Security Regulations allow the President of Zambia to authorize the administrative detention of persons accused of political offences for an indefinite period of time, "for purposes of preserving public security". The author was informed of the charges brought against him on 13 March 1986, that is over one month after his arrest. He was subsequently kept in police detention, on charges of (a) being one of the founding members and having sought to disseminate the views of a political organization, the so-called People's Redemption Organization —an organization considered illegal under Zambia's (then) one-party Constitution, and (b) of preparing subversive activities aimed at overthrowing the regime of (then) President Kenneth Kaunda. The author was released on 3 November 1989, following a Presidential order.

2.3 After his release, the author was placed under surveillance by the Zambian authorities. The latter allegedly denied him his passport, thereby depriving him of his freedom of movement. Moreover, he claims that as a former political prisoner, he was subjected to harassment and intimidation by the authorities, which also reportedly denied him access to governmental and private financial institutions.

The complaint

3.1 Mr Kalenga contends that at the time of his arrest, he was not engaged in any political activities aimed at undermining the Government. Instead, he had been promoting campaigns protesting the Government's national education, military and economic policies. He adds that the subversive activities he was accused of amounted to no more than burning the card affiliating him with President Kaunda's party, UNIP. He claims that, as a prisoner of conscience, he was subjected to unlawful detention, because he was formally informed about the reasons for his detention more than a month following his arrest, contrary to the Regulations mentioned in paragraph 2.1 above and Article 27, paragraph 1(a), of the Zambian Constitution. The latter provision stipulates that the grounds of detention must be supplied within fourteen days following the arrest. In this connection, the author asserts that the charges against him had no basis in fact at the time of his arrest and that they were "fabricated" by the police in order to justify his detention.

3.2 The author further affirms that throughout his detention, he was not brought before a judge or judicial officer to establish his guilt. This allegedly was attributable to the fact that under Zambian legislation regulating public security issues, individuals may be detained indefinitely without being formally charged or tried.

3.3 The author contends that he was subjected to inhuman and degrading treatment during his detention. He claims that he was frequently deprived of food, of access to recreational activities as well as medical assistance, despite the continuing deterioration of his state of health. Moreover, he claims to have been subjected to various forms of "psychological torture". This treatment is said to be prohibited under Articles 17 and 25(2) and (3) of the Zambian Constitution.

3.4 With respect to the requirement of exhaustion of domestic remedies, the author states that he instituted proceedings against the State during his detention. Initially, he filed an application for writ of habeas corpus with the High Court of Zambia. On 23 June 1986, the High Court dismissed his application, on the ground that the author's detention was not in violation of domestic laws. The author then filed another request for writ of habeas corpus with the High Court of Justice, in which he (a) challenged the legality of his detention, (b) complained about the inhuman and degrading treatment suffered during detention, and (c) requested compensation and damages. On 14 April 1989, the application was dismissed by the Court, which declared itself incompetent to deal with the matter on the basis of *res judicata*. The author then petitioned a special tribunal established under the Preservation of Public Security Regulations; this tribunal has the mandate to review periodically the cases of political prisoners and is authorized to recommend either continued detention or release. The tribunal sits, however, in camera, and the President is not obliged to implement its recommendations, made confidentially. On 29 and 30 December 1988, the author was heard by this tribunal. As the State prosecutor could not adduce evidence in support of the charges against the author, the tribunal recommended Mr Kalenga's immediate release. Nonetheless, release did not occur until ten months later, as President Kaunda did not follow up on the recommendation.

The Committee's admissibility decision and the parties' submissions on the merits

4.1 During its forty-third session in October 1991, the Committee considered the admissibility of the communication. It noted with concern the absence of any State Party cooperation on the matter, as the State Party had failed to make submissions on the admissibility of the case in spite of two reminders. On the basis of the information before it, it concluded that the author had met the requirements under Article 5, paragraph 2(b), of the Optional Protocol, and that he had sufficiently substantiated his allegations, for purposes of admissibility.

4.2 On 15 October 1991, the Committee declared the communication admissible in as much as it appeared to raise issues under Articles 7, 9, 10, 12 and 19 of the Covenant.

5.1 In a submission, dated 28 January 1992, the State Party indicated that "Mr Henry Kalenga has been released from custody and is a free person now". No information about the substance of the author's allegations, nor copies of his indictment or of any judicial orders concerning his detention and the alleged legality thereof, have been provided by the State Party. The State Party did not reply to a reminder addressed to it in February 1993.

5.2 In an undated letter received on 24 March 1992, the author requests the Committee to continue consideration of his case. He adds that he continues to suffer from stomach ulcers and a deplorable financial situation as a result of his detention; he further contends that the change in government, in the spring of 1992, has not changed the authorities' attitude towards him.

Examination of the merits

6.1 The Committee has considered the communication in the light of all the information provided by the parties. It notes with concern that, with the exception of a brief note informing the Committee about the author's release, a fact known to the Committee by the time of the adoption of the admissibility decision, the State Party has failed to cooperate on the matter under consideration. It is implicit in Article 4, paragraph 2, of the Optional Protocol that a State Party investigate in good faith the allegations brought against it, and that it provides the Committee with all the information at its disposal, including all available judicial documents. The State Party has failed to provide the Committee with any such information. In the circumstances, due weight must be given to the author's allegations, to the extent that they have been substantiated.

6.2 In respect of issues under Article 19, the Committee is of the opinion that the uncontested response of the Zambian authorities to the author's attempts to express his opinions freely and to disseminate the tenets of the People's Redemption Organization constitute a violation of his rights under Article 19 of the Covenant.

6.3 The Committee is of the opinion that the author's right, under Article 9, paragraph 2, to be promptly informed about the reasons for his arrest and of the charges against him, has been violated, as it took the State Party authorities almost one month to so inform him. Similarly, the Committee finds a violation of Article 9, paragraph 3, as the material before it reveals that the author was not brought promptly before a judge or other officer authorized by law to exercise judicial power. On the other hand, on the basis of the chronology of judicial proceedings provided by the author himself, the Committee cannot conclude that Mr Kalenga was denied his right, under Article 9, paragraph 4, to take proceedings before a court of law.

6.4 The author has claimed, and the State Party has not denied, that he continues to suffer restrictions on his freedom of movement, and that the Zambian authorities have denied him his passport. This, in the Committee's opinion, amounts to a violation of Article 12, paragraph 1, of the Covenant.

6.5 As to Mr Kalenga's claim of inhuman and degrading treatment in detention, the Committee notes that the author has provided information in substantiation of his allegation, in particular concerning the denial of recreational facilities, the occasional deprivation of food and failure to provide medical assistance when needed. Although the author has not shown that such treatment was cruel, inhuman and degrading within the meaning of Article 7, the Committee considers that the State Party has violated the author's right under Article 10, paragraph 1, to be treated with humanity and respect for the inherent dignity of his person.

7. The Human Rights Committee, acting under Article 5, paragraph 4, of the Optional Protocol to the International Covenant on Civil and Political Rights, is of the view that the facts as found by the Committee disclose violations of Articles 9, paragraphs 2 and 3; 10, paragraph 1; 12, paragraph 1; and 19, of the Covenant.

8. Pursuant to Article 2 of the Covenant, the State Party is under an obligation to provide Mr Kalenga with an appropriate remedy. The Committee urges the State Party to grant appropriate consideration to the author; the State Party is under an obligation to ensure that similar violations do not occur in the future.

9. The Committee would wish to receive information, within ninety days, on any relevant measures taken by the State Party in respect of the Committee's Views.

(Done in English, French and Spanish, the English text being the original version.)

[Report: Doc. CCPR/C/48/D/326/1988]

Human rights — Minorities — International Covenant on Civil and Political Rights, 1966, Article 27—Sami reindeer herdsmen in Finland—Whether rights violated by legislation on logging and by road building programmes—Consultation of Sami herdsmen by Government of Finland—Limited impact of Government plans for logging and road building on culture of the Sami

International tribunals—United Nations Human Rights Committee — Competence — Domestic remedies rule — Adequacy of domestic remedies—Ability to invoke International Covenant on Civil and Political Rights before domestic courts — Procedure — Reconsideration of earlier admissibility decision

SARA *et al. v.* FINLAND

(Communication No 431/1990)

United Nations Human Rights Committee.[1]   23 *March* 1994

SUMMARY: *The facts:*—The authors were Finnish citizens and reindeer breeders of the Sami ethnic origin who represented a substantial part of reindeer herding in Finnish Lapland. In November 1990 the Finnish Wilderness Act ("the Act") was passed providing that specifically designated areas were off-limits for logging, whereas in others, defined as "environmental forestry areas", logging was permitted. The Act also entrusted a Central Forestry Board ("CFB") with the planning of the use and maintenance of the wilderness area.

In December 1990 the authors submitted a communication to the Human Rights Committee claiming that the Act jeopardized the future of reindeer herding in general and of their livelihood in particular. They also claimed that since that Act would authorize logging within areas used by them for reindeer husbandry its passage would constitute a serious interference with their rights under Article 27 of the International Covenant on Civil and Political Rights, 1966 ("the Covenant"). The authors were concerned especially in respect of expected logging and road construction activities within the Hammastunturi Wilderness Area, and ongoing road construction activities in the residual area outside the Wilderness Area. They contended that the road constructions into their herding areas had been started without their prior consultation and argued that even partial logging would affect the growth of lichen, which constituted the winter diet for reindeer, and lead to a change in the nutrition balance of the soil, thus rendering the area inhospitable for reindeer breeding for at least a century and possibly irrevocably. Lastly, the authors contended that the Finnish legal system did not provide for remedies to challenge the constitutionality or validity of a Finnish Act of Parliament, nor in respect of a violation of Article 27 of the Covenant.

Finland challenged the admissibility of the communication on the ground that it was incompatible with the provisions of the Covenant. Finland denied that there was a causal link between the measures of protection requested by the authors and the object of the communication itself. Arguing that logging and construction of roads would contribute to the natural development of the forests, Finland also claimed that the communication was inadmissible because the authors could not be considered as victims of a violation of the Covenant. Furthermore, Finland noted that the Covenant had been incorporated into domestic law, and that the authors could submit a complaint to the domestic courts should a plan be approved that would endanger the subsistence of the Sami culture.

[1] The members of the Committee in 1994, with the country of nationality of each member placed in parentheses, were: Francisco José Aguilar Urbina (Costa Rica), Nisuke Ando (Japan), Tamás Bán (Hungary), Marco Tulio Bruni Celli (Venezuela), Christine Chanet (France), Vojin Dimitrijević (Yugoslavia), Omran El Shafei (Egypt), Elizabeth Evatt (Australia), Laurel Francis (Jamaica), Kurt Hendl (Austria), Rosalyn Higgins (United Kingdom), Rajsoomer Lallah (Mauritius), Andreas V. Mavrommatis (Cyprus), Birame Ndiaye (Senegal), Fausto Pocar (Italy), Julio Prado Vallejo (Ecuador), Waleed Sadi (Jordan) and Bertil Wennergren (Sweden).

In July 1991 the Committee declared the communication admissible in so far as it raised issues under Article 27 of the Covenant. As the Committee considered that there was a causal link between the entry into force of the Act and the continuation of road construction in the residual area, the authors had sufficiently substantiated that this road construction could adversely affect their rights under Article 27 of the Covenant. In February 1992 Finland requested a review of the admissibility decision because the Committee's acceptance of this causal link had changed the substance of the communication and introduced new elements in respect of which Finland had not provided any admissibility information.

Held:—(1) Although Article 27 of the Covenant had seldom been invoked before the Finnish courts or its content guided the *ratio decidendi* of Finnish court decisions, the Finnish judicial authorities had become increasingly aware of the domestic relevance of international human rights standards, including the rights enshrined in the Covenant. A recent judgment of the Supreme Administrative Tribunal could not be seen as a negative precedent for the adjudication of the authors' own grievances. Furthermore, the authors' doubts about the Finnish courts' readiness to entertain claims based on Article 27 of the Covenant did not justify their failure to utilize Finnish domestic remedies (p. 346).

(2) The admissibility decision of July 1991 was therefore set aside, and the communication declared inadmissible. The Committee considered that an administrative action challenging road construction activities in the residual area would not have been *a priori* futile, and thus decided that the requirements of Article 5(2)(b) of the Optional Protocol had not been met (p. 346).

The following is the text of the views of the Committee:

Revised decision on admissibility

1. The authors of the communication dated 18 December 1990 are Messrs O. Sara, J. Näkkäläjärvi, O. Hirvasvuopio and Ms A. Aärelä, all Finnish citizens. They claim to be the victims of a violation by Finland of Article 27 of the International Covenant on Civil and Political Rights. They are represented by counsel.

The facts as submitted by the authors

2.1 The authors are reindeer breeders of Sami ethnic origin. Together with the herdsmen's committees (cooperative-type bodies set up to regulate reindeer husbandry in Finland), they represent a substantial part of reindeer herding in Finnish Lapland. Mr Sara is the chief and Mr Näkkäläjärvi, the deputy chief of the Sallivaara Herdsmen Committee; Mr Hirvasvuopio is the chief of the Lappi Herdsmen Committee. In terms of counted reindeer the Sallivaara Herdsmen Committee is the second largest herdsmen's committee in Finland; the Lappi Herdsmen's Committee is the third largest.

2.2 On 16 November 1990, the Finnish Parliament passed Bill 42/1990, called the "Wilderness Act" (ërämaalaki"), which entered into force on 1 February 1991. The legal history of this bill is the result of a delicate compromise reached after protracted discussions between the Samis, environmental protection lobbyists and the Finnish Forest Administration about the extent of logging activities in nothernmost Finland, that is, close to or north of the Arctic Circle. Under the provisions of the Act, specifically designated areas are off-limits for logging, whereas in others, defined as "environmental forestry areas" ("luonnonmukainen metsänhoito"), logging is permitted. Another, third, category of forest areas remains unaffected by the application of the Act.

2.3 An important consideration in the enactment of the Act, reflected in Section 1, is the protection of the Sami culture and particularly of traditional Sami economic activities. Section 3, however, reveals that the *ratio legis* of the Act is the notion and extension of State ownership of the wilderness areas of Finnish Lapland. The authors note that the notion of State ownership of these areas has long been fought by Samis. The implication of Section 3, in particular, is that all future logging activities in the areas used by them for reindeer husbandry will be matters controlled by different Government authorities. In particular, Section 7 of the Act entrusts a Central Forestry Board (CFB) ("metsähallitus") with the task of planning both use and maintenance (hoito-ja käyttösuunnitelma") of the wilderness area. While the Ministry for the Environment ("ympäristöministeriö") may either approve or disapprove the plans proposed by this Board, it cannot amend them.

2.4 The authors indicate that the area used for herding their reindeer during the winter months is hitherto unspoiled wilderness area. The border between the municipalities of Sodankylä and Inari nowadays divides this wilderness into two separate herdsmen's committees. Under the Wilderness Act, the largest part of the authors' reindeer breeding area overlaps with the Hammastunturi Wilderness Area; other parts do not and may therefore be managed by the CFB. Under preliminary plans approved by the Board, only small portions of the authors' breeding area would be off-limits for logging operations, whereas the major part of their areas overlapping with the Hammastunturi Wilderness would be subject to so-called "environ-mental forestry", a concept without a precise definition. Furthermore, on the basis of separate decisions by Parliament, the cutting of forests within the Hammastunturi Wilderness would not begin, until the approval, by the Ministry for the Environment, of a plan for use and maintenance. The Act, however, is said to give the CFB the power to start full-scale logging.

2.5 At the time of the submission in 1990, the authors contended that large-scale logging activities, as authorized under the Wilderness Act, were imminent in the areas used by them for reindeer breeding.

Thus, two road construction projects into the authors' herding areas were started without prior consultation of the authors, and the roads are said to serve no purpose in the maintenance of the authors' traditional way of life. The authors claimed that the roads were intended to facilitate logging activities inside the Hammastunturi Wilderness in 1992 and, in all likelihood, outside the Wilderness as early as the summer of 1991. The road construction had already penetrated over a distance of six miles, at a breadth of 60 feet, into the reindeer herding areas used by the authors. Concrete sink rings have been brought on site, which the authors claim underline that the road is to be built for all-season use by heavy trucks.

2.6 The authors reiterate that the area in question is an important breeding area for the Lappi Herdsmen's Committee, and that they have no use for any roads within the area. For the Lappi Herdsmen's Committee, the area is the last remaining natural wilderness area; for the Sallivaara Herdsmen's Committee, the area forms one-third of its best winter herding areas and is essential for the survival of reindeer in extreme climatic conditions. As to the disposal of slaughtered reindeer, the authors note that slaughtering takes place at places specifically designed for that purpose, located close to main roads running outside the herding area. The Sallivaara Herdsmen's Committee already disposes of a modern slaughterhouse, and the Lappi Herdsmen's Committee has plans for a similar one.

2.7 The authors further note that the area used by them for winter herding is geographically a typical watershed highland, located between the Arctic Sea and the Baltic. These lands are surrounded by open marshlands covering at least two-thirds of the total area. As in other watershed areas, abundant snow and rainfalls are common. The winter season is approximately one month longer than in other areas. The climate has a direct impact on the area's environment, in particular the trees (birch and spruce), whose growth is slow; the trees in turn encourage the growth of the two types of lichen that constitute the winter diet for reindeer. The authors emphasize that even partial logging would render the area inhospitable for reindeer breeding for at least a century and possibly irrevocably, since the destruction of the trees would lead to an extension of the marsh, with the resulting change of the nutrition balance of the soil. Moreover, logging would merely add to present dangers threatening the trees within the authors' herding area, i.e. industrial pollution from the Russian Kola district. In this context, it is submitted that silvicultural methods of logging (i.e. environmentally sensitive cutting of forest areas) advocated by the authorities for some parts of the wilderness area used by the authors would cause possibly irreversible damage to reindeer herding, as the age structure of the forest and the conditions for the lichen growth would change.

2.8 With respect to the requirement of exhaustion of domestic remedies, the authors contend that the Finnish legal system does not provide for remedies to challenge the constitutionality or validity of an Act adopted by Parliament. As to the possibility of an appeal to the Supreme Administrative Tribunal against any future administrative decisions based on the Wilderness Act, the authors point out that the Finnish legal doctrine on administrative law has been applied very restrictively in accepting legal standing on grounds other than ownership. Thus, it is claimed that there are no domestic remedies which the authors might pursue in respect of a violation of Article 27 of the Covenant.

The complaint

3.1 The authors submit that the passage of the Wilderness Act jeopardizes the future of reindeer herding in general and of their livelihood in particular, as reindeer farming is their primary source of income. Furthermore, since the Act would authorize logging within areas used by the authors for reindeer husbandry, its passage is said to constitute a serious interference with their rights under Article 27 of the Covenant, in particular the right to enjoy their own culture. In this context, the authors refer to the Views of the Human Rights Committee in cases Nos 197/1985 and 167/1984[2] as well as to ILO Convention No 169 concerning indigenous and tribal people in independent countries.

3.2 The authors add that over the past decades, traditional methods used for reindeer breeding have decreased in importance and have been partly replaced by "fencing" and artificial feeding, which the authors submit are alien to them. Additional factors enabling an assessment of the irreparable damage to which wilderness areas in Finland are exposed include the development of an industry producing forest harvesting machinery and a road network for wood transport. These factors are said to deeply affect the enjoyment of the authors' traditional economic and cultural rights.

3.3 Fearing that the CFB would approve the continuation of road construction or logging by the summer of 1991, or at the latest by early 1992, around the road under construction and therefore within the confines of their herding areas, the authors requested the adoption of interim measures of protection, pursuant to Rule 86 of the Committee's rules of procedure.

The State Party's observations

4.1 In its submission under Rule 91 of the rules of procedure, the

---

[2] Communication No 197/1985 (*Kitok* v. *Sweden*) [96 *ILR* 637], Views adopted on 25 July 1988, paragraph 9.8; Communication No 167/1984 (*Ominayak* v. *Canada*) [96 *ILR* 667], Views adopted on 26 March 1990, paragraph 32.2.

State Party does not raise objections to the admissibility of the communication under Article 5, paragraph 2(b), of the Optional Protocol, and concedes that in the present situation there are no domestic remedies which the authors should still pursue.

4.2 The State Party indicated that for the Hammastunturi Wilderness, plans for maintenance and use currently in preparation in the Ministry of the Environment would not be finalized and approved until the spring of 1992; nor are there any logging projects under way in the residual area designated by the authors, which does not overlap with the Hammastunturi Wilderness. North of the Wilderness, however, minor "silvicultural felling" (to study the effect of logging on the environment) began in 1990 and would be stopped by the end of the spring of 1991. According to the CFB, this particular forest does not overlap with the area designated in the communication. The State Party added that south of the Wilderness, the gravelling of an existing roadbed would proceed in the summer of 1991, following the entry into force of the Wilderness Act.

4.3 The State Party contends that the communication is inadmissible under Article 3 of the Optional Protocol, as incompatible with the provisions of the Covenant. In particular, it argues that the plans of the CFB for silvicultural logging in the residual area outside the Hammastunturi Wilderness are not related to the passage of the Wilderness Act, because the latter only applies to areas specifically designated as such. The authority of the CFB to approve logging activities in areas other than those designated as protected wilderness is not derived from the Wilderness Act. Accordingly, the State Party denies that there is a causal link between the measures of protection requested by the authors and the object of the communication itself, which only concerns enactment and implementation of the Wilderness Act.

4.4 The State Party further contends that the envisaged forestry operations, consisting merely of "silvicultural logging" and construction of roads for that purpose, will not render the areas used by the authors irreparably inhospitable for reindeer husbandry. On the contrary, the State Party expects them to contribute to the natural development of the forests. In this connection, it points to a report prepared for the Ministry for Agriculture and Forestry by a professor of the University of Joensuu, who supports the view that timber production, reindeer husbandry, collection of mushrooms and berries and other economic activities may sustainably coexist and thrive in the environment of Finnish Lapland. This report states that no single forest or land use can on its own fulfil the income and welfare needs of the population; forest management of the whole area and particularly Northern Lapland must accordingly be implemented pursuant to schemes of multiple use and "strict sustainability".

4.5 The State Party submits that the authors cannot be considered as "victims" of a violation of the Covenant, and that their communication should be declared inadmissible on that account. In this context, the State Party contends that the *ratio legis* of the Wilderness Act is the very opposite from that identified by the authors: its intention was to upgrade and enhance the protection of the Sami culture and traditional nature-based means of livelihood. Secondly, the State Party submits that the authors have failed to demonstrate how their concerns about "irreparable damage" purportedly resulting from logging in the area designated by them translate into actual violations of their rights; they are merely afraid of what might occur in the future. While they might legitimately fear for the future of the Sami culture, the "desired feeling of certainty is not as such protected under the Covenant. There must be a concrete executive decision or measure taken under the Wilderness Act", before anyone may claim to be the victim of a violation of his Covenant rights.

4.6 The State Party further argues that passage of the Wilderness Act must be seen as an improvement rather than a setback for protection of the rights protected by Article 27. If the authors are dissatisfied with the amount of land protected as wilderness, they overlook that the Wilderness Act is based on a philosophy of coexistence between reindeer herding and forest economy. This is not only an old tradition in Finnish Lapland but also a practical necessity, as unemployment figures are exceptionally high in Finnish Lapland. The Act embodies a legislative compromise trying to balance opposite interests in a fair and democratic manner. While the Government fully took into account the requirements of Article 27 of the Covenant, it could not ignore the economic and social rights of that part of the population whose subsistence depends on logging activities: "one cannot do without compromises in a democratic society, even if they fail to satisfy all the parties concerned".

4.7 Finally, the State Party notes that the Covenant has been incorporated into domestic law and that, accordingly, Article 27 is directly applicable before the Finnish authorities and judicial instances. Thus, if, in the future, the Ministry of the Environment were to approve a plan for forest maintenance and care which would indeed endanger the subsistence of Sami culture and thus violate Article 27, the victims of such a violation could submit a complaint to the Supreme Administrative Court.

Admissibility considerations

5.1 During its forty-second session in July 1991, the Committee considered the admissibility of the communication. It noted that the State Party had raised no objection with regard to the admissibility of the communication under Article 5, paragraph 2(b), of the Optional

Protocol. It further took note of the State Party's claim that the authors could not claim to be victims of a violation of the Covenant within the meaning of Article 1 of the Optional Protocol. The Committee reaffirmed that individuals can only claim to be victims within the meaning of Article 1 if they are actually affected, although it is a matter of degree as to how concretely this requirement should be taken.[3]

5.2 Inasmuch as the authors claimed to be victims of a violation of Article 27, both in respect of *expected* logging and road construction activities *within* the Hammastunturi Wilderness and *ongoing* road construction activities in the residual area located *outside* the Wilderness, the Committee observed that the communication related to both areas, whereas parts of the State Party's observations could be read in the sense that the communication *only* related to the Hammastunturi Wilderness.

5.3 The Committee distinguished between the authors' claim to be victims of a violation of the Covenant in respect of road construction and logging *inside* the Hammastunturi Wilderness and such measures *outside* the Wilderness, including road construction and logging in the residual area south of the Wilderness. In respect of the former areas, the authors had merely expressed the fear that plans under preparation by the CFB might adversely affect their rights under Article 27 in the future. This, in the Committee's opinion, did not make the authors victims within the meaning of Article 1 of the Optional Protocol, as they were not actually affected by an administrative measure implementing the Wilderness Act. Therefore, this aspect of the communication was deemed inadmissible under Article 1 of the Optional Protocol.

5.4 In respect of the residual area, the Committee observed that the continuation of road construction into it could be causally linked to the entry into force of the Wilderness Act. In the Committee's opinion, the authors had sufficiently substantiated, for purposes of admissibility, that this road construction could produce effects adverse to the enjoyment and practice of their rights under Article 27.

5.5 On 9 July 1991, accordingly, the Committee declared the communication admissible in so far as it appeared to raise issues under Article 27 of the Covenant.

5.6 The Committee also requested the State Party to "adopt such measures, as appropriate, to prevent irreparable damage to the authors".

The State Party's request for review of the admissibility decision and the authors' reply
6.1 In its submission under Article 4, paragraph 2, dated 10 February 1992, the State Party notes that the Committee's acceptance,

---

[3] See Communication No 35/1978 (*Aumeeruddy-Cziffra* v. *Mauritius*) [62 *ILR* 285], Views adopted on 9 April 1981, paragraph 5; Communication No 61/1979 (*Hertzberg* v. *Finland*) [70 *ILR* 297], Views adopted on 2 April 1982, paragraph 9.3.

in the decision of 9 July 1991, of a causal link between the Wilderness Act and any measures taken outside the Hammastunturi Wilderness has changed the substance of the communication and introduced elements in respect of which the State Party did not provide any admissibility information. It reiterates that in applying the Wilderness Act, Finnish authorities must take into consideration Article 27 of the Covenant, "which, in the hierarchy of laws, is on the same level as ordinary laws". Samis who claim that their Covenant rights were violated by the application of the Act may appeal to the Supreme Administrative Court in respect of the plan for maintenance and care of the Wilderness area approved by the Ministry of the Environment.

6.2 In respect of the activities outside the Hammastunturi Wilderness (the "residual area"), the State Party submits that Article 27 would entitle the authors to take action against the State or the CFB before the Finnish courts. Grounds for such a legal action would be concrete measures taken by the State, such as road construction, which in the authors' opinion infringe upon their rights under Article 27. A decision at first instance could be appealed to the Court of Appeal and from there, subject to certain conditions, to the Supreme Court. The provincial government could be requested to grant provisional remedies; if this authority does not grant such a remedy, its decision may be appealed to the Court of Appeal and, subject to a re-trial permit, to the Supreme Court.

6.3 The State Party adds that the fact that actions of this type have not yet been brought before the domestic courts does not mean that local remedies do not exist but merely that provisions such as Article 27 have not been invoked until recently. Notwithstanding, the decisions of the higher courts and the awards of the Parliamentary Ombudsman in the recent past suggest that the impact of international human rights treaties is significantly on the increase. While the authors do not own the contested area, the application of Article 27 gives them legal standing as representatives of a national minority, irrespective of ownership. The State Party concludes that the communication should be deemed inadmissible in respect of measures taken outside the Hammastunturi Wilderness on the basis of Article 5, paragraph 2(b), of the Optional Protocol.

6.4 Subsidiarily, the State Party reaffirms that current road construction activities in the "residual areas" do not infringe upon the authors' rights under Article 27. It observes that the authors do not specify that the construction has caused real damage to reindeer husbandry. In this context, it observes that the

concept of culture in the sense of Article 27 provides for a certain degree of protection of the traditional means of livelihood for national minorities and can be deemed to cover livelihood and other conditions in so far as they are essential for the culture and necessary for its survival. The Sami culture is closely linked with traditional reindeer husbandry. For the purposes of . . . Article 27 . . . it must be established, however, in addition to the afore-mentioned question of what degree of interference the Article [protects] against, whether the minority practices its livelihood in the traditional manner intended in the Article.

As Sami reindeer husbandry has evolved over time, the link with the natural economy of old Sami tradition has been blurred; reindeer husbandry is increasingly practised with help of modern technology, e.g. snow scooters and modern slaughterhouses. Thus, modern reindeer husbandry managed by herdsmen's committees leaves little room for individual, self-employed, herdsmen.

6.5 The State Party further denies that prospective logging in areas outside the Wilderness will infringe upon the authors' rights under Article 27: "there is no negative link between the entry into force of the Wilderness Act and logging by the CFB outside the wilderness area. On the contrary—enactment of the law has a positive impact on logging methods used in the residual areas." The State Party explains that under the Act on Reindeer Husbandry, the northernmost State-owned areas are set aside for reindeer herding and shall not be used in ways that impair reindeer husbandry. The CFB has decided that highlands (above 300 metres altitude) are subject to the most circumspect forestry. In Upper Lapland, a land and water utilization strategy approved by the CFB that emphasizes the principle of multiple use and sustainability of resources applies.

6.6 It is recalled that the area identified in the authors' initial complaint comprises approximately 55,000 hectares (35,000 ha of the Hammastunturi Wilderness, 1,400 ha of highlands, and 19,000 ha of conservation forest); out of this total, only 10,000 ha or 18 per cent are set aside for logging. The State Party notes that "logging is extremely cautious and the interests of reindeer husbandry are kept in mind". If one considers that logging is practised with strict consideration for the varied nature of the environment, forestry and land use in the area in question do not cause undue damage to reindeer husbandry. Further-more, the significant increase in the overall reindeer population in Finnish Lapland over the past twenty years is seen as a "clear indication that logging and reindeer husbandry are quite compatible".

6.7 In respect of the authors' claim that thinning of the forests destroys lichen (*lichenes* and *usnea*) in the winter herding areas, the State Party observes that other herdsmen have even requested for such thinning to be carried out, as they have discovered that it alters "the ratio of top vegetation to the advantage of lichen and facilitates mobility. The purpose of [such] thinning is, *inter alia*, to sustain the tree population and improve its resistance to airborne pollution."

Furthermore, according to the State Party, lichen is plentiful in the highland areas where the CFB does no logging at all.

6.8 The State Party notes that Sami herdsmen own or co-own forests. Ownership is governed by a variety of legislative acts; the most recent, the Reindeer Farm Act and Decree, also applies to Sami herdsmen. According to the State Party, the authors own reindeer farms. Thinning of trees or logging of private forests is governed by the Private Forests Act. According to the Association of Herdsmen's Committees, the income derived from logging is essential for securing the herdsmen's livelihood and, furthermore, forestry jobs are essential to forest workers and those Sami herdsmen who work in the forests apart from breeding reindeer. In the light of the above, the State Party reaffirms that planned logging activities in the area identified by the complaints cannot adversely affect the practice of reindeer husbandry, within the meaning of Article 27 of the Covenant.

7.1 In their comments, dated 25 March 1992, on the State Party's submission, the authors contend that the State Party's reference to the availability of remedies on account of the Covenant's status in the Finnish legal system represents a novelty in the Government's argumentation. They submit that this line of argument contrasts with the State Party's position in previous Optional Protocol cases and even with that put forth by the Government at the admissibility stage of the case. The authors argue that while it is true that international human rights norms are invoked increasingly before the courts, the authorities would not be in a position to contend that Sami reindeer herdsmen have *locus standi* in respect to plans for maintenance and use of Wilderness areas, or in respect of road construction projects in State-owned forests. Not only is there no case-law in this respect, but Finnish courts have been reluctant to accept standing of any others than the landowners; the authors cite several judgments in support of their contention.[4]

7.2 Inasmuch as the alleged direct applicability of Article 27 of the Covenant is concerned, the authors claim that while this possibility should not theoretically be excluded, there is no legal precedent for the direct application of Article 27; the State Party therefore wrongly presents a hypothetical possibility as a judicial interpretation. The authors reaffirm that *no* available and effective remedies exist in relation to road construction and other measures in the "residual area", which consists exclusively of State-owned lands. The Government's reference to the fact that the Covenant is incorporated into the domestic legal system cannot be deemed to prove that the domestic court practice includes even elementary forms of the approach now put forth by the State Party, for the first time, to a United Nations human rights treaty body.

---

[4] See, for example, judgment of 16 April 1992 of the Supreme Administrative Court in the *Angeli* case.

7.3 The authors challenge the State Party's assessment of the impact of road construction into the area designated in their communication on the enjoyment of their rights under Article 27. Firstly, they object to the State Party's interpretation of the scope of the provision and argue that if the applicability of Article 27 depended solely on whether the minority practises its "livelihood in the traditional manner", the relevance of the rights enshrined in the provision would be rendered nugatory to a large extent. It is submitted that many indigenous peoples in the world have, over time and due to governmental policies, lost the possibility to enjoy their culture and carry out economic activities in accordance with their traditions. Far from diminishing the obligations of States Parties under Article 27, such trends should give more impetus to their observance.

7.4 While Finnish Sami have not been able to maintain all traditional methods of reindeer herding, their practice still is a distinct Sami form of reindeer herding, carried out in community with other members of the group and under circumstances prescribed by the natural habitat. Snow scooters have not destroyed this form of nomadic reindeer herding. Other than in Sweden and Norway, Finland allows reindeer herding for others than Samis; thus, the southern parts of the country are used by herdsmen's committees which now largely resort to fencing and to artificial feeding.

7.5 As to the impact of road construction into their herding area, the authors reiterate that it violates Article 27 because

—construction work already causes noise and traffic that has disturbed the reindeer;
—the two roads form "open wounds" in the forests with, on the immediate site, all the negative effects of logging;
—the roads have changed the pattern of reindeer movements, by dividing the ·wilderness and thereby making it far more difficult to keep the herd together;
—any roads built into the wilderness bring tourists and other traffic disturbing the animals;
—as the government has failed to provide reasonable justifications for the construction of the roads, their construction violates the authors' rights under Article 27, as a mere preparatory stage for logging within their area.

7.6 Concerning the State Party's assessment of logging operations in the areas designated by the communication, the authors observe that although the area is small in comparison with Sami areas as a whole, logging within that area would restart a process that lasted for centuries and brought about a gradual disintegration of the traditional Sami way of life. In this context, it is noted that the area in question remains one of the most productive wilderness areas used for reindeer herding in Finnish Lapland.

7.7 Still in the context of planned logging operations, the authors submit the reports of two experts, according to which (a) under certain conditions, reindeer are highly dependent on lichens growing on trees; (b) lichen growing on the ground are a primary winter forage for reindeer; (c) old forests are superior to young ones as herding areas; and (d) logging negatively affects nature-based methods of reindeer herding.

7.8 The authors insist that the area designated in their communication has remained untouched for centuries, and that it is only in the context of the coming into force of the Wilderness Act that the CFB began its plans for logging in the area. They further contend that if it is true, as claimed by the State Party, that highlands (above 300 metres) are in practice free of CFB activity, then their herding area should remain untouched. However, the two roads built into their area partly run above the 300 metre mark, which shows that such areas are well within the reach of CFB activities. In this context, they recall that all of the area delineated in their complaint is either above the 300 metre mark or very close to it; accordingly, they dismiss the State Party's claim that only 1,400 ha of the area are highlands. Furthermore, while the authors have no access to the internal plans for logging in the area drawn up by the CFB, they submit that logging of 18 per cent of the total area would indeed affect a major part of its forests.

7.9 As to the alleged compatibility of intensive logging and practising intensive reindeer husbandry, the authors note that this statement only applies to the modern forms of reindeer herding using artificial feeding. The methods used by the authors, however, are traditional, and for that the old forests in the area designated by the communication are essential. The winter 1991-2 demonstrated how relatively warm winters may threaten traditional herding methods. As a result of alternating periods with temperatures above and below 0°C the snow was, in many parts of Finnish Lapland, covered by a hard layer of ice that prevented the reindeer from getting their nutrition from the ground. In some areas without old forests carrying lichen on their branches, reindeer have been dying from hunger. In this situation, the herding area designated in the communication has been very valuable to the authors.

7.10 In several submissions made between September 1992 and February 1994, the authors provide further clarifications. By submission of 30 September 1992, they indicate that the CFB's logging plans for the Hammastunturi Wilderness are still in preparation. In a subsequent letter dated 15 February 1993, they indicate that a recent decision of the Supreme Court invalidates the State Party's contention that the authors would have *locus standi* before the courts on the basis of claims brought under Article 27 of the Covenant. This decision, which quashed a decision of the Court of Appeal granting a Finnish citizen who had been successful before the Human Rights Committee compensation,[5] holds that the *administrative*, rather than the *ordinary*, courts are competent to decide on the issue of the complainant's compensation.

7.11 The authors further indicate that the draft plan for use and maintenance of the Hammastunturi Wilderness was made available to them on 10 February 1993, and a number of them were going to be consulted by the authorities before final confirmation of the plan by the Ministry for the Environment. According to the draft plan, no logging would be carried out in those parts of the Wilderness belonging to the area specified in the communication *and* to the herding areas of the Sallivaara Herdsmen's Committee. The same is not however true for the respective areas of the Lappi Herdsmen's Committee: under the draft plan, logging would be carried out in an area of 10 square kilometres (called Peuravaarat) situated in the southernmost part of the Hammastunturi Wilderness and *within* the area specified in the original communication.

7.12 In submissions of 19 October 1993 and 19 February 1994, the authors note that negotiations on and preparation of a plan for use and maintenance of the Wilderness have *still* not been completed, and that the CFB has *still not* made a final recommendation to the Ministry for the Environment. In fact, a delay until 1996 for the finalization of the maintenance plan is expected.

7.13 The authors refer to another logging controversy in another Sami reindeer herding area, where reindeer herdsmen had instituted proceedings against the Government because of planned logging and road construction activities in the Angeli district, and where the Government had argued that claims based on Article 27 of the Covenant should be declared inadmissible under domestic law. On 20 August 1993, the Court of First Instance at Inari held that the case was admissible but without merits, ordering the complainants to compensate the Government for its legal expenses. On 15 February 1994, the Court of Appeal of Rovaniemi invited the appellants in this case to attend an oral hearing, to take place on 22 March 1994. According to counsel, the Court of Appeal's decision to grant an oral hearing "cannot be taken as proof for the practical applicability of Article 27 of the Covenant as basis for court proceedings in Finland, but at least it leaves [this] possibility open".

7.14 In the light of the above, the authors conclude that their situation remains in abeyance at the domestic level.

[3] The case referred to is No 265/1987 (*Antti Vuolanne* v. *Finland*) [96 *ILR* 649], Views adopted on 7 April 1989.

Post-admissibility considerations

8.1 The Committee has taken note of the State Party's information, provided after the decision on admissibility, that the authors may avail themselves of local remedies in respect of road construction activities in the residual area, based on the fact that the Covenant may be invoked as part of domestic law and that claims based on Article 27 of the Covenant may be advanced before the Finnish courts. It takes the opportunity to expand on its admissibility findings.

8.2 In their submission of 25 March 1992, the authors concede that some Finnish courts have entertained claims based on Article 27 of the Covenant. From the submissions before the Committee it appears that Article 27 has seldom been invoked before the local courts or its content guided the *ratio decidendi* of court decisions. However, it is noteworthy, as counsel to the authors acknowledges, that the Finnish judicial authorities have become increasingly aware of the domestic relevance of international human rights standards, including the rights enshrined in the Covenant. This is true in particular for the Supreme Administrative Tribunal, and increasingly so for the Supreme Court and the lower courts.

8.3 In the circumstances, the Committee does not consider that a recent judgment of the Supreme Administrative Tribunal, which makes no reference to Article 27, should be seen as a negative precedent for the adjudication of the authors' own grievances. In the light of the developments referred to in paragraph 8.2 above, the authors' doubts about the courts' readiness to entertain claims based on Article 27 of the Covenant do not justify their failure to avail themselves of possibilities of domestic remedies which the State Party has plausibly argued are available and effective. The Committee further observes that according to counsel, the decision of the Court of Appeal of Rovaniemi in another comparable case, while not confirming the practical applicability of Article 27 before the local courts, at least leaves this possibility open. Thus, the Committee concludes that an administrative action challenging road construction activities in the residual area would not be *a priori* futile, and that the requirements of Article 5, paragraph 2(b), of the Optional Protocol have not been met.

8.4 The Committee takes note of counsel's comment that a delay until 1996 for the finalization of the CFB's plan for use and maintenance is expected and understands this as an indication that no further activities in the Hammastunturi Wilderness and the residual area will be undertaken by the State Party while the authors may pursue further domestic remedies.

9. The Human Rights Committee therefore *decides*:

(a) the decision of 9 July 1991 is set aside;

(b) that the communication is inadmissible under Article 5, paragraph 2(b), of the Optional Protocol;

(c) that this decision shall be communicated to the State Party, to the authors and to their counsel.

(Adopted in English, French and Spanish, the English text being the original version. Subsequently to be issued also in Arabic, Chinese and Russian as part of the Committee's annual report to the General Assembly.)

[Report: Doc. CCPR/C/50/D/431/1990]

Extradition — Capital offences — Offence carrying death penalty in requesting State but not in requested State— Right of requested State to seek assurances that death penalty will not be imposed—Canada–United States Extradition Treaty, 1976, Article 6—Decision by Canada to extradite fugitive without seeking assurances that death penalty would not be imposed—Whether contrary to International Covenant on Civil and Political Rights, 1966

Human rights — Right to life — Inhuman and degrading treatment or punishment — Threat of death penalty — Whether contrary to Article 6 of the International Covenant on Civil and Political Rights, 1966 — Article 6(2) — Application to State which has abolished death penalty— Article 7 — Relevance of "death row phenomenon" — Relevance of fact that author not yet tried or sentenced— Whether execution by lethal injection constituting inhuman or degrading treatment or punishment

Human rights—Scope of human rights treaty—International Covenant on Civil and Political Rights, 1966—Extradition proceedings—Threat of death sentence in requesting State

—Relevance of Article 3 of the Convention against Torture and Other Cruel, Inhuman or Degrading Treatment or Punishment, 1984

COX v. CANADA

(Communication No 539/1993)

United Nations Human Rights Committee.[1]   31 *October* 1994

SUMMARY: *The facts*:—The United States requested the extradition of the author, a United States citizen, from Canada to stand trial for murder in Pennsylvania. If convicted, the author could have been sentenced to death. In July 1991 the Superior Court of Quebec decided that the author should be extradited to the United States. Canada was permitted by Article 6 of the Canada–United States Extradition Treaty, 1976,[2] to seek assurances that the author would not be executed, as the death penalty had been abolished in Canada in 1976. The Minister of Justice, however, decided to proceed with the extradition without seeking such assurances.

The author claimed that the decision by Canada to extradite him violated Articles 6,[3] 7,[4] 14 and 26 of the International Covenant on Civil and Political Rights, 1966, since, if extradited, he maintained he would be treated in a way incompatible with the Covenant. He argued that black people were more likely to be sentenced to death in the United States and that he would suffer from the "death row phenomenon", contrary to Article 7 of the Covenant.

An earlier communication submitted by the author to the United Nations Human Rights Committee had been declared inadmissible on 29 July 1992 for lack of exhaustion of local remedies. Canada maintained that the communication was still inadmissible. The domestic remedies available under Canadian law, which involved an assessment of Canada's human rights obligations, included the availability of all avenues of judicial review to the fugitive before any extradition request was complied with. In this case no

---

[1] For the composition of the Committee, see p. 332, note 1.

[2] Article 6 of the Extradition Treaty provides that:
When the offence for which extradition is requested is punishable by death under the laws of the requesting State and the laws of the requested State do not permit such punishment for that offence, extradition may be refused unless the requesting State provides such assurances as the requested State considers sufficient that the death penalty shall not be imposed, or if imposed, shall not be executed.

[3] Article 6 of the Covenant provides that:
1. Every human being has the inherent right to life. This right shall be protected by law. No one shall be arbitrarily deprived of his life.
2. In countries which have not abolished the death penalty, sentence of death may only be imposed for the most serious crimes in accordance with the law in force at the time of the commission of the crime and not contrary to the provisions of the present Covenant and to the Convention on the Prevention and Punishment of the Crime of Genocide. This penalty can only be carried out pursuant to a final judgment rendered by a competent court.

[4] Article 7 of the Covenant provides that:
No one shall be subjected to torture or to cruel, inhuman or degrading treatment or punishment. In particular, no one shall be subjected without his free consent to medical or scientific experimentation.

exceptional circumstances existed to warrant seeking assurances regarding the death penalty. Canada contended that extradition was outside the scope of the Covenant and that, in any case, on the evidence submitted by the author, the communication was unsubstantiated. The author would not suffer a violation of his rights under Canadian law or under international instruments, including the Covenant, if extradited.

The author submitted that it would have been futile to attempt to exhaust domestic remedies any further, given recent decisions of the Canadian Supreme Court. He highlighted the United States reservation to Article 6 of the Covenant, which reiterated its right to impose the death penalty. He considered that extradition was within the scope of the Covenant and that, in any event, Articles 7 and 10 of the Covenant should be construed in accordance with the more recent and specialized Convention against Torture and Other Cruel, Inhuman or Degrading Treatment or Punishment, 1984, which, in Article 3, prohibited the extradition of a person to another State if there were serious grounds for believing that the person would be subjected to torture. On 3 November 1993 the Committee declared the communication admissible inasmuch as it might raise issues under Articles 6 and 7 of the Covenant.

Held:—(1) (Mrs Higgins and Messrs Francis, Herndl, Mavrommatis, Ndiaye and Sadi and Mrs Evatt dissenting) The Committee upheld its decision of 3 November 1993 on admissibility, having considered further arguments of Canada. The communication had been found admissible inasmuch as it might raise issues under Articles 6 and 7 of the Covenant (pp. 362 and 366).

(a) The author had exhausted all available domestic remedies as required by Article 5(2)(b) of the Optional Protocol to the Covenant (pp. 360-1).

(b) The communication was not excluded from consideration *ratione materiae*. The author had not claimed that extradition, which was outside the ambit of the Covenant, violated the Covenant but that its effects raised issues under certain Covenant provisions (p. 361).

(c) The evidence submitted by the author for admissibility purposes did not suggest that a real and present danger of a violation of Articles 14 and 26 was a foreseeable and necessary consequence of extradition. The Committee was not permitted to assess the compatibility with the Covenant of the laws and practices in another State. As the author had failed to demonstrate that the courts in Pennsylvania would have been likely to violate his rights under those Articles or provide an opportunity for redress in such a situation, this part of the communication was inadmissible under Article 2 of the Optional Protocol (pp. 361-2).

(d) The claim that failure to obtain assurances before extraditing the author violated the Covenant was to be considered on the merits (p. 362).

Individual opinion by Mrs Higgins (dissenting) (co-signed by Messrs Francis, Herndl, Mavrommatis, Ndiaye and Sadi): Although in agreement with the finding that, by reference to Article 2 of the Optional Protocol, the communication was inadmissible in relation to Articles 14 and 16 of the Covenant, it was difficult to see on what jurisdictional basis the Committee had found the communication to be admissible under Articles 6 and 7 of the Covenant. The

Committee should have applied the "foreseeable and necessary consequences" test, in which case, in these particular circumstances, there was no proper legal basis for jurisdiction. The author had failed to satisfy the test of "prospective victim" for the admissibility requirement under Article 1 of the Optional Protocol. Although it was not always necessary for the violation to have already occurred, in the case of the author, there had as yet been no trial and consequently no sentence to render a violation a foreseeable and necessary consequence of extradition (pp. 369-71).

Individual opinion by Mrs Evatt (dissenting): The communication was inadmissible under Articles 1 and 2 of the Optional Protocol. The author had failed to submit facts which substantiated the claim that he was subject to a real risk of a violation of his rights under Articles 6 and 7 of the Covenant if returned by Canada to the United States and was thus found not to be a victim. The author had not shown that there was a real risk that the imposition of the death penalty itself would have violated Article 6, as this was allowed in very specific circumstances and, in any event, his accomplices had only been sentenced to life imprisonment. Regarding Article 7, as there was no real risk of the author being sentenced to death, there was consequently no necessary and foreseeable consequence of a violation of his rights as a result of the "death row phenomenon" (p. 371).

(2) (Messrs Aguilar Urbina and Pocar, Ms Chanet, Messrs Lallah and Wennergren dissenting and Mr Bán partly dissenting): Canada would not violate any provision of the International Covenant on Civil and Political Rights in extraditing the author to the United States to face trial for a capital offence.

(a) A State party to the Covenant, which had abolished the death penalty, was itself at risk of violating the Covenant if it extradited an individual to a State where the death penalty was still applied if there was a real risk of a violation of the individual's rights under Article 6 of the Covenant in that State. There was an obligation for States parties to limit the use of the death penalty where it had not been abolished (p. 366).

(b) Article 6(1) of the Covenant was to be read in conjunction with Article 6(2), which allowed the imposition of the death penalty for the most serious crimes. The author had been charged with complicity in murders, and there was no evidence that he would not receive a fair hearing in the United States in accordance with the Covenant provisions (pp. 366-7).

(c) Given the proceedings, subject to appeal, in the Canadian courts, there was no requirement under Article 6(1) for Canada to seek assurances from the United States that the death penalty would not be imposed (p. 367).

(d) Although States parties had a duty to consider seriously their use of discretion involving the protection of life in the application of extradition treaties, Canada's decision to extradite without assurances had been reached after careful consideration as a result of the absence of exceptional circumstances, the fact that there would have been due process in the State of Pennsylvania and the desire to prevent Canada from becoming a safe haven for fugitives (pp. 367-8).

(e) There would have been no violation of the rights of the author as a result of the plea bargaining procedures which existed in Pennsylvania or as a result of racial discrimination (p. 368).

(f) There was no apparent violation of the author's rights under Article 7 of the Covenant. Regarding the "death row phenomenon", there were no specific factors offered relating to the mental condition of the author and no adverse evidence in relation to the state of prisons in Pennsylvania. The author had not been convicted as yet and his accomplices had only received sentences of life imprisonment. There was evidence from Canada that there was every opportunity to appeal and no contrary evidence that this was not available in a reasonable time. Neither had the potential use of the lethal injection for execution been found to violate Article 7 (p. 368).

Individual opinion by Messrs Herndl and Sadi: The communication should have been declared inadmissible under Articles 1 and 2 of the Optional Protocol as the requirements of the "victim" test had not been met. Given that there had been an examination on the merits, it was to be noted that, taken on the ordinary meaning of the words and in its context, Article 6 did not contain a prohibition on extradition. It was to be concluded that there was no prohibition under international law on extradition to face the death penalty. Regarding Article 7 in relation to the "death row phenomenon", it was agreed that there was no evidence to suggest that the State would have prolonged the wait on death row unreasonably (pp. 372-5).

Individual opinion by Mr Bán (partly concurring, partly dissenting): Although extradition to the United States to face a possible death sentence was not a violation of Article 6, there was a violation of Article 7, if extradition occurred without guarantees, in the prospect of a prolonged wait on death row, as the decisive factor was the psychological as opposed to the physical. The fact that the author had not yet been sentenced was irrelevant. There was no evidence that all of the appellate procedures would have been offered to the author or that Canada would not have been responsible for any unreasonable delay (pp. 375-7).

Individual opinion by Messrs Aguilar Urbina and Pocar (dissenting): There was a violation of Articles 6 and 7 of the Covenant. Having abolished capital punishment itself, Canada was obliged to seek assurances that there would be no imposition of the death penalty on extradition (pp. 377-8).

Individual opinion by Ms Chanet (dissenting): Article 6(1) was to be interpreted separately, and the Committee had erred in law in interpreting it together with Article 6(2). Canada had misread and failed to fulfil its obligations under the Covenant (pp. 379-81).

Individual opinion by Mr Lallah (dissenting): Canada had violated its obligations under Article 6(1) of the Covenant by not seeking assurances that the death penalty would not be imposed. The fact that the charge was punishable by the death penalty in principle rendered the fact that there had as yet been no trial or sentence irrelevant (p. 381).

Individual opinion by Mr Wennergren (dissenting): Canada had violated Article 6(1) when it decided to extradite the author without assurances that the death penalty would not be imposed. It was not possible to determine whether there was a violation of Article 7 with regard to the "death row phenomenon" without further information as to the current practice of the Pennsylvania criminal justice and penitentiary system (pp. 381-2).

The following is the text of the views of the Committee:

1. The author of the communication is Keith Cox, a citizen of the United States of America born in 1952, currently detained at a penitentiary in Montreal and facing extradition to the United States. He claims to be a victim of violations by Canada of Articles 6, 7, 14 and 26 of the International Covenant on Civil and Political Rights. The author had submitted an earlier communication which was declared inadmissible because of non-exhaustion of domestic remedies on 29 July 1992.[5]

The facts as submitted by the author

2.1 On 27 February 1991, the author was arrested at Laval, Quebec, for theft, a charge to which he pleaded guilty. While in custody, the judicial authorities received from the United States a request for his extradition, pursuant to the 1976 Extradition Treaty between Canada and the United States. The author is wanted in the State of Pennsylvania on two charges of first degree murder, relating to an incident that took place in Philadelphia in 1988. If convicted, the author could face the death penalty, although the two other accomplices were tried and sentenced to life terms.

2.2 Pursuant to the extradition request of the United States Government and in accordance with the Extradition Treaty, the Superior Court of Quebec, on 26 July 1991, ordered the author's extradition to the United States of America. Article 6 of the Treaty provides:

When the offence for which extradition is requested is punishable by death under the laws of the requesting State and the laws of the requested State do not permit such punishment for that offence, extradition may be refused unless the requesting State provides such assurances as the requested State considers sufficient that the death penalty shall not be imposed or, if imposed, shall not be executed.

Canada abolished the death penalty in 1976, except in the case of certain military offences.

2.3 The power to seek assurances that the death penalty will not be imposed is conferred on the Minister of Justice pursuant to Section 25 of the 1985 Extradition Act.

2.4 Concerning the course of the proceedings against the author, it

[5] Doc. CCPR/C/45/D/486/1992.

is stated that a habeas corpus application was filed on his behalf on 13 September 1991; he was represented by a legal aid representative. The application was dismissed by the Superior Court of Quebec. The author's representative appealed to the Court of Appeal of Quebec on 17 October 1991. On 25 May 1992, he abandoned his appeal, considering that, in the light of the Court's jurisprudence, it was bound to fail.

2.5 Counsel requests the Committee to adopt interim measures of protection because extradition of the author to the United States would deprive the Committee of its jurisdiction to consider the communication, and the author to properly pursue his communication.

The complaint

3. The author claims that the order to extradite him violates Articles 6, 14 and 26 of the Covenant; he alleges that the way death penalties are pronounced in the United States generally discriminates against black people. He further alleges a violation of Article 7 of the Covenant, in that he, if extradited and sentenced to death, would be exposed to "the death row phenomenon", i.e. years of detention under harsh conditions, awaiting execution.

Interim measures

4.1 On 12 January 1993 the Special *Rapporteur* on New Communications requested the State Party, pursuant to Rule 86 of the Committee's rules of procedure, to defer the author's extradition until the Committee had had an opportunity to consider the admissibility of the issues placed before it.

4.2 At its forty-seventh session the Committee decided to invite both the author and the State Party to make further submissions on admissibility.

The State Party's observations

5.1 The State Party, in its submission, dated 26 May 1993, submits that the communication should be declared inadmissible on the grounds that extradition is beyond the scope of the Covenant, or alternatively that, even if in exceptional circumstances the Committee could examine questions relating to extradition, the present communication is not substantiated, for purposes of admissibility.

5.2 With regard to domestic remedies, the State Party explains that extradition is a two-step process under Canadian law. The first step involves a hearing at which a judge examines whether a factual and legal basis for extradition exists. The judge considers *inter alia* the proper authentication of materials provided by the requesting State, admissibility and sufficiency of evidence, questions of identity and whether the conduct for which the extradition is sought constitutes a crime in Canada for which extradition can be granted. In the case of fugitives wanted for trial, the judge must be satisfied that the evidence is sufficient to warrant putting the fugitive on trial. The person sought for extradition may submit evidence at the judicial hearing, after which the judge decides whether the fugitive should be committed to await surrender to the requesting State.

5.3 Judicial review of a warrant of committal to await surrender can be sought by means of an application for a writ of habeas corpus in a provincial court. A decision of the judge on the habeas corpus application can be appealed to the provincial court of appeal and then, with leave, to the Supreme Court of Canada.

5.4 The second step of the extradition process begins following the exhaustion of the appeals in the judicial phase. The Minister of Justice is charged with the responsibility of deciding whether to surrender the person sought for extradition. The fugitive may make written submissions to the Minister, and counsel for the fugitive may appear before the Minister to present oral argument. In coming to a decision on surrender, the Minister considers the case record from the judicial phase, together with any written and oral submissions from the fugitive, the relevant treaty terms which pertain to the case to be decided and the law on extradition. While the Minister's decision is discretionary, the discretion is circumscribed by law. The decision is based upon a consideration of many factors, including Canada's obligations under the applicable treaty of extradition, facts particular to the person and the nature of the crime for which extradition is sought. In addition, the Minister must consider the terms of the Canadian Charter of Rights and Freedoms and the various instruments, including the Covenant, which outline Canada's international human rights obligations. A fugitive, subject to an extradition request, cannot be surrendered unless the Minister of Justice orders the fugitive surrendered and, in any case, not until all available avenues for judicial review of the Minister's decision, if pursued, are completed. For extradition requests before 1 December 1992, including the author's request, the Minister's decision is reviewable either by way of an application for a writ of habeas corpus in a provincial court or by way of judicial review in the Federal Court pursuant to Section 18 of the Federal Court Act. As with appeals against a warrant of committal, appeals against a review of the warrant of surrender can be pursued, with leave, up to the Supreme Court of Canada.

5.5 The courts can review the Minister's decision on jurisdictional grounds, i.e. whether the Minister acted fairly, in an administrative law sense, and for its consistency with the Canadian Constitution, in particular, whether the Minister's decision is consistent with Canada's human rights obligations.

5.6 With regard to the exercise of discretion in seeking assurances before extradition, the State Party explains that each extradition request from the United States, in which the possibility exists that the person sought may face the imposition of the death penalty, must be considered by the Minister of Justice and decided on its own particular facts.

Canada does not routinely seek assurances with respect to the non-imposition of the death penalty. The right to seek assurances is held in reserve for use only where exceptional circumstances exist. This policy . . . is in application of Article 6 of the Canada–United States Extradition Treaty. The Treaty was never intended to make the seeking of assurances a routine occurrence. Rather, it was the intention of the parties to the Treaty that assurances with respect to the death penalty should only be sought in circumstances where the particular facts of the case warrant a special exercise of the discretion. This policy represents a balancing of the rights of the individual sought for extradition with the need for the protection of the people of Canada. This policy reflects . . . Canada's understanding of and respect for the criminal justice system of the United States.

5.7 Moreover, the State Party refers to a continuing flow of criminal offenders from the United States into Canada and a concern that, unless such illegal flow is discouraged, Canada could become a safe haven for dangerous offenders from the United States, bearing in mind that Canada and the United States share a 4,800 kilometre unguarded border. In the last twelve years there has been an increasing number of extradition requests from the United States. In 1980 there were twenty-nine such requests; by 1992 the number had grown to eighty-eight, including requests involving death penalty cases, which were becoming a new and pressing problem.

A policy of routinely seeking assurances under Article 6 of the Canada–United States Extradition Treaty would encourage even more criminal offenders, especially those guilty of the most serious crimes, to flee the United States into Canada. Canada does not wish to become a haven for the most wanted and dangerous criminals from the United States. If the Covenant fetters Canada's discretion not to seek assurances, increasing numbers of criminals may come to Canada for the purpose of securing immunity from capital punishment.

6.1 As to the specific facts of the instant communication, the State Party indicates that Mr Cox is a black male, forty years of age, of sound mind and body, an American citizen with no immigration status in Canada. He is charged in the State of Pennsylvania with two counts of first degree murder, one count of robbery and one count of criminal conspiracy to commit murder and robbery, going back to an incident that occurred in Philadelphia, Pennsylvania, in 1988, where two teenage boys were killed pursuant to a plan to commit robbery in connection with illegal drug trafficking. Three men, one of whom is alleged to be Mr Cox, participated in the killings. In Pennsylvania, first degree murder is punishable by death or a term of life imprisonment. Lethal injection is the method of execution mandated by law.

6.2 With regard to the exhaustion of domestic remedies, the State Party indicates that Mr Cox was ordered committed to await extradition by a judge of the Quebec Superior Court on 26 July 1991. This order was challenged by the author in an application for habeas corpus before the Quebec Superior Court. The application was dismissed on 13 September 1991. Mr Cox then appealed to the Quebec Court of Appeal, and, on 18 February 1992, before exhausting domestic remedies in Canada, he submitted a communication to the Committee, which was registered under No 486/1992. Since the extradition process had not yet progressed to the second stage, the communication was ruled inadmissible by the Committee on 26 July 1992.

6.3 On 25 May 1992, Mr Cox withdrew his appeal to the Quebec Court of Appeal, thus concluding the judicial phase of the extradition process. The second stage, the ministerial phase, began. He petitioned the Minister of Justice asking that assurances be sought that the death penalty would not be imposed. In addition to written submissions, counsel for the author appeared before the Minister and made oral representations.

It was alleged that the judicial system in the state of Pennsylvania was inadequate and discriminatory. He submitted materials which purported to show that the Pennsylvania system of justice as it related to death penalty cases was characterized by inadequate legal representation of impoverished accused, a system of assignment of judges which resulted in a "death penalty court", selection of jury members which resulted in "death qualified juries" and an overall problem of racial discrimination. The Minister of Justice was of the view that the concerns based on alleged racial discrimination were premised largely on the possible intervention of a specific prosecutor in the state of Pennsylvania who, according to officials in that state, no longer has any connection with his case. It was alleged that, if returned to face possible imposition of the death penalty, Mr Cox would be exposed to the "death row phenomenon". The Minister of Justice was of the view that the submissions indicated that the conditions of incarceration in the state of Pennsylvania met the constitutional standards of the United States and that situations which needed improvement were being addressed . . . it was argued that assurances be sought on the basis that there is a growing international movement for the abolition of the death penalty . . . The Minister of Justice, in coming to the decision to order surrender without assurances, concluded that Mr Cox had failed to show that his rights would be violated in the state of Pennsylvania in any way particular to him, which could not be addressed by judicial review in the United States Supreme Court under the Constitution of the United States. That is, the Minister determined that the matters raised by Mr Cox could be left to the internal working of the United States system of justice, a system which sufficiently corresponds to Canadian concepts of justice and fairness to warrant entering into and maintaining the Canada–United States Extradition Treaty.

On 2 January 1993, the Minister, having determined that there existed no exceptional circumstances pertaining to the author which necessitated the seeking of assurances in his case, ordered him surrendered without assurances.

6.4 On 4 January 1993, the author's counsel sought to reactivate his earlier communication to the Committee. He has indicated to the Government of Canada that he does not propose to appeal the Minister's decision in the Canadian courts. The State Party, however, does not contest the admissibility of the communication on this issue.

7.1 As to the scope of the Covenant, the State Party contends that extradition *per se* is beyond its scope and refers to the *travaux préparatoires*, showing that the drafters of the Covenant specifically considered and rejected a proposal to deal with extradition in the Covenant. "It was argued that the inclusion of a provision on extradition in the Covenant would cause difficulties regarding the relationship of the Covenant to existing treaties and bilateral agreements." (A/2929, Chapt. VI, para. 72). In the light of the history of negotiations during the drafting of the Covenant, the State Party submits

that a decision to extend the Covenant to extradition treaties or to individual decisions pursuant thereto, would stretch the principles governing the interpretation of the Covenant, and of human rights instruments in general, in unreasonable and unacceptable ways. It would be unreasonable because the principles of interpretation which recognize that human rights instruments are living documents and that human rights evolve over time cannot be employed in the face of express limits to the application of a given document. The absence of extradition from the articles of the Covenant when read with the intention of the drafters must be taken as an express limitation.

7.2 As to the author's standing as a "victim" under Article 1 of the Optional Protocol, the State Party concedes that he is subject to Canada's jurisdiction during the time he is in Canada in the extradition process. However, the State Party submits

that Cox is not a victim of any violation in Canada of rights set forth in the Covenant . . . because the Covenant does not set forth any rights with respect to extradition. In the alternative, it contends that even if [the] Covenant extends to extradition, it can only apply to the treatment of the fugitive sought for extradition with respect to the operation of the extradition process within the State Party to the Protocol. Possible treatment of the fugitive in the requesting State cannot be the subject of a communication with respect to the State Party to the Protocol (extraditing State), except perhaps for instances where there was evidence before that extraditing State such that a violation of the Covenant in the requesting State was reasonably foreseeable.

7.3 The State Party contends that the evidence submitted by author's counsel to the Committee and to the Minister of Justice in

Canada does not show that it was reasonably foreseeable that the treatment that the author may face in the United States would violate his rights under the Covenant. The Minister of Justice and the Canadian courts, to the extent that the author availed himself of the opportunities for judicial review, considered all the evidence and argument submitted by counsel and concluded that Mr Cox's extradition to the United States to face the death penalty would not violate his rights, either under Canadian law or under international instruments, including the Covenant. Thus, the State Party concludes that the communication is inadmissible because the author has failed to substantiate, for purposes of admissibility, that the author is a victim of any violation in Canada of rights set forth in the Covenant.

Counsel's submissions on admissibility

8.1 In his submission of 7 April 1993, author's counsel argues that an attempt to further exhaust domestic remedies in Canada would be futile in the light of the judgment of the Canadian Supreme Court in the cases of *Kindler* and *Ng*.

I chose to file the communication and apply for interim measures prior to discontinuing the appeal. This move was taken because I presumed that a discontinuance in the appeal might result in the immediate extradition of Mr Cox. It was more prudent to seize the Committee first, and then discontinue the appeal, and I think this precaution was a wise one, because Mr Cox is still in Canada . . . Subsequent to discontinuation of the appeal, I filed an application before the Minister of Justice, Kim Campbell, praying that she exercise her discretionary power under Article 6 of the Extradition Act, and refuse to extradite Mr Cox until an assurance had been provided by the United States government that if Mr Cox were to be found guilty, the death penalty would not be applied . . . I was granted a hearing before Minister Campbell, on November 13, 1992. In reasons dated January 2, 1993 Minister Campbell refused to exercise her discretion and refused to seek assurances from the United States government that the death penalty not be employed . . . It is possible to apply for judicial review of the decision of Minister Campbell, on the narrow grounds of breach of natural justice or other gross irregularity. However, there is no suggestion of any grounds to justify such recourse, and consequently no such dilatory recourse has been taken . . . all useful and effective domestic remedies to contest the extradition of Mr Cox have been exhausted.

8.2 Counsel contends that the extradition of Mr Cox would expose him to the real and present danger of:

a. arbitrary execution, in violation of Article 6 of the Covenant;

b. discriminatory imposition of the death penalty, in violation of Articles 6 and 26 of the Covenant;

c. imposition of the death penalty in breach of fundamental procedural safeguards, specifically by an impartial jury (the phenomenon of "death qualified" juries), in violation of Articles 6 and 14 of the Covenant;

d. prolonged detention on "death row", in violation of Article 7 of the Covenant.

8.3 With respect to the system of criminal justice in the United States, author's counsel refers to the reservations which the United States formulated upon its ratification of the Covenant, in particular to Article 6:

The United States reserves the right, subject to its Constitutional constraints, to impose capital punishment on any person (other than a pregnant woman) duly convicted under existing or future laws permitting the imposition of capital punishment, including such punishment for crimes committed by persons below eighteen years of age.

Author's counsel argues that this is

an enormously broad reservation that no doubt is inconsistent with the nature and purpose of the treaty but that furthermore . . . creates a presumption that the United States does not intend to respect Article 6 of the Covenant.

9.1 In his comments, dated 10 June 1993, on the State Party's submission, counsel addresses the refusal of the Minister to seek assurances on the non-imposition of the death penalty, and refers to the book *La Forest's Extradition to and from Canada,* in which it is stated that Canada in fact routinely seeks such an undertaking. Moreover, the author contests the State Party's interpretation that it was not the intention of the drafters of the Extradition Treaty that assurances be routinely sought.

It is known that the provision in the extradition treaty with the United States was added at the request of the United States. Does Canada have any evidence admissible in a court of law to support such a questionable claim? I refuse to accept the suggestion in the absence of any serious evidence.

9.2 As to the State Party's argument that extradition is intended to protect Canadian society, author's counsel challenges the State Party's belief that a policy of routinely seeking guarantees will encourage criminal law offenders to seek refuge in Canada and contends that there is no evidence to support such a belief. Moreover, with regard to Canada's concern that if the United States does not give assurances, Canada would be unable to extradite and have to keep the criminal without trial, author's counsel argues that

a state government so devoted to the death penalty as a supreme punishment for an offender would surely prefer to obtain extradition and keep the offender in life imprisonment rather than to see the offender freed in Canada. I know of two cases where the guarantee was sought from the United States, one for extradition from the United Kingdom to the state of Virginia (*Soering*) and one for extradition from Canada to the state of Florida (*O'Bomsawin*). In both cases the states willingly gave the guarantee. It is pure demagogy for Canada to raise the spectre of "a haven for many fugitives from the death penalty" in the absence of evidence.

9.3 As to the murders of which Mr Cox was accused, author's counsel indicates that

two individuals have pleaded guilty to the crime and are now serving life prison terms in Pennsylvania. Each individual has alleged that the other individual actually committed the murder, and that Keith Cox participated.

9.4 With regard to the scope of the Covenant, counsel refers to the *travaux préparatoires* of the Covenant and argues that consideration of the issue of extradition must be placed within the context of the debate on the right to asylum, and claims that extradition was in fact a minor point in the debates. Moreover,

nowhere in the summary records is there evidence of a suggestion that the Covenant would not apply to extradition requests when torture or cruel, inhuman and degrading punishment might be imposed . . . Germane to the construction of the Covenant, and to Canada's affirmations about the scope of human rights law, is the more recent Convention against Torture and Other Cruel, Inhuman or Degrading Treatment or Punishment, which provides, in Article 3, that States parties shall not extradite a person to another State where there are serious grounds to believe that the person will be subjected to torture . . . It is respectfully submitted that it is appropriate to construe Articles 7 and 10 of the Covenant in light of the more detailed provisions in the Convention against Torture. Both instruments were drafted by the same organization, and are parts of the same international human rights system. The Convention against Torture was meant to give more detailed and specialized protection; it is an enrichment of the Covenant.

9.5 As to the concept of victim under the Optional Protocol, author's counsel contends that this is not a matter for admissibility but for the examination of the merits.

Issues and proceedings before the Committee

10.1 Before considering any claims contained in a communication, the Human Rights Committee must, in accordance with Rule 87 of its rules of procedure, decide whether or not the communication is admissible under the Optional Protocol to the Covenant.

10.2 With regard to the requirement of the exhaustion of domestic remedies, the Committee noted that the author did not complete the judicial phase of examination, since he withdrew the appeal to the Court of Appeal after being advised that it would have no prospect of success and, therefore, that legal aid would not be provided for that purpose. With regard to the ministerial phase, the author indicated that he did not intend to appeal the Minister's decision to surrender Mr Cox without seeking assurances, since, as he asserts, further recourse to domestic remedies would have been futile in the light of the 1991 judgment of the Canadian Supreme Court in *Kindler* and *Ng*.[6] The Committee noted that the State Party had explicitly stated that it did not wish to express a view as to whether the author had exhausted domestic remedies and did not contest the admissibility of the communication on this ground. In the circumstances, basing itself on the information before it, the Committee concluded that the requirements of Article 5, paragraph 2(b), of the Covenant had been met.

10.3 Extradition as such is outside the scope of application of the Covenant (Communication No 117/1981 (*MA* v. *Italy*)[7] paragraph 13.4: "There is no provision of the Covenant making it unlawful for a State party to seek extradition of a person from another country"). Extradition is an important instrument of cooperation in the administration of justice, which requires that safe havens should not be provided for those who seek to evade fair trial for criminal offences, or who escape after such fair trial has occurred. But a State party's obligation in relation to a matter itself outside the scope of the Covenant may still be engaged by reference to other provisions of the Covenant.[8] In the present case the author does not claim that extradition as such violates the Covenant, but rather that the particular circumstances related to the effects of his extradition would raise issues under specific provisions of the Covenant. The Committee finds that the communication is thus not excluded from consideration *ratione materiae*.

10.4 With regard to the allegations that, if extradited, Mr Cox would be exposed to a real and present danger of a violation of Articles 14 and 26 of the Covenant in the United States, the Committee observed that the evidence submitted did not substantiate, for purposes of admissibility, that such violations would be a foreseeable and necessary consequence of extradition. It does not suffice to assert before the Committee that the criminal justice system in the United States is incompatible with the Covenant. In this connection, the

[6] The Supreme Court found that the decision of the Minister to extradite Mr Kindler and Mr Ng without seeking assurances that the death penalty would not be imposed or, if imposed, would not be carried out, did not violate their rights under the Canadian Charter of Rights and Freedoms. [98 *ILR* 370 and 473].

[7] 79 *ILR* 242.]

[8] See the Committee's decisions in Communications Nos 35/1978 (*Aumeeruddy-Cziffra et al.* v. *Mauritius*, Views adopted on 9 April 1981 [62 *ILR* 285]) and 291/1988 (*Torres* v. *Finland*, Views adopted on 2 April 1990).

Committee recalled its jurisprudence that, under the Optional Protocol procedure, it cannot examine *in abstracto* the compatibility with the Covenant of the laws and practice of a State.[9] For purposes of admissibility, the author has to substantiate that in the specific circumstances of his case, the courts in Pennsylvania would be likely to violate his rights under Articles 14 and 26, and that he would not have a genuine opportunity to challenge such violations in United States courts. The author has failed to do so. This part of the communication is therefore inadmissible under Article 2 of the Optional Protocol.

10.5 The Committee considered that the remaining claim, that Canada violated the Covenant by deciding to extradite Mr Cox without seeking assurances that the death penalty would not be imposed or, if imposed, would not be carried out, may raise issues under Articles 6 and 7 of the Covenant which should be examined on the merits.

11. On 3 November 1993, the Human Rights Committee decided that the communication was admissible in so far as it may raise issues under Articles 6 and 7 of the Covenant. The Committee reiterated its request to the State Party, under Rule 86 of the Committee's rules of procedure, that the author not be extradited while the Committee is examining the merits of the communication.

State Party's request for review of admissibility and submission on the merits

12.1 In its submission under Article 4, paragraph 2, of the Optional Protocol, the State Party maintains that the communication is inadmissible and requests the Committee to review its decision of 3 November 1993. The State Party also submits its response on the merits of the communication.

12.2 With regard to the notion of "victim" within the meaning of Article 1 of the Optional Protocol, the State Party indicates that Mr Keith Cox has not been convicted of any crime in the United States, and that the evidence submitted does not substantiate, for purposes of admissibility, that violations of Articles 6 and 7 of the Covenant would be a foreseeable and necessary consequence of his extradition.

12.3 The State Party explains the extradition process in Canada, with specific reference to the practice in the context of the Canada–United States Extradition Treaty. It elaborates on the judicial phase, which includes a methodical and thorough evaluation of the facts of each case. After the exhaustion of the appeals in the judicial phase, a second phase of review follows, in which the Minister of Justice is charged with the responsibility of deciding whether to surrender the person for extradition, and in capital cases, whether the facts of the particular case justify seeking assurances that the death

---

[9] Views in Communication No 61/1979, *Leo Hertzberg et al.* v. *Finland*, para. 9.3 [70 *ILR* 297].

penalty will not be imposed. Throughout this process the fugitive can present his arguments against extradition, and his counsel may appear before the Minister to present oral argument both on the question of surrender and, where applicable, on the seeking of assurances. The Minister's decision is also subject to judicial review. In numerous cases, the Supreme Court of Canada has had occasion to review the exercise of the ministerial discretion on surrender, and has held that the right to life and the right not to be deprived thereof except in accordance with the principles of fundamental justice, apply to ministerial decisions on extradition.

12.4 With regard to the facts particular to Mr Keith Cox, the State Party reviews his submissions before the Canadian courts, the Minister of Justice (see paras. 6.2 and 6.3 *supra*) and before the Committee and concludes that the evidence adduced fails to show how Mr Cox satisfies the criterion of being a "victim" within the meaning of Article 1 of the Optional Protocol. Firstly, it has not been alleged that the author has already suffered any violation of his Covenant rights; secondly, it is not reasonably foreseeable that he would become a victim after extradition to the United States. The State Party cites statistics from the Pennsylvania District Attorney's Office and indicates that since 1976, when Pennsylvania's current death penalty law was enacted, no one has been put to death; moreover, the Pennsylvania legal system allows for several appeals. But not only has Mr Cox not been tried, he has not been convicted, nor sentenced to death. In this connection the State Party notes that the two other individuals who were alleged to have committed the crimes together with Mr Cox were not given death sentences but are serving life sentences. Moreover, the death penalty is not sought in all murder cases. Even if sought, it cannot be imposed in the absence of aggravating factors which must outweigh any mitigating factors. Referring to the Committee's jurisprudence in the *Aumeeruddy-Cziffra* case that the alleged victim's risk be "more than a theoretical possibility", the State Party states that no evidence has been submitted to the Canadian courts or to the Committee which would indicate a real risk of his becoming a victim. The evidence submitted by Mr Cox is either not relevant to him or does not support the view that his rights would be violated in a way that he could not properly challenge in the courts of Pennsylvania and of the United States. The State Party concludes that since Mr Cox has failed to substantiate, for purposes of admissibility, his allegations, the communication should be declared inadmissible under Article 2 of the Optional Protocol.

13.1 As to the merits of the case, the State Party refers to the Committee's Views in the *Kindler* and *Ng* cases, which settled a number of matters concerning the application of the Covenant to extradition cases.

13.2 As to the application of Article 6, the State Party relies on the Committee's view that paragraph 1 (right to life) must be read together with paragraph 2 (imposition of the death penalty), and that a State party would violate Article 6, paragraph 1, if it extradited a person to face possible imposition of the death penalty in a requesting State where there was a real risk of a violation of Article 6, paragraph 2.

13.3 Whereas Mr Cox alleges that he would face a real risk of a violation of Article 6 of the Covenant because the United States "does not respect the prohibition on the execution of minors", the State Party indicates that Mr Cox is over forty years of age. As to the other requirements of Article 6, paragraph 2, of the Covenant, the State Party indicates that Mr Cox is charged with murder, which is a very serious criminal offence, and that if the death sentence were to be imposed on him, there is no evidence suggesting that it would not be pursuant to a final judgment rendered by a court.

13.4 As to hypothetical violations of Mr Cox's rights to a fair trial, the State Party recalls that the Committee declared the communication inadmissible with respect to Articles 14 and 26 of the Covenant, since the author had not substantiated his allegations for purposes of admissibility. Moreover, Mr Cox has not shown that he would not have a genuine opportunity to challenge such violations in the courts of the United States.

13.5 As to Article 7 of the Covenant, the State Party first addresses the method of judicial execution in Pennsylvania, which is by lethal injection. This method was recently provided for by the Pennsylvania legislature, because it was considered to inflict the least suffering. The State Party further indicates that the Committee, in its decision in the *Kindler* case, which similarly involved the possible judicial execution by lethal injection in Pennsylvania, found no violation of Article 7.

13.6 The State Party then addresses the submissions of counsel for Mr Cox with respect to alleged conditions of detention in Pennsylvania. It indicates that the material submitted is out of date and refers to recent substantial improvements in the Pennsylvania prisons, particularly in the conditions of incarceration of inmates under sentence of death. At present these prisoners are housed in new modern units where cells are larger than cells in other divisions, and inmates are permitted to have radios and televisions in their cells, and to have access to institutional programmes and activities such as counselling, religious services, education programmes, and access to the library.

13.7 With regard to the so-called "death row phenomenon", the State Party distinguishes the facts of the Cox case from those in the *Soering* v. *United Kingdom*[10] judgment of the European Court of Human

[[10] 98 *ILR* 270.]

Rights. The decision in *Soering* turned not only on the admittedly bad conditions in some prisons in the State of Virginia, but also on the tenuous state of health of Mr Soering. Mr Cox has not been shown to be in a fragile mental or physical state. He is neither a youth, nor elderly. In this connection, the State Party refers to the Committee's jurisprudence in the *Vuolanne* v. *Finland* case, where it held that

the assessment of what constitutes inhuman or degrading treatment falling within the meaning of Article 7 depends on all the circumstances of the case, such as the duration and manner of the treatment, its physical or mental effects as well as the sex, age and state of health of the victim.[11]

13.8 As to the effects of prolonged detention, the State Party refers to the Committee's jurisprudence that the "death row phenomenon" does not violate Article 7, if it consists only of prolonged periods of delay on death row while appellate remedies are pursued. In the case of Mr Cox, it is not at all clear that he will reach death row or that he will remain there for a lengthy period of time pursuing appeals.

Author's comments

14.1 In his comments on the State Party's submission, counsel for Mr Cox stresses that the State of Pennsylvania has stated in its extradition application that the death penalty is being sought. Accordingly, the prospect of execution is not so very remote.

14.2 With regard to Article 7 of the Covenant, author's counsel contends that the use of plea bargaining in a death penalty case meets the definition of torture.

What Canada is admitting . . . is that Mr Cox will be offered a term of life imprisonment instead of the death penalty *if he pleads guilty*. In other words, if he admits to the crime he will avoid the physical suffering which is inherent in imposition of the death penalty.

14.3 As to the method of execution, author's counsel admits that no submissions had been made on this subject in the original communication. Nevertheless, he contends that execution by lethal injection would violate Article 7 of the Covenant. He argues, on the basis of a deposition by Professor Michael Radelet of the University of Florida, that there are many examples of "botched" executions by lethal injection.

14.4 As to the "death row phenomenon", counsel for Mr Cox specifically requests that the Committee reconsider its case-law and conclude that there is a likely violation of Article 7 in Mr Cox's case, since "nobody has been executed in Pennsylvania for more than

[11] Views in Communication No 265/1987, *Vuolanne* v. *Finland*, para. 9.2 [96 *ILR* 649].

twenty years, and there are individuals awaiting execution on death row for as much as fifteen years".

14.5 Although the Committee declared the communication inadmissible as to Articles 14 and 26 of the Covenant, author's counsel contends that Article 6 of the Covenant would be violated if the death penalty were to be imposed "arbitrarily" on Mr Cox because he is black. He claims that there is systemic racism in the application of the death penalty in the United States.

Merits

15. The Committee has taken note of the State Party's information and arguments on admissibility, submitted after the Committee's decision of 3 November 1993. It observes that no new facts or arguments have been submitted that would justify a reversal of the Committee's decision on admissibility. Therefore, the Committee proceeds to the examination of the merits.

16.1 With regard to a potential violation by Canada of Article 6 of the Covenant if it were to extradite Mr Cox to face the possible imposition of the death penalty in the United States, the Committee refers to the criteria set forth in its Views on Communications Nos 470/1991 (*Kindler* v. *Canada*[12] and 469/1991 *Chitat Ng* v. *Canada*[13]). Namely, for States that have abolished capital punishment and are called to extradite a person to a country where that person may face the imposition of the death penalty, the extraditing State must ensure that the person is not exposed to a real risk of a violation of his rights under Article 6 in the receiving State. In other words, if a State party to the Covenant takes a decision relating to a person within its jurisdiction, and the necessary and foreseeable consequence is that that person's rights under the Covenant will be violated in another jurisdiction, the State party itself may be in violation of the Covenant. In this context, the Committee also recalls its General Comment on Article 6,[14] which provides that while States parties are not obliged to abolish the death penalty, they are obliged to limit its use.

16.2 The Committee notes that Article 6, paragraph 1, must be read together with Article 6, paragraph 2, which does not prohibit the imposition of the death penalty for the most serious crimes. Canada, while not itself imposing the death penalty on Mr Cox, is asked to extradite him to the United States, where he may face capital punishment. If Mr Cox were to be exposed, through extradition from Canada, to a real risk of a violation of Article 6, paragraph 2, in the United States, that would entail a violation by Canada of its obligations under Article 6, paragraph 1. Among the requirements of

[12] 98 *ILR* 426.]
[13] 98 *ILR* 479.]
[14] General Comment No 6/16 of 27 July 1982, para. 6.

Article 6, paragraph 2, is that capital punishment be imposed only for the most serious crimes, in circumstances not contrary to the Covenant and other instruments, and that it be carried out pursuant to a final judgment rendered by a competent court. The Committee notes that Mr Cox is to be tried for complicity in two murders, undoubtedly very serious crimes. He was over eighteen years of age when the crimes were committed. The author has not substantiated his claim before the Canadian courts or before the Committee that trial in the Pennsylvania courts with the possibility of appeal would not be in accordance with his right to a fair hearing as required by the Covenant.

16.3 Moreover, the Committee observes that the decision to extradite Mr Cox to the United States followed proceedings in the Canadian courts at which Mr Cox's counsel was able to present argument. He was also able to present argument at the ministerial phase of the proceedings, which themselves were subject to appeal. In the circumstances, the Committee finds that the obligations arising under Article 6, paragraph 1, did not require Canada to refuse the author's extradition without assurances that the death penalty would not be imposed.

16.4 The Committee notes that Canada itself, save for certain categories of military offences, abolished capital punishment; it is not, however, a party to the Second Optional Protocol to the Covenant. As to whether the fact that Canada has generally abolished capital punishment, taken together with its obligations under the Covenant, required it to refuse extradition or to seek the assurances it was entitled to seek under the Extradition Treaty, the Committee observes that the domestic abolition of capital punishment does not release Canada of its obligations under extradition treaties. However, it is in principle to be expected that, when exercising a permitted discretion under an extradition treaty (namely, whether or not to seek assurances that capital punishment will not be imposed) a State which has itself abandoned capital punishment would give serious consideration to its own chosen policy in making its decision. The Committee observes, however, that the State Party has indicated that the possibility to seek assurances would normally be exercised where exceptional circumstances existed. Careful consideration was given to this possibility. The Committee notes the reasons given by Canada not to seek assurances in Mr Cox's case, in particular, the absence of exceptional circumstances, the availability of due process in the State of Pennsylvania, and the importance of not providing a safe haven for those accused of or found guilty of murder.

16.5 While States parties must be mindful of the possibilities for the protection of life when exercising their discretion in the application of extradition treaties, the Committee finds that Canada's decision to extradite without assurances was not taken arbitrarily or summarily. The evidence before the Committee reveals that the Minister of Justice reached a decision after hearing argument in favour of seeking assurances.

16.6 The Committee notes that the author claims that the plea bargaining procedures, by which capital punishment could be avoided if he were to plead guilty, further violate his rights under the Covenant. The Committee finds this not to be so in the context of the criminal justice system in Pennsylvania.

16.7 With regard to the allegations of systemic racial discrimination in the United States criminal justice system, the Committee does not find, on the basis of the submissions before it, that Mr Cox would be subject to a violation of his rights by virtue of his colour.

17.1 The Committee has further considered whether in the specific circumstances of this case, being held on death row would constitute a violation of Mr Cox's rights under Article 7 of the Covenant. While confinement on death row is necessarily stressful, no specific factors relating to Mr Cox's mental condition have been brought to the attention of the Committee. The Committee notes also that Canada has submitted specific information about the current state of prisons in Pennsylvania, in particular with regard to the facilities housing inmates under sentence of death, which would not appear to violate Article 7 of the Covenant.

17.2 As to the period of detention on death row in reference to Article 7, the Committee notes that Mr Cox has not yet been convicted nor sentenced, and that the trial of the two accomplices in the murders of which Mr Cox is also charged did not end with sentences of death but rather of life imprisonment. Under the jurisprudence of the Committee,[15] on the one hand, every person confined to death row must be afforded the opportunity to pursue all possibilities of appeal, and, on the other hand, the State party must ensure that the possibilities for appeal are made available to the condemned prisoner within a reasonable time. Canada has submitted specific information showing that persons under sentence of death in the State of Pennsylvania are given every opportunity to avail themselves of several appeal instances, as well as opportunities to seek pardon or clemency. The author has not adduced evidence to show that these procedures are not made available within a reasonable time, or that there are unreasonable delays which would be imputable to the State. In these circumstances, the Committee finds that the extradition

[15] Views in Communications Nos 210/1986 and 225/1987, *Earl Pratt and Ivan Morgan* v. *Jamaica*, para. 13.6 [98 *ILR* 322]; No 250/1987, *Carlton Reid* v. *Jamaica*, para. 11.6 [98 *ILR* 357]; Nos 270/1988 and 271/1988, *Randolph Barrett and Clyde Sutcliffe* v. *Jamaica*, para. 8.4; No 274/1988, *Loxley Griffith* v. *Jamaica*, para. 7.4; No 317/1988, *Howard Martin* v. *Jamaica*, para. 12.1; No 470/1991, *Kindler* v. *Canada*, para. 15.2 [98 *ILR* 426].

of Mr Cox to the United States would not entail a violation of Article 7 of the Covenant.

17.3 With regard to the method of execution, the Committee has already had the opportunity of examining the *Kindler* case, in which the potential judicial execution by lethal injection was not found to be in violation of Article 7 of the Covenant.

18. The Committee, acting under Article 5, paragraph 4, of the Optional Protocol, finds that the facts before it do not sustain a finding that the extradition of Mr Cox to face trial for a capital offence in the United States would constitute a violation by Canada of any provision of the International Covenant on Civil and Political Rights.

[Adopted in English, French and Spanish, the English text being the original version. Subsequently to be issued also in Arabic, Chinese and Russian as part of the Committee's annual report to the General Assembly.]

APPENDICES

A. *Individual opinions appended to the Committee's decision on admissibility of 3 November 1993*

1. *Individual opinion by Mrs Rosalyn Higgins, co-signed by Messrs Laurel Francis, Kurt Herndl, Andreas Mavrommatis, Birame Ndiaye and Waleed Sadi (dissenting)*
We believe that this case should have been declared inadmissible. Although extradition as such is outside the scope of the Covenant (see *MA* v. *Italy*,[16] Communication No 117/1981, decision of 10 April 1984, paragraph 13.4), the Committee has explained, in its decision on Communication No 470/1991 (*Joseph Kindler* v. *Canada*,[17] Views adopted on 30 July 1993), that a State party's obligations in relation to a matter itself outside the scope of the Covenant may still be engaged by reference to other provisions of the Covenant.

But here, as elsewhere, the admissibility requirements under the Optional Protocol must be met. In its decision on *Kindler*, the Committee addressed the issue of whether it had jurisdiction, *ratione loci*, by reference to Article 2 of the Optional Protocol, in an extradition case that brought into play other provisions of the Covenant. It observed that

if a State party takes a decision relating to a person within its jurisdiction, and the necessary and foreseeable consequence is that the person's rights under the Covenant will be violated in another jurisdiction, the State party itself may be in violation of the Covenant (paragraph 6.2).

[[16] 79 *ILR* 242.]   [[17] 98 *ILR* 426.]

We do not see on what jurisdictional basis the Committee proceeds to its finding that the communication is admissible under Articles 6 and 7 of the Covenant. The Committee finds that the communication is inadmissible by reference to Article 2 of the Optional Protocol (paragraph 10.4) in so far as claims relating to fair trial (Article 14) and discrimination before the law (Article 26) are concerned. We agree. But this negative finding cannot form a basis for admissibility in respect of Articles 6 and 7. The Committee should have applied the same test ("foreseeable and necessary consequences") to the claims made under Articles 6 and 7, before simply declaring them admissible in respect of those Articles. It did not do so—and in our opinion could not have found, in the particular circumstances of the case, a proper legal basis for jurisdiction had it done so.

The above test is relevant also to the admissibility requirement, under Article 1 of the Optional Protocol, that an author be a "victim" of a violation in respect of which he brings a claim. In other words, it is not always necessary that a violation already have occurred for an action to come within the scope of Article 1. But the violation that will affect him personally must be a "necessary and foreseeable consequence" of the action of the defendant State.

It is clear that in the case of Mr Cox, unlike in the case of Mr Kindler, this test is not met. Mr Kindler had, at the time of the Canadian decision to extradite him, been tried in the United States for murder, found guilty as charged and recommended to the death sentence by the jury. Mr Cox, by contrast, has not yet been tried and *a fortiori* has not been found guilty or recommended to the death penalty. Already it is clear that his extradition would *not* entail the possibility of a "necessary and foreseeable consequence of a violation of his rights" that would require examination on the merits. This failure to meet the test of "prospective victim" within the meaning of Article 1 of the Optional Protocol is emphasized by the fact that Mr Cox's two co-defendants in the case in which he has been charged have already been tried in the State of Pennsylvania, and sentenced not to death but to a term of life imprisonment.

The fact that the Committee—and rightly so in our view—found that *Kindler* raised issues that needed to be considered on their merits, and that the admissibility criteria were there met, does not mean that every extradition case of this nature is necessarily admissible. In every case, the tests relevant to Articles 1, 2, 3 and 5, paragraph 2, of the Optional Protocol must be applied to the particular facts of the case.

The Committee has not at all addressed the requirements of Article 1 of the Optional Protocol, that is, whether Mr Cox may be considered a "victim" by reference to his claims under Articles 14, 26, 6 or 7 of the Covenant.

We therefore believe that Mr Cox was not a "victim" within the meaning of Article 1 of the Optional Protocol, and that his communication to the Human Rights Committee is inadmissible.

The duty to address carefully the requirements for admissibility under the Optional Protocol is not made the less necessary because capital punishment is somehow involved in a complaint.

For all these reasons, we believe that the Committee should have found the present communication inadmissible.

[Original: English]

2. Individual opinion by Mrs Elizabeth Evatt (dissenting)

For his claim to be admissible, the author must show that he is a victim. To do this he must submit facts which support the conclusion that his extradition exposed him to a real risk that his rights under Articles 6 and 7 of the Covenant would be violated (in the sense that the violation is necessary and foreseeable). The author in the present case has not done so.

As to Article 6, the author is, of course, exposed by his extradition to the risk of facing the death penalty for the crime of which he is accused. But he has not submitted facts to show a real risk that the imposition of the death penalty would itself violate Article 6, which does not exclude the death penalty in certain limited circumstances. Furthermore, his accomplices in the crime he is charged with were sentenced to life imprisonment, a factor which does not support the contention that the author's extradition would expose him to a "necessary and foreseeable" risk that the death penalty will be imposed.

As to Article 7, the claim that the author has been exposed to a real risk of a violation of this provision by his extradition is based on the death row phenomenon (paragraph 8.2); the author has not, however, submitted facts which, in the light of the Committee's jurisprudence, show that there is a real risk of violation of this Article if he is extradited to the United States. Furthermore, since, in my opinion, the author's extradition does not expose him to a real risk of being sentenced to death, his extradition entails *a fortiori* no necessary and foreseeable consequence of a violation of his rights while on death row.

For these reasons I am of the view that the communication is inadmissible under Articles 1 and 2 of the Optional Protocol.

[Original: English]

B. *Individual opinions appended to the Committee's Views*

1. *Individual opinion by Messrs Kurt Herndl and Waleed Sadi (concurring)*
We concur with the Committee's finding that the facts of the instant case do not reveal a violation of either Article 6 or Article 7 of the Covenant.

In our opinion, however, it would have been more consistent with the Committee's jurisprudence to set aside the decision on admissibility of 3 November 1993 and to declare the communication inadmissible under Articles 1 and 2 of the Optional Protocol, on grounds that the author does not meet the "victim" test established by the Committee. Bearing in mind that Mr Cox has not been tried, let alone convicted or sentenced to death, the hypothetical violations alleged appear quite remote for the purpose of considering this communication admissible.

However, since the Committee has proceeded to an examination of the merits, we would like to submit the following considerations on the scope of Articles 6 and 7 of the Covenant and their application in the case of Mr Keith Cox.

Article 6
As a starting point, we would note that Article 6 does not expressly prohibit extradition to face capital punishment. Nevertheless, it is appropriate to consider whether a prohibition would follow as a necessary implication of Article 6.

In applying Article 6, paragraph 1, of the Covenant, the Committee must, pursuant to Article 31 of the Vienna Convention on the Law of Treaties, interpret this provision *in good faith* in accordance with the ordinary meaning to be given to the terms in their context. As to the ordinary meaning of the words, a prohibition of extradition is not apparent. As to the context of the provision, we believe that Article 6, paragraph 1, must be read in conjunction with Article 6, paragraph 2, which does not prohibit the imposition of the death penalty for the most serious crimes; part of the context to be considered is also the fact that a large majority of States—at the time of the drafting of the Covenant and still today—retain the death penalty. One may not like this objective context, but it must not be disregarded.

Moreover, the notion *in good faith* entails that the intention of the parties to a treaty should be ascertained and carried out. There is a general principle of international law according to which no State can be bound without its consent. States parties to the Covenant gave consent to certain specific obligations under Article 6 of the Covenant. The fact that this provision does not address the link between the protection of the right to life and the established practice of States in the field of extradition is not without significance.

Had the drafters of Article 6 intended to preclude all extradition to face the death penalty, they could have done so. Considering that Article 6 consists of six paragraphs, it is unlikely that such an important matter would have been left for future interpretation. Nevertheless, an issue under Article 6 could still arise if extradition were granted for the imposition of the death penalty in breach of Article 6, paragraphs 2 and 5. While this has been recognized by the Committee in its jurisprudence (see the Committee's Views in Communication No 469/1991 (*Ng* v. *Canada*)[18] and No 470/1991 (*Kindler* v. *Canada*)),[19] the yardstick with which a possible breach of Article 6, paragraphs 2 and 5, has to be measured, remains a restrictive one. Thus, the extraditing State may be deemed to be in violation of the Covenant only if the *necessary and foreseeable consequence* of its decision to extradite is that the Covenant rights of the extradited person wll be violated in another jurisdiction.

In this context, reference may be made to the Second Optional Protocol, which similarly does *not* address the issue of extradition. This fact is significant and lends further support to the proposition that under international law extradition to face the death penalty is not prohibited under all circumstances. Otherwise the drafters of this new instrument would surely have included a provision reflecting this understanding.

An obligation not to extradite, as a matter of principle, without seeking assurances is a substantial obligation that entails considerable consequences, both domestically and internationally. Such consequences cannot be presumed without some indication that the parties intended them. If the Covenant does not expressly impose these obligations, States cannot be deemed to have assumed them. Here reference should be made to the jurisprudence of the International Court of Justice according to which interpretation is not a matter of revising treaties or of reading into them what they do not expressly or by necessary implication contain.[20]

Admittedly, since the primary beneficiaries of human rights treaties are not States or governments but human beings, the protection of human rights calls for a more liberal approach than that normally applicable in the case of ambiguous provisions of multilateral treaties, where, as a general rule, the "meaning is to be preferred which is less onerous to the party assuming an obligation, or which interferes less with the territorial and personal supremacy of a party, or involves less general restrictions upon the parties".[21] Nonetheless, when giving a broad interpretation to any human rights treaty, care must be taken not to frustrate or circumvent the ascertainable will of the drafters.

[18 98 *ILR* 479.]
[19 98 *ILR* 426.]
[20] Oppenheim, *International Law*, 1992 edition, vol. 1, p. 1271.
[21] This corresponds to the principle of interpretation known as *in dubio mitius. Ibid.*, p. 1278.

Here the rules of interpretation set forth in Article 32 of the Vienna Convention on the Law of Treaties help us by allowing the use of the *travaux préparatoires*. Indeed, a study of the drafting history of the Covenant reveals that when the drafters discussed the issue of extradition, they decided not to include any specific provision in the Covenant, so as to avoid conflict or undue delay in the performance of existing extradition treaties (E/CN.4/SR.154, paras. 26-57).

It has been suggested that extraditing a person to face the possible imposition of the death sentence is tantamount, for a State that has abolished capital punishment, to reintroducing it. While Article 6 of the Covenant is silent on the issue of reintroduction of capital punishment, it is worth recalling, by way of comparison, that an express prohibition of reintroduction of the death penalty is provided for in Article 4(3) of the American Convention on Human Rights, and that Protocol 6 to the European Convention does not allow for derogation. A commitment not to reintroduce the death penalty is a laudable one, and surely in the spirit of Article 6, paragraph 6, of the Covenant. But certainly this is a matter for States parties to consider before they assume a binding obligation. Such obligation may be read into the Second Optional Protocol, which is not subject to derogation. But, as of November 1994, only twenty-two countries have become parties—Canada has not signed or ratified it. Regardless, granting a request to extradite a foreign national to face capital punishment in another jurisdiction cannot be equated to the reintroduction of the death penalty.

Moreover, we recall that Canada is not itself imposing the death penalty, but merely observing an obligation under international law pursuant to a valid extradition treaty. Failure to fulfil a treaty obligation engages State responsibility for an internationally wrongful act, giving rise to consequences in international law for the State in breach of its obligation. By extraditing Mr Cox, with or without assurances, Canada is merely complying with its obligation pursuant to the Canada–US Extradition Treaty of 1976, which is, we would note, compatible with the United Nations Model Extradition Treaty.

Finally, it has been suggested that Canada may have restricted or derogated from Article 6 in contravention of Article 5(2) of the Covenant (the "savings clause", see Manfred Nowak's CCPR Commentary, 1993, pp. 100 *et seq.*). This is not so, because the rights of persons under Canadian jurisdiction facing extradition to the United States were not necessarily broader under any norm of Canadian law than in the Covenant and had not been finally determined until the Supreme Court of Canada issued its 1991 judgments in the *Kindler* and *Ng* cases. Moreover, this determination was not predicated on the Covenant, but rather on the Canadian Charter of Rights and Freedoms.

Article 7

The Committee has pronounced itself in numerous cases on the issue of the "death row phenomenon" and has held that "prolonged judicial proceedings do not *per se* constitute cruel, inhuman and degrading treatment, even if they can be a source of mental strain for the convicted persons".[22] We concur with the Committee's reaffirmation and elaboration of this holding in the instant decision. Furthermore we consider that prolonged imprisonment under sentence of death could raise an issue under Article 7 of the Covenant if the prolongation were unreasonable and attributable primarily to the State, as when the State is responsible for delays in the handling of the appeals or fails to issue necessary documents or written judgments. However, in the specific circumstances of the Cox case, we agree that the author has not shown that, if he were sentenced to death, his detention on death row would be unreasonably prolonged for reasons imputable to the State.

We further believe that imposing rigid time limits for the conclusion of all appeals and requests for clemency is dangerous and may actually work against the person on death row by accelerating the execution of the sentence of death. It is generally in the interest of the petitioner to remain alive for as long as possible. Indeed, while avenues of appeal remain open, there is hope, and most petitioners will avail themselves of these possibilities, even if doing so entails continued uncertainty. This is a dilemma inherent in the administration of justice within all those societies that have not yet abolished capital punishment.

[Original: English]

2. Individual opinion by Mr Tamás Bán (partly concurring, partly dissenting)
I share the Committee's conclusion that the extradition of Mr Cox by Canada to the United States to face the possible imposition of the death penalty, under the specific circumstances of this case, would not constitute a violation of Article 6 of the Covenant, and that judicial execution by lethal injection would not, in this case, constitute a violation of Article 7.

I cannot accept the Committee's position, however, that the prospects for Mr Cox being held for a long period of time on death row, if sentenced to death, would not amount to a violation of his rights under Article 7 of the Covenant.

---

[22] Views on Communications Nos 210/1986 and 225/1987 (*Earl Pratt and Ivan Morgan* v. *Jamaica*) adopted on 6 April 1989, paragraph 13.6 [98 *ILR* 322]. This holding has been reaffirmed in some ten subsequent cases, including Nos 270/1988 and 271/1988 (*Randolph Barrett and Clyde Sutcliffe* v. *Jamaica*), adopted on 30 March 1992, paragraph 8.4, and No 470/1991 (*Kindler* v. *Canada*), adopted on 30 July 1993, paragraph 15.2 [98 *ILR* 426].

The Committee based its finding of non-violation of Article 7, regarding the "death row phenomenon" on the following arguments: (1) prison conditions in the State of Pennsylvania have been considerably improved in recent times; (2) Mr Cox has not yet been convicted nor sentenced, the trial of his two accomplices did not end with sentence of death; (3) no evidence has been adduced to show that all possibilities for appeal would not be available within a reasonable time, or that there would be unreasonable delays which would be imputable to the State (*supra*, paragraphs 17.1 and 17.2).

Concerning the prison conditions in Pennsylvania, the State Party, Canada, has in fact shown that substantial improvements in the condition of incarceration of inmates under death sentence have taken place in that State (paragraph 13.6). The measures taken are said to consist mainly of the improvement of the physical conditions of the inmates.

Although I accept the notion that physical conditions play an important role when assessing the overall situation of prison inmates on death row, my conviction is that the decisive factor is rather *psychological* than physical; a long period spent in awaiting execution or the granting of pardon or clemency necessarily entails a permanent stress, an ever-increasing fear which gradually fills the mind of the sentenced individual, and which, by the very nature of this situation, amounts—depending on the length of time spent on death row—to cruel, inhuman and degrading treatment, in spite of every measure taken to improve the physical conditions of the confinement.

Turning now to the second argument, that Mr Cox has not yet been convicted nor sentenced, and that he therefore has no claim under Article 7 (since only *de facto* sentenced-to-death convicts are in a situation to assert a violation of their rights not to be exposed to torture, cruel, inhuman or degrading treatment), I believe this argument is irrelevant when looking into the merits of the case. It could have been raised, and indeed, the State Party did raise it during the admissibility procedure, but it was not honoured by the Committee. I would like to note that the Committee has taken a clear stand in its earlier jurisprudence on the responsibility of States parties for their otherwise lawful decisions to send an individual within their jurisdiction into another jurisdiction, where that person's rights would be violated as a necessary and foreseeable consequence of the decision (e.g. Committee's Views in the *Kindler* case,[23] paragraph 6.2). I will try to show below, discussing the third argument, that in the present case the violation of Mr Cox's rights following his extradition is necessary and foreseeable.

Concerning the third argument, the Committee held that the author adduced no evidence to show that all possibilities for appeal

[²³ 98 *ILR* 426.]

against the death sentence would not be available in the State of Pennsylvania within a reasonable time, or that there would be unreasonable delays imputable to that State, as a result of which Mr Cox could be exposed at length to the "death row phenomenon".

I contest this finding of the Committee. In his submission of 18 September 1994, counsel for Mr Cox contended that "nobody has been executed in Pennsylvania for more than twenty years, and there are individuals awaiting execution on death row for as much as fifteen years".

In its submission of 21 October 1994, the State Party—commenting on several statements made by counsel in his above-mentioned submission of 18 September—remained silent on this point. In other words, it did not challenge or contest it in any way. In my opinion this lack of response testifies that the author has adduced sufficient evidence to show that appeal procedures in the State of Pennsylvania can last such a long time, which cannot be considered as reasonable.

While fully accepting the Committee's jurisprudence to the effect that every person sentenced to death must be afforded the opportunity to pursue all possibilities of appeal in conformity with Article 6, paragraph 4—a right the exercise of which, in capital cases, necessarily entails a shorter or longer stay on death row—I believe that in such cases States parties must strike a sound balance between two requirements: on the one hand all existing remedies must be made available, but on the other hand—with due regard to Article 14, paragraph 3(c)—effective measures must be taken to the effect that the final decision be made within a reasonable time to avoid the violation of the sentenced person's rights under Article 7.

Bearing in mind that in the State of Pennsylvania inmates face the prospect of spending a very long time—sometimes fifteen years—on death row, the violation of Mr Cox's rights can be regarded as a foreseeable and necessary consequence of his extradition. For this reason I am of the opinion that the extradition of Mr Cox by Canada to the United States without reasonable guarantees would amount to a violation of his rights under Article 7 of the Covenant.

I would like to make it clear that my position is strongly motivated by the fact that by Mr Cox's surrender to the United States, the Committee would lose control over an individual at present within the jurisdiction of a State party to the Optional Protocol.

[Original: English]

3. _Individual opinion by Messrs Francisco José Aguilar Urbina, and Fausto Pocar (dissenting)_

We cannot agree with the finding of the Committee that in the present case, there has been no violation of Article 6 of the Covenant. The question whether the fact that Canada had abolished capital punishment except for certain military offences required its authorities to request assurances from the United States to the effect that the death penalty would not be imposed on Mr Keith Cox and to refuse extradition unless clear assurances to this effect are given, must in our view receive an affirmative answer.

Regarding the death penalty, it must be recalled that, although Article 6 of the Covenant does not prescribe categorically the abolition of capital punishment, it imposes a set of obligations on States parties that have not yet abolished it. As the Committee pointed out in its General Comment 6(16), "the article also refers generally to abolition in terms which strongly suggest that abolition is desirable". Furthermore, the wording of paragraphs 2 and 6 clearly indicates that Article 6 tolerates—within certain limits and in view of future abolition—the existence of capital punishment in States parties that have not yet abolished it, but may by no means be interpreted as implying for any State party an authorization to delay its abolition or, *a fortiori*, to enlarge its scope or to introduce or reintroduce it. Accordingly, a State party that has abolished the death penalty is in our view under the legal obligation, under Article 6, paragraph 1, of the Covenant, not to reintroduce it. This obligation must refer both to a direct reintroduction within the State party's jurisdiction, as well as to an indirect one, as is the case when the State acts—through extradition, expulsion or compulsory return—in such a way that an individual within its territory and subject to its jurisdiction may be exposed to capital punishment in another State. We therefore conclude that in the present case there has been a violation of Article 6 of the Covenant.

Regarding the claim under Article 7, we cannot agree with the Committee that there has not been a violation of the Covenant. As the Committee observed in its Views on Communication No 469/1991 (*Charles Chitat Ng v. Canada*),[24] "by definition, every execution of a sentence of death may be considered to constitute cruel and inhuman treatment within the meaning of Article 7 of the Covenant", unless the execution is permitted under Article 6, paragraph 2. Consequently, a violation of the provisions of Article 6 that may make such treatment, in certain circumstances, permissible, entails necessarily, and irrespective of the way in which the execution may be carried out, a violation of Article 7 of the Covenant. It is for these reasons that we conclude in the present case there has been a violation of Article 7 of the Covenant.

[Original: English]

[24 98 *ILR* 479.]

4. *Individual opinion by Ms Christine Chanet (dissenting)*

As in the *Kindler* case, when replying to the questions relating to Article 6 of the Covenant, the Committee in order to conclude in favour of a non-violation by Canada of its obligations under that Article was forced to undertake a joint analysis of paragraphs 1 and 2 of Article 6 of the Covenant.

There is nothing to show that this is a correct interpretation of Article 6. It must be possible to interpret every paragraph of an article of the Covenant separately, unless expressly stated otherwise in the text itself or deducible from its wording.

That is not so in the present case.

The fact that the Committee found it necessary to use both paragraphs in support of its argument clearly shows that each paragraph taken separately, led to the opposite conclusion, namely, that a violation had occurred.

According to Article 6, paragraph 1, no one shall be arbitrarily deprived of his life; this principle is absolute and admits of no exception.

Article 6, paragraph 2, begins with the words: "In countries which have not abolished the death penalty . . .". This form of words requires a number of comments:

It is negative and refers not to countries in which the death penalty exists but to those in which it has not been abolished. Abolition is the rule, retention of the death penalty the exception.

Article 6, paragraph 2, refers only to countries in which the death penalty has not been abolished and *thus rules out the application of the text to countries which have abolished the death penalty.*

Lastly, the text imposes a series of obligations on the States in question.

Consequently, by making a "joint" interpretation of the first two paragraphs of Article 6 of the Covenant, the Committee has, in my view, committed three errors of law:

One error, is that it is applying to a country which has abolished the death penalty, Canada, a text exclusively reserved by the Covenant—and that in an express and unambiguous way—for non-abolitionist States.

The second error consists in regarding as an authorization to re-establish the death penalty in a country which has abolished it what is merely an implicit recognition of its existence. This is an extensive interpretation which runs counter to the proviso in paragraph 6 of Article 6 of that "nothing in this article shall be invoked . . . to prevent the abolition of capital punishment". This extensive interpretation, which is restrictive of rights, also runs counter to the provision in Article 5, paragraph 2, of the Covenant that there shall be no restriction upon or derogation from any of the fundamental human rights recognized or existing in any State party to the present Covenant pursuant to law, conventions, regulations or custom on the pretext that the present Covenant does not recognize such rights or that it recognizes them to a lesser extent.

Taken together, these texts prohibit a State from engaging in distributive application of the death penalty. There is nothing in the Covenant to force a State to abolish the death penalty but, if it has chosen to do so, the Covenant forbids it to re-establish it in an arbitrary way, even indirectly.

The third error of the Committee in the decision results from the first two. Assuming that Canada is implicitly authorized by Article 6, paragraph 2, of the Covenant, to re-establish the death penalty, on the one hand, and to apply it in certain cases on the other, the Committee subjects Canada in paragraphs 14.3, 14.4 and 14.5 as if it were a non-abolitionist country, to a scrutiny of the obligations imposed on non-abolitionist States: penalty imposed only for the most serious crimes, judgment rendered by a competent court, etc.

This analysis shows that, according to the Committee, Canada, which had abolished the death penalty on its territory, has by extraditing Mr Cox to the United States re-established it by proxy in respect of a certain category of persons under its jurisdiction.

I agree with this analysis but, unlike the Committee, I do not think that this behaviour is authorized by the Covenant.

Moreover, having thus re-established the death penalty by proxy, Canada is limiting its application to a certain category of persons: those that are extraditable to the United States.

Canada acknowledges its intention of so practising in order that it may not become a haven for criminals from the United States. Its intention is apparent from its decision not to seek assurances that the death penalty would not be applied in the event of extradition to the United States, as it is empowered to do by its bilateral extradition treaty with that country.

Consequently, when extraditing persons in the position of Mr Cox, Canada is deliberately exposing them to the application of the death penalty in the requesting State.

In so doing, Canada's decision with regard to a person under its jurisdiction according to whether he is extraditable to the United States or not, constitutes a discrimination in violation of Article 2, paragraph 1, and Article 26 of the Covenant.

Such a decision affecting the right to life and placing that right, in the last analysis, in the hands of the Government which, for reasons of penal policy, decides whether or not to seek assurances that the death penalty will not be carried out, constitutes an arbitrary deprivation of the right to life forbidden by Article 6, paragraph 1, of the Covenant and, consequently, a misreading by Canada of its obligations under this Article of the Covenant.

[Original: French]

5. *Individual opinion by Mr Rajsoomer Lallah (dissenting)*
By declining to seek assurances that the death penalty would not be imposed on Mr Cox or, if imposed, would not be carried out, Canada violates, in my opinion, its obligations under Article 6, paragraph 1, of the Covenant, read in conjunction with Articles 2, 5 and 26. The reasons which lead me to this conclusion were elaborated in my individual opinion on the Views in the case of *Joseph Kindler* v. *Canada* (Communication No 470/1991).[25]

I would add one further observation. The fact that Mr Cox has not yet been tried and sentenced to death, as Mr Kindler had been when the Committee adopted its Views on his case, makes no material difference. If suffices that the offence for which Mr Cox faces trial in the United States carries in principle capital punishment as a sentence he faces under the law of the United States. He therefore faces a charge under which his life is in jeopardy.

[Original: French]

6. *Individual opinion by Mr Bertil Wennergren (dissenting)*
I do not share the Committee's Views about a non-violation of Article 6 of the Covenant, as set out in paragraphs 16.2 and 16.3 of the Views. On grounds which I developed in detail in my individual opinion concerning the Committee's Views on Communication No 470/1991 (*Joseph John Kindler* v. *Canada*), Canada did, in my opinion, violate Article 6, paragraph 1, of the Covenant; it did so when, after the decision to extradite Mr Cox to the United States had been taken, the Minister of Justice ordered him surrendered without assurances that the death penalty would not be imposed or, if imposed, would not be carried out.

As to whether the extradition of Mr Cox to the United States would entail a violation of Article 7 of the Covenant because of the so-called "death row phenomenon" associated with the imposition of a capital sentence in the case, I wish to add the following observations to the Committee's Views in paragraphs 17.1 and 17.2. The Committee has been informed that no individual has been executed in Pennsylvania for over twenty years. According to information available to the Committee, condemned prisoners are held segregated from other

[25 98 *ILR* 426.]

prisoners. While they may enjoy some particular facilities, such as bigger cells, access to radio and television sets of their own, they are nonetheless confined to death row awaiting execution for years. And this *not* because they avail themselves of all types of judicial appellate remedies, but because the State party does not consider it appropriate, for the time being, to proceed with the execution. If the State party considers it necessary, for policy reasons, to have resort to the death penalty as such but not necessary and not even opportune to carry out capital sentences, a condemned person's confinement to death row should, in my opinion, last for as short a period as possible, with commutation of the death sentence to life imprisonment taking place as early as possible. A stay for a prolonged and indefinite period of time on death row, in conditions of particular isolation and under the threat of execution which might by unforeseeable changes in policy become real, is not, in my opinion, compatible with the requirements of Article 7, because of the unreasonable mental stress that this implies.

Thus, the extradition of Mr Cox might also be in violation of Article 7. However, there is not enough information in this case about the current practice of the Pennsylvania criminal justice and penitentiary system to allow any conclusion along the lines indicated above. What has been developed above remains hypothetical and in the nature of principles.

[Original: English]

[Report: Doc. CCPR/C/52/D/539/1993]

States — Sovereignty — Transfer of sovereignty — Joint Declaration between People's Republic of China and United Kingdom, 1984 — Hong Kong due to revert to Chinese sovereignty on 1 July 1997 — Hong Kong ceasing to exist as British Colony — Establishment of Hong Kong Special Administrative Region ("HKSAR") — Article 8 of Basic Law of HKSAR providing for continued operation of laws in force before 1 July 1997

Extradition — Treaties — Agreement for the Surrender of Accused and Convicted Persons between the Government of Australia and the Government of Hong Kong, 1993 ("Surrender Agreement")—Surrender Agreement providing for continued extradition relationship after resumption of Chinese sovereignty on 1 July 1997—People's Republic of China consenting to Surrender Agreement — Absence of bilateral extradition relationship between Australia and Poeple's Republic of China—Extradition (Hong Kong) Regulations of 29 June 1997 ("1997 Regulations") giving effect to Surrender Agreement in Australian law

Extradition—Treaties—Extradition Act 1988 (Cth) ("1988 Act")—Proper construction of provisions—Section 12(1) requirement that application to extradite be made on behalf of an extradition country — Whether magistrate acting with authority conferred by Section 12(1) in issuing warrant for arrest of first respondent — Section 5 defining meaning of "extradition country" — Section 5(b)(ii) — Whether HKSAR a "territory"—Whether People's Republic of China responsible for international relations of HKSAR—1997 Regulations—Regulations 4 and 5—Validity of operation of 1997 Regulations after 1 July 1997—Whether sufficient identity between the "Hong Kong" identified in the 1997 Regulations and the HKSAR which came into being on 1 July 1997 — Role of courts in construing and applying legislation — Role of Executive — Relevance of statement in certificate issued by Minister for Foreign Affairs of Government of Australia

State succession—Treaties—Transfer of sovereignty over Hong Kong from United Kingdom to People's Republic of China — Establishment of HKSAR on 1 July 1997 — Classification of HKSAR — Whether "Hong Kong" in Regulation 4 of 1997 Regulations having same relevant identity after 1 July as HKSAR—Section 5(b)(ii) of 1988

Act—Whether HKSAR constituting "territory" within the meaning of Section 5(b)(ii)—Whether HKSAR integral part of China—Whether People's Republic of China responsible for international relations of HKSAR — Whether HKSAR an extradition country for purposes of 1988 Act—The law of Australia

ATTORNEY-GENERAL (COMMONWEALTH) v. TSE CHU-FAI AND ANOTHER[1]

Australia, High Court.　　3 *April* 1998

(Gaudron, McHugh, Gummow, Kirby, Hayne and Callinan JJ)

SUMMARY: *The facts:*—On 1 July 1997 the People's Republic of China ("PRC") assumed sovereignty over the former British Crown Colony of Hong Kong and established the Hong Kong Special Administrative Region ("HKSAR")[2] pursuant to the PRC–United Kingdom Joint Declaration on the Question of Hong Kong, 1984 ("Joint Declaration"). Article 8 of the Basic Law,[3] the constituent document of the HKSAR, provided for the continued operation of the laws in force before the handover. On 14 July 1997 the Chief Executive of the HKSAR requested that the appellant, the Attorney-General for the Commonwealth of Australia, extradite the first respondent, Mr Tse Chu-Fai, to Hong Kong in order to stand trial on various charges including conspiracy to defraud.

Extradition from Australia to extradition countries was governed by the Extradition Act 1988 (Cth) ("1988 Act") and the Extradition (Hong Kong) Regulations of 29 June 1997 ("1997 Regulations"). Section 12(1) of the 1988 Act[4] required that any application to extradite be made on behalf of an "extradition country". Included in the definition of an extradition country contained in Section 5 of the 1988 Act,[5] in paragraph (b)(ii), was "a territory for the international relations of which a country is responsible". Regulation 4 of the 1997 Regulations declared Hong Kong to be an extradition country and Regulation 5 applied the 1988 Act in relation to Hong Kong subject to the Agreement for the Surrender of Accused and Convicted Persons between the Government of Australia and the Government of Hong Kong, 1993 ("Surrender Agreement").[6]

---

[1] The appellant was represented by D. M. J. Bennett QC, M. A. Wigney and N. E. Abadee, instructed by the Australian Government Solicitor. The first respondent was represented by D. F. Jackson QC, I. A. Shearer and D. Jordan, instructed by Deacons Graham & James. There was no appearance for the second respondent. For similar proceedings in the United Kingdom and the United States of America, see pp. 402 and 606 below.

[2] This special administrative region was established under Article 31 of the Constitution of the PRC adopted in 1982 and Article 3(1) of the Joint Declaration. For the texts of Article 31 and Article 3(1), see p. 394 below.

[3] The Basic Law was adopted by the National People's Congress and promulgated by the President of the PRC in 1990 to take effect as of 1 July 1997. For the text of Article 8, see p. 396 below. Article 1 of the Basic Law provided that the HKSAR was "an inalienable part of the [PRC]".

[4] For the text of Section 12(1), see p. 388 below.

[5] For the text of Section 5, see p. 390 below.

[6] For the text of the 1997 Regulations, see p. 390 below.

The Surrender Agreement provided for a continued extradition relationship after the resumption of Chinese sovereignty on 1 July 1997 and was given effect in Australian municipal law by the 1997 Regulations. The PRC consented to the Surrender Agreement but did not itself have a bilateral extradition relationship with Australia.

A magistrate considered the extradition request under the 1988 Act and the 1997 Regulations and issued a warrant for the arrest of the first respondent. The first respondent was arrested on 17 July 1997. He applied to the Supreme Court of New South Wales for a writ of habeas corpus. He contended that the application for the warrant had not been made on behalf of an extradition country as the HKSAR was an integral part of the PRC and, therefore, could not be classed as a territory for the international relations of which the PRC was responsible in accordance with Section 5 of the 1988 Act. He also claimed that the 1997 Regulations ended their valid operation on 1 July 1997. The application for habeas corpus was granted on 21 November 1997 and his release ordered on the ground that the warrant had been issued by the magistrate without the authority conferred by Section 12(1) of the 1988 Act.

The Attorney-General appealed this decision. He claimed that the magistrate had acted with due authority under Section 12(1) as the HKSAR was indeed an extradition country fulfilling the requirements of Section 5(b)(ii) of the 1988 Act. The High Court also had to consider whether a certificate[7] rejected by the primary judge should have been admitted as evidence.

Held:—The appeal was allowed.

(1) The magistrate had issued the warrant in accordance with Section 12(1) of the 1988 Act as the HKSAR was an extradition country within the meaning of Section 5(b)(ii) of the 1988 Act (pp. 397-9).

(2) The facts that the HKSAR had a body of law in force distinct from that in the PRC and that there was a particular judicial structure for the determination of controversies as to respective rights and obligations arising under that body of law indicated that the HKSAR was a "territory" within the meaning of paragraph (b)(ii) of the definition of "extradition country" in Section 5 of the 1988 Act. It was not necessary for the region in question to be geographically separated from the metropolitan area of that country (p. 398).

(3) The PRC was responsible for the international relations of the HKSAR within the meaning of paragraph (b)(ii) of the definition of "extradition country" in Section 5 of the 1988 Act. Notwithstanding the fact that the HKSAR was authorized by the PRC to conduct relevant external affairs on its own in accordance with the Basic Law, Article 13 of the Basic Law stated that the PRC "shall be responsible for the foreign affairs relating to the [HKSAR]". There was no requirement that the country so responsible was itself an extradition country as defined in paragraph (a) of Section 5 (pp. 398-9).

This certificate, dated 9 September 1997, was issued by the Minister for Foreign Affairs of the Government of Australia and stated that the Government of Australia recognized that the HKSAR of the PRC was a territory for the international relations of which the PRC was responsible.

(4) There was sufficient identity between the "Hong Kong" identified in the 1997 Regulations, which came into effect on 29 June 1997, and the HKSAR, which came into being on 1 July 1997, to support the conclusion that the 1997 Regulations had continued their valid operation. Although the legislative and executive institutions had changed, there had been no change in the relevant geographical area and, more importantly, the same body of law remained in force by virtue of Article 8 of the Basic Law, including that law governing the offences allegedly committed by the first respondent (p. 399).

(5) As the certificate in question was authorized by the Minister for Foreign Affairs and not the Attorney-General, it did not constitute prima facie evidence as to the facts therein stated in accordance with Section 52 of the 1988 Act. As a question of law, it was for the Court to decide upon the proper construction and application of paragraph (b)(ii) of the 1988 Act of the definition of "extradition country" and of the term "Hong Kong" in the 1997 Regulations. However, the information furnished by the Executive and contained in the certificate might prove to be helpful and relevant in the Court's determination (pp. 399-401).

The following is the text of the judgment of the Court:

[1]   Gaudron, McHugh, Gummow, Kirby, Hayne and Callinan JJ. By order **[129]** made 22 December 1997 under s 40 of the Judiciary Act 1903 (Cth), the whole of a cause pending in the New South Wales Court of Appeal was removed into this court and a direction was given that the cause be argued before a Full Court. The cause is an appeal by the Attorney-General for the Commonwealth against an order of the Supreme Court of New South Wales made 21 November 1997. By that order, the court directed Mr Ronald Tse Chu-Fai (the first respondent) be released from custody of the Governor of the Metropolitan Reception and Remand Centre (the second respondent).[1] The order, in the nature of a writ of habeas corpus, was made on the footing that the first respondent was unlawfully detained. This was because the warrant under which he had been arrested on 17 July 1997 had been issued by the magistrate without the authority conferred by s 12(1) of the Extradition Act 1988 (Cth) (the 1988 Act). The text of that provision is set out later in these reasons.

[2]   The first respondent has been released from custody upon undertakings which have been given to the Supreme Court and will continue until the disposition of the appeal by the Court of Appeal.

[3]   In March 1997, an information was laid at a Magistrates' Court in Hong Kong alleging that the first respondent had committed 22 offences. The counts included conspiracy to defraud contrary to the common law and the Criminal Procedure Ordinance, conspiracy to falsify an account contrary to the Theft Ordinance and the Criminal Procedure Ordinance, and obtaining services and property by deception contrary to the Theft Ordinance. On 14 March 1997, a magistrate in Hong Kong issued a warrant for the apprehension of the first respondent.

---

1. The reasons for judgment are reported: *Tse Chu-Fai v Governor of the Metropolitan Reception Centre* (1997) 150 ALR 566

[130] [4]   Thereafter, the United Kingdom of Great Britain and Northern Ireland (the UK) ceased to exercise sovereignty in respect of Hong Kong and on 1 July 1997 the People's Republic of China (the PRC) assumed the exercise of sovereignty in Hong Kong and established the Hong Kong Special Administrative Region (the HKSAR). These steps implemented a treaty between the UK and the PRC which was initialled at Peking (now Beijing) on 26 September 1984 and which was identified as "Joint Declaration of the Government of the United Kingdom of Great Britain and Northern Ireland and the Government of the People's Republic of China on the Question of Hong Kong" (the Joint Declaration).[2] Section 1 of the Hong Kong Act 1985 (UK), which came into force on the exchange of instruments of ratification of the Joint Declaration, had provided that, as from 1 July 1997, the Crown was no longer to have "sovereignty or jurisdiction over any part of Hong Kong".

[5]   During the nineteenth century, the UK had concluded three treaties with the then Chinese Government. Under the Treaty of Nanking signed in 1842 and ratified in 1843, Hong Kong Island was ceded in perpetuity; under the Convention of Peking in 1860, the southern part of the Kowloon peninsula and Stonecutters Island were ceded in perpetuity; and under the Convention of 1898, the New Territories were leased to the UK for 99 years from 1 July 1898.[3] The PRC consistently took the view that these were unequal treaties,[4] not concluded on the basis of the sovereign equality of the parties.[5] Paragraphs 1 and 2 of the Joint Declaration stated that the Government of the PRC had "decided to resume the exercise of sovereignty over Hong Kong with effect from 1 July 1997" and the Government of the UK would "restore Hong Kong to the [PRC] with effect from 1 July 1997".

[6]   On 14 July 1997, an extradition request to the appellant, the Attorney-General for the Commonwealth, was made under the hand of the Chief Executive of the HKSAR. This was followed by steps under the 1988 Act leading to the arrest and detention of the first respondent. It should be noted that the laws which founded the offences alleged against the first respondent in the information laid in March 1997 continued in operation in the HKSAR after 1 July 1997. That circumstance will be of primary importance on the disposition of the present appeal. It is convenient first to consider the scope and purpose of the 1988 Act.

The 1988 Act

[7]   Part II of the 1988 Act (ss 12-27) is headed "EXTRADITION FROM AUSTRALIA TO EXTRADITION COUNTRIES" and Pt IV (ss 40-44) is headed "EXTRADITION TO AUSTRALIA FROM OTHER COUNTRIES". Section 4 excludes the operation of two Imperial statutes known as the Extradition Acts 1870 to 1935 and the Fugitive Offenders Act 1881. This exclusion is in aid of several of the principal objects of the 1988 Act stipulated in s 3. One principal object is "to

---

2. (1984) 23 *International Legal Materials* 1366 at 1371
3. (1984) 23 *International Legal Materials* 1366 at 1367
4. McCorquodale, "Negotiating Sovereignty: The Practice of the United Kingdom in Regard to the Right of Self-Determination" (1995) 66 *British Year Book of International Law* 283 at 327. See also (1984) 23 *International Legal Materials* 1366 at 1367
5. See as to this doctrine, Brownlie, *Principles of Public International Law*, 4th ed (1990) pp 615-16

codify" the law relating to the extradition of persons from Australia to extradition countries and New Zealand. Another is to enable Australia to carry out its obligations under extradition treaties. With respect to the first object, it is settled **[131]** that extradition from Australia cannot take place in the absence of statutory authority.[6]

[8] In *United States v Cotroni*,[7] the Supreme Court of Canada identified as follows the importance of such legislation:

> The investigation, prosecution and suppression of crime for the protection of the citizen and the maintenance of peace and public order is an important goal of all organised societies. The pursuit of that goal cannot realistically be confined within national boundaries. That has long been the case, but it is increasingly evident today.

[9] The general principles of extradition law expressed in the concepts of double criminality[8] (s 10(2)), political offence (s 7(a)) and speciality[9] (s 25(2)) appear throughout Pt II of the 1988 Act. They express particular interests of national sovereignty and respect for individual rights. Given the presence of those safeguards, the general scope of Pt II should not be given any narrow interpretation. In particular, the definition in s 5 of "extradition country", upon which this litigation largely turns, should be given a fair reading which facilitates the principal objects of the legislation specified in s 3.

[10] Section 16(1) of the 1988 Act empowers the Attorney-General upon receipt of an extradition request from an extradition country in relation to a person to state, by notice in writing in the statutory form expressed to be directed to any magistrate, that the request has been received. The Attorney-General is not to give the notice unless of a certain opinion with respect to various matters specified in s 16(2). The Attorney-General must be of the opinion that the person in question "is an extraditable person in relation to the extradition country": s 16(2)(a)(i). The Attorney-General must also be of the opinion that, if the conduct of the person constituting the extradition offences for which surrender is sought or "equivalent conduct"[10] had taken place in Australia at the time of receipt of the extradition request, the conduct or equivalent conduct would have constituted an extradition offence in relation to Australia: s 16(2)(a)(ii). Notice is not to be given if the Attorney-General is of the opinion that there is a relevant "extradition objection": s 16(2)(b).[11]

[11] Section 12(1) is of central importance. It states:

> Where:
>
>   (a) an application is made, in the statutory form, on behalf of an extradition country to a magistrate for the issue of a warrant for the arrest of a person; and
>   (b) the magistrate is satisfied, on the basis of information given by affidavit, that the person is an extraditable person in relation to the extradition country;
>
> the magistrate shall issue a warrant, in the statutory form, for the arrest of the person.

[12] It will be apparent that the operation of s 12(1) turns upon the application of two requirements. The first is the making of the application "on behalf of an

---

6. *Barton v Commonwealth* (1974) 131 CLR 477 at 483, 494-5; 3 ALR 70 [55 *ILR* 11.]
7. [1989] 1 SCR 1469 at 1485
8. See *Riley v Commonwealth* (1985) 159 CLR 1 at 15-19; 62 ALR 497 [87 *ILR* 144.]
9. See *Trimbole v Commonwealth* (1984) 155 CLR 186 at 190; 57 ALR 215
10. There is an interpretive provision with respect to "equivalent conduct" in s 10(3)
11. There is an interpretive provision in respect of "extradition objection" in s 7. It includes such matters as political offences and acquittal or pardon in the extradition country.

extradition country". The second is the satisfaction of the magistrate that the person is "an extraditable person in relation to the extradition country". A person
[132] is an "extraditable person" in relation to a country if the criteria in s 6[12] are satisfied. These include the requirement that the offences in respect of which a warrant is in force are "extradition offence[s]" in relation to the country in question.

[13] The term "extradition offence" is defined in s 5 to identify certain offences "against a law" of a country. A reference to "a law of a country includes a reference to a law of, or in force in, a part of the country": s 9. Further, each colony, territory or protectorate of the country, each territory for the international relations of which the country is responsible, and each ship or aircraft of or registered in the country is deemed to be part of the country: s 8(1). This is subject to an exception provided in s 8(1) in the case of a colony, territory or protectorate that itself is an extradition country.[13]

[14] It is apparent from the foregoing, particularly s 9, that the operation of the terms "extradition offence" and "extraditable person" (and thus the second requirement in s 12(1)) may turn upon the law of, or law in force in, a "part" of a country. The term "part" is not defined. The immediate issues on this appeal turn upon the first requirement in s 12(1), that concerned with "extradition country". But, as will become apparent, in dealing with this requirement the territorial operation of a particular body of law is a significant consideration.

The dispute

[15] The case for the first respondent proceeded on the footing that, if the HKSAR is an "extradition country", it was open to the magistrate to be satisfied that the first respondent is an extraditable person in relation to the HKSAR. The first respondent founded his successful application for habeas corpus on the proposition that application for the issue of the warrant for his arrest had not been made "on behalf of an extradition country". The appellant contends that the criterion in s 12(1) was satisfied because the HKSAR is an "extradition country".

[16] The dispute therefore involves the construction of the definition of "extradition country" in s 5 and of regulations giving specific content to that definition. Section 5 states:

---

12. So far as immediately relevant, s 6 states:
  "Where:
  (a) either
      (i) a warrant is or warrants are in force for the arrest of a person in relation to an offence or offences against the law of a country that the person is accused of having committed either before or after the commencement of this Act; ...
  (b) the offence or any of the offences is an extradition offence in relation to the country; and
  (c) the person is believed to be outside the country;
  the person is, for the purposes of this Act, an extraditable person in relation to the country."
13. Section 8(1) states:
  "For the purposes of the application of this Act in relation to a country (other than Australia):
  (a) a colony, territory or protectorate of the country;
  (b) a territory for the international relations of which the country is responsible; and
  (c) a ship or aircraft of, or registered in, the country;
  are, except in the case of a colony, territory or protectorate that is an extradition country, each deemed to be part of the country."

"extradition country" means:

(a) any country (other than New Zealand) that is declared by the regulations to be an extradition country;

(b) any of the following that is declared by the regulations to be an extradition [133] country:

    (i) a colony, territory or protectorate of a country;

    (ii) a territory for the international relations of which a country is responsible; and

(c) until the regulations provide that this paragraph does not apply in relation to the foreign state, any foreign state to which the former Foreign Extradition Act applied by virtue of section 9 of that Act.

[17]   Under the 1988 Act, extradition from Australia to New Zealand is dealt with under the special provisions of Pt III (ss 28-39). The statutory reference in para (c) of the definition of "extradition country" is to the Extradition (Foreign States) Act 1966 (Cth). This was repealed, on the coming into force of the 1988 Act, by s 4 of the Extradition (Repeal and Consequential Provisions) Act 1988 (Cth). Section 4 also repealed the Extradition (Commonwealth Countries) Act 1966 (Cth). The 1988 Act thus replaced two former legislative regimes, one dealing with foreign States and the other dealing with relations between Commonwealth countries. The expression "country" in paras (a) and (b) of the definition of "extradition country" in the 1988 Act is apt to cover all such entities.

[18]   Section 55 of the 1988 Act confers upon the Governor-General the power to make regulations, not inconsistent with the 1988 Act, which prescribe all matters required or permitted by that statute to be prescribed. On 28 May 1997, the Governor-General made two sets of regulations. The first is the Extradition (Hong Kong) Regulations (the 1997 regulations).[14] These comprise regs 1–5 which state:

1. These Regulations may be cited as the Extradition (Hong Kong) Regulations.

2. These Regulations commence on 29 June 1997.

3. In these Regulations, unless the contrary intention appears:
"Surrender Agreement" means the Agreement for the Surrender of Accused and Convicted Persons between the Government of Australia and the Government of Hong Kong, a copy of which is set out in the Schedule.

4. Hong Kong is declared to be an extradition country.

5. The Extradition Act 1988 applies in relation to Hong Kong subject to the Surrender Agreement.

[19]   Regulation 5 is to be read in the light of s 11(1) of the 1988 Act. Section 11(1) states:

The regulations may:

(a) state that this Act applies in relation to a specified extradition country subject to such limitations, conditions, exceptions or qualifications as are necessary to give effect to a bilateral extradition treaty in relation to the country, being a treaty a copy of which is set out in the regulations; or

(b) make provision instead to the effect that this Act applies in relation to a specified extradition country subject to other limitations, conditions, exceptions or qualifications, other than such limitations, conditions, exceptions or

---

14. SR No 123/1997

qualifications as are necessary to give effect to a multilateral extradition treaty in relation to the country.

Provision for regulations in respect of multilateral extradition treaties is made by s 11(1A). The term "extradition treaty" is defined in s 5 as follows:

[134]   "extradition treaty", in relation to a country, means a treaty to which the country and Australia are parties (whether or not any other country is also a party), being a treaty relating in whole or in part to the surrender of persons accused or convicted of offences.

The term "treaty" includes "a convention, protocol, agreement or arrangement": s 5.

[20] The issues which arise in this appeal may be encapsulated by asking whether the "Hong Kong" identified in reg 4 with effect from 29 June 1997 has the same relevant identity after 1 July 1997 as the HKSAR. If the answer is in the negative, s 12(1) of the 1998 Act did not confer the necessary authority upon the magistrate who issued the warrant on 14 March 1997. If it is in the affirmative, the next question is whether the HKSAR is a "territory" or (as the primary judge found) an integral part of the PRC which, not being an extradition country, could not itself have made an application for the issue of a warrant for the arrest of the first respondent in accordance with the 1988 Act.

The status of Hong Kong

[21] In the period between the commencement of the 1988 Act and 29 June 1997, provision in respect of Hong Kong was made by the Extradition (Commonwealth Countries) Regulations (the Commonwealth regulations).[15] The Commonwealth regulations implement what is known as the London Scheme and declare (reg 3) each of the "countries, colonies, territories and protectorates" which were specified in the Schedule to be an extradition country. In respect of each of the above (which have included the UK as well as the entry "Hong Kong"), the Commonwealth regulations make a further special provision pursuant to para (b) of s 11(1) of the 1988 Act. The entry "Hong Kong" in the Schedule to the Commonwealth regulations was omitted by the second set of regulations made on 28 May 1997. These are the Extradition (Commonwealth Countries) Regulations (Amendment).[16] They also were stated to commence on 29 June 1997.

[22] Before 1 July 1997, Hong Kong answered the description in para (b)(ii) of the definition of "extradition country" in s 5 of the 1988 Act of a territory for the international relations of which a country, namely the UK, was responsible. Hong Kong also answered the description in para (b)(i) of a colony or territory of the UK.

[23] The 1997 regulations were stated to commence on 29 June 1997 while that state of affairs applied. The appellant submitted and the first respondent denied that, on and from 1 July 1997, Hong Kong answered the description in para (b)(ii) of a territory for the international relations of which a country, namely the PRC,

---

15. SR No 281/1988. These regulations had been made on 24 November 1988, before the commencement of the 1988 Act on 1 December of that year. The necessary power in that respect was conferred by s 4(1) of the Acts Interpretation Act 1901 (Cth).
16. SR No 122/1997

is responsible. The first respondent appeared to accept that the 1997 regulations were within power when made but submitted that, beginning 1 July 1997, a legislative condition for their continued operation came to an end.[17] This was because the HKSAR is, for the purposes of the definition of "extradition country" in s 5 of the 1988 Act, merely a part of the PRC and not "a territory for the international relations of which" the PRC is responsible. The primary judge accepted this submission. He concluded in favour of the first respondent on the [135] basis that the 1988 Act does not provide for a part of a country to be separately declared as an extradition country.

[24]   There are two corollaries to the above submissions by the first respondent. One is that "Hong Kong", as it is declared in reg 4 of the 1997 regulations to be an extradition country, is not the same "territory", within the meaning of para (b)(ii) of the definition of "extradition country" in s 5 of the 1988 Act, as the HKSAR, so that the 1997 regulations did not operate beyond 30 June 1997. The other is that, in the absence of a declaration under s 5(a) in respect of the PRC itself, the scope of s 5 does not extend to any fresh regulations that might hereafter be made in respect of the HKSAR alone.

The Surrender Agreement

[25]   Before turning to resolve these issues of construction, it is appropriate to consider the circumstances pertaining to the conclusion of the Surrender Agreement and the making of the 1997 regulations. These matters were the subject of detailed evidence, including an affidavit by a deputy principal government counsel of the HKSAR. In large measure the position sufficiently appears from the explanatory statement issued by the authority of the Attorney-General and Minister for Justice in respect of the making of the 1997 regulations. This includes the following:

> The regulations give effect in Australian domestic law to the Agreement for the Surrender of Accused and Convicted Persons between the Government of Australia and the Government of Hong Kong, signed at Hong Kong on 15 November 1993 (the Agreement). The text of this Agreement was tabled in the House of Representatives on 29 June 1994 and in the Senate on 23 August 1994[18]. In accordance with the government's policy of greater parliamentary involvement in Australia's treaty-making processes, a National Interest Analysis (NIA) for the Agreement, prepared by the Attorney-General's Department, was tabled in parliament on 18 June 1996. (The NIA notes the reasons why Australia should become a party to the Agreement.)
>
> On 7 May 1997 the Government of Hong Kong notified Australia, in accordance with Article 21 of the Agreement, that its domestic requirements for the Agreement's entry into force had been complied with. Australia's requirement for the Agreement's entry into force is the making of the proposed regulations. The Agreement enters into force 30 days after the date on which the parties have notified each other that they have complied with their respective requirements for the entry into force of the Agreement. The Government of Hong Kong will be notified on 30 May 1997 that Australia's requirements for the Agreement's entry into force have been complied with. Thirty days after that date, that is, on 29 June 1997, the Agreement will enter into force. Accordingly, 29 June 1997 is also the commencement date of the regulations.
>
> Extradition between Australia and Hong Kong was previously conducted under the

---

17. cf *Mathieson v Burton* (1971) 124 CLR 1 at 10
18. The text appears in *Australian Treaty Series, 1997*, No 11

Commonwealth Scheme for the Rendition of Fugitive Offenders (the London Scheme), an arrangement of less than treaty status in relation to extradition among Commonwealth countries and their dependent territories. The London Scheme is given effect in Australia by the Extradition (Commonwealth Countries) Regulations made under the Extradition Act 1988.

On its reversion to Chinese sovereignty on 1 July 1997 Hong Kong will cease to be part of the Commonwealth and hence will no longer come within the scope of the London Scheme. The Agreement has been negotiated in order to establish a continuing extradition relationship with Hong Kong after 1 July 1997. (Australia has no bilateral **[136]** extradition relationship with the People's Republic of China.) *The Chinese Government has consented to the negotiation and conclusion of the Agreement by Hong Kong.*

From the commencement of the regulations, the Extradition Act will apply to Hong Kong subject to the Agreement. The Extradition (Commonwealth Countries) Regulations (Amendment) will simultaneously omit Hong Kong from the Schedule to the Extradition (Commonwealth Countries) Regulations, so that the Extradition Act will no longer apply to Hong Kong subject to the limitations, conditions, exceptions or qualifications set out in those regulations.

As with all of Australia's extradition treaties, the Agreement contains all the internationally accepted human rights safeguards which are now a part of modern extradition. Under the Agreement, extradition will not be permitted where the fugitive is sought for or in connection with his or her race, religion, nationality or political opinions or would be tried, sentenced or detained for a political offence. In addition, extradition may be refused where the fugitive could be liable to the death penalty, unless satisfactory assurances are given by the requesting party that the death penalty will not be imposed or, if imposed, will not be carried out.

Unlike most other Australian extradition treaties, the Agreement requires presentation of a prima facie case by the requesting party (which is also a requirement of the London Scheme) and permits extradition only in respect of a list of offences. The list has been drawn up to include all offences for which extradition is currently considered appropriate [emphasis added].

[26] It will be noted that the Government of the PRC consented to the negotiation and conclusion of the Surrender Agreement. Further, the Surrender Agreement itself states that the Government of Hong Kong was "duly authorised" to conclude the Surrender Agreement "by the sovereign government which is responsible for its foreign affairs".[19] That sovereign government was the UK. However, the UK took these steps in the negotiation and conclusion of the Surrender Agreement in accordance with procedures agreed with the PRC and implemented through a body known as the Joint Liaison Group.

[27] Annexure II to the Joint Declaration[20] provided for the establishment by the UK and the PRC of a Joint Liaison Group. The matters for consideration of that body had included (Art 4(b)) action to be taken by the two governments "to ensure the continued application of international rights and obligations affecting Hong Kong".

---

19. See *Victoria v Commonwealth* (1996) 187 CLR 416 at 476-7; 138 ALR 129 (*Industrial Relations Act* case); Marston (ed), "United Kingdom Materials on International Law 1993" (1993) 64 *British Year Book of International Law* 579 at 605-6; Marston (ed), "United Kingdom Materials on International Law 1996" (1996) 67 *British Year Book of International Law* 683 at 718-19

20. (1984) 23 *International Legal Materials* 1366 at 1379

[28] Reference also should be made to an exchange of Notes between the PRC and Australia. The PRC Note was received on 12 June 1997. It stated that the Government of the PRC "will resume the exercise of sovereignty in Hong Kong on 1 July 1997, and will establish the [HKSAR]". It went on to state that the Government of the PRC affirmed that the Surrender Agreement "will continue to be applicable in the [HKSAR] from 1 July 1997". The PRC Note continued that, from that date, this and certain other agreements:

> will be regarded as agreements the [HKSAR] has been authorized by the Government of the [PRC] to have signed with the Government of Australia.

Australia replied by confirming that the Surrender Agreement and another **[137]** agreement:[21]

> will be regarded, from 1 July 1997, as agreements the [HKSAR] has been authorized by the Government of the [PRC] to have signed with the Government of Australia.

The Note also confirmed that these agreements "will continue to be applicable in the [HKSAR] from 1 July 1997". The result was that, with respect to the requirements of s 11(1)(a) of the 1988 Act, there were introduced no further "limitations, conditions, exceptions or qualifications" made necessary to give effect to the Surrender Agreement. Further, with respect to the obligations to surrender set out in Art 1 of the Surrender Agreement, the HKSAR was to be treated as the "requesting Party" in a case such as the present.[22]

The Basic Law

[29] It is convenient also briefly to consider some aspects of the constituent document of the HKSAR (the Basic Law).

[30] The Constitution of the PRC was adopted on 4 December 1982 and since has been amended. Article 31 states:

> The state may establish special administrative regions when necessary. The systems to be instituted in special administrative regions shall be prescribed by law enacted by the National People's Congress in the light of the specific conditions.

Paragraphs 1, 2 and 3 of Art 3 of the Joint Declaration stated the following among what the Government of the PRC thereby declared to be the basic policies of the PRC regarding Hong Kong:

> (1) Upholding national unity and territorial integrity and taking account of the history of Hong Kong and its realities, the [PRC] has decided to establish, in accordance with the provisions of Article 31 of the Constitution of the [PRC], a Hong Kong Special Administrative Region upon resuming the exercise of sovereignty over Hong Kong.
> (2) The [HKSAR] will be directly under the authority of the Central People's Government of the [PRC]. The [HKSAR] will enjoy a high degree of autonomy, except in foreign and defence affairs which are the responsibilities of the Central People's Government.

---

21. The Agreement between the Government of Australia and the Government of Hong Kong for the Promotion and Protection of Investments which entered into force on 15 October 1993: *Australian Treaty Series, 1993*, No 30
22. Article 1 states: "The Parties agree to surrender to each other, subject to the provisions laid down in this Agreement, any person who is found in the jurisdiction of the requested Party and who is wanted by the requesting Party for prosecution or for the imposition or enforcement of a sentence in respect of an offence described in Article 2."

(3) The [HKSAR] will be vested with executive, legislative and independent judicial power, including that of final adjudication. The laws currently in force in Hong Kong will remain basically unchanged.

[31] The Basic Law for the HKSAR was adopted by the National People's Congress and promulgated by the President of the PRC on 4 April 1990 to be "put into effect as of 1 July 1997".[23] The Basic Law provides that the HKSAR is "an inalienable part of the [PRC]" (Art 1) and the National People's Congress "authorizes the [HKSAR] to exercise a high degree of autonomy and enjoy executive, legislative and independent judicial power, including that of final adjudication, in accordance with the provisions of [the Basic Law]": Art 2. In addition to the Chinese language, English also may be used as an official [138] language: Art 9. The HKSAR shall have independent finances and the Central People's Government shall not levy taxes in the HKSAR: Art 106. The HKSAR shall maintain the status of a free port (Art 114) and will maintain its own shipping register under the name "Hong Kong, China": Art 125.

[32] Article 13 states:

> The Central People's Government shall be responsible for the foreign affairs relating to the [HKSAR].
> The Ministry of Foreign Affairs of the [PRC] shall establish an office in Hong Kong to deal with foreign affairs.
> The Central People's Government authorizes the [HKSAR] to conduct relevant external affairs on its own in accordance with [the Basic Law].

[33] Chapter VII (Arts 150-157) is headed "External Affairs". Article 157 requires the approval of the Central People's Government to the establishment of foreign consular and other official or semi-official missions in the HKSAR. Consular and other official missions "established in Hong Kong" by States which have formal diplomatic relations with the PRC "may be maintained": Art 157. The application to the HKSAR of international agreements to which the PRC is or becomes a party shall be decided by the Central People's Government "in accordance with the circumstances and needs of the [HKSAR], and after seeking the views of the government of the [HKSAR]": Art 153. This Article also states:

> International agreements to which the [PRC] is not a party but which are implemented in Hong Kong may continue to be implemented in the [HKSAR]. The Central People's Government shall, as necessary, authorize or assist the government of the [HKSAR] to make appropriate arrangements for the application to the [HKSAR] of other relevant international agreements.

Reference should also be made to Art 151 which states:

> The [HKSAR] may on its own, using the name "Hong Kong, China", maintain and develop relations and conclude and implement agreements with foreign states and regions and relevant international organizations in the appropriate fields, including the economic, trade, financial and monetary, shipping, communications, tourism, cultural and sports fields.

The Central People's Government shall, when necessary, facilitate the continued participation of the HKSAR "in an appropriate capacity in those international organizations in which Hong Kong is a participant in one capacity or another, but of which the [PRC] is not a member": Art 152.

---

23. The text of the Basic Law appears in (1990) 29 *International Legal Materials* 1519

[34] The provisions with respect to the legal system in the HKSAR are of particular importance for present purposes. Article 8 is significant for this litigation. It states:

> The laws previously in force in Hong Kong, that is, the common law, rules of equity, ordinances, subordinate legislation and customary law shall be maintained, except for any that contravene [the Basic Law], and subject to any amendment by the legislature of the [HKSAR].

The HKSAR "shall be vested with independent judicial power, including that of final adjudication": Art 19.

[35] The first two paragraphs of Art 18 state:

> The laws in force in the [HKSAR] shall be [the Basic Law], the laws previously in force in Hong Kong as provided for in Article 8 of [the Basic Law], and the laws enacted by the legislature of the [HKSAR].
>
> National laws shall not be applied in the [HKSAR] except for those listed in Annex **[139]** III to [the Basic Law]. The laws listed therein shall be applied locally by way of promulgation or legislation by the [HKSAR].

The national laws listed in Annex III include those with respect to the Territorial Sea, Nationality, and Diplomatic Privileges and Immunities. Article 18 goes on to provide for the Standing Committee of the National People's Congress to delete from the list of laws in Annex III and to add to the list laws relating to defence and foreign affairs "as well as other matters outside the limits of the autonomy of the [HKSAR] as specified by [the Basic Law]". Provision is also made for the application of national laws after a decision that the HKSAR "is in a state of emergency".

[36] On 29 July 1997, the Court of Appeal of the HKSAR ruled that the common law survived the resumption of sovereignty by the PRC and that it was adopted by the Basic Law. The Court of Appeal also ruled that the validity and effect of proceedings commenced under an indictment before 1 July 1997 were preserved by the Basic Law after that date.[24]

Construction of the 1988 Act

[37] Against that background, we turn to the issues of construction of the definition of "extradition country" in s 5 of the 1988 Act.

[38] It will be observed that paras (a) and (b) of the definition of "extradition country" speak of countries rather than States. That usage may be explained, as a matter of legislative history, by reference to the arrangements of less than treaty status which were made with respect to the Commonwealth of Nations under the London Scheme. However, there is nothing on the face of the definition to limit the term "country" in this way. Further, the 1988 Act is designed to provide comprehensively for extradition arrangements as the circumstances require from time to time.

[39] Paragraph (b)(i) of the definition uses the terms "colony, territory or protectorate". These are apt to include the wide range of juridical entities found particularly in the previous systems of European imperial administration.[25] They

---

24. *HKSAR v Ma Wai-Kwan* (29 July 1997, unreported)
25. In Sch 1 to the Interpretation Act 1978 (UK), "[c]olony" is defined as meaning:
    "any part of Her Majesty's dominions outside the British Islands except:

are used, with reference to the Commonwealth of Nations, in the definition of "Commonwealth country" in the Commonwealth regulations.

[40] Under such systems, there was scope for an overlap between the two limbs of para (b). An "extradition country" as declared by the 1997 regulations might answer both (i) and (ii) of para (b).[26] For example, the treaty under which France established a protectorate over Morocco, the Treaty of Fez of 1912,[27] left Morocco as a sovereign State but Morocco "made an arrangement of a [140] contractual character whereby France undertook to exercise certain sovereign powers in the name and on behalf of Morocco, and, in principle, all of the international relations of Morocco".[28]

[41] The term "responsible" in para (b)(ii) suggests authority or control. Nevertheless, responsibilities for the conduct of foreign affairs might be undertaken, and authority or control created, without any element of colonial subordination. The conduct after 1919 by Switzerland of the diplomatic relations of Liechtenstein is an example.[29] Another was the entrusting to Poland of the conduct of the foreign relations of the Free City of Danzig, established by the Treaty of Versailles and placed under the protection of the League of Nations.[30] Circumstances of this character fall within the scope of para (b)(ii).

[42] Further, there may be a bilateral extradition treaty "in relation to" a "specified extradition country", within the meaning of s 11(1)(a), where the parties to the treaty are Australia and the country which has responsibility for the international relations of a territory within the meaning of para (b)(ii) of the definition in s 5. That territory, rather than the country having foreign affairs responsibility, might by regulation validly be declared to be an extradition country under para (b)(ii). In the absence of any empowerment of the extradition country itself, for example by the terms of a treaty, an application for the issue of a warrant under s 12 would be made by the responsible country. It would do so, as that section states, "on behalf of" the extradition country. It would not be to the point that the responsible country itself was not an extradition country.

[43] The position established by the Basic Law for the HKSAR, as a matter of

---

(a) countries having fully responsible status within the Commonwealth;
(b) territories for whose external relations a country other than the United Kingdom is responsible;
(c) associated states [a reference to the West Indies Act 1967 (UK)];
and where parts of such dominions are under both a central and a local legislature, all parts under the central legislature are deemed for the purposes of this definition to be one colony."

26. See Fawcett, "Treaty Relations of British Overseas Territories" (1949) 26 *British Year Book of International Law* 86 at 97-99
27. Parry (ed), *The Consolidated Treaty Series* (1912), vol 216 at 20
28. *Case Concerning Rights of Nationals of the United States of America in Morocco (France v United States of America)* [1952] International Court of Justice Reports 175 at 188 [8]
29. Brownlie, *Principles of Public International Law*, 4th ed (1990) at 74-6; Fawceti, "Treaty Relations of British Overseas Territories" (1949) 26 *British Year Book of International Law* 86 at 102; Oppenheim, *International Law*, 7th ed (1948), vol 1 at 169, fn 4
30. *Case Concerning the Free City of Danzig and the International Labour Organisation* [9] [1929-1930] Annual Digest of Public International Law Cases 410 at 411; Oppenheim, *International Law*, 7th ed (1948), vol 1 at 175-6, fn 4
[8 19 *ILR* 255.]
[9 5 *Ann Dig* 410.]

international law, may be "unusual".[31] It has been suggested that the HKSAR displays the indicia of international legal personality.[32] In particular, we were taken to discussions dealing with the broadening of the previously limited status accorded under international law to regional autonomous entities.[33] It is unnecessary and inappropriate for this court to embark upon these questions. Rather, the issue here concerns the construction of the 1988 Act, with due regard to its scope and purpose. The immediate question is whether the HKSAR as a special administrative region established under Art 31 of the Constitution of the PRC, while within the metropolitan area of the PRC, nevertheless may answer the description within para (b)(ii) of the definition of "extradition country" in s 5 of the 1988 Act of "a territory for the international relations of which [the PRC] is responsible".

[44] The term "territory" may, according to its context, identify no more than a tract of land or an area of the earth's surface. In the law construed in *R v Governor of Brixton Prison; Ex parte Schtraks*[34] "territory" included any area [141] under the effective jurisdiction of a particular State. The term may also identify a geo-political entity with some attributes of a distinct governmental organisation, such as a local administration operating in a particular area. Paragraph (b)(i) of the definition in issue here speaks of a territory "of a country", while para (b)(ii) speaks of "a territory", not of a country, but for the international relations of which a country is responsible.

[45] Central provisions of the 1988 Act, including s 12 and those provisions with respect to the terms "extraditable person" (s 6), "extradition offence" (s 5) and "extradition objection" (s 7), involve consideration of the body of law of or in force in the "extradition country" in question. They thus require consideration, in respect of that which is declared an extradition country under para (b)(ii), of the body of law of or in force in a "territory". The existence of a distinct body of law which is administered within a defined region or area of a country provides, given the purpose and scope of the 1988 Act, a sufficient criterion for the existence of a territory to which para (b)(ii) applies. It is not to the point that this region or area is not geographically divorced from what might be called the metropolitan area of that country.

[46] In the case of the HKSAR, there is in force a body of law distinct from that in force in the balance of the PRC. Further, there is a particular judicial structure for the determination of controversies as to respective rights and obligations arising under that body of law. We have referred in particular to the provisions of Arts 8, 18 and 19 of the Basic Law. These provide the necessary indicia for the character of a "territory" within the meaning of para (b)(ii) of the definition of "extradition country" in s 5 of the 1988 Act.

[47] The question then arises as to whether the HKSAR is a territory "for the international relations of which" the PRC "is responsible". The "high degree of autonomy" referred to in Art 2 of the Basic Law includes the activities with respect to foreign States which are authorised in Art 151. However, the basic

---

31. Shaw, *International Law*, 4 ed (1997) at 716
32. Mushkat, "Hong Kong and Succession of Treaties" (1997) 46 *International and Comparative Law Quarterly* 181 at 193
33. Hannum and Lillich, "The Concept of Autonomy in International Law" in Dinstein (ed), *Models of Autonomy* (1981) at 215
34. [1964] AC 556 at 579, 587, 593, 604 [33 *ILR* 319.]

proposition is stated in Art 13. This is that, while the PRC authorises the HKSAR to conduct relevant external affairs on its own in accordance with the Basic Law, nevertheless the PRC "shall be responsible for the foreign affairs relating to the [HKSAR]".

[48]   It follows that if the 1997 regulations had been made with effect on or after 1 July 1997 and had identified the HKSAR as an extradition country, this would have been within the regulation-making power. This would have been so even if the country having responsibility for the international relations of the HKSAR, namely the PRC, was not itself an extradition country within the meaning of para (a) of the definition of "extradition country" in s 5 of the 1988 Act. It is no requirement of para (b)(ii) that the country there referred to itself has been declared an extradition country under para (a).

[49]   The final question is whether there is sufficient identity between "Hong Kong" as identified in the 1997 regulations as they came into effect several days before 1 July 1997 and the HKSAR to support the conclusion that the 1997 regulations had continued their valid operation.[35] The question should be answered in the affirmative. In light of the explanatory statement issued in respect of the 1997 regulations, it cannot be said that when reg 4 speaks of "Hong Kong" [142] it was intended to refer only to what was the Crown Colony of Hong Kong. Nor has there been such a change as to warrant the conclusion that, beginning 1 July 1997, a legislative condition for the continued operation of the 1997 regulations came to an end. There has been no change in the relevant territorial area. There has been a change in the legislative and executive institutions of government in Hong Kong. Nevertheless, and this is the crucial matter, the body of law in force has, in terms of Art 8 of the Basic Law, been maintained. In particular, the body of law for the alleged contravention of which extradition of the first respondent is sought has remained constant.

[50]   The result is that the magistrate was empowered by s 12 of the 1988 Act to issue the warrant under which the first respondent was detained.

The certificate

[51]   The primary judge rejected the tender of a certificate dated 9 September 1997 by the Minister for Foreign Affairs. This stated:

> I, ALEXANDER JOHN GOSSE DOWNER, Minister for Foreign Affairs, hereby certify that the Government of Australia recognises that the [HKSAR] of the [PRC] is a territory for the international relations of which the [PRC] is responsible.

[52]   Section 52 of the 1988 Act provides that certain certificates by the Attorney-General are, for the purposes of any proceedings under that statute, prima facie evidence of the facts stated in the certificate.[36] Plainly, the above

---

35. cf *R v Governor of Brixton Prison; Ex parte Kahan* [1989] QB 716 at 722-4 [80 *ILR* 10.]
36. Section 52 states:
     "A certificate by the Attorney-General stating that:
       (a) Australia or another specified country is a party to a specified treaty;
       (b) the treaty entered into force for Australia or that other country, as the case may be, on a specified date; and
       (c) as at the date of the certificate, the treaty remains in force for Australia or that other country,
     is, for the purposes of any proceedings under this Act, prima facie evidence of the facts stated in the certificate."

certificate furnished by the Minister for Foreign Affairs was not authorised by
s 52. Rather, it appears to have been tendered as an instance where the court
should take account of the views of the Executive on matters which are the
peculiar responsibility of that branch of government.[37]

[53]   In *Shaw Savill and Albion Co Ltd v Commonwealth*,[38] Dixon J spoke of
"the exceptional rule giving conclusive effect to official statements" and to those
matters of fact "which the Executive is authorised to decide", such as "the
existence of a state of war, the recognition of a foreign State, the extent of the
realm or other territory claimed by the Crown[[39]], or the status of a foreign
sovereign".

[54]   There is a fundamental question under Ch III of the Constitution of the
competence of the Executive (even with respect to those facts identified by
Dixon J) to determine conclusively the existence of facts by certificate where
they are disputed constitutional facts.[40] No such issue arises in this case. The
proper construction of para (b)(ii) of the definition of "extradition country" and
of the term "Hong Kong" in the 1997 regulations is a matter of law. Nor is the [143]
certificate specifically addressed to a fact of the particular category identified by
Dixon J.

[55]   As we have indicated, extradition from Australia requires statutory
authorisation. It is the province and duty of courts exercising jurisdiction with
respect to matters arising under such a statute to construe and apply it. The
Executive, a representative of which is a party to a controversy arising under the
1988 Act, cannot, by a certificate furnished by another representative, "compel
the court to an interpretation of statutory words which it believes to be false".[41]
Nevertheless, as Scarman LJ pointed out in *Re James (An Insolvent)*,[42] in
construing the statutory provision which takes as a factum for its operation a
matter pertaining to the conduct of foreign affairs, the communication of
information by the Executive may be both helpful and relevant.

[56]   That is how the certificate tendered in the present case should be viewed.
That Australia and the PRC conduct international relations with respect to the
HKSAR is readily apparent from an agreement made between them on
26 September 1996, which entered into force on 1 July 1997.[43] It is entitled
"Agreement Between the Government of Australia and the Government of the
People's Republic of China Concerning the Maintenance of the
Consulate-General of Australia in the Hong Kong Special Administrative Region
of the People's Republic of China". This instrument recites the provisions of
Art 157 of the Basic Law, to which reference was made earlier in these reasons.
This concerns the maintenance of consular and other official missions established
in Hong Kong by States which have formal diplomatic relations with the PRC.

37. See *Attorney-General (UK) v Heinemann Publishers Australia Pty Ltd* (1988) 165 CLR 30 at
    51; 78 ALR 449
38. (1940) 66 CLR 344 at 364
39. See also *Ffrost v Stevenson* (1937) 58 CLR 528 at 549 [8 *Ann Dig* 98.]
40. Lindell, "Judicial Review of International Affairs" in Opeskin and Rothwell (eds), *International
    Law and Australian Federalism* (1997), 160 at 196
41. *Re James (An Insolvent)* [1977] Ch 41 at 71 [72 *ILR* 29.]
42. [1977] Ch 41 at 72
43. *Australian Treaty Series, 1997*, No 7

[57]   The certificate should be understood as a statement that, at its date, 9 September 1997, Australia dealt with the PRC on the footing that it was responsible for the international relations of the HKSAR. Given the conclusion of the above agreement with effect from 1 July 1997, it would be a reasonable inference that this state of affairs had been in existence on 14 July 1997, the date of the receipt of the extradition request with respect to the first respondent. The certificate should have been admitted on that basis. However, it remained for the court, against the factual background, including the terms of the Basic Law, to construe and apply the terms of para (b)(ii) of the definition of "extradition country" and the term "Hong Kong" in the 1997 regulations.

Conclusion

[58]   The cause should be remitted to the Court of Appeal for the making of orders to give effect to the reasons for judgment of this court. The appellant and the first respondent should have liberty to file written submissions as to the appropriate order for costs of the cause in this court. The first respondent should file its submissions within seven days and the appellant its submissions within seven days thereafter. Costs in the Court of Appeal should follow the event.

[59]   The orders to be made by the Court of Appeal should provide that:
   (a) the appeal be allowed;
   (b) the first respondent pay the appellant's costs of the appeal in the Court of Appeal; and

[144]   (c) the orders that the first respondent be released from custody by the second respondent and the appellant pay the first respondent's costs be set aside and in place thereof the summons filed 7 August 1997 be dismissed with costs.

[60]   Upon the making of those orders by the Court of Appeal, the undertakings given by the first respondent to the Supreme Court will require him to return to the custody of the second respondent.

Order

(1) The cause be remitted to the Court of Appeal of New South Wales for the making of orders to give effect to the reasons for judgment of this court.

(2) The appellant and the first respondent have liberty, within the periods and in the sequence specified in the reasons for judgment, to file written submissions as to the appropriate order for costs of the cause in this court.

[Report: (1998) 153 ALR 128]

States—Sovereignty—Transfer of sovereignty—Sino-British
Joint Declaration on the Question of Hong Kong, 1984
("Joint Declaration")—Reversion of sovereignty of Hong
Kong to People's Republic of China ("PRC") on 1 July 1997
—Legal consequences of transfer of sovereignty—Extradition request—British Colony of Hong Kong requesting
extradition of applicant from United Kingdom—Trial and
sentence of applicant after transfer of sovereignty—"China
point"—Effect of treaty—Basic Law of the Hong Kong
Special Administrative Region of the PRC ("Basic Law")
implementing treaty obligations owed by the PRC to the
United Kingdom under the Joint Declaration—Whether rule
of law and legal safeguards existing in requesting State
likely to survive handover—Whether successor State likely
to comply with treaty obligations

Extradition — British Colony of Hong Kong requesting
extradition of applicant from United Kingdom—Imminent
return of Hong Kong to PRC—Section 12(1) and (2) of
Extradition Act 1989 conferring discretion on Secretary of
State not to sign surrender warrant — Whether unjust,
oppressive or wrong to return applicant to Hong Kong—
Secretary of State ordering return of applicant to Hong
Kong—Whether Secretary of State applying correct test—
Delicacy of diplomatic relations—Whether decision of
Executive justiciable—Whether errors of law in reaching
decision—Whether collective cabinet or individual decision
—Whether Secretary of State directing himself properly as
to his Section 12 responsibilities—Whether assumption that
the PRC would honour treaty obligations correct—Whether
specialty protection contained in Section 6(4) effective after
1 July 1997—Assessing risks of unfair trial and inhumane
punishment in the individual case of the applicant —
Relevance of evidence of realities of situation—Role of
court in assessing decision of Secretary of State—Whether
Secretary of State acting with procedural fairness—Whether
decision irrational

Human rights—Freedom of movement—European Union
law — Whether applicant's arrest in United Kingdom
contravening Article 48 of Treaty of Rome, 1957—Whether
extradition public policy exception—Whether necessary to
examine scope of public policy exception—Whether relevant
provisions of Treaty of Rome applicable in extradition
cases—Right to fair trial and humane punishment—Risk of

interference with applicant's fundamental human rights—
Necessity for court to scrutinize Secretary of State's
decision to return applicant to Hong Kong — European
Convention on Human Rights, 1950—Whether Secretary
of State's decision to return applicant breaching various
articles of Convention — Whether Secretary of State
overlooking human rights issues in his assessment of
applicant's case—Whether Secretary of State's decision
irrational

Relationship of international law and municipal law—
Treaties—European Union law—Articles 48, 52 and 59 of
the Treaty of Rome, 1957—Provisions having direct effect—
Applicant applying for enforcement of provisions in English
courts pursuant to Section 2 of European Communities Act
1972—Applicant alleging breaches of European Convention
on Human Rights, 1950—Whether United Kingdom courts
to adjudicate on alleged breach of Convention—The law of
England

REGINA *v.* SECRETARY OF STATE FOR THE HOME DEPARTMENT,
ex parte LAUNDER[1]

England, Divisional Court, Queen's Bench Division. 6 *August* 1996

(Henry LJ and Ebsworth J)

House of Lords. 21 *May* 1997

(Lord Browne-Wilkinson, Lord Steyn, Lord Hope of Craighead,
Lord Clyde and Lord Hutton)

SUMMARY: *The facts:*—In October 1993 the Governor of the British Colony
of Hong Kong requested the extradition of the applicant from the United
Kingdom to Hong Kong in order to stand trial on corruption charges. In
April 1994 the applicant was committed by the magistrate, pursuant to
Section 9 of the Extradition Act 1989 ("the Act"), to await the decision of
the Secretary of State for the Home Department on whether to comply
with the extradition request. The applicant applied for a writ of habeas
corpus to challenge his committal under Section 9. Under Section 11 of

---

[1] Before the Divisional Court, the Secretary of State was represented by Kenneth Parker QC.
The applicant was represented by David Vaughan QC and David Perry and the Government of
Hong Kong by James Lewis. Before the House of Lords, the Secretary of State was represented
by Kenneth Parker QC and James Eadie, the applicant by David Vaughan QC and David
Perry, and the Government of Hong Kong by Alun Jones QC and James Lewis. For similar
proceedings in Australia and the United States of America, see pp. 383 and 606.

the Act[2] the Court had the power to discharge the applicant if it considered that it would be unjust or oppressive to return him. The Divisional Court rejected his application in December 1994. Leave to appeal to the House of Lords was refused.

Section 12(1)[3] and (2)[4] of the Act conferred upon the Secretary of State a discretion not to sign the surrender warrant if he considered it inappropriate to do so. Section 12(1) bestowed a general discretion and Section 12(2) specified mandatory requirements: he was not to make an order if it appeared to him that it would be unjust or oppressive to return the applicant having regard to all the circumstances or if the offence carried the death penalty in the requesting State but not in Great Britain. In July 1995, after considering representations from the requesting authority and the applicant, the Secretary of State ordered the return of the applicant to Hong Kong. The applicant invited the Secretary of State to reconsider his decision, on the ground that the return of Hong Kong to the People's Republic of China ("PRC") in 1997 meant he would not receive a fair trial. The Secretary of State, however, confirmed the surrender warrant.

The applicant challenged these decisions and sought judicial review of the exercise of the Secretary of State's discretion, alleging that he had made various errors of law in reaching his conclusion. The applicant's main contention was that, as the sovereignty of Hong Kong was to revert to the PRC on 1 July 1997, the requesting State would no longer exist at the time of his trial and sentence, and thus the legal safeguards providing the right to a fair trial and appropriate humane punishment which existed before that date could not be guaranteed despite arrangements to secure the continuity of the rule of law after the transfer of sovereignty. He also alleged that the Secretary of State had acted irrationally and with procedural impropriety. He questioned the efficacy of the specialty provision contained in Section 6(4) of the Act[5] after 1 July 1997. Concerned by the PRC's human rights record, he claimed that the human rights issues had not been given due consideration in his individual case and alleged an infringement of Article 48 of the Treaty of Rome, 1957,[6] and various breaches of the European Convention on Human Rights, 1950 ("the Convention").

The Government of Hong Kong and the Secretary of State claimed that the applicant was protected by the Joint Declaration which the United Kingdom had concluded with the PRC in 1984. The Joint Declaration provided that the legal system was to remain intact for fifty years after the handover. They also argued that the Basic Law, accepted in the People's Congress in April 1990 as the PRC's constitution for its new Special Administrative Region ("HKSAR") and implementing the treaty obligations owed by the PRC to the United Kingdom under the Joint Declaration, also protected the applicant in that it invested the HKSAR with independent judicial power and preserved legal safeguards. The Secretary of State argued that the United Kingdom Government was bound to proceed on the basis

---

[2] For the text of Section 11(3), see p. 408 below.
[3] For the text of Section 12(1), see p. 408 below.
[4] For the text of Section 12(2), see p. 409 below.
[5] For the text of Section 6(4), see p. 446 below.
[6] For the text of Article 48(3), see p. 460 below.

that the PRC would respect its treaty obligations and that his assessment concerning the future of Hong Kong after the handover was a non-justiciable political judgment by the Executive.

Held (by the Divisional Court):—The applicant's application for judicial review was allowed. The warrant ordering his return was quashed.

(1) There was no reason to conclude that the Secretary of State was improperly taking the seriousness of the offences into account in assessing whether the applicant could have a fair trial in Hong Kong. No error of law was to be inferred from the reference to "serious offences" in the first sentence of the reasons for his decision. Neither was there any reviewable error of law in the way that he assessed the periods of delay and their relevance to the passage of time since the offences allegedly were committed (pp. 415-18).

(2) The Secretary of State had acted with procedural fairness, addressed the correct issues and acted within the confines of his discretion (pp. 418-19).

(3) There was no reason to conclude that the Secretary of State had not taken into account the applicant's claim that his extradition would be oppressive given his lack of connection with Hong Kong and his personal circumstances (p. 419).

(4) The public policy exception to the freedom of movement guaranteed by Article 48 of the Treaty of Rome, a directly effective provision, encompassed extradition and justified the applicant's arrest in the United Kingdom (pp. 419-21).

(5) As the European Convention on Human Rights had not been incorporated into United Kingdom law there could be no adjudication on any alleged breach of that Convention (pp. 421-2).

(6) It was realistic to proceed on the basis that any trial and sentencing of the applicant in Hong Kong would occur after the transfer of sovereignty from the United Kingdom to the PRC. In assessing the risks of there being an unfair trial, inhumane punishment or a failure to comply with the specialty provisions required by Section 6(4) of the Act, it was appropriate to have regard to the evidence advanced on behalf of the applicant, subject to the submissions on justiciability. This evidence encompassed that of human rights abuse, the imposition of the death penalty for corruption offences in the PRC, the wide interpretation given by the PRC to acts of State, over which cases it had jurisdiction, the requirement that the PRC approve of Hong Kong's extradition arrangements and affidavits observing a lack of democracy and rule of law in the PRC (pp. 422-5).

(7) The Section 12 discretion was justiciable, even when a decision was taken on sensitive political or policy grounds. Indeed it was when the interests of the State and the interests of the fugitive were in direct conflict that this protection intended by Parliament was most relevant. The Court was obliged to observe its constitutional role of review whatever the limitations, sensitive to the delicacy of relations with the foreign State and to the advantages possessed by the primary decision taker in relation to the issue (pp. 425-33).

(8) In exercising his discretion, the Secretary of State had been bound by a collective Cabinet decision to proceed on the basis that the PRC would comply with its treaty obligations and that the legal protections would

therefore remain intact and effective. In not exercising his personal judgment he had failed to direct himself properly as to his Section 12 responsibilities and had thus deprived the applicant of his main safeguard at this stage. The matter was remitted to the Secretary of State for further consideration (pp. 433-6).

The Secretary of State appealed to the House of Lords.

Held (unanimously):—The appeal was allowed and applications for judicial review dismissed.

(1) The process of reasoning of the Secretary of State in deciding to return the applicant to Hong Kong in July 1995 and again in December 1995 was evident in the associated letters and affidavits. Although the Court was entitled to examine the Secretary of State's decisions in the normal way, and had a sound basis for doing so, it had to exercise great caution in holding such decisions to be irrational, given the substantial policy content and the sensitivity of the assessment of the effect of treaty obligations undertaken between two sovereign States. The documents revealed that the Secretary of State had given careful consideration to the applicant's representations, giving great weight to the provisions of the Joint Declaration and the Basic Law and proceeding on the basis that the PRC would honour its treaty obligations. There was no evidence of a collective Cabinet decision and the application of the test of whether it was unjust, oppressive or wrong to order the applicant's return showed an awareness that the rights of the individual prevailed over any public interest concern (pp. 447-9).

(2) The test applied by the Secretary of State as to whether it would be wrong, unjust or oppressive to surrender the applicant was the correct one to be applied in an extradition case. The Secretary of State was not entitled to ignore representations, which were responsibly raised, on the assumption that a foreign State would adhere to its treaty obligations. The greater the perceived risk to life or liberty, the greater the importance of detailed scrutiny of the decision (pp. 449-51).

(3) In carefully considering all of the representations made by the applicant, taking advice from the Government of Hong Kong and giving reasons for his decision, the Secretary of State had acted with procedural fairness. It could not be said that he had acted irrationally. Parliament had entrusted him with the discretion whether or not to grant a surrender warrant and thus, whether or not the PRC was to be trusted to implement its treaty obligations was a decision for the Secretary of State and not the Court, which was confined to a supervisory jurisdiction. In the circumstances it was not unreasonable for the Secretary of State to be optimistic about the future for human rights in Hong Kong after the handover. The Secretary of State had not failed to direct himself properly as to his responsibilities under Section 12 of the Act as the evidence revealed that he did not consider himself bound by the Cabinet's assumption that the PRC would comply with its treaty obligations. He had made his own decision after considering all of the representations and examining the risks of injustice and oppression to the applicant as an individual, concluding that the PRC could be relied upon to respect the law in the applicant's case with regard to a fair trial and the imposition of appropriate penalties (pp. 451-4).

(4) The requirements of specialty protection contained in Section 6(4) of the Act were satisfied at the time that the Secretary of State took the decisions and would continue to be satisfied until the date of the handover. It was reasonable to conclude that, in accordance with the fundamental policy enshrined in the Basic Law, the prohibitions necessary to ensure that the applicant would not be surrendered to the PRC would be in place after 1 July 1997. That this had not been considered by the Secretary of State was not fatal to his decisions as he dealt sufficiently with the representations which were made to him at the time and the position was not materially different from that already anticipated (pp. 454-9).

(5) It was unnecessary to examine whether or not the public policy exception permitted extradition in cases where there was a risk of a breach of the Convention as the relevant provisions of the European Community Treaty did not apply to extradition cases (pp. 459-62).

(6) Although the European Convention on Human Rights did not bind the Executive, and only influenced the common law, it was necessary to subject the decision of the Secretary of State to the most anxious scrutiny due to the risk of interference with the applicant's human rights. The evidence revealed that the Secretary of State had shown proper regard to the rights of the applicant and to his individual case in applying the test as to whether in all the circumstances it would be unjust or oppressive to return him to Hong Kong. It was not irrational for the Secretary of State to decide that he was not persuaded that there was a case on human rights grounds for refusing extradition. A reasonable Secretary of State could, on the material available to him, have concluded that the concerns which were indicated by the PRC's actions in other places and in other circumstances were not so serious as to give rise to a serious risk of injustice or oppression in the applicant's case (pp. 462-5).

The text of the opinions delivered in the House of Lords commences at p. 436. The following is the text of the judgment of the Divisional Court, delivered by Henry LJ:

This is the judgment of the Court. By a request dated 7 October 1993, the Governor of Hong Kong seeks the extradition of the applicant Mr Launder to Hong Kong to face trial upon charges of corruption (the receipt of bribes totalling approximately 4.5 million) over the period October 1980 to June 1982.

The Secretary of State issued the authority to proceed on that request on 12 January 1994, and on 7 April 1994 the magistrate committed Mr Launder under Section 9 of the Extradition Act 1989 to await the Home Secretary's decision whether to return him to Hong Kong. Mr Launder challenged that order by applying for a writ of habeas corpus to the Divisional Court. That application was refused by the Court by judgment given on 14 December 1994, and on 9 March 1995 leave to appeal to the House of Lords was refused.

Those events set the stage for the decisions now challenged: the exercise of the Secretary of State's general discretion whether to order the defendant's return under Section 12(1) of the Act:

12(1)Where a person is committed under Section 9 above and is not discharged by order of the High Court . . ., the Secretary of State may by warrant order him to be returned unless his return is prohibited . . . by this Act, or the Secretary of State decides under this Section to make no such order in his case.

Here the Secretary of State considered substantial representations from both the requesting authority and the applicant, and by letter dated 31 July 1995 ordered the return of the applicant to Hong Kong. That is the first decision challenged in these proceedings.

The applicant further contends that significant developments have occurred in Hong Kong, both before as well as after 31 July 1995, which (it is alleged) show he will not get a fair trial if returned to Hong Kong. We refer to these allegations compendiously as the China point. As a consequence, the applicant's solicitors wrote on 29 November 1995 to the Secretary of State inviting him, in the light of the further material presented, to reconsider his order to return. He did so, and by letter dated 21 December 1995 notified the applicant of his decision not to withdraw the order. That decision too is challenged in these proceedings. Mr David Vaughan QC appears for the applicant, Mr Kenneth Parker QC for the Respondents, the Secretary of State, and Mr Alun Jones QC for the Government of Hong Kong, who appear as an interested party.

We consider first the scheme of the Extradition Act 1989, particularly in relation to the respective responsibilities and functions of the Court and the Secretary of State.

Section 11 deals with applications for habeas corpus challenging committal under Section 9. Under this Section the High Court has a primary fact-finding and decision-taking jurisdiction. Section 11(3) reads:

11(3) Without prejudice to any jurisdiction of the High Court apart from this section, the court shall order the applicant's discharge if it appears to the court in relation to the offence, or each of the offences, in respect of which the applicant's return is sought, that:

(a) by reason of the trivial nature of the offence; or

(b) by reason of the passage of time since he is alleged to have committed it or to have become unlawfully at large, as the case may be; or

(c) because the accusation against him is not made in good faith in the interests of justice,

it would, having regard to all the circumstances, be unjust or oppressive to return him.

The significance of this provision was emphasized by Lord Ackner in *R* v. *Governor of Pentonville Prison, ex parte Sinclair* [1991] 2 AC 64, [1991] 2 All ER 366 at pp. 80-1 of the former report:

By this section a radical alteration has been made by giving to the High Court, in part at least, the same kind of discretion as to whether or not to discharge an applicant as the Secretary of State has in deciding whether or not to order a fugitive criminal to be returned to a requesting state.

But those powers of the Court are both given and limited by the Statute. *In re Schmidt* [1995] 1 AC 339, [1994] 3 All ER 65[7] at 378H of the former report, makes that clear:

Accordingly, the position now is that in extradition proceedings under the Act of 1989 the High Court has power to intervene only in the circumstances predicated by the Act and has no inherent Common Law supervisory power as contended for by the applicant. The principal safeguard for the subject of extradition proceedings therefore remains in the general discretion conferred upon the Secretary of State by Parliament in Section 12.

We emphasize the second sentence referring to the Section 12(1) discretion.

The question raised under Section 11 was addressed by the Divisional Court in December 1994, in proceedings which we will examine later. The present challenge relates to the Secretary of State's responsibilities under Section 12 (we speak of his responsibilities because he took the decision here. Section 28 of the Act restricts such decisions to the Secretary of State, or a Minister of State, or an Under-Secretary of State). We have quoted Section 12(1) already—sub-section (2) deals with the more specific aspects of his discretion, sometimes called the mandatory requirements:

12(2) Without prejudice to his general discretion as to the making of an order for the return of a person to a foreign state, Commonwealth country or colony—

(a) the Secretary of State shall not make an order in the case of any person if it appears to the Secretary of State in relation to the offence, or each of the offences, in respect of which his return is sought, that

(i) by reason of its trivial nature; or

(ii) by reason of the passage of time since he is alleged to have committed it or to have become unlawfully at large, as the case may be; or

(iii) because the accusation made against him is not made in good faith in the interests of justice,

it would, having regard to all the circumstances, be unjust or oppressive to return him; and

(b) The Secretary may decide to make no order for the return of a person accused or convicted of an offence not punishable with death in Great Britain if that person could be or has been sentenced to death for that offence in the country by which the request for his return is made.

[7 111 *ILR* 548.]

It will be seen that, while covering in Section 12(2)(a) the ground which the Divisional Court will have covered in Section 11(3), the Secretary of State covers a much wider field having regard to Section 12(1) and 12(2)(b). Both the Court and the Secretary of State may apply the general restrictions on return to be found in Section 6 of the Act. But the Secretary of State's Section 12(1) discretion not to return the fugitive is not only the fugitive's last hope, but the widest in its scope.

We will need to examine the nature of the responsibilities on the Secretary of State when exercising that discretion when we come to consider the relevance of the fact that, if the applicant is returned the likelihood (or so it seems to us) is that any trial of him (and any punishment if he were convicted) would be (and would be served) after the transfer of sovereignty of Hong Kong to the People's Republic of China (PRC). For convenience in this hearing we have referred to the legal issues arising from that transfer as "the China point".

This was a case where the Secretary of State gave his reasons for ordering the surrender in his decision letter of 31 July 1995. We believe that giving reasons represents something of a breakthrough in extradition litigation. Previously, reasons were usually only given after proceedings had been issued for judicial review of the decision. This (as we said in giving leave in *R* v. *Secretary of State for the Home Department, ex parte Chetta* recently) created a logically unsatisfactory situation. Where a decision is very important to the applicant, there is a clear need for reasons for that decision: one reason for that is so the applicant can decide whether he has the basis for an attack on the legality of the decision arising out of those reasons. It creates an Alice in Wonderland situation if you have to mount a reasoned attack on the reasons before you know what they are. But, having decided to give reasons, the Secretary of State sensibly reserved the right to "expand" on those given. That he was clearly entitled to do.

We start by considering the mandatory requirement of Section 12(2)(a)(ii): under which the Secretary of State shall not make an order to return a person if, by reason of the passage of time since he is alleged to have committed the extradition offences it would, having regard to all the circumstances, be unjust or oppressive to return him.

This was the same question that the Divisional Court had to ask themselves under Section 11(3) on the habeas corpus proceedings. The Court was, of course, considering that matter in relation to the situation as it stood up to the date when it gave judgment in December 1994. The Secretary of State was looking at the matter (taking it at the date of the second decision challenged) just over a year later, and so it is necessary to take into account the matters that happened in that year. But, that apart, the Divisional Court were answering the same question that the Secretary of State had to answer.

1. *The Divisional Court's decision of 14 December 1994 (Glidewell LJ and Curtis J)*
On delay generally, the last of the bribes is alleged to have been received by Mr Launder in June 1982, and the first some eighteen months earlier. Therefore at the time of the Divisional Court hearing the offences date from twelve-and-a-half to fourteen years earlier, and at the time of the Secretary of State's final consideration, a year longer. It is said that, on the reported cases, this lapse of time is unprecedented. The cases of *Sinclair (supra)* and *Patel (infra)* suggest that that is right. But where an offender's actions have significantly contributed to such delay, it is not meaningful simply to measure the time in years. Hence the analysis conducted by the Divisional Court:

> It is obvious the time which has elapsed since the offences are alleged to have been committed is very lengthy, and it is therefore necessary to go into the chronology in some little detail.

The Divisional Court divided the time up into four periods. The first period was from the commission of the alleged offences until September 1987, the date of the effective start of the investigation by the Hong Kong Independent Commission against Corruption (ICAC). The reason for that delay is that until the receipt of a letter by an informer purporting to be an investor in the bank, nobody suspected Mr Launder of corruption. The Court absolved the Hong Kong Government and ICAC for any part of that delay, and stated that the delay after 1983 resulted "in part" from Mr Launder's own activities. They considered evidence that steps had been taken to conceal the fact that the trail led to Mr Launder. Some large payments which were made to him and then went on to his company Honeywell were in cash, and where cheques were used, they were not made out to him. And all the money had left Hong Kong by the end of 1983.

The second period was September 1987 to November 1989, when the warrant for the arrest of Mr Launder in Hong Kong was issued. Here the Court found that one year of that two-year period was justified but not the other. The Hong Kong Government and ICAC were responsible for the other year.

Next there was the period from November 1989 to September 1993 when Mr Launder was finally tracked down and arrested at Heathrow in September 1993. He had not been hiding over that period. He had lived openly as a businessman first in Gibraltar, then from some time in 1990 in Berlin. From these bases he travelled the world using his own name and his own credit cards. The prosecution's difficulties were first that if they could discover where Mr Launder last had been, it did not tell them where he was going next. Second, he could only be arrested in a country from which extradition to Hong Kong was a possibility, having regard in particular to the limitation period some countries impose on extradition crime. Warrants were issued for him in Gibraltar and England, but his visits there were infrequent, short-lived and unpredictable. Accordingly, the Divisional Court found that as he was taking pains not to make himself available to the authorities, so he was responsible for that period of delay. As a footnote, it will be seen that when referring (in general terms) to the person whose return to face trial is sought, we refer to him as "the fugitive". In so doing, we are simply following a common usage in extradition law and do not make any assumptions in Mr Launder's case by use of that word.

The fourth period was from September 1993 until the present date. That time had been (and still is being) taken up with the various legal challenges Mr Launder makes to the extradition request.

The Court concluded:

> In summary . . . before September 1987 the Hong Kong Government has no responsibility for the passage of time. Mr Launder has a general responsibility for concealing his part in these offences, if he is guilty of them. By then much of what general prejudice must be caused by the passage of time, that is to say the dimming of memory of potential witnesses, must already have been caused. Secondly, after September 1987 the Hong Kong Government in my view is responsible for, at most, twelve months' of delay during the latter part of the period to September 1989. Thirdly, after September 1989 when the warrant for his arrest was issued, Mr Launder is in my judgment wholly responsible for the delay. (*per* Glidewell LJ, with whom Curtis J agreed).

The Court then went on to consider the effect of the passage of time on whether there could be a fair trial on Mr Launder's return. The Court found that much of the "general prejudice", such as the dimming of the memory of potential witnesses, must have already occurred before the alleged offences were discovered as a result of the informer's letter. The case is that the 4.5 million received by one of Mr Launder's companies from the Carrian Group of companies and the EDA Group of companies were "sweeteners" for past and future favours for loans by Wardley, the investment banking arm of the Hong Kong and Shanghai Bank, of which Mr Launder was Chief Executive. When those groups collapsed in 1982/1983, they owed Wardley approximately 75 million. The prosecution is in a position to prove the passage of the 4.5 million to Mr Launder through his companies.

The applicant denies that an inference of guilt can properly be drawn from the facts that payments made by Tan and Chung or persons connected with them were invested for the benefit of Honeywell, of which he was the sole beneficial owner and that those funds were subsequently realized and removed from Hong Kong. The applicant denies that he was in a position to authorize the relevant loans and says that he was not present at meetings of the Credit Committee of the Bank when they were approved. He complains in non-specific terms about the unavailability of witnesses who could speak to the conduct of the Loans Department and as to the commercial and banking ethos in the early 1980s. With the exception of one Daniel Chung, he does not identify the witnesses, nor explain why no steps were taken to approach them for statements at least by 1989 when he was aware of the warrants, or 1991 when he accepts he knew of the specific charges. The same must apply to documents which he now says may be difficult to trace.

The prosecution say that his real evidential difficulty is that there seems to be no evidence from any quarter of that money going back to either the donors or their companies—and the need for such evidence would have been clear to him a long time ago. The prosecution will ask the Court to infer that these were illegal payments because of the secret and unusual manner in which they were carried out (for instance when large amounts of cash and blank cheques from George Tan were handed over by Launder to an employee of a small finance company in a disposable shopping bag in the foyer of a hotel).

Against this background the Court considered the question of prejudice to the applicant. The Court found that there was no prejudice from any lack of documents. As to any prejudice from lack of witnesses, the Court was handicapped by the fact that Mr Launder did not disclose what his defence was, nor identify the witnesses who would not be available for the defence. The Court did what it could: namely consider the scenario of Mr Launder calling those alleged to be his co-conspirators, Mr Tan and Mr Chung. It was for the defence to decide whether to put any specific difficulties the passage of time caused them before the Court. They were not obliged to, and they chose not to. The Court had before it no sufficient material on which they could say that it was not possible for Mr Launder to have a fair trial on his return. The Court raised the difficulties in its judgment. Those difficulties were not subsequently confronted and dealt with by the applicant. Yet he now seeks to criticize the Secretary of State for not alerting him to this evidential shortcoming. There is nothing in that criticism.

Lastly, the Court then had before it a relatively undeveloped version of the China point. By an affidavit of Alan Colin Byrnes dated 24 October 1994 the applicant placed before the Court:

a) the uncertain situation as to specialty and opportunity to leave after 1st July 1997 when the existing explicit guarantees cease to be part of Hong Kong law;

b) the deteriorating state of relations between the governments of Hong Kong and the PRC which did not justify an assumption that the relevant law/practice in Hong Kong after 1st July 1997 would remain as before. At paragraph 22 he quotes from an address by the Governor of the Colony on 5th October 1994:

> . . . It is the people of Hong Kong who will pay for the failure to complete the Joint Liaison Group's agenda by 1997. To leave uncertainty about arrangements for the return of fugitive offenders will do nothing to inspire confidence.

He raises a further point, namely that if convicted in Hong Kong he might have to serve his sentence in circumstances where:

> there can be no guarantee of the treatment he would then receive. Indeed, part of the penalty is that corruption is met with the death penalty in China.

The Court concluded that while that fear represented "a very serious practical issue", it was not a matter they would take into account because it was a political matter and not one for the Court:

> It is a political matter for the Home Secretary. I say this: not merely can the Home Secretary, but in my view he most certainly should consider this issue seriously . . . when deciding whether to order Mr Launder's return under Section 12(1) of the Act. That decision remains to be made.

Mr Alun Jones QC, for the Hong Kong Government, has made clear to us that the full force of the China point was not one that could realistically be taken at the Section 11 stage of the process—it is a Section 12 point. We will revert to this.

Accordingly, Mr Launder's application failed. Leave to appeal to the House of Lords was sought, but refused.

It is clear from the Secretary of State's decision in this case first, that he gave proper consideration to the Divisional Court's findings on their Section 11 jurisdiction of the issues he had to deal with under Section 12, and second, that he reached a similar conclusion to that Court.

As has already been made clear, his was a task different from theirs in that first, the Secretary of State was viewing the matter from a later date, a year on, and second, he was exercising his own judgment.

But on the common facts that were being considered, it was not seriously contended before us that it could be said that it was irrational (or *Wednesbury* unreasonable: see *Associated Provincial Picture Houses Ltd* v. *Wednesbury Corporation* [1948] 1 KB 223, [1947] 2 All ER 680) for the Secretary of State to have reached the same factual conclusion as had been reached by the Divisional Court when exercising its primary jurisdiction under Section 11. So essentially the attack was necessarily based on his alleged errors of law in reaching that conclusion.

2. *Alleged errors of law on passage of time*
   a) In his decision letter, the Secretary of State opens his reasons for ordering the applicant's surrender with the sentence:

Mr Launder is charged with serious offences in respect of which a prima facie case has been established.

Complaint is made that the Secretary of State:

appears to have taken into account the seriousness of these alleged offences in considering injustice notwithstanding *Kakis* v. *Government of Cyprus* [1978] 1 WLR 779.

In that case, the House of Lords was considering the statutory predecessor to Section 11, namely Section 8(3)(b) of the Fugitive Offenders Act 1967. Lord Diplock said:

The gravity of the offence is relevant to whether changes in the circumstances of the accused which have occurred during the relevant period are such as would render his return to stand his trial oppressive; but it is not, in my view, a matter which should affect the court's decision under Section 8(3)b where the relevant event which happened in that period is one which involves the risk of prejudice to the accused in the conduct of the trial itself—as in the case of Mr Alexandrou's departure from Cyprus.

Mr Alexandrou was a crucial alibi witness for Mr Kakis. However, he could not return to Cyprus for fear of ill-treatment by his political opponents. Lord Diplock was saying that where such an event deprived the applicant of the evidence of a crucial witness, that went to the question of whether it would be unjust to return him, and in dealing with questions of injustice in the trial process, the gravity of the offence was usually not relevant. But, as the passage quoted shows, the gravity of the offence may be relevant in relation to the question of oppression, and in any event the Secretary of State must look to see whether the offence is serious or trivial having relation to Section 12(2)(a)(i). In our judgment no error of law is to be inferred from that bland first sentence of his reasons. We are not persuaded that the Secretary of State illegitimately was taking the seriousness of the offences into account in considering the question as to whether Mr Launder could have a fair trial in Hong Kong.

   b) On the question of passage of time since the dates when it is alleged the offences were committed, the Secretary of State followed the breakdown of the period into four parts, and reached essentially the same conclusion as the Divisional Court had as to the attribution of responsibility for the delay. Like the Divisional Court, he concluded that one year's delay was the sole responsibility of the Hong Kong Government. The rest was either unavoidable, or Mr Launder's responsibility. Those were findings of fact which he was well entitled to reach. But complaint is made as to the way the delay was treated in law.

The first complaint, logically and chronologically, relates to the period from the dates of the offences (October 1980-June 1982) until the receipt in September 1987 of the pseudonymous letter accusing Mr Launder. The Secretary of State amplified his decision letter by affidavit from Mr Ackland (Head of the International Criminal Policy Division in the Home Office) to make clear that the Secretary of State accepted that Mr Launder had concealed the flow of funds to him, that Mr Launder had a general responsibility for that concealment, and that no part of the delay in this period was the fault of the Hong Kong authorities. That passage reflected Glidewell LJ's judgment in the Divisional Court. The alleged error of law is that by that approach the Secretary of State improperly assumed the guilt of Mr Launder.

Reliance is placed on *Attorney-General of Hong Kong* v. *Cheung Wai-Bun* [1994] 1 AC 1, [1993] 2 All ER 510, HL). There the defendant was indicted on charges of conspiracy to defraud and false accounting, the allegation being that the false accounting offences had been committed in order to conceal the conspiracy. The Crown sought to rely on the cover-up they were alleging to show that the defendant had contributed to the delay. Lord Woolf, giving the judgment of the Privy Council, said at 7E of the former report:

However the difficulty in the way of [that submission] is that unless and until the defendant's guilt or innocence was established at the trial, it would not be known whether the defendant had been responsible for concealing the fraud offence. His involvement was the very question around which the trial would revolve . . . In relation to conduct which will be an issue at the trial, the correct approach is for the judge to bear in mind the nature of the Prosecution's case as part of the factual background against which the alleged delay has to be considered and not as necessarily being a bar to the application succeeding. In this case there can be no doubt that Duffy J was well aware of this and there is nothing in his judgment to indicate that he did not give due consideration to the nature of the Prosecution's case in reaching his decision to grant a stay.

It seems to us clear that both the Secretary of State and the Divisional Court followed that approach. The passage in question acknowledges that the significance of the conduct complained of depends on guilt. The nature of the Hong Kong Government's case is that the passage of this money into Mr Launder's account was concealed by activities and devices inconsistent with an above-board business transaction. Mr Launder was free, but not obliged, to offer his explanation for the activities that look like concealment. Absent such explanations, the Secretary of State was entitled, in considering the passage of time, first to have in mind the nature of the prosecution case, and second to reach his conclusion as to where responsibility for the delay lies based on his views of the strength of that case in all the circumstances, taking care not to assume guilt. Concealment is often a badge of fraud, and unexplained concealment does nothing to weaken a prima facie case whereas properly explained concealment might. There is no reason to believe that the Secretary of State assumed guilt in reaching his conclusion. The Secretary of State was entitled to reach the conclusion he did.

That period of delay is of considerable significance, because if and in so far as this may be a case in which memory may be tested (and without any clear idea of the nature of the defence it is not possible to form a view on the importance of memory) most "fading" will, as the Divisional Court found, have occurred by then.

The second period, from September 1987 to November 1989, deals with the time spent by the ICAC investigating the allegations made. While the Secretary of State concluded that the length of this period was primarily due to the difficulty of the task presented, he found that the Hong Kong Government was directly responsible for one year of that delay. The suggestion is made that, when finally considering this question, he treated this application as though there had only been one year's delay. That is a misreading of his decision.

The third period, from November 1989 to September 1993, was after Mr Launder was fully aware, first that he was subject of an ongoing investigation, and, from 1991 onwards, that there was a warrant out for his arrest. The Hong Kong Government in their submissions assert that he was "living the life of a fugitive" over this period. Understandably, Mr Launder objects to that characterization, because there was little if any concealment of his whereabouts by him. True, he was in countries where no warrant had been issued and from which extradition would have been impossible. Physically, he was not hiding, but in law his actions had much the same effect. In *Kakis* v. *Government of Cyprus (supra)* Lord Diplock said (at 783A):

Delay in the commencement or conduct of extradition proceedings which is brought about by the accused himself by fleeing the country, concealing his whereabouts or evading arrest cannot, in my view be relied upon as a ground for holding it to be either unjust or oppressive to return him. Any difficulties that he may encounter in the conduct of his defence and in consequence of the delay due to such causes are of his own choice and making. Save in the most exceptional circumstances it would be neither unjust nor oppressive that he should be required to accept them.

Against that background it seems to us to be impossible to criticize the Secretary of State's conclusion that over that period Mr Launder was responsible for the delay.

The fourth period is the delay from his arrest in September 1993 to date. It seems to us clear that the Secretary of State was treating that delay as unavoidable. We do not read the decision letter, as expanded in Mr Ackland's affidavit, as either ignoring the totality of the time that has passed since the dates of the alleged offences, or the effects of that passage of time. Accordingly, in our judgment there is no force in the criticisms that the Secretary of State simply looked on the only relevant period of delay as that which the Hong Kong Government had been found responsible for, or that he ceased to consider the delay after the applicant's arrest. And, as the citation from Lord Diplock in *Kakis* cited above shows, when looking at the overall length of the delay, there is a fundamental difference between this case and cases such as *R* v. *Secretary of State for the Home Department, ex parte Patel* [1995] 7 Admin LR 56, where all the culpable delay was on the part of the US authorities. Accordingly, we find no reviewable error in the way the Secretary of State dealt with these matters.

3. Procedural improprieties, injustice and perversity

Finally, on the aspects of the case which overlapped with the issues before the Divisional Court on the habeas corpus hearing, it is asserted that:

on the question of injustice and passage of time . . . the decision of the Secretary of State was unlawful, irrational, tainted with procedural impropriety and should be quashed.

Complaint is made of a failure to listen, a failure to give reasons, unfairness in failing to alert the applicant's advisers as to perceived weaknesses in their representations, a failure to conduct an abuse of process type of proceeding here, and the suggestion that in supplementing the reasons originally given, the Secretary of State went beyond anticipated expansion thus impermissibly bolstering his original stated reasons. Complaint is made that the Hong Kong Government's evidence was essentially accepted, it is suggested, uncritically. And the Secretary of State is invited to go into the merits of the criminal case in some detail in a wide-ranging "injustice review".

For the most part, these are procedural matters going to the question of fairness, with perversity and irrationality invoked whenever the submission hits an adverse finding of fact. The process sought emerges as more of an appeal than a *Wednesbury* review.

We are not impressed by these points, whether individually or cumulatively. The Secretary of State gave the applicant great scope for making representations, and the opportunity to do so was fully taken over more than a hundred pages. There is nothing to indicate that these representations were not properly considered. Nor do we consider that any "reasons" objection can here succeed, though the wide-ranging nature of the representations inevitably meant that not every point was dealt with.

Here we are satisfied that, on a "normal" Section 12 challenge, the Secretary of State acted with procedural fairness, addressed himself to the right issues, and acted well within the confines of his discretion. Accordingly, these grounds for judicial review of his decision fail.

4. *The applicant's personal circumstances in relation to the claim based on oppression/change of circumstances since the offences*

The applicant is sixty. He was educated at Rugby and at Heidelberg University. He is married with adult children and grandchildren all of whom live in England; his main home is in England. He is by profession an investment advisor who was based in this country until he went to Hong Kong in 1973, becoming Managing Director and Chief Executive of Wardley Ltd which is the merchant banking branch of the Hong Kong and Shanghai Bank. He was posted back to the UK in August 1983 and resigned from the Bank in the December with effect from March 1984. He has spent only two days in Hong Kong since August 1983. He has no personal or family connections there and, so far as is known, no resources. Since leaving Hong Kong he has established another business, presently based in Germany. He is therefore a British subject, who carries on business within the European Community. He asserts he has no ties with Hong Kong, nor has his wife.

The applicant represented to the Secretary of State that he is facing surrender to a country many thousands of miles from his home; his family would have great difficulty in visiting him. Having regard to the passage of time since the applicant last had contact with Hong Kong, his lack of connection there and the changes in and pending in Hong Kong since 1983 he says it would be oppressive to return him there. The uncertainty as to the conditions under which he might be tried and, if convicted, sentenced add to the strain generated by any return and taken together with the personal circumstances make it oppressive to order his return.

Those matters were fully before the Secretary of State who says he considered them. There is no reason to reject that. This aspect of the application must fail.

5. *The European Community law and European Convention on Human Rights points*

a) The applicant first contends that his arrest at Heathrow was an infringement of his right of freedom of movement given by Article 48 of the Treaty of Rome. That protection is, of course, of direct effect. It is also subject to such limitations as may be justified on grounds of public policy.

His argument is that his working base was Germany at the time, and as he could not have been extradited from Germany, so Article 48 gave him the right notionally to carry that immunity with him wherever he went in the Community.

If his right to freedom of movement achieved that result then, as Mr Parker pointed out, it would apply equally to his liability to be arrested, charged, tried and sentenced for a substantive criminal offence contravening UK laws. If he committed an offence against UK laws for which he could not be extradited from Germany, he could none the less be arrested on arrival here and tried. Public policy would require that, and public policy would also permit a Member State to honour its own wholly non-discriminatory extradition arrangements free from any limitation coming in by way of a side-wind from Article 48.

Unsurprisingly, the English courts have decided that Article 48 did not have that "emasculating" effect on the process of extradition (see *R* v. *Governor of Pentonville Prison, ex parte Budlong and Kember* [1980] 1 All ER 701, [1980] 1 WLR 1110)[8] and the cases which subsequently have followed it, reference to which may be found in *In re Archondakis* (unreported Divisional Court CO/2744/93, 16 November 1994, Glidewell LJ). Referred to there are four Divisional Court authorities to the same effect, which in the ordinary course would be binding on us.

Mr Vaughan, however, submits that all those cases are wrong, because *ex parte Kember* was founded on *R* v. *Saunders* (1979 ECR 1129), and itself was not a Community case. He draws attention to the fact that the well-known case of *Bosman* (1995 ECR 1-1) distinguishes *R* v. *Saunders* on the basis that there was no Community element in that case, and so as the situation was wholly internal, it was plain that Article 48 did not apply. That is right, but we are not satisfied that that fact destroys the reasoning in those cases.

Bosman was concerned with whether football transfer rules formed an obstacle to the freedom of movement for workers and were therefore prohibited by Article 48 of the Treaty. The Court held that provisions which preclude or deter a national of a Member State from leaving his country of origin in order to exercise his right to freedom of movement were such an obstacle, even if applied without regard for the nationality of the workers concerned.

It is difficult in our view to extend that to embrace the application by a Member State of its extradition law. As Griffiths J said in *Budlong/Kember*:[9]

[8 85 *ILR* 72.]　　　　　[9 85 *ILR* 72.]

I regard extradition as far more closely analogous to the implementation of domestic criminal law than to deportation . . . the Extradition Act specifically provides that there will be no extradition unless the foreign state undertakes to allow the accused to return to this country after he has been dealt with for the extradition crime. Extradition is no more than a step that assists in the implementation of the domestic criminal law of the foreign state.

The reliance upon *Saunders* in that case was for the purpose of refusing a reference to the European Court of Justice.

In *Virdee* [1980] 1 CMLR 709, when dealing with the question of whether an applicant for habeas corpus could be lawfully surrendered to a non-EC State under the Visiting Forces Act 1952, the Court held in unambiguous terms that Article 48 had no application. If the intended end result of the "handover" was considered, the situation was closely akin to extradition and "it could not have been the intention of those who drew the Treaty of Rome that it should have the effect of emasculating the process of extradition". In *Virdee* the handover was intended as a step in the implementation of the domestic military law of the foreign State.

In *Healy* [1984] 3 CMLR 575, the court was concerned with whether the detention of an Irish national in the United Kingdom pending extradition infringed Article 48. The Court was specifically (but unsuccessfully) asked not to follow *Kember* and *Virdee*. Goff LJ (at page 583) held that the decision in *Saunders*, from which the other cases have flowed, was based on a purposive interpretation of Article 48.

It was obvious to the court that Article 48 did not aim to restrict the power of member states to lay down restrictions in their own territory on the freedom of movement of all persons subject to their jurisdiction in the implementation of extradition procedure . . . For my part although this court would be free to depart from the decisions of *Kember* and *Virdee*, I can see no ground for departing from those decisions, with which I find myself respectfully in agreement.

We can see nothing in *Bosman* which undermines the principles applied by the courts in the cases cited in *Archondakis* for holding the latter to be wrong.

In our judgment, extradition must come within the public policy exception.

b) Lastly, the European Convention on Human Rights. Every lawyer knows that the Convention has not been incorporated into UK law. The case of *Brind and Others* v. *Secretary of State for the Home Department* [1991] 1 AC 696, [1991] 1 All ER 720[10] so decided. It did so in clear general terms, discouraging any incorporation of the Convention by the back door. That discouragement has not stopped subsequent

[[10] 85 *ILR* 29.]

applications to the tradesman's entrance. That is what Mr Vaughan ingeniously seeks to achieve here. He emphasizes the flexibility of judicial review, the importance of the subject-matter, and draws a novel distinction between policy matters and individual adjudications. However, it is plain to us that we would be wrong to adjudicate on breach of the European Convention here—this case is *a fortiori* the decision of this Court in *R* v. *Secretary of State for the Home Department ex parte Chinoy* (unreported C0/156/91, 10 April 1991, Bingham LJ), as here there is not even the link of the Article V(2) of the Treaty's reference to "law". Mr Vaughan is right to make the point that judicial review is a flexible remedy, and often can achieve the same results as could be achieved in the European Court of Human Rights. But what matters is the route. Unless and until the Convention is incorporated into our law, breaches of the Convention cannot be relied on as such to provide the route.

Accordingly, on all matters other than the China point, this application for judicial review must fail. The China point seems to us to be the crux of this case, and to that we turn next.

6. *The China point*

As we have already said, we regard it as realistic to proceed on the basis that any trial of Mr Launder for these offences, and any sentence imposed were he to be convicted, would take place/be served after the transfer of sovereignty at midnight on 30 June 1997. The reasons why that situation has come about are less important than the fact that it has.

The applicant resists extradition to Hong Kong in circumstances where the Requesting State will cease to exist on midnight of 30 June 1997, when the UK will cede sovereignty to Hong Kong to the PRC. Hong Kong will then become a Special Administrative Region of the PRC (HKSAR). International concern has been expressed over the human rights record of the PRC. Neither the UK nor any European Community or Western country has extradition arrangements with the PRC. It is accepted that the present legal, penal and judicial system in Hong Kong properly protects the applicant's right to a fair trial and appropriate humane punishment if applicable. The applicant's case is that there is a real risk that those existing safeguards will not survive the change. If they do not, the consequences for the applicant if returned for trial are serious.

HM Government and the Government of Hong Kong meet this by saying that the applicant is protected by a treaty, the Joint Declaration, entered into with the PRC in 1984, which aims to preserve the present way of life in Hong Kong for a period of fifty years from hand-over. It specifically provides for the legal system to remain intact:

The laws currently in force in Hong Kong will remain basically unchanged.

Further, the PRC's People's Congress in April 1990 agreed the Basic Law as China's constitution for the HKSAR. This invested that region with independent judicial power, including that of final adjudication. It preserved the principle of trial by jury, and the right to a fair trial without delay, with the presumption of innocence.

The Secretary of State's case is that China has not repudiated that treaty, and that:

The Government (of which the Secretary of State is an important member) must proceed on the basis that the PRC will respect its obligations under the treaty. (Respondent's skeleton, paragraph 25)

That, it is submitted, is a non-justiciable political judgment. That approach is faithfully reflected in the affidavits dealing with the treaty and its effect to be found in the evidence filed by the Government of Hong Kong. Mr Matthews, the Attorney-General of Hong Kong, deposed:

In addition to referring to the law which will govern the change in sovereignty, the affidavits of Mr Palmer and Mr Byrnes contain a great deal of speculation about the political future of Hong Kong. I have not responded to any of this speculation. The political assessment concerning Hong Kong's likely future upon the establishment of HKSAR is a matter solely for the Secretary of State for Home Affairs to evaluate, as a Minister of Her Majesty's Government, in considering whether to order Launder's extradition to Hong Kong.

The applicant criticizes this approach as relying solely on the letter of the treaty, and thus not having regard to the realities of the situation. He has filed evidence relating to those realities and the risk they pose to him if returned from Mr Byrnes, a lawyer with specialist practical and academic experience in human rights and extradition law who from 1989 has taught at the University of Hong Kong, from Mr Palmer, Head of the Law Department of the School of Oriental and African Studies (University of London) and a former Head of the China Law Unit of the Attorney-General's Chambers, Hong Kong, from Professor Yash Ghai, CBE, DCL, Sir Y K Pau, Professor of Public Law at the University of Hong Kong, and from Professor Wade of Cambridge.

At this stage it is not necessary to do more than give the flavour of that body of evidence. The concerns they express are specific, reasoned and supported by argument and evidential material. A number of examples may be given. First, the PRC has a well-documented and bad human rights record. In March 1995 a United Nations' vote co-sponsored by the United Kingdom expressed concerns about *inter alia* "due legal process, and a fair trial" and the need to "improve the impartial administration of justice". This despite the fact that the written constitution of the PRC is, as Mr Vaughan QC for the applicant put it to us, "a model of fairness". The submission is that there is a wide gulf between that document and practice.

Second, though Hong Kong has abolished the death penalty for all crimes, it is available in the PRC for, *inter alia*, corruption offences involving sums in excess of 850 [dollars], and is regularly carried out there. In the six months from July to December 1994, Amnesty International monitored ninety-seven death sentences and executions in the PRC. And, worryingly, the Far Eastern Economic Review for 11 May 1995 reported the execution of a man extradited from Thailand to China following the latter's express assurance that he would face no more than a fifteen-year term of imprisonment.

There is an additional problem raised in relation to the interpretation of the Basic Law. This gives the courts of the HKSAR jurisdiction over all cases in the region where the courts in Hong Kong now have jurisdiction, save where the matter relates to acts of State. The normal interpretation of that phrase would cover matters such as foreign and defence policy. The applicant, relying on an affidavit sworn on 11 July 1995 by Michael Palmer, argues that the interpretation of "act of State" in the PRC is very wide and may extend to cover domestic policy and the "implementation of the policies of the government of the day". That, he says, gives rise to the risk that, given the PRC's drive against economic crime, the applicant could be dealt with under an act of State provision and tried for economic offences whereby he would be used as an example of capitalist corruption and dealt with for crimes which may be capital. The Respondents dispute this possibility: in particular the Attorney-General for Hong Kong challenges the interpretation of the provision relied on by the applicant.

This gives rise to a further concern on behalf of the applicant: namely whether the necessary specialty protections required by Section 6(4) of the Act will be in place and effective after change-over. Under the Treaty there should be no problem. The PRC has agreed that Hong Kong may negotiate and conclude its own arrangements for extradition which can continue beyond the change-over date. But this local legislation requires the approval of the PRC. A local Bill dealing with arrangements between the United Kingdom and HKSAR has been drafted, but not approved. This is puzzling, because local extradition arrangements with other countries have been approved. And time is running out. Further, at a time when it might have been hoped that the Hong Kong Government and the PRC would have been working cooperatively together on matters essential for ensuring a smooth constitutional and legal transition, progress has been disappointing. This has given rise to fears that there is a risk that any law made without the agreement of the PRC will not survive the transfer of powers. Mr Byrnes for the applicant gives by way of example the Hong Kong Bill of Rights 1991, which incorporated the United Nations International Covenant on Civil and Political Rights and the International Covenant on Economic, Social and Cultural Rights: this carried with it a reporting obligation to the United Nations. It was to have been among the protections afforded after transfer. But the Chinese Foreign Ministry have issued a statement regretting the passage of the Bill of Rights into Hong Kong law, and specifically reserving the right to review it on the basis that it will adversely affect the implementation of the Basic Law.

The applicant relies in particular on the affidavits of Professor Yash-Ghai CBE, who observes that "The PRC has no experience of democracy", and with this, no experience of the rule of law as it would operate in a democracy. He fears that there can be no guarantee that any legal framework which would provide for an independent system of justice will survive the transfer, against a background where in the PRC the law has often been seen as an instrument of the Party, and of the Executive.

We have done no more than sketch in the outlines of some of the concerns expressed. Those concerns are expressed over many pages of evidence, are closely reasoned, and supported by press reports and the like. The affidavits come from reputable sources, from those whose competence in the field is not questioned. Their conclusions are disputed. We regard it as necessary for present purposes only to submit the totality of that evidence to one simple test of evaluation: should that evidence be taken into account by one assessing the risks: i) of there being an unfair trial; ii) of such trial being followed by inhumane or inappropriate punishment; and iii) the specialty protections not remaining in place after changeover? Our answer to that composite question would have to be "Yes", but subject to the submissions on justiciability which we consider next.

7. *Justiciability*
a) *The applicant's protections*
The legal protections that the applicant has so far enjoyed are the Section 11 protections considered in the habeas corpus challenge. That challenge did not deal with the full force of this point: first because much of what is relied on has occurred since that hearing took place, and second because this is a matter where the applicant's best and widest protection lies under Section 12(1) in the Secretary of State's general discretion not to sign the warrant ordering his return. His second line of defence lies in the supervisory power in the Court

judicially to review the Secretary of State's exercise of that discretion. We deal with the latter protection first, as the Secretary of State submits that that protection is not available in the circumstances of this case. The submission is that his decision sought to be reviewed is based on a political judgment as to the good faith of a foreign sovereign State, the PRC, and whether it will adhere to the provisions of their 1984 Treaty with the United Kingdom. On this political judgment depend three crucial matters: whether in HKSAR, post-June 1997, there will be protections which should ensure a fair trial; whether there will be appropriate protections as to sentence; and whether the necessary specialty protections required by Section 6(4) of the Act will be in place and effective.

Mr Parker QC on behalf of the Secretary of State submits that this issue is non-justiciable as it is founded on a political judgment by the Executive. Before we consider that question of non-justiciability, it is useful to summarize the protection ordinarily available to those whose return is sought in extradition proceedings.

b) *The normal availability of judicial review of the exercise of the Secretary of State's discretion under Section 12(1)*

What we take to be a non-controversial statement of the law is to be found in the *Soering* case, before the European Court of Human Rights (judgment of 7 July 1989, Series A, Vol. 161).[11] The case dealt with a challenge to the efficacy of the remedy of judicial review of the exercise of the Section 12(1) discretion. Her Majesty's Government set out to and succeeded in satisfying the Court that in extradition matters the fugitive had "an effective remedy before a national authority" (see Article 13 of the Convention) to give the fugitive the protections that the European Convention affords him, the focus in that case being Article 3:

No-one should be subjected to torture or inhuman or degrading treatment or punishment.

Mr Soering was a German national who was detained in England. The United States of America sought his extradition to face charges of murder in the State of Virginia. Article 4 of the Treaty with the United States provided that:

Extradition may be refused unless the requesting Party gives assurances satisfactory to the requested Party that the death penalty will not be carried out.

That assurance was sought, but was given in qualified terms which in the opinion of Lord Justice Lloyd on the judicial review application

[11 98 *ILR* 270.]

"[left] something to be desired". But he refused to grant relief because such relief was premature:

> The Secretary of State has not yet decided whether to accept the assurance as satisfactory and he has certainly not decided whether or not to issue a warrant for Soering's surrender . . . This Court will never allow itself to be put in the position of reviewing an administrative decision before the decision has been made.

But the European Court of Human Rights was concerned with the presence of an effective remedy in the United Kingdom, and the significance of this case for our purposes is first the exposition of the protection available put forward on behalf of HM Government by the Attorney-General, Sir Patrick Mayhew, and second in the Court's reaction to it. HM Government's position as put forward was summarized by the Court as follows:

> 34 Furthermore, under [what is now Section 12 of the 1989 Act] the Secretary of State enjoys a discretion not to sign the surrender warrant (*Atkinson* v. *United States* [1971] AC 197).[12] This discretion may override a decision of the courts that a fugitive should be surrendered, and it is open to every prisoner who has exhausted his remedies by way of application for habeas corpus to petition the Secretary of State for that purpose. In considering whether to order the fugitive's surrender, the Secretary of State is bound to take account of fresh evidence which was not before the magistrates (*Schtraks* v. *Government of Israel, loc. cit.*).
> In addition, it is open to the prisoner to challenge both the decision of the Secretary of State rejecting his petition and the decision to sign the warrant in judicial review proceedings. In such proceedings the court may review the exercise of the Secretary of State's discretion on the basis that it is tainted with illegality, irrationality or procedural impropriety (*Council of Civil Service Unions and Others* v. *Minister for the Civil Service* [1984] 3 All ER 935).
> Irrationality is determined on the basis of the administrative-law principles set out in *Associated Provincial Picture Houses Ltd* v. *Wednesbury Corporation* [1984] 1 KB 223 (the so-called *Wednesbury* principles of reasonableness). The test in an extradition case would be that no reasonable Secretary of State could have made an order for return in the circumstances. As the judgment of Lord Justice Lloyd in the Divisional Court in the present case shows (see paragraph 22 above), the reliance placed by the Secretary of State may be tested to determine whether such reliance is within the confines of reasonableness. According to the United Kingdom Government, on the same principle a court would have jurisdiction to quash a challenged decision to send a fugitive to a country where it was established that there was a serious risk of inhuman or degrading treatment, on the ground that in all the circumstances of the case the decision was one which no reasonable Secretary of State could take. In *R* v. *Home Secretary, ex parte Bugdaycay* [1987] 1 All ER 940[13] at 952, a House

[12 51 *ILR* 288.]   [13 79 *ILR* 642.]

of Lords case concerning a refusal to grant asylum, Lord Bridge, while acknowledging the limitations of the *Wednesbury* principles, explained that the courts will apply them extremely strictly against the Secretary of State in a case in which the life of the applicant is at risk:

> Within those limitations the court must, I think, be entitled to subject an administrative decision to the most rigorous examination, to ensure that it is in no way flawed according to the gravity of the issue which the decision determines. The most fundamental of all human rights is the individual's right to life and, when an administrative decision under challenge is said to be one which may put the applicant's life at risk, the basis of the decision must surely call for the most anxious scrutiny.

Lord Templeman added (at page 956):

> In my opinion where the result of a flawed decision may imperil life or liberty a special responsibility lies on the court in the examination of the decision-making process.

The Court accepted HM Government's submissions, and found that Mr Soering had an effective remedy available in relation to his complaint under Article 3, rejecting arguments that the scope of judicial review was too narrow. They concluded:

According to the United Kingdom Government, a court would have jurisdiction to quash a challenged decision to send a fugitive to a country where it was established that there was a serious risk of inhuman or degrading treatment, on the ground that in all the circumstances of the case the decision was one that no reasonable Secretary of State could take. Although the Convention is not considered to be part of the United Kingdom law . . ., the Court is satisfied that the English courts can review the "reasonableness" of an extradition decision in the light of the kind of factors relied on by Mr Soering before the Convention institutions in the context of Article 3.

The inhuman and degrading treatment that the Court was there concerned with was "the very long period of time spent on Death Row in such extreme conditions".

Founding himself on that, the applicant submits that he must be entitled to attempt to satisfy the Court that no reasonable Home Secretary could conclude that there was not a serious risk that the protections as to due process, fair punishment and specialty (to which he should be entitled) would not be available in HKSAR. If he could not because the issue was non-justiciable, then he was effectively deprived of that part of his Section 12(1) protection.

Before leaving *Soering*,[14] it is useful to add a footnote to *Bugdaycay*, for which I go to the report in [1987] 1 AC 514. This point applies to

[[14] 98 *ILR* 270.]

the appellant Musisi. It was in relation to Mr Musisi that the familiar dicta from the speeches of Lord Bridge and Lord Templeman quoted in *Soering* applied. Mr Musisi sought entry to the United Kingdom as a visitor from Kenya. When that application looked as though it might fail, he claimed political asylum as a refugee from Uganda. His application for asylum was refused on the basis that he had come from a safe third country, Kenya. This decision was challenged on the basis that Kenya was not safe—that in fact he would almost certainly be removed to Uganda. The Minister of State rejected this submission on the grounds that:

It is the respondent's belief that Kenya as a signatory to the United Nations Convention relating to the status of refugees would not knowingly remove a Uganda citizen to Uganda if there was reason to believe he would be persecuted there.

But the Minister of State's confidence that Kenya would adhere to their treaty obligations was not treated as determinative of the issue. Evidence was filed on behalf of the appellant directly alleging breaches by Kenya of that Convention. Accordingly, Lord Bridge concluded:

I cannot escape the conclusion that the Secretary of State's decision in relation to the appellant were taken on the basis of a confidence in Kenya's performance of its obligation under the Convention which is now shown to have been, at least to some extent, misplaced . . . The fact of such breaches must be very relevant to any assessment of the danger that the appellant, if returned to Kenya, would be sent home to Uganda. Since the decision of the Secretary of State appears to have been made without taking that fact into account, [it] cannot, in my opinion, now stand.

c) *Non-justiciability of the judgment that China will adhere to the Treaty: the Secretary of State's submissions*

The nature of the Secretary of State's case is clearly set out in para. 25 of Mr Parker QC's skeleton argument:

On this issue it cannot be too strongly emphasised that the United Kingdom in 1984 entered into a treaty (the Joint Declaration) with the PRC, to the implementation of which both nations, in the judgment of Her Majesty's Government, are dedicated. The PRC has committed no act of repudiation of that treaty, and the Government (of which the S of S is an important member) *must* [emphasis added] proceed upon the basis that the PRC will respect its obligations under the treaty. It would be wholly wrong to speculate upon such a matter as the PRC's supposedly "real" intentions in respect of Hong Kong, and it would be wholly contrary to principle for the courts to seek to carry out some purported factual enquiry on the basis [of] what can only be speculative material at this stage in an effort to ascertain what are the supposedly "real" intentions of the PRC in respect of Hong Kong. On an issue of this kind it is vital that the Crown speaks with a single voice, and that the judicial branch of government defer to the position rightly assumed by the executive touching this area of the executive's prerogative, namely the conduct of relations with another sovereign state and the implementation of treaty obligations with that state: see *R* v. *S of S for the Home Office, ex parte Osman* (Divisional Court unreported 30 July 1992 at Transcript p. 18, *Buttes Gas and Oil Co.* v. *Hammer (No 3)* [1982] AC 888;[15] *Westland Helicopters Ltd* v. *Arab Organisation for Industrialisation* [1995] 2 WLR 126;[16] *Gur Corporation* v. *Trust Bank of Africa Ltd* [1987] 1 QB 599;[17] *Luther* v. *Sagor* [1921] 1 KB 456;[18] *Carl-Zeiss Stiftung* v. *Rayner & Keeler Ltd* (No 2) [1967] 1 AC 853.[19]

It will be seen that the Crown's suggested "single voice" there referred to includes the Secretary of State exercising his Section 12(1) duty as well as the Divisional Court. It will be noted that the only extradition case relied on is one of the unreported *Osman* cases (*R* v. *Secretary of State for the Home Office, ex parte Osman* 30 July 1992), decided by this Court presided over by Lord Justice Woolf. That too was a judicial review of the Secretary of State's exercise of his Section 12 discretion. It was heard five years before HKSAR was to come into existence. The shadow of the unknown falls longer and darker now. Mr Alun Jones QC has pointed out to us that it is only recently that the Section 12 review has become the "business end" of challenges, acknowledging that (as seems to us right) the China point is the crux of these proceedings, and it was a point not fully available at the earlier Section 11 challenge. But this case is not authority for the proposition relied on. See page 20:

While the court is required to scrutinise the Home Secretary's decision with care and should not hesitate to intervene if it appears that an applicant has been prejudiced by the Home Secretary not properly performing his duties, the court must also bear in mind that decisions as to extradition can be highly politically charged. When they are the Home Secretary is in an advantageous position for determining whether in all the circumstances it would be unjust or oppressive to order an applicant's return.

With that statement, we have no quarrel. But that authority conspicuously does not say that that decision is not reviewable. It says in terms that it should be scrutinized with care.

Of the other cases relied on, most assistance is to be derived from *Buttes Gas*, authority for what the editors of De Smith, Woolf and Jowell refer to as

prudent judicial abstention from determining cases that may necessitate ruling on matters which are covered by public international law and involve sovereign acts of foreign states.

[15 64 *ILR* 331.]
[16 108 *ILR* 564.]
[17 75 *ILR* 675.]
[18 1 *Ann Dig* 47.]
[19 43 *ILR* 23.]

Lord Wilberforce (at 938A) gave two possible reasons for such abstention: first the possibility of embarrassment in our foreign relations, and second that the Court may have no judicial or manageable standards by which to judge the issues: "the court would be in a judicial no-man's land". Now, clearly there is in Mr Launder's case the potential for embarrassment in the UK's foreign relations in the evaluation of the risks to which Mr Launder wishes to draw the attention of the Secretary of State and the Court. And, absent seeking assistance from the Foreign Office, the Court may clearly be in difficulty in judging the issues (though in relation to Mr Musisi, there was no such difficulty). And none of those authorities deals with the situation in extradition where first the Secretary of State and then the court are required to form a judgment on the very issue said to be non-justiciable.

Mr Alun Jones QC for the Hong Kong Government did not feel he could support Mr Parker's non-justiciability submission. His position was that the Secretary of State's exercise of his discretion was reviewable, but because of the nature of the discretion it would be rare for such a review to succeed. He sought to support the decision on the basis that the Secretary of State had reached his independent judgment on this matter, and though reviewable, the Court could not go behind it. We must look at all three aspects of that submission.

In an illuminating submission he took us through the statutory development of this branch of the law, culminating in the consolidating Act of 1989.

At the risk of over-simplifying matters, we took the following points from those submissions. The source of most (but not all—the arrangements for the colonies and Commonwealth were governed by the statutory code) extradition arrangements is founded on a treaty with a friendly sovereign State, whom HM Government has trusted with mutual extradition arrangements. But even against that background of trust, HM Government, when the surrendering state, would look to the realities of the request for return: see the general restrictions on return now collected in Section 6 of the 1989 Act. Over the years, these have been developed, and the discretionary judgment as to whether the fugitive should be returned widened, and the final responsibility for that decision (at the Section 12 stage) entrusted to the Secretary of State.

Mr Jones points out that this creates a certain "tension" for the Secretary of State. Under the Treaty, he is responsible for surrendering fugitives to a friendly State, who expects from HM Government what HM Government would expect from them. But under the Act, he has the final responsibility for ensuring, for example, that the requesting State is not acting for an impermissible motive (such as seeking extradition for an offence of a political character), and has the laws in place not only to guarantee certain fundamental aspects of due process (see Section 6(2) and (3)) but also the specialty protections found in Section 6(4), without which the terms on which the fugitive was surrendered could be abused. And all of these matters may require him not necessarily to take at face value the explanation that the requesting State gives. That may be sensitive diplomatically, or even economically. The cause of the tension is that he must bring his own judgement into play in the Section 12(1) discretion, and that may conflict with Government policy.

It is clear from HM Government's exposition of the availability of judicial review in *Soering*[20] (*supra*) that it is accepted that the Section 12 discretion is normally justiciable. It seems to us that there is no warrant for excepting from that general rule those cases where the decision is taken on political or policy grounds, however important or however sensitive those grounds are.

We say this for a reason. Often there will be little or no sensitive or political element in the issue as to whether a fugitive should be surrendered. Then there are no pressures on the Secretary of State to treat the request on anything other than its strict merits. So the fugitive can be sure of the dual protection that Parliament intended him to have: an assessment of the risks by the Secretary of State, with the safety-net of judicial review. But there will be other cases where the interests of the State and the interests of the fugitive are in direct conflict. Mr Vaughan sought to make an analogy. If after Munich in 1938, when HM Government had negotiated the treaty which it was hoped would secure peace for our time, Germany had sought to extradite a Jewish political activist in circumstances where HM Government feared the diplomatic consequences of refusal, if the Secretary of State regarded himself bound by Government policy to surrender the fugitive without regard to the consequent risks to his life and liberty, could it sensibly be suggested that either he had properly exercised his discretion or that that decision was non-justiciable? While not finding the analogy helpful, the hypothesis neatly illustrates the "tensions" already referred to.

When the interests of the State and the interests of the fugitive are in direct conflict, that is when the protection of judicial review is most required. It cannot be right to take away that protection when it is most needed. There is no warrant for doing so to be found in either the Statute or in the extradition cases. In our judgment, this issue is justiciable.

The Court will, of course, be properly sensitive both to the delicacy of relations with the foreign State and the advantages that the primary decision taker, the Secretary of State, has over it in relation to the issue in question. But that is not an argument for making this issue non-justiciable; it is simply a reminder (were it necessary) of the limitations of the constitutional role of the reviewing court. But, whatever the limitations, the Court must observe its constitutional role to ensure that the protection Parliament intended is afforded to the fugitive. As Sir Thomas Bingham MR said in *R* v. *Ministry of Defence, ex parte Smith* and other appeals [1996] QB 517, [1996] 1 All ER 257[21] at 265B of the latter report:

Whilst the Court must properly defer to the exercise of responsible decision makers, it must not shrink from its fundamental duty to do right by all manner of people.

d) *The Secretary of State's responsibilities under Section 12(1)*
When the Secretary of State decides whether or not to sign the warrant ordering the return of the applicant, he must act in the dual role identified by Lord Griffiths in *R* v. *Horseferry Road Magistrates' Court, ex parte Bennett* [1994] 1 AC 42, [1993] 3 All ER 138[22] at 62C of the former report:

Extradition procedures are designed not only to ensure that criminals are returned from one country to another but also to protect the rights of those who are accused of crimes by the requesting country.

It is this dual role that leads to Mr Alan Jones's "tension".
As *In re Schmidt*[23] (*supra*) makes clear, at that stage the exercise of the Secretary of State's discretion is the principal safeguard against the applicant being returned.
At the Section 12 stage the Court's powers in relation to the Secretary of State's discharge of his responsibilities are simply those of review on *Wednesbury* grounds. As this Court (in a constitution of which Henry LJ was a member) said in *R* v. *Secretary of State for the Home Department ex parte Patel* (CO 129/93 unreported dated 9 February 1994):

The statutory question that the Minister had to answer was whether it would be unjust or oppressive to return the applicant . . . in all the circumstances of the case. That was a question profoundly affecting the liberty of the subject and the safeguards against unjust extradition afforded to him (as Lord Griffiths pointed out). Therefore the Minister must exercise his discretion with the greatest care, just as the reviewing court must approach their task with the care that a matter concerning the liberty of the subject requires, while never losing sight of the fact that their task is one of review not appeal.

We are of opinion that that formulation is applicable here, with the *Bugdaycay* amplification that the decision calls for the most anxious

[21] 112 *ILR* 367.]   [22] 95 *ILR* 380.]   [23] 111 *ILR* 548.]

scrutiny because of its plain critical importance to the applicant. In Lord Reid's words, this is a power that the Secretary of State should use whenever it would be "wrong, unjust or oppressive" to return the fugitive. In *Atkinson* v. *United States of America* [1971] AC 197[24] at 233G, Lord Reid said:

> But the Act does provide a safeguard. The Secretary of State always has power to refuse to surrender a man committed to prison by the magistrate. It appears to me that Parliament must have intended the Secretary of State to use that power whenever in his view it would be wrong, unjust or oppressive to surrender the man . . . Then the Secretary of State is answerable to Parliament, but not to the courts, for any decision he may make.

Given the importance of that decision, and given the "tensions" of the balance the Secretary of State must maintain between his treaty commitment and his special responsibility to the applicant, it seems to us inevitable that that anxious decision must be one for the Secretary of State personally—a heavy personal responsibility. It is not unknown for a Minister's individual responsibility (often statutory as here) to conflict with his collective responsibility as a Cabinet member. The Attorney-General, for instance, may on occasion find himself so placed.

Though it was not plain to us at the start of the hearing, and although Mr Alun Jones contested it, it became clear in the course of the proceedings that the Secretary of State's decision was dictated by a collective Cabinet decision and not his individual decision.

First, analysis of Mr Ackland's and Miss Atkins' affidavits filed on behalf of the Secretary of State shows that the formula used throughout in relation to the Treaty was that the Secretary of State "proceeded on the basis that" the PRC would comply with its treaty obligations in relation to each treaty protection questioned. That formula was carefully chosen.

This formula is again used in Mr Parker's skeleton argument at para. 25 (quoted above, with the added emphasis on the word "must"), which makes it clear that the Secretary of State regarded himself as bound by the Cabinet's judgment to proceed on the basis that the treaty protections will be in place and effective. The point is also made in paras. 29 and 30 of the skeleton argument, concluding that:

> The Secretary of State could not conceivably have proceeded on the basis that the PRC would not carry out its international obligations . . . and respect its own Basic Law for the HKSAR insofar as they will govern the judicial system in the HKSAR after July 1997.

The first affidavit of Mr Matthews, the Attorney-General of Hong Kong (quoted above), proceeds on precisely the same basis as that

[24 51 *ILR* 288.]

adopted by the Secretary of State which, it is again there emphasized, can be the only correct approach in the matter.

In a considered passage of his submissions on non-justiciability, Mr Parker made it clear that neither this Court nor the Secretary of State could reach the conclusion that there was a substantial risk that the PRC would not comply with the Treaty. Such a conclusion was off-limits to both. The Secretary of State is a party to, and bound by, that collective Cabinet decision.

Counsel for the applicant prepared a note of the exchange between the Court and Mr Parker, and we have ourselves checked that note against the tape recording of the proceedings.

It is clear that the Secretary of State felt himself bound by the collective Cabinet decision. He felt bound to proceed on the basis of it. Holding the clear opinion as we do that this particular responsibility is a responsibility personal to the Secretary of State, in our judgment he did not properly direct himself as to his Section 12 responsibilities. That misdirection deprived the applicant of his main safeguard at that stage; namely a Minister who would exercise his personal judgement on what the real risks of breach of the treaty safeguards were, so that these could be taken into account in considering whether or not to sign the warrant for extradition.

We regard this a fundamental breach, rather than a technical one. The statute provides who can take the decision. There is good reason for this: responsibilities to an individual are better discharged by another individual than by the Cabinet. Where responsibility for an individual's fate is shared, that responsibility is too easily diluted by the realpolitik of a delicate diplomatic situation. To put it another way, the applicant is entitled to have the risks he has drawn attention to considered, rather than ignored because policy requires them to be ignored. And if the Minister cannot himself form his individual opinion, how can the decision sensibly be reviewed and how can the Section 12(1) protection be delivered? The stance taken is a contradiction of HM Government's stance in *Soering*,[25] and the position that frequently arises in asylum cases. There the Minister must look to the realities of the risk and the Court can review his assessment of the risk—see *Musisi*.

Mr Parker also submitted that while the Secretary of State and the reviewing court could look to the realities of the position after changeover (as in *Soering, Musisi* and the asylum cases) they could not do so before where there had been, in HM Government's view, no acts of repudiation of the Treaty. We do not regard that as a valid ground of distinction. All Section 12(1) decisions involve the decision taker looking into the future and assessing the risk to the fugitive of not receiving the proper protections of a fair trial, appropriate and humane sentencing, and an assurance of the specialty protections.

[25 98 *ILR* 270.]

It follows that in our judgement the Secretary of State erred in his approach to his exercise of his Section 12 discretion, and that (subject to submissions) the warrant ordering the applicant's return be quashed, and the matter remitted to him for further consideration.

Disposition:
Judgment accordingly.

Solicitors:
Treasury Solicitor; Titmuss Sainer Dechert, Crown Prosecution Service, London.

[Report: Transcript]

[The following is the text of the opinions delivered in the House of Lords:]

21 May. LORD BROWNE-WILKINSON. My Lords, I have had the **[842]** advantage of reading in draft the speech to be delivered by my noble and learned friend, Lord Hope of Craighead. For the reasons which he gives, I would allow the appeal.

LORD STEYN. My Lords, I have read in draft the speech to be delivered by my noble and learned friend, Lord Hope of Craighead. For the reasons he gives I would allow the appeal.

LORD HOPE OF CRAIGHEAD. My Lords, this is an appeal against the decision by the Divisional Court of the Queen's Bench Division (Henry L.J. and Ebsworth J.) on 6 August 1996 to quash a warrant under section 12(1) of the Extradition Act 1989 by which the Secretary of State for the Home Department ordered the applicant, Ewan Quayle Launder, **[843]** to be returned to Hong Kong at the request of the Governor to face trial there on charges of corruption for which on 23 November 1989 a warrant had been issued by the Principal Magistrate.

Although the applicant denies the charges which have been laid against him, he accepts for the purposes of this case that a prima facie case against him has been made. The offences fall within the definition of the expression "extradition crime" in section 2(1) of the Act. Arrangements exist between the United Kingdom and the Crown Colony under the Fugitive Offenders (Hong Kong) Order 1967 for securing that the requirements of section 6(4), known as the "specialty protection," are satisfied. It is not suggested that any of the particular matters mentioned in section 12(2) which would make it unjust or oppressive for him to be returned the Hong Kong arise in this case. There is no reason to think that there would have been any other grounds for objecting to the warrant, had it not been for the fact that on 1 July 1997 sovereignty over Hong Kong will be transferred to the People's Republic of China and Hong Kong will then cease to be a Crown Colony.

It has for some time been obvious that the applicant's trial for these offences could not take place until after the transfer of sovereignty. It was plain that questions would be raised about the procedures which would be in place in Hong Kong after 1 July 1997, to ensure that the applicant would receive a fair trial and that he would continue to have the benefit of the specialty protection there were he to be extradited. But the applicant has raised objections to the warrant directed to the future of Hong Kong which are of an even more fundamental character. He maintains that, despite the arrangements which have been made to secure continuity for the rule of law after the transfer, he would be faced with the real risk that the safeguards will not be effective and that he will receive an unfair trial and, if convicted, inhumane punishment. It is these questions which have given rise to the important and difficult issues in this appeal.

It is hard to imagine a more significant event in the history of any state than a transfer of its sovereignty. The transfer of sovereignty over Hong Kong from the United Kingdom to the People's Republic of China ("P.R.C.") will bring to an end more than a century and a half of British rule since Hong Kong island was first occupied by the United Kingdom in 1841 after the Opium War. For the peoples of the region, and for the people of Hong Kong in particular, the resumption of Chinese sovereignty will change many things. That is to be expected and is, indeed, inevitable. But in other respects the transfer will be an unusual one, perhaps unique. It will above all be a negotiated and orderly transfer, the product of 15 years preparation for the event. There are numerous examples in history of transfers of sovereignty by conquest, by treaty or concession or by purchase. But such a long period of negotiation and preparation appears to be unprecedented. The transfer will also involve the creation in Hong Kong of a separate and novel system of government. This has been designed to preserve its own legal system and to provide for it a high degree of legislative and executive autonomy. Under the principle of "one country, two systems" the P.R.C. have decided that, upon its resumption of sovereignty, a Special Administrative Region ("S.A.R.") will be established in Hong Kong and that the socialist system and policies will not be practised there. Not even the United Kingdom, which in other respects is a unique arrangement, provides a precise analogy. For example, the supreme judicial authority for all three jurisdictions in the United [844] Kingdom, save only in respect of decisions of the High Court of Justiciary in Edinburgh, resides in the House of Lords at Westminster. For Hong Kong the supreme judicial authority will reside in Hong Kong, not the P.R.C.

It will be necessary for me later to describe some of the details of these arrangements. At this stage it is sufficient to say that the context for an examination of the issues of law in this case is, even for extradition cases, an unusual one. It placed a heavy responsibility on the Home Secretary whose decisions are under challenge in this case. Your Lordships will be aware of the responsibility which now rests with this House, in view of the critical stage which matters have now reached in the preparation for the handover in only a few weeks time.

Procedural history

It is first necessary to set out briefly a history of the events which have led to this appeal.

The warrant which was issued by the Principal Magistrate on 23 November 1989 was in connection with 14 charges of accepting an advantage, contrary to section 9(1)(*b*) of the Prevention of Bribery Ordinance, Chapter 201 of the Laws of Hong Kong. The charges related to payments made to the applicant between 11 October 1980 and 3 January 1982, during a period when he was resident in Hong Kong and employed there in a senior position in a merchant banking company. They were alleged to have been made in connection with the granting by that company of loans to groups in which the persons who made the payments were shareholders. The payments allegedly so made total HK$45·95m., which is £3·8m. at current exchange rates. A provisional warrant for the applicant's arrest was issued at Bow Street Magistrates' Court on 21 May 1990. He was arrested on 10 September 1993 at Heathrow Airport, having arrived in this country from Berlin. He was granted bail on 30 September 1993 and has been on bail ever since.

On 7 October 1993 the Governor of Hong Kong made a request to the Secretary of State for Foreign and Commonwealth Affairs for the extradition of the applicant to Hong Kong. On 12 January 1994 the Secretary of State issued to the magistrate an authority to proceed under section 7(1) and (4) of the Act of 1989. On the same day he issued a specialty certificate under section 6(7) of that Act to the effect that the Governor of Hong Kong had undertaken that the applicant would receive the protection set out in subsection (4) of that section. On 7 April 1994 the magistrate committed the applicant under section 9 to await the Secretary of State's decision whether or not to order his return. The applicant challenged that order by applying for a writ of habeas corpus to the Divisional Court. That application was dismissed by the Divisional Court on 14 December 1994, and on 9 March 1995 leave to appeal to the House of Lords was refused.

The applicant then made extensive representations to the Secretary of State in an endeavour to persuade him not to order his return to Hong Kong. These were made by him personally by letter to the Home Secretary, through his M.P. and through his solicitor. These representations were supported by lengthy affidavits from experts in this field which raised substantial questions about the prospects of a fair trial and the impartial administration of justice in Hong Kong after the transfer of sovereignty. Following an invitation to comment on a response on these matters from the Hong Kong Government as the requesting authority, the applicant's **[845]** solicitor submitted further material to the Home Secretary. On 31 July 1995 the Secretary of State wrote to the applicant's solicitor informing him that he had decided to order the applicant's return to Hong Kong.

That letter was written on his behalf by Mr. David Ackland, the Head of the International Criminal Policy Division of the Home Office, of which the Extradition Section of the Home Office is a part. He stated that, in the light of the matters raised by the applicant, the Secretary of

State had agreed exceptionally to give his reasons at that stage, reserving the right to expand on them later if leave were to be sought to move for judicial review of the decision. In his statement of the reasons he said that the Secretary of State had considered very carefully all the extensive representations made on the applicant's behalf, but that he did not consider that they were sufficient either individually or cumulatively to justify not surrendering him. After dealing with matters which are no longer in issue, he dealt with the allegations of prejudice arising from the position in Hong Kong after 1 July 1997. He summarised the measures which were to be in place in Hong Kong after that date in the light of the Joint Declaration and the Basic Law to which I shall return later in this speech. He then dealt with representations that the order would be in breach of the applicant's rights under the European Convention on Human Rights and European Community law.

The letter concluded with these paragraphs:

"3. The Secretary of State does not consider that there is anything known about Mr. Launder's personal circumstances that indicates that it would be oppressive or wrong to order his return. 4. The Secretary of State does not consider that it would be unjust or oppressive to order the return of Mr. Launder for any reason in section 12(2)(*a*) of the Extradition Act 1989, or that there are any other statutory bars to surrender. 5. The Secretary of State does not consider that in all the circumstances it would be unjust, oppressive or wrong for any other reason to order Mr. Launder's return. 6. The Secretary of State does not consider, therefore, that there is any reason why he should, in the exercise of his discretion, not order Mr. Launders return."

That is the first decision which was challenged in the proceedings in the Divisional Court. Leave on the application was granted on 7 August 1995. On 8 January 1996 an affirmation by Mr. Ackland was lodged providing a more complete summary of the reasons for the decision taken by the Secretary of State.

Thereafter, in the light of further developments in Hong Kong which the applicant maintains made it clear that he would not get a fair trial after 1 July 1997 if he were to be extradited and that in other respects he would be exposed to oppression and injustice there, his solicitors wrote to the Home Secretary on 29 November 1995 inviting him to reconsider his decision to order the return. They enclosed with their letter a substantial body of further material which the Home Secretary was asked to consider in reviewing his decision. By a letter to the applicant's solicitor dated 21 December 1995, which was written on his behalf by Dr. Susan Atkins, the Head of the Extradition Section of the Home Office, the Home Secretary replied in these terms:

"The Secretary of State has given careful consideration to the representations made by you on behalf of Mr. Launder to determine **[846]** whether they give rise to sufficient grounds for withdrawing the surrender warrant. He has asked me to say, however, that there is nothing contained in these latest representations which leads him to reverse his earlier decision to order the return of Mr. Launder to Hong Kong."

That decision also was challenged in the Divisional Court. An order granting leave on this application was granted on 4 January 1996. On 2 February 1996 an affidavit by Dr. Atkins was lodged setting out the reasons which had guided the Secretary of State in his decision that there were no grounds for reversing his decision of 31 July 1995.

Proceedings in the Divisional Court

The argument in the Divisional Court was directed to six issues, on all of which except one it was held that the application for judicial review must fail. Those on which the decision was adverse to the applicant were (1) the effect of delay, having regard in particular to the provisions of section 12(2)(a)(ii) of the Act of 1989; (2) alleged errors of law on the passage of time; (3) procedural improprieties, injustice and perversity; (4) the applicant's personal circumstances; and (5) the European Convention on Human Rights and European Community law points. On the final point (6), identified in the judgment as the China point, the Divisional Court reached the view that the Secretary of State had erred in his approach to the exercise of his discretion under section 12(1). This was because they understood that he had felt himself bound by a collective Cabinet decision that the P.R.C. would comply with its treaty obligations in regard to each of the treaty provisions which were to be in place in Hong Kong after 1 July 1997 to prevent injustice. It was maintained that his decision on this basis was not reviewable in the courts, but that argument was rejected. The warrant ordering the return of the applicant was quashed, and the matter was remitted to the Secretary of State for further consideration.

As a result of that decision the following question was certified in order to identify the issue of public importance in the case:

"Whether in the exercise of his powers under section 6(4) and/or section 12 of the Extradition Act 1989 the Secretary of State is entitled, on a non-reviewable basis, to proceed on the footing that the requesting state or any successor state, or any other relevant state, will respect its treaty obligations on the sole grounds that this is the collective Cabinet view and that there has been no repudiation of the relevant treaty and thus for this reason alone not to consider evidence which is put forward by the fugitive to show that the Extradition Act 1989 and/or the relevant treaties will not, or may not, be complied with in material respects."

The issues in this appeal

Mr. Parker submitted, in opening the appeal, that the Divisional Court, while right in understanding his submission to be that the issue was non-justiciable, was wrong to conclude that the Secretary of State's decision was dictated by a collective decision by the Cabinet. He said that the court had reached its judgment on the basis of a position which he had not put to them, as his argument had been that the Secretary of State had made a personal decision on these matters. He maintained that the **[847]** Secretary of State had been entitled to rely on the fact that a treaty had been entered into between the United Kingdom and the P.R.C., the basic principles of which had been acted upon when the framework for the future administration of Hong Kong was set up when the Basic Law was promulgated. The real issue therefore was whether the Secretary of State had acted reasonably in reaching his decision, based on all the evidence, that the P.R.C. had not repudiated its obligations under the treaty and that there was no intention on its part not to implement the relevant provisions of the Basic Law.

In making these submissions Mr. Parker was repeating what had been set out in the statement of facts and issues, in which it is recorded that there is an issue between the parties as to the basis of the Secretary of States reasoning. The applicant's position is that the Secretary of State considered himself bound by a collective Cabinet decision to the effect that the P.R.C. would respect its obligations under the treaty and that there had been no acts indicating an intention on its part to repudiate those obligations. In the result he had considered that it was not open to him to examine for himself the question whether there was any risk to Mr. Launder if he were to be extradited. But Mr. Alun Jones for the Government of Hong Kong supported Mr. Parker's submission that the Divisional Court had failed to appreciate that the Secretary of State had made an individual decision in which he had addressed the issues properly. He said that it was clear from the evidence that he had exercised his own discretion in reaching his decision on this matter, and that the only question in the case was whether he had acted irrationally. In the Divisional Court an issue had been raised for the first time about non-justiciablity, but the decision letters and the affidavits for the Home Secretary showed that he had conducted the normal exercise of assessing the competing factors in what was essentially a balancing exercise.

Mr. Vaughan for the applicant maintained that the Divisional Court had been entitled to rely on the submissions of the Secretary of State's counsel, which had been to the effect that the decision taken was non-justiciable. That was why the certified question had, with the agreement of all counsel, been framed in order to identify this issue as the one which was of importance in the case. He agreed that it had not been stated anywhere in the evidence or in the Secretary of State's skeleton argument that the decision had been reached on the basis of a collective decision by the Cabinet. But he said that the evidence was ambiguous on this point and that it required explanation. He referred to a transcript of Mr. Parker's submissions to the Divisional Court in which he made it clear that his argument was that, as there had been a collective decision by the Government that the Joint Declaration and the Basic Law would be complied with by the P.R.C., the issue whether there was a substantial risk to the applicant was non-justiciable.

Mr. Parker conceded that the question as certified did not now arise, in view of his submissions to your Lordships about the state of the evidence. Mr. Vaughan submitted that your Lordships had no jurisdiction to decide any question other that that which had been certified and that, even if your Lordships had jurisdiction to consider the questions of irrationality and illegality, these questions should be directed only to the point whether there had been a repudiation by the P.R.C., not whether a proper assessment had been made of the risks to the applicant. I do not think that I need to expand upon these submissions because, having conferred after listening to them, your Lordships reached the view that we should not decline to hear argument on issues other than on the question **[848]** which had been certified.

In *Attorney-General for Northern Ireland v. Gallagher* [1963] A.C. 349 it was held that the jurisdiction of this House under section 1 of the Administration of Justice Act 1960 in criminal cases is not confined to the point of law set out in the certificate. The same reasoning can be applied to this case. As Lord Reid indicated, at pp. 365–366, the function of the House is to decide the appeal. The only alternative would be to remit to the court below to reopen the case, to hear further argument and to reach a fresh decision in the light of it. There would then have to be a further appeal to bring the matter back before your Lordships' House. In the present case that would not be attractive—it would mean more delay— and it is also unnecessary. All the evidence about the decisions in question is before us, and we were able to hear a full argument on all the issues which the applicant's counsel, in the knowledge that there was a dispute on this point, had set out in their printed case. While it is regrettable that, as Mr. Parker now accepts, the true issues in the case were not clearly identified in argument in the Divisional Court with the result that they were misled into deciding the case on a wrong basis, it would not be in the interests of justice for your Lordships to decline to deal with all the issues now in this appeal.

We must decline to answer the certified question, as it is conceded that that question does not now arise. It is accepted that the question whether the Secretary of State reached a decision which he was entitled to reach is justiciable. So the issues which your Lordships must decide are the familiar ones upon which an administrative decision is subject to review—those of procedural impropriety, illegality and irrationality. In addition there are the issues relating to the applicant's rights under the European Convention on Human Rights and European Community law, which Mr. Vaughan was allowed to develop again before your Lordships in view of the wider scope which it was necessary, in fairness to the applicant, to give to the argument. I shall deal with the issues in that order. But it is first necessary to set the scene by examining the situation in Hong Kong in more detail and identifying the basis on which the Secretary of State reached the decisions which are under challenge in this appeal.

The Joint Declaration and the Basic Law

In 1984, after two years of negotiation, between the United Kingdom and the P.R.C., an international agreement was entered into between these two countries entitled the Sino-British Joint Declaration on the Question

of Hong Kong ("the Joint Declaration"). This is a legally binding bilateral treaty which has been registered with the United Nations both by the United Kingdom and by the P.R.C. The agreement binds the United Kingdom, as the outgoing sovereign state, to transfer sovereignty over Hong Kong to the P.R.C. with effect from 1 July 1997. In the United Kingdom the Hong Kong Act 1985 was passed to make provision for the transfer of sovereignty and other matters consequential on the change of sovereignty and jurisdiction in implement of the Joint Declaration. The P.R.C. for its part undertook, upon the resumption of the exercise of sovereignty, to establish in accordance with article 31 of the Constitution of the P.R.C., a Hong Kong Special Administrative Region which would enjoy a high degree of autonomy, except in foreign and defence affairs
[849] which were to be the responsibility of the Central People's Government. Paragraph 3(3) of the Joint Declaration states:

> "The Hong Kong Special Administrative Region will be vested with executive, legislative and independent judicial power, including that of final adjudication. The laws currently in force in Hong Kong will remain basically unchanged."

Annex I to the Joint Declaration sets out an elaboration by the P.R.C. of its basic policies regarding Hong Kong. Among the many provisions set out in this Annex are those relating to its Constitution, and its legal and judicial systems. In regard to the Constitution Part I of Annex I states, in sentence 42:

> "The National People's Congress of the People's Republic of China shall enact and promulgate a Basic Law of the Hong Kong Special Administrative Region of the People's Republic of China (hereinafter referred to as the Basic Law) in accordance with the Constitution of the People's Republic of China, stipulating that after the establishment of the Hong Kong Special Administrative Region the socialist system and socialist policies shall not be practised in the Hong Kong Special Administrative Region and that Hong Kongs previous capitalist system and life-style shall remain unchanged for 50 years."

In regard to the legal system Part II of Annex I states, in sentence 53:

> "After the establishment of the Hong Kong Special Administrative Region, the laws previously in force in Hong Kong (i.e. the common law, rules of equity, ordinances, subordinate legislation and customary law) shall be maintained, save for any that contravene the Basic Law and subject to any amendment by the Hong Kong Special Administrative Region legislature."

In regard to the judicial system Part III of Annex I states, in sentences 59 to 62:

> "Judicial power in the Hong Kong Special Administrative Region shall be vested in the courts of the Hong Kong Special Administrative Region. The courts shall exercise judicial power independently and free from any interference. Members of the judiciary shall be immune

from legal action in respect of their judicial functions. The courts shall decide cases in accordance with the laws of the Hong Kong Special Administrative Region and may refer to precedents in other common law jurisdictions."

Sentence 68 of the same Part contains this provision:

"The power of final judgment of the Hong Kong Special Administrative Region shall be vested in the court of final appeal in the Hong Kong Special Administrative Region, which may as required invite judges from other common law jurisdictions to sit on the court of final appeal."

Basic Rights and Freedoms are the subject of further provisions which are set out in Part XIII of Annex I, among which are the following provisions in sentences 150, 152 and 153:

"The Hong Kong Special Administrative Region Government shall protect the rights and freedoms of inhabitants and other persons in the Hong Kong Special Administrative Region according to law. . . . The Hong Kong Special Administrative Region Government shall **[850]** protect the rights and freedoms of inhabitants and other persons in the Hong Kong Special Administrative Region according to law. . . . Every person shall have the right to confidential legal advice, access to the courts, representation in the courts by lawyers of his choice, and to obtain judicial remedies. Every person shall have the right to challenge the actions of the executive in the courts."

It can be seen from these necessarily brief quotations that the Joint Declaration provides specifically for the maintenance of Hong Kong's existing judicial system, except for the changes which are required to vest the power of final adjudication in the court of final appeal in place of that vested at present in the Judicial Committee of the Privy Council. Hong Kong is to keep its own legal system based on the common law. That system will, for the next 50 years, be kept entirely separate from that which applies elsewhere in the P.R.C. The power of final adjudication will rest with the court of final adjudication in Hong Kong, not a supreme court in the P.R.C. The provisions of Part XIII of Annex I contain a striking declaration of the P.R.C.'s commitment to the protection of human rights in the Hong Kong S.A.R., bearing in mind the fact that the P.R.C. is not yet a party to either of the multinational treaties referred to at the end of that article.

The Joint Declaration was initialled on 26 September 1984, signed at Beijing on 19 December 1984 and ratified by Parliament on 27 May 1985. In accordance with provisions set out in Annex II a Sino-British Joint Liaison Group was set up to conduct consultations on the implementation of the Joint Declaration and to discuss matters relating to the smooth transfer of government in 1997. In June 1985 a Basic Law Drafting Committee was set up by the P.R.C. which consulted with a liaison committee in Hong Kong. On 4 April 1990 the President of the P.R.C. promulgated the Basic Law for the Hong Kong Special Administrative

Region of the People's Republic of China ("the Basic Law"). On the same date in a Decision of the National People's Congress on the Basic Law it was declared:

"The Basic Law of the Hong Kong Special Administrative Region is constitutional as it is enacted in accordance with the Constitution of the People's Republic of China and in the light of the specific conditions of Hong Kong. The systems, policies and laws to be instituted after the establishment of the Hong Kong Special Administrative Region shall be based on the Basic Law of the Hong Kong Special Administrative Region."

The Basic Law is a lengthy document. It contains 159 articles. It would not be practicable to quote here all the provisions which are relevant to the applicant's case. But in summary it may be said to have implemented in full the treaty obligations owed to the United Kingdom by the P.R.C. under the Joint Declaration. It has also reflected throughout the principle of "one country, two systems" by which it had been declared as a matter of policy that the socialist system and policies would not be practised in the Hong Kong S.A.R. Then there are the provisions in Chapter III relating to the fundamental rights and freedoms of the residents of Hong Kong. Article 28 states that "No Hong Kong resident shall be subjected to arbitrary or unlawful arrest, detention or imprisonment." These rights and freedoms are extended by article 41 to persons other than Hong Kong

[851] residents. Among the provisions in section 4 of Chapter IV relating to the judiciary there are the following articles:

"Article 85. The courts of the Hong Kong Special Administrative Region shall exercise judicial power independently, free from any interference. Members of the judiciary shall be immune from legal action in the performance of their judicial functions.

"Article 86. The principle of trial by jury previously practised in Hong Kong shall be maintained.

"Article 87. In criminal or civil proceedings in the Hong Kong Special Administrative Region, the principles previously applied in Hong Kong and the rights previously enjoyed by parties to proceedings shall be maintained. Anyone who is lawfully arrested shall have the right to a fair trial by the judicial organs without delay and shall be presumed innocent until convicted by the judicial organs."

Article 158 provides that the power of interpretation of the Basic Law shall be vested in the Standing Committee of the National People's Congress, but that the Standing Committee shall authorise the courts of the S.A.R. to interpret on their own, in adjudicating cases, the provisions of the Basic Law which are within the limits of the autonomy of the region. So the power of interpretation of those parts of the Basic Law which relate to matters which have declared to be internal to the S.A.R. is to be devolved to the courts of the S.A.R.

These two documents are impressive both in their attention to detail and in their recognition of fundamental principles. The whole approach is founded on the rule of law. It is entirely consistent with modern concepts of legality. No criticisms have been made in these proceedings on the applicant's behalf about the content of the documents. The question which he has raised is whether the rule of law will turn out to be an illusion in the real world after the handover. The thrust of his attack is that the provisions are still at the executory stage. They have not yet been brought into effect. Their operation in practice has yet to be tested. The applicant contends, by reference to many recent examples of departures from human rights norms within the P.R.C., that there is a substantial risk that in various respects the Joint Declaration will not be adhered to by the P.R.C. after the handover. In so far as his prospects of receiving a fair trial, and of appropriate punishment if found guilty, are concerned he says that the present system in Hong Kong cannot be relied upon to continue beyond 30 June 1997. Questions have also been raised on his behalf as to whether the P.R.C. might so interpret the Basic Law as to deny him a fair trial in view of the provisions of article 19, which declares that the courts of the Hong Kong Special Administrative Region shall have no jurisdiction over acts of state such as defence and foreign affairs. He fears that, as a foreign national, he will be vulnerable to a decision by the Chief Executive that the prosecution in his case is an act of state, which would not be reviewable by the courts of the S.A.R. He also questions the reasonableness of the Secretary of State's judgment that extradition arrangements, and in particular the specialty protection required by section 6(4) of the Act of 1989, will be in place by 1 July 1997.

The decisions by the Secretary of State

The provisions of the Extradition Act 1989 which are relevant to the decisions which are under review in this case are in sections 6 and 12 of that Act. Section 6 imposes general restrictions on the return of a person **[852]** under the procedures set out in Part III of the Act. Subsection (4) of the section provides:

> "A person shall not be returned, or committed or kept in custody for the purposes of such return, unless provision is made by the relevant law, or by an arrangement made with the relevant foreign state, Commonwealth country or colony, for securing that he will not, unless he has first had an opportunity to leave it, be dealt with there for or in respect of any offence committed before his return to it other than—(a) the offence in respect of which his return is ordered; (b) an offence, other than an offence excluded by subsection (5) below, which is disclosed by the facts in respect of which his return was ordered; or (c) subject to subsection (6) below, any other offence being an extradition crime in respect of which the Secretary of State may consent to his being dealt with."

Section 12, which appears in Part III of the Act, provides that the decision to return a person into the custody of the requesting state is at the discretion of the Secretary of State. Subsection (2) sets out various circumstances in which it is provided (a) that the Secretary of State shall not make an order under that section and (b) that he may decline to make an order. The relevant subsection in this case is subsection (1), which confers a general discretion on the Secretary of State in these terms:

"Where a person is committed under section 9 above and is not discharged by order of the High Court or the High Court of Justiciary, the Secretary of State may by warrant order him to be returned unless his return is prohibited, or prohibited for the time being, by this Act, or the Secretary of State decides under this section to make no such order in his case."

The power which is given to the Secretary of State by section 12(1) to make no order in his case is an important part of the protections which the law provides to persons who are the subject of an extradition request. A provisional warrant for his arrest must first be issued under section 8 of the Act. Section 9 provides that, once arrested, he must be brought as soon as practicable before a court for committal to await the decision of the Secretary of State as to his return to the foreign state, Commonwealth country or colony which made the request. His committal is subject to review under the procedures set out in section 11, by which he has the right to make an application for habeas corpus in the High Court. Then there is the Secretary of State's discretion under section 12(1) not to order his return which, as these proceedings have demonstrated, is subject to judicial review by the court in the exercise of its supervisory power. Even after he has issued the surrender warrant the protections are not at an end. The Secretary of State has a continuing duty to keep the matter under review until the person is removed from this country for return to the place which made the request. This is because he has the power, should circumstances change, to withdraw the warrant before it has been implemented. It was in recognition of this duty that, although not obliged to do so by the statute, the Secretary of State agreed to consider the representations made in the light of his original decision letter before issuing his decision of 21 December 1995 not to reverse his earlier decision and withdraw the surrender warrant.

[853]   The evidence as to the basis on which the Secretary of State arrived at his decision on 31 July 1995 that the applicant was to be returned to Hong Kong, and his further decision on 21 December 1995 that there was nothing in the applicant's latest representations which led him to reverse that decision, is to be found in the letters themselves and in the supporting affidavits—the affirmation by Mr. David Ackland, who wrote the first letter, and the affidavit by Dr. Susan Atkins, who wrote the second letter. The structure and content of these documents leads me to the following conclusions about the process of reasoning which the Secretary of State adopted when he took these decisions.

First, it is stated expressly in these documents that the Secretary of State gave careful consideration to all the representations which had been made to him on the applicant's behalf. On the first page of the letter of 31 July 1995 it is stated: "The Secretary of State considered very carefully all the extensive representations made on behalf of Mr. Launder." In paragraph 2 on the second page it is stated: "The Secretary of State does not consider that the representations made by or on behalf of Mr. Launder are sufficient, either individually or cumulatively, to justify not surrendering him." Statements to the same effect are to be found in paragraph 3 of Mr. Ackland's affirmation. In paragraph 34 of his affirmation this statement appears:

> "The Secretary of State has given careful consideration to each of the points raised on behalf of the applicant concerning the position of Hong Kong after 1 July 1997 and has concluded that none of them, taken either individually or cumulatively, would lead him to believe that an order for return was unjust or oppressive."

In the letter of 21 December 1995 it is stated: "The Secretary of State has given careful consideration to the representations made by you on behalf of Mr. Launder to determine whether they give rise to sufficient grounds for withholding the surrender warrant." A statement to the same effect is to be found in paragraph 2 of Dr. Atkin's affidavit. No evidence has been shown to us which casts doubt on the accuracy of these statements by two senior officials of the Home Office.

Secondly, it is clear that great weight has been given by the Secretary of State, in his analysis of what the Divisional Court described as the China Point, to the provisions of the Joint Declaration and the Basic Law. The discussion in paragraphs 2.6 to 2.9 of the letter of 31 July 1995 of the applicant's representations refers throughout only to the Joint Declaration and the Basic Law and, in regard to specialty protection, to an extradition ordinance to be enacted locally. These points are discussed in more detail in paragraphs 23 to 33 of Mr. Ackland's affirmation. In paragraph 34 it is stated: "On all the foregoing matters the Secretary of State has proceeded on the basis that the P.R.C. will honour its obligations and commitments under the established instruments." In her affidavit Dr. Atkins repeats and develops this analysis. In paragraph 5 she states that the Secretary of State "proceeded on the basis" that the P.R.C. would comply with its obligations under the Joint Declaration, and similar statements appear in paragraphs 7, 9, 14, 19 and 20.

Third, no attempt is made to answer in any other way the many detailed representations on the applicant's behalf that, despite what is said in these instruments, the legal, penal and judicial system in Hong Kong after 1 July 1997 would not protect his right to a fair trial and, if convicted, to appropriate punishment. The applicant's argument is that the Secretary of State's approach, which faithfully reflects the evidence**[854]** from Hong Kong through the affidavit of the Attorney General, Mr. Matthews, relies solely on the letter of the treaty and does not begin to address itself to reality. As the Divisional Court put it, the concerns which were expressed about this in the applicant's evidence were specific, reasoned and supported by evidential material and by argument. I shall not attempt to summarise this material. It is sufficient to say that it contains numerous examples of acts done or permitted to be done by the P.R.C. and its officials to illustrate the argument that in the P.R.C. the law is seen as the instrument of the Party and of the Executive, and that any legal framework, however fair and however comprehensive, cannot be expected to guarantee and independent system of justice after the handover. Neither of the decision letters or the supporting affidavits address contain any comments which are addressed to this issue.

Fourth, the test which the Secretary of State has applied in reaching his decision was, as is apparent from the letter of 31 July 1995, whether it was unjust, oppressive or wrong to order the applicant's return. This reflects the wording of section 12(2) of the Extradition Act 1989, which provides that the Secretary of State shall not, in the case to which the paragraph refers, order the return if it appears to him that "it would, having regard to all the circumstances, be unjust or oppressive to return him." The use of this test indicates that the Secretary of State was aware that his primary concern was with the rights of the individual which as Mr. Parker accepted, must prevail over such public interest as there may be in maintaining good relations with the P.R.C.

Fifth, there is no mention in either of the letters or in the affidavits of a collective Cabinet decision about the effects of the treaty arrangements or of any view taken on this matter by the Government. The views expressed are said to be those of the Secretary himself, in the exercise of his discretion. There is therefore a sound basis in the evidence for examining his decisions in the normal way to see whether there was a defect in the decision-making process in the manner described by Lord Greene M.R. in *Associated Provincial Picture Houses Ltd. v. Wednesbury Corporation* [1948] 1 K.B. 223, 233–234. But it has to be said that we are dealing here with decisions in which there is obviously a substantial policy content where, as Sir Thomas Bingham M.R. observed in *Reg. v. Ministry* [26] *of Defence, Ex parte Smith* [1996] Q.B. 517, 556, the court must exercise great caution in holding a decision to be irrational. The area is a particularly sensitive one as it involves an assessment of the effect of treaty obligations undertaken between two sovereign states, as to which Lord Wilberforce's comments in *Buttes Gas and Oil Co. v. Hammer (No. 3)* [1982] A.C. 888, 938 are especially relevant. [27]

The principles to be applied in extradition cases

Atkinson v. United States of America Government [1971] A.C. 197, 232– [28] 233, Lord Reid said of the Extradition Act 1870 (33 & 34 Vict. c. 52) that it provided a safeguard for the fugitive because the Secretary of State always had the power to refuse to surrender a man committed to prison by the magistrate, and that it appeared to him that Parliament must have intended the Secretary of State to use that power whenever in his view it would be wrong, unjust or oppressive to surrender the man. An express power to this effect has now been conferred on the High Court by section 11(3) of the Extradition Act 1989, as Lord Griffiths pointed out in *Reg. v.* **[855]** *Horseferry Road Magistrates' Court, Ex parte Bennett* [1994] 1 A.C. 42, [29] 63. The same test, as to whether it would be unjust or oppressive to return the man, is to be found in section 12(2) of the Act which deals with the powers of the Secretary of State. So there can be no doubt that the test

[[26] 112 *ILR* 367.]   [[28] 51 *ILR* 288.]
[[27] 64 *ILR* 331.]   [[29] 95 *ILR* 380.]

which the Secretary of State applied in this case, as appears from the express references to this test in the concluding paragraphs of his letter of 31 July 1995, was the right one.

But what was the Secretary of State to make of the respondents argument that the treaty arrangements with the P.R.C. could not be relied upon to guarantee his rights to a fair trial and to appropriate punishment? It is clear that an argument in these terms would not be justiciable in the courts. In *Reg. v. Governor of Brixton Prison, Ex parte Kotronis* [1971] A.C. 250 the applicant was a Greek national who had been convicted of [30] an offence in a Greek court for which he had been sentenced to three years' imprisonment. It was contended that, as he was a political opponent of the then Greek government, he had good reason to fear that, should he be returned to Greece, he would be detained either after, or in lieu of, serving his sentence there. Lord Reid dealt with that aspect of his case, at pp. 278–279:

> "Finally, the respondent founds on the political elements in this case. It appears from his evidence that he is a determined opponent of the present Greek Government, that he has spent long periods out of Greece and that when in Greece he has been on three occasions detained without trial and without any charge being made against him. He says he has good reason to fear that if he is returned to Greece he will again be detained either after or in lieu of serving his sentence. But article 7 of our Extradition Treaty with Greece (set out in 1912, S.R & O., No. 193) provides that: 'A person whose surrender has been granted shall in no case be detained or tried ... for any other crime, or on account of any other matters than those for which the extradition shall have taken place.' So it would be a clear breach of faith on the part of the Greek Government if he were detained in Greece otherwise than for the purpose of serving his sentence, and it appears to me to be impossible for our courts or for your Lordships sitting judicially to assume that any foreign Government with which Her Majesty's Government has diplomatic relations may act in such a manner. If that is so, then Kotronis cannot take advantage of any of the provisions in the Act which empower the court to grant relief in a case of a political nature."

The position of the Secretary of State is, of course, different. He cannot ignore representations of that kind on the ground that it must be assumed that a foreign government with which this country has diplomatic relations will adhere to its treaty obligations. If issues of that kind are raised in a responsible manner, by reference to evidence and supported by reasoned argument, he must consider them. The greater the perceived risk to life or liberty, the more important it will be to give them detailed and careful scrutiny. In *Reg. v. Secretary of State for the Home Department, Ex parte Bugdaycay* [1987] A.C. 514, 531 Lord Bridge of Harwich said:[31]

> "The most fundamental of all human rights is the individual's right to life and when an administrative decision under challenge is said to

be one which may put the applicant's life at risk, the basis of the decision must surely call for the most anxious scrutiny."

[856]   In the same case, at p. 537, Lord Templeman extended that duty to the court in its examination of the Secretary of State's decision-making process: "In my opinion where the result of a flawed decision may imperil life or liberty a special responsibility lies on the court in the examination of the decision-making process."

In that case one of the appellants, Musisi, had arrived at Heathrow from Kenya. He was a national of Uganda from which he was a refugee, and he claimed political asylum. The decision to refuse him leave to enter was not based on the denial of his claim to refugee status, but on a conclusion by the Secretary of State that his status as a refugee under the Convention from Uganda did not present an obstacle to his return to Kenya whence he had come. The argument on his behalf was that he would be at risk of being returned to Uganda if he were to be returned to Kenya as a Ugandan national. His appeal was successful, because the evidence showed that the Secretary of State had not adequately considered the question whether there was a danger that his removal to Kenya would result in his return to Uganda. He had not taken into account or adequately resolved the ambiguities and uncertainties which surrounded the conduct and policy of the authorities in Kenya. Lord Bridge explained the approach in this way, at p. 532:

> "For the sake of illustration, I have necessarily taken cases at opposite ends of a spectrum. In the ordinary case of a person arriving here, from a third country, and claiming asylum as a refugee from the country of his nationality, there will be no ground to apprehend that his removal to the third country whence he comes would put him at risk. But at the other end of the spectrum, the risk may be obvious. Between these two extremes there may be varying degrees of danger that removal to a third country of a person claiming refugee status will result in his return to the country where he fears persecution. If there is some evidence of such a danger, it must be for the Secretary of State to decide as a matter of degree the question whether the danger is sufficiently substantial to involve a potential breach of article 33 of the Convention. If the Secretary of State has asked himself that question and answered it negatively in the light of all relevant evidence, the court cannot interfere."

Procedural impropriety, illegality and irrationality

I can deal briefly with the issues of procedural impropriety and irrationality. Mr. Vaughan submitted, after taking us through the evidence, that it was clear that the Secretary of State had completely failed to conduct the proper procedures in his approach to this material. It seems to me however, as it did to the Divisional Court, that the Secretary of State cannot be faulted on the ground that he failed to act with procedural fairness. He gave ample opportunity to the applicant to submit representations. He took advice from the Government of Hong Kong, and he gave the applicant a further opportunity to comment on that advice. He decided, in a commendable departure from the normal procedure in extradition cases, to give reasons for his decision in the letter of 31 July 1995. This enabled the applicant to prepare and submit further representations, which the Secretary of State received and considered before issuing his decision on 21 December 1995 not to withdraw the surrender warrant. He made it clear both in his decision letters and through the affidavits of his officials that he had considered carefully all **[857]** the representations which had been made.

As for irrationality, which Mr. Alun Jones said was the only real issue in the case, this also seems to me to be a complaint which is without any real substance. The question whether it is unjust or oppressive to order the applicant's return to Hong Kong must in the end depend upon whether the P.R.C. can be trusted in implement of its treaty obligations to respect his fundamental human rights, allow him a fair trial and leave it to the courts, if he is convicted, to determine the appropriate punishment.

It cannot be stressed too strongly that the decision in this matter rests with the Secretary of State and not at all with the court. The function of the court in the exercise of its supervisory jurisdiction is that of review. This is not an appeal against the Secretary of State's decision on the facts. His decision has had to be taken amidst an atmosphere of mistrust and suspicion which a court is in no position to penetrate. The visible part is the framework of law which I have described. That part can be explained and analysed. The invisible part is about the hearts and minds of those who will be responsible for the administration of justice in Hong Kong after the handover. This is not capable of analysis. It depends, in the end, upon the exercise of judgment of a kind which lies beyond the expertise of the court. That, no doubt, is why the decision whether or not to grant the warrant has been entrusted to the Secretary of State by Parliament.

On this matter there is room for two quite different views. On one view, which is that taken by the applicant and is supported by a substantial body of evidence from expert witnesses, the P.R.C. has already demonstrated by its conduct in recent years within China that it is incapable of giving effect to the rule of law on which the Basic Law must depend. On this view there is a risk, especially in a case which may be regarded as politically sensitive, that any trial would be unfair and that on conviction the executive would insist on inhuman and excessive punishment. The other view, which is that taken by the Secretary of State, is that the P.R.C. has good reason to make every effort in the Hong Kong S.A.R. to preserve the existing criminal justice system, in recognition that it would not be appropriate to practise the socialist system and policies there. As the preamble to the Basic Law declares, it has been appreciated by the P.R.C. that this is essential if the prosperity and stability of Hong Kong is to be maintained after the transfer. The P.R.C. have an obvious interest in making a success of the new arrangements. A breakdown of the rule of law generally, or even a departure from it in some cases such as this one, would be bound to have a serious effect on confidence throughout the business community on which it depends for that success. In these circumstances optimism about the future for human rights in Hong Kong after the handover, for which such careful arrangements have been made in the Joint Declaration and the Basic Law, cannot be said to be unreasonable. Past conduct within China is not necessarily a good guide to what will happen in Hong Kong after the transfer of sovereignty. The care which has been taken during the long period of preparation for the event to address this issue, which is obvious from the close attention to detail which is revealed by the relevant documents, provides a clear basis for holding that the decision of the Secretary of State to reject the applicant's arguments was not irrational. If there was room for doubt on this matter, I would regard this as a case where great caution would have to be exercised, despite the need for anxious scrutiny, before holding that [858] decision to be one which, in the relevant sense, was unreasonable. But, in all the circumstances, I do not think that there is any real room for doubt.

The real question in the case, as I see it, is whether in taking his decision the Secretary of State asked himself the right question or whether, to put it another way, he fettered his discretion by asking himself the wrong one. This issue has been obscured by the way in which the case was argued on his behalf in the Divisional Court. There can be no doubt that if, as was being suggested, the Secretary of State regarded himself as bound by the Cabinet's judgment on this matter to assume that the P.R.C. would comply with its treaty obligations and on this ground gave no further consideration to the applicant's arguments, he would have failed to direct himself properly to his responsibilities under section 12 of the Act. But, for the reasons already given, I am satisfied that that is not what he did. The evidence shows that he took his own decision after considering all the representations which had been made to him.

But what was the question to which he addressed his mind? If, as was suggested by Mr. Parker at one stage in the argument, he addressed his mind only to the question whether the P.R.C. had repudiated, or was likely to repudiate, its obligations under the treaty, he would have failed to ask himself the right question. The right question, in the light of the representations which had been made to him, was a narrower and more precise one. It goes to the heart of the issue as to whether it would be unjust or oppressive for the applicant to be extradited. It is whether this particular individual would be exposed to the risk of injustice or oppression if he were to be returned to Hong Kong to face trial there after 1 July 1997. If he asked himself the wrong question his decision would be flawed on the ground of illegality. If he asked himself the right one and answered it negatively in the light of all relevant evidence, then, [32] as Lord Bridge said in *Ex parte Bugdaycay* [1987] A.C. 514, the court cannot interfere.

The point requires anxious consideration in the light of the risks which the applicant has identified. An assessment of the risks to the individual after 1 July 1997 is not completed by looking simply for evidence of repudiation by the P.R.C. of its obligations under the treaty. There are passages, especially in the affidavits, which indicate an assumption by the Secretary of State that all the treaty obligations relating to the

[[32] *79 ILR* 642.]

implementation of the Basic Law will be observed. That, no doubt, is why so much of the content of the affidavits has been taken up with an explanation of the measures which will be in place by the date of the handover. There is nothing wrong with that as a starting point. The words of the Joint Declaration and the Basic Law are both relevant and important in the assessment of what the applicant is likely to face if he is returned to Hong Kong. But the question then has to be asked whether these words are likely in practice, in his case, to be meaningless. As the transfer of sovereignty still lies in the future, assumptions about what the future holds for him are inevitable. The P.R.C. cannot be required to serve a probationary period in order to test its behaviour after the handover. The question then is whether the Secretary of State went further in his consideration of the case beyond general assumptions about legality and examined the risks to the applicant as an individual.

The concluding paragraphs of the letter of 31 July 1995 which I quoted earlier provide the best evidence of the question which the Secretary of State had identified. He made it clear here that he had asked himself whether, in all the circumstances, it would be unjust or oppressive or wrong to order the applicant's return to Hong Kong. This was the correct **[859]** test, and I consider that by applying it the Secretary of State can be taken to have applied his mind to the position which the applicant in particular would face under the new arrangements in view of the risks which he had identified. The point to which the applicant had drawn his attention was that the letter of the Basic Law could not be relied upon, at least in his case. The Secretary of State said in his decision letters that he gave careful consideration to the representations which had been made to him. It was not necessary for him to deal with every point which had been raised in the reasons which he gave. Any attempt to deal with only some of them would be open to criticism on the ground that the other points were ignored. There was so much material before him that it would not have been practicable for him to go over the whole ground in the written explanations for the decisions which he took. His statements that he considered the whole matter very carefully must be given due weight. In this unusual case, against the whole background which his letter of 31 July 1995 had identified, that was enough. The emphasis which he gave to the legal framework was not just, as Mr. Vaughan asked us to accept, an assertion that the law is the law. It was the basis for his decision, which as I have said was not an irrational one, that the P.R.C.—despite its actions elsewhere and in other circumstances—could be relied upon to respect the law in the applicant's case and not to interfere in the process of justice in bringing him to trial in Hong Kong and, if he is convicted, imposing and enforcing the appropriate penalties. If that assumption is made it provides a rational and complete answer to all the objections. I do not think that your Lordships would be justified in holding that he failed to address himself to the right question in reaching the conclusion that he should grant a warrant in this case.

There remains however one particular issue in this chapter which must be considered, because if it was clear that the Secretary of State misdirected himself about this it would be necessary to consider whether we should quash his decision and allow him to look at the matter again. This is whether there is substance in the applicant's concern about the absence of specialty protection after 1 July 1997.

Specialty protection

Section 6 of the Extradition Act 1989 imposes a number of general restrictions on the return of a person to a foreign state. If one or more of these restrictions apply the Secretary of State has no discretion in the matter. It is unlawful for the person to be returned to the requesting state or committed or kept in custody for the purposes of return. Among these restrictions is that set out in subsection (4), known as the specialty protection. That subsection provides:

> "A person shall not be returned, or committed or kept in custody for the purposes of such return, unless provision is made by the relevant law, or by an arrangement made with the relevant foreign state, Commonwealth country or colony, for securing that he will not, unless he has first had an opportunity to leave it, be dealt with there for or in respect of any offence committed before his return to it other than—(*a*) the offence in respect of which his return is ordered; (*b*) an offence, other than an offence excluded by subsection (5) below, which is disclosed by the facts in respect of which his return was ordered; or (*c*) subject to subsection (6) below, any other offence being an extradition crime in respect of which the Secretary of State may consent to his being deal with."

[860]

In subsection (7) it is provided that any such arrangement as is mentioned in subsection (4) which is made with a designated Commonwealth country or a colony may be an arrangement for the particular case or an arrangement of a general nature, and that a certificate of the Secretary of State confirming the existence of such an arrangement and stating its terms shall be conclusive evidence of the matters contained in the certificate.

The issues which were raised in regard to the specialty protection fall neatly into two separate chapters, although it is right to add that the whole subject is a complex one in view of the way matters have been developing prior to the handover on 1 July 1997. The first chapter relates to the question whether the specialty protection was in place on the dates when the Secretary of State took the decisions. The second question relates to the question whether the specialty protection will be in place after the handover. The third relates to the question whether, assuming that the specialty protection will be in place after the handover, it will provide effective protection against the applicant's removal from Hong Kong S.A.R. to any other part of the P.R.C. As the argument developed before your Lordships it became clear that the issue which is of primary importance is that raised in the third chapter. But it is necessary to deal with the other two chapters also, if only by way of background, because of the important place which the specialty protection has in extradition law.

(a) The position at present

It is clear, and not disputed by the applicant, that the requirements of section 6(4) were satisfied at the time when the decisions were taken and that they will continue to be satisfied until the date of the handover. The relevant provisions for extradition to the Crown Colony are contained in the Fugitive Offenders (Hong Kong) Order 1967 (S.I. 1967 No. 1911), which was made under the Fugitive Offenders Act 1967 and remains in force notwithstanding the repeal of that Act: see section 34(3) of the Extradition Act 1989. Section 14 of the Schedule to the 1967 Order provides the protection which is required by section 6(4) of the Act of 1989. A certificate to the effect that the specialty protection exists has been issued under section 6(7) of that Act. It is equally clear that the existence of this protection is now, and has for some time been, academic for the purposes of this case as it will cease to exist when sovereignty over Hong Kong is transferred to the P.R.C. For the time being the requirements of section 6(4) are satisfied, but the Secretary of State was also obliged to consider what the position would be on and after 1 July 1997. It would plainly be unjust for the applicant to be returned to Hong Kong until it was clear that there was in place in Hong Kong from and after that date a provision for specialty protection which satisfied the terms of section 6(4).

(b) The position in future

The situation has changed since 1995 when the decisions were taken. So it is necessary first to mention the situation at that time and then to examine the situation at the present stage. Although we are concerned primarily with the reasonableness of the decisions at the time when they were taken we cannot ignore these developments. We are dealing in this **[861]** case with concerns which have been expressed about human rights and the risks to the applicant's life and liberty. If the expectations which the Secretary of State had when he took his decisions have not been borne out by events or are at risk of not being satisfied by the date of the applicant's proposed return to Hong Kong, it would be your Lordships' duty to set aside the decisions so that the matter may be reconsidered in the light of the changed circumstances.

At the date when the decisions were taken in 1995 the matter had to be based upon a reasonable expectation of what would be arranged in the future. As Mr. Ackland has explained in paragraph 31 of his affirmation, the P.R.C. had agreed that Hong Kong might negotiate and conclude, under authorisation by the P.R.C., its own extradition arrangements prior to the date of the handover which would remain in force after that date. By the date of his affirmation a number of such agreements had already been signed with other countries which contained the specialty protection. A draft of an Ordinance to be enacted locally in Hong Kong had been prepared and was awaiting approval by the P.R.C. Mr. Ackland said that it was reasonably expected that the P.R.C. would give its approval, as Hong Kong's independent extradition arrangements were fully accepted by the P.R.C.

Since that date there have been further developments. We were shown a copy of an Order in Council made on 8 April 1997 under paragraph 3(2) of the Schedule to the Hong Kong Act 1985, called the Hong Kong (Extradition) Order 1997 (S.I. 1997 No. 1178). That Order is subject to the negative resolution procedure. It had not yet been laid before Parliament. We were also shown a copy of Hong Kong Ordinance No. 23 of 1997 which was made on 26 March 1997, to be known as the Fugitive Offenders Ordinance. This is designed to regulate extradition between Hong Kong and places outside Hong Kong after 1 July 1997. Section 17 of the Ordinance will provide the specialty protection in Hong Kong S.A.R. after that date for persons who are surrendered to Hong Kong under such extradition arrangements. In order to complete the necessary arrangements with the United Kingdom it will be necessary for an agreement to be entered into in accordance with the statutory scheme contained in the Ordinance. Provision is made by section 3(1) of the Ordinance for these agreements, once made, to be enacted as part of the law of Hong Kong. The procedures in the Ordinance will then apply as between Hong Kong and the United Kingdom subject to the limitations, restrictions, exemptions and qualifications, if any, contained in the Order.

Two affidavits were shown to us to explain the stage which matters have now reached in finalising these arrangements. In her affirmation dated 18 April 1997 Clare Checksfield, head of the Extradition Section of the Home Office, states that the text of the agreement is close to being finalised and that there remained only two outstanding minor issues neither of which is relevant to this case. She says that she has no reason to believe that the agreement, when it is concluded, will not contain articles dealing with the specialty protection which is required for fugitive offenders surrendered to Hong Kong. In his affidavit dated 21 April 1987 Wayne Walsh, Acting Deputy Principal Crown Counsel in the Attorney-General's Chambers, Prosecutions Division of the Legal Department of the Government of Hong Kong, states that to date Hong Kong has signed new agreements with six countries for the surrender of fugitive offenders, all of which contain a provision restricting resurrender of the fugitive to a [862] place outside the jurisdiction of Hong Kong. These six countries are the United States, Canada, Australia, the Philippines, Malaysia and The Netherlands. The new arrangements to govern the surrender of fugitives between Hong Kong and the United Kingdom have not yet been concluded, but they are in negotiation and the Chinese have already approved the model form of agreement in the Joint Liaison Group and no difficulties are expected. As the new arrangements with Hong Kong must be concluded between the United Kingdom and Hong Kong S.A.R. the agreement cannot be signed and brought into effect until 1 July 1997. But this is what the parties are working towards and it is likely that express protection against resurrender will be in place by that date.

For the applicant an affidavit was produced from Professor Yash Pal Ghai of Hong Kong who had been asked to provide his opinion on whether the specialty protection contained in the Fugitive Offenders Ordinance would prevent the fugitive offender from being removed from Hong Kong S.A.R. to the P.R.C. He makes the point that the international arrangements which Hong Kong S.A.R. has entered into or which may be entered into on its behalf will not apply in its relations with the rest of the P.R.C. I shall deal with this point in the next chapter. As for the question whether arrangements will be in place on 1 July 1997 or shortly thereafter to provide the specialty protection in place of the present arrangements, it appears that matters have developed as the Secretary of State anticipated when he took his decisions in 1995.

(c) Protection against surrender to the P.R.C.

The important question, which has only emerged as a special point of concern very recently in the light of the terms of the Fugitive Offenders Ordinance, is whether the provisions of that Ordinance will be effective to prevent the transfer of a person from Hong Kong S.A.R. to the P.R.C. It is plain that the present arrangements are effective to prevent such a transfer, but with effect from 1 July 1997 Hong Kong will be part of the P.R.C. Not surprisingly, the Ordinance has been framed on this basis. As Mr. Walsh has explained in his affidavit, it is designed to regulate extradition between Hong Kong and places outside Hong Kong other than the P.R.C. Section 17(2) of the Ordinance deals with the resurrender of the fugitive to a third jurisdiction, and it provides that the fugitive shall not be surrendered to any other "prescribed place" unless conditions similar to those in section 17(1) apply. The P.R.C. cannot be a prescribed place under the Ordinance, so section 17(2) is silent about the resurrender of a fugitive to China.

Professor Yash Ghai has therefore correctly identified a gap in the proposed arrangements which is of particular importance to the applicant's position were he to be returned to Hong Kong. Two questions then arise. The first is whether other protections will be available to him to prevent his surrender to the P.R.C. whether before or after any trial on the charges which have been made against him. The second is whether the existence of this gap, which was not observed by the Secretary of State when he took his decisions, vitiates these decisions and makes it necessary for the matter to be remitted to him for further consideration.

The answer to the first point lies partly in the terms of the agreement which is being negotiated by the United Kingdom with Hong Kong prior to its enactment under section 3(1) of the Ordinance, and partly in the Basic Law. The draft agreement contains in article 18(1) a provision by which the surrender of the fugitive "to any other jurisdiction" is restricted **[863]** on terms which are consistent with the specialty protection in section 6(4) of the Act of 1989. Mr. Walsh states that all six of the agreements which have been made to date contained an article in similar terms. That safeguard will become part of the Ordinance once the agreement with the United Kingdom has been enacted under section 3(1). Persons returned from the United Kingdom to the jurisdiction of Hong Kong S.A.R. after 1 July 1997 will therefore have the benefit of that protection, in the same way as persons returned to the jurisdiction of Hong Kong S.A.R. from the other six countries with whom agreements have already been made.

Then there are the provisions of the Basic Law relating to the rights and freedoms of persons in Hong Kong and to the judiciary. Mr. Walsh has explained in his affidavit that there is no operative legal basis for the surrender of fugitives from Hong Kong S.A.R. to the P.R.C. after the handover. The Chinese Extradition Ordinance (c. 235) which was originally enacted in Hong Kong in 1889 dealt only with the surrender from Hong Kong to China of Chinese nationals, not fugitives, and it is being repealed. Professor Yash Ghai has expressed concern about the risk of informal surrender from Hong Kong to the P.R.C., but Mr. Walsh states that Hong Kong has to date never informally, or otherwise, extradited a person from Hong Kong to the P.R.C. It does on a regular basis repatriate illegal immigrants, but it is the stated policy of the present Hong Kong Government and of the incoming Government of the S.A.R. that it does not and will not surrender or resurrender persons to places outside its jurisdiction either to face trial or to serve sentences unless it is pursuant to a law and subject to safeguards.

I think that it is reasonable to conclude therefore that, in accordance with the fundamental policy which has been enshrined in the Basic Law, the prohibitions which are needed to ensure that the applicant is not surrendered to the P.R.C. will be in place on and after 1 July 1997. As I have already said, there is room for two views as to whether the P.R.C. can be relied upon to respect this policy. But it cannot be said to be irrational to prefer the view that sufficient commitment to that policy has already been demonstrated by the P.R.C. and that sufficient incentives exist to ensure the continuation of that commitment after the handover.

As for the second point, I do not think that the fact that this gap appears to have been overlooked by the Secretary of State is fatal to the decisions. It was not clearly identified until the Fugitive Offenders Ordinance had become available and the argument was well under way in your Lordships' House. The Secretary of State dealt sufficiently with the representations which were made to him at the time. There is nothing in the present information to suggest that the position is now materially different from that which, taking his decisions overall, he had anticipated.

European Community law and human rights

In the Divisional Court the applicant contended that his arrest at Heathrow Airport, on his arrival there from Berlin, was an infringement of his right of freedom of movement under article 48 of the European Community Treaty and that the Secretary of State's decisions were in breach of various articles of the European Convention on Human Rights. These arguments were rejected by the Divisional Court. The applicant then applied to the Divisional Court for certification of these issues as raising matters of general public importance and for leave to cross-appeal. [864] These applications were opposed by the Secretary of State and they were rejected by the Divisional Court. As I have already mentioned however, Mr. Vaughan was allowed to develop these arguments again before your Lordships in view of the wider scope which it was necessary to give to the whole matter.

(a) European Union law

The applicant had established a place of business in Germany. It was necessary for him to travel extensively between the member states for the purposes of that business, and he had done so frequently before his arrest. Article 48.3 of the European Community Treaty provides:

> "[Freedom of movement for workers] shall entail the right, subject to limitations justified on grounds of public policy, public security or public health: . . . (*b*) to move freely within the territory of member States for this purpose; . . ."

The applicant's argument is that the effect of his arrest and of any subsequent order for his extradition would be to prevent him from continuing with his business activities in Germany, from which he could not have been extradited to Hong Kong, and elsewhere in the Community. Although he relies principally on article 48 which applies to workers, he refers also to article 52 which relates to the right to establishment of the self-employed and to article 59 which relates to the provision of services. These articles also are subject to such limitations as may be justified on grounds of public policy: see articles 56 and 66 of the European Community Treaty. The effect of these provisions is to prevent discriminatory restrictions imposed by a member state, other than that of which the person is a national, in which he wishes to carry out business activities. They can also extend to non-discriminatory restrictions imposed by his state of origin on movement to another member state in which the person proposes to pursue or is pursuing his work or business activities: *Union Royale Belge des Sociétés de Football Association ASBL v. Bosman* (Case C-415/93) [1995] E.C.R. I-4921, 4959–4965. As these provisions have direct effect the applicant is entitled to apply to the courts of this country for their enforcement under section 2 of the European Communities Act 1972.

The question which the applicant has raised is whether his detention and extradition can be justified on grounds of public policy. The Divisional Court held that extradition must come within the public policy exception. In his argument to your Lordships Mr. Vaughan said that the applicant had never contended that European Union law prevents extradition in all circumstances. His submission is that, whereas in normal circumstances public policy will justify extradition, in exceptional circumstances it will not do so. He maintains that such exceptional circumstances exist in this case because of the evidence which has been produced to show that the applicant's extradition to Hong Kong would expose him to the risk of violations of the European Convention on Human Rights, and that public policy could never justify such a restriction on his fundamental rights under European Union law.

In *Reg. v. Governor of Pentonville Prison, Ex parte Budlong* [1980] 1 W.L.R. 1110 the applicant, Kember, was a U.K. national who had been [33] charged with burglary in the United States of America. The United States Government made a request for her surrender under the Extradition Treaty between the United Kingdom and the U.S.A. The applicant then

[865] sought a reference to the European Court of Justice for a preliminary ruling on the question whether her extradition had to be justified on public policy grounds under article 48(3). If her submission had been right on that point it would have meant that her extradition could only have been ordered on grounds of public policy based exclusively on her own personal conduct: see article 3 of Council Directive (64/221/E.E.C.) of 25 February 1964. Her argument was rejected and, as the point was held to be reasonably clear and free from doubt, no reference was made to the European Court. Griffiths J. observed, at p. 1127, in regard to the argument which relied on the decision of the European Court of Justice in *Reg. v. Bouchereau* [1978] Q.B. 732 that a recommendation for deportation made by a criminal court in this country was a measure within the meaning of article 3(1) and (2) of the Directive and could only be made on grounds of public policy, that if this submission was right it would impose a formidable fetter upon extradition:

> "The whole basis of extradition is that the accused has offended against society in another country; in all probability he is no threat to our society. Does that then mean he is not to be extradited to face justice where he has committed the crime? I cannot believe that it can have been the intention of those who drew the Treaty of Rome that it should have the effect of so emasculating the process of extradition."

The decision in *Ex parte Budlong* was followed in *In re Habeas Corpus Application of Navinder Singh Virdee* [1980] 1 C.M.L.R. 709, in which it was held that article 48 did not apply to a case where the applicant was to be surrendered to a non-European Community state under the Visiting Forces Act, and in *In re Habeas Corpus Application of Carthage Healy* [1984] 3 C.M.L.R. 575, in regard to the detention of an Irish national pending his extradition from the United Kingdom. Mr. Vaughan has criticised the decisions in these cases on the ground that *Ex parte Budlong* was founded on the opinion of the Advocate General in *Reg. v. Saunders* (Case 175/78) [1974] E.C.R. 1129. He has pointed out that it was made clear in *Union Royale Belge des Sociétés de Football Association ASBL v. Bosman* that there was no Community element in *Reg. v. Saunders* [1995] E.C.R. I-4921, as the situation there was a purely internal one. He has also pointed out that in none of these cases before the Divisional Court was it suggested that there was a risk of a breach of the European Convention on Human Rights by virtue of the surrender. But I do not think that either of these points affects the substance of the opinion which Griffiths J. expressed in *Ex parte Budlong*.

It is true that Griffiths J. relied in that case on the decision in *Reg. v. Saunders* that article 48 did not aim to restrict the power of the member states to lay down restrictions, within their own territory, on the freedom of movement of all persons subject to their jurisdiction in the implementation of domestic criminal law. That case was concerned with a matter which was wholly internal to the United Kingdom, as Miss Saunder's case was concerned with the breach by her of a condition of a binding-over order requiring her to return to her place of residence in Northern Ireland. It did not involve travel between member states. But the point which Griffiths J. was making was that in *Reg. v. Saunders* a clear distinction had been drawn between deportation, which was the subject of the decision in *Reg. v. Bouchereau*, and restrictions on the freedom of movement of individuals imposed by the criminal court in the ordinary course of the administration of justice. He said that extradition was far more closely analogous to the implementation of domestic criminal **[866]** law than to deportation.

In my opinion the recognition in *Union Royale Belge des Sociétés de Football Association ASBL v. Bosman* that there was no Community element in *Reg. v. Saunders* adds nothing new which is relevant to this point. There is no indication in what Griffiths J. says about *Reg. v. Saunders* that he had overlooked the fact that it was dealing with a matter which was purely internal to the United Kingdom. On the contrary his repeated use of the phrase "domestic criminal law" shows that he was well aware of this point. His main reason for regarding extradition as outside the scope of article 48 was that, if that was so, the process of extradition would be emasculated if it was to be necessary to justify the decision in each case on grounds of public policy, and he also said that it would produce anomalies between member states whose extradition treaties had been entered into before the Treaty of Rome and those whose treaties were made or amended after that date. His reasoning on these points seems to me, with respect, to be entirely satisfactory. As Goff L.J. explained in *Healy* [1984] 3 C.M.L.R. 575, 583 the significance of *Reg. v. Saunders* is that in that case the court took a purposive approach to article 48. He said that it was obvious that that article did not aim to restrict the power of member states to lay down restrictions within their own territory from the freedom of movement of all persons subject to their jurisdiction in the implementation of extradition procedures. In my opinion the same can be said of the implementation by member states of their obligation to extradite persons from their territory under treaty obligations entered into with other states. The result is that it is not necessary for the Secretary of State to justify the respondent's detention and his decision to extradite him on the grounds of public policy.

Mr. Vaughan's argument that the public policy exception does not permit extradition in cases where there is a risk of a breach of the European Court of Human Rights does not therefore arise. The decision in *Ex parte Budlong* was not that extradition could always be justified on [34] grounds of public policy, but that the relevant provisions of the European Community Treaty did not apply to extradition cases at all. As I consider that *Ex parte Budlong* was correctly decided on this point, I consider it unnecessary to examine the scope of the public policy exception in this case.

European Convention on Human Rights

The applicant's argument in the Divisional Court was that, in the light of what Mr. Vaughan has described as the exceptional circumstances of this case, the provisions of the European Convention itself provided a

[34] 85 *ILR* 72.]

remedy. That argument was rejected by the Divisional Court on the ground that the Convention has not been incorporated into United Kingdom law: _Reg. v. Secretary of State for the Home Department,_ [35] _Ex parte Brind_ [1991] 1 A.C. 696. Mr. Vaughan's argument in that court that judicial review is a flexible remedy which can often achieve the same results as could be achieved in the European Court of Human Rights was accepted. But, as Henry L.J. put it, "what matters is the route. Unless and until the Convention is incorporated into our law, breaches of the Convention cannot be relied on as such to provide the route."

Mr. Vaughan renewed his argument before your Lordships on a number of grounds which I think require more careful examination. The [867] way in which they were expressed does not enable them to be dismissed simply on the ground that he has chosen the wrong route. Indeed, two features of this case seem to me to indicate that the applicant's arguments under the Convention are directly relevant to the remedy which he seeks by way of judicial review. The first is the argument which he presented to the Secretary of State in his representations. This was that the rights which would be put at risk if he were to be returned to Hong Kong were his rights under the Convention—in particular his rights to life and liberty, to a fair trial and not to be subjected to inhuman or degrading treatment or punishment: see articles 2, 3, 5 and 6. The second is that the Secretary of State himself, as Mr. Ackland has told us in paragraph 36 of his affirmation, took account of the applicant's representations that his extradition to Hong Kong would be a breach of the Convention in reaching his decision that he should be extradited.

It is often said that, while the Convention may influence the common law, it does not bind the executive. This view was reflected in the observation by Sir Thomas Bingham M.R. in _Reg. v. Ministry of Defence,_ [36] _Ex parte Smith_ [1996] Q.B. 517, 558E that exercising an administrative discretion is not of itself a ground for impugning that exercise. That is so; but the whole context of the dialogue between the Secretary of State and the applicant in this case was the risk of an interference with the applicant's human rights. That in itself is a ground for subjecting the decisions to the most anxious scrutiny, in accordance with the principles laid down by this House in _Reg. v. Secretary of State for the Home_ [37] _Department, Ex parte Bugdaycay_ [1987] A.C. 514, as Sir Thomas Bingham M.R. also recognised in _Ex parte Smith,_ at p. 554H. Then there is the question whether judicial review proceedings can provide the applicant with an effective remedy, as article 13 requires where complaints are raised under the Convention in extradition and deportation [38] cases: see _Soering v. United Kingdom_ (1989) 11 E.H.H.R. 439; _Vilvarajah_ [39] _v. United Kingdom_ (1991) 14 E.H.R.R. 248; _D. v. United Kingdom,_ The Times, 12 May 1997. If the applicant is to have an effective remedy against a decision which is flawed because the decision-maker has misdirected himself on the Convention which he himself says he took into account, it must surely be right to examine the substance of the argument. The ordinary principles of judicial review permit this approach because it

[35 85 _ILR_ 29.]   [37 79 _ILR_ 642.]   [39 108 _ILR_ 321.]
[36 112 _ILR_ 367.]   [38 98 _ILR_ 270.]

was to the rationality and legality of the decisions, and not to some independent remedy, that Mr. Vaughan directed his argument.

That argument was directed to three issues. The first was whether the Secretary of State correctly took into account the scope and content of the Convention. It was maintained that it was not sufficient for him merely to assert that he took the Convention into account if he had failed to do so correctly. In a life and liberty case a bare assertion that the Convention was considered was insufficient, especially where the decision-maker had stated that his decision was based wholly on political policy considerations. The second was whether the Secretary of State had personally and properly considered the applicant's individual case and circumstances. It was pointed out that the Convention protects the individual and that it must be applied to his individual circumstances. It would not be sufficient for the Secretary of State to rely on a political decision of the Cabinet or to reach a decision not related to the applicant's contentions or to his individual circumstances. The third was directed to the rationality of the Secretary of State's decisions. In this regard the argument was that, in a case concerning the personal circumstances of an individual and not the creation or operation of a rule to be applied **[868]** generally, the Convention was directly relevant.

It can be seen from this summary that much of the substance of the objection is directed to an aspect of the argument in the Divisional Court which has been departed from expressly in this House. I have already dealt with this point in my outline of the issues in this appeal and in my analysis of the decisions by the Secretary of State as revealed by his decision letters and the affidavits. The evidence which is before us does not support the proposition that his decision was based wholly on political policy considerations. It shows that he took his own decision, having proper regard to the rights of the applicant as an individual. The test which he applied was whether it would in all the circumstances be unjust or oppressive for the applicant to be extradited to Hong Kong. The application of this test shows that he was aware that his concern was with the rights of the individual, not with political considerations. The applicant's allegation in his printed case that the Secretary of State washed his hands of the applicant's fate without detailed scrutiny of his allegations is not made out by the evidence. The case would have been different, if the evidence had shown that the decisions were wholly political and that proper regard had not been paid to the applicant's human rights. If that had been the position there would have been no need, in a case of this kind, for Mr. Vaughan to rely on the Convention. The Secretary of State would have failed to address himself to the right question, and on that ground at least it would have been open to review as to its legality. As it is, that is not the state of the evidence and there are no longer any grounds for maintaining this criticism.

The remaining part of Mr. Vaughan's argument can be dealt with under the heading of irrationality. He maintained that the Convention required detailed scrutiny and evaluation of the facts in an extradition

[40] case where the person's human rights were at risk. He referred to *Soering v. United Kingdom*, 11 E.H.R.R. 439 to illustrate his point that confidence in a legal system was not enough. There had to be an examination of the domestic law and practice as it was applied in reality. In that case, on the facts, practice in the United States was at serious risk of failing to conform to the standards of the Convention, so the decision to order the detainee's surrender to that country was held to involve a breach of the Convention. Mr. Vaughan said that the Secretary of State had based his decision on a formal interpretation of the Joint Declaration, asserting that the law was the law, rather than an analysis of practice in Hong Kong.

Here again, however, the argument raises points which I have already dealt with under previous headings, and in particular in my examination of the question whether the decisions could be said to be irrational. I do not think that it is necessary to go over these points again. It is enough to say that the argument which Mr. Vaughan presented under this heading seemed to me to be inextricably linked to those which he had already presented under the heading of irrationality. No new points of substance were raised in this branch of his argument. The decision which he says should have been taken would have had to have been based on the conclusion that, despite the provisions of the Joint Declaration and the Basic Law, the practice of the P.R.C. in the field of human rights to date within its own territory showed that there was a serious risk that the provisions of these instruments would be departed from in Hong Kong S.A.R. But the arguments are not all one way on this point, as I have already sought to demonstrate. A reasonable Secretary of State could, on

[869] the material available to him, have concluded that the concerns which were indicated by the P.R.C.'s actions in other places and in other circumstances were not so serious as to give rise to a serious risk of injustice or oppression in the applicant's case. The human rights context has not been overlooked in this assessment. On the contrary, it lies at the heart of the whole argument. It is precisely because it was not irrational for the Secretary of State to say that he was not persuaded that there was a case on human rights grounds for refusing extradition to Hong Kong that his decisions stand up to the required degree of scrutiny.

Conclusion

For these reasons I would allow this appeal and dismiss the applications for judicial review. In view of the fact that the argument for the Secretary of State in the Divisional Court was departed from, I would not alter the order as to costs which was made in that court. I would make no order as to costs in the appeal to this House.

LORD CLYDE. My Lords, I have had the advantage of reading in draft the speech to be delivered by my noble and learned friend, Lord Hope of Craighead. For the reasons which he gives, I, too, would allow the appeal.

[[40] 98 *ILR* 270.]

LORD HUTTON. My Lords, I have had the advantage of reading in draft the speech of my noble and learned friend, Lord Hope of Craighead. I agree with it and for the reasons which he gives I would allow the appeal.

Appeal allowed.
No order as to costs.

Solicitors: Treasury Solicitor; Crown Prosecution Service; Titmuss Sainer Dechert.

[Reports: [1997] 1 WLR 839; [1997] 3 All ER 992]

Governments—Recognition—Change of government following *coup d'état*—Criteria for determining whether organizers of *coup* now the government — Constitutional status — Degree, nature and stability of control over the territory of the State—Dealings between United Kingdom Government and new regime—Extent of international recognition of regime — Board of directors of company appointed by government of foreign State—Company possessing bank account with London bank — Directors appointed as signatories for bank account—New regime purporting to dismiss directors and appoint replacements—New directors giving fresh instructions to bank—Whether bank obliged to honour instructions from original board of directors or newly appointed board of directors

Recognition—Governments—United Kingdom policy on recognition—1980 statement—*Coups d'état*—Letters from Foreign and Commonwealth Office indicating attitude of

United Kingdom Government towards new regime — Approach to be taken by courts—The law of England

SIERRA LEONE TELECOMMUNICATIONS CO. LTD v. BARCLAYS BANK PLC[1]

England, High Court, Queen's Bench Division. 6 *February* 1998

(Cresswell J)

SUMMARY: *The facts*:—Sierra Leone Telecommunications Co. Ltd ("Sierratel") was a company incorporated in Sierra Leone and was wholly owned by the Sierra Leone Government. Under its articles of association, the board of directors of Sierratel consisted of eight members appointed by the Government of Sierra Leone. Sierratel had a bank account with the defendant bank in London and had completed a bank mandate authorizing four signatories to sign payment requests on its behalf. In May 1997 there was a military *coup* in Sierra Leone and the democratically elected Government fled into exile. The government of the United Kingdom condemned the *coup* and continued to deal with the exiled elected Government. Letters from the Foreign and Commonwealth Office, which were put before the Court, stated that the United Kingdom Government continued to have dealings with the exiled Government of Sierra Leone and had no dealings with the regime installed in Sierra Leone following the *coup d'état*.

After the *coup*, the defendant bank continued to honour payment instructions made by the original signatories. In December 1997, however, the bank received a letter purporting to come from the Secretary of State, Transport and Communications in the regime installed in Sierra Leone following the *coup*, and the Executive Chairman of the board of Sierratel. This letter notified the bank that the new regime in Sierra Leone had dismissed the board of directors of Sierratel and replaced them with new directors and that three of the signatories on the bank account had been suspended. A subsequent communication from the Executive Chairman instructed the bank not to honour payment instructions which had been issued by the original signatories. The bank therefore refused to meet a number of payment requests on the basis that it had reasonable grounds to believe that those requests had been made without authority. The High Commissioner of Sierra Leone in London, who continued to act on behalf of the exiled Government, then instructed lawyers to bring an action in the name of Sierratel against the defendant bank seeking a declaration that the bank account remained subject to the terms of the mandate and to instructions given by the signatories named in that mandate. Counsel for Sierratel argued that the regime installed in the capital of Sierra Leone following the *coup* was not the Government of Sierra Leone and that, accordingly, its purported replacement of the board of directors and suspension of the signatories from the bank account were

---

[1] The plaintiff company was represented by Mr Timothy Saloman QC, instructed by Stephenson Harwood. The defendant bank was represented by Mr Richard de Lacy, instructed by Lovell White Durrant.

ineffective. He contended that the exiled Government continued to be the Government of Sierra Leone and that Sierratel's affairs continued to be managed by the directors appointed by that exiled Government.

Held:—The declaration was granted.

(1) Applying the Rome Convention on the law applicable to contractual obligations, which was given the force of law in the United Kingdom by the Contracts (Applicable Law) Act 1990, the proper law of the contract between Sierratel and the defendant bank was the law of the country with which the contract was most closely connected. In the case of a banking contract, the law of the country of the banking establishment with which the transaction was made normally governed the contract. Accordingly, the governing law of the contract between Sierratel and the defendant company was English law (p. 472).

(2) The capacity of a company to enter into any legal transaction was governed by the constitution of the company and the law of the State in which that company was incorporated, in this case Sierra Leone (p. 473).

(3) The relevant provisions of Sierra Leone law stated that the board of directors of Sierratel was to be appointed by the Government. The question, therefore, was who was to be regarded as the Government of Sierra Leone, following the *coup* of May 1997: the exiled elected Government or the regime which had staged the *coup* (p. 473).

(4) In the field of foreign relations, the Crown in its executive and judicial functions ought to speak with one voice and the recognition of a foreign State or government was a matter of foreign policy on which the Executive was in a markedly superior position to form a judgment. Since 1980, however, the policy of the United Kingdom had been not to confer recognition on governments as opposed to States. It was therefore for the Court to determine, in the light of evidence about the dealings of the United Kingdom Government, the constitutional status of the rival regimes in Sierra Leone, the degree, nature and stability of administrative control which each regime exercised and the extent of international recognition as to which was the Government of Sierra Leone (pp. 474-5).

(5) It was clear that the military junta in Sierra Leone was not the constitutional Government. The evidence showed that it was not in control of the country outside the capital, Freetown, and that forces loyal to the exiled Government controlled larger parts of the country. In those areas which were under the control of the military junta, there was nothing resembling law and order. The United Kingdom Government had no dealings with the military junta and continued to deal, on a government-to-government basis, with the exiled Government. The United Nations had imposed sanctions and the *coup* had been condemned by the Commonwealth, the Organization of African Unity and the European Community. Accordingly, the military junta was not the Government of Sierra Leone. The new directors were not validly appointed and the affairs of Sierratel continued to be managed by the original board of directors. The bank was therefore obliged to honour payment instructions given by the original signatories under the mandate (pp. 475-8).

The text of the judgment of the Court commences on the opposite page.

[823] CRESSWELL J. This cases raises important issues as to international recognition and international banking. It reflects the problems faced by an international bank when it holds an account of a company wholly owned by a foreign government and there is a military coup in the country in question.

This matter came before me on 23 January 1998 on an application by the plaintiff company, Sierra Leone Telecommunications Co Ltd (to whom I shall refer as 'Sierratel'), for a mandatory injunction. On that occasion it was accepted by both parties that the appropriate relief to be claimed by those representing the plaintiff company was a declaration. Accordingly I gave leave to serve amended points of claim seeking declaratory relief and in addition gave directions for a speedy trial of the issue whether the plaintiff is entitled to declaratory relief.

The trial has come on for hearing today two weeks after the first application to the court. In this way the court has demonstrated its readiness to bring on a trial in a very short period of time, so as to resolve questions of immediate importance in the commercial and international field. By letter dated 29 January Messrs Lovell White Durrant gave notice of today's hearing to The Secretary, Sierratel, Freetown, Sierra Leone. Sierratel's claim as pleaded in the amended points of claim is for—

[824]   'a declaration that the Plaintiff's US Dollar account no. 83051922 held at the Defendants' Knightsbridge International Banking Centre remains subject to the original terms of the Mandate dated 31 July 1996 and, in particular, remains subject to instructions given on behalf of the Plaintiffs by the named signatories identified therein (and no others) ...'

The background

Sierratel is a company incorporated in Sierra Leone as a parastatal company, ie a company wholly owned by the Sierra Leone government which controls its business dealings. Sierratel holds a US dollar account at Barclays Bank plc's (Barclays) Knightsbridge International Banking Centre, London, SW1. On 25 May 1997 a coup took place in the Republic of Sierra Leone. The democratically elected government of President Kabbah has since then continued as the government of Sierra Leone from Conakry, Republic of Guinea. The British government has consistently condemned the military coup and continues to deal with the democratically elected government of Sierra Leone under President Kabbah.

Sierratel was incorporated in Sierra Leone on 1 April 1995. Since the coup in May 1997 the company has continued to carry on its business activities from Washington, London and Guinea. In mid-1996 Sierratel opened the US dollar bank account with Barclays. The account became operational in October 1996. On 31 July 1996 a bank mandate was completed authorising the following signatories to sign payment requests on the company's behalf: (1) F E Jarrett, managing director; (2) S R Tumoe, deputy managing director; (3) A R Wurie, financial controller; (4) A E O Brima, manager, financial accounts. Two signatures from the above are required by the mandate for any payments. A security code system was established between Sierratel and Barclays with each payment request carrying this code. After the coup a new security code was established in London in August 1997. This new code is still in operation.

Sierratel by the above signatories continued to use, and Barclays continued to authorise the use of, the account following the coup. The bank has, however, not met several payment requests issued by Sierratel recently and presented to the bank. These requests, which total approximately $US1,080,000 and DM108,192, are in respect of outstanding payments to creditors. All the payment requests relate to contracts entered into prior to the coup.

The reason for Barclays' failure to meet the payment requests is as follows. On 24 December 1997 Barclays received a letter dated 22 December purportedly from Sierratel in Freetown as follows:

> 'At the Board meeting of the New Board of Directors of ... (SIERRATEL)— minutes attached ... it was resolved that the Signatories of the following be suspended with immediate effect:—(1) Mr. Frank E. Jarrett, Managing Director (2) Mr. Sahr R. Tumoe, Deputy Managing Director (3) Mr. Allmamy Wurie, Financial Controller ...'

The letter was signed by Mr Osho Williams (described as Secretary of State, Transport and Communications) and Mr Victor B Foh (described as executive chairman, board of directors, Sierratel). Enclosed with that letter were what purport to be minutes of a meeting of the board of directors of Sierratel on Wednesday, 3 December 1997. At para 1 of the minutes it is stated: '... the old Board was dissolved by letters from the Ministry of Transport and**[825]** Communications on the 28 August 1997 ...' At para 3(2) it is stated:

> '... It was resolved that in the interim, the signatures of the first three senior members of staff currently out of the country be suspended from all Local and Foreign Accounts.'

Barclays replied by fax on 31 December 1997. A response of the same date was received in the form of a handwritten fax from Mr Foh, which stated: 'Your fax of 31 December 1997 refers. Payments outlined not authorised by Board and must not be honoured without reference to Board ...'

Since that date Barclays has not responded to the payment requests referred to above. Barclays denies that the position it has taken amounts to a breach of contract. Mr Timothy Saloman QC, who is instructed by the Sierra Leone High Commissioner, who represents the government of President Kabbah, has not suggested that the initial stance taken by Barclays in freezing the account was other than reasonable. The affidavit of Mr Matthew Harrison, international corporate manager with Barclays, puts the matter in this way:

> 'Barclays has been effectively asked by the original signatories to make a difficult choice whether to ignore completely the letter of 22 December 1997 addressed to Barclays from the head office of Sierratel, or the conflicting instructions emanating from the original signatories.'

Barclays says that the payment instructions of Sierratel will be honoured immediately once this court has decided and declared how and by whom instructions are to be given on behalf of Sierratel.

The evidence

I record that the evidence before the court comprises (a) the first and second affidavits of Mr Gibbons and the first affidavit of Mr Solomon Berewa, the

Attorney General and Minister of Justice in President Kabbah's government, on behalf of Sierratel and (b) the first affidavit of Mr Harrison, on behalf of the bank. In accordance with the directions that I gave on 23 January 1998 those affidavits stand as evidence for the purpose of this trial. Neither party has given notice to the other requiring any deponent to attend for cross-examination.

The submissions by Mr Saloman on behalf of Sierratel

Mr Saloman (instructed by the Sierra Leone High Commissioner, Professor Foray, who represents the government of President Kabbah) submitted as follows. The defendant bank's duty is based on contract or agency. On either basis, its duty was to comply with the terms of its mandate, paying sums and debiting its accounts as therein authorised. The terms of the mandate were agreed by Sierratel's board of directors on 31 July 1996. The mandate has not been determined or varied as a matter of the proper law of the contract (English law). Prima facie, therefore, the plaintiff's account remains subject to the terms of the mandate dated 31 July 1996 and to instructions given by the signatories named therein (and no others) and they are entitled to a declaration accordingly. As to any defence or question that the authority of the named signatories to represent the plaintiff has been validly revoked, this is unsustainable for two reasons. (1) The 'new Board of Directors' (including Mr Victor B Foh, signatory of the letters of 22 and 31 December 1997) was not appointed by the government of Sierra Leone or the President. The acts of the 'new Board' in purportedly [826] suspending the named signatories are not valid acts binding upon the plaintiff company. (2) The authority of the signatories and directors named in the mandate (Mr Jarrett, Mr Tumoe and Mr Wurie) has never been validly revoked. The first two mentioned (at least) are directors and they have never been validly removed from their positions.

The submissions by Mr de Lacy on behalf of the bank

Mr de Lacy on behalf of the bank submitted as follows. A bank's obligation to its current account customer is generally to honour its customer's orders in the ordinary course of business with reasonable skill and care, subject to the availability of funds or credit. Where the bank has reasonable grounds (falling short of proof) for believing that a payment order has been made without authority, although it is regular and in accordance with the mandate, it is justified in refusing to honour the order: *Barclays Bank plc v Quincecare Ltd* (1988) [1992] 4 All ER 363 at 375–376 per Steyn J and *Lipkin Gorman (a firm) v Karpnale Ltd* (1989) [1992] 4 All ER 409 at 421, [1989] 1 WLR 1340 at 1356 per May LJ and [1992] 4 All ER 409 at 439, 441, [1989] 1 WLR 1340 at 1376, 1378 (particularly the reference to 'serious or real possibility albeit not amounting to a probability') per Parker LJ. A case where a bank has reasonable grounds for believing that there is a possibility that the existing mandate has been revoked is a case a fortiori to the case of a regular order complying with a mandate but in fact unauthorised by the customer (e g because of the customer's agent's fraud).

Where the issue is as sensitive and important as the question of the continued authority of a foreign government, the bank was entitled to take the stand which it did, and effectively freeze the account. In all the circumstances of this case, however, the evidence shows that Sierratel, acting through the agency of the former board, is entitled to a declaration that the former board has not been effectively displaced and is able to control the terms of the bank's mandate and hence the accounts of Sierratel. In the special circumstances of this case the bank (1) claims no interest of its own in the issue; (2) seeks to assist the court impartially to determine whether the declaration as to the control of Sierratel should be granted; (3) leaves it to the court to make that determination.

The law governing the contract between Sierratel and Barclays

Rule 180 in *Dicey and Morris on the Conflict of Laws* (12th edn, 1993) vol 2, p 1259 states:

> '(1) The law applicable to a contract by virtue of Rules 175 and 176 governs in particular: (a) interpretation; (b) performance; (c) within the limits of the powers conferred on the court by its procedural law, the consequences of breach, including the assessment of damages in so far as it is governed by rules of law; (d) the various ways of extinguishing obligations, and prescription and limitation of actions. (2) In relation to the manner of performance and the steps to be taken in the event of defective performance regard is to be had to the law of the country in which performance takes place.'

It was held in *Libyan Arab Foreign Bank v Bankers Trust Co* [1989] 3 All ER 252 at 266, [1989] QB 728 at 746 that as a general rule the contract between a bank and its customer is governed by the law of the place where the account is kept, in the absence of agreement to the contrary. The rule was reaffirmed in *Libyan Arab Foreign Bank v Manufacturers Hanover Trust Co* [1988] 2 Lloyd's Rep 494 at 502, in which it was said that solid grounds are needed for holding that this general rule **[827]** does not apply. It is a rule of the greatest commercial importance, and there is a risk of grave difficulty and confusion if some other law is the governing law.

These cases must now be reconsidered in the light of the Rome Convention on the law applicable to contractual obligations, which was given the force of law in the United Kingdom on 1 April 1991 by the Contracts (Applicable Law) Act 1990. The basic rule under the convention is that in the absence of a choice of law, a contract is governed by the law of the country with which it is most closely connected: art 4(1). The rule is qualified by a number of rebuttable presumptions. It is presumed that the contract is most closely connected with the country where the party who is to effect 'characteristic performance' has its central administration. In the case of a bank account, such party will be the bank. However, if the contract is entered into in the course of that party's trade, the governing law will be that of the country in which the principal place of business is situated or, where performance is to be effected through a place of business other than the principal place of business, the country in which that other place of business is situated: art 4(2). As to bank accounts it seems to me that the principle established in the Libyan assets cases is substantially unchanged. Performance, ie repayment of the sum deposited, is to be effected through the branch where the account is kept. It is the law of the country where the account is kept which governs the contract. This view appears to be consistent with that expressed in the Giuliano and Lagarde Report (see OJ 1980 C282 p 21), which states that 'in a banking contract the law of the country of the banking establishment with which a transaction is made will normally govern the contract'. The governing law of the contract between Sierratel and Barclays is thus English law.

Payment within mandate

It is a basic obligation owed by a bank to its customer that the bank will honour on presentation a cheque drawn by the customer on the bank provided that there are sufficient funds in the customer's account to meet the cheque or the bank has agreed to provide the customer with overdraft facilities sufficient to meet the cheque. Where the bank honours such a cheque or other instructions it acts within its mandate, with the result that the bank is entitled to debit the customer's account with the amount of the cheque or other instruction.

Capacity and internal management of Sierratel

The law of Sierra Leone determines who are Sierratel's officials authorised to act on its behalf. Rule 156 in *Dicey and Morris* vol 2, p 1111 states:

'(1) The capacity of a corporation to enter into any legal transaction is governed both by the constitution of the corporation and by the law of the country which governs the transaction in question. (2) All matters concerning the constitution of a corporation are governed by the law of the place of incorporation.'

The law of the place of incorporation determines who are the corporation's officials authorised to act on its behalf: *Carl-Zeiss-Stiftung v Rayner & Keeler Ltd (No 2)* [1966] 2 All ER 536 at 556, 568 and 588, [1967] 1 AC 853 at 919, 939 and 972. [2]

[828] *The new board of directors was not appointed by the government of Sierra Leone: its purported acts are accordingly invalid*

Sierratel has a memorandum and articles in many respects similar to those of companies incorporated in England and Wales. Under Sierratel's articles of association only 'the Government of Sierra Leone' may appoint the directors. Article 71(I) provides:

'The Board of Directors of the Company shall consist of eight members appointed by the Government of Sierra Leone: one of whom shall be appointed Chairman of the Board.'

According to the evidence of Mr Berewa, pursuant to s 70 of the Constitution of Sierra Leone 1991 the appointment of the directors of all parastatals must be made by the President and approved by Parliament. Section 70 of the Constitution provides:

'The President may appoint, in accordance with the provisions of this Constitution or any other law the following persons ... (e) the Chairman and other Members of the governing body of any corporation established by an Act of Parliament, a statutory instrument, or out of public funds, subject to the approval of Parliament.'

See further ss 40(3) and (4), 46(4) of and Sch 2 to the Constitution.

Mr Berewa further states that the junta has not lawfully set aside or revised the constitution itself.

[[2] 43 *ILR* 23.]

In the field of foreign relations the Crown in its executive and judicial functions ought to speak with one voice and the recognition of a foreign state or government is a matter of foreign policy on which the executive is in a markedly superior position to form a judgment: see *GUR Corp v Trust Bank of Africa Ltd* [3] (*Government of the Republic of Ciskei, third party*) [1986] 3 All ER 449 at 454, [1987] QB 599 at 604 per Steyn J, and see further [1986] 3 All ER 449 at 459 and 466–467, [1987] QB 599 at 616 and 625 per Donaldson MR and Nourse LJ.

The policy of the United Kingdom is now not to confer recognition on governments as opposed to on states. The new policy of Her Majesty's government was stated in parliamentary answers in April and May 1980: see 48 HL Official Report (5th series) cols 1121–1122, 28 April 1980; 983 HC Official Report (5th series) written answers cols 277–279, 25 April 1980 and 985 HC Official Report (5th series) written answers col 385, 23 May 1980:

> 'In future cases where a new régime comes to power unconstitutionally our attitude on the question whether it qualifies to be treated as a Government will be left to be inferred from the nature of the dealings, if any, which we may have with it, and in particular on whether we are dealing with it on a normal Government to Government basis.'

In *Republic of Somalia v Woodhouse Drake & Carey (Suisse) SA, The Mary* [1993] 1 [4] All ER 371 at 382, [1993] QB 54 at 65–66 Hobhouse J stated:

> 'Where Her Majesty's government is dealing with the foreign government on a normal government to government basis as the government of the relevant foreign state, it is unlikely in the extreme that the inference that the foreign government is the government of that state will be capable of being rebutted and questions of public policy and considerations of the interrelationship of the judicial and executive arms of Government may be paramount: see *The Arantzazu Mendi* [1939] 1 All ER 719 at 722, [1939] AC 256 **[829]** at 264 and *GUR Corp v Trust Bank of Africa Ltd* (*Government of the Republic of* [5] *Ciskei, third party*) [1986] 3 All ER 449 at 466, [1987] QB 599 at 625. But now that the question has ceased to be one of recognition, the theoretical possibility of rebuttal must exist.'

Hobhouse J pointed out that it would be contrary to public policy for the court not to recognise as a qualified representative of the head of state of a foreign state the diplomatic representative recognised by Her Majesty's government (see [1993] 1 All ER 371 at 382, [1993] QB 54 at 66).

Hobhouse J stated ([1993] 1 All ER 371 at 383, [1993] QB 54 at 67):

> '... it is relevant to distinguish between regimes that have been the constitutional and established government of a state and a regime which is seeking to achieve that position either displacing a former government or to fill a vacuum. Since the question is now whether a government *exists*, there is no room for more than one government at a time nor for separate de jure and de facto governments in respect of the same state. But a loss of control by a constitutional government may not immediately deprive it of its status, whereas an insurgent regime will require to establish control before it can exist as a government.' (Hobhouse J's emphasis.)

[3 75 *ILR* 675.]   [4 94 *ILR* 608.]   [5 9 *Ann Dig* 60.]

The factors to be taken into account in deciding whether a government exists as the government of a state are set out by Hobhouse J as follows:

'Accordingly, the factors to be taken into account in deciding whether a government exists as the government of the state are: (a) whether it is the constitutional government of the state; (b) the degree, nature and stability of administrative control, if any, that it of itself exercises over the territory of the state; (c) whether Her Majesty's government has any dealings with it and if so what is the nature of those dealings; and (d) in marginal cases, the extent of international recognition that it has as the government of the state.' (See [1993] 1 All ER 371 at 384, [1993] QB 54 at 68.)

See further *The Arantzazu Mendi* [1939] 1 All ER 719 at 722, [1939] AC 256 at 264 as to 'exercising effective administrative control'.

I turn to consider the factors identified by Hobhouse J in turn.

(a) *Whether it is the constitutional government of the state*

On 27 June 1997 Mr Tony Lloyd, Minister of State at the Foreign and Commonwealth Office, issued the following statement on Sierra Leone:

'The British Government has followed the events in Sierra Leone since the illegal overthrow of President Kabbah's government on 25 May with serious concern. It has been actively involved in attempts to find a peaceful resolution which will lead to the restoration of the legitimate government of President Kabbah. In this regard it welcomes the meeting of ECOWAS states held in Guinea on 26 June, and looks forward to the report of the Committee established by ECOWAS to take the process forward. In recognition of the close ties which have always existed between United Kingdom and Sierra Leone, the Government underlines its continued support to the courageous people of Sierra Leone who have so steadfastly rejected this attempt to reverse the progress to democracy achieved last year. It looks forward to recommencing its assistance to the reconstruction, **[830]** rehabilitation and development of Sierra Leone once, but not until, constitutional order has been restored.'

On 28 November 1997 the Foreign and Commonwealth Office wrote to Messrs Stephenson Harwood as follows:

'You asked me to set out the British Government's policy towards Sierra Leone ... The British Government welcomed the election in Sierra Leone of President Ahmad Tejan Kabbah in February 1996. We have consistently condemned the military coup of 25 May 1997 which overthrew the democratically elected government of Sierra Leone. We look forward to the restoration of constitutional order in that country. We continue to deal with the democratically elected government of Sierra Leone under President Kabbah. We have no dealings with the military junta in Freetown.'

In a letter to Professor Foray, Sierra Leone High Commissioner, dated 13 January 1998 the Foreign and Commonwealth Office stated:

'... I attach a copy of my letter to Stephenson Harwood of 28 November 1997. British Government policy on Sierra Leone has not changed since then. I also attach for your information an extract from Hansard showing a written answer to the House of Lords of 12 January 1998. This sets out the British Government's position on Sierra Leone.'

The written answer to the House of Lords of 12 January 1998 stated:

'Baroness Symons of Vernham Dean: Where democratic governments have been overthrown by violence we have often worked with them in exile as part of our global support for democracy. Tejan Kabbah is not the "former" President of Sierra Leone; he remains the legitimate leader of that country.'

(b) *The degree, nature and stability of administrative control, if any, that it of itself exercises over the territory of the state*

According to the Sierra Leone High Commissioner the military junta presently has no control whatsoever over the country outside of Freetown and there are civil unrest problems in Freetown. There are still defence units loyal to President Kabbah throughout the country. These units have imposed an internal blockade. A soldier loyal to the junta visited a shop in Freetown recently and made various demands to the shopkeeper. The shopkeeper refused to bow to the soldier's demands and the shopkeeper was then shot. A local crowd subsequently lynched the soldier. This sort of thing has happened on a number of occasions recently. The junta has very little real control over the administrative affairs of the country. There were some civil servants left after the coup who had not managed to flee the country. They only number approximately a quarter of the full complement under the legitimate government and therefore none of the departments of government are functioning properly, if at all.

According to the affidavit of Mr Berewa, Attorney General and Minister of Justice in President Kabbah's government, it is precisely because there is in fact no semblance of order in Freetown that the expatriate community and diplomatic missions, which were evacuated following the coup, still remain out of the country. Looting and robbery still remain the order of the day in Freetown and are often perpetrated by members of the junta itself. It has been the clear aim of the junta to coerce the civil population to collaborate with them. They have **[831]** failed in this aim, and to such an extent that there has been a very significant defection by members of the Sierra Leone army and civilian police to the forces of the West African Peace Keeping Force ECOMOG, and the Civil Defence Militia, which is loyal to President Kabbah.

Of the three tiers of superior courts (the High Court, Court of Appeal and Supreme Court), none are sitting or hearing cases. Over 80% of the judges of the superior courts have fled the country since the coup. Of the inferior (ie magistrates) courts only three are nominally sitting in Freetown. These three courts are not functioning properly, since the junta is a law unto itself and settles matters arbitrarily. It often hands down sentences of summary execution, which are carried out indiscriminately.

The situation described in para 9(d) of Mr Harrison's affidavit is accurate:

'The Bank of Sierra Leone (Central Bank) and Sierra Leone Commercial Bank Limited (wholly owned by Government) are operating. The other commercial banks namely Barclays Bank of Sierra Leone Limited, Standard Chartered Sierra Leone Limited and Union Trust Bank Limited, accounting for over 75% of the banking sector business, have remained closed since the coup. The manufacturing sector has virtually ceased production. The majority of the working population has not returned to work and numerous Sierra Leoneans, including many professionals, have fled the country.'

This situation results from the lack of a semblance of order in Sierra Leone and the refusal by the civil population, both manual workers and professionals, to co-operate with the junta. The majority of the citizens of Sierra Leone are waiting for the democratically elected government to be restored. The infrastructure of the country has collapsed. Basic amenities such as water and electricity are virtually non-existent. Owing to the embargo on postal activities by the Universal Postal Union there is no postal communication between Sierra Leone and the outside world. Hospitals function only at the behest of Médecin Sans Frontières or the International Red Cross. The junta itself is not providing medical services. Despite strenuous attempts by the junta to reopen schools, the majority of schools have remained closed since the coup because parents do not co-operate with the junta and are afraid that their children may be kidnapped, harmed or raped. Petrol is in extremely short supply and although the diesel that runs generators is sometimes available, a shortage of essential fuels has meant that Freetown has had rotating power cuts ever since the coup. The junta has no control over more than two-thirds of the country. They do not control the country's only international airport situated at Lungi, near Freetown, nor the main internal airfield at Hastings. Both these airfields are controlled by the forces of ECOMOG. The Port of Freetown at Queen Elizabeth II Quay is also under the control of the ECOMOG Forces. Similarly ECOMOG controls the main routes to and from the capital city, Freetown, and even members of the junta are not allowed to move freely from Freetown to the provinces and back. The civil defence units which remain loyal to President Kabbah and which are fighting for the restoration of democracy are in control of a very significant portion of the territory up-country. There have been some armed hostilities recently and the government of President Kabbah has received reports of some casualties. The most recent reports show that forces loyal to President Kabbah are in control of the most important areas up-country.

[832] (c) *Whether Her Majesty's government has any dealings with it and if so what is the nature of those dealings*
    See under (a) above.

(d) *In marginal cases, the extent of international recognition that it has as the government of the state*
    The United Nations has imposed sanctions relating to the supply of arms and petroleum products to Sierra Leone: see United Nations Resolution SCR 1132 of 8 October 1997. The resolution has been enacted in England by various statutory instruments. In addition the coup has also been condemned by the Commonwealth, the Organisation of African Unity and the European Community. A number of West African states, which together formed the Economic Community of West African States (ECOWAS), have been involved

in attempts to stabilise the situation in Sierra Leone. ECOWAS troops are presently in Freetown and ECOWAS' representatives have met with representatives of the military junta. At a meeting in Conakry, Guinea, on 22/23 October 1997 a peace plan between ECOWAS Ministerial Committee of Five on Sierra Leone, and representatives of the military junta leader, Major Johnny Koroma, adopted a ECOWAS peace plan for Sierra Leone. This peace plan provides for the reinstatement of the legitimate government of President Kabbah within a period of six months. The peace plan remains operative and it is fully expected that the legitimate government of President Kabbah will be reinstated in Sierra Leone within the stated timeframe.

In the light of my analysis of the factors in *The Mary* [1993] 1 All ER 371, [1993] QB 54 I conclude that the military junta are not 'the Government of Sierra Leone'. The mandate to Barclays of 31 July 1996 stands. Nothing that the military junta has purported to do since May 1997 affects that mandate. The letters of 22 December 1997 and 31 December 1997 from those associated with the junta to the bank are of no effect. The military junta is not the government of Sierra Leone. The 'new directors' were not validly appointed. It follows that Sierratel is entitled to the declaration sought and I order accordingly.

Declaration granted.

[Report: [1998] 2 All ER 821]

Diplomatic relations—Diplomatic immunity—Diplomatic agents—Family of diplomatic agent—Extent of immunity— Child custody dispute between diplomatic agent and spouse —Jurisdiction of courts of receiving State—Waiver—Vienna Convention on Diplomatic Relations, 1961, Articles 1, 31, 32 and 37 — Relevance of human rights agreements — European Convention for the Protection of Human Rights

and Fundamental Freedoms, 1950 — United Nations Convention on the Rights of the Child, 1989—The law of England

Re P (No 1)[1]

England, High Court, Family Division.   7 August 1997

(Stuart-White J)[2]

SUMMARY: *The facts:*—The father was a United States national, who was a member of the United States diplomatic mission to the United Kingdom. The mother was a German national. There were two daughters who resided with the parents in London. The mother commenced divorce proceedings in Germany. Fearing that the father intended to remove the two children to the United States of America, the mother applied to the High Court in London for orders under the Children Act 1989, restraining the father from removing the two children from the United Kingdom and seeking the leave of the Court to take the children to Germany. An interim order was granted prohibiting the father from removing the children from the United Kingdom. The father and the United States of America, which intervened in the proceedings, applied for a declaration that the Court had no jurisdiction because the father, as a diplomatic agent, and the children, as members of the family of a diplomatic agent forming part of his household, were entitled to diplomatic immunity.

Held:—The application by the father and the United States of America was granted. The Court had no jurisdiction.

(1) In accordance with Articles 31 and 37 of the Vienna Convention on Diplomatic Relations, 1961, which had been given effect in English law by the Diplomatic Privileges Act 1964, the father and the children were immune from the jurisdiction of the English courts. That immunity could be waived only by the sending State, the United States of America, which had indicated that it did not waive the immunity in the present case. The Court accordingly had no discretion which it could exercise on behalf of the mother (pp. 480-2).

(2) The European Convention on Human Rights, 1950, and the United Nations Convention on the Rights of the Child, 1989, did not alter this conclusion. Neither had been incorporated into English law. They did not assist in construing the provisions of the Diplomatic Privileges Act 1964, which were clear and unambiguous (pp. 483-4).

The text of the judgment of the Court commences on the following page.

---

[1] For related proceedings, see p. 486 below.
[2] The applicant mother was represented by Mr Henry Setright, instructed by Margaret Bennett; the respondent father and the United States of America were represented by Ms Jennifer Roberts, instructed by Clifford Chance.

STUART-WHITE J: The proceedings before me concern two children – R, **[625]** who is 12½, and C, who is 9½.

The children are the children of married parents. The father is a US national, the mother is a German national and she has commenced divorce proceedings in Germany on 24 July 1997.

The first of the applications before me is an application by the mother in Children Act proceedings by which she claims a residence order, specific issue and prohibited steps order and leave to remove the children permanently from England and Wales to Germany. Her application came before Sumner J ex parte on 25 July 1997 and an interim prohibited steps order was granted prohibiting the father from removing the children from their present address or from England and Wales. The order was expressed to last until yesterday, 6 August 1997, which was the return date for her application.

The second application before me is on a summons by the USA and the father, which asserts, and invites the court to hold, that the court has no jurisdiction to entertain the mother's application because both the father and the children enjoy immunity from process by reason of the diplomatic immunity which derives from the Vienna Convention on Diplomatic Relations 1961, the relevant Articles of which were incorporated into English law by the Diplomatic Privileges Act 1964 and which are set out in Sch 1 to that Act.

It is plainly appropriate to deal first with the summons by the USA and the father. Indeed Mrs Roberts, who appears for the USA and the father, has instructions only in relation to that summons and not in relation to the mother's applications. The facts relating to that summons can be succinctly stated.

The father is a senior diplomat in the service of the USA. He is employed as a member of the diplomatic staff at the US Embassy in London. He, the mother and the two children all live at the same address in London, at premises provided by the Embassy. The mother fears that the father intends to remove the children to the USA. She asserts that R has made known her wish that this should not take place. The mother, on the other hand, wishes to take the children permanently to Germany.

Article 31 of the Vienna Convention provides (subject to certain irrelevant exceptions) as follows:

'A diplomatic agent shall enjoy immunity from the criminal jurisdiction of the receiving State. He shall also enjoy immunity from its civil and administrative jurisdiction ...'

and then follow the exceptions. The words 'diplomatic agent' are defined by Art 1 of the Convention as follows:

'(e) a "diplomatic agent" is the head of the mission or a member of the diplomatic staff of the mission;
(d) the "members of the diplomatic staff" are the members of the staff of the mission having diplomatic rank ...'

By a certificate issued on behalf of the Secretary of State for Foreign and Commonwealth Affairs it is certified that the father is a member of the diplomatic staff. Section 4 of the Diplomatic Privileges Act provides:

[626] 'If in any proceedings any question arises whether or not any person is entitled to any privilege or immunity under this Act a certificate issued by or under the authority of the Secretary of State stating any fact relating to that question shall be conclusive evidence of that fact.'

Article 37(1) of the Convention provides:

'The members of the family of a diplomatic agent forming part of his household shall, if they are not nationals of the receiving State, enjoy the privileges and immunities specified in Articles 29 to 36.'

That of course means that they enjoy the privileges and immunities specified in Art 31.

A certificate provided under s 4 of the Diplomatic Privileges Act certifies that the children with whom I am concerned are the dependants of the father. It is to be noted that the certificate does not follow the wording of Art 37. It is possible to conceive of dependants who are members of a diplomat's family not forming part of his household and for this reason the certificate does not, in my judgment, provide conclusive proof that the children fall within the provisions of Art 37. Nevertheless, it is not (and of course cannot be) disputed that the children are members of the father's family. Moreover they, together with the mother, live in the same house as that in which he lives.

Mr Setright on behalf of the mother does not concede that the children form part of the father's household, pointing out that serious matrimonial disagreements exist and that divorce proceedings have been commenced by the wife. These facts however do not, in my judgment, constitute a basis for rejecting the natural inference to be drawn from the facts as I have recited them, namely the inference that these children (whatever may be the position of the mother) do form part of the father's household.

The arguments deployed on behalf of the mother, to which I shall refer in a little more detail shortly, prompt consideration of whether diplomatic immunity enjoyed by an individual can be waived by that individual. It is provided by Art 32(1) as follows:

'1. The immunity from jurisdiction of diplomatic agents and of persons enjoying immunity under Article 37 may be waived by the sending State.

2. Waiver must always be express.'

The 'sending State' of course in the instant case is the USA and that State has not waived immunity. There exists neither in the Diplomatic Privileges Act nor in the Vienna Convention any provision for waiver by the individuals enjoying such immunity. That immunity is effectively the property of the sending State and not of those individuals.

Article 32(3), which provides for the situation in which a person enjoying immunity himself initiates proceedings, precludes him from invoking immunity in respect of any counterclaim directly connected with the principal claim. This provision is not material to the situation which arises in this case and I hold that neither the father nor the children has any right to waive the immunity with which they are invested by Art 31 and Art 37 respectively.

This view of the law coincides precisely with that expressed by Laws J in *Propend Finance v Sing* (unreported) 17 April 1997, in which he said at p 38 [3] of the transcript, whilst dealing it is true with the position of a diplomat and **[627]** not that of a member of his household (though it seems to me the same principle must apply):

'Subject to the 1978 Act [ie the State Immunity Act 1978] a sovereign State is immune in its right as such. A diplomat by contrast is immune only in right of his sending State. His immunity is conditional, because by definition there exists a higher authority, his own State, which can cancel it: something he has no power to do himself. In the case of the State's own actions, there is of course no higher authority. So it is at the State's choice whether, for its own ends, to accept in any proceedings the legal power of a foreign court: hence the question as regards the State will be whether it has submitted to the jurisdiction. But the diplomat *cannot* by submitting himself to the jurisdiction be stripped of his immunity. It does not belong to him in any right of his own. So the test for loss of immunity is necessarily a different one. However far the diplomat has himself bowed to the foreign court's jurisdiction, he remains immune (subject of course to the exceptions in the 1964 Act, which in this case I have discounted), unless his sending State says otherwise: unless it waives his immunity. This is well illustrated by *Bolasco v Wolter* (1957) 24 ILR 525, a decision of the Tribunal of Luxembourg (an appellate court). An Italian diplomat had contested an action brought against him on the merits, without raising any plea to the jurisdiction. The first instance court treated his defence on the merits as a waiver of immunity, and gave judgment for the plaintiff. On any view, no doubt, the defendant had for his part submitted to the jurisdiction. But the appeal court quashed the judgment: the diplomat had had no authority from his government to waive immunity.'

Laws J's decision was subject to consideration by the Court of Appeal, of whose judgment I have also seen a transcript, and on this point the ruling of Laws J was expressly approved by the Court of Appeal. Thus it is submitted on behalf of the USA and the father that this court has no jurisdiction to entertain the mother's application and must so hold, and accordingly must dismiss the mother's application.

It is submitted on the basis of the facts in this case and the clear statutory provisions that the court's hands are tied in this way and that it has no discretion which it could exercise on behalf of the mother were it minded to do so.

[3 111 *ILR* 611 at 642.]

Mr Setright, however, on behalf of the mother, in a characteristically skilful and attractively presented submission, has argued that the court does possess such a discretion and should have regard, in deciding how to construe, and whether and the extent to which to implement, the 1964 Act and the Convention, to modern thinking, both domestically and internationally, as to the position of children. He points out the apparent irony inherent in the proposition that a provision which is expressed as conferring a privilege to be enjoyed may operate against the interests and against the wishes of the person for whose ostensible benefit it exists. This is, he argues, a particularly poignant irony if it operates contrary to the welfare of a child. He further submits that a provision which may operate in a way adverse to the welfare of a child and ignores the child's wishes is contrary to the spirit of the Children Act 1989. Whether or not that be so, it would have been possible for Parliament to **[628]** include in the Children Act an amendment or repeal of the material parts of the Diplomatic Privileges Act 1964, but it chose not to do so. Accordingly, in my judgment, this part of Mr Setright's submission does not impact on the question whether or in what way I should give effect to the 1964 Act.

Persuasive support for that view, if support is needed, can be found in a Canadian case *Laverty v Laverty* decided by Cunningham J in September 1994. In that case, which concerned a dispute relating to the matrimonial home of a US diplomat serving in the Embassy in Ottawa the question arose whether, because Art 31(4) of the Convention expressly provides that the immunity of a diplomatic agent from the jurisdiction of the receiving State does not exempt him from the jurisdiction on the sending State, diplomatic immunity was effectively removed in private law family matters by reason of the arrangements for reciprocal enforcement of family law orders. Cunningham J said at p 7 of the transcript:

'Let me briefly comment upon a point raised by counsel for Mrs Laverty, that Art 31(4) of the Vienna Convention, read in conjunction with the Reciprocal Enforcement of Support Orders Act, RSO 1990 CR7 removes immunity in private law family matters. It is argued that international recognition of domestic support orders is now, through this and other such statutes, being achieved such that any "artificial barriers" to jurisdiction are removed. In my view, the Reciprocal Enforcement of Support Orders Act does not confer substantive powers but merely sets out a scheme by which proper domestic orders are to be enforced outside the jurisdiction. The entire statute is premised on the fact that the host country (Canada in this case) has jurisdiction to make the order. Unfortunately, as I have determined, we do not.'

Much the same situation seems to me to apply in relation to the interface between the Children Act and the Diplomatic Privileges Act.

Mr Setright's final and I think his principal submission is that since the ratification of the Vienna Convention and its incorporation into the Diplomatic Privileges Act, two other important international Conventions have been agreed, signed and ratified by the British Government. They are the European Convention on Human Rights 1950 and the United Nations Convention on the Rights of the Child 1989. Mr Setright has drawn my attention to a number of Articles in each of these Conventions which emphasise the rights and the welfare of children, the importance of the integrity of family life and the undesirability of unjustified interference by the State incompatible with these principles and objectives.

However, there is, it seems to me, a fatal flaw in this part of Mr Setright's argument. It is clearly established that nothing in any Treaty or Convention can become part of English law unless it is expressly incorporated into English law by statute. Clear authority for this proposition is to be found in the House of Lords' decision, in *British Airways v Laker Airways* [1985] AC [4] 58. Lord Diplock delivered the leading speech with which their Lordships all agreed and at 85H–86A he said this:

'The interpretation of treaties to which the United Kingdom is a party but the terms of which have not either expressly or by reference been incorporated in English domestic law by legislation is not a matter that falls within the interpretative jurisdiction of an English court of law. In this House the **[629]** contrary has not been contended and no arguments have been addressed to your Lordships directed to the construction of the language of Bermuda 2.'

Bermuda 2 was the Treaty which was the subject of those proceedings.

The British Parliament could have incorporated either or both of the Conventions relied upon by Mr Setright, or parts of them, into English statute law. But it has not done so. Accordingly, I hold that their provisions are of no assistance to the court in construing the provisions of the Diplomatic Privileges Act which are clear and unambiguous. Nor do the provisions of those Conventions confer on the court any discretion as to the implementation of those provisions. Accordingly, the claim for diplomatic immunity succeeds. Service of the mother's application will be set aside and her application dismissed for want of jurisdiction. For the same reason, the order of Sumner J will be set aside but not, I think, discharged as asked for in the summons because it has expired.

In the summons issued by the USA and the father, there is also sought a declaration. In the terms in which it is sought in the summons, it seems to me that the declaration sought is too widely drawn. In any event, in the light of my decision on the question of immunity and the jurisdiction of the court to entertain the mother's application, I regard the granting of a declaration in those or other terms as unnecessary and otiose and I do not grant one.

Before I part from the case I do, however, make the following observations. The mother is effectively debarred from arguing her case relating to the children in the English courts. It is not for me to say what would be the appropriate forum in which he should or could do so. One possible forum is the courts of the USA. Before she can avail herself of the jurisdiction of the US courts, she has a number of practical hurdles to overcome, not least the fact that (I am told) she is without funds to enable her

to initiate proceedings there. In that connection I can, I think, do no better
than to quote the passage in Cunningham J's judgment in *Laverty v Laverty*
which immediately followed the passage that I have already cited:

'What then is the effect of all this upon Mrs Laverty? Clearly the US
Government has an obligation to ensure that Mrs Laverty and the children
are not left out in the cold. They were sent here by the US Government
which has declined the waiving of diplomatic immunity. That being the
case, I should think that the US Federal authorities would ensure Mrs
Laverty easy and cost-effective access to the appropriate US court. She
should not have to chase Mr Laverty around the USA seeking to enforce
rights which, were it not for diplomatic immunity, she might do easily.'

I quote that not as a proposition at law nor even as an exhortation, but
merely as an observation.

Subject to any question of costs, that concludes my judgment.

[Report: [1998] 1 FLR 625]

**Diplomatic relations—Diplomatic immunity—Diplomatic
agents—Family of diplomatic agent—Extent of immunity—
Child custody dispute between diplomatic agent and spouse
—Jurisdiction of courts of receiving State—Immunity of
diplomatic agent after termination of appointment —
Immunity in respect of official acts — Limits — Vienna
Convention on Diplomatic Relations, 1961, Articles 1, 31,
32 and 37 — Relevance of human rights agreements —
European Convention for the Protection of Human Rights
and Fundamental Freedoms, 1950**

**State immunity—Jurisdictional immunity—Immunity of
State officials for official acts—Extent—Diplomat returning
to sending State with children—Whether an official act—
Whether official immune in action in courts of receiving
State—Relationship between State immunity and diplomatic
immunity**

Treaties—Effect in national law—Hague Convention on the Civil Aspects of International Child Abduction, 1980—The law of England

Re P (No 2)[1]

England, High Court, Family Division.   22 *January* 1998

(Sir Stephen Brown, *President*)

Court of Appeal, Civil Division.   11 *March* 1998

(Lord Woolf MR, Butler-Sloss and Simon Brown LJJ)[2]

SUMMARY: *The facts:*—The father was a United States national, who was a member of the United States diplomatic mission to the United Kingdom. The mother was a German national. There were two daughters who resided with the parents in London. The mother commenced divorce proceedings in Germany. Fearing that the father intended to remove the two children to the United States of America, the mother applied to the High Court in London for orders under the Children Act 1989, restraining the father from removing the two children from the United Kingdom and seeking the leave of the Court to take the children to Germany. The father and the United States of America, which intervened in the proceedings, maintained that the English courts lacked jurisdiction, because the father and the children possessed diplomatic immunity. The High Court upheld that argument and dismissed the mother's application (p. 479 above).

The day after the judgment in the first proceedings, the father, mother and children left the United Kingdom for the United States of America in accordance with arrangements made by the United States Embassy. Although the family travelled together, the mother's solicitors wrote to the father's solicitors stating that the mother did not consent to the father taking the children to the United States of America. On arrival in the United States of America, the father and mother lived separately. The father's diplomatic functions in the United Kingdom ended when he returned to the United States of America. Child custody proceedings were begun in a court in the United States of America. In those proceedings, the mother contended that the father had removed the children from the United Kingdom in violation of the Hague Convention on Civil Aspects of International Child Abduction, 1980 ("the Hague Convention"). While those proceedings were pending, the mother commenced separate proceedings in the High Court in London, seeking a declaration that the father had wrongfully removed the children from the United Kingdom in breach of the Hague Convention and the Child

---

[1] For related proceedings, see p. 478 above.
[2] The applicant mother was represented by Mr Peter Duffy QC and Mr Henry Setright, instructed by Dawson Cornwell & Co.; the respondent father and the United States were represented by Professor Christopher Greenwood, instructed by Clifford Chance; Mr David Lloyd Jones appeared as *amicus curiae*.

Abduction and Custody Act 1985, which gave effect to the Hague Convention in English law.

The father and the United States of America, which intervened in the English proceedings, contended that the English courts lacked jurisdiction on the ground that the father had returned to the United States of America with the children on the orders of the United States Government so that:

(i) his act was therefore one performed in the exercise of his functions as a member of the United States diplomatic mission in the United Kingdom, with the result that he was entitled to diplomatic immunity under Article 39(2) of the Vienna Convention on Diplomatic Relations, 1961,[3] notwithstanding that he was no longer a diplomat accredited to the Government of the United States; and

(ii) since the act was one ordered by the State and in respect of which the State was immune from the jurisdiction of the English courts, the father benefited from the State immunity of the United States of America.

Held (by the High Court):—The application by the father and the United States of America would be granted. The Court lacked jurisdiction.

(1) Diplomatic immunity was immunity from jurisdiction, not immunity from legal liability. The fact that the father had been entitled to immunity from suit at the time he left the United Kingdom did not mean that he could not now be held to have acted contrary to English law. The act of taking the children to the United States of America could not be regarded as an exercise of his official functions as a diplomat. Accordingly, he was not now entitled to diplomatic immunity (pp. 494-5).

(2) The father was, however, entitled to State immunity. The agent of a foreign State enjoyed immunity in respect of his acts of a sovereign or governmental character. In the case of an agent who was a member of a diplomatic mission, diplomatic immunity and State immunity did not necessarily coincide. In the present case, the act of taking the children back to the United States of America was performed under orders from the United States Government and was an act of a sovereign governmental character (pp. 495-6).

The mother appealed to the Court of Appeal.

Held (by the Court of Appeal):—The appeal was dismissed. The final decision in the present case had to be made by the courts in the United States of America. It would serve no useful purpose for an English court to grant the declaration sought and prolonged proceedings in England might well be contrary to the interests of the children. Accordingly the Court would not hear the appeal (p. 501).

The text of the judgments delivered in the Court of Appeal commences at p. 496. The text of the judgment of the High Court commences on the following page.

_____

[3] The text of Article 39(2) is set out at p. 494 below.

SIR STEPHEN BROWN P: The plaintiff is the mother of two children **[1027]** towhom I shall refer for the purpose of these proceedings as A and B born in 1984 and 1987. The defendant father is the husband of the mother. The father is and was at all material times a member of the diplomatic service of the USA. He is an American citizen. The mother is a German national who married the father in Germany in October 1982 when he was serving in Germany. In 1994 the father was posted to London where he served as a senior member of the diplomatic staff of the US embassy until August 1997. The father and the mother and their two children lived as a family in a house provided by the US embassy. By the spring of 1997 marital difficulties had arisen between the mother and father. The situation according to the mother reached the point of breakdown and she made known her wish to return to Germany with the children and not to go back to the USA. It appears that in July 1997 the mother commenced divorce proceedings in Germany. The following day the mother issued applications for residence orders in respect of the children pursuant to the provisions of the Children Act 1989 in London. She also applied for leave to remove the children to Germany and at the same time she sought a prohibited steps order in order to seek to prevent the father from taking the children to the USA. At an ex parte hearing she obtained an interim order from Sumner J prohibiting the father from removing the children to the USA. The **[1028]** USA and the father than issued a summons seeking the dismissal of the 'English' proceedings, if I may so term them, on the grounds of diplomatic immunity. On 7 August 1997 Stuart-White J heard the application made by the [4] USA and the father and held that their claim for diplomatic immunity succeeded. He set aside the service of the mother's applications and dismissed them for want of jurisdiction. Since the previous order made by Sumner J was an interim order which had expired on 6 August 1997 he made no separate order in respect of that matter. He refused leave to appeal. Very shortly after the order, in pursuance of travel arrangements made by the US embassy, the father, the mother and the children returned to the USA in the same aircraft. The mother complains and asserts that her return to the USA with the children was against her wishes and that she went under protest. It appears that the mother and the father and the children have since resided in the USA although the mother and father are separated. The father has petitioned a court in the USA for custody of the children and the mother has cross petitioned. In addition, it appears that the mother petitioned the US court for an order for the return of the children to the UK pursuant to the Hague Convention. The father has filed a response contesting that application which is awaiting a hearing in the USA.

On 7 November 1997 the mother issued an originating summons in this jurisdiction seeking a declaration pursuant to s 8 of the Child Abduction and Custody Act 1985 that the removal of the minors from the jurisdiction of the UK and from England and Wales by the defendant father in August 1997 was a 'wrongful removal' within the meaning and terms of Art 3 of the Hague Convention. It appears that an ex parte application was also made to Stuart-White J for a declaration in such terms and that it was granted ex

[⁴ See p. 478 above.]

parte by the judge with liberty to the defendant father to apply. When the notice of the declaration was received by the father in the USA he sought to suspend or discharge the order of Stuart-White J. Singer J adjourned his application to a date in 1998. On 14 November 1997 the father supported by the USA applied to the Court of Appeal for leave to appeal against the order of Singer J declining to suspend or discharge the order of Stuart-White J and at the same time the USA applied for leave to intervene. The Court of Appeal allowed the father's appeal and set aside the order of Singer J and the declaration made ex parte by Stuart-White J was suspended pending an inter partes hearing. On 26 November 1997 a summons was formally issued by the USA for leave to intervene in the English proceedings together with a summons by the father seeking the dismissal of the proceedings on grounds of both State and diplomatic immunity. On 1 December 1997 Bracewell J gave leave to the USA to intervene and ordered that the question of immunity from jurisdiction should be dealt with at a preliminary hearing.

The present hearing is accordingly concerned solely with the question whether diplomatic and/or State immunity should preclude the English court from exercising jurisdiction to determine the issues raised by the plaintiff mother in her originating summons by which she seeks the declarations to which I have referred. The court is not presently concerned with the substance of the issues which would fall for consideration under the provisions of the Hague Convention application.

At this hearing the father and the USA have common representation by counsel on the issue of the jurisdiction of this court. The mother is
[1029] represented by leading and junior counsel and in addition at the request of the court the Attorney-General has made available counsel as amicus curiae. It should be emphasised that the Attorney-General is not a party to these proceedings and has not himself sought to intervene. The amicus is an independent counsel who will seek to assist the court in the light of his own experience. He does not represent or speak for the Attorney-General or the Government of the UK.

The defendant father and the USA as intervener jointly submit that the defendant father is entitled to diplomatic immunity in respect of the removal of the minors from the UK. It is further submitted this was done on the direct orders of the USA and that in asking the court to make a declaration that the removal of the minors from the UK was a 'wrongful removal' the plaintiff mother is in effect impugning a sovereign act of the USA. It is submitted that under the provisions of the State Immunity Act 1978 the USA is immune from the jurisdiction of the English courts and that that immunity extends to the acts of the defendant in his capacity as an official of the USA. Linda Jacobson is an assistant legal adviser for Diplomatic Law and Litigation in the Office of the Legal Adviser of the US Department of State. She has sworn an affidavit dated 9 December 1997 in which she states:

'I am authorised by the Government of the USA to make this affidavit in support of an application on the part of the USA and on behalf of the defendant disputing the jurisdiction of this honourable court on the grounds of immunity.'

In para 4 of the affidavit she explains the regulations which govern an employee of the foreign service of the USA. She deposes inter alia that a foreign service employee may be issued with orders to travel on duty to an assignment at any location and is subject to disciplinary action in the event of a failure or refusal to comply. In para 5 of the same affidavit she states:

'Foreign service employees assigned to overseas missions and family members forming part of their household (if also US citizens) travel to the relevant posts on diplomatic passports issued by the Government of the USA.

Mr P and his two minor children travelled to the UK on such diplomatic passports when he assumed his position at the US embassy in London in August 1994.'

I interpolate that it will be recalled that although the wife is not a US citizen the children are both citizens of the USA as well as enjoying German nationality. In para 9 of the same affidavit she states that:

'The decision to curtail Mr P's tour of duty was taken by the Director of the Office of Career Development and Assignments in the Bureau of Personnel in the State Department on 7 August 1997, acting under the delegated authority of the Director General of the Foreign Service.'

In para 10 she states:

'In accordance with that decision, on 7 August 1997, the Department of **[1030]** State authorised the embassy to incur the necessary travel expenditure to return the P family to the USA, curtailment of the assignment having been ordered. Since Mr P's assignment to his posting at the embassy in London as a diplomatic representative of the USA included provision for him to be accompanied by his wife and children, for whose entry into and residence in the UK the USA was responsible as a matter of international law, the intended effect of these orders was to return the P family as a unit to the USA.'

Paragraph 13:

'The decision by the State Department to recall Mr P and his family was an official act of the US Government. The implementation of the State Department decision and of the travel orders issued by it by embassy officials in London were also official acts of the US Government; as was Mr P's departure from the UK with his family in accordance with them. Moreover Mr P's departure from his post was undertaken in the exercise of his diplomatic functions as a member of the mission.'

Paragraph 14:

'In my respectful submission, the USA could not conduct its foreign policy effectively and, in particular ensure appropriate representation of its interests abroad if it were not able freely to assign and withdraw diplomats and their dependants to and from overseas postings. The USA does so in accordance with the mutual rights and obligations of States contained in the Vienna Convention and in the exercise of its sovereign authority. The departure of Mr P and his family from the UK in August 1997 was on the express orders of the Government of the USA and I am advised that as a matter of public international law and of English law Mr P is accordingly immune from the jurisdiction of this honourable court in respect of these proceedings.'

James Alan Williams, Director of the Office of Career Development and Assignments in the Bureau of Personnel of the US Department of State in Washington, DC, swore two affidavits the first of which is dated 5 January 1998 in which he states that he dealt with the request for the termination or curtailment of Mr P's tour and communicated the decision to the embassy in London on 7 August 1997. He personally authorised the embassy to incur the necessary travel expenditure to return the P family to the USA. In para 5 of this affidavit he states:

'The intended effect of the orders issued by me on 7 August 1997 on behalf of the Department of State to the embassy in London was to return the P family as a unit to the USA. The implementation of this decision and of the travel orders by embassy officials in London (who, as foreign service employees, were required to act in accordance with my decision) were official acts of the US Government, as was Mr P's departure from the UK with his family in accordance with them. Moreover, Mr P's **[1031]** departure from his post was undertaken in the exercise of his functions as a member of the mission.'

In para 6:

'Mr P's actions in departing the UK in August with his family were directed and authorised by the government of the USA and fell within the course and scope of Mr P's duties as an employee of the Department of State and were undertaken in the exercise of his functions as a member of the US mission to the UK.'

Mr Williams has submitted a further draft affidavit during the progress of the hearing which has been admitted with the consent of the plaintiff and is the subject of an undertaking to have it sworn by the defendant. In para 3 of this second affidavit Mr Williams states:

'I ordered that Mr P's tour be curtailed. I also directed that orders be issued for the family to be returned to the USA. The orders communicated to the embassy in London were unequivocal and mandatory: both the embassy in London and Mr P were required to comply with them. The fact that the embassy wrote to Mr and Mrs P in terms solicitous to the distressing circumstances in which they found themselves did not and could not change the nature and effect of the underlying orders I had issued.'

Paragraph 4:

'Having received his orders Mr P's only choice was either to comply with them or to disobey them. In order to comply with them, he had to return to the USA at the time and in the manner directed by the embassy *and to bring his family with him*. Mr P complied.'

Paragraph 5:

'The foreign service of the USA could not operate efficiently and effectively if the US Government were not able freely to assign and re-assign diplomats and their dependants in accordance with the needs of the service. As a member of the diplomatic staff of the mission representing the USA in the UK Mr P's acts in compliance with his recall orders were an essential part of his functions as a member of the mission albeit his final exercise of those functions before departing his post and taking up a new position at the Department of State in Washington, DC.'

On the basis of that evidence counsel for Mr P and for the USA submits first that the act of taking his children from the UK when he left to return to the USA in August 1997 was an act done in the necessary course of his diplomatic duties. It is further submitted that it was an act which he was *ordered* to perform by his government. Accordingly, counsel submits this is a situation which gives rise to both diplomatic and to State immunity from the jurisdiction of the courts of the UK.

For the plaintiff mother it is submitted that the act of taking his children **[1032]** with him when he left the UK was a private action which fell outside the performance of Mr P's diplomatic duty and furthermore was an action which took place at a stage when his diplomatic immunity ceased to have effect. The plaintiff relies on the correspondence which was addressed personally to Mr P and to his wife by the officials of the embassy of the USA in London. Counsel refers to the affidavit of Mr James Anthony Gresser, the attorney in charge of the Civil Division European Office of the US Department of Justice in the embassy in London, and to the exhibits to his affidavit and in particular to a letter written on 7 August 1997 by the acting deputy chief of mission Mr Charles Ries to Mr P. In that letter the deputy chief of mission states that he was writing an identical letter to the plaintiff wife and in the course of the letter he said:

'I want to stress that it is not our intention to take sides in your dispute with your wife or to make any decisions relative to provisional custody of the children. These are matters in which we have no competence or responsibility and your disagreements in this respect really should be settled by competent family law authorities as soon as possible. It is our hope that the family would travel together and that you and your wife would agree on this in the children's best interest.'

It concluded:

'I urge you to come to an agreement with your wife on how to manage your family situation and your travel from the UK. I must reiterate that, notwithstanding our international legal rights to immunity as diplomats, it is the firm policy of the US Government that we respect local law. Both of you have our sympathy and best wishes at this difficult time in your lives. With warm personal regards. Sincerely, signed Charles Ries acting deputy head of mission.'

Counsel for the plaintiff submits that the terms of that letter do not accord with the concept of an 'order' suggested in the affidavits of Miss Jacobson and Mr Williams. Counsel also relies on the fact that Mr P had personally engaged solicitors in relation to his marital problems. In a letter dated 8 August 1997 Mr P's solicitors wrote to the mother's solicitors in terms which commenced as follows:

'We are the solicitors who have now been asked to write to you on behalf of Mr P in relation to the family's return to America. We are told that your client is concerned about her position on her return to the USA. Mr P has no wish to make matters worse between the parties which would only be seriously detrimental to the well-being of the children. In order to facilitate the return, our client would agree ...'

There followed seven paragraphs of proposed undertakings which Mr P would give in relation to the residence of the children in the USA and the provision inter alia of maintenance support. It concluded with the following passage upon which counsel placed reliance:

[1033]   'Our client would also require your client to agree:

(a) not to travel to the USA for 14 days after his departure with the children;
(b) not to institute or pursue any proceedings against our client of any nature (including proceedings under the Hague Convention) save any proper inter partes domestic application arising out of the breakdown of the marriage.'

Counsel relies on those documents in particular for his submission that contrary to Mr Williams' and Miss Jacobson's evidence the removal of the

children from the UK by Mr P in August 1997 cannot be considered as an
act of a sovereign or governmental nature but in reality was a private act in
the family context. Accordingly, counsel submits it cannot be regarded as an
act of the USA performed on its behalf by Mr P as its agent.

The Diplomatic Privileges Act 1964 implements in part the Vienna
Convention on Diplomatic Relations 1961. This governs diplomatic
privileges and immunity. The State Immunity Act 1978 governs State
immunity. As Mr Lloyd-Jones, amicus curiae, pointed out diplomatic
privileges and immunities are functional in character. Their purpose is not to
benefit individual diplomats but to ensure the efficient performance of the
functions of diplomatic missions as representing States. See the preamble to
the Vienna Convention. Article 29 of the Vienna Convention provides that
the person of a diplomatic agent shall be inviolable. He shall not be liable to
any form of arrest or detention. Article 37 extends this immunity to
members of his family. Article 39 (1) provides:

'Every person entitled to privileges and immunities shall enjoy them from
the moment he enters the territory of the receiving State on proceeding to
take up his post ...'

However Art 39(2) provides:

'When the functions of a person enjoying privileges and immunities have
come to an end, such privileges and immunities shall normally cease at
the moment when he leaves the country, or on the expiry of a reasonable
period in which to do so, but shall subsist until that time, even in case of
armed conflict. However, with respect to acts performed by such a person
in the exercise of his functions as a member of the mission, immunity
shall continue to subsist.'

Diplomatic immunity as such is not immunity from legal liability but
immunity from suit. Where therefore proceedings have been brought against
a defendant who enjoys immunity, the proceedings may be allowed to
continue once that immunity has been lost. The original proceedings in the
Family Division for a residence order were commenced whilst Mr P was still
in post. Accordingly, as the judge held, Mr P enjoyed diplomatic privilege
and immunity including his personal inviolability at that time. The present
originating summons was issued on 7 November 1997 after Mr P had left
the UK and after his diplomatic status in the UK had been terminated.
Accordingly, in the present case attention must be directed to Art 39(2) and **[1034]**
in particular to the final sentence which states:

'However, with respect to acts performed by such a person in the exercise
of his functions as a member of the mission, immunity shall continue to
subsist.'

The plaintiff argues that at the time that the originating summons was issued Mr P's diplomatic status had been terminated and that any immunity could only apply to acts carried out or performed in the exercise of his functions as a member of the mission. The taking by him of his children with him from this country at the end of his mission could not amount to an act performed by Mr P in the exercise of his functions as a member of the mission. Therefore it is submitted diplomatic immunity could not continue to subsist at the time the originating summons was issued. The rationale of the continuing immunity is that the acts of a diplomatic agent in the exercise of his official functions are in [5] law the acts of the sending state. See the case of *Zoernsch v Waldock* [1964] 1 WLR 675; further see *Denza on Diplomatic Law*, p 250 and Professor Dinstein's work 'Diplomatic Immunity from Jurisdiction Ratione Materiae' (1966 Vol 5 ICLQ 76 at p 82). Mr Lloyd Jones as amicus curiae has strongly submitted that in this case it would be difficult if not impossible to take the view that the action of taking the children from the jurisdiction at the end of his posting was an act performed in the exercise of Mr P's functions as a member of the mission. I accept that submission. Whilst Mr P could not have been prevented at the time from taking his children with him from this country nevertheless after he had returned to the USA and his diplomatic status had been determined so far as the UK was concerned his action in taking the children cannot be considered to have been the exercise of a function as a member of the mission within Art 39(2).

State immunity is a separate concept. The immunity usually applies in cases where the foreign State is named as a defendant. However it has been accepted by the Court of Appeal in the case of *Propend Finance Pty Ltd v* [6]*Sing* (unreported) 17 April 1997 that the agent of a foreign State will enjoy immunity in respect of his acts of a sovereign or governmental nature. Accordingly there may be cases where the diplomatic agent may enjoy both diplomatic and State immunity. These immunities will not be co-extensive.

The US Government has insisted in this case that the removal by Mr P of his family from the UK and their return to the USA was done in compliance with a direct order of government. It is plainly put on a high plane by Mr Williams in both his affidavits. Paragraph 5 of his second affidavit states:

'The foreign service of the USA could not operate efficiently and effectively if the US Government were not freely able to assign and reassign diplomats and their dependants in accordance with the needs of the service. As a member of the diplomatic staff of the mission representing the USA in the UK, Mr P's acts in compliance with his recall orders were an essential part of his functions as a member of the mission albeit his final exercise of those functions before departing his post and taking up a new position at the Department of State in Washington, DC.'

And in para 4 he states:

[5 41 *ILR* 438.]   [6 111 *ILR* 611.]

'Having received his orders Mr P's only choice was either to comply with **[1035]** them or to disobey them. In order to comply with them he had to return to the USA at the time and in the manner directed by the embassy and to *bring his family with him.* Mr P complied.'

In the light of that evidence, which I accept, I am driven to conclude that the act of taking his children back to the USA at the end of his mission was an act of a governmental nature and as such is subject to State immunity from legal process.

Whilst this court is not concerned today with the substance of the mother's application for a declaration made pursuant to the Child Abduction and Custody Act 1985 it may be observed that the allegation of wrongful removal is now pending for determination by a court in the USA.

In the circumstances I propose to set aside the originating summons and its service upon the defendant and to discharge the proceedings on the ground that the USA and the defendant are immune from the jurisdiction of this court.

COURT OF APPEAL
11 March 1998

LORD WOOLF MR: Before this court today is an appeal from a decision given by the President on a preliminary issue which arose in these circumstances. The respondent was an official of the US Government. From 1994 to 1997 he served as a diplomat at the US embassy in London. Unfortunately, during the period that he was in this country, marital problems commenced.

There are two children of the family, one born on 23 December 1984 and the other born on 18 December 1987. While the parties were in England, the children were with them and at all times they were living together as a family. The mother is a German national and the children had dual nationality.

As a result of the marital problems, divorce proceedings were started by the mother in Berlin. The mother was concerned that the children might be removed from this country. She wanted to protect her position and, as she saw it, the position of the children. On 25 July 1997 the mother issued an application in this country for a prohibited steps order to prevent the father taking the children to the USA. She also sought leave to remove the children to Germany. An ex parte order was originally made by Sumner J prohibiting the father from removing the children from the UK.

On 4 August 1997 the USA and the father issued a summons seeking to dismiss the English proceedings because of immunity from the jurisdiction of these courts. On 7 August 1997 the mother's application was dismissed for want of jurisdiction and the order of Sumner J was set aside. The mother's application for leave to appeal and a stay was refused. On 8 August 1997 the father was posted back to the USA and the mother and the children also returned there.

The mother has petitioned the court in Virginia for an order for the return of the children to the UK on the basis that the children had been abducted contrary to the Hague Convention. On 7 November 1997 the mother issued an originating summons in the UK seeking a declaration pursuant to s 8 of **[1036]** the Child Abduction and Custody Act 1985 that the removal of the children from the UK by the father was a wrongful removal within the meaning of Art 3 of the Hague Convention. An order was granted ex parte by Stuart-White J with liberty to the father to apply. That application was subsequently adjourned and eventually an order was made for the determination of a preliminary issue, again as to the question of immunity, in relation to these proceedings.

The preliminary issue was heard by the President, and on 22 January 1998 he gave a decision. He came to the conclusion that there was no immunity under the Diplomatic Privileges Act 1964 based on the Vienna Convention on Diplomatic Relations 1961, but there was State immunity based on the State Immunity Act 1978. It was against his decision (which meant that the application for a declaration was dismissed) that this appeal comes before this court. The matter has been expedited so that this court could determine the preliminary issue, bearing in mind that the matter is due to come again before the Virginia court on 19 March 1998.

Skeleton arguments in some detail, together with appropriate authorities, have been placed before this court by those acting on behalf of the mother, those acting on behalf of the father and the US Government, and also by Mr David Lloyd-Jones, who has, at short notice, appeared to assist this court as amicus curiae, as he assisted the President in the court below.

Although the time available for this court to deal with the matter was limited, the court would have been able to do so due to the excellent material in writing which has been put before the courts by all parties. However, at the outset of the appeal, the court raised the issue with counsel as to the appropriateness of our hearing the appeal.

This court has been mindful throughout that, quite apart from interesting and difficult issues considered by the President in relation to the preliminary issue to which I have made reference, there are two children involved whose future has to be determined. The mother's wish for those children is that they should reside with her in Germany, not in this country. The father's wish is that the children should not go to Germany. Presumably it is his wish, although this is not clear, that the children should remain in the USA.

The danger in this case is that the courts, both in this jurisdiction and in the USA, are going to become weighed down with issues of complexity and difficulties arising out of the father's diplomatic status, and, as is contended by the father, the diplomatic status of the mother and the children at the time that they left this country.

The jurisdiction which the court would be exercising, if it had the right to do so, comes under s 8 of the Child Abduction and Custody Act 1985 which is in these terms:

'The High Court or Court of Session may, on an application made for the purposes of Article 15 of the Convention by any person appearing to the court to have an interest in the matter, make a declaration or declarator that the removal of any child from, or his retention outside, the United Kingdom was wrongful within the meaning of Article 3 of the Convention.'

An application for the declaration has to be made for the purposes of Art 15 of the Convention. It reads:

'The judicial or administrative authorities of a Contracting State may, **[1037]** prior to the making of an order for the return of the child, request that the applicant obtain from the authorities of the State of the habitual residence of the child a decision or other determination that the removal or retention was wrongful within the meaning of Article 3 of the Convention, where such a decision or determination may be obtained in that State. The Central Authorities of the Contracting States shall so far as practicable assist applicants to obtain such a decision or determination.'

Article 15 of the Hague Convention raises an interesting point which would have to be determined by this court if it had jurisdiction, which may also have to be determined by the US court in Virginia because of the Hague Convention proceedings taking place there, as to the impact upon the applicability of the Convention that when the father was in this country he was here as a diplomat serving in a senior post.

There would also have to be determined the question as to whether children who accompany their parents (who are here because of the diplomatic status of the father) are to be regarded as habitually resident within this jurisdiction. Those are not matters which are before this court on this appeal and would not be determined as part of our consideration of the preliminary issue. As to the decision of the President in relation to the preliminary issue, although we have not heard argument, we can say with confidence that the points raised by the mother and the father, to which I will refer, are, at least, arguable.

The mother says that the decision of the President, who granted immunity on the basis of State immunity, was wrong, but his decision in relation to diplomatic immunity was right. The father and the US Government say that the decision of the President was right on the question of State immunity but wrong on the question of diplomatic immunity. It is our view that if this appeal had been argued to determination there were three possible outcomes:

(1) the President's judgment would be upheld;
(2) the appeal would be successful and the mother would succeed; and
(3) the US Government and the father would succeed on their cross-appeal on a respondent's notice in relation to the issue upon which he and the US Government were unsuccessful before the President.

It is certainly possible that if we had, as we would have done, given a decision before 19 March 1998, that would not have been of any help to the court in Virginia because, (a) the situation is such that there could well have been a further appeal within this jurisdiction; and (b) it would only have dealt with the preliminary issue and would not have gone on to consider, assuming the decision was adverse to the father, the question as to whether or not this was an appropriate case to grant a declaration. That would only come at a later stage. In those circumstances this court considered whether there was any benefit to be achieved in these proceedings by us considering the appeal, or whether our decision was only going to complicate an already complex situation. We have also considered carefully as to whether or not, by considering the appeal, there was any useful contribution that we could **[1038]** make to assist the court which inevitably is going to have to consider the issue in Virginia.

The conclusion we reached was that we could not provide any assistance. One advantage that we have over the court in Virginia in considering the issues involved here, is that this court could, because of the European argument which Mr Duffy on behalf of the mother relies to a substantial extent, have referred the matter to Europe for a decision under Art 177 of the Treaty. If such a reference had been made, it would have had the advantage of determining finally the validity° of Mr Duffy's arguments, which are not accepted as being correct by Mr Lloyd-Jones in his capacity as amicus.

However a reference under Art 177 would be wholly impractical in the timescale of determining the issue as to where these children are to reside. A substantial period would elapse before the European court could give us the benefit of their assistance. As Mr Duffy submitted, the courts in this country are now more familiar with dealing with European points than the courts in the USA. I doubt in this context whether there would be much advantage to this court considering European points advanced by Mr Duffy purely for that purpose.

There is also a real risk that if we decided that we had jurisdiction, and if we decided to go on to consider the merits of granting a declaration, that there could be an unattractive result produced. This is because our decision would not be binding on the Virginia court, the Virginia court could take a different view from ourselves. One could have a conflict as to the correct approach in relation to the application of the Hague Convention. The US Government has become involved in the Virginia proceedings, seeking to canvas before the judge in Virginia the very same issues that arise here to which I have already made reference.

In the end it seems to me important that this court should bear in mind that what is being sought is a declaration, a remedy which is discretionary. There are situations where the courts have granted declarations under s 8, but they have been granted only in very limited circumstances. There is certainly no precedent of which we are aware where a declaration has been granted under s 8 where the issue only indirectly concerns this country.

As already stated, ultimately, the conflict is as to whether the children should be with the mother in Germany or whether they should remain in the

USA. The only purpose of the result of the Hague Convention proceedings is that the children would be returned to the UK so that this country can deal with the issue as to whether the children should go with the mother to Germany. As to this, the Virginian court is in a better position than this court because all the parties are in the USA.

There has been a previous case under s 8 considered by this court, namely *Re P (Abduction: Declaration)* [1995] 1 FLR 831. In that case, a division of this court presided over by Butler-Sloss and Millett LJJ and Sir Ralph Gibson, had to consider a situation where a father had made an application under s 8. In that case the courts in California had wanted the help of the English courts, albeit that there had not been compliance with the strict requirements of the Hague Convention. This court said that, in the circumstances that existed, which did not include the complication of a German national being involved, as in this case, there is jurisdiction in this court which is absolutely right, to make a declaration under s 8. It is true to say that the jurisdiction under s 8 may be more extensive than that under Art 15, at least to the extent that it is not confined to a situation where Art 15 **[1039]** has been complied with where the court can make a declaration under s 8.

However, in her judgment, my Lady said at 835H:

'Should such a declaration be made? Section 8 presupposes that this court will tread the path which will also be trodden by the Californian court and we would not presume to do so unless asked.'

In saying that, as I understand it, my Lady was regarding the request as having been made by the Californian court although the correct procedure had not been carried out. She went on to say:

'The purpose of Art 15 goes to the obligation of the State to comply with the request. In a situation falling directly within Art 15 the requested State may have made a firm or provisional finding or made an assumption that the habitual residence is English. In the present appeal the request is at an earlier stage where the Central Authority of the USA faced with the 1992 English order and a complicated matrimonial history seeks our assistance before placing the application before the judicial authorities. In the interests of comity it is proper for us to assist when called upon to do so. In the general run of cases on such a request made before there is a decision or an assumption by the requested State as to where is the habitual residence of the child, it would be preferable for the English court, if the facts permit, to make a declaration upon the assumption that the habitual residence is in England, rather than making a specific finding on an issue still in dispute in the other State. The issue properly to be the concern of the English court under the Convention is whether an applicant parent had rights of custody according to English law at the time of the removal.'

Millett LJ also gave a judgment, which is very helpful in giving guidance as to the circumstances when it is appropriate for an English court to make a declaration.

I would not go so far as to say that there can be no situation, where you have a father who is of one nationality and a mother who is of another nationality and neither are nationals of this country, where it would be appropriate to make a declaration under s 8 (at least if asked to do so by a foreign court). However, I am quite satisfied that a declaration in these proceedings has no contribution to make to the proceedings in the USA. I strongly suspect that if we were to grant a declaration that would not do other than delay the proceedings in the USA, and would be contrary to the interests of the children.

Accordingly it would serve no purpose, indeed it would be contrary to the interests of the children which the Hague Convention procedure is designed to assist, if we were to proceed with this appeal. It would only result in examination of legal issues which, in any event, will have to be examined in the USA, even if, which is by no means certain, we were to come to the conclusion that the courts of this country have jurisdiction.

Accordingly I would at this preliminary stage dismiss this appeal notwithstanding the attractive arguments advanced by Mr Duffy and Mr **[1040]** Setright suggesting that it would be appropriate for us to continue with the appeal.

BUTLER-SLOSS LJ: I respectfully agree with the judgment of the Master of the Rolls. This application for a declaration under s 8 is ancillary to the proceedings which are going ahead in Virginia. The situation which arises before this court is entirely different from that in the case of *Re P (Abduction: Declaration)* [1995] 1 FLR 831 to which my Lord, the Master of the Rolls, has referred. In my judgment also, this court has nothing to contribute on any of the issues which fall directly to be decided by the Virginian court. I agree that this appeal should be dismissed.

SIMON BROWN LJ: I agree that this appeal should be dismissed for the reasons given by my Lord.

Appeal dismissed. No order as to costs. Legal aid taxation of mother's costs. Leave to appeal to House of Lords refused. Liberty to apply to this court to restore appeal if US court decides to return children to this country under Hague Convention.

[Report: [1998] 1 FLR 1027]

State immunity — Jurisdictional immunity — National of sending State employed as member of technical and administrative staff of consulate of foreign State — Dismissal—Claim for damages for unlawful dismissal— Whether foreign State entitled to jurisdictional immunity— Restrictive theory of immunity — Scope of application to disputes concerning employment contracts—Employment involving performance of subordinate consular functions— Whether exercise of jurisdiction would constitute inter-ference with performance of sovereign functions

Consular relations — Consular employee — Whether performing consular functions — Vienna Convention on Consular Relations, 1963, Article 5

Sources of international law—Customary international law —Rules on State immunity relating to employment contracts —Scope of application of rules in the absence of applicable international treaty—The law of the Federal Republic of Germany

X *v.* ARGENTINA

(Case No 2 AZR 513/95)

Federal Republic of Germany, Federal Labour Court (BAG). 3 *July* 1996

(Etzel, *President*; Bitter and Fischmeier, *Judges*)

SUMMARY: *The facts*:—The plaintiff, an Argentinian national, was employed as a member of the administrative and technical staff of the Consulate General of Argentina in Düsseldorf from 1964 to 1991, when the relationship was terminated. She instituted proceedings against her employer before the German courts, seeking a declaration that her employment had subsisted until the end of 1991, arguing that there were no grounds for her dismissal, and claiming damages. At first instance and on appeal the action was dismissed on the ground that the defendant was entitled to jurisdictional immunity as a foreign State. The plaintiff appealed to the Federal Labour Court.

Held:—The appeal was dismissed.

(1) In the absence of international agreements or other legal provisions, the question of whether and to what extent a foreign State was subject to German jurisdiction was to be decided in accordance with the general rules of public international law. There was no rule of public international law which excluded German jurisdiction for actions brought against a foreign State

relating to its non-sovereign activities. The decisive factor in making the distinction between sovereign and non-sovereign acts was their nature rather than their purpose. Whilst this classification was, in principle, a matter for national law, certain limits were imposed by public international law in cases where it was necessary to classify an activity of a foreign State as performed *jure imperii* because it belonged to the core sphere of State authority, even though under national law it would be regarded as a private law activity.

(2) Where an employment relationship with a foreign State involved the performance of consular functions, within the definition contained in Article 5 of the Vienna Convention on Consular Relations, 1963, including the issue and extension of passports and the processing of visas, even though the employee had a subordinate role in the performance of those functions, the employment belonged to the core sphere of sovereign activity of the State concerned and was exempt from national jurisdiction so far as the conduct and termination of the relationship were concerned. Any examination of the circumstances of the dismissal of such an employee would conflict with the principle that consular relations should not be impeded (*ne impediatur legatio*).

The following is the text of the judgment of the Court:

OPERATIVE PART OF THE JUDGMENT

The plaintiff's appeal on points of law against the judgment of the Labour Court of Appeal of Düsseldorf of 10 May 1995 (No 2 (11) Sa 182/95) is dismissed with costs.

Facts and Procedure

The plaintiff was born on 24 February 1926. She is an Argentinian national and was employed as a member of the administrative and technical staff of the Consulate General of the defendant from 1 March 1964 until 28 February 1991 at a monthly salary which last amounted to DM 3,500. Her tasks included, among other things, the issuing and extension of Argentinian passports, the processing of visa applications, and attestations.

The plaintiff, who has drawn a pension from the Federal Insurance Institution for Salaried Employees (*Bundesversicherungsanstalt für Angestellte* (*BfA*)) since 1 January 1992, argues that there were no facts justifying the termination of her employment relationship prior to 28 February 1991. In her view, the defendant could not plead immunity because German local embassy staff were employed on the basis of ordinary contracts of employment and not appointed by an act of sovereignty. The conclusion of a contract of employment did not form part of consular tasks. Accordingly, the defendant had acted in this context like a private person. The plaintiff asserted that she did not have a special position of trust which could lead to a different assessment. For this reason, the decision on the dispute as to the continued existence

(*Bestandsstreitigkeit*) of her contract of employment fell within the scope of German labour law jurisdiction and German labour law was authoritative.

The plaintiff has requested:

(1) a finding that the employment relationship between the parties continued to exist beyond 28 February 1991, until 31 December 1991, under the same conditions as before;

(2) judgment against the defendant, specifying that the defendant should pay to the plaintiff the sum of DM 35,000, plus 4 per cent interest over the period from 1 January 1992.

The defendant has applied for the action to be rejected as inadmissible.

The defendant asserted that the plaintiff at first worked without a permanent employment relationship, as was usual for consular employees. The Consul at the time only proposed a permanent employment relationship to his Government on 7 June 1966. This proposal was then implemented by Resolution No 427 of 7 December 1971. In establishing the applicability of German jurisdiction, it was irrelevant which concrete activities the plaintiff carried out within the Consulate. Any subjection of the Defendant Republic to German jurisdiction would lead to organizational power being transferred from the sending State of the Consulate to the receiving State (the Federal Republic of Germany) which was impermissible.

The Labour Court dismissed the action. The Labour Court of Appeal of Düsseldorf dismissed the plaintiff's appeal. The plaintiff now pursues her application further by an appeal on points of law which the Labour Court of Appeal of Düsseldorf gave leave to file.

Grounds of the Judgment

The plaintiff's appeal on points of law is unfounded. The Labour Court of Appeal of Düsseldorf correctly denied German jurisdiction (Section 20(2) of the Law on the Constitution of the Courts) (*Gerichtsverfassungsgesetz—GVG*).

I. The Labour Court of Appeal assumed that the defendant, as a foreign State, was not subject to German jurisdiction according to general customary international law if the subject-matter of the legal dispute relates to the sovereign activity of the defendant. If the content of the employment relationship was the direct fulfilment of tasks which fall within the sphere of State authority in its narrow and specific sense, questions in dispute which are connected with the establishment and termination of the employment relationship must be excluded from German jurisdiction, because the connection with the fulfilment of sovereign tasks of the foreign State outweighs the (in principle) private law character of the establishment and termination of an employment relationship. This was the case here because the plaintiff was responsible for carrying out consular tasks in the narrow sense. It was thus irrelevant whether the plaintiff's employment relationship was established by a sovereign act.

II. This Court agrees with this position, so far as both the result and the reasoning are concerned.

1. In the absence of international agreements or other legal provisions, the question of whether and to what extent the defendant, as a foreign State, is subject to German jurisdiction is to be decided in accordance with the general rules of public international law (Section 20(2) *GVG*). The Labour Court of Appeal correctly assumed that, whilst States are not subject to the jurisdiction of other States under general customary international law wherever the subject-matter of the legal dispute relates to their sovereign activities, there is no rule of public international law (which would form part of German federal law by reason of Article 25 of the German Constitution (*GG*)) which excludes German jurisdiction for actions brought against a foreign State in relation to its activities of a non-sovereign nature (judgment of the Federal Constitutional Court (*BVerfG*) of 30 April 1963, 2 *BvM* 1/62, 16 *BVerfGE* 27).[1] The decisive factor for the distinction between sovereign and non-sovereign State activities is not their motive or purpose, but rather the nature of the disputed State act or legal relationship, although the classification must in principle be made under national law if there are no criteria for delimitation under public international law (16 *BVerfGE* 27, 61 *et seq.*). However, there are limits under public international law to the classification of the State activity or legal relationship in dispute as non-sovereign. National law may only be called upon to make the distinction subject to the proviso that State activities, or legal relationships determined by them, may not be taken out of the sovereign sphere, and consequently no longer qualify for immunity if, according to the predominant opinion of States, they belong to the sphere of State authority as defined in the narrow and specific sense. By way of exception, it may be necessary under public international law to classify the activity of a foreign State as an act performed *jure imperii* because it is to be attributed to the core sphere of State authority, although under national law it would be viewed as private law activity and not public law activity (16 *BVerfGE* 27, 63 *et seq.*).[2]

It is unimportant whether the legal relationship in dispute was established by a private law declaration of intent, as would automatically be the case where an employment relationship under German law was concerned, or by an act of sovereignty, as Resolution No 427 of 7 December 1971 may indicate. A legal relationship which imposes an obligation to perform tasks which are to be attributed to the activity of

[[1] 45 *ILR* 57.]   [[2] *Ibid.*]

the foreign power, police power or the administration of justice (see also 16 *BVerfGE* 27, 63,[3] with further references) normally cannot be the subject-matter of a dispute as to the continued existence (*Bestandsstreitigkeit*) of the relationship before German courts, without breaching the immunity of the foreign State concerned, irrespective of how the relationship was formed. In this context, the appeal on points of law is wrong in criticizing the Labour Court of Appeal for not giving concrete consideration to the tasks performed by the plaintiff in the defendant's Consulate. On the contrary, the Labour Court of Appeal found that the plaintiff's tasks in the defendant's Consulate included, amongst other things, the issuing and extension of Argentinian passports, the processing of visas and arranging attestations, all of which is undisputed. These are basic consular functions as defined in Article 5(d) and (f) of the Vienna Convention on Consular Relations of 24 April 1963 (*BGBl*, 1969 II, 1585, 1587, 1595). Even if the plaintiff acted in accordance with instructions, the tasks specified belong to the core sphere of sovereign activity of the defendant, contrary to the view put forward in the appeal on points of law (see Labour Court of Appeal of Hamburg decision of 30 January 1978, 2 Sa 119/77, *IPRspr.* 78 No 132 Sp. 314; Seidl-Hohenveldern, *ZfRV* 1990, 302, 305; see also *BVerfG* judgment of 13 December 1977, 2 BvM 1/76, 46 *BverfGE* 342, 397).[4] Accordingly the defendant is to be exempted from German jurisdiction so far as the legal relationship in dispute and its termination are concerned (see Labour Court of Appeal of Hamburg, *loc. cit.*; Geimer, *Internationales Zivilprozesrecht*, 2nd edn, margin note No 582; Seidl-Hohenveldern, *loc. cit.*, p. 304; . . .).

This Court does not regard the contrary view (Gamillscheg, *Internationales Arbeitsrecht*, pp. 401 *et seq*. . . .) as convincing. Along with the need to respect foreign sovereignty, State immunity in contentious proceedings is also based on the principle of non-interference with the exercise of sovereign powers of the foreign State (Schack, *Internationales Zivilverfahrensrecht*, margin note No 148). If an employee acts in a sovereign capacity for a foreign State, then the examination of his or her dismissal by the national courts would conflict with the principle that diplomatic or consular relations should not be impeded (*ne impediatur legatio*, see 46 *BVerfGE* 342, 397 *et seq*.;[5] Seidl-Hohenveldern, *ZfRV* 1990, 302 *et seq*. and *RIW* 1993, 239). In this case, the examination could require an assessment of the sovereign act, with the consequence that the unimpeded fulfilment of the tasks of the embassy or consulate would be adversely affected (see the decision of the Labour Court of Appeal of Hamburg cited above, p. 317).

It need not be considered whether the result would be different if the plaintiff fulfilled her consular tasks without any margin of

[3 *Ibid*.]   [4 65 *ILR* 146.]   [5 *Ibid*.]

discretion to act, only in accordance with specific instructions in each individual case. The plaintiff, who bears the burden of proof of the preconditions for the application of German jurisdiction (see Rosenberg/Schwab/Gottwald, *Zivilprozessrecht*, 15th edn, paragraph 19, p. 91; Stein/Jonas/Schumann, *ZPO*, 20th edn, p. 323 . . .) did not make substantiated submissions, or at least not sufficiently substantiated submissions, in this respect. Since the defendant did not waive its immunity, the action was correctly dismissed as inadmissible.

2. This Court holds that the immunity of foreign States is clearly established with regard to disputes concerning the continued existence of legal relationships which impose obligations for the fulfilment of basic consular sovereign tasks. The existence of the rule of public international law mentioned at the outset is evidenced by the case-law of the Federal Constitutional Court referred to above. For the reasons specified in section 1 above, its significance does not give rise to doubts which would make a submission to the Federal Constitutional Court under the terms of Article 100(2) of the Federal Constitution (*GG*) appropriate (in this context, see *BVerfG* judgment of 30 October 1962,[6] 2 *BvM* 1/60, 15 *BVerfGE* 25; Labour Court of Appeal of Hamburg, *loc. cit.*, pp. 318 *et seq.*; Münch Komm-Wolf, *ZPO*, Section 20 *GVG*, margin note No 8).

[Report: 83 *BAGE* 262 (in German)]

State immunity — Jurisdictional immunity — Consular employee—Caretaker—Contract of employment—Termination—Express subjection to provisions of local law—Employee suffering from disability—Requirement under local law for public authorities to consent to dismissal—Whether applicable to consular employee of foreign State—Whether application of such rule would infringe sovereignty of foreign State

Consular relations—Immunity—Jurisdictional immunity—Dismissal of disabled consular employee — Requirement under local law for consent by public authorities to

dismissal—Whether enforceable against sending State— Whether such requirement constituting interference with performance of consular functions—Vienna Convention on Consular Relations, 1963, Article 5—The law of the Federal Republic of Germany

FRENCH CONSULATE DISABLED EMPLOYEE CASE

(Case No AZ 1K 4/88)

Federal Republic of Germany, Administrative Court (VG) of Mainz.   5 *May* 1988

SUMMARY: *The facts*:—The respondent was employed as a caretaker at a French consulate in Germany from 1981 until 1986, when he was dismissed for unsatisfactory performance of his duties following repeated warnings. Since 1983 he had suffered from 50 per cent disability and he now challenged his dismissal on the ground that the consent of the local Welfare Office, which was required under German law because he was disabled, had not been obtained. The Welfare Office took a decision refusing to give its consent to the dismissal. The French Government challenged that decision in administrative proceedings before the German courts, seeking a declaration that the dismissal of their consular employee did not require the consent of the Welfare Office.

Held:—The complaint was well founded, the decision of the Welfare Office was quashed and the declaration sought was granted.

(1) Under the restrictive doctrine of State immunity, such immunity applied only to sovereign acts and not to acts of a private-law character. Thus, in principle, when a foreign State entered into a contract of employment it submitted itself to the regime of private law applicable in that jurisdiction.

(2) Nevertheless, it did not follow that the provisions of the German Law on Disabled Persons were applicable in this case. Those provisions were not concerned with the effect of an agreement under private law but rather required, for reasons of employment policy, the consent of the public authorities in any case of dismissal of a disabled employee. To allow the German State such far-reaching influence where the employer was a foreign State would be contrary to the principle of sovereign immunity.

(3) The French Consulate served the interests of the French State by fulfilling consular functions as defined in Article 5 of the Vienna Convention on Consular Relations 1963. It thereby fulfilled sovereign functions of the sending State and accordingly the receiving State was debarred from intervening in the internal affairs of the Consulate which, in the interests of the proper representation of the sending State, had to be able to organize its services in accordance with its specific requirements in an unimpeded manner.

The text of the relevant part of the judgment of the Court commences on the opposite page.

[389]   OPERATIVE PART OF THE JUDGMENT

The . . . decisions [of the Welfare Office (*Hauptfürsorgestelle*)] of 3 December 1986 and 17 November 1987 are hereby quashed and it is declared that the complainant's dismissal of the co-respondent (*Beigeladene*) does not require the consent of the [respondent] Welfare Office.

The respondent and the co-respondent shall each bear one half of the costs of the proceedings.

[. . .]

Facts and Procedure
The complainant seeks a declaration that the consent of the respondent is not required before the co-respondent [employee] may be dismissed.

Under a contract concluded in 1981 between the complainant and the co-respondent, the latter was engaged as caretaker of the French Consulate in . . ., and was allocated a service flat within the consular building. The contract, which was drawn up in French, provided for its tacit annual renewal and was terminable by either party in accordance with the conditions laid down by local law.

[390] Since . . . 1983 the co-respondent has been severely handicapped, suffering from 50 per cent disability.

On 9 May 1985 the complainant gave the co-respondent written notice requiring him to perform his contractual duties in a proper manner. On 21 May 1986 he was given a written warning, alleging an increasing neglect of duty. The following specific allegations were made: the co-respondent was not cleaning properly; he was storing electrical goods on the consular premises, raising the suspicion that he was engaging in some illicit activity on his own account; he was consuming excessive amounts of alcohol; he was neglecting his clothing; because of his asthma, he was unable to work as a driver. Finally it was alleged that despite the fact that his wife, who was employed to do the cleaning, had left the matrimonial home, he was continuing to draw her salary.

On 25 July 1986 the complainant gave the co-respondent written notice of termination, with effect from 31 December 1986, both of his employment and of his tenancy of the service flat.

On 14 August 1986 the co-respondent lodged an application with the Labour Court (*Arbeitsgericht*) for relief against dismissal (*Kündigungsschutzklage*), claiming *inter alia* that he was 50 per cent disabled by asthma . . .

[The Court then gave a detailed account of the subsequent proceedings. The co-respondent's application for relief was referred to the local Welfare Office, which refused to give its consent to his dismissal, ruling that his contract of employment was subject to the statutory protection afforded to disabled persons by German law. The complainant's appeal against this decision having failed, it now sought an order against the Welfare Office to have both its initial decision and the appeal quashed, together with a declaration that the Office's consent to the co-respondent's dismissal was not required. After setting out the arguments of the parties, the Court continued:]

[392] . . .

Grounds of the Judgment
The complaint is admissible and well founded.

The fact that the complainant itself initiated these proceedings is sufficient to give the German courts jurisdiction (see von Schönfeld, 1986 *NJW*, 2980, 2983) . . .

[The Court then dealt with the question of admissibility from the standpoint of German administrative law and continued:]

The complaint is not only admissible but also succeeds on the merits.

The complainant is entitled to the declaration sought. Its dismissal of the co-respondent did not require the consent of the Welfare Office.

[The Court examined in detail the relevant provisions of the German Law on Disabled Persons (*Schwerbehindertengesetz—SchwbG*). It ruled that the co-respondent fell within the category of persons entitled to the protection of that Law, but that the latter must be interpreted as applying only to domestic employers and not to foreign States or consulates. The Court continued:]

[393] . . . This is the only interpretation of the above Law which is also compatible with the applicant's legal status. The principle of the immunity of foreign States under international law is founded on a belief that all States are equal under international law and that in consequence no individual State has the legal authority to make the activities of another sovereign State subject to the acts of its Legislature, Judiciary or Executive. Under the doctrine of restricted State immunity as currently recognized, this principle must be qualified in the sense that immunity applies only to sovereign acts (*acta jure imperii*) and not to activities of a private-law character (*acta jure gestionis*) (16 *BVerfGE* 34,[1] 46 *BVerfGE* 342,[2] 64 *BVerfGE* 1;[3] see also Verdross/Simma, *Universelles Völkerrecht, Theorie und Praxis*, 3rd edn, 1984, pp. 762 ff.). Thus, when a foreign State enters into a contract of employment, in principle it submits itself to the regime of private law. However, it does not follow that Sections 15 ff. *SchwbG* must apply in the present case. It must be borne in mind, in accordance with the principle established by decision of the Federal Labour Court (*Bundesarbeitsgericht—BAG*), that the private-law right of relief against dismissal is overlaid by a predominantly public-law element.

[1 45 *ILR* 57.]   [2 65 *ILR* 146.]   [3 65 *ILR* 215.]

The effectiveness of an expression of intention under private law is made subject to the consent of a domestic public authority. Thus the regime provided for in Sections 15 ff. *SchwbG* is not primarily of a private-law nature, since it deals not with the effect in terms of private law of the parties' intentions, but rather, for reasons of social welfare, requires the involvement of a public authority in any case of involuntary dismissal of a disabled person (*BAG*, Decision of 30 April 1987, Case No 2 *AZR* 192/86, 1987 *NJW* 2766-7).

The requirement of consent reserves an administrative power of decision to the [Welfare Office], thereby enabling it to exercise extensive influence over the internal organization of the Consulate. This power does not derive primarily from the terms of the contract of employment (which were agreed quite independently of the right of the labour courts to grant relief), but is founded essentially on employment policy considerations. To allow the German State such far-reaching influence would be contrary to the principle of sovereign immunity. The French Consulate serves the interests of the French State (see, in relation to consular **[394]** duties, Article 5 of the Vienna Convention of 24 April 1963, 1969 *BGBl*. II, 1585) and thereby fulfils that State's sovereign functions. Such a legal status accordingly debars the receiving State from intervening in the Consulate's internal staff affairs (a point never even touched upon by the respondent Welfare Office) since the Consulate must enjoy full freedom, in the interests of the proper representation of the sending State, to organize its services in accordance with its own individual requirements (see also Steinmann, 1965 *MDR* 795-6).

There is also nothing in the terms of the agreement concluded in . . . 1981 between the complainant and the co-respondent to make Section 15 *SchwbG* applicable in this case. That agreement, which is in French, contains the following clause: *Le présent contrat est renouvelable chaque année par tacite reconduction. Il peut être dénoncé de part et d'autre dans les conditions fixées par la législation locale.* "This contract may be renewed each year by tacit agreement. It may be terminated by either party in accordance with the conditions laid down by local law." The agreement contains no specific provision dealing with the point at issue here and therefore requires interpretation. Sections 133 and 157 of the Civil Code (*BGB*) provide that agreements are to be interpreted in accordance with the requirements of good faith (*Treu und Glauben*) and having regard to normal *commercial* practice (*Verkehrssitte*). The clause has been drawn in wide terms. Taking the words used in isolation, it would certainly appear that termination of the agreement is to be governed by local law as a whole, which would include both Federal and Regional *Land* law, and hence also the *Schwerbehindertengesetz*. However, to interpret the agreement in so broad a manner would be contrary to the particular nature of the legal relationship between the parties. In the first place, it

could hardly have been intended that the *Schwerbehindertengesetz* should apply to the agreement, since at the time of its conclusion there was no indication that the co-respondent was disabled. Moreover, there is nothing to suggest that the form of words chosen necessarily included the requirement of the respondent's consent pursuant to Section 15 *SchwbG*. As has already been pointed out, this requirement must be characterized as a provision of public law. There is nothing in the overall context to suggest that it was the complainant's intention that the terms of the contract should include such a provision . . . Furthermore, the final decisive point is that if the complainant had intended to include such a requirement, given the public-law nature of the consent procedure described above, it would in effect have been submitting itself to the sovereign power of the German State. This would necessarily have entailed a corresponding waiver of immunity. Such waiver may be express or implied, but is always required (see von Schönfeld, *loc. cit.*, 2983). On the facts before this Court there is absolutely no evidence that, in signing the contract of employment, the complainant intended to make so far-reaching a commitment.
. . .

[Report: 27 *Archiv des Völkerrechts* 1989-90, p. 389 (in German)]

State immunity — Jurisdictional immunity — Consular employee—National of receiving State employed as financial assistant — Dismissal — Claim for unlawful dismissal — Whether foreign State entitled to jurisdictional immunity— Whether assistant performing sovereign functions—Whether assistant integrated into organizational structure of consulate —Whether enquiry by municipal courts into lawfulness of dismissal would infringe sovereignty of foreign State

Consular relations—Consular employee—Financial assistant — Whether performing consular functions — Vienna Convention on Consular Relations, 1963, Article 5 —

Whether judicial enquiry into circumstances of dismissal would interfere with consular functions—The law of the Federal Republic of Germany

MULLER *v.* UNITED STATES OF AMERICA

(Case No 10 Sa 1506/97)

Federal Republic of Germany, Regional Labour Court (LAG) of Hesse

(Niedenthal, *President*; Henninger and Mayer, *Judges*)

11 *May* 1998

SUMMARY: *The facts:*—Mr Muller, a German national, was employed from 1992 to 1996 as a financial assistant responsible for analysis and budgetary preparation at the United States Consulate General in Frankfurt. In 1996 his employment was terminated for reasons of "organizational restructuring" and he was offered new employment at a lower grade. He instituted proceedings before the German courts seeking a declaration that the termination of his employment was void since it was unjustifiable on social grounds. The United States argued that the German courts had no jurisdiction over the claim because the plaintiff was responsible for the fulfilment of sovereign functions. The Labour Court *(AG)* of Frankfurt accepted the plea of lack of jurisdiction and the plaintiff appealed.

Held:—The United States was entitled to jurisdictional immunity.

(1) The plaintiff clearly had a staff function within the consular administration. The preparation and drafting of budget plans for the financing of the work of a consulate fell within the core area of consular activity since they determined and limited the scope of that work. A person performing such tasks was entrusted with a function directly related to the fulfilment of consular functions. It was therefore not relevant to consider the necessary limits imposed upon the doctrine of State immunity (p. 518).

(2) The question of the social justification for the alteration of the terms and conditions of the employment of the plaintiff related to the organizational structure of the Consulate of the Defendant State. Any examination of whether the decision at issue was reasonable or arbitrary would necessarily involve the danger that the administrative and organizational structure of the Consulate would be subjected to judicial review involving an assessment of how it worked. The manner in which a foreign State provided for the fulfilment of consular tasks from an organizational standpoint was a matter for sovereign decision and could not be subject to judicial review. Such an examination would adversely affect the guarantee under international law of the unimpeded fulfilment of consular functions (pp. 518-19).

The text of the judgment of the Court commences on the following page.

OPERATIVE PART OF THE JUDGMENT

The plaintiff's appeal against the judgment of the Labour Court of Frankfurt am Main of 6 March 1997 (No 3 Ca 4355/96) is dismissed with costs. Leave to appeal on points of law is granted.

Facts and Procedure

The parties are in dispute concerning a notice of termination of employment pending a change of contract.

The plaintiff has been employed at the Consulate General of the United States of America in Frankfurt am Main since 1 July 1992, on the basis of a contract dated 24 June 1992, most recently with an annual gross remuneration of DM 87,000.00. He is employed as a so-called Financial Assistant and is classified in Remuneration Category FSN 9. According to the contract, the conditions of employment are determined by the "FSN Handbook" and a "Compensation Plan". The plaintiff's tasks at work are regulated by a job description relating to Job No N53405. He is there described as first financial adviser to the managing administrative officials and as head of department. As such, his tasks include the analysis of financial information of the Consulate relating to both past financial years and the various current budget programmes, as well as the formulation of the Consulate's budget plan for submission to the Embassy. For further details, reference is made to the translation of the job description submitted by the plaintiff (pp. 56-7 of the writ) and the copy of the employment contract (pp. 3-4 of the writ).

In a letter dated 10 May 1996, the Defendant State terminated the employment relationship with the plaintiff from 31 January 1997, on the basis of the abolition of the plaintiff's position for organizational reasons. At the same time it offered the plaintiff continued employment under different conditions, down-grading him to the position of Financial Management Analyst at the remuneration level FSN 8. The plaintiff accepted the change of working conditions offered, subject to their social justification. The plaintiff applied for the position of Supervisory Financial Management Analyst, remunerated at level FSN 10, which was a new post at the Consulate General created in the course of the same organizational rearrangement. This application was unsuccessful.

In his action the plaintiff objects to the legal validity of the notice of termination pending a change of contract. He believes that German jurisdiction applies and that German labour law is applicable.

In particular, the plaintiff argues that the formation, alteration or cancellation of an employment relationship with a consular employee is attributable to the private-law sphere and does not constitute sovereign activity for which a foreign State can claim immunity and consequently cannot be sued in a German court. In addition, the plaintiff submits that the tasks assigned to him according to his job description did not form part of the core area of the exercise of foreign power of the Defendant State. He did not make any decisions nor did he perform any sovereign acts. Furthermore, he argues that, under the same conditions, the Defendant State would not grant immunity to a foreign State which was sued before an American court. He also maintains that the same conclusion results from the European Convention on State Immunity (Council of Europe). The plaintiff finally argues that his former position has not been abolished but has been filled by someone else after minimal changes.

The plaintiff seeks a ruling that the notice of termination pending a change of contract, dated 10 May 1996, is invalid.

The Defendant State asks for the dismissal of the claim.

The United States of America argues that German jurisdiction is excluded for the present claim, because sovereign activity is involved. It submits that the plaintiff's tasks in particular relate to the financial sovereignty of the sending State and the shaping of consular policy. In addition, the notice of termination pending a change of contract was based on organizational changes in the course of a reorganization of all diplomatic and consular offices in anticipation of the forthcoming move of the United States Embassy from Bonn to Berlin. German jurisdiction is excluded because a foreign State could not be prohibited by German labour courts' jurisdiction from creating certain consular organizational structures, which led to the abolition of the plaintiff's former position, without encroaching on the core area of sovereign activity. Likewise, according to the United States, a foreign State cannot be given directions as regards the persons to which it must entrust specific tasks.

The Defendant State has also submitted that the plaintiff's department has been totally reorganized, so that he no longer had to perform monitoring functions. Accordingly, the plaintiff did not have a claim to promotion to the newly created position with a broader sphere of responsibility.

The Labour Court rejected the claim on the ground that it was not competent to decide the issue because the Defendant State was not subject to German jurisdiction in the dispute between the parties concerning the validity of the notice of termination pending a change of contract. For further details, reference is made to the judgment under appeal of 6 May 1997.

The plaintiff's appeal against this judgment, served on him on 3 July 1997, was lodged on 4 August 1997 and substantiated on 6 October 1997, after an extension of the deadline for the substantiation of the appeal . . .

The plaintiff repeats and expands on his legal arguments at first instance, in accordance with which the present case does not involve sovereign acts of the Defendant State and, in particular, the plaintiff did not perform any consular tasks as defined in the Vienna Convention of 24 April 1963 and the Act of 26 August 1969 which implements the Convention. In support of his argument he refers to the rules which, since 1976, apply in the United States and those applicable in the United Kingdom since 1978. He asserts that these result in there being no immunity for foreign States in comparable cases in those countries.

The plaintiff requests that the Court allow the appeal and quash the judgment of the Labour Court of Frankfurt am Main dated 6 March 1997 (No 3 Ca 4355/96).

The Defendant State requests that the appeal be dismissed with costs.

The United States of America defends the judgment under appeal, repeating and expanding on its submissions at first instance regarding the facts and the law. In addition, the United States submits that the question of how the finance department of a consulate is organized, and which persons shall be entrusted with managerial tasks involving personnel management and internal administrative responsibility, falls within the core area of State immunity and is therefore not subject to German jurisdiction. As far as further details of the submissions of the parties are concerned, reference is made to the contents of the writs exchanged.

Grounds of the Decision
The plaintiff's appeal is admissible so far as the subject-matter of the complaint is concerned and the appeal was lodged and substantiated in the proper form and in good time. However, the appeal is unfounded. The Labour Court correctly stated that German jurisdiction did not apply and rejected the claim as inadmissible.

The Labour Court correctly based its assessment on the principles of State immunity developed in the case-law of the Federal Constitutional Court and the Federal Labour Court. In the event of a lack of international treaty law or other legal provisions the question as to whether and to what extent a foreign State is subject to German jurisdiction must be assessed in accordance with the general rules of international law (Section 20 paragraph 2 of the Judicature Act (*Gerichtsverfassungsgesetz—GVG*)). According to general customary international law foreign States are not subject to German jurisdiction to the extent to which the subject-matter of the dispute relates to the sovereign activity of those States. The decisive factor in distinguishing between sovereign and non-sovereign State activity is not the motive or purpose of the activity, but rather the nature of the act in dispute or the disputed legal relationship. The delimitation between the two areas of activity must be made according to national law (Federal Constitutional Court (*BVerfG*), 30 April 1963, 16 *BVerfGE* 27).[1] Nevertheless, national law may only be used for making this distinction subject to the proviso that State activities or relevant legal relationships may not be excluded from the sovereign sphere if, according to the opinion predominantly held by States, they belong to the sphere of State authority in the narrower and true sense. Thus, activities regarded as falling within the private-law sphere under national law must be viewed as sovereign if they are attributable to the core area of State authority (*BVerfG*, *loc. cit.*). The case-law of the Federal Labour Court is also based on these principles (*BAG*, 3 July 1996, No 2 AZR 513/95;[2] *BAG*, 20 November 1997, No 2 AZR 631/96).

Doubt is not cast on the application of these principles, and in particular the content of customary international law as found by the Federal Constitutional Court (*loc. cit.*), by the references of the plaintiff to provisions of national and European treaty law. The European Convention on State Immunity of 1972 (Council of Europe) cannot unilaterally sweep aside applicable customary international law and have effect against the United States of America. The same would apply to national statutory rules, dating respectively from 1976 and 1978, in the United States of America and the United Kingdom, although it remains unclear on which individual provisions the plaintiff bases his opinion that the United States would not grant immunity to a foreign State in comparable cases. The case-law of the Federal Labour Court in any case is still based on the findings of the Federal Constitutional Court regarding customary international law and the principles developed therefrom on the determination of the limits of the immunity to be granted to foreign States, including the Defendant State in the case (*BAG*, 20 November 1997, *loc. cit.*).

It is beyond doubt that the formation, alteration and termination of an employment relationship take place in private-law form under national law. It is likewise beyond doubt that this fact alone is not decisive according to the principles described above. If the core area of State authority is affected, the private-law character of the relationship takes on secondary importance.

An effect on the core area of State activity can result, on the one hand, from the fact that the subject-matter of the employment relationship is the fulfilment of tasks which in themselves are to be attributed to the exercise of State authority of the foreign State concerned. On the other hand, such an effect can arise from the fact that the act or measure of that State at issue (in this case the

[1 45 *ILR* 57.]   [2 See p. 502 above.]

notification of termination pending a change of contract) cannot be brought before a German court, and thus be the subject-matter of judicial review there, without an infringement of State immunity.

As regards the first point, reference can be made to the accurate comments of the Labour Court (p. 5 of the judgment), with which this Court agrees (see Section 64(6) of the Labour Courts Act (*ArbGG*) and Section 543(1) of the Code of Civil Procedure (*ZPO*)). In performing the task entrusted to him in the past the plaintiff clearly had a staff function within the consular administration. Amongst other things, he was responsible for analysing the financial data of the Consulate and formulating the current budget plan on the basis of that data. The preparation and drafting of budget plans for the purposes of carrying out and financing the work of the Consulate, in particular as defined by the Vienna Convention on Consular Relations of 24 April 1963 (cf. Act on the Convention of 26 August 1969, *BGBl.* II, 69, 1585), falls within the core area of consular activity in the receiving State. It determines and limits the actual scope of the Consulate's work. Decisions within this area are sovereign in nature. Any person performing a staff function as "first financial assistant to the managing administrative officials", devising instructions which the management of the Consulate cannot simply ignore, is entrusted with a function which directly relates to the fulfilment of consular tasks. Given such a function it is no longer relevant to consider the effect of the necessary limits to State immunity caused by the fact that States nowadays assert ever-increasing influence in areas which were formerly the preserve of private individuals.

This Court in fact considers that the need to grant immunity arises from an examination of the social justification of the notice of termination pending a change of contract, which is required assuming the applicability of German law in accordance with the plaintiff's submissions (see *BAG*, 20 November 1997, *loc. cit.*).

According to the assertion of the Defendant State the triggering circumstance and justification, for the notice of termination pending a change of contract, is the reorganization of all diplomatic and consular offices, which in turn is caused by the forthcoming move of the Embassy to Berlin. The Defendant State further asserts that the position formerly occupied by the plaintiff has been abolished, new administrative structures have been established and that a new higher-paid job with more extensive responsibilities and powers has been created, alongside which there is no longer any need for a position like the one formerly held by the plaintiff. The notice of termination pending a change of contract is thus justified for reasons of business organization. It may be assumed that the employer is in principle free in his decision as to how to structure and organize his business in order to achieve his business aims in the most effective and cost-efficient way possible. This also includes the freedom to group functions together and to take organizational decisions which lead to the abolition of jobs in the business. Even the pursued aim of concentrating work amongst the remaining jobs is in principle not objectionable from the point of view of the law on unfair dismissal (see, however, *contra*, Preis, *NZA* 1995, pp. 241-5). Such entrepreneurial organizational decisions should not be examined for their material legal justification and their expediency, but rather only to establish whether they are obviously unreasonable or arbitrary (*BAG*, 24 April 1997, cited above). Such an examination is necessary but sufficient in order to recognize feigned excuses, hidden "substitution" dismissals and similar types of cases. This examination in turn requires complete disclosure of the changed concept and the main considerations supporting it by the employer, on the one hand, and also an assessment of its plausibility and amenability to review by the Labour Court. In the present case, the labour courts would also have to examine the newly created internal administrative and organizational structure of the Consulate to see whether its suitability for the fulfilment of the tasks of the Consulate is plausible, understandable and convincing. The result of such an examination is open, even given the restricted scope of review, because there are uncertain legal and factual concepts. Such an examination would therefore necessarily involve the danger that the labour courts would exercise review powers with regard to the internal adminis-tration and organizational structure of the Consulate in a manner which assessed and judged them. The way in which a foreign State seeks to ensure the fulfilment of consular tasks from an organizational standpoint is a matter of sovereign decision. It does not have to account to the German courts for the creation of organizational structures and their plausible suitability for the fulfilment of tasks in the consular field. If the opposite view were taken, this would constitute an encroachment on consular activity because such an examination would adversely affect the guarantee under international law of the unimpeded fulfilment of the tasks of the Consulate.

The decision as to costs is based on Section 97 of the Code of Civil Procedure (*ZPO*).

Leave to appeal on points of law is granted in accordance with Section 72(2)(1) of the Labour Courts Act (*ArbGG*).

[Report: Unpublished]

State immunity — Jurisdictional immunity — National of receiving State employed by information agency of foreign State as secretary and telephonist—Contract of employment —Claim for arrears of salary following termination of contract—Whether foreign State entitled to jurisdictional immunity—Whether employee integrated into the organizational structure of foreign State—Nature of work done by information agency—Whether inquiry by court into nature of employment tasks violating jurisdictional immunity— The law of Italy

LIBYAN ARAB JAMAHIRIYA *v.* TROBBIANI

(Decision No 145/1990)

Italy, Court of Cassation (Plenary Session). 16 *January* 1990

(Brancaccio, *President*)

SUMMARY: *The facts*:—Ms Trobbiani was employed by the Libyan State and worked for the Jana Information Agency from 1984 to 1986 as a secretary and telephonist, her duties including the preparation of newspaper cuttings. In 1987 she instituted proceedings against Libya before the Examining Magistrate (*Pretore*) of Rome, claiming arrears of salary allegedly payable under Italian law because she had been wrongly graded. Libya objected that the Italian courts lacked jurisdiction and applied to the Court of Cassation for settlement of the jurisdictional issue as a preliminary question.

Held:—The Italian courts lacked jurisdiction.

(1) Employment contracts between Italian citizens and foreign States were not excluded from the jurisdiction of the Italian courts where their purpose was the provision of services of a manual nature, merely auxiliary to the activities of a public-law character of the foreign sovereign entity. But this was not the case where a person was employed in an administrative capacity within a foreign State's information agency, and was accordingly fully integrated into the public-law organizational structure of that State, which directed its information policy through that agency.

(2) Under customary international law, whenever the substantive relationship on which the courts were called upon to adjudicate was properly to be regarded, by virtue of its nature, functions or other effective links, as coming within the ambit of a foreign State's sovereign power, then it was excluded from the jurisdiction of national courts. In such circumstances the courts were excluded from conducting an enquiry into the facts as well as from handing down judgments.

(3) Accordingly, the courts had no jurisdiction with regard to a dispute concerning a job description which was claimed to justify a higher grading within the foreign State's administrative structure, since this would entail an

encroachment on activities coming within the scope of the State's right of self-organization so far as the substance or confidentiality of its sovereign activities were concerned. Such a dispute went beyond the purely financial aspects of the employment relationship and was therefore covered by jurisdictional immunity.

The following is the text of the relevant part of the judgment of the Court:

Course of the Proceedings—In an application lodged on 26 February 1987 with the Rome Magistrate (*Pretore*) sitting as a labour judge, Rossana Trobbiani stated that she had been employed from 5 August 1984 to 4 May 1986 by the diplomatic mission, or People's Office, of the Libyan Arab Socialist Jamahiriya, working for the Jana Agency as a fourth-level employee with duties of secretary and telephonist and responsibility for the preparation of newspaper cuttings for press-review purposes. She further stated that, under the National Labour Code (*CCNL*) for embassy employees, administrative staff were automatically classified as fifth-level employees, and accordingly she sought a declaration from the Court that the respondent was under a duty, "in accordance with the law and by virtue of the relevant provisions of the National Labour Code, applicable by analogy in accordance with Article 36 of the Constitution", to pay her an additional amount of 8,924,314 lire, representing difference in salary and compensation in lieu of notice.

In the course of the proceedings before the lower court, Libya lodged a request for a preliminary ruling on jurisdiction, claiming that the Italian courts had no jurisdiction in the matter . . .

Grounds of the Decision—The People's Libyan Arab Socialist Jamahiriya argues that in this dispute it is immune from Italian jurisdiction by reason of the combined effect of a number of qualifying circumstances, namely: the fact that the contract of employment was performed on its premises; the nature of its organ, the Jana Agency, for which the applicant carried out her duties, and the functions of that organ, whose purpose was to give official voice to its political stance in relation to foreign States; and the fact that the duties carried out by the applicant were closely linked with that State purpose.

In response, Rossana Trobbiani argues that the duties which she was employed to perform were of a merely routine nature, and thus failed to satisfy the requirement of being directed to the achievement of the institutional purposes of a public-law nature of the foreign State, such a requirement being a prerequisite, according to the jurisprudence of this Court, for the existence of jurisdictional immunity.

In these proceedings the Italian courts lack jurisdiction.

From the parties' submissions it is clearly not in dispute that the plaintiff was employed by the Libyan State, and that the activities of the Jana Agency, where she carried out her duties, are directly referable to that State. This second point of agreement is moreover one generally accepted. It is common knowledge how much importance is currently attached to information policy, particularly by sovereign States, who take a special interest in instruments serving to reflect the complexity of their views within the international community, to the point where they may well insist on exercising absolute control over the means assigned by them to projecting their image abroad.

The plaintiff, an employee of the Libyan State, worked for the Jana Agency as a secretary and telephonist. Her duties also involved the "preparation" of newspaper cuttings for purposes of a review of the press. The exact nature of this latter duty is not clear. "Preparation" could refer either to purely material duties or to work substantially greater in scope, more closely connected with the agency's functions. On the other hand, the first two types of duty clearly denote a position of trust within the organization, inasmuch as they are directly bound up with the work of its officials and also inevitably involve access in practice to information concerning the agency's official activities and business (for a similar view, in relation to the work of an embassy secretary, see Plenary Decision No 1282 of this Court of 15 March 1989). It may accordingly be concluded that there was an objective internal link, both immediate and direct, between the employment relationship and the institutional aims of the Jana Agency, and hence that the applicant was fully integrated into the public-law organizational structure of the foreign State, which conducted its information policy through that Agency.

However, this is not necessarily conclusive of the matter.

Under the most recent jurisprudence of this Court (first expressed in Plenary Decision No 2329 of 15 May 1989[1]) the jurisdiction of the receiving State must be upheld, in accordance with the trend of customary international law, even where the employee's duties involve collaboration in public functions of the sending State, if the claim concerns "purely financial aspects of the employment relationship out of which the dispute arose". In such cases, it has been held that the receiving State's jurisdiction does not constitute an interference with the organization and functions of the official agency of the foreign State.

We must therefore now define what constitutes for present purposes a "purely financial aspect of the employment relationship" with the foreign State that does not involve interference with its sovereignty.

To this end we must consider the effect of acts by the receiving State in exercise of its power of jurisdiction, in so far as these are liable to

[1 101 *ILR* 380.]

encroach upon the internal domain of the sending State's sovereignty, and hence to impugn that sovereignty by interfering in some way with the relationships through which it is expressed.

The jurisdiction which a State articulates and expresses by virtue of its *jus imperii* consists of two elements: the power of decision or *jus dicere*, and the power of enquiry or *jus facta conoscere*. In both cases the "justiciary State" (*Stato judice*), by virtue of its sovereign power, exercises authority over the parties, effectively obliging them to undergo examination and then to have the facts in their disputes definitively and "judicially" established and the law determined. This system cannot operate where one of the parties claims that, because of the close link between the relationship at issue and its own sovereignty, it is entitled to be accorded equal status with the court. That is to say, it is by definition subject only to its own law (*auto-legittimata*), in the fullest sense of the term, and hence cannot be expected to submit to requests for information imposed upon it by the court. Inasmuch as customary international law (which under Article 10 of the Constitution is applicable within the Italian legal order) enshrines the principle that one sovereign State shall be immune from the jurisdiction of another, then it protects such sovereignty in the widest sense, safeguarding not only a State's freedom of action but also the confidentiality of that action. Thus immunity from jurisdiction (the right not to be judged) signifies freedom from the obligation to submit, as a party to legal proceedings, to examination by a foreign court and then to the judgment consequent upon that examination. This remains the true view of the law, it being by no means established that the "restrictive" approach to State immunity has been superseded as a result of the modern tendency (noted in Decision 2329/89 *supra*[2]) on the part of certain States to reduce its scope still further.

The dividing line between the receiving State's right of jurisdiction and jurisdictional immunity is determined by the connective features (*requisiti connettivi*) of the substantive issue on which the court is called upon to adjudicate: whenever these place the matter, by virtue of its nature, function or other effective links, within the ambit of the foreign State's sovereign power, then it is excluded from the receiving State's jurisdiction, in the full sense of the term, that is to say from both the court's power to make enquiry into the facts and the power to hand down judgments.

Thus, where it is impossible to evaluate the financial consequences of a matter presenting these connective features without at the same time adjudicating, in the wide sense referred to above, upon the relationship out of which the claim is alleged to arise, then in effect the relationship itself becomes the subject of the court's enquiry. The court examines what the relationship actually involves and should

[² *Ibid.*]

involve and passes judgment on both aspects. In such circumstances the subject-matter of the dispute passes out of the realm of the merely financial.

On the other hand, where, on the basis of the *causa petendi* and the *petitum* taken together, it is clear that, over and above its pecuniary nature, the matter into which the court is called upon to enquire and to pass judgment is in substance wholly dissociated from any of the connective features referred to above, then it may be said that it is purely the financial aspect that is at issue. In other words, the matter at issue is such that, *a priori*, there is no possibility of encroachment—not just by the court's *jus dicere* but also by its *jus facta cognoscere*—upon the substance, or even the confidentiality, of the sovereign activities and transactions of the foreign State.

This will be the case, for example, where the claim is for payment of sums due in respect of remuneration whose amounts are not in dispute, or for additional amounts on account of late payment of sums whose exact amounts are known.

Applying this distinction, it is clear that there is a close dependence, both in logic (in relation to the power of judicial enquiry) and, particularly, in law (in relation to the power of adjudication) between the financial aspects of a relationship covered by immunity and the relationship itself. This is the case where, in a staff dispute which interferes (or has interfered) with the public-law organizational structure of the foreign State, the plaintiff requests the national court, in proceedings brought against that State, to pass judgment on acts of the defendant coming within the scope of its right of self-organization (for example where it is alleged, as in the present case, that the duties performed by the plaintiff entitled her to a higher grading within the foreign State's administrative structure). We would emphasize that this is the case, even where the claim involves only a factual enquiry (and not the handing down of a judgment) into the sovereign internal activities of the foreign State, such as those relating to the scope of the duties performed by the plaintiff. In effect, even here the investigative and inquisitorial implications of the proceedings necessarily involve an intrusion by the jurisdictional power of the justiciary State into the sovereign domain of the foreign State (for example through the admission, taking and evaluation of evidence as to the duties which the plaintiff employee of the foreign State claims to have performed).

Having declared that the Italian courts do not have jurisdiction in this case, we consider it fair and reasonable that the costs of the entire proceedings should be borne by the respective parties.

[Report: *RDI* 1990, p. 402 (in Italian)]

State immunity — Jurisdictional immunity — National of receiving State employed by commercial office of foreign State as secretary and administrative officer—Dismissal—Claim for reinstatement and unpaid allowances—Whether foreign State entitled to jurisdictional immunity—Restrictive theory of immunity — Scope of application to disputes concerning employment contracts — Limitation to cases where there is actual likelihood of interference with performance of sovereign functions — Types of claims involving such interference — Distinction between claims for reinstatement or damages and claims for unpaid allowances

Sources of international law—Customary international law —European Convention on State Immunity, 1972—Whether evidence of established customary international law — Doctrine of restrictive immunity in relation to employment contracts—Application in State which has signed but not ratified the Convention—The law of Italy

NORWEGIAN EMBASSY *v.* QUATTRI

(Decision No 12771/1991)

Italy, Court of Cassation (Plenary Session).   28 *November* 1991

(Zucconi Galli Fonseca, *President*)

SUMMARY: *The facts:*—Ms Quattri was employed by the Commercial Office of the Royal Norwegian Embassy as a secretary and administrative officer from the beginning of 1987 until the end of 1989, when she was dismissed for unspecified "organizational reasons". In 1990 she brought proceedings against Norway before the Examining Magistrate (*Pretore*) of Milan, claiming reinstatement, damages and various allowances payable under Italian law. The Norwegian Embassy claimed immunity from the jurisdiction of the Italian courts and applied to the Court of Cassation for a preliminary ruling on the jurisdictional issue.

Held:—The Italian courts lacked jurisdiction over the claim for reinstatement and damages but they were competent to exercise jurisdiction over the claim for unpaid allowances.

(1) Under customary international law, a foreign State was immune from the jurisdiction of other States in respect of employment relationships created for purposes of the achievement of its institutional aims, but such immunity was restricted to acts carried out in exercise of its public-law functions. Thus there was no immunity in respect of acts carried out by the foreign State on

the territory of another State in the capacity of an ordinary individual governed by the private law of the receiving State, even where those acts were necessary for the establishment, organization and proper operation of an official agency of the foreign State (pp. 527-8).

(2) The Italian State was not entitled to interfere in the performance of duties which were intrinsic to a public-law entity of a foreign State. The essential question was therefore whether the decision sought from the court was actually likely in practice to interfere with the essential core of the foreign State's functions. Such interference did not occur where the court exercised jurisdiction in respect of disputes arising out of employment relationships in which the employee carried out duties of a merely auxiliary nature. The same applied where the claim involved purely financial issues, unless there was direct interference with the public-law powers of the foreign State with regard to the manner in which it organized its ambassadorial offices or services, as where acceptance of the claim would imply a declaration that an employee's dismissal was invalid (pp. 528-9 and 531).

(3) This approach, which was in line with and further developed the jurisprudence of the Italian courts, reflected the current trend in international practice to restrict still further the scope of jurisdictional immunity in relation to employment contracts between foreign States and citizens of the receiving State, although in the current state of the law a new practice at variance with the old could not yet be regarded as fully established. A significant indication of this trend was contained in the European Convention on State Immunity, 1972, which had been ratified by a number of major European States and signed but not ratified by Italy. At the very least, it recognized the current position in international law with regard to the progressive restriction of the scope of State immunity in the case of employment contracts (pp. 529-30).

The following is the text of the relevant part of the judgment of the Court:

Course of the Proceedings—In an application lodged on 16 January 1990 with the Milan Magistrate (*Pretore*) sitting as a labour judge, Monica Quattri, a [former] employee of the Italo-Norwegian Chamber of Commerce of Milan under the collective regime for the commercial sector, stated that on 15 January 1987 she had been hired by the Commercial Office of the Royal Norwegian Embassy with duties of secretary, technical-administrative officer, etc., under a contract which referred expressly to the laws and regulations currently in force [in Italy], particularly as regards pregnancy and maternity. It was further provided that, in the event of her employment being terminated, she was to be given notice of not less than three calendar months. On 16 June 1989 she had married and on 1 December of the same year she had been dismissed without notice for unspecified "organizational reasons". She contended that her dismissal, which she strongly disputed, was invalid, in that (i) it was contrary to Section 7 of the Law of 9 January 1963 and (ii) it had been notified to her without an accompanying statement of grounds or adequate reasons, in breach of the contractual regime governing her employment. She further alleged that she had not been paid the cashier's till allowance (*indennità di cassa*) due in respect of the duties carried out by her.

She accordingly requested the *Pretore*:

(1) to declare her dismissal invalid and order that she be reinstated in her former post;

(2) to order the Embassy to pay her a till allowance;

(3) to order the Embassy to pay her salary from the date of her dismissal until the date of her reinstatement;

(4) to order that she be compensated for the loss suffered in consequence of her unlawful dismissal, in accordance with Section 18 of Law No 300 of 1970;

(5) to order that the Embassy pay her the allowance due to her in lieu of notice, termination allowance, and thirteenth and fourteenth month and holiday allowance in respect of the year 1989, plus interest and revaluation costs.

Having entered an appearance, the Norwegian Embassy, by way of preliminary point, claimed immunity from the jurisdiction of the Italian courts. In the course of the first-instance proceedings it lodged an application for a preliminary ruling on jurisdiction, supported by a written memorial and opposed by Ms Quattri with a counter-petition.

Grounds of the Decision—The Royal Norwegian Embassy contends that Monica Quattri, being a permanently integrated member of its organizational structure, albeit in the commercial sector, with administrative duties including decision-making powers, involving special responsibility and a duty of secrecy, had become part of the public-law organizational structure of the Kingdom of Norway, with whose aims the activities of the Commercial Office were closely connected. Accordingly, it invokes the principle of customary international law *par in parem non habet jurisdictionem*, applicable in Italian law by virtue of Article 10 of the Constitution, and hence contends that the Italian courts have no jurisdiction in the proceedings brought by Ms Quattri before the Milan *Pretore* sitting as a labour judge. It further argues that such immunity from jurisdiction is not precluded by the fact that the employment contract is specifically stated to be governed by Italian law.

On the question of jurisdiction . . . we would begin by stating that, under customary international law, it is recognized that there is an area within which a foreign State enjoys immunity from the jurisdiction of another State with regard to relationships entered into for purposes of the achievement of its institutional aims, but this is restricted to acts carried out by the State in exercise of its public functions.

With regard to acts carried out by a foreign sovereign power on the territory of another State in the capacity of a private-law subject under the internal legal order of the receiving State, that is to say transactions (not falling within the ambit of the *jus imperii*) which take the form of private-law relationships necessary for purposes of the establishment, organization and proper functioning of an official agency of the foreign State, but which are only indirectly connected with the exercise of public functions, it has been held that these in principle fall outside the scope of [jurisdictional] immunity. They include, for example, a contract for the rental of a building to be used as consular offices and contracts for the supply of goods.

More delicate problems arise in relation to employment contracts concluded on the territory of the receiving State between citizens of that State and the sending State and covering activities to be performed on that territory. Such contracts have special characteristics, which derive from the fact that . . . the relationship thus created concerns . . . not an object but a human being, charged with the performance of a human task, to be carried out subject to, and for purposes of, the aims of the [foreign] State to which the official agency established on another State's territory belongs.

It has been pointed out (see Decision No 2329 of 15 May 1989[1]) that the special nature of such contracts resides in the fact that the use which the foreign State derives from them (by contrast with those for the supply of some material item) is based on a collaborative relationship in the true sense of the term. It has also been stated (see Decision No 3374 of 18 July 1989) that the problem does not arise— contrary to the situation here, where there was clearly an agreement to make the contract of employment subject to Italian law, but (only) with regard to its substance—where there has been an agreement (in that case between the Association of Italian Knights of the Sovereign Order of Malta and the Region of Lazio), in the sense of an acceptance, that the contract of employment should be *entirely* governed by the law of the Italian State, that is to say not merely as to substance but also in its procedural aspects, with a consequent waiver . . . of [jurisdictional] immunity.

Where, as in the present case, no such waiver can be inferred, then it must be determined whether and how far the local court may intervene, by conducting proceedings, gathering evidence and handing down decisions concerning the relationship between the employee/ citizen and the employer/foreign State, given that such intervention touches very closely on the essential core of that State's activities and functions.

In this regard we have no difficulty in reaffirming the rule that the receiving State, and hence its courts, may not interfere in the performance of duties which are intrinsic to the foreign public-law entity, and that this will not be the case where the employee's duties are of a merely auxiliary nature.

However, Decision No 2329 of 1989[2] also lays down an additional criterion, although it shares the same rationale, that the Italian court must consider whether the decision sought from it by the employee is actually likely to interfere in practice with the functioning of the foreign public-law entity. Thus where the potential for such interference does not exist, immunity is excluded, even in the case of employees carrying out high-level duties.

This jurisprudence . . . reflects the current trend in international practice (although, in the current state of the law, a practice markedly at variance with that previously obtaining cannot yet be regarded as established) to restrict still further the scope of jurisdictional immunity in relation to employment contracts between foreign States and citizens of the receiving State.

A significant indication of this trend is the Basle Convention of 16 May 1972 (which entered into force on 16 May 1976), which Italy has signed but not yet ratified, but which has been ratified by certain major European States, such as the United Kingdom and Germany, and also by Switzerland, Belgium, the Netherlands, Austria, Luxembourg and Cyprus, and has been accorded the status of a document which, at the very least, recognizes the current position in international law with regard to the progressive restriction of the scope of State immunity (see Decisions Nos 4502 of 21 October 1977[3] and 5819 of 23 November 1985[4]). The Convention, which excludes immunity in the case of employment contracts concluded and to be performed within the receiving State, has been implemented by the United Kingdom through the State Immunity Act of 1978, following the precedent set by the United States with its Foreign Sovereign Immunities Act of 1976.

It was in this context that Decision No 2329 of 1989[5] established the aforementioned criterion as the limit to immunity. In so doing it was attempting to reconcile the need to ensure respect for the foreign State (by recognizing its right to immunity within the essential core area of its functions) with the need to ensure that, within their own State, former employees possess the means to protect their rights, in particular through access to their own courts, an essential requirement in order to enable them to obtain justice through means readily accessible to them. Thus the question is whether the decision sought from the court is actually likely to interfere in practice with that essential core of the foreign State's functions. On this basis it was decided that no such potential for interference exists, and hence

[2 *Ibid.*]
[3 77 *ILR* 602.]

[4 87 *ILR* 20.]
[5 101 *ILR* 380.]

immunity is excluded, whenever the claim and the decision upholding it concern purely financial aspects of the employment relationship which gave rise to the dispute brought before the Italian courts.

However, since that Decision a new tendency has emerged (see Decision No 145 of 16 January 1990[6]), which suggests that the area of immunity could be wider than previously indicated. This latter Decision, while excluding immunity in the case of an employee performing duties linked to the public-law activities of the foreign sovereign body (and thus integrated into its organizational structure) where the dispute satisfies the condition of being purely financial in essence, nonetheless ruled that jurisdiction must be refused where the employee occupied a position of trust within the organizational structure (working for the Embassy press office) and her claim, notwithstanding its essentially financial nature, nonetheless affected the sovereign powers of the foreign State, or entailed an assessment or enquiry into the exercise of those powers, as when she claimed that the nature of the duties performed by her entitled her to a higher grading or increased salary. A similar approach was also adopted in Decision No 3248 of 19 April 1990.

Clearly, even where the content of a claim is purely financial, the source of the disputed obligation is always the employment relationship between the foreign State and its employee (and that relationship inevitably remains bound up with the decision sought from the national court). This Court accordingly takes the view that it is important to avoid a situation where (with the exception of cases where the employee's duties are of a merely auxiliary character) every claim, even those of a purely financial nature, ends up falling outside the jurisdisction of the Italian courts, to an extent going beyond the reasonable limits imposed by the need to respect the essential core of the foreign State's functions. Effectively, those limits could largely be determined by the grounds of objection taken by the defendant State or sovereign entity, depending on how far these involved a thoroughgoing enquiry into the relationship on which the claim was based. The result would be that the said State or entity would become the final arbiter of its own refusal of jurisdiction.

The content of a claim is ascertained not just from the statement of claim (*petitum*), but also from the legal relationship underlying it (*causa petendi*), and it is for the court to determine (over and above the submissions of the parties) what the proceedings actually involve, and to decide, in the context of the *causa petendi* (the employment relationship) relied on by the plaintiff or disputed by the defendant, which aspects of the latter it is entitled to consider. Thus there is nothing to prevent the court from holding that the link between the

[6 See p. 520 above.]

causa petendi and the financial claim may in some cases constitute a bar to jurisdiction, while in others it has no such effect.

Applying these principles, this Court, sitting in plenary session, will now rule on the question of jurisdiction submitted to it . . . The plaintiff, who was already working as secretary to the commercial counsellor of the Norwegian Embassy, was formally recruited by the Embassy on 15 January 1987. Her duties were those of secretary and technical-administrative officer, in other words duties not merely of an auxiliary nature but closely connected with the public-law activities of an official agency of a foreign State.

After being dismissed on 1 December 1989, she brought proceedings before the Milan *Pretore* sitting as a labour judge, requesting that he: (1) declare her dismissal invalid and order that she be reinstated in her former post; (2) order the Embassy to pay her a till allowance; (3) order the Embassy to pay her salary from the date of her dismissal until the date of her reinstatement; (4) order that she be compensated for the loss suffered in consequence of her unlawful dismissal, in accordance with Section 18 of Law No 300 of 1970; (5) and order that the Embassy pay an allowance in lieu of notice, termination allowance, and thirteenth and fourteenth month and holiday allowance in respect of the year 1989.

It is clear from an examination of the content of heads of claim (1), (3) and (4) that these must be excluded from the jurisdiction of the Italian courts, inasmuch as any enquiry into the lawfulness of the dismissal constitutes a direct interference with the public-law powers of the foreign State with regard to the manner in which it organizes its ambassadorial offices and services, which are matters not susceptible of examination by the Italian courts. This lack of jurisdiction (i.e. as to the lawfulness of the dismissal) accordingly extends to those claims whose acceptance would imply a declaration that the dismissal was invalid, namely the claims for reinstatement, consequential loss, and payment of salary from the date of dismissal until reinstatement.

By contrast, examination of the other heads of claim—payment of the till allowance, of the allowance in lieu of notice, termination allowance, and thirteenth and fourteenth month and holiday allowance in respect of the year 1989—do not involve any violation of the [foreign State's] immunity from examination by the Italian courts, which must accordingly be declared to have jurisdiction, since such an examination can be halted when it reaches the threshold of the domain covered by the public-law powers of the foreign State, into whose exercise the courts are not entitled to enquire. (*Omissis.*)

[Report: *RDI* 1991, p. 993 (in Italian)]

State immunity—Jurisdictional immunity—Foreign national employed as driver/interpreter by embassy of foreign State—Contract of employment—Claim against embassy for salary arrears — Whether foreign State entitled to jurisdictional immunity—Subordinate nature of employment — Claim relating to purely financial matters — Whether foreign nationality of claimant relevant—The law of Italy

ZAMBIAN EMBASSY *v.* SENDANAYAKE

(Decision No 5941/1992)

Italy, Court of Cassation (Plenary Session). 18 *May* 1992

(Carotenuto, *President*)

SUMMARY: *The facts*:—Mr Sendanayake was employed by the Zambian Embassy as a driver/interpreter from 1983 to 1987. He claimed arrears of salary on the ground that his remuneration had been incorrectly calculated on the basis of a national collective agreement. The Zambian Embassy invoked jurisdictional immunity and requested a preliminary ruling on this issue from the Court of Cassation.

Held:—The Italian courts were competent to exercise jurisdiction over the claim.

(1) In view of the secondary, auxiliary nature of the duties of a driver/interpreter in relation to the functions and purposes of the embassy of a foreign State, a dispute concerning his terms of employment lay within the jurisdiction of the Italian courts. Moreover, the fact that the dispute was concerned only with financial issues meant that the courts would in any event have had jurisdiction.

(2) The plaintiff's foreign nationality was irrelevant since, under Article 24(1) of the Constitution, all persons were given the right of recourse to the courts to protect their rights and legitimate interests.

The following is the text of the relevant part of the judgment of the Court:

Course of the Proceedings—In an application lodged on 7 September 1990 with the Rome Magistrate (*Pretore*) sitting as a labour judge, Gamin R. Sendanayake stated that he had been employed by the Zambian Embassy from January 1983 to December 1987 as a driver/interpreter. He claimed payment of various sums, representing the difference between the salary due to him under the national collective agreement for embassy employees and that payable in accordance with Article 36 of the Constitution.

The Embassy claimed immunity from the jurisdiction of the Italian courts, both by virtue of its capacity as the representative of a sovereign State and on the ground that Sendanayake was himself a foreigner. In the course of the initial proceedings on the merits, the Embassy sought a preliminary ruling from this Court on the matter of jurisdiction . . .

Grounds of the Decision—The fact that the duties carried out by Sendanayake as driver/interpreter were of a secondary, auxiliary nature in relation to the purposes and functions of the Embassy of the Zambian Republic in Rome brings the dispute within the scope of the jurisdiction of the Italian courts. Under the doctrine of restrictive immunity as accepted in international law and followed by the case-law of this Court (see, *inter alia*, plenary Decision No 5628 of 17 October 1988), it in no sense impugns the sovereignty of the foreign State concerned. Moreover, the dispute is essentially concerned solely with financial matters, the only question at issue between the parties being whether the plaintiff's remuneration is to be calculated by reference to the national collective agreement or the Constitution (Article 36). This fact would in any event have brought the case within the scope of the jurisdiction of the Italian courts, even if Sendanayake's duties had been more closely bound up with the Embassy's institutional functions (see Plenary Decision of this Court No 145 of 16 January 1990[1]).

The Court cannot accept the Embassy's objection based on the fact that the employee is himself non-Italian, being a citizen of Sri Lanka. In fact the Constitution of the Italian Republic (Article 24(1)), grants to "all persons"—and not just to Italian citizens—the right of recourse to the courts to protect their rights and legitimate interests. It has been authoritatively stated (see Constitutional Court Decision No 48 of 1986) that this provision is formulated in terms so general as to cover any form of exclusion from judicial protection, whether subjective or objective. As has been formally recognized (see Constitutional Court Decision No 18 of 1982), it reflects an overriding principle of our legal order, intimately bound up with that of democracy itself, namely "to ensure that, in any dispute of whatever nature, all persons shall at all times have access to a judge and to a judgment".

We accordingly find that the Italian courts have jurisdiction in this case. (*Omissis.*)

[Report: *RDI* 1992, p. 402 (in Italian)]

[1 See p. 520 above.]

State immunity — Jurisdictional immunity — National of receiving State employed as assistant in embassy of foreign State—Contract of employment—Claim against embassy for non-payment of social security contributions required by Italian law — Whether foreign State entitled to jurisdictional immunity — Whether claim relating to purely financial matters—The law of Italy

CARBONAR *v.* MAGURNO

(Decision No 9675/1993)

Italy, Court of Cassation (Plenary Session).   24 *September* 1993

(Montanari Visco, *President*)

SUMMARY: *The facts:*—Miss Magurno was employed at the Brazilian Consulate, first in Naples and then in Milan, from 1976 to 1989. She instituted proceedings against the Brazilian Ambassador, as representative of Brazil, for losses arising from the non-payment of social security contributions in relation to her second post. Brazil claimed jurisdictional immunity and applied to the Court of Cassation for a preliminary ruling on the jurisdictional issue.

Held:—The Italian courts were competent to exercise jurisdiction over the claim.

In proceedings brought by employees of foreign States, or of entities equivalent thereto, the Italian courts were competent to exercise jurisdiction where the employment was merely auxiliary to the institutional functions of the defendant State or entity. They were also competent, even where the employee performed duties closely bound up with such functions, if the decision sought from the court related solely to financial aspects of the employment relationship and was therefore not liable to affect or interfere with those functions.

The following is the text of the relevant part of the judgment of the Court:

Course of the Proceedings—In an application lodged on 23 October 1991 [with the Milan Magistrate (*Pretore*)], Maria Teresa Magurno stated the following: She had been employed as an assistant (*ausiliaria*) at the Brazilian Consulate, first in Naples—from 7 June 1976 to 31 December 1985—and then, from 1 January 1986 to 2 May 1989, in Milan. She had received a termination allowance in respect of the first period of employment, but not for the second. During her period of employment in Milan her employer had failed to pay her social security contributions. She now brought proceedings before the *Pretore* against the Federative Republic of Brazil, in the person of its Ambassador *pro tempore* in Italy, seeking: (a) an order that the defendant pay to the INPS (*Istituto Nazionale della Previdenza Sociale*) [National Social Security Agency] the contributions due in respect of the sums received by her by way of salary; (b) an order that she be compensated for any loss suffered by reason of the effect of prescription in relation to the unpaid contributions and that the defendant be required to purchase an annuity on her behalf pursuant to Law No 1338 of 1962; and (c) an order that the defendant pay her the sum of 5,247,106 lire by way of termination allowance for the period 1 January 1986 to 2 May 1989.

The Brazilian Republic, having entered a defence, claimed immunity from jurisdiction and applied to this Court in plenary session for a preliminary ruling on the matter.

. . .

Grounds of the Decision—The applicant Ambassador, in his capacity as representative of the State of Brazil, contends that the Italian courts do not have jurisdiction, relying on the principle of the jurisdictional immunity of foreign States, which is recognized under Article 10 of the Constitution, in respect of contracts concluded by them with citizens of the receiving State for purposes of the fulfilment of their institutional functions.

The Court would point out that the case-law cited by the applicant (including a number of decisions of this same Court in plenary session), which is founded on a distinction based on the nature of the duties carried out by the employee, with the Italian courts being accorded jurisdiction only in respect of those disputes where the duties concerned were of a purely manual nature, has been clearly superseded, with effect from Decision No 2329 of 1989,[1] quickly followed, *inter alia*, by Decisions Nos 4909 and 4968 of the same year.

Those decisions established that, in the case of contracts of employment between Italian citizens and foreign States, or entities equivalent thereto, the jurisdiction of the Italian courts in proceedings brought by such employees applies, under the principle of so-called "restrictive immunity" now generally accepted in international law, not only where the employment is merely auxiliary to the institutional functions of the defendant State or entity, but also to those cases where the employee performs duties closely bound up with those functions, but the decision sought from the court relates solely to financial aspects of the employment relationship and hence is not liable to affect or interfere with the said functions.

Subsequent decisions having resolved certain doubts with regard to the effect, for purposes of jurisdiction, of proceedings and judgments

[1 101 *ILR* 380.]

involving employees belonging to the second of the above two categories (see Decisions Nos 145 of 1990[2] and 7548 of 1991), the case-law of this Court in plenary session has definitively confirmed that the decisive factor in all such cases is that the dispute be essentially concerned solely with financial matters (see, most recently, Decisions Nos 5941 of 1992,[3] 1716 of 1992 and 12771 of 1991;[4] *contra*, 12315 of 1992).

In accordance with the reasoning underlying this view of the law, which this Court would make clear that it shares and adopts as its own, it must follow that the Italian courts have jurisdiction in this case, given that the purely financial nature of Mrs Magurno's claim—including that relating to the payment of social security contributions (see Decision No 4909 of 1989 cited above)—is not in dispute. (*Omissis.*)

[Report: *RDI* 1993, p. 812 (in Italian)]

State immunity — Jurisdictional immunity — Employee of cultural institute of foreign State—Job involving administrative and managerial responsibility—Dismissal—Claim for reinstatement and damages—Whether entity of foreign State entitled to jurisdictional immunity—Whether employee integrated into organizational structure of entity of foreign State—Whether enquiry into lawfulness of dismissal would infringe sovereignty of foreign State—The law of Italy

PERRINI *v.* ACADÉMIE DE FRANCE

(Decision No 5126/1994)

Italy, Court of Cassation (Plenary Session). 26 *May* 1994

(Montanari Visco, *President*)

SUMMARY: *The facts:*—Ms Perrini was employed from 1986 to 1990 in an administrative post with managerial responsibility by the *Académie de France* in

[2 See p. 520 above.]   [3 See p. 532 above.]   [4 See p. 525 above.]

Rome, a cultural institution established by the French Government within the framework of cultural cooperation between France and Italy under a Cultural Agreement signed in 1949. Having been abruptly dismissed in 1990, without any proper reason being given, she instituted proceedings before the Italian courts for damages and reinstatement. The defendant disputed the jurisdiction of the Italian courts on the ground that it was an administrative body of a foreign State, and applied to the Court of Cassation for a preliminary ruling on the jurisdictional issue.

Held:—The Italian courts had no jurisdiction over the claim.

(1) The Italian courts had no jurisdiction in relation to an employment dispute between an Italian citizen and a public-law entity of a foreign State where the employee concerned was integrated into the entity's organizational structure and performed duties which were not merely manual or subordinate but closely linked with the entity's public-law activities in pursuance of its institutional functions.

(2) The jurisdiction of the Italian courts was excluded in the case of proceedings where the plaintiff sought a declaration of unlawful dismissal and an order for reinstatement, since this would involve an enquiry directly impugning the public-law powers of the foreign State with regard to the manner in which it organized its official agencies and services.

The following is the text of the relevant part of the judgment of the Court:

Course of the Proceedings—In an application lodged [with the Rome Magistrate (*Pretore*)] on 21 July 1992, Anna Felice Perrini stated the following: On 26 April 1986 she had been hired by the *Académie de France* in Rome in an administrative post with managerial responsibilities, on the standard terms of employment for civil servants. She had in fact been working since December 1982 as archivist and cataloguing assistant to the "art history" department, as well as carrying out general secretarial duties. Between 1982 and 1986 her employment had been artificially interrupted for short periods, in order to preserve its part-time character. On 1 February 1990 the plaintiff had been abruptly dismissed, on the ground that her work as secretary/documentary assistant to Mr André Castel at the Villa Medici had come to an end. In fact, her work had also involved a whole series of other duties. In the absence of any proper ground for her dismissal, she had requested the *Académie* to withdraw it, but to no avail. Invoking the provisions of Law No 300 of 1970, she accordingly requested the *Pretore*, sitting as a labour judge, to declare her dismissal unlawful, to order her immediate reinstatement, and to order the *Académie* to pay damages.

The defendant, having entered an appearance, disputed the jurisdiction of the Italian courts, on the ground that it was a public administrative body of a foreign State, and lodged an application for a preliminary ruling on the matter . . .

Grounds of the Decision—The applicant, the *Académie de France*, contests the jurisdiction of the Italian courts in this dispute under three main heads: the public-law nature of the employment in question; the type of duties carried out by the plaintiff, Ms Perrini; and the specific content of her claim.

The application is well founded.

With regard to the first head, this Court finds that the *Académie de France* constitutes an integral part of the administration of the French State, as is clear from the terms of Decree No 71-1140 of 21 December 1971, which defines it as a "national public establishment of an administrative character, possessing legal personality and financial autonomy, and answerable to the Minister for Cultural Affairs" (Article 1: "*établissement public national à caractère administratif doté de la personnalité civile et de l'autonomie financière . . . placèe sous la tutelle du ministre des affaires culturelles*").

Under the Franco-Italian Cultural Agreement, signed in Paris on 4 November 1949 and implemented by Law No 1177 of 30 July 1952, and the Exchange of Notes of 17 May 1965, implemented by Law No 875 of 4 October 1966, the *Académie de France* is one of the "establishments of high culture" which the Italian and French Governments have agreed to recognize, "each promising to accord to the other every facility for the creation and operation of such establishments", within the framework of cultural cooperation and "the development of relations in the field of science and the arts" (Article 1 of Law No 1177 of 1952, as cited above, extended to the *Académie* by Law No 875 of 4 October 1966).

The public-law purposes of the *Académie* are thus clearly established: it directly represents the French Ministry for Cultural Affairs operating in Italy; it pursues the institutional aims of the French State (the diffusion of national culture abroad); and in fact, as the documents before us show, the annual French Budgetary Law makes provision for a sum to cover its operating costs.

Thus in this case there exists an *ad hoc* agreement between two States, ratified and given effect in domestic law, which reinforces the principle of international law "*par in parem non habet jurisdictionem*" (a cardinal principle, recognized by Article 10 of the Constitution and reaffirmed by this Court on numerous occasions in relation to foreign cultural establishments: see Plenary Decisions of this Court No 9322 of 16 December 1987, *Lycée Châteaubriand*;[1] and No 979 of 15 February 1979, *Danish Cultural Institute*).[2]

As to the second head it is clear, on Ms Perrini's own admission, that she was recruited to a post carrying managerial responsibilities. Officially archivist and cataloguing assistant to the art history department, in practice she carried out secretarial duties of a particularly

[1 87 *ILR* 53.]   [2 65 *ILR* 325.]

skilled and specialized nature (research, loans of works for exhibitions, organization of lectures and conferences, collaboration in the André Castel exhibition at the Villa Medici, etc.). Clearly these were not merely manual or subordinate duties, but involved a position of trust, closely linked with the *Académie*'s public-law activity in pursuance of its institutional functions, and hence characterized by her integration into that entity's organizational structure. Under the case-law of this Court, such a situation excludes the jurisdiction of the Italian courts in relation to employment disputes between Italian citizens and foreign States (see Plenary Decisions of this Court No 1282 of 15 March 1989—secretary working directly with [consular] officials; No 12771 of 28 November 1991[3]—secretary/technical-administrative officer). The fact that the employment was governed by the terms of a standard collective contract is irrelevant (see Plenary Decision No 12315 of 18 November 1992).

Finally, as regards the content of the claim, Ms Perrini sought a declaration that her dismissal was unlawful, an order for her reinstatement and damages for loss of salary. All three heads of claim fall outside the jurisdiction of the Italian courts, inasmuch as any examination of them directly impugns the public-law powers of the foreign State with regard to the manner in which it organizes its official agencies and services (see Decision No 12771/91 cited above).

We accordingly conclude that the Italian courts do not have jurisdiction in this case. (*Omissis.*)

[Report: *RDI* 1995, p. 229 (in Italian)]

International organizations — Immunity — Jurisdictional immunity — National of receiving State employed by international organization in managerial role — Whether integrated into organizational structure — Contract of employment—Termination—Claim for unlawful dismissal and reinstatement — Whether international organization entitled to jurisdictional immunity—Whether examination of legality of dismissal of employee involving interference with public functions of international organization—Bari Institute of International Centre for Advanced Mediterranean

[3 See p. 525 above.]

Agronomic Studies—Legal status—Whether engaged in ordinary commercial or public-law activities — Whether entitled to jurisdictional immunity — Paris Agreement establishing the International Centre, 1962 — Additional Protocol — Italian reservation—Whether recognition of jurisdictional immunity by municipal courts may violate guarantee of judicial protection for individuals under Italian Constitution, Article 24—Requirement for international organizations to make adequate provision for settlement of employment disputes—Whether independent internal appeals procedure acceptable—The law of Italy

NACCI v. BARI INSTITUTE OF THE INTERNATIONAL CENTRE FOR ADVANCED MEDITERRANEAN AGRONOMIC STUDIES

(Decision No 5565/1994)

Italy, Court of Cassation (Plenary Session). 8 *June* 1994

(Brancaccio, *President*)

SUMMARY: *The facts:*—Mr Nacci was employed from 1979 to 1990 by the Bari Institute of the International Centre for Advanced Mediterranean Agronomic Studies, first as Institute Manager and later as Head of Documentation. In 1990 he was dismissed, following the abolition of his post. He brought proceedings against the Institute before the Examining Magistrate (*Pretore*) of Bari for unlawful dismissal, seeking reinstatement and damages. The Institute claimed immunity from the jurisdiction of the Italian courts. The *Pretore* gave judgment in favour of Mr Nacci but, on appeal, the Tribunal of Bari held that the Institute was entitled to jurisdictional immunity pursuant to the Agreement establishing the International Centre, which had been ratified by Italy. Mr Nacci appealed to the Court of Cassation.

Held:—The appeal was dismissed.

(1) The International Centre for Advanced Mediterranean Agronomic Studies was an international inter-governmental organization. Such organizations served as instruments of the participitating States with a view to the fulfilment of specific functions of common interest. They constituted new international entities which operated alongside, but distinct from, those States as autonomous subjects of international law (p. 544).

(2) Pursuant to Articles 2 and 3 of Additional Protocol No 2 to the Agreement establishing the Centre, as modified by the Italian Reservation, the Centre enjoyed immunity in Italy in respect of jurisdiction and the enforcement of judgments, subject to the same limits and in accordance with the same general principles applicable under international law with regard to foreign States. Those immunities applied also to the Agronomic Institute established by the Centre at Bari (pp. 544-5).

(3) Where a subject of international law entered into an agreement with an entity operating under Italian domestic law, it waived its right to invoke its own powers of autonomy in respect of relationships deriving from that agreement. However, this applied only to disputes with staff hired in order to carry out activities in pursuance of the agreement and not to disputes with employees participating in the international body's organizational and decision-making structure, who thus performed duties closely bound up with that body's institutional public-law functions (pp. 545-6).

(4) There was no general principle of international law whereby a contract of employment between an international body and a citizen of the receiving State could in no circumstances involve the exercise of sovereign power and must thus necessarily be subject to the jurisdiction of that State (pp. 547-8).

(5) The fact that the activities of the Institute involved services and research in the agricultural sector did not transform it into a commercial undertaking. The provision of services of this kind (albeit for payment) came within the public-law purposes of the International Centre. The value to be placed upon services provided by the Institute in pursuance of the Centre's aims was a matter for the Centre alone and was of no concern to the Italian courts (pp. 548-9).

(6) Any examination of the lawfulness of the termination by an international body of a contract of employment necessarily involved direct interference with the exercise of that body's public-law powers in relation to the manner in which it organized its departments and services. Such an examination clearly fell outside the scope of the jurisdiction of the courts of the receiving State, which were likewise excluded from adjudicating upon a consequential claim for damages (p. 552).

(7) There was nothing in the provisions of the Constitution to make the jurisdiction of the Italian courts proof against any form of exemption. In practice, where the rules of an international body provided for the establishment of an internal agency endowed with independence and objectivity, for the purpose of hearing appeals in disputes concerning the rights of their employees, this constituted sufficient guarantee of the overriding principle of judicial protection laid down in Article 24 of the Constitution (pp. 553-4).

The following is the text of the relevant part of the judgment of the Court:

Course of the Proceedings—On 10 July 1979 Giuseppe Nacci was hired as Institute Manager (_amministratore_) by the Mediterranean Agronomic Institute (IAM) of Bari, a local agency of the International Centre for Advanced Mediterranean Agronomic Studies. Subsequently, on 17 December 1986, he was transferred to a different post and assigned the task of reorganizing the Institute's library, documentation and audio-visual systems and generally improving its management by making its services to users more efficient. By letter of 28 June 1990 he was dismissed, following the abolition of the post of Head of Department of the Documentation Centre.

Nacci contended that the Institute's conduct in this regard amounted to persecution directed at him personally. On 2 October 1990 he instituted proceedings against the Institute before the Bari Magistrate (*Pretore*), in which he sought a declaration that his dismissal was void and an order for reinstatement, together with damages in respect of the loss suffered by him, calculated on the basis of his salary from the date of cessation of his employment to that of his effective reinstatement, plus social security contributions.

The Institute entered an appearance and, by way of preliminary point, raised an objection to the jurisdiction of the Italian courts. On the merits, it claimed that Nacci's employment was such, in view in particular of its managerial nature, that it could be terminated at any time.

On 29 April 1991 the Bari *Pretore* gave judgment in Nacci's favour. The IAM appealed against that judgment, repeating its claim *inter alia* that the Italian courts lacked jurisdiction.

In a decision given on 24 April 1992 the Bari Tribunal held that the Italian courts lacked jurisdiction in the matter and ordered each party to bear its own costs. The Tribunal pointed out that the Bari Institute is an organ of the International Centre and, as such, enjoys immunity from jurisdiction and execution pursuant to the terms of the international Agreement establishing the Centre, ratified in Italy by Law No 932 of 13 July 1965.

The Tribunal ruled that an employment relationship fell outside the ambit of jurisdictional immunity only where the duties involved were manual, or merely auxiliary to the public-law activities of the entity concerned, or where the claim was concerned solely with financial issues. In this case, however, Nacci was permanently integrated into the IAM's organizational structure and participated, first as Institute Manager and then as Head of Department, in primary essential functions closely bound up with the Institute's basic activities, namely research and training. Moreover his claim, inasmuch as it sought an enquiry into the lawfulness of his dismissal and an order for his reinstatement, directly impugned the Institute's exercise of its public-law powers, which were not susceptible of enquiry before the Italian courts.

The Tribunal held further that it was irrelevant that the IAM ran training and conversion courses financed by the Region, since Nacci was not involved with those activities, but integrated into the Institute's organizational structure for purposes of the fulfilment of its public institutional functions.

Nacci has appealed in cassation against this decision, invoking four grounds, against which the IAM has counter-petitioned. Both parties have presented written submissions.

Grounds of the Decision—In his first ground of appeal, in which he alleges a violation of Article 2 of the Additional Protocol to the Agreement establishing the International Centre, the appellant contends that the Tribunal failed to take account of the fact that the IAM had renounced any claim to jurisdictional immunity and had voluntarily and spontaneously submitted itself to Italian law and to Italian jurisdiction.

This argument is founded on the fact that the Staff Rules of the International Centre provide that the legislation applicable to employees in respect of social security and family allowances shall be that obtaining in the country where they are employed. The Staff Rules of the IAM further provide that Italian law shall apply not only to the above matters, but also to long-service allowance, special leave for pregnancy and maternity, medical inspections, trade-union rights and leave of absence for military service, while Article 45 provides that disputes shall be dealt with by a Conciliation and Arbitration Board, with the Director of the Bari Provincial Labour Office acting as independent arbitrator. Finally, under an agreement with the trade unions signed on 20 January 1979, provision was made for specific categories of individual employment dispute to be submitted for conciliation and arbitration to the said Provincial Office. The regime applicable to staff possessing international status is expressly stated to be subject to these Rules, although this has never been formally approved. The fact that local staff are made subject to the law of the receiving State implies acceptance of Italian jurisdiction.

In support of his contention that the respondent has waived jurisdictional immunity, the appellant further relies on the fact that almost every year the IAM signs contracts with the Puglia Region for the organization of training, conversion and re-training courses, whose content is prescribed by the Region. Under these contracts the IAM is obliged to comply not only with the regime established by regional Law No 54 of 17 October 1978 and by national Law No 845 of 21 December 1978, making itself subject to State and regional control in the matter, but also to apply to employees the terms of the relevant collective bargaining agreement.

The contracts provide that disputes shall be submitted to the Bari courts.

Nacci accordingly contends that even if, by virtue of his initial duties, he was to be regarded as a member of staff possessing international status, the effect of the activities carried on by the IAM was such that it had become integrated into the Italian legal order and subject to the jurisdiction of the Italian courts.

The Institute objects to any consideration of these heads of claim, on the ground that these are new matters, involving an enquiry and evaluation of facts (statements by the IAM, Staff Rules, etc.) that should not be admitted in proceedings on the issue of jurisdiction.

This objection is unfounded. As a rule, it is for the lower court to assess the evidence submitted to it and to determine the nature of the employment relationship. However, exceptionally, the Court of Cassation ruling on jurisdiction in plenary session (whether as a preliminary issue or by way of appeal) may also do so, where such determination is essential in order to enable the Court to decide whether or not the [Italian] courts have jurisdiction in respect of the employment relationship in question.

In this case, the Staff Rules on which the appellant now relies were produced from the start of the proceedings, and must be deemed to have been taken into account by the courts below in reaching their decisions as to whether or not the Italian courts have jurisdiction. In the present proceedings those same Rules are now relied on as representing an implied waiver of jurisdictional immunity, but this merely involves a re-interpretation of evidence already before the Court.

Nevertheless, this Court finds that the appellant's objections are in substance unfounded.

At no point does Nacci's claim call into question the case-law of this Court, which has consistently upheld the jurisdictional immunity of the Bari Institute of the International Centre for Advanced Mediterranean Agronomic Studies (see Cassation Decisions Nos 2425 of 27 April 1979,[1] 2316 of 4 April 1986,[2] 3732 and 3733 of 4 June 1986[3] and 1513 of 13 February 1991).

The Centre is an international inter-governmental organization, established by various Mediterranean States (Spain, Portugal, France, Italy, Yugoslavia, Greece and Turkey) for purposes of the development of agronomic studies and of international cooperation between agricultural management and advisory personnel in the countries concerned.

International organizations of this type on the one hand serve as an instrument of the member States for the fulfilment of specific functions of common interest, while on the other they constitute new international entities, which operate alongside those States, in a manner distinct from them and with their own autonomous internal legal order.

They conduct relations on equal terms with other independent entities and are subject to the same rules of international law, both customary and treaty, that govern relations between States.

In this case the International Centre enjoys both jurisdictional immunity and immunity from execution (Articles 2 and 3 of Additional Protocol No 2 to the Agreement). Italy, in the Reservation annexed to that Agreement, has undertaken to respect those immunities, subject to the limits and in accordance with the general

[¹ 78 *ILR* 86.]   [² 87 *ILR* 29.]   [³ 87 *ILR* 37.]

principles applicable under international law to foreign States. These privileges clearly apply to the Bari Institute which, under the terms of Article 3(c) of the Agreement and of the latter's Additional Protocol No 1, is regarded, together with that at Montpellier, as an institution of the signatory States themselves.

The appellant does not dispute this, but argues that the Bari Institute, in adopting Staff Rules whose forms and institutions in the matter of welfare and social security are typical of those of the Italian system, has not only made the terms of employment of its staff subject to the substantive regime of Italian law, but as a result has also accepted the jurisdiction of the Italian courts and implicitly waived its jurisdictional immunity in this regard. In support of this argument he cites certain plenary decisions of this Court (Decisions Nos 2173 of 1981, 110 of 1987[4] and 3374 of 1989).

However, looking beyond the necessarily somewhat general terms of the statements of principle set out in the headnotes (*massime*) to those Decisions, if we examine the factual context in which they were made, we find that their value as precedents is quite different from that claimed.

Thus, Decision No 2173 of 13 April 1981 states that making provision for a welfare and social security regime prescribed by Italian law implies acceptance by the Supreme Allied Command Europe of the jurisdiction of the Italian courts in respect of disputes involving such social security obligations. However (as is moreover clear from the terms in which the principle is stated), that Decision is concerned with "local workforce" employees who, under Article 8(f) of the Paris Agreement of 26 July 1961, ratified by Presidential Decree No 2083 of 18 September, are (by contrast with international personnel, who are dealt with in the first part of the Article) expressly made subject to Italian jurisdiction.

Decision No 110 of 12 January 1987,[5] which concerns an Italian citizen hired in Italy by the Federal German television authority, upheld the jurisdiction of the Italian courts, notwithstanding the employer's immunity from jurisdiction as a subject of international law, "where it was clear that the parties had expressly provided that the contract of employment should be subject to the private-law regime of Italian law in matters of employment, and had thus agreed to submit any disputes in this regard to the Italian courts". From the tenor of this headnote it would seem that jurisdiction of the Italian courts is a necessary consequence of the fact that the contract of employment is made subject to the private-law regime of Italian law. But this is not the case. In fact, the text of the judgment makes it clear that the contract provided not only that "Italian labour law" should apply, but also that any disputes should be heard by the Rome

[4 87 *ILR* 38.]   [5 *Ibid.*]

Tribunal. Thus the jurisdiction of the Italian courts was expressly provided for, and not simply to be inferred from the provision that the contract was to be governed by Italian law.

The last of the decisions cited by the appellant deals with a different question, namely that raised in the second head of the first ground of appeal.

In its Decision No 3374 of 18 July 1989 this Court in plenary session held that where, under an agreement with a Region with regard to healthcare activities . . ., an international sovereign entity (in this case the Order of Malta) undertook to apply the substantive rules [of Italian labour law] to disputes with its employees, this implied acceptance of the jurisdiction of the Italian courts with regard to all employment disputes, and a consequent waiver of jurisdictional immunity.

This principle, upheld on a number of occasions in both the previous and subsequent case-law (see Cassation Decisions Nos 1326 of 17 March 1989, 3360 of 18 March 1992 and 13702 of 30 December 1992), is based on the notion that, where a subject of international law enters into an agreement with an entity operating within the Italian legal order (in all these cases the agreement was in respect of healthcare provision), then, in relation to the subject-matter of that agreement, it waives its sovereign powers and agrees to act as a subject of Italian law, thus submitting with regard to relationships arising out of the agreement (whether with users [of its services] or with employees) to the jurisdiction of the Italian courts.

But these principles apply only to staff hired to carry out the activities covered by the agreement (in Decision No 3360 of 18 March 1992, this is specifically made clear in the judgment, but all the other decisions referred to above involve similar situations) and not to staff employed in the organizational and decision-making structure of the international entity, whose duties are thus closely bound up with its institutional and public-law functions (see Cassation Decision No 2415 of 26 February 1993 concerning the Order of Malta).

In this case Nacci was not hired to carry out duties in connection with the professional training courses covered by the agreements between the IAM and the Puglia Region, but was a member of the IAM management, occupying a post at managerial grade within the official organizational structure and answering directly to the Secretary-General of the International Centre, with a legal and economic status quite distinct from that of so-called "local workforce" employees.

It follows that the activities carried out by the IAM under agreements with the Regions are of no relevance to Nacci's case. Nor is it of any relevance for purposes of jurisdiction that his employment was contractually subject to provisions typical of employment relationships governed by Italian law.

The second ground of appeal alleges a breach of Article 2 of Additional Protocol No 2 to the Agreement establishing the International Centre, in view of the Italian Reservation (as recorded in Law No 932 of 13 July 1965), which refers the matter [of jurisdiction] to the rules of customary international law. The appellant argues that the jurisdictional immunity of foreign States under international law applies only to relationships standing totally outside the internal legal order, where the State in question is acting within [the territory of] another State either as a subject of international law or by virtue of its position as the holder of sovereign power. He contends that the tendency, both in international practice and in the legislative practice of other States, is to apply the jurisdiction of the receiving State to disputes arising out of employment relationships to be performed on its territory by its own citizens under contracts with foreign States. They are to be treated as private-law relationships not constituting an exercise of sovereign power. Article 5 of the European Convention on State Immunity, signed at Basle in 1972, treats the matter in this way, and that Convention is regarded by both doctrine and case-law as declaratory of customary international law. Similarly, the London Agreement of 19 June 1951 on the Status of NATO Forces provides that where an employee of a foreign State is a national of the receiving State, then his employment will be governed by local law. Analogous provisions are to be found in the Treaty of Washington of 19 January 1960 between the United States and Japan, in the Bonn Agreement of 3 August 1959 between the member States of NATO and the German Federal Republic and in the Agreement signed on 12 June 1982 between Italy and the MFO, ratified by Law No 968 of 29 December 1982. He points out further that a number of States (United Kingdom, Australia, United States, South Africa, etc.) have adopted legislation excluding jurisdictional immunity in the case of employment relationships to be performed on their territory by their own citizens under contracts with foreign States. Moreover, the Italian Ministry of Foreign Affairs has itself on a number of occasions requested diplomatic representatives and international organizations operating in this country to respect Italian labour and social security legislation in regard to their employment contracts with Italian nationals. It must therefore be concluded, he argues, that employment relationships do not involve the exercise of sovereign power, and that disputes concerning such relationships should be subject to the jurisdiction of the forum State.

This ground, however, also fails.

As the appellant himself recognizes, the European Convention on State Immunity, adopted at Basle on 16 May 1972, Article 5 of which provides for the jurisdiction of the receiving State to apply to employment relationships to be performed on its territory by its own citizens under contracts with foreign States, has never been ratified by

Italy and accordingly cannot be applied by this Court as if it were a norm of Italian law.

In ratifying the Treaty establishing the International Centre, Italy expressly bound itself to recognize the [latter's] immunity from jurisdiction and execution, subject to the limits and in accordance with the general principles applicable under international law to foreign States.

Nor is it helpful to the appellant to invoke the London Agreement concluded on 19 June 1951 by the member States of NATO with regard to the status of forces of one signatory State stationed on the territory of another (or the analogous agreements with other States cited by the appellant). The purpose of those agreements was not to regulate relations among subjects of international law, but to reconcile the independence of headquarters of foreign armed forces with the desire of the receiving State to suffer the minimum degree of restriction of its own sovereignty on its own territory compatible with the Atlantic Alliance. And even this Agreement did not make all employment relationships entered into by nationals of the receiving State subject to the latter's jurisdiction, but distinguished between employees hired with international status, in respect of whom immunity from jurisdiction applied, and those with local status, who remained subject to the substantive and procedural laws of the State where their employment was to be performed.

Equally without relevance are the internal laws adopted by individual States, which have no force in international terms, but apply only within those States' own respective legal orders.

Finally, no effect can be accorded for jurisdictional purpose to our own Foreign Ministry's various requests to foreign diplomatic representatives and international organizations operating in Italy to respect Italian labour and social security legislation in the case of disputes with employees who are Italian nationals. These are matters of substantive law, affecting rights recognized and protected by the Constitution.

Thus there is no general principle of international law laying down that employment relationships entered into by subjects of international law with citizens of the receiving State can never involve the exercise of sovereign power and are therefore necessarily subject to the jurisdiction of that State.

In his third ground, alleging violations of the same provisions, the appellant argues that the International Centre was accorded jurisdictional immunity only for the purposes of fulfilling the objectives indicated in the Agreement, namely to provide additional instruction of an economic and technical nature and to foster a spirit of international cooperation among agricultural advisory and management personnel in Mediterranean countries. He claims that the activities of the Bari Institute actually bore no relation to these objectives, inasmuch as they consisted either in the organization of training courses commissioned by the Ministry of Foreign Affairs or by the Puglia Region, or in research on behalf of public and private bodies paid for on a normal basis. The practical result of these activities was the production and distribution of plant and crop materials, the provision of services to farmers, the conduct of trials and tests commissioned by the Region or by the *Cassa del Mezzogiorno*, the publication of a magazine, which was offered for sale in the normal way, and publication of the texts of course lectures and exercises. These activities were conducted on a profit-making basis, and in fact each year's accounts showed very substantial profits. Thus this was a commercial business, falling totally outside the official purposes of the International Centre.

The appellant contends that his own duties, both initially and subsequently, related to these commercial activities of the Institute.

This ground also fails.

The activities described above, the organization of courses, services to farmers, chemical tests, etc., all fall within the scope of the International Centre's aims, which consist in the provision of instruction in economic and technical matters, the development of agriculture in Mediterranean countries and the training of agricultural management and advisory staff (see the preamble to the Agreement). The fact that these activities may be financed wholly or in part by national public entities, under appropriate agreements, does not transform the Institute into a commercial undertaking, because the provision of services of this kind (which were never envisaged as free) comes within the public-law purposes of the Centre.

The value to be placed upon the practical services provided by the Bari Institute in pursuance of the International Centre's institutional aims is a matter which concerns only the Institute and not the Italian courts.

In his final ground of appeal the appellant contends that the duties performed by him were not connected with the furtherance of the Institute's established aims, but were of an auxiliary and subordinate nature and, accordingly, remained within the jurisdiction of the Italian courts. This applied, moreover, even to his initial post as Institute Manager, given that the Institute's Director himself only had the power to make proposals. The appellant further states that, in any event, in order for the jurisdiction of the Italian courts to be excluded, the judicial order sought must be such as to interfere with the public functions of the entity concerned, there being no such interference where the claim is concerned only with financial issues, even where the employee carries out high-level tasks. He adds that the latter was in fact not the case here, his duties being of a merely executive nature.

He further contends that any judgment that he might obtain concerning the unlawfulness of his dismissal is irrelevant to the present proceedings, which are concerned merely with the specific form in which that judgment might be enforced. He argues that, in effect, in all cases where an employee seeks annulment of his dismissal and reinstatement in his former post, his claim also covers the lesser remedy provided for in Article 8 of Law No 604 of 15 July 1966, whereby the court may restrict itself to ordering an international employer to make good the financial consequences of the unlawful dismissal.

This ground also fails.

In an international body whose purpose is the professional training and instruction of agricultural management and advisory staff, the duties of first managing the Institute and then "reorganizing the Institute's library, documentation and audio-visual systems and generally improving its management by rendering its services to Institute students and other users more efficient" are among the most important of the duties necessary for the purposes of the organization and its operation.

Notwithstanding the efforts made in these proceedings (for obvious litigational purposes) to devalue the duties carried out by Nacci in his final posting, the fact is (as the *Pretore* found) that the Documentation Centre of which the appellant was in charge contained books and periodicals, together with an electronic archive of projects and studies concerning land reclamation, irrigation and national and international systems of water management (covering twenty-two different countries) and provided assistance and advice, both of a general bibliographical nature and on specific subjects, with regard to the subject-matter of courses and research projects.

Proof of the managerial status enjoyed by Nacci, who was directly answerable under the official organizational structure only to the Centre's Secretary-General in Paris, can be seen from the high salary paid to him and from his special status as an international employee, by contrast with that of staff recruited locally.

As has already been pointed out, the jurisdictional immunity of the International Centre and of its dependency, the Institute, was recognized by Agreement of the Contracting States. That Agreement has, by ratification, been incorporated into the national law of every one of those States.

However, Italy entered a Reservation to the Agreement, in which it is provided that immunity from jurisdiction shall apply within the Italian national legal order subject to the limits and general principles under which international law accords such immunity to foreign States.

It follows that the issue of jurisdiction in this case has to be decided not on the basis of the unlimited jurisdictional immunity provided for in the Agreement, but in accordance with the rule of customary international law "*par in parem non habet jurisdictionem*", which has been held to be compatible with the Constitution (see Constitutional Court Decision No 48 of 18 June 1979)[6] and has been incorporated into Italian law by Article 10 of the Constitution.

That rule of international law has been held by the case-law of this Court in plenary session to be limited to relationships totally extrinsic to the internal legal order, that is to say where foreign States or entities assimilated to them carry on activities on Italian territory in their capacity as subjects of international law or exercise the sovereign powers with which they are endowed under their own legal order.

Where, on the other hand, foreign States or international entities act outside the scope of their sovereign powers, carrying on activities of a private-law or commercial nature, or in satisfaction of material or auxiliary needs *jure gestionis*, the jurisdiction of the forum State cannot be excluded.

This is so-called "restrictive immunity", which covers only transactions performed with a view to the achievement of the institutional aims of the entities concerned, as opposed to "absolute immunity" which reflects the desire of foreign States to protect their independence and autonomy from the jurisdictional authority of individual receiving States.

As far as employment relationships are concerned, there has been a dispute of principle as to whether they can be dealt with on the basis of the standard dichotomy (between acts *jure imperii* and *jure gestionis*). But the case-law of this Court has applied a distinction based on whether the relationship is with a foreign State or with an international organization. In the former case, in order to exclude Italian jurisdiction, the individual concerned must be both formally employed in an administrative capacity and participate in the State's public-law activities, which are essential conditions to bring the relationship within the scope of [the State's] public functions (see most recently: Cassation Decisions Nos 3248 of 19 April 1990, 1282 of 15 March 1989 and 6172 of 15 July 1987).[7] In the case of international organizations, in order to exclude Italian jurisdiction it is sufficient that the employee be permanently or continuously integrated into the organization's organic structure, irrespective of the nature and level of his duties. What the Court has to consider are those organizational aspects (administrative structure, allocation of tasks, salary structure) which are directly instrumental to the achievement of the organization's institutional aims (see most recently: Cassation Decisions Nos 1513 of 13 February 1991, 8433 of 18 August 1990 and 5819 of 23 November 1985[8]).

[6 78 *ILR* 101.]   [7 87 *ILR* 42.]   [8 87 *ILR* 20.]

It is true that recently, with a view to providing a measure of reconciliation between two conflicting requirements—namely, on the one hand, that of ensuring respect for subjects of international law in the exercise of their functions and, on the other, the need to ensure that Italian citizens working for those entities in their own country are able to protect their rights through access to their own courts—the case-law of this Court, albeit not without opposition (see Cassation Decision No 7548 of 9 July 1991), has shown a tendency to restrict the scope of jurisdictional immunity to those cases where the judgment sought is liable to interfere with the entity's public-law activities.

Thus it has been held, following this jurisprudential trend, that the jurisdiction of the Italian courts extends to proceedings brought by an employee performing duties connected with the employer's public-law activity where the issues raised are of a purely financial nature (see Cassation Decisions Nos 2329 of 15 May 1989,[9] 4968 of 20 November 1989, 12771 of 28 November 1991,[10] 9675 of 24 September 1993[11]).

It is unnecessary for the Court in these proceedings to adopt a position on this partial conflict in the case-law, since even the most liberal approach in any event excludes the jurisdiction of the Italian courts in all cases where an employee challenges his or her dismissal and seeks reinstatement and an order against the employer for payment of salary and damages (see Cassation Decisions Nos 12315 of 18 November 1992 and 12771 of 28 November 1991[12] already cited; and with regard to the International Centre for Agronomic Studies, in relation to the enforcement aspects of a reinstatement order, Decisions Nos 1513 of 13 February 1991 and 3733 of 4 June 1986[13]). The present case does indeed concern a challenge to a dismissal.

Any examination [by the courts] of the lawfulness of the termination of a contract of employment by an international entity (in the present case, as a result of the abolition of Nacci's post as Director of the Documentation Centre) necessarily entails direct interference with the exercise of that entity's public-law powers in terms of the manner in which it organizes its departments and services, and as such clearly falls outside the jurisdiction of the courts of the receiving State.

Nor is there any force in the appellant's contention that the Court could restrict itself to ordering the IAM to pay him damages. Quite apart from the fact that the appellant's claim in these proceedings is for a declaration that his dismissal was unlawful, together with orders for his reinstatement and for payment of damages, it should be pointed out that, even if the claim were limited to a request for damages, this would still depend upon a finding that his dismissal was unlawful, and the Court cannot examine or accept the one head of claim without first dealing with the other.

[9 101 *ILR* 379.]   [11 See p. 534 above.]   [13 87 *ILR* 37 (note).]
[10 See p. 525 above.]   [12 See p. 525 above.]

In his written submission Nacci contends by way of subsidiary claim that Law No 932 of 13 July 1965 [ratifying the Agreement establishing the Centre] is unconstitutional on the grounds of conflict with Articles 2, 3, 11, 24 and 25 of the Constitution, in that it seeks to incorporate into the Italian legal order the provisions according jurisdictional immunity to the Bari Institute of the International Centre for Advanced Mediterranean Agronomic Studies. He contends that the principles of Italian constitutional law impose certain inviolable limits to the automatic acceptance by our legal order of norms of international law. Specifically, if the IAM were to be accorded absolute jurisdictional immunity, its employees would be debarred from seeking to protect their rights before the courts, leaving them reliant on the discretionary decisions of their employer.

We would point out that this argument, put forward in proceedings against this same employer, has already been dismissed by this Court a number of times as manifestly unfounded (see Cassation Decisions Nos 3732 and 3733 of 13 June 1986[14] and 1513 of 13 February 1991).

Moreover, as already stated, the jurisdictional immunity accorded to the respondent is not the full immunity provided for in the Agreement but, in consequence of Italy's Reservation, is limited to that accorded to foreign States under the rules of customary international law.

It is true that jurisdiction is a typical feature of sovereignty, and indeed one of the latter's constituent elements, nonetheless, as the Constitutional Court has pointed out on a number of occasions, there is no rule of the Constitution protecting the jurisdiction of the [Italian] State against any form of exemption, nor can any such protection be deduced, with particular reference to civil matters, from the general principle of Italian law whereby any exemption from a rule must be founded on an "ordinary law" (*legge ordinaria*).

In fact the Constitution itself, in Article 80, provides for the ratification by ordinary law of international agreements concerning matters of arbitration or jurisdiction (see Constitutional Court Decisions Nos 175 of 11 December 1973 and 18 of 2 February 1982).

The [right to judicial] protection provided for in Article 24 of the Constitution is thus no bar to the jurisdictional immunity of foreign States and other subjects of international law, and the principles laid down in that Article are compatible with the (reciprocal) obligations arising out of international agreements and under customary international law with regard to the protection of the immunity of foreign States.

Problems can arise in determining whether there exists in practice a court competent to safeguard the right invoked by the party concerned. The question [does not] arise in the case of foreign States, inasmuch

[14 *Ibid.*]

as, where the jurisdictional protection of the Italian courts is not available, it is always possible to seek a remedy before those States' own domestic courts.

However, it could arise in the case of proceedings against international bodies (which have no judicial system of their own), if the protection of the rights of their employees depended, as the appellant contends, on decisions in regard to which the employer enjoyed absolute discretion.

But this is not the case here.

Under the Rules of the International Centre of 4 December 1989 (submitted in evidence by the appellant himself), there is an Appeals Committee, with authority to hear appeals lodged by employees against the Centre's decisions.

That Committee "may annul any decision of the Secretary-General or of the Board of Directors where this is contrary to the terms of engagement of the individual concerned or to the provisions of these Rules or of the relevant regulations or instructions. The Committee may order the Centre to make compensation in respect of any loss resulting from a wrongful act perpetrated against an employee" (Article 61).

The Committee is composed of a Chairman and two members of different nationalities, nominated by the Board from outside the staff of the Centre, and who must be either lawyers or other highly qualified persons, with extensive experience in administrative matters (Article 60).

Thus we are dealing here with an internal agency of an international entity, endowed with independence and objectivity guaranteed by the high competence of its members and by the fact that they have been appointed from outside the Centre. This is sufficient to safeguard the overriding principle of judicial protection pursuant to Article 24 of the Constitution (see Constitutional Court Decision No 18 of 2 February 1982 already cited). It is irrelevant that the Committee does not consist of judges covered by a formal guarantee of independence (a condition not always present even within the judicial order of foreign States) and that this is in effect a form of "private court", which has no powers with regard to the production of evidence or to the enforcement of its decisions.

The appeal accordingly fails. It is fair and proper that each party should bear its own costs in respect of the present proceedings.

[Report: *RDI* 1994, p. 837 (in Italian)]

State immunity — Jurisdictional immunity — Consular employee — National of receiving State employed as telephonist — Dismissal — Claim for reinstatement and damages—Whether foreign State entitled to jurisdictional immunity—Whether duties of telephonist merely subordinate — Whether telephonist integrated into organizational structure of foreign State—Whether enquiry by municipal courts into lawfulness of dismissal would infringe sovereignty of foreign State

Consular relations — Consular employee — Telephonist — Whether performing consular functions—Vienna Convention on Consular Relations, 1963

Relationship of international law and municipal law — Rules of customary international law — Rules on State immunity — Whether incorporated into municipal law — Effect of Article 10 of Italian Constitution—The law of Italy

UNITED STATES OF AMERICA *v.* LO GATTO

(Decision No 4483/1995)

Italy, Court of Cassation (Plenary Session).   21 *April* 1995

(Bile, *President*; Di Cio' and Taddeucci, *Presidents of Chambers*; Rapone, Sgroi, Sommella, Giustiniani, Borre and Amirante, *Judges*)

SUMMARY: *The facts*:—Ms Lo Gatto, an Italian national, was employed as a clerk and subsequently as a telephonist at the United States Consulate in Palermo between 1963 and 1991, when she was dismissed. She instituted proceedings before the Italian courts for unlawful dismissal, reinstatement and damages. The United States claimed jurisdictional immunity and applied to the Court of Cassation for settlement of the jurisdictional issue as a preliminary question.

Held:—The United States was entitled to jurisdictional immunity.

(1) Any examination of the lawfulness of the dismissal would directly interfere with the exercise of the sovereign powers of a foreign State in relation to the organization of its representative office and therefore violate the principle of customary international law "*par in parem non habet jurisdictionem*", incorporated into Italian law pursuant to Article 10 of the Constitution. It would also interfere with the independence of the organization of a consular office, contrary to the principle of reciprocity.

(2) It was argued that a telephone operator performed merely "duties of execution" which were secondary and subordinate to typical consular functions.

However, the duties of a consular or embassy telephone operator were based on trust and involved integration into the organizational structure of the foreign State concerned, so that the employment relationship itself involved the exercise of sovereign functions.

The following is the text of the relevant part of the judgment of the Court:

Course of the Proceedings—In an application lodged before the Magistrate (*Pretore*) of Palermo, sitting as a labour judge, on 19 August 1992, Franca Maria Lo Gatto brought proceedings against the Embassy in Italy of the United States of America, asking for the annulment or withdrawal of her dismissal, with an order to be made against the Embassy of the United States, in the person of its Ambassador, to "reinstate her in her place of work and to pay compensation pursuant to Section 18 of Law No 300 of 20 May 1970 to cover her wages for the period from her dismissal until reinstatement".

Ms Lo Gatto has stated that she worked at the United States Consulate in Palermo from May 1963, firstly as a clerk in the Commercial Office and then, from 1 April 1989, at another posting due to the closure of that office.

From 25 March 1990 the applicant carried out the duties of telephone operator and receptionist until the termination of the employment relationship on 31 May 1991. A decision of 27 January 1991, according to which she would have been appointed a "Special Consular Service Assistant", was not implemented.

The applicant has specified that, in a letter of 2 April 1991, she was notified of her dismissal with effect from 31 May 1995, due to the withdrawal of the position of Special Consular Service Assistant. However, since she was carrying out the duties of a telephone operator and not those corresponding to the position which was withdrawn, she considered that her dismissal, justified on the basis of the withdrawal of that position, was totally unjustified.

The United States Embassy appeared in order to raise, as a preliminary question, the lack of jurisdiction of the Italian court and, in the alternative, argued on the merits that the claim was unfounded.

In an application dated 24 November 1993 the United States of America requested a preliminary ruling on the jurisdictional issue by the Court of Cassation . . .

Grounds of the Decision—The application for a preliminary ruling on the jurisdictional issue lodged by the United States seeks a declaration that the Italian court is not competent to exercise jurisdiction over the claim brought by Ms Lo Gatto before the *Pretore* of Palermo. The

United States argues that the claim interferes with the sovereign functions of a foreign State and in particular with the organization of its diplomatic/consular offices. This interference results from both the request for a declaration that the dismissal was unlawful and void, and the request for reinstatement in employment, as well as the request for compensation if the other relief sought is granted.

The application is well founded.

The plenary session of this Court has affirmed, in relation to disputes concerning employment relationships of Italian employees of embassies and foreign consulates in Italy, involving collaboration in the performance of the functions of the foreign State in question, that the Italian courts have no jurisdiction because of the effect of diplomatic or consular immunity, whenever the judgment would interfere with the organization of the diplomatic or consular office. Such is the case, *inter alia*, where dismissal is met with a request for reinstatement in employment (see the Decisions in plenary session of the Court of Cassation No 3248 of 19 April 1990, No 12771 of 28 November 1991,[1] No 12315 of 18 December 1992,[2] No 5126 of 26 May 1994,[3] and No 5565 of 8 June 1994[4]).

In the case at issue, as the applicant points out, the employee started the proceedings in order to establish the unlawfulness of her dismissal, and thereby claim compensation and reinstatement in her employment. Such claims necessarily and directly affect the exercise of the public powers of the foreign State concerned so that their acceptance would be in clear conflict with the principle of customary international law "*par in parem non habet jurisdictionem*" (a basic principle incorporated by Article 10 of the Constitution and re-affirmed on many occasions by this Court). Equally, acceptance of such claims would conflict with the autonomy and independence of the organization of diplomatic/consular offices, based on the principle of reciprocity.

In this connection, the Court feels that it ought to refer specifically to the statement made by Ms Lo Gatto that, as a telephone operator, she merely carried out duties of execution, that is to say tasks which were secondary and accessory to the typical functions of a consulate. Consequently, according to Ms Lo Gatto, there could be no interference with the organization of the office in question and certainly not with the public and sovereign powers of the foreign State concerned.

On the contrary, the Court of Cassation in plenary session, by Decisions No 3248/90, No 7548/91 and No 12315/92,[5] has affirmed that the duties of a telephone operator in embassies and consulates of foreign States fall within those tasks which are based on trust and belong to the public organization of the office itself.

[1 See p. 525 above.]   [3 See p. 536 above.]   [5 See Note at p. 558 below.]
[2 See Note at p. 558 below.]   [4 See p. 536 above.]

Accordingly, in the case at issue, this Court can only confirm, on the one hand, that Ms Lo Gatto was inserted into the organization of the Consulate in Palermo with qualified duties of cooperation. Furthermore, the application which she has lodged, which is aimed in substance at obtaining reinstatement in her employment, necessarily affects the sovereign powers of a foreign State. The claim is therefore barred by application of jurisdictional immunity on the basis of Article 43 of the Vienna Convention on Consular Relations of 24 April 1963, which was ratified in Italy by Law No 804 of 9 August 1967.

The Italian judge therefore has no jurisdiction over the claim . . .

[Report: *Diritto Pratica del Lavoro* 1995, p. 2625 (in Italian)]

NOTE.—An earlier decision of the Court of Cassation (Plenary Session) in *Giaffreda* v. *French Republic* involved an almost identical dispute between a consular employee who was a national of the receiving State (Italy) and a foreign State. Mr Giaffreda was employed as an usher and telephonist from 1982 to 1989, when he was dismissed. He brought proceedings before the Italian courts for unlawful dismissal, reinstatement and damages. France claimed jurisdictional immunity and applied to the Court of Cassation for settlement of the jurisdictional issue as a preliminary question. The Court of Cassation held that immunity applied. It was true that the jurisdiction of the Italian courts in a dispute between a foreign State and a consular employee had been upheld by the Court of Cassation in an earlier judgment of 15 May 1989 (101 *ILR* 380). But that decision was to be distinguished since it was concerned purely with the financial aspects of an employment relationship which had been terminated without reinstatement being sought, whereas the present claim required a determination of the legality of the dismissal with a view to possible reinstatement. This would have necessitated an examination of the reasons for the dismissal, which had their origin in the managerial and organizational activity of the representative office of a foreign State. The decision sought would therefore have constituted unacceptable interference with consular activity (judgment of 18 November 1992, Case No 12315/1992, *RDI* 1994, p. 340 (in Italian)).

State immunity — Jurisdictional immunity — Consular employee — Citizen of receiving State employed as commercial officer—Contract of employment—Termination —Claim for unlawful dismissal—Whether foreign State entitled to jurisdictional immunity — Whether employee integrated into organizational structure of foreign State— Whether enquiry by municipal courts into lawfulness of dismissal would infringe sovereignty of foreign State

Consular relations — Consular employee — Commercial officer—Whether performing consular functions—Vienna Convention on Consular Relations, 1963, Article 5

Relationship of international law and municipal law — Rules of customary international law — Compatibility of rules on State immunity with principles of Italian Constitution —Incorporation of rules of customary international law into municipal law—Article 10 of Constitution—The law of Italy

CANADA v. CARGNELLO

(Decision No 4017/1998)

Italy, Court of Cassation (Plenary Session). 20 *April* 1998

(La Torre, *President*; Pontrandolfi and Cantillo, *Presidents of Chambers*; Amirante, Garofalo, Ianniruperto, Orestano, Vittoria and Ravagnani, *Judges*)

SUMMARY: *The facts:*—Mr Cargnello, an Italian citizen, was employed as a commercial officer by the General Consulate of Canada in Milan from 1982 until 1993, when he was dismissed for "incompetence". He instituted proceedings against his employer for a declaration that his dismissal was unlawful and for compensation in lieu of reinstatement. The Examining Magistrate (*Pretore*) upheld his claim and awarded compensation. An appeal to the Court of Milan was dismissed, a plea of lack of jurisdiction put forward by the Canadian Consulate being rejected on the grounds that Mr Cargnello had performed commercial rather than consular duties and the claim did not seek the reinstatement of his employment relationship but merely damages. Canada appealed to the Court of Cassation.

Held:—The appeal was allowed. Italian courts had no jurisdiction over the claim.

(1) The appeal lodged by the State of Canada was admissible even though the party to the earlier stages of the proceedings had been the Consulate itself. A consulate was not a body independent of its sending State, but rather

its representative, so that the State itself was not excluded from choosing to defend its interests directly since consulate and sending State were one and the same subject of international law (p. 564).

(2) The promotion of commercial transactions between private firms was included amongst consular functions, as defined in Article 5 of the Vienna Convention on Consular Relations, 1963. Accordingly, contrary to the finding of the Court of Milan, the activities of the respondent as a commercial officer did form part of consular functions. The duties of a commercial officer therefore entailed his inclusion in the institutional structure of the consulate with the result that he participated in the public functions of the foreign State which employed him (pp. 564-5).

(3) Particular problems arose, so far as the scope of the jurisdictional immunity of foreign States was concerned, in disputes concerning employment relationships involving the performance of functions for the sending State on the territory of the receiving State, where the protection of the rights of workers who were not nationals of the sending State was at stake. The jurisprudence recognized that immunity should be limited to cases where the exercise of jurisdiction would interfere with the essential core of sovereign functions. Thus jurisdiction was certainly excluded where reinstatement in an employment position was sought. It was also consistent with the jurisprudence to exclude jurisdiction where, as here, a claim for compensation would require an investigation into the behaviour of the foreign State as employer and thus directly concern the exercise of public powers related to the organization of the administration of the foreign State and the management of its employment relationships. In other words, immunity applied even to claims with a purely financial content, where the exercise of sovereign powers by the foreign State was affected by the claim (pp. 565-6).

(4) Such a rule was not incompatible with provisions of the Italian Constitution[1] enshrining the right to work (Article 2), the right to equality before the law (Article 3) and the right to legal protection (Article 24) since the principle of specialty applied. Derogations from jurisdiction were justified if they were necessary to ensure the fulfilment of diplomatic or consular functions, which were a fundamental institution of international law and as such recognized by Article 10 of the Italian Constitution as rules to which the Italian legal order should conform (pp. 566-7).

The following is the text of the judgment of the Court:

Course of the Proceedings—Mr Joes Cargnello was hired by the General Consulate of Canada in Milan by a letter dated 5 May 1982 and appointed to work for the Commercial Division with the duties of Commercial Officer for the sector of advanced technology products, mineral oil and gas, as well as industrial machinery and equipment. In accordance with the tasks entrusted to him, he was responsible for commercial cooperation between Italy and Canada, promoting investments in Canada by Italian companies and providing assistance to Canadian exporters in the regions of Northern Italy. By a letter

---

[1] The text of these provisions appears in nn. 9 and 10 below.

dated 28 May 1993 he was dismissed due to "incompetence". On the basis of the above facts the plaintiff asked that the termination of his employment should be declared null and void, since the procedure provided by Section 7 of Law No 300 of 20 May 1970 had not been complied with and, in any event, there were no grounds. Consequently he asked for the Canadian Consulate to be ordered to pay his accrued salary from the date of his dismissal until he found another equivalent job or, in the alternative, to pay damages in the amount of accrued salary from the date of his dismissal until the date of the Court's decision, as well as an indemnity in lieu of reinstatement.

Since the defendant did not appear, the Examining Magistrate (*Pretore*), by a decision dated 21 September 1994, declared the dismissal illegal and, upholding the claim in the alternative, ordered the Canadian Consulate to pay damages and an indemnity in lieu of reinstatement. The above decision was the subject of appeal, primarily by the General Consulate of Canada and incidentally by Mr Cargnello. The Court of Milan, by a judgment dated 2 September/11 November 1995, dismissed the two appeals.

In so far as is relevant for these proceedings, the Court stated that there was no lack of jurisdiction, both because the activity performed by Mr Cargnello did not form part of actual consular duties and because the claim submitted involved judicial review of the termination of employment and protection of the plaintiff's right to damages, and was not aimed at setting aside the effects of that termination.

So far as the incidental appeal is concerned, the Tribunal held that the termination could not be considered null and void because of infringement of the guarantees provided by Section 7 of Law No 300/1970.

Canada, representing the General Consulate of Canada in Milan, has lodged a petition for the cassation of that judgment on two grounds discussed below.

Mr Cargnello has lodged a counterclaim involving an incidental appeal based on one ground.

Reasons for the Decision

1. This Court orders the consolidation of the principal petition with the incidental petition, since they both challenge the same judgment (Article 335 of the Italian Code of Civil Procedure).

2. In the ground of his appeal in cassation the principal petitioner invokes the infringement and wrong application of Article 10 of the Italian Constitution, Article 4 of the Italian Code of Civil Procedure, Article 43 of the Vienna Convention of 24 April 1963 (ratified and implemented in Italy by Law No 804 of 19 August 1967), as well as inadequate justification (by the Court) on a critical issue of the dispute,

in relation to Article 360, paragraphs 1, 3 and 5 [of the Code of Civil Procedure] in the part of the judgment in which the Court deemed it appropriate to assert its jurisdiction.

The petitioner points out, in the first place, that consular functions must not be evaluated pursuant to the Italian legal order, but rather according to foreign rules based on the principles and norms of customary international law and treaty law, whereby it is prohibited for a court of the forum State to verify whether the nature of the activity performed by the employee belongs to the domain of public or private law, since the court is only permitted to verify whether the duties assigned to the employee of a foreign State are considered as pertaining to public law according to that State's own law and regulations.

The Court of Milan concluded that there was no undue interference in the sphere of sovereignty and independence of the State concerned since, on the basis of the Italian system, it considered that the activity performed by Mr Cargnello was of a private nature. It supported this conclusion by remarking that the Italian State had entrusted Italy's foreign commercial activity to the ICE [Foreign Trade Agency], which operates separately and outside the framework of Italian consular offices, as is also the case with Canada's commercial offices, which do not involve diplomatic representation.

The petitioner argues, however, that Canadian law supports his view, since it entrusts to the Ministry of International Commerce the duty of promoting the expansion of Canada's international trade, assisting Canadian exporters in their initiatives in international markets and promoting exports. Consequently, the promotional activity of commercial trade performed locally by commercial divisions of Canadian consulates is clearly of a public nature.

In this situation, according to the principal petitioner, the promotion of commercial relations between Canadian and Italian operators, which is included amongst the public functions of the Consulate's Commercial Division, must be distinguished from commercial activities themselves which businessmen (or the foreign State itself) perform, as part of this promotion.

On the other hand, in making this distinction, the competent Court must not resort to an unacceptably arbitrary choice in classifying those acts which a foreign State may perform within its sphere of sovereignty. Rules of custom and treaty exist in international law, which enable the Court to ascertain the applicability of the principle "*par in parem non habet jurisdictionem*". Indeed, Article 5(b) and (c) of the Vienna Convention on Consular Relations, implemented in Italy by Law No 804 of 1967, specifically lists, amongst consular functions, the following:

—"furthering the development of commercial, economic, cultural and scientific relations between the sending State and the receiving State":

—"ascertaining conditions and developments in the commercial, economic, cultural and scientific life of the receiving State, reporting thereon to the Government of the sending State and giving information to persons interested".

Consequently, according to the petitioner, the conclusion reached in the judgment under appeal is not based on a correct criterion, since the duty to offer assistance to private entities within the framework of commercial cooperation is clearly included amongst consular functions, and the fact that Italy avails itself of the ICE for the performance of the above duties is irrelevant.

The principal petitioner raises a further objection, arguing that the Court of Cassation has identified a number of criteria for categorizing a labour relationship. Italian jurisdiction is accordingly excluded when the employment relationship . . . requires that the employee participate in a public activity (Court of Cassation Decision No 3248/1990). This occurs, according to the jurisprudence of the Court of Cassation (Decisions Nos 3063/1979 and 3468/1988), when the employment relationship has as its object managerial or white-collar duties and entails the inclusion of the employee in the public organization of the [foreign] State for the achievement of its institutional purposes. All these features are present in this case, according to the petitioner.

The petitioner also raises an additional objection against the judgment being challenged, in so far as the Court of Milan stated that, since the object of the claim was damages, this entailed the jurisdiction of the Italian courts because it did not [seek to] withdraw the effects of the termination notice. According to the petitioner, this statement conflicts with the principle, asserted in this Court's case-law (Court of Cassation Decisions Nos 145/1990[2] and 7548/1991), that jurisdiction must be denied where financial aspects of the employment relationship are at issue and the employee wants to make a claim for damages, which requires appraisals and investigations of the exercise of the powers of the foreign State concerned.

3.-4. [In his second ground of appeal the petitioner challenged the award by the Court of Milan to the plaintiff of fifteen months' salary under Article 18 of the Italian Workers' Statute. The petitioner argued that this benefit was only available where an employee was reinstated in the job from which he had been dismissed, which could not be ordered in this case because the employer was the consulate of a foreign State. Mr Cargnello argued that, if the Court found that his right under Article 18 was indeed unenforceable, then his dismissal should be declared null and void in law since in any event it was without cause. The Court continued:]

5. The first issue which this Court must examine is whether the petition filed by the State of Canada is admissible even though, in the

[2 See p. 520 above.]

earlier stages of the proceedings, the defendant was the General Consulate of Milan. Mr Cargnello's attorney points out that the actor in the material legal relationship was the Consulate, which provided for the establishment and termination of the employment and, having been absent from the first stage of the proceedings, appealed to the Court of Milan. The State of Canada, on the other hand, in filing the petition before the Court of Cassation, offered no documentation or suitable data to "provide the reasons for replacing the Consulate in these proceedings".

6. This Court believes that it is not appropriate to uphold the plea of inadmissibility against the State of Canada.

First, it must be pointed out that consular offices are entities of their sending State and their position in relation to that State can only be governed by the domestic legal system of that State.

By a memorial filed pursuant to Article 378 of the Italian Code of Civil Procedure, Canada relied upon the rules of its domestic legal system (which were not challenged by the defence in the course of the oral proceedings), according to which the Ministry of Justice (the Attorney-General, who may delegate this function to the Deputy Attorney-General) has full standing to represent the State in any dispute concerning Canadian ministerial offices, including consulates which are classified as offices of the Ministry of Foreign Affairs. It follows that the General Consulate of Milan is not a subject different from the sending State, but constitutes a representative body of that State. As such, the Consulate has standing to sue and be sued in disputes concerning its functions and this does not exclude the possibility that the State itself, through its institutional bodies (here the Ministry of Justice), may decide directly to defend its interests, which are usually looked after, according to the Canadian system, by its consuls.

Accordingly, there are not two different subjects, which might suggest that one subject replaced another in the current lawsuit, but rather one single subject, the State of Canada, which is party to the relationship, created through one of its offices, from which the present dispute arose.

7. With regard to the principal petition, this Court holds that Italian courts lack jurisdiction over the matter at issue.

In the first place it must be stated that, contrary to what is held in the judgment under appeal, the duties entrusted to, and performed by, Mr Cargnello fall completely within consular functions, as provided for by Article 5, paragraphs (b) and (c), of the Vienna Convention of 24 April 1963, implemented in Italy by Law No 804 of 9 August 1967. In fact, these provisions expressly list, amongst consular functions, "furthering the development of commercial, economic, cultural and scientific relations between the sending State and the receiving State" (paragraph (b)) and "ascertaining conditions and developments in the commercial, economic, cultural and scientific life of the receiving State, reporting thereon to the Government of the sending State and giving information to persons interested therein" (paragraph (c)). The Court of Milan started from the above rules, to which it also made reference, but added that the specific duties of Mr Cargnello (to fulfil requests for assistance received from Canadian companies interested in concluding business deals on the Italian market; to describe to Italian companies Canadian products and the benefits to be derived from commercial deals with Canada . . .) were not part of "consular functions" since this term did not include the "satisfaction of particular requirements of corporate bodies wishing to perform such activities in their homeland or abroad".

The above statement is clearly erroneous, since promoting commercial deals between private entities is also included in the duties of consular offices, as is disclosed by the paragraph of Article 5 of the Convention mentioned above. It appears from this paragraph that any activity in support of the commercial transactions of the "persons interested therein" (irrespective of whether they are private or public entities) between the territory of the forum and the sending State, is amongst the duties which, according to the rules of international law, may be entrusted to consular offices. Equally, Article 45 of Presidential Decree No 18 of 5 January 1967 on the rules governing the administration of foreign affairs lists amongst consular functions, "to promote in the most appropriate manner any economic activity concerning Italy, taking particular interest in the development of commercial exchanges", a provision which shows that, also according to the Italian legal order, the duty of promoting commercial transactions is included amongst the duties of Italian consular offices.

Accordingly, the duties of Commercial Officer entailed the inclusion of Mr Cargnello in the typical structure of the Consulate and his duties were therefore institutional in nature and, in accordance with international custom, typical of the activities of those bodies entrusted with the representation of the interests of the sending State in the receiving State.

The next question which arises is [bearing in mind the nature of the duties performed by Mr Cargnello] whether a claim, aimed exclusively at obtaining compensation for loss arising from an allegedly unlawful dismissal, can be pursued before a court of the forum State.

It must first be pointed out that, pursuant to customary international law, the immunity of a foreign State from the jurisdiction of another State is recognized, in relationships established for the achievement of the foreign State's institutional aims, although it is limited to acts through which the foreign State performs public functions.

Particular problems arise in connection with employment relationships established on the territory of the receiving State, for activities to be carried out on that territory, in the performance of functions typical of an office belonging to a foreign State. Initially, in a decision of the Court of Cassation No 2329 of 15 May 1989,[3] an effort was made to mediate between the requirement of ensuring recognition of the immunity of a foreign State and the protection of the rights of citizens in employment. The criterion adopted limited immunity to cases where a judicial decision would actually and concretely interfere with the essential core of the functions of the foreign State concerned.

In later decisions it has been pointed out that, in the presence of duties related to the institutional functions of a sovereign State, immunity also applies to claims with a financial content, but only in cases where the exercise of sovereign powers of the foreign State is involved. Thus Italian jurisdiction is certainly excluded in the case of claims seeking reinstatement in employment (see, *inter alia*, Court of Cassation Decisions No 3248 of 19 April 1990; No 12315 of 18 November 1992;[4] No 5565 of 8 June 1994;[5] and No 4483 of 21 April 1995),[6] or more favourable economic treatment because of the performance of duties of greater responsibility (Court of Cassation Decisions No 145 of 16 January 1990;[7] and No 8768 of 9 September 1997). Decision No 12771 of 28 November 1991[8] is to be included in the same trend of jurisprudence covering cases which . . . require an evaluation of the facts by the Court resulting in a denial of jurisdiction. This occurs in the event that a purely monetary claim requires an investigation of the behaviour of the employer in having recourse to dismissal, since such an investigation directly concerns the exercise of public-law powers relating to the organization of the offices [of the foreign State] and the management of its employment relationships.

In this situation, bearing in mind the case-law on the identification of the essential core of consular functions with regard to which immunity from jurisdiction arises, the decision under appeal was rightly challenged by the petitioner as a violation of the immunity from jurisdiction enshrined in Article 43 of the Vienna Convention on Consular Relations, as interpreted above. The counterclaimant argues that the rules in fact conflict with certain principles of the Italian Constitution, specifically Article 2 (the right to work), Article 3[9] (discrimination, with respect to a Canadian company operating in Italy) and Article 24[10] (denial of legal protection to the employee by the Italian State). The doubt raised by the counterclaimant is clearly unfounded.

---

[3] 101 *ILR* 379.]   [4] See Note at p. 558 above.]
[5] See p. 540 above.]   [6] See p. 555 above.]
[7] See p. 520 above.]   [8] See p. 525 above.]
[9] Article 3 provides: "All citizens are equal before the law."]
[10] Article 24 provides: "All citizens may bring judicial proceedings for the protection of their rights."]

The Constitutional Court has pointed out that the freedom of an employer to terminate any employment relationship and the right of an employee to maintain his position are opposing values, which must be balanced by the Legislature . . . (see, for example, decision of the Constitutional Court No 2 of 14 January 1986). Consequently, statutes drafted in a differentiating manner do not affect the principle of equality nor the right to work.

In addition, the other doubt expressed by the counterclaimant is also unfounded, as the Constitutional Court ruled in connection with a similar case concerning diplomatic immunity which was governed by Article 31 of the Vienna Convention of 18 April 1961, implemented in Italy by Law No 804 of 9 August 1967. In Decision No 48 of 18 June 1979[11] the Constitutional Court stated that there was no conflict with the rules of the Constitution in that case because the principle of specialty applied. International law recognized that derogations from jurisdiction arising from diplomatic immunity were justified if they were necessary to ensure the performance of the functions of diplomatic missions. Even though that case was concerned with different [treaty] rules, there is no doubt that the same rationale applies to the [treaty] rule applicable here since, pursuant to Article 10 of the Italian Constitution, our legal system "shall conform with the generally acknowledged rules of international law" which include, as is well known, the rule *par in parem non habet jurisdictionem*.

Finally, the alleged violation of the principle of equality has not been established. This principle, which requires similar treatment of similar situations, is not applicable here since the functions, guarantees and rights/duties of an employee are different depending on whether he is employed by a consulate or a company of the same foreign State.

8. The principal petition must therefore be upheld with a declaration of lack of jurisdiction of the Italian courts so far as the application to the case at issue of Article 18 of Law No 300 of 20 May 1970[12] is concerned . . .

For the above reasons, the Court:
—Consolidates the petitions;
—Upholds the principal petition;
—Declares that the Italian courts lack jurisdiction over the claim and counterclaim;
—Annuls the judgment under appeal . . .

[Report: Unpublished]

[11 78 *ILR* 106.]
[12 Article 18 deals with the right of an employee to be reinstated in his employment if unlawfully dismissed.]

NOTE.—This decision may be compared with an earlier judgment of the Italian courts rendered in 1981 in *Bulli* v. *Foreign and Commonwealth Office*, which also involved an employment dispute between a commercial officer and a consulate, printed in 65 *ILR* 343.

Human rights—Refugees—Applicants for refugee status— Test to be applied—Geneva Convention relating to the Status of Refugees, 1951, and Protocol, 1967—Relevance of other human rights treaties

Treaties — Effect in national law — Geneva Convention relating to the Status of Refugees, 1951, and Protocol, 1967—The law of New Zealand

BUTLER *v.* ATTORNEY-GENERAL AND REFUGEE STATUS APPEALS AUTHORITY[1]

New Zealand, Court of Appeal. 30 *September* 1997

(Richardson P, Henry, Keith, Tipping and Williams, JJ)

SUMMARY: *The facts:*—The appellant, who was a citizen of the United Kingdom and of the Republic of Ireland, had travelled to New Zealand while on bail pending appeal from his most recent conviction. In May 1991 the appellant had arrived in New Zealand with his elder son and his partner, who was pregnant. He failed to disclose his convictions and was wrongly granted a visitor's permit. In August 1991 he was informed about the discovery of the facts about his convictions, following which he filed an application for refugee status. In October 1991 the New Zealand Immigration Service obtained a removal warrant, but undertook not to execute it until the appellant's refugee status had been determined. Shortly afterwards, a daughter was born to the appellant and his partner. In 1992 the appellant's wife and their other son had arrived in New Zealand and they too had applied for refugee status. The application was declined and the appellant appealed to the Refugee Status Appeals Authority ("the Authority"). The Authority dismissed his appeal in December 1992.

---

[1] The appellant was represented by R. Harrison QC; the first respondent was represented by E. D. France and C. Geiringer.

In 1993 the appellant filed an application at the High Court for review of the Authority's decision, claiming that he was entitled to refugee status under the 1951 Convention relating to the Status of Refugees ("the Convention") as supplemented by its 1967 Protocol ("the Protocol"). The application was dismissed in July 1997. The appellant appealed on matters of law relating to the tests applied by the Authority.

Held:—The appeal was dismissed. There was no error of law in the Authority's determination of the present case.

(1) The issue in this case was one of law relating to the definition of "refugee" in Article 1(A)(2) of the Convention as supplemented by the Protocol. Although the provisions of the Convention had been incorporated into the executive machinery for considering applications for refugee status, the New Zealand Legislature had not given express effect to the Convention nor the Protocol in the law of New Zealand upon accession to both treaties (p. 571).

(2) In view of the way the case had been presented to the Authority, it could not be said that the Authority had committed an error of law in not separately addressing a distinct reasonableness element (pp. 577-80).

(3) Furthermore, the members of the Authority had incorporated the notion of reasonableness into their tests relating to relocation as that matter had arisen from the definition of "refugee" as stated in Article 1(A)(2) of the Convention. In addressing the role of reasonableness in the relocation element of the definition of "refugee", the basic concept of protection was central to the definition of "refugee". The test for reasonableness had to be seen in context and had to be related to the primary obligation of the country of nationality to protect the claimant. While the relocation element was inherent in the definition of "refugee", it was not distinct. Having regard to the Convention's purposes of original protection or surrogate protection for the avoidance of persecution, the question was whether it was unreasonable in a relocation case to require a claimant to avail him- or herself of the available protection of the country of nationality (pp. 580-2).

(4) While the members of the Authority had included a reasonableness element in their decisions in a manner which was appropriate in the circumstances of the appeal, the rights and interests of the family as found in the Universal Declaration of Human Rights, the International Covenant on Civil and Political Rights and the Convention on the Rights of the Child did not have to be considered on the basis of those circumstances and the definition of refugee in the Convention (pp. 582-3).

The following is the text of the judgment of the Court, delivered by Keith J:

The Issue and the Proceedings

Daniel Martin Butler, the appellant, claims that he is entitled to refugee status under the 1951 Convention relating to the Status of Refugees as supplemented by its 1967 Protocol, 189 UNTS 150; 606 UNTS 267. He contends, in terms of the Convention, that owing to well-founded fear of being persecuted for reasons of political opinion he is outside the countries of his nationality (the United Kingdom of Great Britain and Northern Ireland, and the Republic of Ireland), and that, owing to that fear, he is unwilling to return to those countries. His fears relate to death threats made against him by the Irish People's Liberation Organization (IPLO) and to his relations with the Royal Ulster Constabulary (RUC). He wishes to avoid being removed from New Zealand and returned to the United Kingdom.

Officials of the New Zealand Immigration Service (NZIS) declined his application for refugee status and, in a decision given on 14 December 1992, the Refugee Status Appeals Authority (RSAA) dismissed his appeal from that decision. He seeks review of the Authority's decision and, as formulated in the submissions made to us, an order requiring the Authority to consider the appeal afresh on a different basis from that which it is said to have adopted. Robertson J heard the application for review, initially filed four-and-a-half years earlier on 18 January 1993, on 18 July 1997 and dismissed the application in a judgment given on 29 July 1997. He mentioned some of the reasons given by the parties for the inordinate delay in getting the case to trial.

Mr Butler gave notice of appeal on 14 August 1997. The only issues before us are matters of law, relating to the tests applied by the RSAA to Mr Butler's appeal. For the reasons given in this judgment we do not consider that the Authority erred in law and, accordingly, we dismiss the appeal.

A New Case on Appeal

In the High Court phase of the proceedings Mr Butler also sought relief in respect of decisions taken by officials and the Minister of Immigration under the Immigration Act 1987 but these matters are no longer before us. The case on appeal is distinct from that in the High

Court in a second sense. The grounds for the challenge to the Authority's decision as presented to us are markedly different from those argued below.

The Crown, while not formally opposing the Court dealing with the new grounds, submits that we should, in deciding whether to exercise our discretion in the interests of justice to consider those fresh matters, consider certain cautionary propositions. We do accept that it is unsatisfactory for an essentially new case to be mounted on appeal: the parties and the Court do not have advantage of the issues being refined through the first instance hearing and decision, with the consequence of the argument being presented in a more developed and considered way. As well, the cost and delay associated with an appeal might have been avoided had the new matters been raised and disposed of at first instance along with the other issues considered. And, although it is not in issue here, different evidence might have been required or called to meet the new grounds. The issue in this case is however a narrow one of law relating to the definition of "refugee" in the Convention and Protocol. As well, the importance to the appellant and his family of the decision to execute (or not) the removal warrant which he faces and the possibly grave consequences of that action have led us to consider the new grounds.

The case has been argued on the basis of the 1951 Convention and the 1967 Protocol but Parliament did not give express effect to the Convention in the law of New Zealand either in 1960 when New Zealand acceded to it nor in 1973 when New Zealand acceded to the 1967 Protocol nor at any later time. Rather, as explained later, the provisions of the Convention were incorporated into the executive machinery for considering applications for refugee status. We come back to the absence of legislation at the end of the judgment. In the meantime we proceed simply on the basis of the treaty texts.

The Definition of "Refugee"

The Convention and Protocol define "refugee" and then set out the status (or the rights and duties) of a refugee and regulate certain administrative matters. At the heart of the Convention and this case is the definition of "refugee" in Article 1. We set out most of that Article. The emphasized words are those principally in issue. The words in square brackets were deleted by the 1967 Protocol:

For the purposes of the present Convention, *the term "refugee" shall apply to any person who*: . . .
A (2) [As a result of events occurring before 1 January 1951 and] *owing to well-founded fear of being persecuted for reasons of race, religion, nationality, membership of a particular social group or political opinion, is outside the country of his nationality and is unable or, owing to such fear, is unwilling to avail himself of the protection of that country;* or who, not having a nationality and being outside the country of his former

habitual residence [as a result of such events], is unable or, owing to such fear, is unwilling to return to it.

In the case of a person who has more than one nationality, the term "the country of his nationality" shall mean each of the countries of which he is a national, and a person shall not be deemed to be lacking the protection of the country of his nationality if, without any valid reason based on well-founded fear, he has not availed himself of the protection of one of the countries of which he is a national.

. . .

C. This Convention shall cease to apply to any person falling under the terms of section A if:

(1) He has voluntarily re-availed himself of the protection of the country of his nationality; or

(2) Having lost his nationality, he has voluntarily reacquired it; or

(3) He has acquired a new nationality, and enjoys the protection of the country of his new nationality; or

(4) He has voluntarily re-established himself in the country which he left or outside which he remained owing to fear of persecution; or

(5) He can no longer, because the circumstances in connection with which he has been recognized as a refugee have ceased to exist, continue to refuse to avail himself of the protection of the country of his nationality.

. . .

D. This Convention shall not apply to persons who are at present receiving from organs or agencies of the United Nations other than the United Nations High Commissioner for Refugees protection or assistance.

When such protection or assistance has ceased for any reason, without the position of such persons being definitively settled in accordance with the relevant resolutions adopted by the General Assembly of the United Nations, these persons shall *ipso facto* be entitled to the benefits of this Convention.

E. This Convention shall not apply to a person who is recognized by the competent authorities of the country in which he has taken residence as having the rights and obligations which are attached to the possession of the nationality of that country.

F. The provisions of this Convention shall not apply to any person with respect to whom there are serious reasons for considering that:

(a) He has committed a crime against peace, a war crime, or a crime against humanity, as defined in the international instruments drawn up to make provision in respect of such crimes;

(b) He has committed a serious non-political crime outside the country of refuge prior to his admission to that country as a refugee;

(c) He has been guilty of acts contrary to the purposes and principles of the United Nations.

It was the 1 January 1951 temporal limit stated in the first line of Article 1(A)(2) which led to the preparation of the 1967 Protocol. In its preamble the Contracting States recalled that limit, stated "that new refugee situations have arisen since the Convention was adopted and that the refugees concerned may therefore not fall within the scope of the Convention" and declared that it was desirable that equal status should be enjoyed by all refugees covered by the definition irrespective of the date of 1 January 1951. Accordingly when New Zealand became party to the Protocol its obligations were very considerably extended especially in respect of refugee claims made at the border or within New Zealand, for instance by someone who, as in the current case, entered on a visitor's permit.

The substantive provisions of the 1951 Convention setting out the status of refugees begin with the obligations of refugees in Article 2:

Every refugee has duties to the country in which he finds himself, which require in particular that he conform to its laws and regulations as well as to measures taken for the maintenance of public order.

The remaining substantive provisions concern the rights of refugees and the corresponding duties of the Contracting States relating to matters such as non-discrimination, religion, legal status, employment, welfare, travel documents (see Immigration Act 1987 Section 18(b)) and administrative assistance. Some rights are conferred in absolute terms (such as the right of access to the courts) while others are conferred by reference to a standard. The standard is either national treatment (for instance in respect of religion and elementary education) or the rights of aliens (for instance in respect of religion and elementary education) or the rights of aliens (for instance in respect of property and employment). An important right included in Chapter V (Administrative Measures) is the right of a refugee lawfully in the territory of the Contracting State not to be expelled save on the grounds of national security or public order (Article 32; see also the non-expulsion —"non-refoulement"—provision in Article 33).

The Refugee Status Appeals Authority

In early 1991 the RSAA was established by Cabinet decision with the power "to make a final determination on appeal from decisions of officers of the Refugee Status Section (RSS) of the New Zealand Immigration Service of claims of refugee status, that is, to determine whether persons are refugees within the meaning of Article 1, Section A(2) of the 1951 Convention . . . as supplemented by the 1967 Protocol . . .".

The terms of reference in force at the relevant time provided that for the purposes of any appeal two members were to sit, with the possibility of a representative of the United Nations High Commissioner for Refugees (UNHCR) sitting as a non-voting participant. In this case, in fact three members and the UNHCR representative sat. Nothing was made of that fact. A related rule was that "A decision of the Authority shall be a decision of the members hearing an appeal.

Where members are unable to agree on a decision, the outcome shall be in favour of the claimant (that is, refugee status shall be granted)."

The claimant was to be given at least ten days' notice of the hearing and the RSS was to be responsible for providing an independent interpreter if required. The Authority's procedure included considering the written decision of officers of the RSS and any written material submitted by the claimant and the RSS, interviewing the claimant and considering any other evidence presented by the claimant who might be represented. Officers of the RSS could give evidence if the claimant was interviewed and could be required by the Authority to obtain further information or carry out further investigations. Otherwise the Authority could regulate its procedures, receive such evidence and conduct its hearings in such manner as it thought fit.

The Authority's decision on an appeal, together with the reasons for it, was to be put in writing and provided to the claimant. The RSS was to inform the Minister of Immigration and the Minister of Foreign Affairs and Trade of the outcome of every appeal.

Under the procedures approved by Cabinet on 17 December 1990:

The Minister of Immigration agrees to be bound by the decisions of the RSAC [*sic*] in favour of the appellant in all but exceptional cases. He would direct the Immigration Service to consider successful appellants for residence in line with current policy which provides for a grant of residence in all but exceptional cases.

By contrast the *Refugee Status Determination Procedures* published by the NZIS in August 1993 (after the relevant date in this case) takes an apparently more absolute position:

The Authority's decision on any matter properly before it shall be final and there shall be no right of appeal or rehearing on that matter, and the Minister of Immigration agrees to be bound by the decision.

Nothing turns on the difference in this appeal since the application for review is now directed solely at the Authority's decision. The two provisions do however help highlight the fact that what is in issue in the work of the RSS and the RSAA is distinct in law from the grant of temporary or residents' permits or the making of a special direction under the Immigration Act. A further decision remains to be made if the successful appellant is to remain in New Zealand, with the rights conferred by and flowing from that Act.

There is no legislation establishing the RSAA, providing for its membership, its procedures, its functions and its powers, or creating rights of appeal against or review of its decisions. The only reference to it in the statute book is its inclusion in the list of tribunals in respect of

which legal aid may be granted, Legal Services Act 1991 Section
19(1)(j). As already noted we return to that matter at the end of this
judgment.

The Facts

We can state the facts briefly since review of the Authority's decision is
sought solely on the basis of error of law. The appellant was born in
Belfast in 1951. He is a citizen of both the United Kingdom and the
Republic of Ireland. In 1973 he was sentenced in Belfast to five years'
imprisonment for false imprisonment and possession of a firearm and
in early 1991 again in Belfast to eighteen months' imprisonment for
the suspicious possession of ammunition. We were informed from the
bar that he has recently sought a pardon in respect of the 1991
conviction. In 1980 he married Collette Butler and they have two sons
who are now sixteen and fifteen. While on bail pending appeal from
his 1991 conviction he travelled to New Zealand with his older son
and his *de facto* pregnant partner, Bernadette Daly, and on 31 May
1991 he was granted a three months' visitor's permit. That grant was
in breach of Section 7 of the Immigration Act under which no permit
is to be granted to anyone who has been convicted at any time of any
offence and has been sentenced to imprisonment for a term of five
years or more or who within the preceding ten years has been
convicted of an offence and sentenced to a term of twelve months or
more. Mr Butler did not disclose those convictions and when the New
Zealand Immigration Service discovered the facts about his convictions
it advised the appellant of this, on 29 August 1991. On the next day
Mr Butler filed his application for refugee status.

On 9 October 1991 the NZIS obtained a removal warrant from
the Auckland District Court and undertook not to execute it until Mr
Butler's refugee status was determined. Two days later a daughter was
born to Mr Butler and Ms Daly. On 17 January 1992 Mrs Butler and
their other son arrived in New Zealand and they too applied for
refugee status.

The refugee application was being processed throughout this period,
with an interview being conducted and documentation and submissions
being presented. On 10 March 1992 the application was declined and
Mr Butler appealed on the same day to the RSAA. The appeal was
heard over three days in May and June by three members of the
Authority, along with a representative of the UNHCR participating as
a non-voting member. Mr Butler was represented by experienced counsel,
and with his wife and their two sons gave evidence. The appeal was
dismissed on 14 December 1992 with Judge B. O. Nicholson giving his
reasons and Dr J. M. Priestley giving his reasons with which Mr R. P. G.
Haines agreed. The reasons differed on two matters, as will appear.

The Decision of the RSAA

Mr Butler's case before the RSAA was twofold. First, he had a genuine fear of being murdered as an alleged informer by the IPLO. According to a publication of a research group which was before the RSAA, the Irish Republican Socialist Party broke from the official Irish Republican Army in 1974. It spawned a paramilitary wing, the Irish National Liberation Army, later that year. Following internal feuding and killings a further splinter group, the IPLO, had emerged by 1987 (Research Institute for the Study of Conflict and Terrorism *Northern Ireland: Reappraising Republican Violence—a special report* (1991) 19). Secondly, he had a genuine fear of death and harassment from the Royal Ulster Constabulary (RUC) because of a ruse he used against them on the issue of acting as an informer.

It is helpful in considering the way the RSAA decided these two claims to use the six-step approach its members used in this case as in earlier ones. The issues before us related to steps 3 and 4:

1. Is the appellant genuinely in fear?
2. Is the harm he fears of sufficient gravity to amount to persecution?
3. Is there a real chance that the appellant will suffer persecution if he returns to either of his countries of nationality?
4. Will both the United Kingdom and the Republic of Ireland fail in their duty to protect the appellant from persecution?
5. Is the persecution feared for a Convention reason?
6. Is the appellant excluded from refugee status by the provisions of Article 1F of the Convention?

On step 1, Judge Nicholson held that the test was satisfied in relation to both the IPLO and the RUC, Dr Priestley and Mr Haines only the former.

They agreed that the feared harm did amount to persecution—step 2.

They agreed as well that the persecution was for a Convention reason—"political opinion"—step 5—and that Mr Butler was not excluded by Article 1F—step 6.

On steps 3 and 4 the members agreed that Mr Butler could be confined safely in prison in Northern Ireland (given that he had yet to serve the eighteen months' sentence) but that there was a real chance of persecution were he to stay in Northern Ireland after that. They all considered however that there was no such real chance were he to go to Great Britain at the end of the sentence or, according to Dr Priestley and Mr Haines (but not Judge Nicholson), to the Republic of Ireland. That is to say, they all agreed that adequate provision was available in the United Kingdom outside Northern Ireland.

The Alleged Errors of Law

The various findings of fact were not challenged before us. Rather the attack was on the Authority's understanding of the law involved in the findings just summarized. Mr Harrison QC (who did not appear in the High Court) submitted that if the Authority held, as it had, that the appellant had a well-founded fear for Convention reasons in respect of part, but not all, of the country of nationality it must consider the reasonableness in all the circumstances of any resulting location to another part of the country. As well, in a case involving family members like the present, the Authority in carrying out that reasonableness inquiry must have regard to rights in respect of the family as found in the Universal Declaration of Human Rights (UNGA Resolution 217A(III)), the International Covenant on Civil and Political Rights (999 UNTS 171) and the Convention on the Rights of the Child (1993 NZTS No 3). The second argument was based on *Tavita* v. *Minister of Immigration* [1994] 2 NZLR 257[2] and later decisions of this Court.

The submission was that the RSAA had not formulated those two tests for itself and had failed to apply them. That, it was argued, was a reviewable error of law. For reasons relating to (1) the process followed before the Authority, (2) the decisions given by its members, and (3) the interpretation of the definition we cannot accept that submission. We consider those matters in relation to the two proposed tests.

1. *The process followed before the Authority*

A person claiming refugee status has the burden of establishing the elements of the claim. That rule should however not be applied mechanically. Those making a decision which may put an individual's right to life at risk and courts reviewing any such decision have a special responsibility to see that the law is complied with, e.g. *R* v. *Home Secretary, ex parte Bugdaycay* [1987] AC 514,[3] 531, 537.

The evidence given and the submissions made to the Authority covered the whole of the United Kingdom and in particular what was referred to in the submissions as "internal flight". (The RSAA prefers the expression "relocation", in part on the basis that the refugee status decisions look forward, while the expression "internal flight" contemplates alternative action that the claimants might have taken in the past instead of leaving their country of nationality.) That evidence and submission was in response to "one of the major reasons" which the RSS gave for refusing the application:

Following his release from prison, Mr Butler may relocate himself and his family in any part of Ireland, the British Isles or in a member country of the European Economic Community, if he is uncomfortable with the prospect of resuming life in Belfast.

[[2] 101 *ILR* 455.]   [[3] 79 *ILR* 642.]

The written submission then referred to an earlier decision of the Authority and quoted from the work of a Canadian scholar whose opinion the Authority had earlier adopted:

The logic of the internal protection principle must, however, be recognized to flow from the absence of a need for asylum abroad. It should be restricted in its application to persons who can *genuinely access* domestic protection, and for whom the reality of protection is *meaningful*. In situations where, for example, financial, logistical or other barriers prevent the claimant from reaching internal safety; where the quality of internal protection fails to meet basic norms of civil, political and socio-economic human rights; or where internal safety is otherwise illusory or unpredictable, state accountability for the harm is established and refugee status is appropriately recognized. James C. Hathaway, *The Law of Refugee Status* (1991) 134 (original emphasis)

(The passage has also been adopted by the Canadian Federal Court of Appeal, *Thirunavukkarasu* v. *Canada (Minister of Employment and Immigration)* [1994] 1 FC 589, 597; and by the English Court of Appeal, *R* v. *Home Secretary, ex parte Ikhalk*, 16 April 1997.)

In a note to the second sentence of that passage, Professor Hathaway quotes the following paragraph from the UNHCR *Handbook on Procedures and Criteria for Determining Refugee Status*:

The fear of being persecuted need not always extend to the *whole* territory of the refugee's country of nationality. Thus in ethnic clashes or in cases of grave disturbances involving civil war conditions, persecution of a specific ethnic or national group may occur in only one part of the country. In such situations, a person will not be excluded from refugee status merely because he could have sought refuge in another part of the same country, if under all the circumstances it would not have been reasonable to expect him to do so. (Para. 91, original emphasis; the passage is identical in the 1997 edition and is also quoted in a recent judgment by the English Court of Appeal, *R* v. *Home Secretary, ex parte Robinson*, 11 July 1997, para. 12, *The Times*, 1 August 1997.)

The *Handbook* has been issued since 1979 for the guidance of governments and especially of officials concerned with the determination of refugee status. It is "based on the knowledge accumulated by the High Commissioner's office", including knowledge of State practice, exchanges between the Office and State officials, principles defined by the Executive Committee of the UNHCR's Programme and relevant literature. It is often referred to in judgments (e.g. *Canada (Attorney-General)* v. *Ward* [1993] 2 SCR 689,[4] 713-14; for the role of subsequent State practice in interpretation, see the Vienna Convention on the Law of Treaties, 1969, Article 31(3)(b)), but sometimes caution is expressed, e.g. Mason CJ in *Chan* v. *Minister for Immigration and Ethnic Affairs* (1989) 87 ALR 412,[5] 420.

[4 104 *ILR* 222.]   [5 90 *ILR* 138.]

Counsel before the RSAA did not refer to that passage in her submissions. Rather she went immediately from the quotation from Professor Hathaway to the reasons for Mr Butler's contention that he did not have the option of internal flight either within Ireland or within the United Kingdom:

(1) he would not be able to obtain meaningful protection from the ILPO anywhere else in the United Kingdom
(2) a return to Ireland or the United Kingdom would lead to his immediate arrest and imprisonment in Ireland (perhaps that should read Northern Ireland) and
(3) he was not guaranteed entry to Britain, given the power of the United Kingdom Home Secretary to exclude persons suspected of links with terrorists.

The Authority made clear findings of fact against Mr Butler on those matters, and concluded that there was not a real chance of persecution in Great Britain. Those findings are not in issue before us.

To return to the alleged errors of law, the appellant's submission to the RSAA did not go beyond the specified issues of protection and exclusion to any wider issues of the unreasonableness or harshness of relocation. Nor did the evidence. All that Mr Harrison could refer us to beyond those two matters was evidence relating to the quality of life and family circumstances, but that evidence was not directed either to any unreasonableness or harshness element or (to refer to the second alleged error of law) to any international standard relating to the family in the definition of refugee as it was to be applied by the Authority. He accepted that the appellant's case before the Authority was not directed at any second element of reasonableness, the reason being, he said in his reply, that there was no such second element established in the law applied by the RSAA at the time of its 1992 hearing and decision.

We later consider one aspect of that submission—the developing interpretation of the definition. At this stage we conclude that given the way the case was presented to the RSAA it cannot be said that it committed an error of law in not separately addressing a distinct reasonableness element. No such element was presented to it as arising from the facts. Indeed so far as we understand the facts it would have been very difficult for the appellant to have done that. This is not the kind of case when either the law or the factual situation before the Authority requires it of its own motion to take up any such additional element; see the statements to similar effect of Black CJ and Whitlam J in *Randhawa* v. *Minister for Immigration, Local Government and Ethnic Affairs* (1994) 124 ALR 265, 270-1, 280 FCA.

It cannot be an error of law for a tribunal considering a matter (here location) which is properly before it to fail to rule on some particular aspect of that matter if the particular aspect is not referred to by the interested party and if it does not stand out as requiring decision.

That in itself is a sufficient basis for dismissing the appeal, but we consider as well the other two reasons mentioned.

2. *The decisions of the members of the RSAA*

Judge Nicholson in considering the third and fourth matters in his list—the real chance of persecution if Mr Butler returned, and the likelihood of failure by the countries of nationality in their duty of protection—concluded his discussion of the former in relation to the United Kingdom in this way:

In summary on the third issue I find that the appellant can safely be returned to a Northern Ireland prison to serve his sentence but that if he were to attempt to live in Northern Ireland upon his release from prison, there is a real chance of his being killed by the IPLO. However, the appellant can safely relocate within the United Kingdom by taking up residence in Great Britain upon his release. *I cannot accept that it would be unreasonable to expect him to do so.* His fear of persecution is therefore not well-founded. (emphasis added)

He then found in terms of the fourth matter that Mr Butler could obtain the protection of the United Kingdom if he lived in Great Britain.

Dr Priestley, in summarizing his understanding of the test to be applied when the feared persecutor was a non-State agency, also included an element of reasonableness:

Sometimes, of course, the inability of the state to provide adequate protection may be limited to a certain locality or region (the protection available to victims of terrorist groups in the Punjab springs to mind). In such instances, however, refugee status is not available if adequate protection *can reasonably be accessed elsewhere in the state.* (emphasis added)

As well, he had begun his decision by saying that his route to the decision was not markedly different from Judge Nicholson's.

It is true that neither decision treats "reasonableness in all the circumstances" as a distinct matter but, to repeat, that was not put to the Authority and, to anticipate the next part of his judgment, such a reading may not have been required in any event.

The fact that the members of the Authority did incorporate the notion of reasonableness into their tests relating to relocation as that matter arose from the definition of "refugee".

3. The role of reasonableness in the relocation element of the definition of "refugee"
Mr Harrison put a 1995 decision of the Authority at the centre of his argument on the interpretation of the definition of "refugee" as it relates to relocation. According to the Authority in that case relocation turned on two issues:

1. Can the individual *genuinely access* domestic protection which is *meaningful*?
2. Is it reasonable, in all the circumstances, to expect the individual to relocate?

Indeed, said the Authority, that had been so since it began sitting in June 1991, *Refugee Appeal No 523/92 Re RS* (17 March 1995) 31. By contrast, Mr Harrison's argument was in part that that two-step test was not available in 1992 when Mr Butler's appeal was decided. Natural justice, the argument continued, required that he now be entitled to the benefits of the later development of the law.

An application for review on the ground that a body has made an error of law would seem by its very nature to require that the assessment be made by reference to the law of the time (as compared with an appeal by way of rehearing where the evolving law can be invoked), but such an approach in the present context might be thought to be technical. Accordingly we prefer to address the matter of interpretation directly (while recalling the conclusions that we have reached under the two preceding headings).

Central to the definition of "refugee" is the basic concept of protection—the protection accorded (or not) by the country of nationality or, for those who are stateless, the country of habitual residence. If there is a real chance that those countries will not provide protection, the world community is to provide surrogate protection either through other countries or through international bodies. So both paragraphs of Article 1(A)(2) define refugees in part by reference to their ability or willingness to avail themselves of the protection of their country of nationality or of habitual residence. Similarly the reasons for the cessation of refugee protection in Article 1(C) are based on the protection of a country becoming available. Article 1(E) is to the same effect. And Article 1(D) as well turns on protection or assistance being available from a United Nations body other than the UNHCR. The Supreme Court of Canada recently stated the rationale underlying international refugee protection in this way in a case involving a claim relating to feared persecution by the Irish National Liberation Army:

International refugee law was formulated to serve as a back-up to the protection one expects from the state of which an individual is a national. It was meant to come into play only in situations when that protection is unavailable, and then only in certain situations. The international community intended that persecuted individuals be required to approach their home state for protection before the responsibility of other states becomes engaged. For this reason, James Hathaway refers to the refugee scheme as "surrogate or substitute protection", activated only upon failure of national protection: see *The Law of Refugee Status* (1991), at p. 135. (*Canada (Attorney-General)* v. *Ward* [1993] 2 SCR 689,[6] 709).

As it said later in that judgment the lynch-pin is the State's inability to protect (722), or in the words of Lord Goff the true object of the Convention is not just to assuage fear, however reasonably and plausibly entertained, but to provide a safe haven for those unfortunate people when fear of persecution is in reality well founded (*R* v. *Home Secretary, ex parte Sivakumaram* [1989] AC 958,[7] 1000).

The various references to and tests for "reasonableness" or "undue harshness" (a test stated by Linden JA in *Thirunavukkarasu* v. *Canada (Minister of Employment and Immigration)* [1994] 1 FC 589, 598 FCA) must be seen in context or, to borrow Brooke LJ's metaphor, "against the backcloth that the issue is whether the claimant is entitled to the status of refugee", *R* v. *Home Secretary, ex parte Robinson*, para. 18. It is not a stand alone test, authorizing an unconfined inquiry into all the social, economic and political circumstances of the application including the circumstances of members of the family. The test is for instance sharply different from the humanitarian tests provided for in the Immigration Act Sections 63B and 105. It does not in particular range widely over the rights and interests in respect of the family: the refugee inquiry is narrowly focused on the persecution and protection of the particular claimant. In no case to which we were referred were international obligations in respect of the family seen as being linked to the definition of refugee. While family circumstances might be relevant to the reasonableness element, there is no basis for such a link on the facts of the present case. We note as well that New Zealand had not become bound by the Convention on the Rights of the Child at the time of the decision of the Authority.

Rather than being seen as free standing (as more recent decisions of the Authority appear to suggest), the reasonableness test must be related to the primary obligation of the country of nationality to protect the claimant. To repeat what Professor Hathaway said in the passage relating to relocation quoted earlier, *meaningful* national State protection which can be *genuinely accessed* requires provision of basic norms of civil, political and socio-economic rights. To the same effect Linden JA in the Canadian case cited above, [1994] 1 FC at 598-9, stresses that it is not a matter of a claimant's convenience or of the attractiveness of the place of relocation. More must be shown. The reasonableness element must be tied back to the definition of "refugee" set out in the Convention and to the Convention's purposes of original protection or surrogate protection for the avoidance of persecution. The relocation element is inherent in the definition; it is not distinct. The question is whether, having regard to those purposes, it is unreasonable in a relocation case to require claimants to avail themselves of the available protection of the country of nationality.

It follows from the above discussion that we see no error of law in the Authority's determination in the present case. Its members did include a reasonableness element in their decisions that Mr Butler was not a refugee within Article 1(A)(2) of the Convention, in a manner which was appropriate in the circumstances of the appeal. As well, there was no basis arising from those circumstances and the definition of "refugee" for an argument that the rights and interests of the family as referred to in the relevant international texts had to be considered.

The Reviewability of Decisions of the RSAA
The parties were in agreement both in the High Court and in this Court that the courts have the power to review determinations of the RSAA for error of law. Accordingly their submissions dealt with the matter only briefly. For instance the appellant's written submission said that

The nature of the functions [the RSAA] performs and the fact that it has been established as part of New Zealand's compliance with its obligations under international law plainly make it open to judicial review by way of the prerogative writs (under Part VII of the High Court Rules); see *Singh* v. *Refugee Status Appeals Authority* [1994] NZAR 193, 212 [where RSAA decisions were held to be subject to judicial review for error of law]; contrast *Burt* v. *Governor-General* [1992] 3 NZLR 672 [about the prerogative of mercy in respect of a criminal conviction].

Counsel also referred to decisions in this country and the United Kingdom in which judicial review and the prerogative writs were held to be available in respect of a range of non-statutory functions; see e.g. *Electoral Commission* v. *Cameron* (1997) 10 PRNZ 440, 447-8 and the cases referred to there.

Because the issue was not fully argued and because of the conclusions we have reached on the substance, we do not express a final view on it. We do no more than note the following matters:

(1) the non-statutory powers exercised in the cases mentioned (with the exception of the *Singh* case) appear to have had legal effect under the law of the country in question—for instance by way of the exercise of the prerogative to grant a pardon, or of the power to

grant compensation, or to recognize (or not) the bargaining power of a trade union, or to approve or not a proposed commercial transaction for stock exchange purposes; by contrast, as noted earlier in the judgment, the RSAA determination is not in law effective in respect of immigration status;

(2) while the entering into a treaty is the exercise of a prerogative power and some prerogative powers are subject to judicial review (although in respect of treaty making see *R* v. *Foreign Secretary, ex parte Rees-Mogg* [1994] QB 552[8]) the carrying out of its obligations might or might not involve prerogative powers; legislative or general common law powers might be used; we note that while Section 40 of the Immigration Act 1964 expressly saved the prerogative there is no such provision in the 1987 Act;

(3) if the courts can consider applications for review in cases such as this the basic principle that the Executive cannot change the law by entering into treaties in the absence of securing any necessary legislative change would appear to be avoided, e.g. *New Zealand Airline Pilots Association Inc.* v. *Attorney-General* (CA300 and 301/96, 16 June 1997) 18 referring to *Attorney-General for Canada* v. *Attorney-General for Ontario* [1937] AC 326,[9] 347.

Legislation, such as that enacted in Australia, Canada and the United Kingdom—or in New Zealand in respect of other immigration matters—would remove any doubts about reviewability and could be expected as well to regulate aspects of the courts' powers, for instance by way of rights of appeal to them.

The facts also suggest the value of legislative attention, especially the changes in them since 1960 when New Zealand acceded to the 1951 Convention. The absence of legislative action at that time is perhaps to be explained first by the fact that the only people the Convention covered were identified through the processes of the UN High Commissioner for Refugees largely followed in refugee camps in Europe by reference to events that had occurred at least ten years earlier. As well, the means of travel to New Zealand then available reduced the prospect of disputes about refugee status arising in New Zealand. Finally, the substantive rights to which duly admitted refugees were entitled under the Convention were presumably considered as already being guaranteed under the law of New Zealand (subject to one reservation which New Zealand made).

Refugees continue to come to New Zealand under such resettlement programmes (the quota since 1987 has been 800 per year). Since the UNHCR recognizes their status no New Zealand procedure is needed to deal with them. But so far as refugee applications being

[8 98 *ILR* 166.]   [9 8 *Ann Dig* 41.]

made from within New Zealand are concerned, the situation has changed markedly since 1960 with, first, the removal (in 1973) of the temporal limit on those who might claim refugee status, second, the large increases in the numbers of refugees including many from countries much closer to New Zealand, third, the much greater availability of means of travel, especially by air, to New Zealand, and, fourth, the great increase in visitors to New Zealand (for many applicants for refugee status arrived earlier on regular permits as visitors or students). Issues about refugee status now arise frequently within New Zealand. The two years may not be typical, but in 1991 when Mr Butler arrived and in 1992 when his application was considered and appeal heard, 1,977 refugee status applications were made in New Zealand (R. P. G. Haines, *The Legal Condition of Refugees in New Zealand* (1995) 4). A Cabinet paper of December 1991 recorded that about 100 applications were being lodged each month (about a fifty-fold increase since 1987 when only twenty-seven had been made in the whole year) and that nearly all the 50 per cent which were declined went to the RSAA on appeal. "For the foreseeable future the Authority will need to process some 60 cases each month . . .".

Legislation would not only clarify and regularize the position in respect of review or appeal. It would also (as with the statutory immigration tribunals) provide binding rules relating to the appointment, status, tenure and protection of the members of the tribunal; their powers for instance in respect of the calling of evidence; the protection of parties and witnesses; the status of the RSS within the process; the public or private nature of its procedure; time limits and other aspects of the tribunal's procedure; and its independent servicing. There are also problems of the type indicated in the judgment of this Court given during the Gulf War in *D* v. *Minister of Immigration* [1991] 2 NZLR 673 and addressed, although not expressly by reference to refugees, by Parliament later that year, Immigration Amendment Act 1991 Section 38. Legislation might in addition provide for the cessation of refugee status. The residence permit provisions of the Act cannot be matched with that aspect of the Convention definition.

We have no reason at all to doubt that the Authority has exercised its functions with independence and judgment notwithstanding its lack of legislative basis. But if there is good reason for the other immigration tribunals to be established by legislation there is at least equal reason in the case of the Authority. Parliament went part of the way in 1991 when in the Legal Services Act 1991 it recognized the Authority's particular significance, compared with other immigration tribunals in respect of which legal aid is not in general available, Section 19(1)(j) and (4A). The distinction it drew then might be seen as emphasizing the obligations which New Zealand has under the

Convention and Protocol, matters to which Mr W. M. Wilson QC referred in his *Report to the Rt Hon W. F. Birch, Minister of Immigration, on the Processes of Refugee Status Determination* (29 April 1992) 18-22 in which he recommended legislation.

Result

For the reasons given, the appeal is dismissed. In the circumstances we make no order for costs.

[Report: Transcript]

Jurisdiction—Extraterritorial jurisdiction—Murder committed in Mexico by United States national—Whether offence within jurisdiction of court in United States — Whether Arizona court acting contrary to international law in imposing death penalty when Mexican law did not provide for death penalty—The law of the State of Arizona

STATE OF ARIZONA *v.* WILLOUGHBY[1]

United States, Supreme Court of Arizona.   23 *March* 1995

(Feldman, *Chief Justice*; Moeller VCJ; Zlaket, Martone and Corcoran JJ)

SUMMARY: *The facts*:—In 1991 the defendant, who was a United States citizen who resided in the State of Arizona, murdered his wife during a family trip to Mexico. The defendant was convicted by a State court in Arizona for premeditated first-degree murder and conspiracy. The Court sentenced him to death. He appealed, contending, *inter alia*, that the Arizona courts lacked jurisdiction.

[1] The State of Arizona was represented by the Attorney-General, Mr Grant Woods, by Paul J. McMurdic; Mr Willoughby was represented by Mr John W. Rood, III.

Held:—The defendant's convictions and death sentence were affirmed.

(1) Although the fatal blow and the victim's death had occurred in Mexico, there was sufficient evidence that premeditation had been committed in Arizona, thus supporting jurisdiction to prosecute the defendant for first-degree murder. There was also sufficient evidence of conduct in Arizona to support jurisdiction to prosecute for conspiracy (pp. 590-6).

(2) As substantial parts of the crime had taken place in Arizona it was unnecessary to consider whether the murder in Mexico had had a substantial effect in Arizona to assert jurisdiction over the crimes. Arizona had therefore not violated international law nor exceeded its sovereign powers by prosecuting the defendant for conspiracy and murder (p. 596).

(3) There was no conflict between international law and the portion of Arizona law which allowed the imposition of the death penalty for murder which had been planned in Arizona but committed in Mexico which did not have the death penalty (pp. 598-9).

(4) Arizona's imposition of the death penalty for a murder that had been premeditated in Arizona and committed in Mexico which had no death penalty, did not conflict with the 1978 Mexico–United States Extradition Treaty under which a party could refuse extradition in death penalty cases. Mexico had not invoked the Extradition Treaty, thus removing the issue of extradition. Even if Mexico had wished to have Arizona's assurance that it would not impose the death penalty, Mexico could only have done so if it had had custody of the defendant (pp. 598-600).

Per Justice Martone (concurring): The Court, and not the jury, decided the question of territorial jurisdiction. Additionally, the jurisdictional standard of proof was by the preponderance of the evidence as territorial jurisdiction was not an element of the offence (p. 605).

Per Justice Corcoran (concurring): The Court should not decide upon the jurisdictional question as the defendant had not raised it and the parties had not briefed that question. The jurisdictional standard of proof was of a preponderance standard (p. 606).

The following is the text of the opinion of the Court, delivered by Chief Justice Feldman:

[1321]

On May 19, 1992, a Maricopa County jury convicted Daniel Hayden Willoughby (Defendant) of premeditated first-degree murder and conspiracy to commit murder, fraudulent schemes and artifices, armed robbery, obstructing a criminal investigation, and filing a fraudulent insurance claim. The court sentenced him to death for the murder conviction and to life in prison for the conspiracy offenses. Appeal of the judgment and sentence is automatic. Ariz.R.Crim.P. 26.15 and 31.2(b). This court has jurisdiction under Ariz. Const. art. 6, § 5(3) and A.R.S. §§ 13–4031 and 13–4033(A).

FACTS AND PROCEDURAL HISTORY

Defendant and his wife, Trish, were residents of Phoenix, Arizona. In late 1990, Defendant arranged a trip to Puerto Peñasco (Rocky Point), Mexico, ostensibly as a Christmas gift for Trish. The couple and their three children rented a condominium at Las Conchas beach for a weekend in February 1991. The day after the family arrived, Defendant and the children went to visit a nearby museum. Trish stayed behind because she was tired and wanted to rest.

After Defendant and the children boarded their van for the museum, Defendant returned to the condo, saying he forgot his passport. He remained in the condo for about five minutes. While he was inside, his oldest daughter tried to enter, but the door was locked. When Defendant came out of the condo, he was adjusting his belt and tucking in his shirt. After Defendant returned to the van, he and the children went on their trip.

When they returned some two hours later, Defendant's ten-year-old daughter Thera rushed in to tell her mother about the trip. She found her mother unconscious in the bedroom. Trish had been stabbed, bludgeoned, and strangled, and a knife was protruding from her head. Defendant gathered the children outside for prayer and then drove to the Red Cross station for help. Trish died that evening.

Mexican authorities questioned Defendant, who told them that he and his wife were happily married. They eventually released Defendant, and he arranged for the return of Trish's body to Arizona for burial. No autopsy was performed until Arizona authorities exhumed the body several months later.

After the murder, Defendant's mother-in-law told several people, including an investigator from the Arizona Attorney General's Office, that Defendant might have committed the murder. This prompted an investigation which revealed that, although he had appeared happily married, Defendant had been unhappy with his wife for the past several years. **[1322]**

Investigators discovered that in late 1990, Defendant met Ysenia Patino Gonzalez, a Mexican transsexual who was then "married" to Jack Mielke. After the purported marriage ceremony between Ysenia and Mielke, Mielke paid for Ysenia to have a male-to-female sex change operation. At all relevant times, Ysenia was a resident alien living in Arizona.

Defendant began an affair with Ysenia, took her on vacations, and paid the rent for her apartment. Trish eventually learned of the affair and confronted Ysenia. Defendant moved Ysenia to a different apartment. He also bought her an expensive engagement ring and told others, including Jack Mielke, that he wanted to marry Ysenia. He told Ysenia, however, that he could not divorce his wife because she "had too much on him."

Defendant, in fact, depended on Trish's income. She and her mother were sole partners in a business worth over $2.5 million, with a 1990 income of $324,000. Defendant, meanwhile, had lost his job, and he told Ysenia he would be "taken to the cleaners" if he tried to divorce Trish.

Defendant began to talk about killing his wife. Ysenia testified at trial that at various times Defendant discussed buying a firearm silencer in Mexico, drowning Trish while scuba diving, or pushing her off a cliff at the Grand Canyon. In May 1990, during a dinner with Ysenia and Jack Mielke at a Tempe restaurant, Defendant said, "I think I will take her to Mexico and get rid of her." He later made similar statements to them at a restaurant in Cottonwood, Arizona. He also discussed having his "Mafia connections" kill her.

Defendant began discussing with Trish and her mother the disposition of their business should one of them die. He eventually con-

[1323] vinced them to adopt an insurance-funded buyout agreement. Several insurance policies covered Trish, including a $750,000 policy purchased just months before her murder.

Defendant began to plan the murder in more detail. He told Ysenia that he wanted the satisfaction of killing Trish. Ysenia was instructed to come in after the killing and make it look like a robbery by stabbing Trish, strangling her with a rope he bought, ransacking the condo, and taking her rings and money. Defendant rented a condo in Rocky Point, somewhat removed from others in the area, and paid in cash. Defendant and Ysenia made two trips from Phoenix to Rocky Point before the killing to reconnoiter the area and go over their plans. In Phoenix, Defendant showed Ysenia a weapon, described as a homemade mace consisting of a heavy ball attached by rope to a handle, he would use to kill Trish. He arranged for Ysenia's brother to take Ysenia to Rocky Point on the day of the murder.

On the afternoon of the killing, Defendant met Ysenia and her brother on the beach at Rocky Point. After Defendant and Ysenia talked, Defendant returned to the condo. Ysenia left her brother at a park and drove to a spot with a view of the condo. After Defendant and the children left for the museum, she went to the condo and entered through the unlocked back door. Taking knives from the kitchen, Ysenia went to the bedroom and saw Trish lying comatose in a pool of blood. Trish was still breathing, each breath making a gurgling sound. Following Defendant's plan, Ysenia stabbed and strangled Trish but was unable to kill her. After taking Trish's rings and money and scattering the contents of Trish's purse, Ysenia fled, meeting her brother for the return trip to Arizona.

At the border, a United States Customs agent understood Ysenia to say that she and her brother were going to a store just across the border. When the agent saw that they did not go there, she had them returned to the port of entry and searched. Trish's rings were discovered in Ysenia's pocket, but because no contraband was discovered, Ysenia and her brother were released. They immediately returned to Phoenix.

After the murder, Defendant took steps to cover his tracks. He told Ysenia to leave Phoenix, and she returned to Mexico. Defendant called a meeting of his neighbors, at which he denied involvement in the killing and tried to dissuade them from talking to police. He asked Ysenia's brother to lie to police about seeing Defendant in Mexico. He threatened Jack Mielke and told him not to get involved. He called his travel agent to have the trip information removed from the agent's computer. He asked his former secretary to tell police he was a wonderful family man and told her to threaten a co-worker to prevent him from telling police about Defendant and Ysenia. He lied to investigators, saying that guards at the condo had seen three Indians in a black pickup truck in the area. He collected on an older life insurance policy for his wife but was unsuccessful in collecting on the policy purchased to fund the buyout agreement between Trish and her mother.

A Maricopa County grand jury indicted Defendant for premeditated first-degree murder and conspiracy to commit one or more of the following offenses: murder, fraudulent schemes and artifices, armed robbery, obstructing a criminal investigation or prosecution, and filing a fraudulent insurance claim. Ysenia was charged with murder by the Mexican authorities, pleaded guilty, and was sentenced to life in prison. During the investigation, the Mexican government cooperated with Arizona officials by allowing them to interview Ysenia and giving them temporary custody of her so that she could testify at the three-week trial. In return for turning state's evidence, the state agreed to not prosecute Ysenia and to try to have her sentence in Mexico reduced.

The defense called no witnesses and rested immediately after the state's case concluded. The jury convicted Defendant of both the murder and conspiracy counts. After the aggravation/mitigation hearing, the trial judge found one aggravating circumstance—that the murder was committed in expectation of pecuniary gain—and no mitigating circumstances. He sentenced Defendant to death for the murder and life imprisonment for the conspiracy conviction.

JURISDICTION ISSUES

The fact that the fatal blow and the victim's death occurred in Mexico raises jurisdictional issues not present in the great majority of cases. The trial court asserted jurisdiction under A.R.S. § 13–108,[1] which gives Arizona extra-territorial jurisdiction under certain conditions, including cases in which a defendant commits an element of an offense within the state. The state invoked jurisdiction on the ground that Defendant had planned the crime in Arizona, premeditation being an element of the charges.

Before trial, Defendant challenged the constitutionality of A.R.S. § 13–108 and moved to dismiss the murder charge on the ground that Arizona lacked subject matter jurisdiction to try him for crimes committed in Mexico. The trial judge denied the motion. At the close of evidence, Defendant asked the trial judge to instruct the jury that it must decide beyond a reasonable doubt that an element of the crime was committed in Arizona. After hearing arguments on who decides the jurisdictional question and by what quantum of proof, the judge refused Defendant's request to instruct the jury on the jurisdictional issue, holding that the court would resolve the jurisdictional facts under a preponderance of the evidence standard.

On appeal, Defendant does not renew his argument that the jurisdictional question was for the jury. He does argue, however, that the evidence was insufficient to prove that essential elements of first-degree murder or conspiracy occurred in Arizona, that the court erred in finding jurisdiction, that the Arizona statute conferring jurisdiction is un-

constitutional, and that Arizona law cannot **[1324]** be applied because it conflicts with Mexican law, which has no death penalty. In essence, Defendant contends that because both Trish's death and the act directly causing it occurred in Mexico, there is neither a factual nor constitutional basis for Arizona's assertion of jurisdiction to try him or to impose the death penalty.

In the past, we have reviewed the facts of cases to decide whether the trial court properly exercised jurisdiction, but we have not provided any guidance to trial courts about how to resolve disputed factual issues necessary for exercising territorial jurisdiction. *E.g., State v. Poland,* 132 Ariz. 269, 275, 645 P.2d 784, 790 (1982), *aff'd,* 476 U.S. 147, 106 S.Ct. 1749, 90 L.Ed.2d 123 (1986); *State v. Bussdieker,* 127 Ariz. 339, 341, 621 P.2d 26, 28 (1980). The need for guidance on who decides jurisdictional facts and by what standard is illustrated by cases such as this and *State v. Vaughn,* 163 Ariz. 200, 202, 786 P.2d 1051, 1053 (App.1989), which the court of appeals remanded, without discussing the appropriate standard of proof, to give the defendant an opportunity to prove at a post-trial hearing that the state did not have jurisdiction. The facts and trial record of this case squarely raise the issue of who properly resolves jurisdictional facts in a criminal case and by what standard. Because Defendant's right to a jury trial may have been violated, raising the possibility of fundamental error, and because our previous decisions provide no guidance, we address this issue before considering the merits of Defendant's other arguments.[2]

---

1. A.R.S. § 13–108(A) provides in relevant part:

    A. This state has jurisdiction over an offense that a person commits by his own conduct or the conduct of another for which such person is legally accountable if:

    1. Conduct constituting any element of the offense or a result of such conduct occurs within this state; or

    .   .   .   .   .

    3. The conduct within this state constitutes an attempt, solicitation, conspiracy or facilitation to commit or establishes criminal accountability for the commission of an offense in another jurisdiction that is also an offense under the law of this state....

2. We emphasize that the question was not first raised by this court. It was raised and argued in the trial court. The concurring opinion argues that because this issue was not raised on appeal, we should not decide it. We disagree. Until we determine whether the judge or jury decides jurisdictional facts, we cannot decide whether the trial judge committed error or fundamental error in appropriating the jurisdictional question. Thus, fundamental error doctrine requires us to reach this issue. Moreover, experience teaches that the issue eventually will be decided in this case—if not now, then in post-conviction proceedings. We see no purpose in delaying the inevitable. Our present consideration of the issue, therefore, is also motivated by concerns for finality and efficiency.

[1325] A. **Jurisdictional decisions in Arizona**

Under A.R.S. § 13–108(A)(1), Arizona has jurisdiction to try a defendant if conduct constituting one or more elements of the charged offenses occurred in Arizona. According to § 13–1105(A)(1), a "person commits first degree murder if . . . [i]ntending or knowing that his conduct will cause death, such person causes the death of another with premeditation. . . ." A.R.S. § 13–1101(1) defines premeditation to mean "that the defendant acts with either the intention or the knowledge that he will kill another human being, when such intention or knowledge precedes the killing by a length of time to permit reflection." To invoke jurisdiction in this case, the state sought to prove that Defendant committed premeditation in Arizona.

In the usual case, there is no question but that the crime charged was committed entirely in Arizona. In this unusual case, Defendant is charged with an offense only part of which is alleged to have taken place in Arizona: the fatal blow and the death occurred in Mexico, and only acts of preparation allegedly took place in Arizona. To prosecute and convict Defendant for first-degree murder in Arizona, the state had to prove that acts of premeditation were committed in Arizona.[3] A.R.S. § 13–108(A). Thus, the jurisdictional facts appear to be intertwined with the substantive facts and might not be capable of separate resolution: to convict, the state had to prove premeditation, and to exercise jurisdiction, the state had to prove that if premeditation occurred, it took place in Arizona.

1. *The identity of the factfinder and the standard of proof*

If jurisdictional facts are intertwined with the merits of the case, the jurisdictional and substantive issues are difficult to resolve separately *only if the jurisdictional facts are controverted by evidence.* In the civil arena, we addressed the issue in *Bonner v. Minico, Inc.,* 159 Ariz. 246, 253–54, 766 P.2d 598, 605–

06 (1988), and followed the approach of the United States Supreme Court in *Land v. Dollar,* 330 U.S. 731, 735, 67 S.Ct. 1009, 1011, 91 L.Ed. 1209 (1947) (trial court generally has the authority to decide jurisdiction; if jurisdictional facts are controverted and intertwined with the merits, they must be left to the trier of fact). Although the court itself cannot resolve the substantive issue by resolving disputed jurisdictional facts, the "jurisdictional factual issues, like other factual issues, remain subject to the usual rules of summary judgment." *Bonner,* 159 Ariz. at 254, 766 P.2d at 606.

Although summary judgment procedure as such is not available in criminal cases, if factual questions unrelated to the elements of an offense are not disputed, courts do not submit them to the jury. *E.g., State v. Wood,* 180 Ariz. 53, 65, 881 P.2d 1158, 1170 (1994) (lesser-included offense instruction not required if not supported by the evidence). The jury's role, as guaranteed by our state and federal constitutions, is to decide the factual issues of a defendant's guilt or innocence. *State v. Bible,* 175 Ariz. 549, 567, 858 P.2d 1152, 1170 (1993), *cert. denied,* —— U.S. ——, 114 S.Ct. 1578, 128 L.Ed.2d 221 (1994). The issue then is this: if jurisdictional facts are controverted and their resolution intertwined with proof of elements of the crime, who should resolve the factual question of jurisdiction—judge or jury—and by what standard?

In the absence of controlling federal authority, states are of course free to determine their own rules for resolving jurisdictional facts in criminal cases. Our legislature has not addressed this matter.[4] We have not decided it and look, therefore, to other authority for guidance. Most states have held that if the facts on which jurisdiction depends are controverted, resolution of those disputed facts must be left to the jury. *Sheeran v. State,* 526 A.2d 886, 890 (Del.1987); *Lane v. State,* 388 So.2d 1022, 1028 (Fla.1980); *Conrad v. Indiana,* 262 Ind. 446, 317 N.E.2d 789, 792 (1974); *State v. Liggins,* 524 N.W.2d 181,

---

3. The state did not charge Defendant with felony murder, no doubt because none of the elements of the underlying felony occurred in Arizona.

4. The legislative record for the enactment of A.R.S. § 13–108 offers no guidance on court procedures for deciding questions of jurisdiction.

184 (Iowa 1994); *State v. Batdorf,* 293 N.C. 486, 238 S.E.2d 497, 502–03 (1977) (reversing previous decisions and requiring the state to prove jurisdiction beyond a reasonable doubt, with proper jury instructions); *People v. McLaughlin,* 80 N.Y.2d 466, 591 N.Y.S.2d 966, 606 N.E.2d 1357, 1359–60 (1992); *Commonwealth v. Bighum,* 452 Pa. 554, 307 A.2d 255, 258 (1973). Only two jurisdictions have expressly held that the issue is not for the jury but for the court. *Connecticut v. Beverly,* 224 Conn. 372, 618 A.2d 1335, 1339 (1993); *Mitchell v. United States,* 569 A.2d 177, 180 (D.C.App.) (the location of an offense is not a factual question for the jury), *cert. denied,* 498 U.S. 986, 111 S.Ct. 521, 112 L.Ed.2d 532 (1990). However, as one respected authority observed, the general rule is: "At least when the matter has been put into issue by the defendant, whether the prosecuting government actually has criminal jurisdiction over the conduct of the defendant is a matter to be determined by the trier of fact." 1 WAYNE R. LaFAVE & AUSTIN W. SCOTT, SUBSTANTIVE CRIMINAL LAW § 2.7(b), at 163 (1986) (citations omitted) (hereinafter LA-FAVE & SCOTT).[5]

Some courts actually treat jurisdiction like an element of the crime, at least when there is evidence controverting jurisdiction.[6] *E.g., Sheeran,* 526 A.2d at 890; *Lane,* 388 So.2d at

1028; Annotation, *Comment Note—Necessity of Proving Venue or Territorial Jurisdiction of Criminal Offense Beyond Reasonable Doubt,* 67 A.L.R.3D §§ 10–12 (1975 and Supp. 1994). In those states, the prosecution must prove beyond a reasonable doubt that an element of the crime occurred in the state for the state to exercise its jurisdiction. *E.g., State v. Ross,* 230 Conn. 183, 646 A.2d 1318, 1331 (1994), *cert. denied,* — U.S. —, 115 S.Ct. 1133, 130 L.Ed.2d 1095 (1995); *Lane,* 388 So.2d at 1028; *McLaughlin,* 591 N.Y.S.2d at 969 n. *, 606 N.E.2d at 1360 n. * (citing 22 jurisdictions holding that proof of territorial jurisdiction must be proven beyond a reasonable doubt and two that have adopted the proof by a preponderance standard). The Florida Supreme Court reasoned that broad jurisdiction conferred by a statute like A.R.S. § 13–108 requires the highest level of proof. *Lane,* 388 So.2d at 1028.

Even when jurisdictional facts are not contested by controverting evidence and are decided by the trial judge, in some jurisdictions the judge must decide those facts beyond a reasonable doubt. *Mitchell,* 569 A.2d at 180. A lesser standard has been allowed in cases in which the question of territorial jurisdiction is identified with the issue of venue.[7] *See, e.g., Cauley v. United States,*

---

5. The concurrence takes the minority view, concluding that jurisdiction is always a question of law for the court. The concurrence fails to take into account those rare cases addressed by our rule where controverted jurisdictional facts cannot be resolved without reaching the merits of the case. The rule we adopt is no different than that applied in *Bonner* where our civil courts are prohibited from deciding controverted jurisdictional facts when they are intertwined with the substantive issues in the case.

The procedure is analogous to instructing the jury on facts pertaining to probable cause in a malicious prosecution or false arrest case. Probable cause is a legal issue for the judge, but where there is conflicting probable cause evidence, the jury must decide the facts and the judge instructs on the law as to what constitutes probable cause. *Bradshaw v. State Farm Mut. Auto. Ins. Co.,* 157 Ariz. 411, 419, 758 P.2d 1313, 1321 (1988) ("the court may instruct the jury hypothetically, telling them what facts will constitute probable cause."); *Sarwark Motor Sales, Inc. v. Woolridge,* 88 Ariz. 173, 177–78, 354 P.2d 34, 36–37 (1960) (setting forth two methods of instructing the jury); *see also* W. PAGE KEETON ET AL. PROSSER AND KEETON ON THE LAW OF TORTS § 119, at

882 (5th ed. 1984) (judge can either require special verdict or instruct on what facts, if found, would constitute probable cause).

6. We suspect the reason for this is simply because in almost every case in which the issue is raised, as in the present case, proof of the facts essential to establishing jurisdiction is inextricably intertwined with proof of an element of the crime.

7. At trial, the prosecutor persuaded the judge that jurisdiction was an issue for the court by citing Arizona venue cases. *E.g., State v. Mohr,* 150 Ariz. 564, 566, 724 P.2d 1233, 1235 (App. 1986). The two concepts are different in very important ways. Venue is a question of whether the trial court exercises jurisdiction in the proper locality. By art. 2, § 24, the Arizona Constitution requires that the court's jurisdiction be invoked in the county where the crime occurred, but such venue may be waived or changed. *State v. Girdler,* 138 Ariz. 482, 490, 675 P.2d 1301, 1309 (1983), *cert. denied,* 467 U.S. 1244, 104 S.Ct. 3519, 82 L.Ed.2d 826 (1984); *see also Lane,* 388 So.2d at 1026. Subject matter jurisdiction, on the other hand, may not be waived or

[1327] 355 F.2d 175 (5th Cir.), *cert. denied*, 384 U.S. 951, 86 S.Ct. 1572, 16 L.Ed.2d 548 (1966). Only one state court has adopted a preponderance standard for deciding whether the state has territorial jurisdiction. *People v. Cavanaugh*, 44 Cal.2d 252, 282 P.2d 53, 59 (1955) (approving jury instruction that proof of territorial jurisdiction could be established by a preponderance of the evidence), *cert. denied*, 350 U.S. 950, 76 S.Ct. 325, 76 S.Ct. 325 (1956); *see also* Utah Code 1953 § 76-1-501(3) (Michie 1994) ("The existence of jurisdiction and venue are not elements of the offense but shall be established by a preponderance of the evidence.").

In drafting the Model Penal Code (MPC), the textual basis for much of Arizona's criminal code, the American Law Institute (ALI) broadly defined jurisdiction as an element of an offense. MPC § 1.13(9)(e). The ALI recommends, therefore, that jurisdiction be proved beyond a reasonable doubt. MPC § 1.12(1) cmt. at 188–89; *see also Liggins*, 524 N.W.2d at 184 (citing cases); *McLaughlin*, 591 N.Y.S.2d at 969 n. *, 606 N.E.2d at 1360 n. *; LaFave & Scott § 2.7(b), at 163. Although our legislature adopted many sections of the MPC, it did not advert to this jurisdictional provision. Thus, we are not required to follow the ALI's recommended procedure for deciding jurisdiction.

Nevertheless, we believe the position taken by the ALI and the vast majority of states is, for the most part, a good rule: jurisdictional facts must be established beyond a reasonable doubt in all cases in which jurisdictional facts are questioned. *See, e.g., Sheeran*, 526 A.2d at 890; *Lane*, 388 So.2d at 1029; *Liggins*, 524 N.W.2d at 184; *McLaughlin*, 591 N.Y.S.2d at 969 n. *, 606 N.E.2d at 1360 n. *; *see also* Annotation, 67 A.L.R.3D § 10, at 988. The view requiring the lesser standard, espoused by the concurrence, is not only a distinct minority view but cannot be logically applied to cases such as this. It simply makes no sense in a single

trial to require the factfinder to determine the existence of facts on the reasonable doubt standard for guilt purposes and the same facts on the preponderance standard for jurisdiction purposes. Thus, beyond simply being the majority rule, the view requiring the higher quantum of proof has much to commend it:

> Even if [the highest standard of proof] is not compelled under *In re Winship* [8] because jurisdiction is not one of "those facts essential to establishing criminality of the defendant's conduct," it is nonetheless sound. Use of the beyond a reasonable doubt standard minimizes the possibility that a defendant will be tried in one state for a crime actually committed elsewhere. Moreover, it makes it more likely that other states will afford full faith and credit to decisions regarding criminal jurisdiction, even though they are not constitutionally required to do so. There is also the practical consideration that using a lesser standard for a portion of the prosecution's case and the beyond a reasonable doubt standard for the rest would doubtless create confusion in the minds of jurors.

LaFave & Scott § 2.7(b), at 163 (citations omitted). We agree with this reasoning and the position taken by most courts. In the very rare case in which jurisdiction is legitimately in issue because of contradicting jurisdictional facts, Arizona's territorial jurisdiction must be established beyond a reasonable doubt by the jury.

We do not, however, equate jurisdiction with elements of the offense, although some states have treated it as such. If the jurisdictional facts are undisputed, as in almost all cases, the court may decide the issue. *See Graham v. State*, 34 Ark.App. 126, 806 S.W.2d 32, 34 (1991) (state not required to prove jurisdiction absent evidence affirmatively showing court may lack jurisdiction); *Liggins*, 524 N.W.2d at 184; *Bighum*, 307 A.2d at 258–59. In the absence of

---

changed. *State v. Avila*, 147 Ariz. 330, 334, 710 P.2d 440, 443 (1985); *State v. Baldwin*, 305 A.2d 555, 559 (Me.1973). Venue and sovereign jurisdiction therefore are governed by different policy considerations. *Lane*, 388 So.2d at 1026; *see Liggins*, 524 N.W.2d at 184 (territorial jurisdiction treated

as an essential element of an offense; venue is a nonjurisdictional issue); *Baldwin*, 305 A.2d at 558.

8. 397 U.S. 358, 90 S.Ct. 1068, 25 L.Ed.2d 368 (1970).

evidence contradicting jurisdiction, then, only the issues pertaining to criminality must go to the jury. LaFave & Scott § 2.7(b), at 163.

2. Did the evidence raise any issue whether conduct constituting an element of the crime occurred in Arizona?

Normally, the question of where premeditation occurred would be irrelevant. But because the fatal blow and death occurred outside of Arizona, in order to exercise jurisdiction and try Defendant for premeditated first-degree murder the state had to establish both that premeditation occurred and that it occurred in Arizona. Consequently, a substantive issue of this case was inextricably bound with the jurisdictional issue. However, that fact alone is not sufficient to require the jury to resolve the jurisdictional question. If there is no evidence that the acts of premeditation alleged by the state might have taken place outside Arizona, then there is no material dispute about where premeditation occurred and no requirement to send the question of jurisdiction to the jury. We thus look to see whether there was any jurisdictional dispute to be resolved by the jury.

Premeditation is established by evidence of a plan to murder formed after deliberation and reflection. *State v. Tostado*, 111 Ariz. 98, 101, 523 P.2d 795, 798 (1974). Thus, if the murder scheme was hatched in Arizona, Arizona can assert jurisdiction. *Id.* Other states with similar statutes have taken the same approach. *Lane*, 388 So.2d at 1027–28 (evidence of premeditation or a predicate felony for conspiracy in Florida confers jurisdiction to try defendant although fatal blow and death occurred in Alabama); *Conrad*, 317 N.E.2d at 791–92 (jury properly instructed that it must find killing in Ohio was intended and planned in Indiana to convict defendant in Indiana).

In the present case, there was substantial evidence of deliberation and reflection—a considered, planned agreement to kill. Testimony from Ysenia, her brother, Jack Mielke, and other witnesses showed that much of the planning took place in Arizona. For example, during a conversation

between Defendant and Ysenia in Chandler, **[1328]** Defendant explained the plan to Ysenia in detail. Defendant's Arizona acts included discussing with Ysenia where, when, and by what means he would kill his wife; securing Ysenia's cooperation in making the murder look like a robbery; arranging with a Phoenix vacation rental agency to rent a condo in Rocky Point for the murder; obtaining his mother-in-law's cooperation to ensure that his wife would be free from business responsibilities on the weekend of the planned murder; arranging with Ysenia's brother to drive her to Rocky Point; and showing the murder weapon to Ysenia. After the killing, Defendant followed through with his plan to cover his tracks and collect the insurance money.

Nor was proof of the scheme entirely dependent on Ysenia's challenged testimony. There were other, unimpeached witnesses who heard Defendant plotting. There was, for example, the evidence from Ysenia's brother, Jack Mielke, travel agents, insurance agents, and others. Certainly, these facts are sufficient evidence of premeditation to establish Arizona's jurisdiction under § 13–108(A)(1).

There was no controverting evidence on the jurisdictional issue. Although Defendant argued about the interpretation of his conduct, claiming the discussions were only hypothetical and not actual planning for a real murder, he did not dispute the location of these discussions. He argued that merely discussing the desire to kill his wife did not prove that he actually planned to follow through. He points out, for instance, that at various times he discussed pushing Trish off a cliff, drowning her, purchasing a firearms silencer in Mexico, and arranging a Mafia hit. He does not argue that these discussions occurred outside Arizona; instead he claims they did not show a real intent to commit the murder as it actually occurred. The state, however, showed that at least one of the methods discussed—bludgeoning with a homemade mace followed by Ysenia's attack—was consistent with the forensic and other evidence of Trish's death. There is no evidence indicating that the final plan to kill was discussed anywhere else but in Arizona.

[1329] We conclude, therefore, that all of the evidence establishes, beyond doubt, that if an actual murder was planned, the plan was hatched in Arizona and brought to fruition in Mexico. The jury verdict on both the murder and conspiracy counts settled any question of whether the plan formulated was real. The evidence raised no question about where it was formulated. Premeditation being "part of the corpus delicti" of premeditated first-degree murder, *Poland,* 132 Ariz. at 276, 645 P.2d at 791, and the verdict having established that actual premeditation occurred, there was no question but that it occurred in Arizona.

Based on the foregoing, we conclude that the trial judge was not required to send the question of jurisdiction to the jury. We note that in taking the issue of jurisdiction from the jury, the trial judge applied the preponderance of evidence standard to determine whether the facts supported the state's authority to prosecute this case. Although this is an incorrect statement of the state's burden to establish sovereign jurisdiction, the error is harmless on this record because the evidence established beyond any doubt that an element of the charged offense was committed in Arizona, and there was no evidence to the contrary.

Therefore, we find that there was no error, fundamental or otherwise, in refusing Defendant's request to instruct the jury on the jurisdictional prerequisites and only harmless error in the judge's statement that he found jurisdiction by a preponderance. Thus, we hold that the state had power to try Defendant for the murder committed in Mexico.

3. *Was there sufficient evidence of conduct in Arizona to support jurisdiction to prosecute for conspiracy?*

Defendant was also charged with conspiracy to commit any or all of the following: murder, fraudulent schemes and artifices, armed robbery, obstructing a criminal investigation or prosecution, and filing a fraudulent insurance claim. Jurisdiction on these counts was predicated on A.R.S. § 13-108(A)(3). *See supra* note 1.

Conspiracy is defined in A.R.S. § 13-1003(A):

A person commits conspiracy if, with the intent to promote or aid the commission of an offense, such person agrees with one or more persons that at least one of them or another person will engage in conduct constituting the offense and one of the parties commits an overt act in furtherance of the offense, except that an overt act shall not be required if the object of the conspiracy was to commit any felony upon the person of another. . . .

Although the elements of conspiracy are intent, an agreement, and, in some cases, an act in furtherance of a substantive offense, *State v. Newman,* 141 Ariz. 554, 559, 688 P.2d 180, 185 (1984), reviewing courts generally focus on the agreement element. *State v. Gessler,* 142 Ariz. 379, 383, 690 P.2d 98, 102 (App.1984). The agreement may be proven by circumstantial evidence. *State v. Avila,* 147 Ariz. 330, 336, 710 P.2d 440, 446 (1985).

Testimony amply demonstrated that a number of conversations in Arizona focused on a scheme to murder, perpetrate a fraud, commit armed robbery, obstruct a criminal investigation, and receive insurance money. In addition to those facts already mentioned, Defendant's insistence that his wife and mother-in-law insure a buy-sell agreement for their business and Ysenia's bragging to others that she was "going to be a millionaire" indicated that an agreement for criminal conduct was made. On this count, as on the murder count, the guilty verdict defeats Defendant's claims that his discussions with Ysenia, Jack Mielke, Ysenia's brother, the travel agent, and others were no more than idle talk. The jury found beyond a reasonable doubt that Defendant and Ysenia actually planned the killing. Here, as on the murder count, the evidence is unquestioned that if a real agreement was reached, it was made in Arizona.

We hold, therefore, that the trial court had sovereign power to try Defendant for conspiracy. *See State v. Streater,* 233 N.J.Super. 537, 559 A.2d 473, 476–77 (Ct.1989) (New Jersey had jurisdiction to try conspiracy count even though acts constituting substantive offense occurred solely in Connecticut), *review denied,* 117 N.J. 667, 569 A.2d 1358 (1989); *accord Commonwealth v. Kloss,* 253 Pa.Super. 559, 385 A.2d 480, 483 (1978).

B. Is assertion of jurisdiction unreasonable and therefore in violation of principles of international law?

Defendant also contends that Arizona's assertion of jurisdiction in this case violates an important principle of international law. Relying on the RESTATEMENT (THIRD) OF FOREIGN RELATION LAWS OF THE UNITED STATES § 402 cmt. k (1986) (hereinafter RESTATEMENT),[9] he argues that killing an American citizen in a foreign country does not have a sufficiently substantial result within the state to give the state jurisdiction to prosecute the homicide. Defendant claims that the effect in Mexico, on the other hand, is substantial, making Mexico the only sovereign with power to try Defendant.

Arizona's exercise of jurisdiction in this case is not, as Defendant assumes, based on the effect or results of the crime in Arizona. *Cf. State v. Miller,* 157 Ariz. 129, 755 P.2d 434 (App.1988). It is based instead on the evidence that elements of the charged offenses took place in Arizona. RESTATEMENT § 402(1)(a) expressly recognizes that a state may exercise its authority to regulate conduct that occurs within the state: A "state has jurisdiction to prescribe law with respect to conduct that, wholly or in substantial part, takes place within its territory...."

A state's criminal law may have extra-territorial effect. *See Strassheim v. Daily,* 221 U.S. 280, 285, 31 S.Ct. 558, 560, 55 L.Ed. 735 (1910) (upholding Michigan prosecution for acts of bribery and obtaining public money under false pretenses in Illinois); *Ross,* 646 A.2d at 1332–32. Long ago states recognized the need and right to enforce their criminal laws to protect themselves and their citizens from the injurious acts of others, "wherever committed." *People v. Tyler,* 7 Mich. 161, 221 (1859). Because substantial elements of the crimes took place in Arizona, we need not consider whether the murder

committed on foreign soil had a substantial **[1330]** effect in Arizona to assert jurisdiction over the crimes. We hold only that, on the facts of this case, Arizona did not violate international law or exceed its sovereign power by prosecuting Defendant for conspiracy and murder, even though the blow was struck and death occurred in Mexico.

C. Even if Arizona had sovereign power, does A.R.S. § 13–108 confer jurisdiction over acts that take place in a foreign country?

Defendant next argues that if a legislative body does not expressly extend the reach of a statute to a foreign country, courts should construe the statute narrowly to apply it only within the United States, citing *Foley Bros. v. Filardo,* 336 U.S. 281, 285, 69 S.Ct. 575, 577, 93 L.Ed. 680 (1949), and *United States v. Bowman,* 260 U.S. 94, 98, 43 S.Ct. 39, 41,[2] 67 L.Ed. 149 (1922). He points out that A.R.S. § 13–108 and MPC § 1.03, the textual basis for A.R.S. § 13–108, do not expressly apply to foreign nations. Thus, Defendant posits, MPC § 1.10 implies that A.R.S. § 13–108 only covers acts committed in other states of the union. Accordingly, Defendant says, § 13–108 should be interpreted as conferring extra-territorial jurisdiction only for crimes within other states, not for a crime in Mexico.

The cases Defendant cites do not carry his argument. *Bowman* reaches the opposite result, holding that a federal fraud statute applies to a crime consummated outside the territorial limits of the United States, even though the statute itself did not expressly say so. 260 U.S. at 98, 43 S.Ct. at 41. *Foley Bros.,* a civil case, held the Eight–Hour Workday law inapplicable to the employees of an American company doing business in Iraq and Iran. The Court explained that congressional intent and the legislative scheme may be considered in addition to the statute's text. 336 U.S. at 285, 69 S.Ct. at 577 ("[The] legislation of Congress, *unless a contrary intent appears,* is meant to apply

---

9. A state of the United States "may exercise jurisdiction on the basis of territoriality, *including effects within the territory,* and, in some respects at least, on the basis of citizenship, residence, or domicile in the State." (Emphasis added).

[1331] only within the territorial jurisdiction of the United States.").

We do not find these cases helpful. When interpreting nonjurisdictional, substantive statutes like those in *Foley Bros.* and *Bowman*, we ordinarily assume the substantive reach of a law is contained within the territorial borders of the enacting jurisdiction to avoid conflicts with other jurisdictions. But when jurisdiction is the very substance of a statute, we must look carefully at its language to determine its intended reach. The statutes examined in the cases cited by Defendant concerned substantive matters, not jurisdiction.

Section 13–108, however, specifically addresses extra-territorial jurisdiction. It is worded broadly, referring to "conduct outside this state" and conduct "in another jurisdiction." Its text does not expressly limit jurisdiction to other states. Had the intent been to apply the statute only to other states of the United States, appropriate limiting words could have easily been used. To ascertain legislative intent, we look first to the text and purpose of the statute. *Hernandez–Gomez v. Leonardo*, 180 Ariz. 297, 301, 884 P.2d 183, 187 (1994), *petition for cert. filed*, 63 U.S.L.W. (U.S. Jan. 27, 1995). In the absence of express limiting language or apparent contrary intent, we should not limit the extra-territorial reach of a statute intended to confer extra-territorial jurisdiction. Because the text of § 13–108 may fairly be construed to give Arizona jurisdiction "over crimes having any 'contact' with this state," *see* 1 RUDOLPH J. GERBER, CRIMINAL LAW OF ARIZONA 108–1 (2d ed. 1993), criminal jurisdiction should reach the extent permitted under federal and international law. There being no textual limit on the reach of this statute conferring extra-territorial power, we conclude that the statute includes, on its face, offenses consummated in foreign countries as well as in other states and that it was properly applied by the trial court.

D. So construed, does A.R.S. § 13–108 violate the Constitutions of the United States and Arizona by extending territorial jurisdiction beyond Arizona's borders?

Defendant offers two arguments for the proposition that § 13–108 violates the Sixth Amendment of the United States Constitution [10] and art. 2, § 24 of the Arizona Constitution.[11] The first is that both constitutions require that a criminal defendant be tried in the district or county where the crime was committed. Defendant argues that this assures that the state where a crime was completed can punish the offender or extradite the offender to another jurisdiction. *Huntington v. Attrill*, 146 U.S. 657, 669, 13 S.Ct. 224, 228, 36 L.Ed. 1123 (1892).

Standing alone, the Sixth Amendment protects individuals against action taken by the United States, not against state action. *Dodge v. Nakai*, 298 F.Supp. 17, 22 (D.Ariz.1968). Although other provisions of the Sixth Amendment have been incorporated into the Fourteenth Amendment as limitations on state action, *see Duncan v. Louisiana*, 391 U.S. 145, 148–49, 88 S.Ct. 1444, 1447, 20 L.Ed.2d 491, *reh'g denied*, 392 U.S. 947, 88 S.Ct. 2270, 20 L.Ed.2d 1412 (1968), the venue, or vicinage, provision at issue here has not. Therefore, the Sixth Amendment provision arguably is not applicable to state prosecutions.[12] *Caudill v. Scott*, 857 F.2d 344, 345 (6th Cir.1988); *Cook v. Morrill*, 783

---

10.   In all criminal prosecutions, the accused shall enjoy the right to a speedy and public trial, by an impartial jury *of the State and district wherein the crime shall have been committed*, which district shall have been previously ascertained by law.... (Emphasis added.)

11.   In criminal prosecutions, the accused shall have the right to appear and defend in person, and ... to have a speedy public trial by an impartial jury *of the county in which the offense is alleged to have been committed*.... (Emphasis added.)

12.   The Sixth Amendment's vicinage provision technically prescribes that jurors will be selected from the geographical area in which the crime occurred. 2 CHARLES WRIGHT, FEDERAL PRACTICE & PROCEDURE § 301, at 190 (2d ed. 1982). The Supreme Court has interpreted this provision additionally as a requirement to fix "the situs of the trial in the vicinage of the crime," thereby establishing venue. *Johnston v. United States*, 351 U.S. 215, 220, 76 S.Ct. 739, 742, 100 L.Ed. 1097 *reh'g denied*, 352 U.S. 860, 77 S.Ct. 23, 1 L.Ed.2d 69 (1956).

F.2d 593, 596 (5th Cir.1986) ("right to a trial in the district where the defendant committed the crime is not ... fundamental and essential to a fair trial").

Further, Defendant erroneously assumes that the crime occurred in and only in Mexico. In fact, essential elements of offenses defined in Arizona's criminal code occurred in Arizona. *Poland,* 132 Ariz. at 275, 645 P.2d at 790 ("When the elements of a crime are committed in different jurisdictions, any state in which an essential part of the crime is committed may take jurisdiction."). Premeditation, an element of first-degree murder, and an agreement to commit a felony, an element of conspiracy, occurred in Arizona.

Arizona's extra-territorial jurisdiction statute accomplishes precisely what Defendant alleges to be the purpose of art. 2, § 24 and the Sixth Amendment: it gives Arizona the power to prosecute and punish those who engage in criminal conduct within Arizona's territory, whether or not the crime was fully completed here. *See, e.g., State v. Suarez,* 137 Ariz. 368, 375, 670 P.2d 1192, 1199 (App. 1983). Any other rule would make Arizona's interest in deterring criminal conduct subject to the prosecutorial whim of whatever jurisdiction happened to be the locus of the final act.

Defendant's second argument is that § 13-108 effectively amends the Sixth Amendment and art. 2, § 24 by replacing the terms "crime" and "offense" with the words "conduct constituting an element of the offense," thereby giving Arizona courts the power to unilaterally seize a defendant and try him for crimes committed outside its geographic jurisdiction. This argument fails to recognize the distinction between venue and jurisdiction.[13] We do not read the constitutional text to concern anything other than vicinage. These provisions are designed to guarantee a criminal defendant the right to trial by an impartial jury. *See State ex rel. Sullivan v. Patterson,* 64 Ariz. 40, 47, 165 P.2d 309, 313 (1946) ("[I]t is *the right of trial by an impartial jury* in the county in which the offense is alleged to have been

committed that is preserved rather than the **[1332]** absolute right to a trial in the county.") (emphasis added); *State v. Mohr,* 150 Ariz. 564, 566, 724 P.2d 1233, 1235 (App.1986); *accord People v. Caruso,* 119 Ill.2d 376, 116 Ill.Dec. 548, 554, 519 N.E.2d 440, 446 (1987), *cert. denied,* 488 U.S. 829, 109 S.Ct. 83, 102 L.Ed.2d 59 (1988). The purpose of requiring a criminal defendant to be tried before a jury of "the State and district wherein the said crime shall have been committed" was to prohibit the government from choosing a tribunal favorable to its case and give the defendant the right to be tried by jurors from the locality in which criminal conduct occurred. *Travis v. United States,* 364 U.S. 631, 634, 81 S.Ct. 358, 360, 5 L.Ed.2d 340 (1961).

Clearly, vicinage is a venue rather than a jurisdictional question. While jurisdiction is the power of a court to try a case, venue concerns the locale where the power may be exercised. *Caruso,* 116 Ill.Dec. at 554, 519 N.E.2d at 446; *Lane,* 388 So.2d at 1026; 2 WAYNE R. LaFAVE & JEROLD H. ISRAEL, CRIMINAL PROCEDURE § 16.1(a), at 334–35 (1984). The constitutional provisions in question do not impose limits on the state's jurisdictional authority, only on the place where the defendant may be tried. *See United States v. Johnson,* 323 U.S. 273, 276, 65 S.Ct. 249, 250–51, 89 L.Ed. 236 (1944).

Thus, Defendant *was* tried in the Arizona vicinage in which his alleged criminal conduct occurred, and this is all the constitution guarantees. A defendant who commits only part of an offense in Arizona cannot invoke the vicinage clause as a shield from prosecution in Arizona. Without extra-territorial jurisdiction, a defendant such as Willoughby could occasionally escape justice altogether.[14]

E. Can Arizona impose the death penalty for a murder committed in a country that has no death penalty?

Defendant next argues that because Mexico has no death penalty, Arizona may not exercise jurisdiction or impose the death

---

13. *See supra* note 6.

14. One such scenario is the placement of a bomb on an airplane by a terrorist, causing the airplane to explode over the ocean.

[1333] penalty in this case. First, Defendant cites *Miller*, 157 Ariz. 129, 755 P.2d 434, for the proposition that international law controls if state law conflicts with international law or the laws of another country. Thus, Defendant submits, imposition of the death penalty conflicts with international law.

Miller is inapplicable both factually and in principle. *Miller* was arrested in Utah, extradited to Arizona, and charged here with theft for receiving stolen property. The property had been stolen in Arizona by others, and Miller helped the original thieves dispose of the stolen property in Nevada. Miller was not an Arizona resident and had not entered Arizona. While noting that under § 13–108(A)(1) the results of a person's extra-territorial criminal conduct could subject him to prosecution in Arizona,[15] the court concluded that Miller's extra-territorial conduct was not sufficiently related to the crime in Arizona. He caused only a continuing deprivation of an Arizona resident's property. *Id.* at 134, 755 P.2d at 439. Because the relationship between conduct and results was too attenuated, Arizona had no jurisdiction; "Arizona must conform to international law in its exercise of extra-territorial jurisdiction." *Id.*

This case presents no such conflict with international law. The state does not premise its jurisdiction over Defendant on the results theory it sought to apply in *Miller*. Instead, the state asserts jurisdiction pursuant to the element clause in § 13–108(A)(1), which is a proper basis for exercising jurisdiction. *See* RESTATEMENT § 402(1)(a); MPC § 1.03(1)(a); ARIZONA CRIMINAL CODE COMMISSION COMMENTARY at 20. We see no conflict between this portion of Arizona's law and international law.

Next, Defendant argues that Arizona's imposition of the death penalty conflicts with the Mexico–United States extradition treaty, which, in Art. 8, permits a party to refuse extradition in death penalty cases.[16] The treaty establishes a mechanism for surrendering individuals from the custody of one country to the custody of another under prescribed circumstances and only when the treaty is invoked. *United States v. Alvarez–Machain*, 504 U.S. 655, ——, 112 S.Ct. 2188, 2194, 119 L.Ed.2d 441 (1992). Parties to an [3] extradition treaty may exert their legislative policies on each other by enumerating the offenses for which a person may be extraditable. *Hu Yau–Leung v. Soscia*, 500 F.Supp. 1382, 1384 (E.D.N.Y.1980), *rev'd on other grounds*, 649 F.2d 914 (2d Cir.), *cert. denied*, 454 U.S. 971, 102 S.Ct. 519, 70 L.Ed.2d 389 (1981). But unless the treaty is invoked by one of the countries, there can be no basis for claiming that the policies of one country impermissibly conflict with the policies of the other. *See United States v. Verdugo–Urquidez*, 939 F.2d 1341, 1357 (9th Cir.1991) [4] (rights under a treaty are recognized only when the affected foreign government registers a protest), *judgment vacated on other grounds*, —— U.S. ——, 112 S.Ct. 2986, 120 L.Ed.2d 864 (1992).

Mexico did not invoke the treaty. Mexico cooperated with Arizona's prosecution of Defendant. Extradition was not an issue because Mexican authorities made no effort to extradite or prosecute Defendant, an Arizona resident arrested in Arizona. Even if Mexico wished to have Arizona's assurance that Arizona would not impose the death penalty, it was not in a position to obtain it. Such a right belongs only to the party having custody of the defendant.[17] We conclude that the

---

15. Again, in relevant part, A.R.S. § 13–108(A)(1) provides:

This state has jurisdiction ... if ... [c]onduct constituting any element of the offense or a *result* of such conduct occurs within this state. (Emphasis added.)

16. Article 8 of the extradition treaty between the United States and Mexico, which was signed May 4, 1978, states:

When the offense for which extradition is requested is punishable by death under the laws

of the requesting Party and the laws of the requested Party do not permit such punishment for that offense, extradition may be refused unless the requesting Party furnishes such assurances as the requested Party considers sufficient that the death penalty shall not be imposed, or, if imposed, shall not be executed.

31 U.S.T. 5059, 5065 (1979).

17. *See supra* note 15.

application of A.R.S. § 13–108 to this case does not violate international law.

TRIAL ISSUES

A. Did the court err in denying Defendant's motion for acquittal?

Defendant claims the trial court erred in denying his motion for acquittal on both counts. *See* Ariz.R.Crim.P. 20. In reviewing the evidence, this court examines the facts in the light most favorable to sustaining the verdict and resolves all reasonable inferences against the defendant. *State v. Atwood*, 171 Ariz. 576, 596, 832 P.2d 593, 613 (1992), *cert. denied*, — U.S. —, 113 S.Ct. 1058, 122 L.Ed.2d 364 (1993). We will reverse a trial court's denial of a Rule 20 motion if probative facts in support of a conviction were absent. *State v. Mathers*, 165 Ariz. 64, 66, 796 P.2d 866, 868 (1990).

1. First-degree murder

The record provides ample evidence to support the conviction for premeditated murder. The facts already recited and others in the record clearly establish not only Defendant's desire to be rid of his wife but a motive for the killing (insurance money), a means (a homemade weapon), and a scheme (a family vacation in Mexico and a mock robbery) to accomplish that result. The uncontroverted facts show that the plan was consummated.

There was substantial evidence that Defendant was the killer. From a distance, Ysenia saw Defendant and his children file out of the condo and get into the family van; Defendant go back inside the house, leaving his children in the van; and Defendant's daughter Marsha get out of the van and go to the condo. Marsha told several people that the door to the condo was locked and that shortly after she tried to open the door Defendant reappeared and strongly discouraged her from going inside. Ysenia then observed Marsha and Defendant get back into the van and drive away. Ysenia said that she then drove to the house, opened the back door left unlocked by Defendant, called to Trish, grabbed some blunt knives from the kitchen, found Trish lying unconscious on the bed,

tried to stick the knives into her, took some rings and money, scattered the contents of Trish's purse, and left. Ysenia's fingerprints were found inside the house, and she had Trish's rings in her possession when she was stopped at the border. **[1334]**

There was strong evidence of each element of first-degree murder—intent, premeditation, and an act that caused the death of the victim.

2. Conspiracy

Defendant was charged with one count of conspiracy with five predicate offenses enumerated. If the conspiracy to commit murder is sufficiently supported, we need not discuss the other conspiracy allegations. *See State v. Ortiz*, 131 Ariz. 195, 205, 639 P.2d 1020, 1030 (1981) ("When an indictment charges a single conspiracy with multiple objects, a conviction will stand if the prosecution proves the defendant guilty of conspiracy to commit any one of the objects."), *cert. denied*, 456 U.S. 984, 102 S.Ct. 2259, 72 L.Ed.2d 863 (1982).

The elements of conspiracy to commit murder are intent to promote the offense of murder and an agreement with another that one will do the actual killing. A.R.S. § 13–1003(A); *State v. Apelt*, 176 Ariz. 349, 360, 861 P.2d 634, 645 (1993), *cert. denied*, — U.S. —, 115 S.Ct. 113, 130 L.Ed.2d 59 (1994). Because murder is a felony upon the person of another, an overt act in furtherance of the offense is not required to convict for conspiracy. A.R.S. § 13–1003(A). The evidence described above clearly supports a jury finding that Defendant intended and agreed with Ysenia to commit murder. The overt acts jointly performed by Defendant and Ysenia confirm that there was an agreement between them. Thus, the court did not err in denying Defendant's motion for acquittal.

B. Did the court err in questioning jurors about their views on the death penalty?

Defendant alleges that the court violated his Sixth Amendment right to a fair and impartial jury by asking voir dire ques-

[1335] tions seeking jurors' views on the death penalty. Two prospective jurors were excused after they said that they could not convict at all, knowing that Defendant might be given a death sentence. Death qualifying jurors, he argues, is a religious qualification that begets a jury biased in favor of capital punishment and therefore violates art. 2, § 12 of the Arizona Constitution.

This argument runs contrary to our past rulings. *State v. White,* 168 Ariz. 500, 509, 815 P.2d 869, 878 (1991), *cert. denied,* 502 U.S. 1105, 112 S.Ct. 1199, 117 L.Ed.2d 439 (1992); *State v. Fisher,* 141 Ariz. 227, 249, 686 P.2d 750, 772, *cert. denied,* 469 U.S. 1066, 105 S.Ct. 548, 83 L.Ed.2d 436 (1984). Article 2, § 12 of the Arizona Constitution prohibits disqualifying a juror because of his or her religious views. Although religious beliefs may motivate one's opinion about the death penalty, the beliefs themselves are not the basis for disqualification. In *Fisher,* we stated that a "person whose religious beliefs prevent him or her from finding a defendant guilty, notwithstanding proof beyond a reasonable doubt . . ., is not impartial." 141 Ariz. at 249, 686 P.2d at 772. We echoed these words recently in *State v. West,* 176 Ariz. 432, 440, 862 P.2d 192, 200 (1993), *cert. denied,* — U.S. —, 114 S.Ct. 1635, 128 L.Ed.2d 358 (1994), and continue to believe that the crux of a fair trial is the ability of the trier of fact to render a verdict based on the facts and applicable law. Excusing a juror whose religious beliefs prevent him from meeting that standard does not violate art. 2, § 12 of the Arizona Constitution. *White,* 168 Ariz. at 509, 815 P.2d at 878.

C. Was it reversible error for the prosecutor to ask a witness about Defendant's "Mafia connections"?

The prosecution elicited testimony from witnesses concerning Defendant's alleged connection with the Mafia. Defendant claims that this improperly referred to bad character and violated Ariz.R.Evid. 404(a). Defendant argues that the Mafia link question was so prejudicial that it constituted fundamental error.

Because Defendant did not object to the questioning at trial, he waived his objection, and we review only for fundamental error. *West,* 176 Ariz. at 445, 862 P.2d at 204. Error is fundamental when it deprives the defendant of a right essential to the defense or to a fair trial. *State v. Cornell,* 179 Ariz. 314, 329, 878 P.2d 1352, 1367 (1994).

Ysenia testified that Defendant told her his Mafia connections refused to kill Trish. Jack Mielke testified that he did not warn Trish of the murder scheme out of fear for his life after learning from Defendant that Defendant was connected with the Mafia. An investigator from the Attorney General's Office testified that he did not uncover any evidence that the Mafia owed Defendant any favors, although he did find evidence of Mafia connections. Admission of some or all of this testimony over proper objection might constitute error or even abuse of discretion. *See* Ariz.R.Evid. 404(a). There was, however, no objection. Moreover, Ysenia's testimony was relevant to prove intent or premeditation before the murder. Jack Mielke's testimony explained why he failed to tell Trish or authorities about his discussions with Defendant and supported his credibility. The investigator's testimony regarding Mafia ties was elicited by Defendant during cross-examination to attack Ysenia's credibility and by the prosecutor on redirect to rehabilitate her credibility.

We conclude that the danger of unfair prejudice on this record was not so great that any error could be described as fundamental.

SENTENCING ISSUES

A. Summary Issues

1. *Constitutionality of non-jury sentencing*

Arizona excludes jurors from the sentencing process. A.R.S. § 13–703(B). Defendant argues this violates the Equal Protection Clause of the Fourteenth Amendment. This same claim was recently rejected in *State v. Landrigan,* 176 Ariz. 1, 6, 859 P.2d 111, 116, *cert. denied,* — U.S. —, 114 S.Ct. 334, 126 L.Ed.2d 279 (1993).

2. Constitutionality of Arizona's death penalty scheme

Defendant next argues that Arizona's death sentencing procedure is unconstitutional because it fails to objectively channel the trial court's discretion. We recently rejected this argument in *West,* 176 Ariz. at 454, 862 P.2d at 214.

B. Were Defendant's due process rights violated by denial of his motion for a continuance to allow more witnesses at the sentencing hearing?

The jury returned its verdict on May 19, 1992. The sentencing hearing did not begin until August 5, 1992. The state called no witnesses, but Trish's mother gave a statement as a victim. Defendant called twelve witnesses the first day of the hearing and five more the next day. Another witness was scheduled but did not testify because Defendant's counsel did not feel there was enough time left that day. Instead, the court ordered a continuance for a psychological examination of Defendant. The sentencing hearing reconvened on September 22 to examine the psychologist's report. Defense counsel requested another continuance so that he could talk with the psychologist and file an untimely motion for a new trial. The judge granted the request over the state's objection and continued the hearing to October 26, stating his intention to conclude the process without further delay. Defense counsel indicated he intended to call only the psychologist as his final witness.

At the October 26 hearing, defense counsel said that he was prepared only to argue the motion for a new trial. The judge reminded him of the court's previous admonition that he would conclude the sentencing hearing that day, and counsel agreed that he had told the court he would be prepared to do so. The following exchange then occurred:

The Court: If there were other witnesses like the many people that you produced in the two days of our previous session, I would think it would be unnecessary to produce more of the same. If you have other witnesses on other issues, please tell me who they are and give me some indication of what you expect them to say, so that I can evaluate whether we **[1336]** need to recess to hear what they would have to say.

Defense Counsel: Your honor, the witnesses that I had intended to call were basically of the same type and character of the ones that I had previously produced. I did not subpoena a couple of them. They are not here. But I will state to the court that they would not be raising or bringing up any new issues that had not been previously raised at my prior, earlier mitigation hearing.

The judge then informed defense counsel that he would only hear final arguments from the state and defense counsel and any statement Defendant wished to make. At the end of the hearing, the judge sentenced Defendant to death.

Defendant correctly argues that a court must consider all mitigating aspects of a defendant's character and circumstances before imposing a capital sentence. *State v. Brewer,* 170 Ariz. 486, 504, 826 P.2d 783, 801, *cert. denied,* — U.S. —, 113 S.Ct. 206, 121 L.Ed.2d 147 (1992). Thus, defense counsel argues, rejection of relevant proffered testimony was clear error, violating Defendant's due process rights.

We disagree. The judge had already granted several continuances, which delayed sentencing for more than five months after the jury verdict, and had heard seventeen mitigation witnesses. It was well within the court's discretion to deny a further continuance for cumulative evidence, especially when counsel knew that the judge intended to proceed with sentencing that day. The court did not abuse its discretion in denying a continuance.

C. Independent Review

When the death sentence is imposed by the trial judge, this court conducts a thorough and independent review of the record and of the aggravating and mitigating evidence to determine whether the sentence is justified. *Brewer,* 170 Ariz. at 500, 826 P.2d at 797.

At the sentencing hearing for first-degree murder, the trial court weighs aggravating

[1337]and mitigating circumstances to determine whether the death sentence is warranted. A.R.S. § 13–703. The state must prove aggravating circumstances beyond a reasonable doubt. *See* A.R.S. § 13–703(C); *Brewer,* 170 Ariz. at 500, 826 P.2d at 797. The defendant must prove mitigating circumstances by a preponderance of the evidence, but the trial court may consider evidence that tends to refute a mitigating circumstance. *State v. Lopez,* 174 Ariz. 131, 145, 847 P.2d 1078, 1092 (1992), *cert. denied,* —— U.S. ——, 114 S.Ct. 258, 126 L.Ed.2d 210 (1993).

1. Did the trial court err in finding that Defendant committed homicide for pecuniary gain?

The trial court found only one statutory aggravating circumstance [18]—murder in expectation of financial gain [19]—and no mitigating circumstances sufficiently substantial to call for leniency. Defendant challenges both findings.

Although the mere receipt of proceeds from an existing insurance policy will not satisfy the requirements of § 13–703(F)(5), *State v. Madsen,* 125 Ariz. 346, 353, 609 P.2d 1046, 1053, *cert. denied,* 449 U.S. 873, 101 S.Ct. 213, 66 L.Ed.2d 93 (1980), evidence is sufficient to support a finding of the (F)(5) factor if it shows that the defendant killed for financial gain. *White,* 168 Ariz. at 511, 815 P.2d at 880.

Evidence showed that Defendant pressed for a buyout agreement between Trish and her mother to ensure that Trish's share of their business would be liquidated on her death and distributed under her will. Integral to the agreement was the purchase of additional insurance on Trish's life. After the murder, Defendant received proceeds under one life insurance policy and tried to obtain proceeds from the policy used to fund the buyout agreement. The financial gain finding was also supported by Defendant's stated reason for killing rather than divorc-

ing his wife: she would have taken him "to the cleaners." We affirm the finding that Defendant murdered for financial gain.

2. Mitigating evidence

Defendant presented seventeen witnesses who testified that he has been a generous and compassionate co-worker, friend, neighbor, and family member. One witness related how Defendant offered monetary and moral support when the witness became too disabled to work. Another witness who had been out of work told the court that, without being asked, Defendant twice loaned him money, asking only that the witness repay the loans when he was able. A neighbor testified that Defendant helped her financially and in other ways to ensure her six children had shoes to wear, bicycles on their birthdays, and a decent house to live in. The witnesses believed Defendant performed these deeds without any expectation of collecting on them later.

Defendant was described as an active member in his church who often volunteered to conduct spiritual and educational visits to other members. Until Trish's death, her mother considered Defendant a good parent to his three children, two of whom he had adopted, and a good provider. Many witnesses observed Defendant to be patient, loving, and engaged with his own children and those of his neighbors. The bishop of his ward commended Defendant for his faithful service as counselor, church school teacher to young children, and Boy Scout leader. In brief, many people portrayed Defendant as a person who contributed substantially to their community.

The trial judge found this evidence credible. Acknowledging the evidence, he nevertheless concluded that it was not

sufficiently substantial to call for leniency. With the defendant's concurrence, the court asked for a psychological "profile"

---

18. Although the prosecutor attempted to prove that Defendant committed the murder in an especially heinous, cruel, or depraved manner as another aggravating circumstance, the trial judge carefully reasoned that the evidence did not support such a finding beyond a reasonable doubt.

19. A.R.S. § 13–703(F)(5) establishes as an aggravating circumstance proof that "the defendant committed the offense as consideration for the receipt, or in expectation of the receipt, of anything of pecuniary value."

evaluation of the defendant; the same was done by Dr. K. Thomas Nelson, Ph.D., with assistance of his colleague, clinical psychologist David Biegen, Ph.D. The report, made available to counsel but now sealed to protect the privacy of the many people to whom Dr. Nelson talked, demonstrates that Defendant's essential character is fundamentally self-centered, with certain aggressive impulses to control other people, with defense mechanisms to compensate for perceived loss of control. Dr. Nelson and Dr. Biegen conclude that Defendant's apparently altruistic acts, described by witnesses at the presentence hearing before the court, are probably manifestations of these "defenses" to loss of control as well as elements of defendant's "over-controlled" personality. Thus, with the aid of this excellent report, the court concludes that the correct inference from the "good character" evidence is not that defendant had a good character (and thus was "a good man gone bad"), but that his acts were merely manifestations of the character traits which eventually led him to plan and execute the murder of his wife.

Special Verdict, Oct. 26, 1992, at 6. We believe that proof of a great number of past good deeds, even if prompted by impure psychological motives, has considerable mitigating value. Thus, a long record of significant good deeds for others and the community as a whole is entitled to substantial weight even if not entirely engendered by virtuous motives.[20]

On the other side of the scale, however, is the quality of the aggravating factor. In weighing, we do not simply count the number of aggravating or mitigating factors. *State v. Stuard,* 176 Ariz. 589, 610, 863 P.2d 881, 902 (1993). The quality and strength of each must also be considered. *State v. Barreras,* 181 Ariz. 516, 521, 892 P.2d 852, 857 (1995). This murder for pecuniary gain is not comparable to some crimes that might fall under that rubric. *Cf. State v. Fierro,* 166 Ariz. 539, 551, 804 P.2d 72, 84 (1990)

(defendant, caught burglarizing home and fired upon by homeowner, fired back and killed homeowner while escaping). **[1338]**

The killing in this case did not arise out of the heat of passion, fear, struggle, or attempt to escape. This killing was not just the result of momentary premeditation but of Defendant's deliberate, carefully conceived, meticulously planned, and cold-blooded scheme to kill, rather than divorce, his unsuspecting wife. In this respect it was very much like the cold and callous contract killing that may have prompted the promulgation of § 13–703(F)(5). *See State v. Clark,* 126 Ariz. 428, 437, 616 P.2d 888, 897 (Gordon, J., specially concurring and arguing that § 13–703(F)(5) applies only to circumstances in which the defendant is a hired killer), *cert. denied,* 449 U.S. 1067, 101 S.Ct. 796, 66 L.Ed.2d 612 (1980).

In conclusion, although we disagree to some extent with the trial judge's evaluation of the mitigating facts and acknowledge that in many cases Defendant's record of significant good deeds and community service would weigh heavily in favor of leniency, given the strength and quality of the aggravating circumstance in this case, we agree with the trial judge that leniency is not appropriate. On balance, we conclude that Defendant's record of good deeds does not outweigh the aggravating factor.

DISPOSITION

None of the issues raised by Defendant warrant reversal of his convictions. We have reviewed the entire record for fundamental error pursuant to A.R.S. § 13–4035 and have found none. We find one aggravating circumstance beyond a reasonable doubt. We find the mitigating circumstances are substantial, but under these facts not substantial enough to call for leniency. Accordingly, we affirm Defendant's convictions and death sentence.

MOELLER, V.C.J., and ZLAKET, J., concur.

---

20. Indeed, the psychologists did not pretend to understand or explain Defendant's past conduct or behavior in relation to the ghastly crime he committed. They could identify character and personality traits, but they did not claim that this provided a sufficient explanation of Defendant's conduct. Psychological Profile Report on Daniel Willoughby, Sept. 7, 1992.

[1339]   MARTONE, Justice, concurring.

I join the court in affirming this conviction and sentence. I write separately to express my disagreement with the court's resolution of two important legal issues, one not raised on appeal by the defendant, and both unnecessary to the resolution of this case. I refer to the question of territorial jurisdiction: Who gets to decide it and by what standard?

The court concludes that "[i]n the very rare case in which jurisdiction is legitimately in issue because of contradicting jurisdictional facts, Arizona's territorial jurisdiction must be established beyond a reasonable doubt by the jury." *Ante,* at 538, 892 P.2d at 1327. But the court also concedes that "[o]n appeal, Defendant does not renew his argument that the jurisdictional question was for the jury." *Ante,* at 535, 892 P.2d at 1324. The court also concedes that "[t]here was no controverting evidence on the jurisdictional issue." *Ante,* at 539, 892 P.2d at 1328.

Thus, the court decides two important substantive issues, one of which is not raised by the defendant on appeal, and neither of which is presented by the facts of this case. I do not believe we should decide complex issues unless we must. We never know what the next case will present. The court says that "fundamental error doctrine requires us to reach this issue," *ante,* at 535 n. 2, 892 P.2d at 1324 n. 2. On the contrary, the court must decide whether there is error, and then whether it is fundamental. *State v. King,* 158 Ariz. 419, 424, 763 P.2d 239, 244 (1988). "Since there is no error, there is no occasion to reach the doctrine of fundamental error." *State v. Youngblood,* 173 Ariz. 502, 505 n. 2, 844 P.2d 1152, 1155 n. 2 (1993).

Nor does the nonwaivability of subject matter jurisdiction require us to reach these issues. First, subject matter jurisdiction is not in dispute. The Superior Court of Arizona is a trial court of general jurisdiction with subject matter jurisdiction over the offense as charged. But even if one categorized territorial jurisdiction under the heading of subject matter jurisdiction, the question of territorial jurisdiction has been raised

by the defendant and we are deciding it. What has not been raised is the discrete legal issue of whether the judge or jury decides it.

Even if this case were an appropriate occasion to decide these complex issues, I would decide each of them differently. I subscribe to the view that the court, and not the jury, decides the question of territorial jurisdiction. *State v. Beverly,* 224 Conn. 372, 618 A.2d 1335 (1993); *Mitchell v. United States,* 569 A.2d 177 (D.C.App.1990). Jurisdiction is a question of law and thus the judge ought to make the findings necessary to support a conclusion that there is jurisdiction. *Cf.* Rule 43(i), Ariz.R.Civ.P. Many motions in both civil and criminal cases require the taking of evidence. These include motions to dismiss for lack of subject matter jurisdiction, motions to dismiss for lack of *in personam* jurisdiction, motions for transfer of venue, and many others. These sorts of motions raise legal issues and it is up to the judge to find whatever facts are necessary to support the appropriate legal conclusion. It seems anomalous to me to allow a jury to tell the court whether it has jurisdiction or not.

Nor do I agree that the better rule is that jurisdictional facts must be established beyond a reasonable doubt. Proof beyond a reasonable doubt is necessary to establish the elements of a crime but, as the court acknowledges, "[w]e do not, however, equate jurisdiction with elements of the offense." *Ante,* at 538, 892 P.2d at 1327. The jurisdiction of the court has nothing to do with the elements of a crime.[1]

Does the standard of proof really matter? I believe it can. It may well be that there is no proof beyond a reasonable doubt that any state has jurisdiction. But there may be proof by a preponderance of the evidence that one or more. states have jurisdiction. Having imposed the reasonable doubt standard on jurisdiction, there may now be instances in which a criminal charge could be heard nowhere, even though the offense itself can be proven beyond a reasonable doubt. I

---

1. The court says that it "makes no sense in a single trial to require the factfinder to determine the existence of facts on the reasonable doubt standard for guilt purposes and the same facts on the preponderance standard for jurisdiction pur-

poses." *Ante,* at 538, 892 P.2d at 1327. But under my view, it is not the *same* fact finder. The jury decides guilt. The judge decides jurisdiction.

thus favor a rule that, because territorial jurisdiction is not an element of the offense, the jurisdictional standard of proof is by the preponderance of the evidence. *People v. Cavanaugh*, 44 Cal.2d 252, 282 P.2d 53 (1955).

CORCORAN, Justice.

I concur with the majority and affirm both defendant's convictions and sentences, including the death sentence. However, because the defendant has not raised in this court, **[1340]** and the parties have not briefed, the question whether the judge or the jury is to determine the jurisdictional question, I would not decide it. I would await an appropriate case where the issue is both raised and briefed.

As to the issue of whether jurisdictional facts must be proved beyond a reasonable doubt or by a preponderance of the evidence, I agree with Justice Martone that the standard should be a preponderance standard.

[Report: 892 P2d 1319 (1995)]

Editorial Footnotes:

[2] 1 *Ann Dig* 159.
[3] 95 *ILR* 355.

[4] 90 *ILR* 668.

NOTE.—The United States Supreme Court denied an application for *certiorari* without giving an opinion (133 L Ed 2d 677; 116 S Ct 725).

States — Sovereignty — Transfer of sovereignty — Joint Declaration between People's Republic of China and United Kingdom, 1984 — Hong Kong due to revert to Chinese sovereignty on 1 July 1997—Hong Kong ceasing to exist as British Colony—Hong Kong becoming part of China on date of reversion—Article 3 of Joint Declaration— Establishment of Hong Kong Special Administrative Region ("HKSAR")—Basic policies to remain intact for fifty years after handover — Whether requesting sovereign able to comply with terms of United Kingdom–United States Extradition Treaty, 1972

Extradition—Treaties—Scope and effect—United Kingdom–
United States Extradition Treaty, 1972—Extended to Hong
Kong in 1976—Supplementary Treaty, 1986—Whether terms
of Treaty permitting extradition of petitioner to Hong
Kong—Whether requesting State able to try and punish
petitioner before 1 July 1997—Whether change of sovereignty
over Hong Kong affecting applicability of Treaty—Absence
of extradition treaty between United States and China—
Intention of United States Senate—Doctrine of non-inquiry
—Doctrine of separation of powers—Whether Court having
independent role—Whether Court able to depart from Treaty
and wishes of Executive — Non-justiciability of evaluation
of contingent political events—Whether certain provisions
of Treaty rendering Treaty inapplicable to present case

Relationship of international law and municipal law —
United States Congress passing Hong Kong Policy Act
1992—United Kingdom–United States Extradition Treaty,
1972—Act providing that all treaties with Hong Kong to
remain in force until reversion — Provision of means to
continue treaties after 1 July 1997—Whether Act evidence of
Congressional intent that Treaty should extend to petitioner
—Whether Act amending Treaty

State succession — Transfer of Hong Kong from United
Kingdom to China—Whether doctrine applicable—Effect
on extradition treaty—The law of the United States

UNITED STATES OF AMERICA *v.* LUI KIN-HONG, A.K.A. JERRY LUI[1]

United States District Court, District of Massachusetts. 7 *January* 1997

(Tauro, *Chief Judge*)

[1] In the District Court the petitioner was represented by Andrew Good, Harvey A.
Silverglate, Silverglate & Good, Boston, MA. The United States was represented by Alex
Whiting, Susan C. Hanson-Philbrick, United States Attorney's Office, Michael Surgalla, United
States Department of Justice, Office of International Affairs, Boston, MA.

Andrew Y. Au, Greenbelt, MD, for Alliance of Hong Kong Chinese appeared as *amicus curiae.*
Michael Posner, Lawyers' Committee for Human Rights, New York City, for Lawyers'
Committee for Human Rights appeared as *amicus curiae.* John Reinstein, Civil Liberties Union of
Massachusetts, Boston, MA, for American Civil Liberties Union of Massachusetts appeared as
amicus curiae.

In the Court of Appeals the United States was represented by Alex Whiting, Assistant United
States Attorney, with whom Donald K. Stern, United States Attorney, Susan Hanson-Philbrick,
Assistant United States Attorney, and Michael Surgalla, United States Department of Justice,
Office of International Affairs, were on brief. The appellee was represented by Andrew Good,
with whom Harvey A. Silverglate, Silverglate & Good, were on brief.

Michael Posner and John Reinstein on brief for Lawyers' Committee for Human Rights and
American Civil Liberties Union of Massachusetts, *amici curiae* in support of appellee.

For similar proceedings in Australia and the United Kingdom, see pp. 383 and 402 above.

United States Court of Appeals, First Circuit.   20 *March* 1997

(Aldrich, *Senior Circuit Judge*; Boudin and Lynch, *Circuit Judges*)

Order denying rehearing en banc.   10 *April* 1997

(Torruella, *Chief Judge*; Selya, Boudin, Stahl and Lynch, *Circuit Judges*)

SUMMARY: *The facts:*—The petitioner, a citizen of the British Dependent Territories (Hong Kong) and of Canada, was arrested in the United States in 1995 as the result of an extradition request by the United Kingdom on behalf of the British Colony of Hong Kong ("Hong Kong"). The Extradition Treaty, 1972 ("the Treaty"), which governed extradition arrangements between the United States and the United Kingdom, was officially extended to Hong Kong in 1976 and modified by the Supplementary Treaty, 1986. In 1996 the Magistrate Judge authorized the surrender of the petitioner to Hong Kong. He petitioned for a writ of habeas corpus.

Pursuant to the Joint Declaration between the People's Republic of China ("China") and the United Kingdom, 1984 ("the Joint Declaration"), Hong Kong was due to revert to Chinese sovereignty on 1 July 1997. Under the terms of the Joint Declaration China declared its basic policies with respect to Hong Kong. It stated its intention to establish a Hong Kong Special Administrative Region ("HKSAR") which was to be vested with a high degree of autonomy and independent judicial power. The laws in force in Hong Kong were to remain basically unchanged.[2] Article 3(12) stipulated that these basic policies were to remain the same for fifty years after the handover.

The petitioner alleged that his extradition to Hong Kong was not permitted under the Treaty as it was not possible for him to be tried and punished by the requesting sovereign before Hong Kong reverted to China. He maintained that the United States Senate, in approving the Treaty, had not intended that the regime which tried and punished the fugitive should be different from that which had given its assurances in the Treaty. Accordingly, he maintained that he could not be surrendered as the Treaty did not permit his extradition and there was no extradition treaty between the United States and China.

The United States asserted that the literal terms of the Extradition Treaties between the United States and the United Kingdom clearly allowed the petitioner's extradition to Hong Kong and that in the circumstances of the case the Court was not permitted to deviate from the Treaties.

Held (by the District Court):—The petition for a writ of habeas corpus was granted. The Magistrate Judge lacked jurisdiction to authorize the petitioner's extradition.

(1) The Court had the jurisdiction to examine whether the requesting sovereign was able to fulfil its obligations under the Treaty (p. 615).

(2) As it would be impossible for the United Kingdom to try and punish the petitioner through its Colony of Hong Kong before Hong Kong's reversion to China, the United Kingdom was unable to comply with the terms of the

[2] See Article 3 of the Joint Declaration at p. 625 below.

Treaty. As such, and as no valid extradition treaty existed between the United States and China, the extradition of the petitioner could not be permitted (pp. 615-17).

(3) In ratifying the Treaty the United States Senate had not intended that the petitioner should be tried and punished by China, a non-democratic country, but by the United Kingdom as requesting sovereign. Extradition to Hong Kong in these circumstances would, therefore, contravene the will of the Senate, as well as the terms of the Treaty. The Hong Kong Policy Act 1992 did not amend the Treaty and was only evidence of the fact that Congress supported the continuation of treaties with Hong Kong according to their own terms (pp. 617-21).

(4) The doctrine of State succession, whereby a sovereign could assume all of the responsibilities and duties of a predecessor sovereign if all parties agreed, was not applicable as China, being a non-democratic regime, was not able to meet the political offence requirements, as amended by the Supplementary Treaty (pp. 621-2).

(5) The non-inquiry doctrine, which forbade judicial authorities from investigating the fairness of a requesting nation's justice system when considering whether to permit extradition to that nation, had not been violated. The Court's interpretation of the Treaty was in fact consistent with this doctrine as it was based on its acceptance that the Executive and Legislature had deemed the justice system of the United Kingdom and its Colony fair enough to send the accused for trial (p. 622).

(6) As the Court had concluded that the Magistrate Judge lacked jurisdiction, it was unnecessary to consider whether he had also erred in finding probable cause for the crimes charged (p. 622).

The United States appealed.

Held (by the Court of Appeals):—The appeal was allowed. The order of the District Court granting the writ of habeas corpus was reversed.

(1) The approval by the United States Senate of the Supplementary Treaty in 1986, while aware of the reversion of Hong Kong to China on 1 July 1997, and its lack of comment on the issue indicated that it did not intend the Treaty to be inapplicable where trial and punishment was to be carried out by China as opposed to Hong Kong. Governments of State parties changed frequently but this did not excuse non-compliance with the terms of the agreement (p. 623).

(2) The doctrine of the separation of powers meant that the Judiciary was not at liberty to rewrite treaties which had been approved by the Executive. As there was no denial of due process and the petitioner was facing prosecution for an ordinary crime, not for political reasons, the Court's independent role was restricted (p. 623).

(3) One of the principles developed by the courts to ensure that judicial enquiry did not impinge upon executive prerogative and expertise was the rule which prohibited investigation into the fairness and procedures of a requesting nation's justice system. Whether the new treaty between the United States and the new Hong Kong Government, providing for reciprocal post-reversion extradition, would be approved by the Senate, whether the current treaty was to be extended by executive agreement and whether China was to adhere to the terms of the Joint Declaration were questions which

involved the evaluation of contingent political events and were thus non-justiciable. The Executive had already provided a statutory scheme under which the validity of the extradition of the petitioner could be ascertained (pp. 626-9).

(4) As the Senate had chosen not to modify or abrogate the Treaty, the Court could not interfere with its terms. On the plain language of the Treaty, the obligation of the United States to extradite the petitioner expressed in Article I of the Treaty was not undermined by four treaty provisions which the petitioner claimed rendered the Treaty inapplicable in his case. The warrant requirement in Article VII(3) of the Treaty and the dual criminality requirement in Article III were satisfied. Neither did the political offence exception contained in Article 3(a) of the Supplementary Treaty nor the rule of specialty apply (pp. 630-3).

(5) The Magistrate Judge was fully warranted in finding probable cause to support the petitioner's extradition (pp. 633-8).

The petitioner requested a rehearing before the full bench of the Court of Appeals.

Held (by the Court of Appeals, Circuit Judge Stahl dissenting):—The petition for *en banc* review was dismissed.

Per Circuit Judge Stahl (dissenting): (1) In the circumstances a certification of extraditability constituted a violation of the Treaty as it was to be inferred from the language of Article XII of the Treaty that extradition was only permitted if the offences were to be tried and punished by the requesting sovereign (pp. 639-42).

(2) The United Kingdom's surrender of sovereignty over Hong Kong to China on 1 July 1997 would effect an impermissible re-extradition with respect to the petitioner under the terms of Article XII of the Treaty as his prosecution would take place under the judicial system of a third-party sovereign State (pp. 642-5).

(3) The certification of the petitioner for extradition did not comport with the intent of the Legislature in ratifying the Treaties between the United States and the United Kingdom as it would result in a third sovereign State, China, with which there was no extradition treaty, trying and punishing the petitioner (pp. 645-9).

The Order of the *En Banc* Court commences at p. 638. The text of the judgment of the Court of Appeals, delivered by Circuit Judge Lynch, commences at p. 623. The following is the text of the judgment of the District Court:

Before the court is a petition for a writ of *habeas corpus* seeking the unconditional release of Petitioner Lui Kin–Hong ("Lui"), who has been in the custody of the United States since his arrest in Boston on Decem-

[1281]

[282] ber 20, 1995. That arrest was precipitated by an extradition request of the United Kingdom on behalf of the Crown Colony of Hong Kong ("Hong Kong").

On August 29, 1996, Magistrate Judge Zachary Karol issued an opinion authorizing the surrender of Lui to Hong Kong. In response, Lui filed the pending petition.

I.

HISTORICAL BACKGROUND

The complex legal issues involved in this petition and the underlying extradition request must be examined in the context of the unique colonial relationship between the United Kingdom and Hong Kong. That relationship originated in 1898 when the United Kingdom leased the New Territories of Hong Kong from China for a term of ninety-nine years. Convention of Beijing, June 9, 1898, in 1 *Treaties and Agreements with and Concerning China,* 1894–1919, 130, No. 1898/11 (1921). The remaining Hong Kong territory was subsequently ceded to the United Kingdom. *See* Comment, *The Reversion of Hong Kong to China: Legal and Practical Questions,* 21 Willamette L.Rev. 327 (1985).

Accordingly, extradition to Hong Kong from the United States has been governed by the Extradition Treaty between the Government of the United States of America and the United Kingdom of Great Britain and Northern Ireland (the "Treaty"). U.S.-U.K., 28 U.S.T. 227, June 8, 1972. The reach of the Treaty was officially extended to Hong Kong by an exchange of notes in Washington, D.C. on October 21, 1976. The Treaty was subsequently modified by the Supplementary Treaty Concerning the Extradition Treaty Between the Government of the United States of America and the Government of the United Kingdom of Great Britain and Northern Ireland (the "Supplementary Treaty") on December 23, 1986. S. Treaty Doc.

No. 99–8, 99th Cong., 1st Sess., 132 Cong. Rec. 16557 (1986).[1]

Central to the issues underlying this petition are the facts that, on July 1, 1997, Hong Kong will revert to the sovereignty of the People's Republic of China ("China"),[2] and that the United States does not have an extradition treaty with China. *See* 18 U.S.C.A. § 3181 (West 1985 & Supp.1996) (listing countries with whom the United States has an extradition treaty).

II.

THE PETITIONER

Lui, a citizen of both Hong Kong and Canada, was employed by Brown & Williamson Tobacco Corporation ("B & W") from August 1988 to May 1993. B & W is a wholly-owned subsidiary of British–American Tobacco Industries PLC ("BAT PLC"). On January 1, 1992, Lui, while still employed by B & W, became Export Director at the British American Tobacco Corporation in Hong Kong ("BAT–HK"), also a wholly-owned subsidiary of BAT PLC. At the time, BAT–HK had exclusive rights to distribute cigarettes in several Asian countries, and Lui was allegedly responsible for allocating cigarettes to selected Hong Kong trading companies.

In its extradition request, the Crown Colony of Hong Kong claims that Lui, in conjunction with other BAT–HK executives, solicited and accepted bribes in excess of three million American dollars from one trading company in particular, Giant Island Ltd. ("GIL"), and certain GIL affiliates, namely Wing Wah Company ("Wing Wah") and Pasto Company Ltd. GIL allegedly paid the bribes to secure a monopoly over the export of BAT–HK cigarettes.

While Lui admits to having received the money, he contends that it was legitimate business income, paid to him in exchange for his assistance in establishing GIL's profitable trading relationships. In support of his posi-

---

1. All of the treaties relevant to this case have been reprinted in 2 *Extradition Laws and Treaties, United States* 920.1–920.30 (compiled by Igor I. Kavass & Adolf Sprudzs, 1980 & Rev. 6, 1989).

2. Hong Kong's sovereignty will change pursuant to the Joint Declaration of the Government of the

United Kingdom of Great Britain and Northern Ireland and the Government of the People's Republic of China on the Question of Hong Kong with Annexes, Beijing, December 19, 1984, ratified and entered into force on May 27, 1985, T.S. No. 26 (1985), Cmnd. 9543.

tion, Lui points to the undisputed fact that it was not until several years after 1988—when GIL made the first payment to him—that he had or knew he would have any influence over BAT–HK's cigarette allocations.

In Hong Kong, Lui faces one charge of bribery conspiracy and nine substantive bribery charges.

Sometime prior to 1993, Lui began preparations to open a business in the Philippines. He became a partner of the Subic International Cargo Center, Inc. ("SICCI"), which was incorporated in May 1993 and is involved in the warehousing and shipping of cigarettes into Asia. Lui is a primary partner of SICCI. He owns approximately 35% of the issued stock and, until his arrest, managed its day to day operations.

Hong Kong, through the Independent Commission Against Corruption (the "ICAC"), began an investigation of Lui's business activities. ICAC attempted to arrest Lui on April 26, 1994, about one year after his business in the Philippines had been established. He was then out of the country on an overseas business trip.

Although Lui apparently has not returned to Hong Kong since the spring of 1994, ICAC agents were invited to meet with him in the Philippines. For some unknown reason, the meeting never occurred, even though the agents did go to the Philippines.

A Hong Kong magistrate issued a warrant for Lui's arrest on January 23, 1995. Another warrant was issued on December 12, 1995.

Prior to his arrest, Lui and his family had **[1283]** spent the summer of 1995 in Canada. They had purchased a house in Toronto in 1991, and became citizens in June 1994. The purpose of their December 1995 trip to Boston was to visit a hospitalized friend. It was on their arrival at Boston's Logan Airport that Lui was arrested.

III.

PROCEDURAL HISTORY

On December 19, 1995, the United States Attorney's office filed an extradition complaint in the District Court pursuant to 18 U.S.C.A. § 3184 (West Supp.1996).[3] The complaint set forth the United Kingdom's request for the extradition of Lui on behalf of Hong Kong. A provisional warrant was issued, and Lui was arrested upon his arrival at Logan Airport in Boston, Massachusetts on December 20, 1995.

At Lui's initial appearance before Magistrate Judge Karol on December 21, 1995, the Government moved to detain him for the duration of the extradition proceedings. On February 2, 1996, after hearings, Magistrate Judge Karol issued an order allowing the Government's detention motion.

On April 3, 1996, Lui first appeared before this court in order to challenge the Magistrate Judge's detention order.[4] In an April 25, 1996 opinion, this court concluded that "special circumstances" overrode the presumption against bail in extradition cases,

---

3. 18 U.S.C.A. § 3184 provides:
    Whenever there is a treaty or convention for extradition between the United States and any foreign government, any justice or judge of the United States, or any magistrate authorized so to do by a court of the United States, or any judge of a court of record of general jurisdiction of any State, may, upon complaint made under oath, charging any person found within his jurisdiction, with having committed within the jurisdiction of any such foreign government any of the crimes provided for by such treaty or convention, issue his warrant for the apprehension of the person so charged, that he may be brought before such justice, judge, or magistrate, to the end that the evidence of criminality may be heard and considered. Such complaint may be filed before and such warrant may be issued by a judge or magistrate of the United States District Court for the District of Columbia if the whereabouts within

the United States of the person charged are not known or, if there is reason to believe the person will shortly enter the United States. If, on such hearing, he deems the evidence sufficient to sustain the charge under the provisions of the proper treaty or convention, he shall certify the same, together with a copy of all the testimony taken before him, to the Secretary of State, that a warrant may issue upon the requisition of the proper authorities of such foreign government, for the surrender of such person, according to the stipulations of the treaty or convention; and he shall issue his warrant for the commitment of the person so charged to the proper jail, there to remain until such surrender shall be made.

4. On the same day, this court converted Lui's Rule 16(a) appeal of the bail order to a writ of *habeas corpus* pursuant to 28 U.S.C.A. § 2241 (West 1995). *See, e.g., Argro v. United States,* 505

1284] and that Lui's proffered conditions of release would reasonably assure his presence at future proceedings. The court, therefore, ordered Lui's release from Plymouth County Correctional Center. *Kin-Hong v. United States*, 926 F.Supp. 1180 (D.Mass.1996).

The Court of Appeals reversed this court's bail decision on May 14, 1996, holding that no special circumstances existed sufficient to override the presumption against bail. *United States v. Kin-Hong*, 83 F.3d 523 (1st Cir.1996) (per curiam). Lui, therefore, has been detained in United States custody for more than one year, since December 20, 1995.

On May 28, 1996, Magistrate Judge Karol began a three day hearing to consider Lui's extraditability. Three months later, on August 29, 1996, he issued his opinion in which he found the evidence against Lui sufficient to sustain the bribery conspiracy charge and eight of the nine substantive bribery charges. The Magistrate Judge, thereafter, certified Lui's extraditability to Hong Kong.

Here, in his September 3, 1996 Amended Petition for a Writ of *Habeas Corpus*,[5] Lui alleges, in part, that the Treaty does not permit his extradition because he cannot be tried and punished by the requesting sovereign, the Crown Colony of Hong Kong, prior to its reversion to China. For the reasons set forth below, this court agrees.[6]

IV.

THE HONG KONG REVERSION TIMETABLE

Central to the pending *habeas corpus* petition and the related extradition request is the fact that the Crown Colony of Hong Kong reverts to Chinese control in less than six months, on July 1, 1997. This raises the threshold factual issue as to whether the Crown Colony of Hong Kong will be able to try and to punish Lui prior to that reversion date.

Magistrate Judge Karol did not reach the question of which sovereign, the Crown Colony of Hong Kong or China, would be the one to try and to punish Lui if he is extradited. He did speculate that Lui might not be tried by either Hong Kong or China, because he might be released after a pre-trial procedure known as a "committal hearing." Given the enormous amount of resources the Government has devoted to the task of extraditing Lui, this court rejects the unsubstantiated notion that Hong Kong would drop the charges against him upon his return.

In any event, Magistrate Karol's surmise is not relevant to the controlling issue under the Treaty: whether it is possible for the Crown Colony of Hong Kong to try and to punish Lui before reversion, should they choose to do so.[7]

The uncontradicted evidence before the court establishes conclusively that Hong Kong will be unable to try and to punish Lui before reversion.

In an affidavit, former Hong Kong Senior Assistant Crown Prosecutor Kevin Barry Egan[8] asserts that a trial of Lui could not be concluded within fourteen months of Lui's

---

F.2d 1374, 1378 (2nd Cir.1974) (parolee's appeal of revocation proceeding treated as *habeas corpus* petition); *Caporali v. Whelan*, 582 F.Supp. 217, 219 (D.Mass.1984) (deportee's complaint seeking review of Immigration and Naturalization Service's detention order treated as petition for *habeas corpus*).

5. The petition was taken under advisement by this court on December 4, 1996, following an extensive briefing schedule by the parties.

6. Lui also challenges Magistrate Judge Karol's finding of probable cause. Given its disposition with respect to Lui's Treaty theory, this court does not reach the probable cause issue.

7. The Government consistently suggests that Lui is arguing that the Treaty does not authorize his extradition because he *might* be tried and punished by a non-signatory to the Treaty. This is a mischaracterization of Lui's claim. Lui actually argues that the Treaty does not authorize his extradition because it is impossible for him to be tried and punished by the requesting sovereign, the Crown Colony of Hong Kong, prior to reversion.

8. Mr. Egan was employed by the Hong Kong Attorney-General's Chambers (Prosecutions Division) from April 1980 through January 1991. While there, he held the positions of Crown Counsel, Senior Crown Counsel, Assistant Principal Crown Counsel, Senior Assistant Crown

surrender to Hong Kong.[9] (Egan Aff. ¶ 25). Considering that reversion will occur in less than six months, this evidence demonstrates that no trial or punishment by the Crown Colony of Hong Kong is possible prior to then.

The Government's own evidence requires the same conclusion. The Assistant Crown Prosecutor, Lena Chi Hui-ling, stated in an affidavit, dated January 12, 1996, that, "[i]f ... extradition were to be substantially delayed as a result of various legal proceedings taken after the extradition hearing, then it would be likely that Lui Kin-hong would not be tried until after June 30, 1997, [the day before reversion]...." (Chi Aff. ¶ 3). The extradition hearing was completed on May 30, 1996. Magistrate Judge Karol's opinion was issued three months later on August 29, 1996. Significantly, more than seven months have already passed since the Magistrate Judge's hearing.[10] And appeals will inevitably follow this court's decision with respect to the *habeas corpus* petition. The reality, therefore, is that the Crown Colony of Hong Kong will not be able to try and to punish Lui by the time of reversion. There is no evidence to the contrary.

If, nonetheless, Lui is extradited now, but the Crown Colony of Hong Kong is unable to

try and to punish him prior to reversion, he will then be in the custody of China, not the United Kingdom. China could, therefore, try Lui before the courts of the Hong Kong Special Administrative Region (the "HKSAR"). *Id.* If found guilty, Lui would be punished, not by the Crown Colony of Hong Kong or the United Kingdom, but by China.

At oral argument, the Government contended that this court lacks jurisdiction to examine the reality of whether Hong Kong would be competent to satisfy its obligation under the treaty to try and to punish Lui prior to reversion. Transcript of November 18 hearing at 8. In support, the Government cited the case of *Terlinden v. Ames,* 184 U.S. 270, 22 S.Ct. 484, 46 L.Ed. 534 (1902). In *Terlinden,* the Supreme Court stated that:

> Undoubtedly treaties may be terminated by the absorption of powers into other nationalities and the loss of separate existence, as in the case of Hanover and Nassau, which became by conquest incorporated into the Kingdom of Prussia in 1866. Cessation of independent existence rendered the execution of treaties impossible. But where sovereignty in that respect is not extinguished, and the power to execute remains unimpaired, outstanding treaties

[1285]

Prosecutor, and on occasion, acting Deputy Crown Prosecutor.

9. Egan bases his opinion on the timing of Hong Kong criminal procedure. He explains that after his extradition to Hong Kong, Lui would appear in court every eight days until the prosecutor seeks a "return date." The "return date," when finally sought, must be scheduled for between ten and forty-two days after the prosecutor's request. Egan explains that Lui's "return date" would inevitably be scheduled for forty-two days after the request, due to the case's complexity.

Moreover, Egan avers that a "return date" can be vacated and rescheduled at any time. Egan states that, in complex cases such as Lui's, such rescheduling often occurs.

On the "return date," Lui would have the right to demand a committal hearing. According to Egan, that hearing would happen four to six months after the "return date." He bases this opinion on his experience and the case of Lui's co-defendant, Chong Tsoijun, who did not have his committal hearing until ten months after he was charged.

10. The process has moved expeditiously. The critical dates are as follows:

Lui's arrest:	December 20, 1995
Detention Hearing:	January 10, 1996
Magistrate Judge Orders Detention:	February 4, 1996
Hearings on Habeas Petition:	April 4 and April 22, 1996
District Court's Opinion:	April 25, 1996
Court of Appeals Opinion:	May 14, 1996
Magistrate Judge's Hearing:	May 28–30, 1996
Magistrate Judge's Opinion	August 29, 1996
Scheduling Conference:	September 5, 1996
Initial Brief's Received:	November 8, 1996
Habeas Corpus Hearing:	November 18, 1996
Final Brief Received:	December 4, 1996

1286] cannot be regarded as avoided because of impossibility of performance.

Id. at 283, 22 S.Ct. at 489.

Contrary to the Government's contention, this court interprets *Terlinden* to authorize inquiry into Hong Kong's ability to try and to punish Lui. The fact is that, in less than six months, the Crown Colony of Hong Kong will experience "cessation of independent existence" as a colony of the United Kingdom. This means that, upon reversion, it will be impossible for the United Kingdom, through the Crown Colony of Hong Kong, to try and to punish Lui pursuant to its extradition request.

Terlinden involved a case in which the German Empire requested extradition under a treaty between the United States and the Kingdom of Prussia. The Court found that the Kingdom of Prussia, while part of the German Empire, continued to have an independent existence, and could still execute its responsibilities under the treaty. *See id.* at 285, 22 S.Ct. at 490.

Here, however, the Crown Colony of Hong Kong will be no more as of July 1, 1997. It will be in the same position as a sovereign taken by conquest. It will cease to have any existence beyond that as a part of China. In such a situation, *Terlinden* teaches that this court has jurisdiction to examine whether Hong Kong is able to fulfill its obligations as a requesting sovereign under the Treaty. As discussed earlier, the evidence shows that it cannot. China is the only sovereign that will be able to try and to punish Lui. China is not a signatory to the Treaty. As shall be discussed below, the Treaty, by its own terms, does not allow the extradition of a person to Hong Kong if the Crown Colony of Hong Kong is unable to try and to punish that person.

V.

THE LAW

A. *"Extradition" Defined*

No person may be extradited absent a valid treaty between the requesting

sovereign and the requested sovereign.[11] *See Factor v. Laubenheimer,* 290 U.S. 276, 287, 54 S.Ct. 191, 193, 78 L.Ed. 315 (1933); *In re Howard,* 996 F.2d 1320, 1329 (1st Cir. 1993). The Supreme Court has defined "extradition" as "the surrender by one nation to another of an individual accused or convicted of an offense outside of its own territory, and within the territorial jurisdiction of the other, which, *being competent to try and to punish him,* demands the surrender." *Terlinden,* 184 U.S. at 289, 22 S.Ct. at 491 (emphasis supplied). And so, to be a competent requesting party, under the terms of an extradition treaty, a sovereign must be able to try and to punish the subject of the request, the relator.[12]

B. *Jurisdiction*

There is a valid treaty between the United States and the United Kingdom that covers the Crown Colony of Hong Kong. The United States has no extradition treaty with the Peoples Republic of China.

Hong Kong reverts to China in 174 days, on July 1, 1997. Lui asserts that, because of this time constraint, it is impossible for the United Kingdom, as the requesting party, to try and to punish him, through its Crown Colony of Hong Kong, prior to reversion. Under the doctrine of *Terlinden,* therefore, the United Kingdom is incompetent to live up to the terms of its extradition agreement with the United States, because Hong Kong will have reverted to China before he can be tried and punished by the Crown Colony. For these reasons, Lui argues, Magistrate Judge Karol had no jurisdiction to permit extradition.

A Magistrate Judge's allowance of extradition, pursuant to 18 U.S.C. § 3184, is not a final order. *Koskotas v. Roche,* 931 F.2d 169, 171 (1st Cir.1991). A relator,[3] therefore, may not directly appeal such a

---

11. The "requesting sovereign" is the one seeking extradition of the accused. The "requested sovereign" is the one with custody of the accused.

12. In an extradition case, such as the one presently before the court, the "relator" is the party seeking to stop extradition through a writ of *habeas corpus.*

decision. *Id.* It is appropriate, however, to attack the Magistrate Judge's order collaterally by seeking a writ of *habeas corpus*, which is what Lui has done here. *Id.*

VI.

THE LANGUAGE OF THE TREATY

The language of the Treaty itself prohibits a person from being extradited to Hong Kong if Hong Kong, as a Crown Colony of the United Kingdom, is unable to try and to punish him. Specifically, 1) the Warrant provision, 2) the Dual Criminality provision, 3) the Political Offense provisions, and 4) the Specialty provisions of the Treaty all establish that Lui cannot be extradited to a sovereign that is not able to try and to punish him, any more than he could be extradited to a non-signatory nation.

A. Warrant Requirement

Articles VII(3) and VII(5) of the Treaty impose a Warrant requirement for extradition.[13] The requesting sovereign must present a warrant to the requested sovereign signifying that the relator is charged with, or has been convicted of, an extraditable offense in the courts of the requesting sovereign. The Warrant requirement permits the requested sovereign to know that the relator has been accused or convicted pursuant to the laws of the requesting sovereign, and that he will be tried and punished in accordance with that sovereign's laws.

B. Dual Criminality Requirement

Pursuant to its Dual Criminality provisions, the Treaty requires that the courts of the requested sovereign examine the criminal laws of the requesting sovereign. The court of the requested sovereign must decide whether the charged offense fits "the descriptions [of extraditable offenses] listed in the Schedule annexed to [the] Treaty, ... or

[is] any other offense" that is a felony under **[1287]** the laws of both signatories. Article III.

The purpose of the Dual Criminality requirement is to provide the requested sovereign with the opportunity to examine the substantive law of the requesting sovereign in the context of the Treaty. *See also* Article VII(2)(b), (c) and (d). Here, it underscores the expectation running through the Treaty that the relator, Lui, is to be tried, judged, and punished in accordance with the laws of the requesting sovereign, the Crown Colony of Hong Kong.

C. The Political Offense Provisions

Article 3(a) of the Supplementary Treaty reads as follows:

> Notwithstanding any other provision of this Supplementary Treaty, extradition shall not occur if the person sought establishes to the satisfaction of the competent judicial authority by a preponderance of the evidence that the request for extradition has in fact been made with a view to try or punish him on account of his race, religion, nationality, or political opinions, or that he would, if surrendered, be prejudiced at his trial, or punished, detained or restricted in his personal liberty by reason of his race, religion, nationality or political opinions.

This article requires the court to examine the reasons for the requesting sovereign's desire to try and to punish the relator. It looks to the motive of the requesting sovereign, not some non-signatory nation. And it underscores again the Treaty's requirement and expectation that extradition, here, may not take place if the requesting sovereign, the Crown Colony of Hong Kong, is unable to try and to punish Lui in the relatively few days left before its reversion to China.

---

13. The provision of Article VII requiring a warrant reads as follows:

  (3) If the request [for extradition] relates to an accused person, it must also be accompanied by a warrant of arrest issued by a judge, magistrate or other competent authority in the territory of the requesting Party and by such

evidence as, according to the law of the requested Party, would justify his committal for trial if the offense had been committed in the territory of the requested Party, including evidence that the person requested is the person to whom the warrant of arrest refers.

[1288] *D. Specialty Provisions*

Article XII of the Treaty [14] prohibits the requesting sovereign from trying and punishing the relator for crimes other than those for which he has been extradited, or from extraditing the relator to a third-party sovereign.[15] This section demonstrates once again that the Treaty allows only for extradition for offenses that can be tried and punished by the requesting sovereign.

The United States cannot enforce the Specialty provisions once extradition takes place. The adoption of these provisions, and of the Treaty itself, is premised on the trust running between the United States and the United Kingdom. The United Kingdom is promising that it, and only it, will try and will punish Lui for specified crimes, and no others. By its adoption of the Treaty, the United States manifests its belief in that promise of the United Kingdom.

China has made no such promises to the United States. Indeed, as has been pointed out, the United States has no extradition treaty with China.

The Treaty is exclusively between the signatories. Hong Kong reverts to China on July 1, 1997. The terms of the Treaty do not.

VII.

THE LEGISLATIVE HISTORY

Not only does the language of the Treaty support the view that the United States may not extradite Lui, so, too, does the history of the Senate's ratification.[16]

The version of the Supplementary Treaty initially presented to the Senate greatly narrowed the usual Political Offense exception found in other United States extradition treaties. *Supplementary Extradition Treaty Between the United States and the Kingdom of Great Britain and Northern Ireland: Hearing Before the Subcommittee on the Constitution of the Senate Committee on the Judiciary,* 99th Cong., 1st Sess. 16–22 (1985) (letter from the President transmitting Supplementary Treaty to the Senate). The new version narrowed the Political Offense exception to apply only to "pure political and nonviolent crimes." *Supplementary Extradition Treaty Between the United States and the Kingdom of Great Britain and Northern Ireland: Hearing Before the Senate Committee on Foreign Relations,* 99th Cong., 1st Sess. 4–5 (1985) (statement of Abraham D. Sofaer, Legal Advisor, Department of State). Apparently, the proposed change arose from a controversy regarding the United States' failure to extradite three Provisional Irish Republican Army members to the United Kingdom.

In the Senate Foreign Relations Committee, some Senators expressed concern over the narrow Political Offense exception. The proponents of the narrowed exception believed that it was appropriate in view of the United States' trust in the judicial and penal systems of the United Kingdom. They assured the questioning Senators that the United Kingdom would grant fair trial and punishment.

Later, other Senators expressed the same concern about the narrowed exception on the floor of the Senate during debate over ratifi-

---

14. Article XII(1), the specialty provision, reads as follows:

   (1) A person extradited shall not be detained or proceeded against in the territory of the requesting Party for any offense other than an extraditable offense established by the facts in respect of which his extradition has been granted, or on account of any other matters, nor be extradited by that Party to a third State—
   (a) until after he has returned to the territory of the requested Party; or
   (b) until the expiration of thirty days after he has been free to return to the territory of the requested Party.

15. Lui is not alleging that the reversion of Hong Kong to Chinese rule would constitute "extradition" to China in violation of Article XII. The court, therefore, does not reach the question of whether reversion, itself, results in the violation of the Specialty provisions.

16. It is entirely proper for this court to go beyond the words of the Treaty and Supplementary Treaty to examine "the negotiations and diplomatic correspondence of the contracting parties relating to the subject matter, and to their own practical construction of it." *Factor v. Laubenheimer,* 290 U.S. 276, 294–95, 54 S.Ct. 191, 196, 78 L.Ed. 315 (1933).

cation. 99th Cong., 2d Sess., 132 Cong.Rec. 9119–71 (daily ed. July 16, 1986). Once again, they were assured by the Supplementary Treaty's proponents that the United States could trust the United Kingdom and its judicial process to be fair and just. *See*, *e.g.*, *id.* at 9166–67. The Senate then ratified the Supplementary Treaty, with a narrowed version of the political offense exception, by the required two-thirds vote.

The Senate's ratification was clearly premised on its trust in the judicial and penal systems of the United Kingdom. To permit the benefits of that trust to be assumed by any non-signatory nation would undermine the clear and unequivocal intent of the Senate. It is clear beyond rational dispute that the Senate would not have ratified had there been any suggestion that the Treaty provisions could be extended, even by circumstance, to China.

This court's interpretation of the legislative record is bolstered by the Senate's Declaration in its Resolution of Ratification of the Supplementary Treaty. The Declaration reads:

> The Senate of the United States declares that it will not give its advice and consent to any treaty that would narrow the political offense exception with a totalitarian or other non-democratic regime and that nothing in the Supplementary Treaty with the United Kingdom shall be considered a precedent by the executive branch or the Senate for other treaties.

Id. at 9120 (enacted). The Senate could not have intended a treaty which contains such language to be used to extradite a relator for

eventual trial and punishment in China, a **[1289]** non-democratic regime.[17]

The Government suggests that the legislative history of the Political Offense provisions should not be used as persuasive authority regarding the other sections of the Treaty and Supplementary Treaty. The court disagrees. The court considers it powerful evidence that the Senate wished the Treaty to apply only to relators who could be tried and punished by a signatory sovereign whose credentials and trust had been weighed and judged by the United States.

This court is not making a judgment about the judicial and penal systems of China or of the HKSAR. Under this court's analysis, it would not matter if China's legal system were *more* efficient and humane than either the United States' or the United Kingdom's. The bottom line is that the terms of the Treaty do not allow extradition when the requesting sovereign is unable to try and to punish the relator. The Crown Colony of Hong Kong will be unable to try and to punish Lui prior to reversion. If Lui is in Hong Kong after reversion, China would be in a position to try and to punish him. To permit such an untoward result would be to ignore the clear language of the Treaty and to contravene the will of the Senate.

VIII.

THE GOVERNMENT'S VARIOUS RESPONSES

A. Consequences of Interpretation

The Government argues that a parade of horribles would result from an interpretation

---

17. Considering the information regarding China's judicial and penal systems now in the public domain, it strains credulity to suggest that the Senate would approve of the Treaty's application, with its narrowed Political Offense provisions, to a relator who can only be tried by the Chinese judiciary.

The Chinese judicial system, for example, gave an eleven year sentence to Wang Dan for the "crime" of writing articles critical of the Chinese government. Steven Mufson, *Sentencing Is Blow To China Dissidents; Movement Drained as Leader Gets 11 Years.* Wash. Post, October 31, 1996, at A23. Wang Dan's trial only lasted three or four hours. *Id.* In a recent article on China's "Strike Hard" anti-crime campaign, the Washington

Post reported that, "the time from arrest to trial is often a matter of days; the time from sentencing to execution can be measured in the minutes it takes to walk a prisoner to a field, level a pistol at his head and pull the trigger." Keith B. Richburg, *China Executes Hundreds in Crackdown; Crime Wave Brings Arrests, Quick Trials,* Wash. Post, July 6, 1996, at A1.

Already, there are signs that the HKSAR judicial system will appear very much like the Chinese judicial system. *See* Simon Winchester, *Hong Kong: On Trial,* Nat'l L.J., December 16, 1996, at A1. The Senate, concerned as it was with the narrowness of the political offense exception, did not intend for the Treaty to apply to such a judicial system.

1290] of the Treaty as adopted by the court today. The court disagrees.

The Government is concerned that the court's interpretation will halt all extraditions to Hong Kong. Citing the *Howard* case, 996 F.2d at 1331, it argues that a court should not interpret an extradition treaty in such a way that it becomes a "non-extradition treaty." First and foremost, an extradition treaty must be interpreted according to its terms. Here, the terms of the Treaty do not allow for Lui's extradition. The court, therefore, is not eviscerating the Treaty as the Government suggests. The court is enforcing the Treaty as written and ratified.

The court's interpretation does not lead to the Government's conclusion that all extraditions to Hong Kong over recent years have been in violation of the Treaty. Extradition is permitted in all cases except those where Hong Kong is unable to try and to punish the relator. In any case in which Hong Kong, at the time of extradition, was able to try and to punish a relator, regardless of whether it did try and did punish him, the Treaty could apply, and the extradition could be lawful.

It is also incorrect that this court's interpretation will require the United States, at the time of reversion, to insist on the release of those relators who are still on trial or are incarcerated awaiting trial. Those who were extradited when it was *possible* for the Crown Colony of Hong Kong to try and to punish them get no comfort from this court's conclusions today. Here, the uncontroverted evidence shows that it is *impossible* for Hong Kong to try and to punish Lui prior to reversion.

In any event, even if the court were to agree with the Government regarding the logistical consequences of its interpretation

of the Treaty, such concerns would be irrelevant. The court's responsibility in examining Lui's *habeas corpus* petition is solely to determine whether the Treaty authorizes his extradition. It does not. The court must adhere to the law, regardless of the consequences.

B. Four Treaty Provisions

The Government contends that none of the four provisions of the Treaty mentioned in Section VI should be considered with respect to Lui's petition. Again, this court disagrees.

The court refers to the Warrant requirement, the Dual Criminality requirement, the Political Offense provision, and the Specialty provision only to demonstrate that the Treaty and the Supplementary Treaty, as ratified by the Senate, do not, by their own terms, allow for the extradition of Lui when it is certain that his trial and punishment would not be at the hands of the requesting sovereign, the Crown Colony of Hong Kong.

C. The Hong Kong Policy Act

In 1992, the Congress passed, and the President signed, the Hong Kong Policy Act (the "Act"), 22 U.S.C.A. §§ 5701–32 (West Supp.1996). The Act provides that all treaties with Hong Kong will remain in force at least until reversion. 22 U.S.C. § 5721(b) (West Supp.1996).[18] It also gives the President means by which he may continue treaties post-reversion. *Id.*

The Government is not claiming that the Act, in and of itself, extends the Treaty in such a way that it applies to Lui. The Government conceded at oral argument that, should the President and Congress do nothing between now and reversion, Lui would go

---

18. 22 U.S.C. § 5721(b) reads as follows:

(b) International agreements

For all purposes, including actions in any court in the United States, the Congress approves the continuation in force on and after July 1, 1997, of all treaties, and other international agreements, including multilateral conventions, entered into before such date between the United States and Hong Kong, or entered into before such date between the United States and the United Kingdom and applied to Hong Kong, unless or until termi-

nated in accordance with law. If in carrying out this subchapter, the President determines that Hong Kong is not legally competent to carry out its obligations under any such treaty or other international agreement, or that the continuation of Hong Kong's obligations or rights under any such treaty or other international agreement is not appropriate under the circumstances, such determination shall be reported to the Congress in accordance with section 5731 of this title.

free. *See* Transcript of November 18 hearing at 41. The Government, rather, is suggesting that the Act is evidence of Congressional intent that the Treaty should extend to relators in Lui's position. The court disagrees.

The Government argues that if Congress had intended that the Treaty not permit extradition of a relator who, like Lui, could not be tried and punished by the Crown Colony of Hong Kong prior to reversion, some member of Congress would have raised the issue during debate over the Act. Such a contention implicitly assumes, however, that Congress had intended the Act to extend the Treaty past reversion even absent any further action on its part. But, there is strong evidence that Congress did not so intend and, indeed, intended the contrary.

At hearings preceding the passage of the Act, the State Department's Deputy Legal Advisor informed a Congressional committee that:

> on extradition—we are now negotiating with the Hong Kong Government on a new treaty, to replace the existing U.S.-U.K. agreement, which would continue in force after reversion to [China]. *Consistent with U.S. practice in the extradition area, we intend to seek Senate advice and consent to such a treaty if negotiations are successful.*

Hong Kong's Reversion to China and Implications for U.S. Policy: Hearing Before the Subcommittee on East Asian and Pacific Affairs of the Senate Committee on Foreign Relations, 102nd Cong., 2d Sess., 17 (1992) (prepared statement of Jamison M. Selby, Deputy Legal Advisor, Department of State) (emphasis supplied). It is apparent, therefore, that Congress passed the Act with the understanding that any extradition to China for trial and punishment would require the approval of a new treaty with Senate advice and consent.

Moreover, the Act is only evidence that Congress supports the continuation of treaties with Hong Kong *according to their own terms.* The terms of the Treaty at issue here do not authorize the extradition of Lui where it is impossible for the Crown Colony of Hong Kong to try and to punish him prior

to reversion. *See supra* Part VI. The Act **[1291]** does not amend the Treaty. A substantive change that would allow Lui to be tried and punished by China, as opposed to the Crown Colony of Hong Kong, would require the advice and consent of the Senate pursuant to the Constitution. U.S. Const. art. II, § 2. *See New York Chinese TV Programs, Inc. v. U.E. Enterprises, Inc.,* 954 F.2d 847, 853–54 (2nd Cir.1992). [4]

D. *Case Law*

The Government contends that every court that has interpreted the Treaty has rejected this court's interpretation, and allowed extradition even though a relator *might* be tried by China. The Government is incorrect. None of the three cases cited are inconsistent with this court's analysis.

In *Oen Yin–Choy v. Robinson,* 858 F.2d 1400 (9th Cir.1988), *cert. denied,* 490 U.S. 1106, 109 S.Ct. 3157, 104 L.Ed.2d 1020 [5] (1989), the court examined two arguments similar to Lui's. First, it rejected the contention that Hong Kong's reversion acted as an extradition to China in violation of the specialty provision of the Treaty. *Id.* at 1403–04. Second, it held that, although the United Kingdom could not guarantee that China would honor all the provisions of the Treaty after reversion, extradition to Hong Kong with the possibility of trial and punishment by China *eight years in the future* was not barred. *Id.* at 1404. Lui raises the same issue that the *Oen* court thought proper to examine. But, Lui's claim is different. Lui does not argue that the *possibility* of trial and punishment by China bars extradition. He argues that the *certainty* that the Crown Colony of Hong Kong *cannot* try and punish him prior to reversion, *in 174 days*— not eight years—bars his extradition pursuant to the Treaty.

The Government also cites *Extradition of Tang Yee–Chun,* 674 F.Supp. 1058 (S.D.N.Y. 1987). *Tang* is not contrary to this court's rationale today. Indeed, the court there noted that any concern about the effects of reversion were "too speculative and too remote to justify any action by this Court." *Tang,* 674 F.Supp. at 1068. That was a

[1292] reasonable observation nine years before reversion. But, today, with less than six months left before reversion, it is clear that the Treaty's violation is no longer "too speculative" or "too remote" for remedial action.

The Government, lastly, relies on *Cheng Na–Yuet v. Hueston,* 734 F.Supp. 988 (S.D.Fla.1990), *aff'd* 932 F.2d 977 (11th Cir. 1991). There, the court thought it proper to examine the same issue raised by Lui here. But, as in *Tang,* the court noted that looking to China's potential actions after reversion was "too speculative and too remote to justify any action by this court." *Id.* at 993. That view, while arguably legitimate seven years ago, is inapposite to the reality of today, less than six months before reversion.

E. Reviewability

Habeas corpus review in an extradition case is very limited. *See Koskotas* [6] *v. Roche,* 931 F.2d 169, 171 (1st Cir.1991). Its purpose is "only to inquire whether the magistrate had jurisdiction, whether the offense charged is within the treaty, and . . . whether there was any evidence warranting the finding that there was reasonable ground to believe the accused guilty." *Id.* (quoting *Fernandez v. Phillips,* 268 U.S. 311, 312, 45 [7] S.Ct. 541, 542, 69 L.Ed. 970 (1925)). The Government argues that this court lacks jurisdiction to examine Lui's claim that the Treaty does not permit his extradition to a sovereign which is unable to try and to punish him.

The Government also contends that, because Lui's argument regarding the inapplicability of the Treaty to him is non-jurisdictional and non-constitutional, he has waived it by not raising it before the Magistrate Judge. *See Lo Duca v. United States,* 93 F.3d 1100, 1111 (2nd Cir.1996) (citing *Jhirad v. Ferrandina,* 536 F.2d 478, 486 (2nd Cir.1976); *Austin v. Healey,* 5 F.3d 598, 601 (2nd Cir.1993)).

The court rejects the Government's contentions on the grounds that Lui's argument regarding the applicability of the Treaty is jurisdictional and is, therefore, an appropriate issue for this court to consider in a *habeas corpus* proceeding.

This court has the responsibility of determining whether the Treaty, together with 18 U.S.C. § 3184, grants the Magistrate Judge the authority to permit extradition. If the Magistrate Judge lacks the authority to do so, he lacks jurisdiction. The other courts which have examined the effect of reversion on extradition have found that whether a party to a treaty will be able to fulfill its obligations is fundamental to the Magistrate Judge's authority and jurisdiction. *See, e.g., Oen,* 858 F.2d at 1403 (reached merits when relator "argues that the district court lacked jurisdiction to order his extradition because the Hong Kong Government has not satisfied requirements of the extradition Treaty"); *Cheng,* 734 F.Supp. at 992 (reached merits when relator argued that "Magistrate lacked jurisdiction to certify extradition since the Reversion of the government of Hong Kong to the People's Republic of China in 1997 makes it impossible for Hong Kong to comply with various terms of the Treaty"). Whether the Treaty allows for the extradition of Lui to the Crown Colony of Hong Kong, a sovereign that can neither try nor punish him prior to reversion, is, therefore, a question of the Magistrate Judge's jurisdiction, which this court may address.

IX.

STATE SUCCESSION

The Government has not explicitly relied upon the doctrine of state succession. But, in its opposition brief it mentions that the Sino–British Joint Liaison Group recently approved a new extradition agreement. This agreement may lay the groundwork for a claim that a new treaty with China, approved by two-thirds of the Senate, is not necessary in order to extradite Lui. The court disagrees.

Under the doctrine of state succession, a sovereign may take upon itself all the responsibilities and duties under a treaty of a predecessor sovereign if all parties agree. *See Terlinden,* 184 U.S. at 282–88, 22 S.Ct. at 489–91. State succession cannot occur here. In order for China to accept all responsibilities of the Treaty, it must accept the Supplementary Treaty as well. The Supplementary

Treaty includes the Senate's Declaration o Ratification, which states that:

> The Senate of the United States de clares that it will not give its advice an consent to any treaty that would narrov the political offense exception with a totali tarian or other non-democratic regime an that nothing in the Supplementary Treat with the United Kingdom shall be consid ered a precedent by the executive brancl or the Senate for other treaties.

132 Cong.Rec. S 9120 (daily ed. July 1€ 1986). China, being a non-democratic re gime, cannot meet the Political Offense re quirements as amended by the Supplementa ry Treaty.

X.

THE NON-INQUIRY DOCTRINE

The Government argues that, under the non-inquiry doctrine, the court should not inquire into the effect of reversion on Lui. The doctrine "forbids judicial authorities from investigating the fairness of a request-ing nation's justice system when considering whether to permit extradition to that nation." *Howard,* 996 F.2d at 1329.

But, this court's analysis has not violated the non-inquiry doctrine. Indeed, this

19. Lui also asserts that reversion requires the court to examine the treatment he is likely to receive at the hands of the Chinese judicial and penal systems. He claims that the conditions would be so terrible that the court should bar his extradition even if the Treaty would normally permit it.

court's interpretation of the Treaty is consis- **[1293]** tent with the purposes behind the non-inqui-ry doctrine. The non-inquiry doctrine teaches that the Judicial Branch should not interfere with a judgment by the Executive and Legislative Branches that, "the treaty partner's justice system [is] sufficiently fair to justify sending accused persons there for trial." *Id.* Here, the court's interpretation of the Treaty is based in large measure on its recognition that the Executive and Legis-lative Branches have judged the justice sys-tem of the United Kingdom and the Crown Colony of Hong Kong to be sufficiently fair to send accused persons there for trial. But, no such judgment was made as to Chi-na, the sovereign which, in reality, will try and will punish Lui if the extradition is al-lowed.

XI.

CONCLUSION

For the reasons discussed above, this court concludes that Magistrate Judge Karol lacked jurisdiction to authorize the extradi-tion of Lui. The court, therefore, grants Lui's Amended Petition for a Writ of *Habeas Corpus.* [19]

An order will issue.

Lui's claim is not frivolous. *See supra* note 17. The court, however, does not reach this issue, or, as noted earlier, the issue of whether Magistrate Judge Karol erred in finding probable cause for the crimes charged, because of its holding that Magistrate Judge Karol lacked jurisdiction.

[Report: 957 F Supp 1280]

Editorial Footnotes:

[3] 104 *ILR* 110.
[4] 96 *ILR* 81.
[5] 104 *ILR* 43.

[6] 104 *ILR* 110.
[7] 3 *Ann Dig* 307.

[The text of the judgment of the Court of Appeals, delivered by Circuit Judge Lynch, commences on the opposite page.]

[106]

The United States District Court granted a writ of habeas corpus to Lui Kin–Hong ("Lui"), who sought the writ after a magistrate judge certified to the Secretary of State that she may, in her discretion, surrender Lui for extradition to the Crown Colony of Hong Kong. The United Kingdom, on behalf of Hong Kong, had sought Lui's extradition on a warrant for his arrest for the crime of bribery. Lui's petition for habeas corpus was premised on the fact that the reversion of Hong Kong to the People's Republic of China will take place on July 1, 1997, and it will be impossible for the Crown Colony to try and to punish Lui before that date. The United States appeals. We reverse the order of the district court granting the writ of habeas corpus.

The United States argues that Lui is within the literal terms of the extradition treaties between the United States and the United Kingdom, that the courts may not vary from the language of the treaties, and that the certification must issue. Lui argues that the language of the treaties does not permit extradition, an argument which is surely wrong. Lui's more serious argument is that the Senate, in approving the treaties, did not mean to permit extradition of someone to be tried and punished by a government different from the government which has given its assurances in the treaties.

Lui does not claim that he faces prosecution in Hong Kong on account of his race, religion, nationality, or political opinion. He does not claim to be charged with a political offense. The treaties give the courts a greater role when such considerations are present. Here, Lui's posture is that of one charged with an ordinary crime. His claim is that to surrender him now to Hong Kong is, in effect, to send him to trial and punishment in the People's Republic of China. The Senate, in approving the treaties, could not have intended such a result, he argues, and so the court should interpret the treaties as being inapplicable to his case. Absent a treaty permitting extradition, he argues, he may not be extradited.

While Lui's argument is not frivolous, neither is it persuasive. The Senate was well aware of the reversion when it approved a supplementary treaty with the United Kingdom in 1986. The Senate could easily have sought language to address the reversion of Hong Kong if it were concerned, but did not do so. The President has recently executed a new treaty with the incoming government of Hong Kong, containing the same guarantees that Lui points to in the earlier treaties, and that treaty has been submitted to the Senate. In addition, governments of our treaty partners often change, sometimes by ballot, sometimes by revolution or other means, and the possibility or even certainty of such change does not itself excuse compliance with the terms of the agreement embodied in the treaties between the countries. Treaties contain reciprocal benefits and obligations. The United States benefits from the treaties at issue and, under their terms, may seek extradition to the date of reversion of those it wants for criminal offenses.

Fundamental principles in our American democracy limit the role of courts in certain matters, out of deference to the powers allocated by the Constitution to the President and to the Senate, particularly in the conduct of foreign relations. Those separation of powers principles, well rehearsed in extradition law, preclude us from rewriting the treaties which the President and the Senate have approved. The plain language of the treaties does not support Lui. Under the treaties as written, the courts may not, on the basis of the reversion, avoid certifying to the Secretary of State that Lui may be extradited. The decision whether to surrender Lui, in light of his arguments, is for the Secretary of State to make.

This is not to say American courts acting under the writ of habeas corpus, itself guaranteed in the Constitution, have no independent role. There is the ultimate safeguard that extradition proceedings before United States courts comport with the Due Process Clause of the Constitution. On the facts of this case, there is nothing presenting a serious constitutional issue of denial of due process. Some future case may, on facts amounting to a violation of constitutional guarantees, warrant judicial intervention. This case does not.

I.

We repeat the facts essentially as we stated them in our earlier opinion. *United States v. Lui Kin–Hong*, 83 F.3d 523 (1st Cir.1996) (reversing district court's decision to release Lui on bail).

Lui is charged in Hong Kong with conspiring to receive and receiving over U.S. $3 million in bribes from Giant Island Ltd. ("GIL") or GIL's subsidiary, Wing Wah Company ("WWC"). Lui, formerly a senior officer of the Brown & Williamson Co., was "seconded" in 1990 to its affiliated company, the British American Tobacco Co. (Hong Kong) Ltd. ("BAT–HK"), where he became Director of Exports in 1992. The charges result from an investigation by the Hong Kong Independent Commission Against Corruption ("ICAC"). The Hong Kong authorities charge that GIL and WWC, to which BAT–HK distributed cigarettes, paid bribes in excess of HK $100 million (approximately U.S. $14 to $15 million) to a series of BAT–HK executives, including Lui. The bribes were allegedly given in exchange for a virtual monopoly on the export of certain brands of cigarettes to the People's Republic of China ("PRC") and to Taiwan. Among the cigarettes distributed were the popular Brown & Williamson brands of Kent, Viceroy, and Lucky Strike. GIL purchased three-quarters of a billion dollars in cigarettes from 1991 to 1994, mostly from BAT–HK.

A former GIL shareholder, Chui To–Yan ("Chui"), cooperated with the authorities and, it is said, would have provided evidence of Lui's acceptance of bribes. Some of Lui's alleged co-conspirators attempted to dissuade Chui from cooperating. Chui was later abducted, tortured, and murdered. The ICAC claims that the murder was committed to stop Chui from testifying. Lui is not charged in the murder conspiracy. Lui was in the Philippines (which has no extradition treaty with Hong Kong) on a business trip when the Hong Kong authorities unsuccessfully sought to question him in April 1994.

Lui has not returned to Hong Kong since **[107]** then.

At the request of the United Kingdom ("UK"), acting on behalf of Hong Kong, United States marshals arrested Lui as he got off a plane at Boston's Logan Airport on December 20, 1995. The arrest was for the purpose of extraditing Lui to Hong Kong.[1] The government asked that Lui be detained pending completion of the extradition proceedings. The magistrate judge, after a hearing, denied Lui's request to be released on bail.

The district court, on April 25, 1996, reversed the order of the magistrate judge and released Lui on bail and conditions. *Lui Kin–Hong v. United States*, 926 F.Supp. 1180 (D.Mass.1996). The district court held that the reversion of Hong Kong to the PRC on July 1, 1997, raised complex legal issues that would result in protracted proceedings and presented a "special circumstance" overriding the presumption against bail. *Id.* at 1189. That court also found that there were conditions of release that would adequately ensure Lui's presence at future proceedings. *Id.* at 1196. This court reversed the district court and, on May 14, 1996, ordered Lui held pending the resolution of the extradition certification issue. *Lui*, 83 F.3d at 525.

The magistrate judge commenced extradition hearings on May 28, 1996. Those proceedings, during which evidence was taken, lasted three days. The magistrate judge found that there was probable cause to believe that Lui had violated Hong Kong law on all but one of the charges in the warrant.[2] Magistrate Judge Karol, pursuant to 18 U.S.C. § 3184, issued a careful decision certifying Lui's extraditability on August 29, 1996. *In re Extradition of Lui Kin–Hong ("Lui Extradition")*, 939 F.Supp. 934 (D.Mass. 1996). On September 3, 1996, Lui filed an amended petition for a writ of habeas corpus, the only avenue by which a fugitive sought for extradition (a "relator") may attack the

---

1. The most recent warrant for Lui's arrest from the Hong Kong authorities is dated February 5, 1996; there were earlier warrants.

2. The magistrate judge found the government had not met its burden of showing probable cause as to Count 2, concerning a payment of HK $1,953,260 made on or about October 21, 1988.

[108] magistrate judge's decision,[3] with the district court.

After a hearing, the district court issued a memorandum and order granting the writ on January 7, 1997. *Lui Kin–Hong v. United States* ("*Lui Habeas*"), 957 F.Supp. 1280, (D.Mass.1997). The district court reasoned that, because the Crown Colony could not try Lui and punish him before the reversion date, the extradition treaty between the United States and the UK, which is applicable to Hong Kong, prohibited extradition. *Id.* at 1285–86. Because no extradition treaty between the United States and the new government of Hong Kong has been confirmed by the United States Senate, the district court reasoned, the magistrate judge lacked jurisdiction to certify extraditability. *See id.* at 1286–92. The district court denied the government's motion for reconsideration on January 13, 1997. This court then stayed the district court's order and expedited the present appeal.

At the time Lui was arrested in Boston in December 1995, more than eighteen months remained before the reversion of Hong Kong to the PRC on July 1, 1997. The various proceedings in our court system have now occupied fifteen of those months, as the magistrate judge and district judge have given careful consideration to the issues.

II.

The extradition request was made pursuant to the Extradition Treaty Between the Government of the United States of America and the Government of the United Kingdom of Great Britain and Northern Ireland, June 8, 1972, 28 U.S.T. 227 (the "Treaty"), as amended by the Supplementary Treaty Between the Government of the United States of America and the Government of the United Kingdom of Great Britain and Northern Ireland, June 25, 1985, T.I.A.S. No. 12050 (the "Supplementary Treaty").[4] The original Treaty was made applicable to Hong Kong, among other British territories, by an exchange of diplomatic notes on October 21, 1976. 28 U.S.T. at 238–41.[5] The Supplementary Treaty is applicable to Hong Kong by its terms. Supplementary Treaty, art. 6(a) & Annex.

Hong Kong's status as a Crown Colony is coming to an end on July 1, 1997, when Hong Kong is to be restored to the PRC. The impending reversion, at the expiration of the UK's ninety-nine year leasehold, was formally agreed upon by the UK and the PRC in 1984; the United States was not a party to this agreement. *See* Joint Declaration of the Government of the United Kingdom of Great Britain and Northern Ireland and the Government of the People's Republic of China on the Question of Hong Kong, Dec. 19, 1984, ratified and entered into force May 27, 1985, T.S. No. 26 (1985) (the "Joint Declaration"). Under the terms of the Joint Declaration, the PRC "declares" its "basic policies" with respect to Hong Kong. *Id.* art. 3. The PRC states that it intends to establish a "Hong Kong Special Administrative Region" ("HKSAR"), *id.* art. 3(1), which will enjoy a "high degree of autonomy except in foreign and defence affairs." *Id.* art. 3(2). In addition, the PRC states that the HKSAR "will be vested with … independent judicial power, including that of final adjudication" and that the "laws currently in force in Hong Kong will remain basically unchanged." *Id.* art. 3(3). These "basic policies" are, accord-

---

3. Due to the limited function of an extradition proceeding, there is no direct appeal from a judicial officer's certification of extraditability. *See Collins v. Miller*, 252 U.S. 364, 369–70, 40 S.Ct. 347, 349, 64 L.Ed. 616 (1920). A habeas petition is therefore the only mechanism by which a relator may seek review.

4. We refer to the Treaty and the Supplementary Treaty as "the Treaties."

5. By its terms, the Treaty applies to the UK, and, in addition, to "any territory for the international relations of which the United Kingdom is responsible and to which the Treaty shall have been extended by agreement between the Contracting Parties embodied in an Exchange of Notes." Treaty, art. II(1)(a).

The Treaty permits either the UK or the United States, upon six months written notice, to terminate the application of the Treaty as to any territory to which the Treaty was extended under article II(1)(a). *Id.* art II(2). To date, to our knowledge, neither party has attempted to invoke this provision to terminate the application of the Treaty to Hong Kong.

ing to the Joint Declaration, to "remain unchanged for 50 years." *Id.* art. 3(12).

United States Senate ratification of the Supplementary Treaty occurred on July 17, 1986, well after the widely publicized signing of the Joint Declaration. *See* 132 Cong.Rec. 16,819 (1986). Clearly, the Senate was aware of the planned reversion when it approved the applicability to Hong Kong of the Supplementary Treaty.[6] The Supplementary Treaty does not contain an exception for relators who can show that their trial or punishment will occur after the date of reversion. Indeed, the Supplementary Treaty is entirely silent on the question of reversion.

The United States does not have an extradition treaty with the PRC. However, on December 20, 1996, the United States signed an extradition treaty with the government of the nascent HKSAR, which provides for reciprocal post-reversion extradition. *See* Agreement Between the Government of the United States of America and the Government of Hong Kong for the Surrender of Fugitive Offenders, Dec. 20, 1996 (the "New Treaty"). The New Treaty will not enter into force until the Senate gives its advice and consent. It was submitted to the Senate on March 3, 1997. *See* 143 Cong.Rec. S1846 (daily ed. Mar. 3, 1997).

A. *United States Extradition Procedure*

In the United States, the procedures for extradition are governed by statute. *See* 18 U.S.C. ch. 209. The statute establishes a two-step procedure which divides responsibility for extradition between a judicial officer[7] and the Secretary of State. The judicial officer's duties are set out in 18 U.S.C. § 3184. In brief, the judicial officer, upon

complaint, issues an arrest warrant for an **[109]** individual sought for extradition, provided that there is an extradition treaty between the United States and the relevant foreign government and that the crime charged is covered by the treaty. *See id.* If a warrant issues, the judicial officer then conducts a hearing to determine if "he deems the evidence sufficient to sustain the charge under the provisions of the proper treaty." *Id.* If the judicial officer makes such a determination, he "*shall* certify" to the Secretary of State that a warrant for the surrender of the relator "*may* issue." *Id.* (emphases added). The judicial officer is also directed to provide the Secretary of State with a copy of the testimony and evidence from the extradition hearing. *Id.*

It is then within the Secretary of State's sole discretion to determine whether or not the relator should actually be extradited. *See* 18 U.S.C. § 3186 ("The Secretary of State *may* order the person committed under section[ ] 3184 ... of this title to be delivered to any authorized agent of such foreign government ....") (emphasis added). The Secretary has the authority to review the judicial officer's findings of fact and conclusions of law *de novo*,[8] and to reverse the judicial officer's certification of extraditability if she believes that it was made erroneously.[9] *See* 4 Abbell & Ristau, *International Judicial Assistance: Criminal—Extradition* § 13–3–8(2), at 266–69 (1995); Note, *Executive Discretion in Extradition*, 62 Colum.L.Rev. 1313, 1316–25 (1962). The Secretary may also decline to surrender the relator on any number of discretionary grounds, including but not limited to, humanitarian and foreign policy considerations. *See* 4 Abbell & Ristau, *supra*, § 13–3–8(3), at 269–73; II Bassiouni,

---

6. *See, e.g.,* 132 Cong.Rec. 16,598 (1986) (statement of Sen. Hatch) (commenting on applicability of Supplementary Treaty to Hong Kong).

7. The judicial officer may be any federal judge, any authorized magistrate, or any state judge of a court of general jurisdiction. *See id.* § 3184.

8. While not required to by statute, the Department of State routinely accepts written submissions from relators in conjunction with its review of extraditability. 4 Abbell & Ristau, *International Judicial Assistance: Criminal—Extradition,* § 13–3–8(5), at 274 (1995).

9. Although at first glance, this procedure might appear to be of questionable constitutionality because it subjects judicial decisions to executive review, rendering them non-final, *cf. Hayburn's Case,* 2 U.S. (2 Dall.) 408, 1 L.Ed. 436 (1792), it has been held that the judicial officer in an extradition proceeding "is not exercising 'any part of the judicial power of the United States,'" and instead is acting in "a non-institutional capacity." *United States v. Howard,* 996 F.2d 1320, 1325 (1st Cir.1993) (quoting *In re Kaine,* 55 U.S. (14 How.) 103, 120, 14 L.Ed. 345 (1852)).

[110] *International Extradition: United States Law and Practice* 601–04 (1987). Additionally, the Secretary may attach conditions to the surrender of the relator. *See Jimenez v. United States District Court,* 84 S.Ct. 14, 19, 11 L.Ed.2d 30 (1963) (Goldberg, J., chambers opinion) (denial of stay) (describing commitments made by Venezuelan government to United States Department of State as a condition of surrender of fugitive); 4 Abbell & Ristau, *supra,* § 13–3–8(4), at 273–74; II Bassiouni, *supra,* at 604.[10] The State Department alone, and not the judiciary, has the power to attach conditions to an order of extradition. *See, e.g., Emami v. United States District Court,* 834 F.2d 1444, 1453 (9th Cir.1987); *Demjanjuk v. Petrovsky,* 776 [8] F.2d 571, 584 (6th Cir.1985), vacated on other grounds, 10 F.3d 338 (6th Cir.1993). Of course, the Secretary may also elect to use diplomatic methods to obtain fair treatment for the relator. *See,* Note, *supra,* at 1325–26; *cf. In re Normano,* 7 F.Supp. 329, 329 (D.Mass.1934). [9]

Thus, under 18 U.S.C. § 3184, the judicial officer's inquiry is limited to a narrow set of issues concerning the existence of a treaty, the offense charged, and the quantum of evidence offered. The larger assessment of extradition and its consequences is committed to the Secretary of State. This bifurcated procedure reflects the fact that extradition proceedings contain legal issues peculiarly suited for judicial resolution, such as questions of the standard of proof, competence of evidence, and treaty construction, yet simultaneously implicate questions of foreign policy, which are better answered by the executive branch. Both institutional competence rationales and our constitutional structure, which places primary responsibility for foreign affairs in the executive branch, *see, e.g., United States v. Curtiss-Wright Export Corp.,* 299 U.S. 304, 319–22, 57 S.Ct. 216, [10] 220–22, 81 L.Ed. 255 (1936), support this division of labor.

In implementing this system of split responsibilities for extradition, courts have developed principles which ensure, among other things, that the judicial inquiry does not unnecessarily impinge upon executive prerogative and expertise. For example, the executive branch's construction of a treaty, although not binding upon the courts, is entitled to great weight. *Factor v. Laubenheimer,* 290 U.S. 276, 295, 54 S.Ct. 191, 196, 78 L.Ed. 315 (1933); *cf. United States v. Howard,* 996 F.2d 1320, 1330 n. 6 (1st Cir. 1993) (deference to executive in extradition context stems, at least in part, from fact that executive wrote and negotiated operative documents). Another principle is that extradition treaties, unlike criminal statutes, are to be construed liberally in favor of enforcement because they are "in the interest of justice and friendly international relationships." *Factor,* 290 U.S. at 298, 54 S.Ct. at 197. These principles of construction require courts to:

> interpret extradition treaties to produce reciprocity between, and expanded rights on behalf of, the signatories: "[Treaties] should be liberally construed so as to effect the apparent intention of the parties to secure equality and reciprocity between them. For that reason, if a treaty fairly admits of two constructions, one restricting the rights which may be claimed under it, and the other enlarging it, the more liberal construction is to be preferred."

Howard, 996 F.2d at 1330–31 (quoting *Factor,* 290 U.S. at 293–94, 54 S.Ct. at 195–96).

Another principle that guides courts in matters concerning extradition is the rule of non-inquiry. More than just a principle of treaty construction, the rule of non-inquiry tightly limits the appropriate scope of judicial analysis in an extradition proceeding. Under the rule of non-inquiry, courts refrain from "investigating the fairness of a requesting nation's justice system," *id.* at 1329, and from inquiring "into the procedures or treatment which await a surrendered fugitive in the requesting country." *Arnbjornsdottir-Mendler v. United States,* 721 F.2d 679, 683 (9th Cir.1983). The rule of [11] non-inquiry, like extradition procedures generally, is shaped by concerns about institutional competence and by notions of separation of powers. *See United States v. Smyth,*

---

10. The United States has, for example, imposed conditions as to the type of trial the relator would receive (*e.g.,* in civil, rather than martial law, court) and as to security arrangements for the relator. 4 Abbell & Ristau, *supra,* § 13–3–8(4), at 273 n.1.

61 F.3d 711, 714 (9th Cir.1995).[11] It is not that questions about what awaits the relator in the requesting country are irrelevant to extradition; it is that there is another branch of government, which has both final say and greater discretion in these proceedings, to whom these questions are more properly addressed.[12]

Lui contends that, on July 1, 1997, the reversion of Hong Kong to the PRC will result in his being subjected to trial and punishment by a regime with which the United States has no extradition treaty. This future event, Lui argues, operates retroactively to render his extradition illegal, *as of today*, because, he says, extradition is only legitimate where trial and punishment will be administered by the regime with which the United States has a treaty.

Although Lui is correct that the government has conceded that he will not be tried before reversion, it is also quite possible that the scenario he depicts will not arise. The new extradition treaty with the HKSAR may be approved by the United States Senate, establishing a continuity of treaties through and beyond July 1, 1997.[13] The United States government may choose to extend the current Treaty by executive agreement.[14] To the extent that Lui's argument depends on the fairness of the procedures he will be subjected to, he asks this court to decide that the PRC will not adhere to the Joint Declaration with the UK, in which it declared its intention to maintain Hong Kong's legal system for fifty years.

[111]

All of these questions involve an evaluation of contingent political events. The Supreme Court has said that the indicia of a non-justiciable political question include:

> a textually demonstrable constitutional commitment of the issue to a coordinate political department; or a lack of judicially discoverable and manageable standards for resolving it; or the impossibility of deciding without an initial policy determination of a kind clearly for nonjudicial discretion; or the impossibility of a court's undertaking independent resolution without expressing lack of respect due coordinate

---

11. One commentator has analogized the rule of non-inquiry to the "act of state" doctrine, which prohibits United States courts from judging the governmental acts of a foreign country performed within its own territory. *See* Semmelman, *Federal Courts, The Constitution, and The Rule of Non-Inquiry in International Extradition Proceedings*, 76 Cornell L.Rev. 1198 (1991). The "act of state" doctrine, the Supreme Court has said, "arises out of the basic relationships between branches of government in a system of separation of powers. It concerns the competency of dissimilar institutions to make and implement particular kinds of decisions in the area of international relations." *Banco Nacional de Cuba v. Sabbatino*, 376 U.S. 398, 423, 84 S.Ct. [12] 923, 938, 11 L.Ed.2d 804 (1964). This court has doubted, in dicta, that the rule of non-inquiry is constitutionally mandated. *Howard*, 996 F.2d at 1330 n. 6. Whether the doctrine is constitutionally mandated is immaterial here.

12. Nor is it true, as Lui suggests, that the rule of non-inquiry is only appropriate where the existence of a treaty reflects a substantive judgment about the fairness of another nation's procedures. The United States has maintained, over time, extradition treaties with some of the world's most oppressive and arbitrary regimes. *See* 18 U.S.C. § 3181 (listing treaties of extradition and dates entered into). The rule of non-inquiry expresses *no* judgment about a foreign nation's ability and willingness to provide justice;

it simply defers that assessment to the second part of every extradition proceeding—review of extraditability and determination of the appropriateness of surrender by the Secretary of State. Indeed, a leading commentator, in discussing the scope of the Secretary's discretion under 18 U.S.C. § 3186, has argued that it is precisely *"because of* the rule of non-inquiry" that it is appropriate for the Secretary to exercise discretion on humanitarian grounds. II Bassiouni, *supra*, at 602 (emphasis added).

13. The government does not argue that, absent any other action and of their own accord, the Treaties would continue beyond reversion to apply to Hong Kong. Accordingly, on the facts of this case, we find the discussion of the state succession doctrine in *Terlinden v. Ames*, 184 U.S. 270, 22 S.Ct. 484, 46 L.Ed. 534 (1902), a case heavily relied upon by the district court, *see Lui Habeas*, 957 F.Supp. at 1285–86, to be of little assistance to Lui. Of course, the discussion in *Terlinden* of the rule of non-inquiry is relevant, and supports our analysis.

14. It may be argued that this alternative infringes upon the Senate's prerogative, under the Treaty Clause, U.S.Const., art. II, § 2, to give its advice and consent. But it is hardly an appropriate judicial task to attempt to resolve a hypothetical and not ripe dispute between the legislature and the executive.

[112] branches of government; or an unusual need for unquestioning adherence to a political decision already made; or the potentiality of embarrassment from multifarious pronouncements by various departments on one question.

Baker v. Carr, 369 U.S. 186, 217, 82 S.Ct. 691, 710, 7 L.Ed.2d 663 (1962). While not all of these ingredients are present here, several are. Moreover, unlike many "political questions," whose resolution, absent judicial determination, must await the vagaries of the political process, here there is a statutory scheme which provides for the resolution of these questions by an identified member of the executive branch. The case for judicial resolution is thus weaker than with many such questions.

The principles of reciprocity and liberal construction also counsel against construing the Treaties so as to prohibit Lui's extradition. Hong Kong, through the United Kingdom, has entered bilateral treaties with the United States. The United States has sought extradition of criminals from Hong Kong in the past, and may wish to continue to do so up until July 1, 1997. If the executive chooses to modify or abrogate the terms of the Treaties that it negotiated, it has ample discretion to do so. However, if this court were to read a cut-off date vis-a-vis extraditions to Hong Kong into the Treaties, it would risk depriving both parties of the benefit of their bargain.

None of these principles, including noninquiry, may be regarded as an absolute. We, like the Second Circuit, "can imagine situations where the relator, upon extradition, would be subject to procedures or punishment so antipathetic to a federal court's sense of decency as to require reexamination of the principle[s]" discussed above. *Gallina* [13] *v. Fraser,* 278 F.2d 77, 79 (2d Cir.1960). This is not such a case. Lui is wanted for economic, not political, activities whose criminality is fully recognized in the United States. His extradition is sought by the *current* Hong Kong regime, a colony of Great Britain, which, as Lui himself points out, is one of this country's most trusted treaty partners. Moreover, Lui has been a fugitive from Hong Kong since 1994. He has

been subject to extradition since entering the United States in December 1995. That now only a few months remain before the reversion of Hong Kong is partly attributable to strategic choices made by Lui himself. There is nothing here which shocks the conscience of this court.

B.   *The Treaties*

There is no dispute that the Treaty, as supplemented by the Supplementary Treaty, is currently in effect and is applicable to Hong Kong. The district court, in granting Lui's habeas petition, reasoned that "the Treaty, by its own terms, does not allow the extradition of a person to Hong Kong if the Crown Colony of Hong Kong is unable to try and to punish that person." *Lui Habeas,* 957 F.Supp. at 1286. The government counters that the terms of the Treaty clearly allow Lui's extradition. There is nothing in the plain language of the Treaties that would permit the construction made by the district court. The principles discussed above argue persuasively against reading judicially created limitations into the Treaties' unambiguous text.

1.   *Overview*

We begin our analysis of the Treaties with a brief overview of the Treaties' operative provisions. Article I of the Treaty states the basic reciprocal compact, providing that:

> Each Contracting Party undertakes to extradite to the other, in the circumstances and subject to the conditions specified in this Treaty, any person found in its territory who has been accused or convicted of any offense within Article III, committed within the jurisdiction of the other Party.

Treaty, art. I.

Article III contains the "dual criminality" requirement, a requirement that is "central to extradition law and [one that] has been embodied either explicitly or implicitly in all prior extradition treaties between the United States and Great Britain." *Brauch v. Raiche,* 618 F.2d 843, 847 (1st Cir.1980). Article III, in relevant part, provides that:

> Extradition shall be granted for an act or omission the facts of which disclose an

offense within any of the descriptions listed in the Schedule annexed to this Treaty ... or any other offense, if: (a) the offense is punishable under the laws of both Parties by imprisonment or other form of detention for more than one year or by the death penalty....

Treaty, art. III(1). The annexed Schedule lists twenty-nine general crimes, including bribery, the crime of which Lui is accused. *See* Treaty, Schedule, No. 23.

Article V contains various affirmative defenses, including the "political offense" exception. As a general matter, the political offense exception "is now a standard clause in almost all extradition treaties of the world." I Bassiouni, *supra*, at 384. The political offense exception in the Treaty prohibits extradition where "(i) the offense for which extradition is requested is regarded by the requested Party as one of a political character; or (ii) the person sought proves that the request for his extradition has in fact been made with a view to try or punish him for an offense of a political character." Treaty, art. V(1)(c).

The Supplementary Treaty narrows the availability of this political offense exception. It lists a range of crimes—all crimes of violence—that may not be regarded as political offenses for the purpose of raising the political offense exception. *See* Supplementary Treaty, art. 1. The Supplementary Treaty also offers an affirmative defense to fugitives sought for crimes of violence who, by virtue of its article 1, are unable to raise the political offense exception. *See* Supplementary Treaty, art. 3(a), (b). Such a fugitive may block extradition by establishing:

> by a preponderance of the evidence that the request for extradition has in fact been made with a view to try or punish him on account of his race, religion, nationality, or political opinions, or that he would, if surrendered, be prejudiced at his trial or punished, detained or restricted in his personal liberty by reason of his race, religion, nationality or political opinions.

Id. art. 3(a).

The procedural requisites of an extradition request are specified in article VII of the Treaty. The request must be accompanied **[113]** by, *inter alia,* a description of the fugitive, a statement of facts of the offense, and the text of the law under which he is charged. *See* Treaty, art. VII(2). For accused (as opposed to already convicted) fugitives, the request must also include a valid arrest warrant and "such evidence as, according to the law of the requested Party, would justify his committal for trial if the offense had been committed in the territory of the requested Party, including evidence that the person requested is the person to whom the warrant of arrest refers." *Id.* art. VII(3).[15]

Article XII contains the "specialty" requirement, a common feature of extradition treaties. Specialty has two basic components. First, the requesting state may not try the fugitive for any crimes other than the specific crime for which extradition was sought and granted. Second, the requesting state may not re-extradite the fugitive to a third state. *See* Treaty, art. XII.

2. *Analysis*

Both the district court and Lui focus on four Treaty provisions in concluding that the Treaty is inapplicable to Lui. *See Lui Habeas,* 957 F.Supp. at 1286–89. We address these provisions in turn, concluding that the obligation of the United States to extradite Lui, specified in article I of the Treaty, is not undermined by any of these provisions. We base our analysis on the plain language of the Treaty. *United States v. Alvarez–Machain,* 504 U.S. 655, 663, 112 S.Ct. 2188, [14] 2193, 119 L.Ed.2d 441 (1992); *Sumitomo Shoji Am., Inc. v. Avagliano,* 457 U.S. 176, 180, 102 S.Ct. 2374, 2377, 72 L.Ed.2d 765 [15] (1982). Underlying this analysis is the court's awareness of the limited role of the judiciary in extradition proceedings.

The Warrant Requirement

The district court understood the warrant requirement of article VII(3) to serve the purpose of permitting "the request-

---

15. Article IX(1), in turn, states that extradition shall not be granted if the evidentiary showing required by article VII(3) is not made by the requesting party.

[114] ed sovereign to know that the relator has been accused ... pursuant to the laws of the requesting sovereign, and that he will be tried and punished in accordance with that sovereign's laws." *Lui Habeas,* 957 F.Supp. at 1287. In this case, the district court reasoned, since Lui would not be tried in accordance with the present Hong Kong regime's laws, the warrant requirement was not met. *Id.*

There is nothing in the language of article VII(3), or the rest of article VII, which indicates that the warrant requirement serves the greater function attributed to it by the district court. Indeed, the warrant requirement appears to do nothing more than to help the judicial officer in the requested country to confirm that there are in fact charges properly pending against the relator in the requested country, and that the relator is actually the person sought. It does not authorize the investigation which the district court envisioned, and indeed such an investigation is foreclosed by the rule of non-inquiry. A warrant was provided by the Hong Kong authorities here, and Lui does not attack its validity or authenticity. The warrant requirement was plainly satisfied.

The Dual Criminality Requirement

The district court understood the purpose of the dual criminality requirement, as stated in article III of the Treaty, to be "to provide the requested sovereign with the opportunity to examine the substantive law of the requesting sovereign in the context of the Treaty." *Lui Habeas,* 957 F.Supp. at 1287. The court stated that the requirement serves to "underscore[ ] the expectation running through the Treaty that [Lui] is to be tried, judged, and punished in accordance with the laws of the requesting sovereign." *Id.*

There is nothing in the text of article III of the Treaty that supports this sweeping conclusion. The dual criminality requirement, by its plain terms, is satisfied if the crime of which the relator is accused appears on the annexed Schedule or is punishable in both countries by at least one year's imprisonment. Bribery, as noted above, appears on the annexed Schedule.

The purpose of the dual criminality requirement is simply to ensure that extradition is granted only for crimes that are regarded as serious in both countries. *See United States v. Saccoccia,* 58 F.3d 754, 766 (1st Cir.1995) ("The principle of dual criminality dictates that, as a general rule, an extraditable offense must be a serious crime (rather than a mere peccadillo) punishable under the criminal laws of both the surrendering and the requesting state."), *cert. denied,* — U.S. —, 116 S.Ct. 1322, 134 L.Ed.2d 474 (1996); *Restatement (Third) of the Foreign Relations Law of the United States* § 476, cmt. d (1987); *id.* § 475, cmt. c.

The dual criminality requirement is satisfied here.

The Political Offense Exception

The district court also relied on article 3(a) of the Supplementary Treaty, which, it stated, requires the judicial officer "to examine the reasons for the requesting sovereign's desire to try and to punish the relator." *Lui Habeas,* 957 F.Supp. at 1287. In this case, stated the district court, article 3(a) "underscores again the Treaty's requirement and expectation that extradition ... may not take place if the requesting sovereign ... is unable to try and punish Lui in the relatively few days left before its reversion to China." *Id.*

The Supplementary Treaty article 3(a) defense is simply inapplicable here. Supplementary Treaty article 3(a) describes a defense which is available only to fugitives charged with one of the crimes specified in article 1 of the Supplementary Treaty, all of which are crimes of violence. Lui's alleged crime—bribery—is not among the crimes enumerated in the Supplementary Treaty's article 1.

Indeed, the very purpose of the Supplementary Treaty was to cabin the political offense exception so that perpetrators of certain violent offenses would be precluded from avoiding extradition simply because their criminal activity was inspired by political motivation. *See Howard,* 996 F.2d at 1324–25. Because this contraction of the time-honored political offense exception stirred up a great deal of controversy during negotiations, a compromise position was ultimately agreed upon, so that fugitives barred from invoking the political offense defense might still claim the protection of the more limited defense of article 3(a). *See id.* at 1324 (discussing negotiating history and legislative history).

Lui properly does not claim that he is entitled to the article V(1)(c) political offense exception.[16] The Supplementary Treaty article 3(a) defense was unavailable to him, and thus, however much article 3(a) might ever, as the district court stated, "require[ ] the court to examine the reasons for the requesting sovereign's desire to try and to punish the relator," *Lui Habeas,* 957 F.Supp. at 1287, it certainly does not do so here.

Moreover, article 3(a) allows the judicial officer to make only a narrowly circumscribed inquiry. "[A]n extradition target must establish by a preponderance of the evidence that, if he were surrendered, the legal system of the requesting country would treat him differently from other similarly situated individuals because of his race, religion, nationality, or political opinions." *Howard,* 996 F.2d at 1331. Lui made no such showing of discrimination, and the district court, in making its own predictions about the post-reversion justice system in Hong Kong, exceeded the narrow inquiry permitted by article 3(a).

The Rule of Specialty

The district court understood the Treaty's specialty provision to signify that "the Treaty allows only for extradition for offenses that can be tried and punished by the requesting sovereign." *Lui Habeas,* 957 F.Supp. at 1288. Because the specialty obligation cannot be enforced by the United States after reversion, reasoned the district court, article XII is violated *ab initio,* and Lui cannot be extradited. *Id.* at 1288–89.

The rule of specialty literally has no application here. The rule has two basic requirements: that the relator be tried for

the crimes charged in the extradition warrant and that the relator not be re-extradited **[115]** to another country. There is no claim that either of these is violated. Indeed, as the district court properly recognized, Lui is not arguing that the reversion itself would constitute a de facto re-extradition from Hong Kong to China in violation of the specialty provision. *Lui Habeas,* 957 F.Supp. at 1288 n. 15; *see also Oen Yin–Choy v. Robinson,* 858 F.2d 1400, 1403–04 (9th Cir.1988).[17]

The essence of Lui's argument is rather different: it is that the fact that he cannot be tried and punished by the same government which gave the Treaty assurances contravenes the rationale behind the specialty provisions and so undermines confidence that this is the result the Senate intended in giving its consent. The responses to that argument are largely those outlined at the beginning of this opinion. We add only our thoughts directed to the specialty clause itself.

If Lui's position were correct, the enforceability of many extradition treaties to which the United States is a party would be thrown into grave doubt. Regimes come and go, as, indeed, do states. Moreover, 18 U.S.C. § 3184, which defines the role of the courts in the extradition process, gives no discretion to the judicial officer to refuse to certify extraditability on the ground that a treaty partner cannot assure the requested country that rights under a treaty will be enforced or protected. *See Saccoccia,* 58 F.3d at 766–67.

The Ninth Circuit, writing in 1988, also rejected a similar argument made by a fugitive who fought extradition by arguing that the United States would be unable to compel Hong Kong's compliance with the specialty obligation because, although he would face trial in the Crown Colony, his imprisonment might extend past the reversion date. "Were the Treaty to be interpreted as [the fugitive] asks, extradition to Hong Kong would be the exception rather than the rule because it would be limited in practice only

---

16. Even if he had attempted to assert the political offense exception, he would likely have been unsuccessful since "[c]riminal conduct in the nature of financial fraud ... traditionally has been

considered outside the 'political offense' exception." *Koskotas v. Roche,* 931 F.2d 169, 172 (1st Cir.1991) (citing cases). [16]

[116] to extraditions for crimes which could be punished for a term expiring before the reversion date." *Oen Yin–Choy,* 858 F.2d at 1404. Indeed, if we interpreted the specialty provision in this way, we would be forced to conclude that any relator extradited from the United States to Hong Kong at any point since the signing of the Joint Declaration, was, if he faced a term of imprisonment upon conviction that could conceivably extend past the date of reversion, sent to Hong Kong in violation of the Treaty.

Of course, Lui may express his concerns about the post-reversion enforceability of specialty to the Secretary of State, who, in her discretion, may choose not to surrender him. We note that the newly signed, as yet unratified, extradition treaty between the United States and the HKSAR provides that specialty protection "shall apply to fugitive offenders who have been surrendered between the parties prior to the entry into force" of the new treaty. New Treaty, arts. 16, 20. It is not the role of the judiciary to speculate about the future ability of the United States to enforce treaty obligations.

III.

Lui also challenges the determination of the magistrate judge that there was probable cause to believe that Lui had violated Hong Kong law on eight of the nine charges in the warrant. Although the district court declined to review this issue, we do reach it.

Lui protests that we lack power to reach this issue, and that we must remand to the district court for further findings. However, the issue was fully briefed and argued to the district court. The record is complete. This is a habeas corpus appeal, in which the district court was not the fact finder but had only a review function over the findings made by the magistrate judge. The function to be exercised by the district court is more akin to appellate review, and is done on the same

record as is before us. Under these circumstances, the district court had no greater institutional competence to perform this review task than do we. That the district court declined to reach the issue does not deprive us of the power to do so.

While it is true that, as a general matter, federal courts of appeals do not rule on issues not decided in the district court, *Singleton v. Wulff,* 428 U.S. 106, 120, 96 S.Ct. 2868, 2877, 49 L.Ed.2d 826 (1976), we do have discretion to address issues not reached by the district court when the question is essentially legal and the record is complete. *Quinn v. Robinson,* 783 F.2d 776, 814 (9th [18] Cir.1986); *cf. Howard,* 996 F.2d at 1329 ("That the district court failed to afford plenary review on this aspect of the case does not mean that we must remand.... Rather, because the question is quintessentially legal and this court is fully capable of deciding it without any further development of the record, we can simply address and resolve it.") (citations omitted). Such is the case here. We have before us the parties' memoranda on probable cause to the district court and the magistrate judge as well as the completed evidentiary record. In the interest of conserving judicial resources and mindful of the policy that extradition matters be handled expeditiously, we see no reason for further delay.[17] *Cf. Fernandez v. Phillips,* 268 U.S. 311, 312, 45 S.Ct. 541, 542, 69 L.Ed. 970 [19] (1925) (Supreme Court reviews probable cause determination of judge certifying extradition without intermediate court passing on the question).

The traditional formulation is that, on habeas corpus review of a certification of extraditability, the court only examines the magistrate judge's determination of probable cause to see if there is "any evidence" to support it. *Fernandez,* 268 U.S. at 312, 45 S.Ct. at 542; *see also Sidali v. INS,* 107 F.3d 191, 199–200 (3d Cir.1997); *Then v. Melendez,* 92 F.3d 851, 854 (9th Cir.1996). This

---

17. There is no unfairness to Lui. He has had full opportunity to address the issue of whether there is probable cause for extradition before the magistrate judge and full opportunity to address the magistrate judge's determination before the district court. In the extradition proceedings before the magistrate judge, Lui filed a 45 page memorandum on the probable cause issue accompanied by a copious appendix. He also filed motions to exclude certain of the government's evidence, called witnesses, and presented both live testimony and testimony by affidavit.

circuit has interpreted the "any evidence" standard quite literally, conducting a fairly deferential review of the magistrate's find-[20] ings. *See Koskotas* v. *Roche*, 931 F.2d 169, 176 (1st Cir.1991); *United States v. Manzi*, 888 F.2d 204, 205 (1st Cir.1989); *Brauch*, 618 F.2d at 854; *Greci v. Birknes*, 527 F.2d 956 (1st Cir.1976).

Recently, some other appellate courts, while retaining the traditional formulation, have apparently engaged in a more rigorous review of the evidence presented before the judicial officer, thus raising questions about the actual content of the "any evidence" standard. *See, e.g., Sidali*, 107 F.3d at 199–200; *Ludecke v. Marshal*, 15 F.3d 496, 497–98 (5th Cir.1994); *Peters v. Egnor*, 888 F.2d 713, 717–18 (10th Cir.1989). The Supreme Court last addressed the scope of a court's authority on habeas corpus review of a finding of extraditability in 1925, when it said that "the alleged fugitive from justice has had his hearing" and that "habeas corpus is available only to inquire" into a very limited list of issues. *See Fernandez*, 268 U.S. at 312, 45 S.Ct. at 542. The existence of "any evidence warranting the finding that there was reasonable ground to believe the accused guilty" was one of only three issues that the *Fernandez* court said might permissibly be reached on habeas. *Id.* At that time, the scope of habeas corpus review of *all* proceedings was very limited, and *Fernandez's* strictures on review in extradition proceedings, including the deferential "any evidence" standard, may simply reflect that generally narrower view of the writ. *See In re Extradition of Burt*, 737 F.2d 1477, 1484 (7th Cir.1984) ("[T]he broad language of *Fernandez*, which on its face would appear to restrict the scope of inquiry here, must be construed 'in the context of its time and in the context of subsequent development of the scope of habeas corpus review.'" (citation omitted)). Since 1925, and until the enactment of the AEDPA in 1996,[18] habeas corpus in other contexts has expanded to become a "second look" at most substantive and procedural issues. Similarly, courts reviewing certifications of extraditability, while continuing to cite *Fernandez*, have

actually engaged in review of issues beyond **[117]** those enumerated by the Supreme Court in 1925. *See* Kester, *Some Myths of United States Extradition Law*, 76 Geo.L.J. 1441, 1473 (1988); *see also* 4 Abbell & Ristau, *supra*, § 13–3–6, at 255–57. Thus, it is arguable that the "any evidence" standard is an anachronism, and that this court should engage in a more searching review of the magistrate's probable cause findings.

There is no reason to predict a resolution of this issue here. Whatever the prism through which this record is reviewed, ranging from a strictly construed "any evidence" standard to *de novo* review, our conclusion is that the government has met its burden.

The purpose of the evidentiary portion of the extradition hearing is to determine whether the United States, on behalf of the requesting government, has produced sufficient evidence to hold the person for trial. The standard of sufficiency is derived from United States law, including the Treaty between the United States and the UK. Under 18 U.S.C. § 3184, the judicial officer must determine whether the evidence of criminality is "sufficient to sustain the charge under the provisions of the proper treaty or convention." The Treaty requires that:

> Extradition shall be granted only if the evidence be found sufficient according to the law of the requested Party ... to justify the committal for trial of the person sought if the offense of which he is accused had been committed in the territory of the requested Party....

Treaty, art. IX(1). "United States courts have interpreted this provision in similar treaties as requiring a showing by the requesting party that there is probable cause to believe that the accused has committed the charged offense." *Quinn*, 783 F.2d at 783 (separate opinion of Reinhardt, J.) (citing cases). The Supplementary Treaty defines probable cause:

> Probable cause means whether there is sufficient evidence to warrant a man of reasonable caution in the belief that ... an

---

18. Antiterrorism and Effective Death Penalty Act ("AEDPA"), Pub.L.No. 104–132, 110 Stat. 1214

(1996)

[118] offense has been committed by the accused.

Supplementary Treaty, art. 2. The actual trial, if any, is in the foreign court, and it is not the purpose of the extradition hearing to determine whether the evidence is sufficient to justify conviction. Thus it is the probable cause determination which is subject to our review.

There is no dispute that payments of over HK $21 million (approximately U.S. $3 million) and unsecured loans of HK $10 million (approximately U.S. $1.4 million) were made to Lui, that the payments were made into foreign bank accounts in Lui's name, and that the payments were not made directly by check but through a series of steps which made them more difficult to trace. There is also no dispute that the payments were made on the dates charged. The timing is significant. The payments coincided with the knowledge that Lui was being considered as Director of Exports for BAT-HK and with his appointment to that position in 1992.[19] The loans were made within three days of Lui's leaving his employment at Brown & Williamson and BAT-HK. It is not contested that BAT-HK was the major supplier of cigarettes to GIL and WWC, that Brown & Williamson prohibits its employees from accepting "inducements" from those with whom it does business and requires disclosure statements to be completed, and that Lui failed to disclose any of these payments on his disclosure form. The dispute between the government and Lui is basically over the purpose of these payments.

Two competing theories explaining the purpose of the payments were presented to the magistrate judge. The government argued that the payments were bribes. Although Lui had no burden to produce any evidence at all and the burden of showing probable cause rested entirely on the government, Lui did present an explanation for the loans and payments, primarily in the affidavit

of Hung Wing Wah ("Hung"), a former GIL director and sole proprietor of GIL's subsidiary, WWC.[20] In essence, Hung said that, in or around 1987, prior to Lui's employment with Brown & Williamson, he and Lui first began discussing "cigarette business matters." Hung stated that these discussions eventually led to the establishment of a profitable business relationship in which Hung purchased Japanese cigarettes and resold them at a profit for the account of Chen Ying–Jen ("Chen"), a former GIL principal. The payments to Lui's foreign bank accounts were filtered through Chen's account.

Hung stated he was told by Chen that, because of the substantial profits generated by the business relationship Lui had been instrumental in establishing, Chen had agreed to pay Lui for his assistance and would continue paying Lui as long as the relationship continued to generate such substantial profits. Hung indicated that the sums paid to Lui bore a reasonable relationship to the magnitude of Chen's profits. And finally, Hung stated that the unsecured short term loans had been made to Lui so that Lui could invest in the then-booming Hong Kong stock market. Hung stated that both the principal and interest were repaid shortly after the loans were made. During the hearing before the magistrate judge, Lui's counsel indicated that Lui would testify, and described what that testimony would be. This description matched the testimony given by Hung. Lui ultimately declined to testify.

Lui argued that the government's evidence was insufficient to support an inference of bribery and that there was, in any event, an innocent explanation. The government argued that the undisputed facts were sufficient to establish probable cause, and that the explanation was inherently implausible. In addition, the government argued, it had two "smoking gun" statements directly saying the payments were bribes. We return to

---

19. The one exception to this was the October 1988 payment alleged in Count II, as to which the magistrate judge found a lack of probable cause.

20. Lui chose not to testify on his own behalf, as was his prerogative. The magistrate judge prop-

erly excluded the polygraph evidence offered by Lui to corroborate his testimony. The polygraph evidence was not relevant, there being no such testimony in evidence to corroborate. Whether it would be admissible if he did testify, we do not address.

these two statements and Lui's attack on them later.

The magistrate judge concluded that the explanation proffered by Lui's counsel—"to the effect that the payments represented a gratuitous gesture of gratitude by one of GIL's former principals for Lui's assistance in introducing him to a supplier of Japanese cigarettes in 1987, some six years before the last payments were made"—was inherently implausible. *Lui Extradition,* 939 F.Supp. at 955.[21] The implausibility of the explanation does give credence to the government's theory. *See United States v. Burgos,* 94 F.3d 849, 867 (4th Cir.1996) (implausible tales to the finder of fact can rationally be viewed as circumstantial evidence of guilt), *cert. denied,* —— U.S. ——, 117 S.Ct. 1087, 137 L.Ed.2d 221 (1997). Without consideration of the two "smoking gun" statements, the magistrate judge was fully warranted in finding probable cause.

In addition, the two statements, which Lui argues were inadmissible, were properly admitted at the probable cause stage of the extradition hearing and further support a finding of probable cause.

The first statement was given to Hong Kong investigators in July 1994 by Chui, one of Lui's alleged coconspirators. Chui was one of the principals of GIL until April 1993. In his statement, Chui implicated himself and other principals of GIL in a scheme to bribe Lui and others to secure favorable allocations of cigarettes from BAT–HK. According to Chui, GIL began paying bribes to Lui when they first anticipated that Lui might eventually become an important BAT–HK decision-maker. Chui was murdered in Singapore nine months after giving this statement.

The second statement was made by Francis McNamara Haddon–Cave, who worked with Chui. Haddon–Cave testified in Hong Kong in October 1995 at a hearing to determine the sufficiency of the evidence to commit one of Lui's alleged coconspirators for

trial on a charge of conspiracy to bribe Lui. **[119]** Haddon–Cave testified that he was hired by Chui to work as a consultant for GIL and began working there in October 1992. One of Haddon–Cave's responsibilities was to foster relationships between GIL and major suppliers like BAT–HK. Haddon–Cave testified that Chui told him in Lui's presence that Lui was "our man" and an important link with GIL. Lui, then BAT–HK's Director of Exports, did not deny it. Haddon–Cave further testified that later, outside of Lui's presence, Chui told him that Lui was "on the take" and had become wealthy as a result of the payments that distributors made to him to secure favorable allocations of cigarettes.

The framework for determining admissibility of evidence here is determined by the Treaty itself and by United States legal rules governing admissibility in extradition proceedings. Pursuant to federal statute, documents offered as evidence in an extradition hearing:

> shall be received and admitted as evidence ... for all the purposes of such hearing if they shall be properly and legally authenticated so as to entitle them to be received for similar purposes by the tribunals of the foreign country from which the accused party shall have escaped....

18 U.S.C. § 3190.[22] Proof of such authentication is the certificate of the principal diplomatic or consular officer of the United States resident in such foreign country. *Id.* Additionally, article VII(5) of the Treaty provides that any evidence given upon oath or affirmation "shall be received in evidence in any proceedings for extradition" if it is duly authenticated. Treaty, art. VII(5). Both the Haddon–Cave testimony and the Chui statement meet this authenticity requirement and were thus admissible at the extradition hearing by the terms of the relevant statute and treaties.

---

21. The statement in the magistrate's opinion that Lui adduced only counsel's argument and not explanatory evidence, *Lui Extradition,* 939 F.Supp. at 955, is obviously an oversight. Among other items, the Hung Wing Wah affidavit was admitted into evidence and considered by the magistrate judge.

22. Lui does not rely on the language of 18 U.S.C. § 3190. Most courts reviewing the language have concluded that § 3190 requires only that the evidence meet any authentication requirement imposed by a foreign tribunal, not that it be admissible, much less that it be admissible at trial. *See Oen Yin–Choy,* 858 F.2d at 1406; *Lui*[21] *Extradition,* 939 F.Supp. at 934 (citing cases).

[120]   Lui argues nonetheless that the two statements were improperly admitted because they would be inadmissible at trial under Hong Kong law. Lui argues that it is inherently unfair to certify that he is extraditable on the basis of evidence that would be inadmissible in the court where he would face trial. He also argues that failure to consider the Hong Kong High Court's declaratory judgment (later reversed) that the Chui statement would be inadmissible would evince great disrespect for the judicial system of Hong Kong. Both of these arguments are misplaced.

In probable cause hearings under American law, the evidence taken need not meet the standards for admissibility at trial. Indeed, at a preliminary hearing in federal court a "finding of probable cause may be based upon hearsay in whole or in part." Fed.R.Crim.P. 5.1(a). This is because a "preliminary hearing is not a minitrial of the issue of guilt," *Coleman v. Burnett*, 477 F.2d 1187, 1201 (D.C.Cir.1973); rather, "its function is the more limited one of determining whether probable cause exists to hold the accused for trial." *Barber v. Page*, 390 U.S. 719, 725, 88 S.Ct. 1318, 1322, 20 L.Ed.2d 255 (1968). An extradition hearing similarly involves a preliminary examination of the evidence and is not a trial. *Charlton v. Kelly*, 229 U.S. 447, 461, 33 S.Ct. 945, 949–50, 57 L.Ed. 1274 (1913); *Romeo v. Roache*, 820 F.2d 540, 544 (1st Cir.1987). An extradition hearing does not require a higher standard of evidence than a probable cause hearing. The special and limited nature of extradition hearings is manifested in a more lenient standard for admissibility of evidence. Neither the Federal Rules of Criminal Procedure, *see* Fed.R.Crim.P. 54(b)(5), nor the Federal Rules of Evidence, *see* Fed.R.Evid. 1101(d)(3), apply to extradition hearings. The evidence may consist of hearsay, even entirely of hearsay. *Collins v. Loisel*, 259 [22] U.S. 309, 317, 42 S.Ct. 469, 472, 66 L.Ed. 956 (1922). So American domestic law has already resolved against Lui any claim that there is a violation of Constitutional rights from the admission of hearsay evidence at a probable cause hearing which would not be admitted at trial.

Under Hong Kong law, the Haddon–Cave statement and the Chui statement present separate and distinct issues. The Haddon–Cave statement was ruled inadmissible at the Hong Kong trial of Chong Tsoi–Jun ("Chong"), an alleged co-conspirator, on an objection that it was not made in furtherance of the conspiracy.

As to the Chui statement, a Hong Kong High Court judge issued a declaration that the statement was inadmissible hearsay. On appeal, the Hong Kong Court of Appeal vacated this ruling, finding that Lui's request for a declaratory judgment was not justiciable in the Hong Kong courts, but that even if it were, the judge's grant of the declaration would be an abuse of discretion. The Court of Appeal reasoned that the issue of the admissibility of the Chui statement in the extradition proceeding was a matter for the United States court to decide. The court noted, however, that the parties agreed that the statement was inadmissible hearsay under Hong Kong law. In light of the Hong Kong court's statement that the admissibility of the Chui statement in the extradition hearing is a matter for the United States court to decide, admission of the statement into evidence cannot be viewed as a sign of disrespect for a sister court.

The focus on admissibility is, we think, misplaced, both based on these facts and on larger, institutional concerns about the operation of habeas corpus in extradition certifications. While in *Manzi* we "recognized that serious due process concerns may merit review beyond the narrow scope of inquiry in extradition proceedings," there is no serious due process issue here. *See Manzi*, 888 F.2d at 206; *see also Koskotas*, 931 F.2d at 174; [23] cf. *Burt*, 737 F.2d at 1481; *Gallina*, 278 F.2d [24] at 78. Lui's liberty interests are protected by the very existence of "an unbiased hearing before an independent judiciary." *In re Kaine*, 55 U.S. (14 How.) 103, 14 L.Ed. 345 (1852).

Inherent in the probable cause standard is the necessity of a determination that the evidence is both sufficiently reliable and of sufficient weight to warrant the conclusion. The probable cause standard does not even require that the government make its showing by a preponderance of the evidence. But neither is it toothless. All evidence does not have the same importance even if it is authentic and admissible. For example, a confession obtained by duress is inherently unreliable and would be given little weight even if the confession were authenticated. *See Gill v. Imundi,* 747 F.Supp. 1028, 1042–47 (S.D.N.Y.1990). The reliability of the evidence is a factor for the reviewing court to consider as well, and potentially unreliable evidence may be accorded reduced weight by the court. *Restatement, supra,* § 478.

No such concerns about reliability are implicated here. First, the statements themselves were neither involuntary nor obtained under questionable circumstances. Further, the Hong Kong courts did not rule that either statement was untrue or otherwise cast doubt on the statements' credibility. Each statement was thought inadmissible in Hong Kong on grounds pertaining to hearsay. The Haddon–Cave statement was deemed inadmissible because it did not meet one of the requirements for admissibility of a co-conspirator's statement. The Chui statement was thought inadmissible because the declarant was dead. The Hong Kong government alleges that Chui was involved in the conspiracy until he became a government informant and witness and that he was murdered in order to prevent him from testifying. GIL directors, including Hung and Chong, allegedly tried to dissuade Chui from cooperating with the ICAC. We need not reach the issue of whether the statement of a declarant, murdered to keep him from testifying, might be admissible at a criminal trial in the United States, *cf. United States v. Houlihan,* 92 F.3d 1271 (1st Cir.1996), *cert. denied,* — U.S. —, 117 S.Ct. 963, 136 L.Ed.2d 849 (1997), whatever the consequence of these facts under Hong Kong law. Nevertheless, we note that the Chui statement might well be admissible under United States law as a statement against interest. *See* Fed.R.Evid. 804(b)(3). The magistrate judge correctly ruled that the two statements were not unreliable.

One final argument need not detain us long. Lui argues, from his counsel's tactical decision not to present his testimony at the

extradition hearing, that he was precluded **[121]** from testifying. He argues that the magistrate judge drew an unfavorable inference, in violation of his Fifth Amendment rights, from his failure to testify. The argument misapprehends what happened. The magistrate judge did no such thing. Lui presented testimony from Hung and five other affiants, as well as argument of counsel attempting to explain the payments and loans. The magistrate judge disbelieved the explanation, as it was within his discretion to do. There is nothing in this objection.

For these reasons we reverse the grant of habeas corpus by the district court. We continue in effect the requirement that Lui be held without bail. If Lui wishes to file a petition for rehearing and/or a petition for rehearing en banc with this court, he must do so within 14 calendar days. *See* Fed. R.App.P. 40(a) & 35(c). We stay, in any event, delivery of the certification of extraditability to the Secretary of State during this 14 calendar day period to permit Lui to seek relief from the United States Supreme Court.

So ordered.

Before TORRUELLA, Chief Judge, and SELYA, BOUDIN, STAHL *, and LYNCH, Circuit Judges.

ORDER OF EN BANC COURT

The suggestion for the holding of a rehearing en banc having been carefully considered by the judges of this Court in regular active service and a majority of said judges not having voted to order that the appeal be heard or reheard by the Court en banc,

It is ordered that the suggestion for rehearing en banc be denied.

STAHL, Circuit Judge, (dissenting).

Because I do not believe that the panel's opinion reaches the correct result, and because I believe that this case raises numerous difficult and complex questions of law that warrant the full court's considered attention, I would grant the petition. I there-

* Dissent follows.

[122] fore respectfully dissent from the court's decision to deny rehearing en banc.

I. The Treaty Language

The extradition request in this case was made by authorities of the British Crown Colony of Hong Kong pursuant to two bilateral treaties dating from 1972—a primary agreement and a supplemental treaty—that both the United States and the United Kingdom have signed and ratified.[1] The main treaty applies to Hong Kong by an exchange of diplomatic notes made in October 1976, see 28 U.S.T. at 238–41, while the supplemental treaty by its terms applies to the United Kingdom and "the territories for whose international relations the United Kingdom is responsible," which, as listed in an annex, includes Hong Kong.[2] In 1984, the United Kingdom and the People's Republic of China issued a Joint Declaration, which was ratified and entered into force in 1985, under which sovereignty over Hong Kong will revert to China on July 1, 1997.[3] In 1985, the United States signed the supplemental treaty and the United States Senate ratified it the following year. Despite being ratified after the well-publicized Sino–British Joint Declaration regarding Hong Kong's future status, the supplemental treaty says nothing about fugitives sought for extradition ("relators") to Hong Kong, like Lui Kin–Hong, who can demonstrate that their trial will occur after Hong Kong's reversion to China.

"In construing a treaty, as in construing a statute, we first look to its terms to determine its meaning." *United States v. Alvarez–Machain*, 504 U.S. 655, 663, 112 S.Ct.[25] 2188, 2193, 119 L.Ed.2d 441 (1992) (citing *Air France v. Saks*, 470 U.S. 392, 397, 105 S.Ct.[26] 1338, 1341, 84 L.Ed.2d 289 (1985); *Valentine v. United States ex rel. Neidecker*, 299 U.S. 5, 11, 57 S.Ct. 100, 103–04, 81 L.Ed. 5 (1936)).[27] Article I of the primary US–UK bilateral extradition treaty provides that "[e]ach Contracting Party undertakes to extradite to the other" persons accused or convicted of certain enumerated offenses "subject to the conditions specified in this Treaty." Among the conditions that the treaty specifies are those found in Article XII, which incorporates a "specialty" provision, a common feature of extradition treaties,[4] and contains a prohibition against a relator's re-extradition to stand trial in a third state. Article XII in relevant part provides:

(1) A person extradited shall not be detained or proceeded against in the territory of the requesting Party for any offense other than an extraditable offense established by the facts in respect of which his extradition has been granted, or on account of any other matters, nor be extradited by that Party to a third State—

(a) until after he has returned to the territory of the requested Party; or

(b) until the expiration of thirty days after he has been free to return to the territory of the requested Party.

1. *See* Extradition Treaty Between the Government of the United States of America and the Government of the United Kingdom of Great Britain and Northern Ireland, June 8, 1972, 28 U.S.T. 227 [hereinafter "the treaty"] *and* Supplemental Treaty Between the Government of the United States of America and the Government of the United Kingdom of Great Britain and Northern Ireland, June 25, 1985, T.I.A.S. No. 12050 [hereinafter "the supplemental treaty"].

2. The supplemental treaty specifically applies to Great Britain and Northern Ireland, the Channel Islands, the Isle of Man, Anguilla, Bermuda, the British Indian Ocean Territory, the British Virgin Islands, the "Cayman Islands, the Falkland Islands, the Falkland Island Dependencies, Gibraltar, Hong Kong, Montserrat, Pitcairn, Henderson, Ducie and Oeno Islands, St. Helena, the St. Helena Dependencies, the Sovereign Base Areas of Akrotiri and Dhekelia in the Island of

Cyprus, Turks and Caicos Islands. *See* Art. 6 & Annex.

3. *See* Joint Declaration of the Government of the United Kingdom of Great Britain and Northern Ireland and the Government of the People's Republic of China on the Question of Hong Kong, Dec. 19, 1984, 1984 Gr. Brit. T.S. No. 20 (Cmd.9352) [hereinafter "the Joint Declaration"].

4. *See* Kenneth E. Levitt, Note, *International Extradition, The Principle of Specialty, and Effective Treaty Enforcement*, 76 Minn. L.Rev. 1017, 1022–24, 1027–28 (1992) ("The principle of specialty allows requesting states to try or punish defendants only for the offenses for which they were extradited.... Most United States extradition treaties currently in force, and all negotiated within the last one hundred years, incorporate the principle of specialty.").

Lui's case raises the difficult question of the proper interpretation to be given to this Article of the extradition treaty and the specialty provision incorporated therein in the peculiar situation that the record reveals. The evidence shows and the government concedes that Lui will be tried in the court system of a sovereign other than that of the requesting Party and different than the one he would have been tried by but for the reversion of sovereignty over Hong Kong to China. As the district court found in granting habeas relief, the "uncontradicted evidence" establishes, as the government now concedes, that "[t]he reality ... is that the Crown Colony of Hong Kong will not be able to try and to punish Lui by the time of reversion." *Lui Kin–Hong v. United States*, 957 F.Supp. 1280, 1285 (D.Mass.1997) (as corrected January 9, 1997).

The difficult question Lui's case presents is whether a certification of extraditability pursuant to the US–UK bilateral extradition treaty and 18 U.S.C. §§ 3181, 3184 can issue in these circumstances. For the reasons that follow, I believe it cannot.

On its face, Article XII of the treaty prohibits a requesting Party from trying and punishing the relator for crimes other than those for which he has been extradited. Moreover, it prohibits a requesting Party from extraditing the relator to a third-party sovereign. As I read Article XII, therefore, the fairest and most reasonable inference to be drawn from the treaty's language is that it allows only for extradition for offenses that will be tried and punished by the requesting sovereign.

This is not the case we have before us. Thus, in my view, the district court correctly concluded that the most reasonable inference from Article XII's language is that the treaty "prohibits a person from being extradited to Hong Kong if Hong Kong, as a Crown Colony of the United Kingdom, is unable to try and to punish him." 957 F.Supp. at 1287. I believe that the logical inference to be drawn from the quoted treaty language is that Article XII requires the requesting Party to retain exclusive jurisdiction and custody over

relators extradited to it by the requested [123] Party. To me, the natural meaning of the language in Articles I and XII suggests that a "condition" to extradition under the treaty is that a relator is to be tried and punished in the courts and prisons of the Contracting Party requesting extradition. This requirement is subject solely to the exceptions provided for in subsections (1)(a) and (b), which do not apply here because the realty in this case is that Crown Colony authorities will neither return Lui to United States territory nor give him 30 days' freedom to leave Hong Kong prior to surrendering him to their Chinese successors, as those subsections would alternately require. On the facts revealed, therefore, I believe the district court correctly concluded that Lui cannot be certified for extradition because the United Kingdom fails to "live up to the terms of its extradition agreement with the United States." *Id.* at 1286.

The purpose to be gleaned behind Article XII's words also supports the position that Lui cannot be certified for extradition in the current circumstances. This circuit has indicated that "[t]he existence of such [an extradition] treaty between the United States and another country indicates that, at least in a general sense, the executive and legislative branches consider *the treaty partner's* justice system sufficiently fair to justify sending accused persons there for trial." *In re Extradition of Howard*, 996 F.2d 1320, 1329 (1st Cir.1993) (emphasis added) (citing *Glucksman v. Henkel*, 221 U.S. 508, 512, 31 S.Ct. 704, 705, 55 L.Ed. 830 (1911); *Neely v. Henkel (No. 1)*, 180 U.S. 109, 123, 21 S.Ct. 302, 307, 45 L.Ed. 448 (1901)).

In this particular instance, I agree with the district court that the US–UK bilateral treaties are "premised on the trust running between the United States and the United Kingdom." *Lui*, 957 F.Supp. at 1288. In my view, the district court rightly noted that Article XII's language manifests an exchange of promises between our nation and a trusted treaty partner: "[t]he United Kingdom is promising that it, and only it, will try and will punish [relators like] Lui for specified crimes, and no others. By its adoption of the Treaty, the United States manifests its belief

[124] in that promise of the United Kingdom." *Id.* Because the Crown Colony's extradition request in this case fails to live up to this promise by the United Kingdom, I believe that the district court properly concluded that a certification for Lui's extradition to Hong Kong cannot issue. As this court has recently explained, in extradition cases "[t]he requesting state must 'live up to whatever promises it made in order to obtain extradition.'" *United States v. Saccoccia*, 58 F.3d 754, 766 (1st Cir.1995) (quoting *United States* [28] *v. Najohn*, 785 F.2d 1420, 1422 (9th Cir.) (per curiam), *cert. denied*, 479 U.S. 1009, 107 S.Ct. 652, 93 L.Ed.2d 707 (1986)).[5]

In arriving at my conclusion I am mindful of the Supreme Court's seminal extradition decision in *Terlinden v. Ames*, 184 U.S. 270, 289, 22 S.Ct. 484, 491-92, 46 L.Ed. 534 (1902). In *Terlinden*, the Court explained that a state requesting a relator's extradition must be "competent to try and to punish him." *Id.* at 289, 22 S.Ct. at 492. The *Terlinden* Court was asked to determine whether the German Empire could successfully request a relator's extradition on the basis of a treaty between the United States and the Kingdom of Prussia, where the two sovereigns, King and Emperor, were one and the same. *See id.* at 284, 22 S.Ct. at 489-90. The Court concluded that the Kingdom of Prussia, although part of the subsequently formed German Empire, continued to enjoy "its identity as such," and treaties that it had entered could still be performed "either in the name of its King or that of the Emperor." *Id.* at 285, 22 S.Ct. at 490. In making its determination, the Court explained that "the question whether power remains in a foreign State to carry out its treaty obligations is in its nature political and not judicial, and that the courts ought

not to interfere with the conclusions of the political department in that regard." *Id.* at 288, 22 S.Ct. at 491.

The situation in *Terlinden*, however, is different than the one raised by Lui's case. In *Terlinden*, the question was whether or not the Kingdom of Prussia continued to have an independent existence and whether its treaty obligations could be exercised in the name of its King notwithstanding the fact that he had subsequently acquired "the title of German Emperor." *Id.* at 284, 22 S.Ct. at 490. The impending reversion of sovereignty over Hong Kong does not raise this question. No one doubts—and the government does not dispute—that the Crown Colony of Hong Kong will cease to exist beyond reversion to China. If some doubt existed on this score, *Terlinden* counsels that the judicial department would have to defer to the judgment of the political branches because the action of the political branches of government "must be regarded as of controlling importance" on the question of "whether [a] treaty has ever been terminated." 184 U.S. at 285, 22 S.Ct. at 490. Lui's case frames an entirely different question. The extradition request from the Crown Colony of Hong Kong does not raise the issue of whether or not the US–UK extradition treaties have been terminated. Instead it raises the question of whether the requesting sovereign is "competent to try and to punish him." *Id.* at 289, 22 S.Ct. at 492.

In my view, the Supreme Court in *Terlinden* makes a distinction between a state's "power ... to carry out its treaty obligations" (a determination on which the judiciary must defer to the political branches), *id.* at 288, 22 S.Ct. at 491, and a state's "competen[ce] to try and to punish" a relator. *Id.* at 289, 22 S.Ct. at 492. The first issue

---

5. The panel opinion relies upon *Saccoccia*, a case that involved the interpretation of an extradition treaty between the United States and Switzerland, to argue that federal extradition procedures do not give judicial officers the discretion to refuse the issuance of certificates of extraditability "on the ground that a treaty partner cannot assure the requested country that rights under a treaty will be enforced or protected." Op. at 115 (citing *Saccoccia*, 58 F.3d at 766-67). My research fails to find support for the proposition for which the panel cites *Saccoccia*. On my

reading, *Saccoccia* indicates that Article XII's "specialty" provision does not require an exact mirror-image between the precise indictment that prompts an extradition and the subsequent prosecution. *See* 58 F.3d at 766-67. Because that is not the problem that I believe to be fatal to the extradition request in Lui's case, and as I indicate in the main body of my dissent, I believe that *Saccoccia* is properly read, if at all, to support an interpretation of Article XII that would preclude the issuance of a certificate of extraditability in the unique circumstances present here.

goes to the question of whether a treaty partner—and hence a treaty relationship—still exists. On this issue, *Terlinden* informs us that courts must defer to the determination of the political branches. *See id.* at 285, 288, 22 S.Ct. at 490, 491. The second issue goes to the question of whether a treaty partner is fulfilling the promises and obligations it has undertaken with the United States. *See id.* at 289, 22 S.Ct. at 491–92. The Court's discussion in the paragraphs following its reference to sovereign competency makes clear that courts retain the authority and duty to ascertain that the treaty-established prerequisites to extraditability have been met in a particular case. The Court noted that no question existed in the case before it that the treaty-created preconditions for extradition had been met. As the Court explained,

> *If it be assumed in the case before us, and the papers presented on the motion for a stay advise us that such is the fact, that* the commissioner, on hearing, deemed the evidence sufficient to sustain the charges, and certified his findings and the testimony to the Secretary of State, and a warrant for the surrender of Terlinden on *the proper requisition was duly issued, it cannot be successfully contended that the* courts could properly intervene on the ground that the *treaty under which both governments had proceeded, had terminated* by reason of the adoption of the constitution of the German Empire, notwithstanding the judgment of both governments to the contrary.

Id. at 289–90, 22 S.Ct. at 492 (emphasis added).

Therefore, contrary to the panel opinion's suggestion, the district court correctly concluded that *Terlinden* teaches that this court has jurisdiction to examine whether the Hong Kong extradition request fulfills the obligations undertaken by the United Kingdom under the treaty. *See Lui*, 957 F.Supp. at 1285–86. Unlike *Terlinden*, the relator in this case does not argue that the extradition treaty under which he has been sought has been terminated because the requesting sovereign no longer exists. Instead Lui argues and the record reveals that the Crown Colo-

ny of Hong Kong, though it currently exists, **[125]** will not try or punish him before reversion and thus does not meet the conditions imposed by Articles I and XII of the treaty and the *Terlinden* requirement that an authority requesting a relator's extradition must be "competent to try and to punish him." 184 U.S. at 289, 22 S.Ct. at 492.

As I read it, Article XII indicates that the United States and the United Kingdom undertook an agreement to extradite relators but only for trial and punishment in the courts and prisons of each other. Because it is conceded that the extradition request in this case will result in Lui's being tried and punished under the courts of another sovereign, my reading of Articles I and XII of the treaty convince me that the British Hong Kongese authorities fail to live up to the obligations undertaken by the United Kingdom. If Lui may be extradited at all pursuant to the bilateral US–UK extradition treaties, I read the relevant treaty provisions to say that this may occur only if the United Kingdom or authorities accountable to it retain exclusive jurisdiction over Lui's person following Hong Kong's reversion to China. Because the Crown Colony will surrender custody over Lui and jurisdiction over his criminal case to the Chinese successor regime, I am of the opinion that the extradition request in this peculiar set of circumstances constitutes a violation of the relevant treaty terms. As such, I believe that no certification of extraditability can issue from this court pursuant to the US–UK extradition treaty and 18 U.S.C. §§ 3181, 3184.

II. The Re-extradition Prohibition

Lui's case also presents a difficult question with respect to whether the United Kingdom's surrender of sovereignty over Hong Kong to China in July 1997 would effect an impermissible re-extradition with respect to Lui under the terms of Article XII. For the reasons that follow, I believe it would.

Article XII in relevant part provides that "[a] person extradited [to a requesting Party] shall not . . . be extradited by that Party to a third State." Here, upon reversion, the United Kingdom will surrender sovereignty

[126] and responsibility for the administration of justice in Hong Kong to China. In the event that Lui is extradited to Hong Kong prior to reversion, the record shows beyond question that he will be surrendered to the courts and judicial system of a third-party sovereign state for prosecution. The difficulty lies in determining whether reversion and Lui's surrender to the Chinese regime that will succeed the Crown Colony amounts to another extradition.

The plain meaning and derivations of the words "extradite" and "extradition" help lead me to conclude that the surrender contemplated for Lui would constitute another extradition. The dictionary definition of "extradite" is, "To deliver up, as to another state or nation." *Funk & Wagnalls New Comprehensive International Dictionary of the English Language* 450 (1978). "Extradition" is alternatively defined in dictionaries as, "The surrender of an accused person by a government to the justice of another government, or of a prisoner by one authority to another," *id.*, as "the surrender of an alleged fugitive from justice or criminal by one state, nation, or authority to another," *The Random House Dictionary of the English Language* 685 (2d ed.1987), and as, "The surrender or delivery of an alleged criminal usu[ually] under the provisions of a treaty or statute by one country, state, or other power to another having jurisdiction to try the charge." *Webster's Third International Dictionary* 806 (1986).[6]

Legal usage has followed the word's plain meaning. Black's Law Dictionary defines "extradition" by closely paraphrasing the formula given in *Terlinden*, wherein the Supreme Court defined "[e]xtradition" as *"the surrender by one nation to another of an individual* accused· or convicted of an offence outside its own territory, and within the territorial jurisdiction of the other, which, being competent to try and to punish him, demands the surrender."* 184 U.S. at 289, 22 S.Ct. at 492 (emphasis added); *Black's Law Dictio-*

nary 526 (5th ed.1979) (replacing the word "nation" with "state or country").

International practice is consistent with this legal usage of the term. Prohibitions on re-extradition, like that found in Article XII, are fundamental features of "many [extradition] treaties" that are generally interpreted to give force to the broad principle of international law that "a person extradited to one state may not be *extradited or otherwise surrendered to a third state for prosecution."* Restatement (Third) of Foreign Relations Law § 477 cmt. d.

The operative plain meaning of the word, its legal usage, international practice, and its etymological derivation all indicate that the surrender which the record shows and the government concedes is contemplated for Lui would constitute another extradition. Upon reversion, the United Kingdom will surrender sovereignty to China as well as surrender jurisdiction over and custody of criminal defendants like Lui. Using the *Terlinden* definition, on the peculiar circumstances in this case, upon reversion: (1) Lui will be "surrender[ed] by one nation to another"; (2) he will be "an individual accused ... of an offence outside [the extraditing authority's] own territory," because authority over that territory will pass from the United Kingdom to China; (3) the offenses for which Lui is accused "will be within the territorial jurisdiction" of the receiving authority, *viz.*, China; and (4) the receiving authority, under Sino–British international agreements, specifically the Joint Declaration regarding reversion, will be "competent to try and to punish him." 184 U.S. at 289, 22 S.Ct. at 492.

Having canvassed the relevant sources that help to illuminate the meaning of the word "extradition," I believe that the revealed reality that the Crown Colony will surrender custody over Lui and jurisdiction over his criminal case to the Chinese successor regime contemplates another extradition in violation of Article XII of the US–UK bilateral extradition treaty. A decision of

---

6. The derivation of the English word is from the French, Old French and ultimately Latin equivalents. Specifically, the English "extradition" stems from a Latin union of the prefix *ex-* [out] and *traditio* [a delivery or surrender], the latter word flowing from *traditus*, the past participle of tradere [to deliver], which, in turn, stems from the conjunction of *trans-* [across] and *dare* [give]. *See Funk & Wagnalls New Comprehensive International Dictionary of the English Language* 450, 1330 (1978).

the Ninth Circuit, on which the panel opinion in the instant case relies, reaches a contrary result. *See Oen Yin–Choy v. Robinson,* 858 [29] F.2d 1400, 1403–04 (9th Cir.1988). Starting from the premise that this case is not controlling in this court, this circuit should decline to follow this decision because I believe that its argument is neither thorough nor persuasive. Moreover, the Ninth Circuit was faced by a fact pattern quite unlike the heightened and unique circumstances present in Lui's case and thus was not required to squarely face the issue presented here.

In *Oen,* the United States Attorney, acting on behalf of the United Kingdom and the Crown Colony of Hong Kong, initiated extradition proceedings against Oen in April 1987, a full decade before the scheduled date of reversion. *Id.* at 1403. Oen was charged with false accounting and publishing a false statement, extraditable offenses under Article III of the US–UK extradition treaty. *Id.* at 1405. Oen argued that if he was extradited and convicted then the possibility existed that he would remain incarcerated beyond July 1, 1997, the date of reversion. He argued that this hypothetical scenario would have the effect of extraditing him to China in violation of Article XII of the treaty. *Id.* at 1403.

The Ninth Circuit disagreed and concluded that the *Terlinden* definition of "extradition" meant that "[n]either deportation nor surrender other than in response to a demand pursuant to Treaty constitutes extradition." *Id.* at 1404. Having thus rephrased the *Terlinden* definition, the Ninth Circuit panel concluded that "*even if* Oen becomes subject to Chinese authority pursuant to a reversion of sovereignty upon cession and termination

of the British lease of Hong Kong, he will not **[127]** have been extradited to China." *Id* (emphasis added).

I find the *Oen* court's conclusion unsatisfactory for three reasons. First, as my previous discussion elaborates, it does not follow from either the commonly settled meaning of the word "extradition" or the term's operative legal usage, as manifested by the Supreme Court's definition in *Terlinden.* Instead it proceeds upon a rearticulated and truncated sense of the term that does not correspond to *Terlinden* and that cuts against international practice and the meaning that the term and its French and Latin cognates have carried since Roman antiquity.

Second, even on its own terms, the *Oen* court misapplied the meaning of the word "extradition." Specifically, even if one accepts the *Oen* view that a surrender must be effectuated in response to a demand pursuant to treaty in order for it to constitute an extradition, then a Hong Kong relator's postreversion surrender would qualify. In view of the treaty architecture that surrounds the impending reversion and the provisions in the Joint Declaration that address the juridical and legal transfer of sovereignty, it is difficult to see how the Crown Colony will surrender custody over Lui and jurisdiction over his criminal case to the Chinese successor regime in the absence of the demands on his person *qua* criminal defendant that owe their legal status solely to treaty. *See, e.g.,* Sino–British Joint Declaration, para. 1 ("The Government of the People's Republic of China declares ... that it has decided to resume the exercise of sovereignty over Hong Kong with effect from 1 July 1997.").[7]

---

7. The surrender of sovereignty and Chinese demands on Hong Kongese criminal defendants upon reversion all flow from treaty provisions. The United Kingdom's sovereignty over Hong Kong stems from cessions of territory made in 1842 (pursuant to the Treaty of Nanking) and 1860 (pursuant to the Convention of Peking) and a ninety-nine year lease contained in the Convention of Beijing, June 9, 1898. *See* Shawn B. Jensen, *International Agreements Between the United States and Hong Kong Under the United States–Hong Kong Policy Act,* 7 Temp. Int'l & Comp. L.J. 167, 168–69 (1993); *see also* 1 *Treaties and Agreements with and Concerning China, 1894–1919,* 130, No. 1898/11 (1921) (*cited in*

Oen, 858 F.2d at 1403). Moreover, the three constitutive parts of Hong Kong—Hong Kong proper (1842), Kowloon (1860), and the New Territories (1898)—are scheduled to revert to China on July 1, 1997 pursuant to the Sino–British Joint Declaration which was signed on December 19, 1984 and entered into force on May 27, 1985. *See* Jensen, *supra,* at 170–73. That international agreement, by addressing the Chinese successor regime's executive, legislative, and judicial powers, provides for the transfer of jurisdiction over persons accused of criminal offenses and in custody in Hong Kong at the date of reversion. See Joint Declaration, para. 3(3).

[128] Third, the factual pattern in *Oen* was radically dissimilar to the one that the court faces in this case. In *Oen*, the relator raised only a distant hypothetical possibility that he would remain incarcerated in Hong Kong prisons following reversion some ten or nine years later. No one doubted that Oen, upon extradition, would be tried and, if necessary, sentenced by courts of the British Crown Colony and imprisoned in Crown Colony gaols.

The *Oen* court thus did not address itself to the situation in this case, where it is certain as a practical matter and conceded by the government that the relator's trial would not be under the courts of the British Crown Colony. Therefore, the *Oen* decision did not fully address the issue that squarely confronts us today, whether Lui's surrender to Chinese authorities after reversion *for trial* will amount to another extradition. Read closely, *Oen* simply refuses to conclude that a previously convicted, already incarcerated prisoner is extradited upon reversion. This is not the predicament with Lui. I thus believe that *Oen* is unpersuasive and not on point.

III.

Legislative Intent, Judicial Deference, and Separation of Powers

Lui's case also presents a difficult question with respect to whether certification of extradition in the circumstances known to the court and conceded by the government would comport with the legislature's intent in ratifying the US–UK extradition treaties. For the reasons that follow, I do not believe certifying Lui for extradition would accord with legislative intent.

The legislative history surrounding the United States Senate's ratification of the supplementary treaty, which the district court

ably canvassed, indicates that the Senate was concerned about the extent and degree to which it could trust the United Kingdom and its judicial system to be fair and just, ultimately concluding that the United Kingdom's courts were worthy of confidence. *See* 99th Cong., 2d Sess., 132 Cong. Rec. 9119–71 (daily ed. July 16, 1986) (reprinting the Senate floor debate on ratification) (*cited in Lui*, 957 F.Supp. at 1287–88). In my view, to interpret the bilateral treaties between the United Kingdom and the United States so as to allow the benefits of such specially placed trust to be assumed by a non-signatory sovereign would fail to adhere to the Senate's intent. As the district court explained, "[i]t is clear beyond rational dispute that the Senate would not have ratified had there been any suggestion that the Treaty provisions could be extended, even by circumstance, to China." *Lui*, 957 F.Supp. at 1289.

I reach this conclusion understanding full well that the United States signed an agreement on December 20, 1996 with the government of the fledgling Hong Kong Special Administrative Region ("HKSAR"), the British Crown Colony's successor, which provides for reciprocal post-reversion extradition. *See* Agreement Between the Government of the United States of America and the Government of Hong Kong for the Surrender of Fugitive Offenders, Dec. 20, 1996. However, the new treaty constitutes a different bargain than the one voted upon by the Senate when it ratified the US–UK bilateral treaties. Moreover, the new agreement will not enter into force, if it indeed does so, until such time as the Senate, to which the new treaty was submitted on March 3, 1997, gives its advice and consent by a constitutionally required two-thirds vote. *See* U.S. Const. art. II, § 2; 143 Cong. Rec. § 1846 (daily ed. Mar. 3, 1997).[8]

---

8. In reaching this conclusion, I am mindful of the United States–Hong Kong Policy Act of 1992 (commonly known as the McConnell Act), codified at 22 U.S.C. §§ 5701–5732. As commentators have explained, this congressional enactment "allows the United States to treat Hong Kong, where appropriate, as a separate entity from the PRC for purposes of U.S. domestic law." Christopher K. Costa, Comment, *One*

Country—Two Foreign Policies: United States Relations With Hong Kong After July 1, 1997, 38 Vill. L.Rev. 825, 855 (1993). Under the McConnell Act's provisions, "the areas in which separate treatment is appropriate are determined by the terms of the [Sino–British] Joint Declaration .... [which] grants Hong Kong a 'high degree of autonomy' in nine areas: economic policy, trade, finance, monetary policy, shipping, communica-

In my view, therefore, the recently signed US–HKSAR extradition treaty is itself highly probative of the proper interpretation that must be given to the existing bilateral extradition treaties between the United States and the United Kingdom under which Lui's extradition to Hong Kong is being sought. Put simply, these treaties do not survive the surrender of sovereignty to China and do not contemplate the surrender of relators to stand trial in courts under the sovereign aegis of China. *See* Janice M. Brabyn, *Extradition and the Hong Kong Special Administrative Region*, 20 Case W. Res. J. Int'l L. 169, 173 (1988) ("Hong Kong's extradition relationships with other states ha[ve] always been exclusively vested in the British Crown.... Hong Kong's present extradition powers and relations are [thus] a direct consequence of, and are dependent upon, its colonial status. If nothing is done between now and 1997, both powers and relations will end when that colonial status ends.").

In ratifying the US–UK bilateral extradition treaties, I believe the political branches have judged the justice system of the United Kingdom and of the British Crown Colony of Hong Kong to be sufficiently fair to send accused persons there for trial. Until such time as the Senate ratifies the US–HKSAR extradition treaty no such similar expression of faith or trust has been made by the political branches with respect to China or to the Chinese successor to the British Crown Colony, which, if he is extradited, will try and punish Lui. The United States currently has no extradition treaty with China, which enjoys extradition relations with but one other country, Russia. Separation of powers principles and judicial self-restraint counsel that this court is not at liberty to interpret Article XII of the US–UK extradition treaty in such a way so as to yield a result for which the Senate did not bargain in ratifying the US–UK extradition treaty and which it is currently debating in the form of the recently

submitted US–HKSAR agreement. *See* 143 **[129]** Cong. Rec. § 1846 (daily ed. Mar. 3, 1997).

Of special import is the fact that the supplemental US–UK treaty was ratified by the Senate in 1986 at a time when it was fully aware of the widely publicized Sino–British Declaration regarding Hong Kong's reversion in 1997. The supplemental treaty nonetheless does not limit or otherwise circumscribe the terms of Article XII of the main treaty. As the panel's opinion explains, the supplemental treaty, as ratified by the Senate in 1986, "is entirely silent on the question of reversion." Op. at 109. Because Article XII, on my reading, allows only for extradition for offenses that can be tried and punished by the requesting sovereign, and because the supplemental treaty does not create any exception for reversion-affected relators like Lui, the treaty, as I read it and as the district court found, indicates that no right to demand extradition and no corresponding duty to surrender Lui exists where it is conceded that Lui will not be tried under courts of the United Kingdom or its dependent territories.

This silence in the face of Article XII's apparent requirement that relators are only to be tried by the judicial authorities of the two Contracting Parties is telling because the presumption in American and international law is against extraditability in the absence of any treaty-created right or obligation. Applicable Supreme Court precedent and "[t]he principles of international law recognize no right to extradition apart from treaty. While a government may, if agreeable to its own constitution and laws, *voluntarily* exercise the power to surrender a fugitive from justice to the country from which he has fled ... *the legal right to demand* his extradition *and the correlative duty to surrender* him to the demanding country *exist only when created by treaty.*" *Factor v. Laubenheimer*, 290 U.S. 276, 287, 54 S.Ct. 191, 193, 78 L.Ed. 315 (1933) (emphasis added); *see also* 18

---

tions, tourism, culture and sport." *Id.* The McConnell Act would not appear to have any direct bearing on this case, which involves foreign affairs and international law enforcement,

because "[t]he Act does not establish a U.S. policy toward Hong Kong in the two areas reserved to PRC control by the Joint Declaration—defense

[130] U.S.C. §§ 3181, 3184; Restatement (Third) of Foreign Relations Law § 475 & cmt. a.[9]

Despite the foregoing, the panel opinion construes the US–UK treaties as requiring Lui's extradition to Hong Kong by invoking, *inter alia*, the principles that extradition treaties are to be construed liberally in favor of enforcement, see op. at 110 (citing *Laubenheimer*, 290 U.S. at 298, 54 S.Ct. at 197), and with great deference to executive branch interpretation. *See id.* at 110 (citing *Laubenheimer*, 290 U.S. at 295, 54 S.Ct. at 196; *Howard*, 996 F.2d at 1330–31 & n. 6).

These arguments, while worthy of consideration, ultimately fail to justify a result that does not correspond to the relevant treaty provisions in Articles I and XII or to the congressional intent reflected therein, *viz.*, that the United States agrees to extradite fugitives sought by authorities in the United Kingdom and its dependent territories to be prosecuted in the courts and under the law of those jurisdictions. I agree with the district court that a refusal to certify Lui for extradition requires no untoward judicial interference with prerogatives constitutionally entrusted in the executive branch of government. On the contrary, separation of powers principles and the prevention of undue encroachment upon the Senate's constitutional prerogatives counsel against certifying Lui for extradition under the peculiar circumstances present in his case.

Specifically, I do not agree that refusing certification in Lui's case along the lines that the district court established implies any judicial arrogation of the executive's power over our affairs with foreign nations. Under

the analysis ably laid out by the district court, the refusal to certify Lui's extraditability does not stem from any assessment or judgment about the fairness or trustworthiness of the Chinese judicial or penal systems, a determination that the third branch of government is not generally empowered or as qualified as the political branches to make. The district court correctly concluded that the certification question is an entirely legal one and that

> it would not matter if China's legal system were more efficient and humane than either the United States' or the United Kingdom's. The bottom line is that the terms of the Treaty do not allow extradition when the requesting sovereign is unable to try and to punish the relator. [And t]he Crown Colony of Hong Kong will be unable to try and to punish Lui prior to reversion.

Lui, 957 F.Supp. at 1289.

I therefore cannot agree with an interpretation of the US–UK bilateral treaties that would permit circumstances to conspire so as to allow a relator to be extradited to Hong Kong where the practical reality is that China, a sovereign state with which the United States has no extradition treaty, will try and punish Lui. Neither can I agree with the panel opinion's conclusion that, because Lui's extradition is sought by the current Hong Kong regime, the right to demand extradition and the correlative duty to surrender him in fact do exist, regardless of what is

---

and foreign affairs." *Id.* at 856; *see also* Jensen, *supra* note 7, at 180–81.

9. The United States recognizes only one statutory exception to this principle. Specifically, 18 U.S.C. § 3181(b) permits "the surrender of persons, other than citizens, nationals, or permanent residents of the United States, who have committed crimes of violence against nationals of the United States in foreign countries without regard to the existence of any treaty of extradition" upon the fulfillment of certain criteria. The instant case involves allegations of economic crimes and thus does not implicate this recently and narrowly drawn exception to the generally operative principle of American and public international law.

As the quotation from *Laubenheimer* indicates, it should be understood that this opinion draws a distinction between voluntary extradition and extraditability as of right or obligation. "[I]t now clear that apart from a treaty a state has no duty to deliver up a person who has sought asylum within its boundaries. If the state wishes, it can afford him a refuge and protection.... Of course, a state is under no duty to afford asylum to a fugitive; it may expel him from its territories if it choose, and without complaint from the individual who is expelled." *United States ex rel. Donnelly v. Mulligan*, 74 F.2d 220, 222 (2d Cir.1934). This distinction [30] may appear academic in light of the government's expressed desire to extradite Lui in this case, but it is a distinction that is not without significance.

conceded will transpire upon his arrival in Hong Kong.

The opinion correctly notes that "governments of our treaty partners often change, sometimes by ballot, sometimes by revolution or other means, and the possibility or even certainty of such change does not itself excuse compliance with the terms of the agreement embodied in the treaties between the countries." Op. at 106. But the instant case does not raise the question presented by a mere change in government, whether peacefully or violently accomplished. Instead it represents a situation in which *sovereignty* over a particular territory, Hong Kong, will revert from one sovereign, the United Kingdom, with whom the United States has signed and ratified an extradition treaty, to another sovereign, the People's Republic of China, with which the United States currently has no such treaty relationship.

In my view, this court cannot fail to differentiate between a change in government, which ordinarily does not affect treaty-based obligations, and a change in sovereignty brought about when territory of one sovereign state is ceded and becomes part of the territory of another preexisting state, which generally terminates the effect of treaties of the predecessor state with respect to the territory in question. *See* Vienna Convention on Succession of States in Respect of Treaties, art. 15. U.N. Doc. A/CONF. 80/31 (1978), 72 Am. J. Int'l L. 971 (1978).[10]

Whatever difficulties may arise in sorting out succession questions in other contexts,[11] in this case it is clear—and the executive branch does not question—that Hong Kong will not succeed to the rights and obligations contained in the US–UK extradition treaties, as might have been the case had Hong Kong become an independent state in its own right rather than reverting to Chinese sovereignty.

See, e.g., Brabyn, *supra* at 174 ("For treaty-**[131]** based relations, ex-colonies can often rely upon the general principles of treaty succession [to secure continuity in international legal relations].... Hong Kong [however] is not moving from colonial status to independence. It is being restored to the sovereignty, or resuming its place as part, of the PRC.... [After reversion, existing international treaties involving Hong Kong] must be read as subject to incompatibility with the sovereignty of the PRC.").

Accordingly, I believe that this court must recognize that the Crown Colony's present ability to fulfill the requirements imposed by the US–UK extradition treaties can only be assessed in light of the concession that the Crown Colony will not in fact try or punish him and with an eye to the fact that the Chinese successor regime in Hong Kong will not succeed to the Crown Colony's extradition rights and obligations. *See id.* Because of these facts, this court cannot certify Lui for extradition because the Crown Colony's extradition request fails to live up to the United Kingdom's promise, as I believe memorialized in the terms of the extradition treaties, to try all relators extradited from the United States in courts under its jurisdiction.

Finally, I am unpersuaded by the panel's argument that refusing to certify Lui for extradition would be improper because it might mean that "any relator extradited from the United States to Hong Kong at any point since the signing of the Joint Declaration, was, if he faced a term of imprisonment upon conviction that could conceivably extend past the date of reversion, sent to Hong Kong in violation of the Treaty." Op. at 116.

In the first place, as I explained earlier in discussing *Oen*, Lui's case raises a peculiar set of circumstances. The record indicates and the government concedes that Lui will

---

10. Although the Convention on Succession presently lacks the requisite signatories for it to enter into force, and although the United States is not a signatory, the Convention is nonetheless viewed as an authoritative statement of the rule governing the succession of states under public international law. *See* Jensen, *supra* note 7, at 180–81 (citing Michael Akehurst, *A Modern Introduction to International Law* 159 (1987) (noting that while the Convention on Succession "is not

yet in force ... many of its provisions codify the customary international law on the subject")).

11. *See generally* D.P. O'Connell, *State Succession in Municipal Law and International Law* (2 vols. 1967); D.P. O'Connell, *The Law of State Succession* (1956); Louis Henkin et al., *International Law* 286 (3d ed.1993); Restatement (Third) of Foreign Relations Law § 208, Reporters' Note 1.

[132] be both tried and, if convicted, punished under a judicial and penal system not under the jurisdiction of the United Kingdom. Second, I am not persuaded by the panel's argument that refusing to certify Lui might cast aspersions on the rectitude of other near-reversion extraditions and thus "make extradition to Hong Kong ... the exception rather than the rule." Op. at 115 (quoting *Oen*, 858 F.2d at 1404). The implication would appear to be that this cannot be what the Senate intended. In view of the legislative considerations and determinations that I have outlined above, I do not believe that this court can speculate that the unavailability of extradition to Hong Kong in the circumstances of this case fails to uphold the Senate's expressed concerns and legislated intent. The US–UK extradition treaties do not just implicate Hong Kong; they are comprehensive agreements that encompass the United Kingdom and all the territories dependent upon it.[12] I cannot agree with the panel's implication that the district court's interpretation would have been a deal-breaker and the Senate would have refused to ratify the treaties if it had

been told that their terms would be interpreted to prevent Lui's extradition in these circumstances. On the contrary, I believe that the district court was much nearer the mark when it concluded that "[i]t is clear beyond rational dispute that the Senate would not have ratified had there been any suggestion that the Treat[ies'] provisions could be extended, even by circumstance, to China." *Lui*, 957 F.Supp. at 1289.

To conclude, this court faces a situation that my research indicates has no truly analogous counterpart in the annals of modern international law. Because I do not believe that the panel's opinion reaches the correct result, and because I believe that the full court should hear and consider the numerous difficult legal questions that this case raises, I would grant the petition for en banc review.

For the foregoing reasons, I respectfully dissent from the denial of the petition.

12. *See supra* note 2.

[Report: 110 F 3d 103 (1997)]

Editorial Footnotes:

8 79 *ILR* 534.
9 7 *Ann Dig* 358.
10 8 *Ann Dig* 48.
11 96 *ILR* 104.
12 35 *ILR* 2.
13 31 *ILR* 356.
14 95 *ILR* 355.
15 101 *ILR* 570.
16 104 *ILR* 110.
17 104 *ILR* 43.
18 79 *ILR* 490.
19 3 *Ann Dig* 307.

20 104 *ILR* 110.
21 104 *ILR* 43.
22 1 *Ann Dig* 272.
23 104 *ILR* 110.
24 31 *ILR* 356.
25 95 *ILR* 355.
26 96 *ILR* 113.
27 8 *Ann Dig* 352.
28 104 *ILR* 7.
29 104 *ILR* 43.
30 7 *Ann Dig* 338.

INDEX

For references to particular articles of treaties, see the Table of Treaties, p. xxxv.

A

Acquiescence. *See also* Estoppel
  protest—
    —factors mitigating failure 83-5, 102-3, 108, 136
    ——*force majeure* 112-13
Ancient title. *See* Title, historic
Applicable law—
  contract—
    —place where account kept 472
    —Rome Convention on the Law Applicable to Contractual Obligations 472
  corporation—
    —authority to act on its behalf—
    ——place of incorporation 473
  intertemporal principle 46, 115
Arbitral award. *See also* Arbitral tribunal
  annulment 243-311
    —appeal, distinguished 267, 290, 299-300
    —automatic where ground established, whether 309-10
    —excess of powers 245
    ——lack of jurisdiction under arbitration clause 246, 252-65
    ——lack of jurisdiction under ICSID Convention 246
    ——manifest, need to be 246, 248, 251-2, 265
    ——failure to observe due process 276-7. *See also* serious departure from a fundamental rule of procedure *below*
    ——award beyond legal framework established by parties 277
    ——decision based on arguments not advanced 276-7
    ——equality of parties 277
    —failure to state reasons 245, 284-91, 307
    ——burden of proof 289
    ——contradiction of reasons 287-9
    ——failure to deal with every question submitted 285, 291-304
    ——hypothetical 289
    ——inadequacy of reasons 285-6, 290-1
    ——sufficient and relevant as test 286-7
    ——unelaborated arguments 298
    —grounds—
    ——error of law 267-8, 306-7
    ——failure to apply appropriate applicable law 266-7, 268-73
    ——failure to state reasons. *See above*
    ——failure to substantiate legal basis for award 270-3, 297, 307-9
    ——manifest excess of powers. *See* excess of powers *above*
    ——serious departure from a fundamental rule of procedure. *See below*
    ——solution based unjustifiably on equity 267, 272-3, 304, 307-9
    —guidelines—
    ——*in favorem validitatis sententiae* 264, 273
    —partial 273-4
    —serious departure from a fundamental rule of procedure 245, 274-84

F

G

J

Judicial review—
  appeal, distinguished 418, 452
  extradition. *See* Extradition, judicial review
  grounds—
    —change in applicant's personal circumstances 419
    —error of law 415-25
    —illegality 453, 464
    —irrationality 414, 449, 452, 464-5
    —procedural impropriety 418-19
  non-statutory body 583-6
Jurisdiction. *See also* State immunity, jurisdiction
  conspiracy—
    —to commit crime abroad 595-6
  effects doctrine—
    —separable elements of crime, distinguished 596, 599
  extraterritorial—
    —death penalty, relevance 598-600
    —legislation conferring, interpretation 596-7
    —offence planned in forum State 590, 594-9, 605-6
  responsibility for determining 591-4, 605-6
  standard of proof 591-4, 605-6
  territorial—
    —effects doctrine. *See above*
  venue, distinguished 592, 597-8
Justiciability—
  decision based on political judgement—
    —foreign State's adherence to treaty 422-3, 425-6, 429-33, 450-1

L

Law—
  body of rules 269
  rules/principles, distinction 269
Legislation, interpretation—
  phrases. *See* Words and phrases
  presumptions—
    —extraterritorial effect. *See* territorial limitation *below*
    —territorial limitation 596-7
  responsibility—
    —judicial 400

M

Maps—
  accuracy—
    —admission against interest 99-100
    —colour 96
  evidence of—
    —title to territory 97
    ——"approximate tentative international boundary" 102-3
  pecked lines, significance 98
  relevance—